# THE PSYCHOLOGY OF RESOLVING

# GLOBAL CONFLICTS

# THE PSYCHOLOGY OF RESOLVING

# GLOBAL CONFLICTS

## From War to Peace

### Volume 1: Nature vs. Nurture

*Edited by Mari Fitzduff and Chris E. Stout*

Contemporary Psychology

PRAEGER SECURITY INTERNATIONAL

Westport, Conn. · London

## Library of Congress Cataloging-in-Publication Data

The psychology of resolving global conflicts : from war to peace / edited
   by Mari Fitzduff and Chris E. Stout.
       v. cm.—(Contemporary psychology, ISSN 1546–668X)
   Includes bibliographical references and index.
   Contents: v. 1. Nature vs. nurture—v. 2. Group and social factors—
       v. 3. Interventions.
   ISBN 0–275–98201–7 (set : alk. paper)—ISBN 0–275–98208–4
       (v. 1 : alk. paper)—ISBN 0–275–98209–2 (v. 2 : alk. paper)—
       ISBN 0–275–98210–6 (v. 3 : alk. paper)
   1. War—Psychological aspects.  2. Peace—Psychological aspects.
       I. Fitzduff, Mari.  II. Stout, Chris E.  III. Series: Contemporary
       psychology (Praeger Publishers)
       U22.3.P79 2006
       327.1′72—dc22          2005025487

British Library Cataloguing in Publication Data is available.

Library of Congress Catalog Card Number: 2005025487
ISBN:  0–275–98201–7 (set)
   0–275–98208–4 (vol. 1)
   0–275–98209–2 (vol. 2)
   0–275–98210–6 (vol. 3)
ISSN:  1546–668X

First published in 2006

Praeger Security International, 88 Post Road West, Westport, CT 06881
An imprint of Greenwood Publishing Group, Inc.
www.praeger.com

Printed in the United States of America

∞™

The paper used in this book complies with the
Permanent Paper Standard issued by the National
Information Standards Organization (Z39.48–1984).

10 9 8 7 6 5 4 3 2 1

# Contents

Foreword *by Chris E. Stout*                                                      vii

Introduction: **Ending Wars: Developments, Theories, and Practice**                ix
*Mari Fitzduff*

1 **Human Nature, Ethnic Violence, and War**                                        1
  *Melvin Konner*

2 **Tribal, "Ethnic," and Global Wars**                                            41
  *R. Brian Ferguson*

3 **Neuropsychology of Conflict: Implications for Peacemaking**                    71
  *Douglas E. Noll*

4 **Becoming Evil: How Ordinary People Commit Genocide and**                       89
  **Mass Killing**
  *James Waller*

5 **Fundamentalism, Violence, and War**                                           109
  *J. Harold Ellens*

6 **Humiliation, Killing, War, and Gender**                                       137
  *Evelin Gerda Lindner*

7 **Lessons for the Rest of Us: Learning from Peaceful Societies**                175
  *Bruce D. Bonta and Douglas P. Fry*

 8  **Integrative Complexity and Cognitive Management in International**   211
    **Confrontations: Research and Potential Applications**
    *Peter Suedfeld, Dana C. Leighton, and Lucian Gideon Conway III*

 9  **Emotion, Alienation, and Narratives in Protracted Conflict**         239
    *Suzanne Retzinger and Thomas Scheff*

10  **The Capacity for Religious Experience Is an Evolutionary**           257
    **Adaptation to Warfare**
    *Allen D. MacNeill*

11  **Conflict Transformation: A Group Relations Perspective**             285
    *Tracy Wallach*

12  **Psychology of a Stable Peace**                                       307
    *Daniel Shapiro and Vanessa Liu*

Conclusion: **What Can We Do?**                                           331
    *Mari Fitzduff*

Index                                                                     337

About the Series                                                          345

About the Series Editor and Series Advisory Board                         347

About the Contributors                                                    349

# FOREWORD

First of all, it is an honor to have been able to work with Mari, and I have Deborah Carvalko to thank for being our matchmaker (I certainly got the better part of that deal). It has been a humbling experience to read the contributed works of the scholars, researchers, theorists, clinicians, and activists herein and to add some perspective in my own minor ways. And it is a prideful opportunity to include this set in my Contemporary Psychology series with Praeger Security International.

As I have previously noted elsewhere concerning terrorism, there is no proverbial "unified field theory" concerning the complexity of conflict, or war, or even peace for that matter. This set thus gives voice to various perspectives and conceptualizations of contributory factors of not only conflict and war, but thankfully, also of peace.

Marshall McLuhan once said that "propaganda ends where dialog begins," and I believe that this set can foster dialogs and conversations across disciplines and perspectives. I have spent time with some who operate in the comfort zone of smirking condescension: the so-called cognacenti or self-proclaimed experts. I would dare say that those folks are absent from these pages, for herein readers will be treated to real issues, real facts, real experiences. There is no pseudointellectual sleight of hand, no moral carpet bombing from 10,000 feet, no preachy nonalignment. Such writing can come across as a lovely amorphous mishmash of ideas like extruded marshmallows.

At the other extreme, these topics can serve as literary vehicles (if not crucibles) of rage unhinged from facts, of infantile rebelliousness written within a cordon of comfort, or sophistry masquerading as protest. Militants enjoy outrage; that is their art form. But there is no indoctrination of readers into the theater of outrage by the authors of this work. We hope that our peer review process has served to minimize such contamination, but by definition, it is difficult to see one's own blind spot—so we hope the vetting of manuscripts through a gauntlet of capable peer reviewers has served us and readers well. We thank them for their critically important efforts in ensuring the quality of this work—thanks to Steve Fabick, Paul Kimmel, Steven Kouris, and Malini Patel, truly great work, my friends. We are in your debt.

In globally considering issues of conflict, warring, and peace, there are not only various approaches and perspectives, but thankfully many disciplines are on the job. One of the most difficult tasks in producing this work was the fact that there are a finite number of manuscripts and topical areas that we were able to include. As a result, we were forced to turn away good works by skilled authors to other publication venues that would be a better topical fit. Such speaks to the broad spectrum of approaches that these topics draw from. Even so, we have likely pushed the traditional boundaries of editorial scope with this set to include works that may not typically be considered synchronous with typical editorial perspectives. We hope you, the reader, find benefit in our having done so.

Chris E. Stout
Kildeer, Illinois
May 2005

# ENDING WARS: DEVELOPMENTS, THEORIES, AND PRACTICE

### Mari Fitzduff

## Wars Forever?

Is human nature such that nations and communities are destined forever to be involved in permanent warfare with each other? Or can we, through a more thorough understanding of ourselves and our social contexts, and a willingness to act upon such understandings, diminish our use of deadly violence to resolve our local and global conflicts?

Such questions are the substance of the issues addressed in these three volumes by 51 of the leading psychological scholars of conflict and war in today's world. They are writing in response to a world where the end of the Cold War appears to have brought little respite to the ravages of violent conflict, and where there is an increasing concern about the local and global use of nonstate terrorist tactics to solve ideological and social conflicts. They are also writing in the hope that the understandings and suggestions gleaned from these chapters can help to inform the decisions of policy makers and others with a responsibility for preventing and solving intranational, international, and global conflicts.

## The Need

The last century has been aptly named "The Age of Genocide" (Power, 2002). It has been estimated that 60 million men, women, and children have been the casualties of mass killing and genocide in the last century alone (Smith, 2000). The International Peace Research Unit has calculated that between the end of the Second World War and 2001, there were 226 armed conflicts (PRIO, 2002). Most of these wars were what Kaldor (1999) calls the "new wars," which are wars of an intrastate nature, where a government turns upon its people, a people turns upon its government, or people turn upon each other. Most of the casualties of these wars are civilians. Despite hopes that the end of the Cold War would herald a time of peace, the years since its ending have unfortunately continued to be extremely deadly ones. Wars such as those in Rwanda, the former Yugoslavia, East Timor, the Democratic Republic of the Congo, Sri Lanka, Sierra Leone, Somalia, Ivory Coast, Nepal, Indonesia, Liberia, Haiti, and the Sudan have all significantly dented such hopes. Many wars, such as those in Columbia, the Middle East, or India and Pakistan, have now lasted for decades and appear to be "intractable" conflicts. Within the last few years, the threat of nuclear usage has again reappeared, as in Pakistan and India, and has newly appeared in places such as North Korea.

To add to our fears, the last decade has also brought a new and terrifying variation of war in the form of globalized terrorist actions, perpetrated by nonstate groups that are fighting out their particular kind of fundamentalist perspectives on a national and world stage (Stout, 2002). Although as yet the figures for death from such activities are relatively small in comparison to the figures for other wars, the fact that a major attack was perpetrated against the United States on September 11, 2001, has had significant consequences for the sense of security in peoples and nations around the world.[1] It has also increased the willingness of some states, such as the United States and the United Kingdom, to involve themselves in preemptive wars when they feel their security to be under threat. The development of such preemptive wars is likely to increase the number of possible scenarios for further war interventions over the next few decades.

Such wars have come at a huge cost. World military spending in 2003 was calculated to be $956 billion (U.S.) (SIPRI, 2004), which is an increase on previous years of about 11 percent in real terms. While this cost is mainly borne by the United States, which accounts for almost half of the world's total military expenditure, it has huge consequences for lesser developed countries, whose military budgets have also continued to increase, often at great cost to their education, heath, and economic development agendas.

Must such violence and counterviolence be addressed through continuing such expenditure on armies and increasingly sophisticated forms of military technologies? Or can our responses to conflicts be better dealt with by increasing the strategies and programs through which many more conflicts can be prevented, managed, and resolved less destructively? Such questions have been at the heart of the research agenda for the conflict-resolution field since the beginnings of its development.[2]

## The Study of Conflict Resolution

The domain of the study of war has traditionally been the domain of the discipline of international politics, in which war was seen as an exemplification of the power of the state, through the use of force and military technology to serve the interest of the states in defense or expansion. It was not until after the horrors of the Second World War that the study of nonmilitary approaches to the resolution of conflicts and war, and the study of human nature and behavior in relation to this, began to develop as a discipline of study. Initial research tended to be characterized by the study of the development of peace advocacy movements (Van Denguen, 2003). Many of these movements were associated with the Quakers, the Mennonites, and the Brethren who began their work of unofficial diplomacy and their work of peace education in the early decades of the twentieth century. Many of their ideas were garnered from the work of Gandhi and his approach to the resolution of the conflict in India between Britain and the Indian independence movement.

The incubation of the field within the context of peace movements means that many conflict researchers today often have a double agenda. The first is the desire on the part of many scholars to be relevant to particular ongoing challenges of conflict in the world today. Their work is thus openly value laden (Wessells, Schwebel, & Anderson, 2001) with many being transparent about their commitment to ending conflict and war. In addition to undertaking research, many conflict researchers will involve themselves as mediators in particular conflicts, in advocacy work for particular groups, against particular wars, or in favor of particular solutions to certain conflicts. For other scholars, the priority has been to bring critical analysis and rigorous methodological approaches to their research in the hope of developing more generic theories that can be of broader use to the field. These strands often overlap. As Kelman (1991, p. 251) suggested, "A behavioral science perspective has been the backbone of the peace research movement and the peace research movement in turn has provided much of the motivating force behind the behavioral study of war and peace." Within the field there is often a healthy cross-fertilization of practice and reflection, although many critics would say such cooperation has yet to be sufficiently developed and utilized (Church, 2005, Fitzduff, 2000).

## The Development of the Field

The development of the field has not always been politically easy. Many people, particularly in the United States (Montgomery, 2003), have been suspicious that such studies might signal a "softer" approach to ongoing conflicts, leaving a country open to the suspicion of its enemy that it was not willing to fight for its interests. Such critiques were inevitably heightened by states of fear and defensiveness during two world wars. However, a gradual aggregation of individuals in the 1950s, particularly in the United States, began to ask serious questions about how to address the continuing re-emergence of violent conflicts throughout the world. In pursuit of this agenda, scholars in the field came from many disciplines: those within the International Relations field who began to feel that the international relationship perspective was insufficient in and of itself to address issues of conflict, as well as historians, anthropologists, mathematicians, sociologists, and social and individual psychologists.

The new ideas began to attract increasing interest, and the field grew and spread rapidly during the following decades. Today, there are hundreds of academic modules dealing with conflict and its resolution at the undergraduate level, and there are approximately 20 graduate programs in the field. The uncertainty about the field as a distinct discipline continues, with the result that these programs are variously located within faculties of politics, sociology, history, law, anthropology, or psychology and usually reflect such orientations in their priorities for research and teaching. Some programs address business, environmental, domestic, neighborhood, or individual conflicts, whereas others concentrate on issues of war and conflict. A major shortcoming of such programs is that apart from the programs in South Africa, most of the programs are in the more economically developed Western countries, although the last decade has begun to see their development in other countries as well, particularly in areas of ongoing conflict.[3]

## Psychologists and Conflict Resolution

Researchers involved in the social sciences, and particularly in the field of psychology, have played a very significant part in the development of the conflict-resolution field. What inspired many of the early pioneers in the field of peace and conflict studies was the rapidly burgeoning field of the behavioral sciences, with its implications for the study of conflict. They saw the potential of applying the concepts that were emerging in social psychology, group theory, systems behavior, and sociology theory to the challenge of averting, or at least limiting, war. These researchers also drew from the growing fields of organizational conflict studies, group process analysis, and the fields of industrial conflict.

What characterized a behavioral science approach to the study of war and peace was defined by Herb Kelman (1991) in terms of three assumptions: (a) that war and peace are forms of human behavior, (b) that they can thus be studied scientifically, and (c) that as they were essentially group activities, they must be studied from a "systemic," rather than from an individualistic perspective. The first assumption, that war and peace are forms of human behavior, was seen as a correction to some of the reductionist tendencies which had gained currency following the genocide of the Second World War. Such tendencies had shown particular national proclivities toward war, and in some nations tendencies toward more peaceful behavior. The second assumption was that peace and war behavior could be studied scientifically and yield propositions that could be empirically tested. The third proposition, that war and peace must be studied from a "systems" perspective, was very much an assertion of the importance of contextual and situational factors in stimulating war, as opposed to the determinants of personal or even group characteristics.

This approach was not intended to provide a comprehensive or even a prioritized theory for the field; rather, it was an additional perspective through which to complement existing approaches. Social science researchers believed that theories of international relations that failed to take psychological and social-psychological theories into account were incomplete and failed sufficiently to explain the causes of conflict. Their approach does not deny, for example, the influence of state processes, the politics and power dynamics at all levels, or the effect of structural factors such as elite based economic development throughout the course of a conflict. It does, however, suggest that an understanding of these factors is not enough without also understanding the social-psychological needs that underpin the responses to such factors.

The aggregation of scholars willing to address the topic of peace and war from a sociological and social-psychological perspective was significantly assisted when, in 1951, Arthur Gladstone and Herb Kelman published a letter in the *American Psychologist* in which they argued that some of the assumptions about human behavior that underline foreign policy needed to be evaluated in the light of psychological knowledge. The response to this letter led to the formation of a group of psychologists and social scientists interested in researching possible alternatives to the use of war to solve conflict. In 1952, this group eventually became the Research Exchange for the Prevention of War; it began to publish the *Bulletin of the Research Exchange on the Prevention of War* and to hold workshops and undertake research on issues of conflict. Subsequently, in 1954, the Ford Foundation established the Center for the Advanced Study of the Behavioral Sciences at Stanford, which was to be a prime resource in establishing the ideas behind behavioral science. Under its auspices, a group that included Herb Kelman, Kenneth Boulding, Anatol Rapoport, and Stephen Richardson began to revitalize the work of the exchange. They transformed the *Bulletin* into a new publication that emerged in 1957 called the *Conflict Resolution Journal: A Quarterly for Research Related to War and Peace*. The publication of the journal was a significant factor in helping to define the field and in beginning to validate conflict resolution as a professional concern (Kelman, 1981).

Within the conflict-resolution field, there have been only a few institutions that have focused specifically on researching psychological understandings of conflict and war.[4] However, within many of the existing conflict-resolution programs, there are psychologists working alongside their colleagues in other disciplines, attempting to complement their understanding of conflict and war using psychological approaches. Many of these individuals have found challenge and collegiality within the American Psychological Association's Division 48, the Society for the Study of Peace, Conflict, and Violence. This division was set up to promote peace in the world at large and within nations, communities, and families, and it encourages psychological and multidisciplinary research on the causes, consequences, and prevention of violence and destructive conflict. It also promotes education and training on issues concerning peace, nonviolent conflict resolution, and reconciliation. It fosters communication among researchers, teachers, and practitioners who are working on these issues and are applying the knowledge and methods of psychology in the advancement of peace and prevention of violence and destructive conflict.

As with the field in general, one of the limitations is that over half of the world's psychologists live in the United States and other industrialized societies, and therefore psychological approaches to conflicts and war are inevitably informed by such perspectives. In addition, the majority of the work is published in English, thus decreasing its accessibility to the insights of the non English speaking world.[5] As Dawes (1997) and Wessells (1999) have pointed out, this poses a problem of both the marginalization of indigenous research and understanding and the possibility of inappropriate and imperialist approaches to strategic conflict interventions in situations of war and conflict.

## Theories

### A History of Diverse Perspectives

Inevitably, the history of the development of conflict resolution as a behavioral science has been challenged and enriched throughout its development by varying perspectives in the field about the causes and nature of conflict. Given that conflict resolution is a relatively young field, it is inevitable that differing perspectives should flourish. In the main, research has focused on four possible areas for consideration when addressing the causes of conflict.

The first of these has been a contentious one, i.e., the question of whether or not violence and war, which appear to be so ubiquitous, are "natural" to humankind. Is conflict a relic, perhaps, of evolution where gain for particular groups and the overall robustness of humanity is best served by competition, including war? Although discredited for a variety of reasons in the 1980s, discussion of such theories is now making a comeback due to both a review of some previous assumptions made by anthropologists about the pacific or otherwise nature of human communities and also by the rising ascendancy of the biological sciences with their increasing sophistication and capacity for understanding the possible genetic and chemical aspects of human nature, some of which may be related to conflict tendencies.

The second focus for many researchers, particularly in the early days of the field, has been on individual human and personality factors. For these researchers the question is whether or not there are certain individuals who, for reasons of upbringing or intrinsic personality characteristics, are prone either to a rigidity in their character or emotional or cognitive values which make it easy for them to identify those who are different as the enemy, to follow leaders with similar rigidity, or to more easily find meaning and importance, as well as personal gain in their lives in involving themselves in a war.

The third focus for other researchers has been their exploration of the group nature of human beings, their need to belong to a group, to feel themselves to have a distinctive identity, to feel threatened if their group is in any way threatened, and to simplify such belonging in a way that makes it easy for them to go to war, or to be led to war.

The fourth theory comes from those who, while not necessarily disregarding the other approaches, suggest that, in fact, the roots of war often lie primarily in structural issues that disregard the needs of human beings for fairness and respect. They suggest that such exclusion, exemplified by societies, nations, or an increasingly globalized world that favors certain groups over others, provides an explosive conflict-prone situation, particularly when combined with group and individual needs. This is particularly true when such factors are combined with an increasingly easy availability of arms. As will be evidenced in these volumes, there is often a considerable overlap between these varying perspectives.

### Are War and Conflict Natural?

Work on developing possible alternatives to violence and war is viewed with skepticism by many people, and particularly by some Darwinian scholars, who believe that such efforts will come to naught, given the nature of human beings. Such cynicism was underpinned by the work of early researchers such as Lorenz (1970) who believed that aggressive impulses are innate, and by Wynne-Edwards (1962), who viewed human aggression as a necessary mechanism to ensure the best usage of territory. They applied concepts such as "the survival of the fittest" to conflict between differing groups.

Consideration of the idea that human beings have inherited a tendency to make war from our animal ancestors and that such violent behavior is genetically programmed into our human nature has been vigorously rejected by many who fear that such a pessimistic view of human nature will be cited as proof that war is inevitable and will therefore be used to justify it. There are also many scholars and others who are concerned that any form of natural or "genetic" determinism could unwittingly or otherwise provide support for certain forms of racism (Christie & Dawes, 2001, p. 138).

This fear of determinism was particularly to the fore, and therefore particularly understandable, in the 1980s, when theories of biological difference were being used to explain and justify both gender and racial differentials and to implicitly or otherwise justify discrimination. In response to such concerns, psychologists and other social scientists from 14 different countries came together in 1986 and produced what became known as the Seville Statement on Violence, which emphasized the fact that although humans have the potential to undertake violent war, such undertakings are not inevitably determined (UNESCO, 1986).

Given the political sensitivities of the time, this debate continued only in a muted fashion for the subsequent decade. However, new research findings, alongside an increasingly refined capacity for investigating human neural and biochemical mechanisms mean that the debate as to how far human beings are constrained by what Waller (Vol. 1, chap. 4) calls their "ancestral shadow" continues with some vigor in several chapters in these volumes. Waller suggests in his chapter on genocide and mass violence that the very ubiquity of wars almost everywhere human beings are present suggests that we need to recognize that there are some powerful, innate, "animal" influences on human behavior that represent evolved social capacities lying at the core of human nature. "In short, natural selection has left deep traces of design in our minds and at least some of those designs leave us evolutionarily primed with the capacity to perpetrate extraordinary evil against each other." MacNeill (Vol. 1, chap. 10) also argues that participating in warfare (along with religion) is an evolutionary adaptation, which has provided selective advantages for both winners and losers in so far as the overall benefits exceed the average costs. "In other words, the human capacities for religious experience and warfare have adapted to each other in a coevolutionary spiral that has made individual and group mass murder and suicide virtually inevitable, given prevailing ecological subsistence patterns."

For his part, Konner (Vol. 1, chap. 1) suggests that "there is in human nature a natural tendency to violence and, additionally, to war, and that the failure to fully recognize this tendency—a common failure in academic circles—increases the risk." Konner suggests that any remainders of the myth of human beings as innately peaceful has been demolished through recent research and that "the whole of human history since the hunter-gatherer era can be largely understood as a process of relentless, expansionist tribal warfare." Konner also points to the emerging research that suggests that there are biological mechanisms, and in particular, male-specific mechanisms, that demonstrate their role in aggressive tendencies and activities. He also suggests that there is increasing evidence that genetic factors related to aggression exist. B. Ferguson (Vol. 1, chap. 2), while recognizing that cross-cultural comparisons do show men to be more aggressive, claims that there are solid societal theories that explain such regular gender differences such as culturally elaborated outgrowths of social task segregation, based on physical factors such as strength, pregnancy, and requirements of infant care.

Ferguson also refutes the idea that anthropological evidence suggests that war has been ubiquitous and that violence has been a basic human pattern of human society. And, while acknowledging that individual or collective propensities to violence can play a significant part in the discussions surrounding war, he points out that decisions that lead to war are typically long considered and debated collectively. They are also usually considered within contexts that are rational in terms of a group's interest (e.g., the development of permanent settlements, growing population, social segmentation of clans or lineage, increasing status hierarchy, increased trade, and climate disturbance). In other words, wars occur not through any natural propensity to them, but because those who make the decision to fight do so because they believe it is in their self-interest. He therefore proposes a new term, "identerest," to call attention to how material interest, in combination with cultural and symbolic understanding often involve groups in lethal struggles.

Noll (Vol. 1, chap. 3) points to the need to recognize that human beings are essentially emotional beings with rational thoughts suggesting that "humans rationalize and justify after the fact and do not consciously choose much of what they do." He suggests that most conflict arises from the fear system, which originally protects humans from danger. "This system is outside conscious control, is always on during consciousness, and cannot be turned off without extensive programming and training."

However, while pointing to the ubiquitous nature of violence and the challenges it poses, none of the above authors are disposed to be deterministic about the possibly darker side of human nature. Waller points out that prosocial tendencies have also been favored by natural selection and that we can and should, therefore, identify those elements of our human nature that can most usefully serve cooperative and peaceful goals and build on them. "We can foster cultural practices and resources that activate these adaptations and produce mutually beneficial outcomes for formerly antagonistic groups." Noll also points to the fact that the human brain has also been adapted to form social attachment and that there is a clear neurological substrate for cooperative, harmonious behavior, much of which is modulated by the neurochemical systems in the brain.

Konner, too, makes it clear that there are many variations evident in the extent and ways in which societies utilize violence and that cultural values and practices are often a significant factor in limiting the use of aggression. He also emphasizes that all genetic study is developmental genetics and assumes environmental influences in the growing fetus, infant, and child. There is, therefore, no excuse for not attempting to limit the almost universal use of violence to address conflict, and he points to the need to understand it also as a behavioral science problem and to commit to addressing it on that basis.

Bonta and Fry (Vol. 1, chap. 7) for their part are particularly reluctant to endorse the suggestion that there are limitations on humans' capacity to live peacefully with each other. Using anthropological evidence, they point instead to the many current societies that commit themselves to solving conflicts without violence. As their study of "peaceful" societies shows, societies have often very different beliefs about the appropriateness and inappropriateness of using violence and about how conflicts should be handled. They point out that a cross-cultural perspective reveals that the amount of physical aggression manifested within societies is highly variable, that the peacefulness-aggressiveness of a given society is not immutably fixed through time, and that it can be changed. Whether or not people believe in using violence to solve conflict is determined by their values and belief systems. Their work suggests that a positive relationship exists between the intensity of belief and commitment to peacefulness and the actual lack of violence in societies. They claim,

> an important insight from peaceful societies that is directly relevant to creating a more peaceful world is that their very existence demonstrates that humans have a substantial capability to prevent, limit, and handle conflicts nonviolently. The existence of peaceful societies shows that violence and warfare are not inevitable. This insight offers hope for breaking away from a long-standing self-fulfilling prophecy.

Pedersen (Vol. 2, chap. 2) also challenges the prevailing belief in Western cultures that aggression and warfare are inevitable consequences of conflict. He points to the very differing ways in which conflict is addressed within differing societies. He contrasts the existence of cultures that are "Low Context," that seek an "objective" and "fair" solution to a problem, that value independence, autonomy, freedom, and personal rights, and are linear and focused on problem solving, with those of a "High Context," which value inclusion, approval, and associations and understand conflict from a more holistic and inclusive reality. His emphasis on a culture-centered approach to conflict, as opposed to the usefulness of any universal interventionist model, challenges the notion of any fixed propensity to violence in human societies.

An important additional factor in the debate as to whether or not violence is natural or not is that the evidence clearly shows that the use of violence and the conducting of war is mainly a male occupation. As long ago as 1949, Mead's work confirmed that in all cultures violence is overwhelmingly used by the males (Mead, 1949), and recent work confirms that this is still the case (Goldstein, 2002). Konner, in his chapter, shows that the role of hormonal and genetic factors as well as structural brain differences may account for at least some of the male tendencies toward violence. He notes, however, that certain social dynamics such as the segregation of males in certain societies appears to foster violence. This factor would certainly suggest that perhaps the male propensity is less innate than might be implied by the statistic, and that it, too, is very open to the influence of societal and cultural pressures.

### Are Wars Caused by Individual Human Variables?

#### Personality

Is it possible that differences in personality and individual human functioning are the causes of aggression and war? The Second World War, with the rise of fascism and the genocidal Holocaust in Germany, led to a great deal of research that was an attempt to understand what kind of person could be responsible for, or participate in, such horrific acts. This research led, in particular, to the idea of the Authoritarian Personality (Adorno, Frenkel-Brunswik, & Levinson, 1950), which suggested the existence of a personality type who was susceptible to prejudice toward the out-group. It was suggested that such personalities were the result of oppressive child-rearing practices and that their emergence could be assisted by certain socio-economic factors, which increased the individual's insecurity (Rokeach, 1950).

However, subsequent critiques (Brown, 1995) of the concept of the Authoritarian Personality claimed that the initial research had underestimated the power of the group and relationships in shaping such attitudes. It was also argued that the idea of an authoritarian personality type failed to explain situations where there was collective aggression and out-group hostility by many thousands of people of variable personality types. In particular, the theory fails to account for emergences over a relatively short period of collective group hostility. This may suggest, therefore, that

> authoritarianism may actually be the effect of changing social conditions, rather than deriving from particular child-rearing relations. If this is so, then … the commonly observed correlation between authoritarianism and prejudice, rather than indicating a causal relationship between them, may actually stem more from their joint dependence on these wide societal factors. (p. 36)

#### Categorization

While Adorno's suggestion of a personality type that is susceptible to prejudice may be too simple to explain many factors in the continuing occurrence of conflict, several chapters in these volumes point to the need to take into account at least one variable of individual cognitive functioning that is evidently relevant to our human tendency to so easily identify the "other" as an enemy. Categorization is the activity by which we simplify and reduce the complexity of our world and the groups of people within it. It is an inescapable feature of human functioning, as our worlds are often too complex for us to survive without such categorization. Such a need almost inevitably means simplifying and discriminating between those groups we belong to and other groups.

In his chapter on fundamentalism (Vol. 1, chap. 5), Ellens claims that such cognitive simplification is a characteristic of those who have a limited ability to live with the ambiguity inherent in life. "Fundamentalism is a psychopathology that drives its components to construct orthodoxies in whatever field it is in which these proponents work." Furthermore, he claims that it "is a psychology that insists addictively that its view of reality and truth is the only authentic one, and the whole truth." In his chapter, Ellens also raises the question as to whether or not such addictive dichotomization into the in-group and the out-group in fundamentalism is genetically or socially based, given his claim that fundamentalism appears to run in families.

Konner, too, in his chapter, sees a tendency toward dichotomization of one's social world as a significant contributing factor to the ease with which conflicts and war emerge. He points to the apparent need, when confronted with a stimulus, to classify it as either familiar or strange, and then to decide between approach or avoidance. He also addresses the fact that no community in the world that is free of such dichotomies, that all communities have groups whom they see as "strange" or "different," and in a situation of fear and anxiety, the masses can easily fix their minds upon an enemy.

In their chapter on integrative complexity that refers to how an individual processes new information or ideas, flexible thinking, and cognitive nuances, Suedfeld, Leighton, and Conway (Vol. 1, chap. 8) point to research that shows that low integrative complexity is sometimes associated with reduced effectiveness in resolving conflicts and increased other-directed attributions of blame. In addition, people with lower levels of integrative complexity are more likely to resort to competitive actions like war and are more likely to use violence when frustrated, whereas individuals with higher integrative complexity may have enhanced chances for successful negotiation and nonviolent conflict resolution. They also assert, however, that such factors are not necessarily determinant and that the actual level of integrative complexity at which an individual functions is affected by his or her environment.

Shapiro and Liu (Vol. 1, chap. 12) point to a particular version of dichotomization often prevailing in situations of conflict, which they call *vertigo*. They see *vertigo* as a polarized perception of a group's relationship with another group. Such a perception can have a powerful inhibiting force on intergroup cooperation. "In vertigo, a person becomes preoccupied with a single relationship, failing to consider alternative or expanded perspectives of the relationship or of other relationships." Inevitably, such a narrow focus limits an individual's capacity to see beyond the hostile relationship with an enemy group and to elicit any mutual gain and exit strategies from their conflict.

### Psychoanalytic Perspectives

Psychoanalysts bring their particular perspective to intergroup conflict. They focus in particular on the intraindividual tensions and their relationship to the challenges of developmental growth. At an early stage, psychoanalysts suggest that infants begin to differentiate themselves from their world and other people. This is a function of the *ego*, which, while becoming separate from the *id*, acquires certain functions including the function of creating its own self-image. Finding it difficult to accept that both pleasure and pain can result from the one person, they come to believe in a simplistic world of "good" and "bad" people through a process called "splitting." Maturity can help to address this simplicity, but too often humans retain a dangerous capacity to externalize or to project positive qualities on those whom they see as idealized good people and negative qualities on those whom they demonize as bad people. Such negative externalization is often functional to the individual in that it helps the individual to differentiate herself/himself and group from the other and thus helps to consolidate an individual's cohesiveness and identity. The above processes, which Freud calls defense mechanisms, usually function at the unconscious level of the individual and are therefore rarely available for rational inspection by the individual. Bion (1961) adapted Freud's theories and applied them to the life of a group, which he believed often served as a "container" for the defense mechanisms of the individuals who made up the group. Subsequently, Volkan's work (1988) suggested the idea that externalization of "badness" can also be attached to what he calls STE's, or suitable targets for externalization, which can be projected onto the symbols, flags, icons, or songs of the enemy group, as well as the groups themselves. He suggests that such STE's are often formed in early and mid adolescence and can be significant in contributing to the continuation of the cycles of hostility and violence. Volkan also points to the fact that groups often adopt "chosen glories," which are often mythologized achievements that have taken place in the group's history; accordingly, groups may also adopt "chosen traumas," which are events that help to define the borders of a group's identity and consolidate their negative externalization against the enemy.

As Wallach also notes in her chapter (Vol. 1, chap. 11), a group may attempt to avoid or deny its own internal conflicts by finding an external group or enemy onto which it can project its unacceptable, split-off parts. She suggests that this is the root of stereotyping, sexism, racism, and other "isms." Wallach suggests that "the less personal contact we have with other groups or individuals who represent different group identities, the more they may serve as a blank screen onto which we project our own images, ideas, desires, longings, anxieties, and prejudices." She also points to the use of splitting and projective techniques which are used by leaders who often invoke an external enemy in order to mobilize public sentiment against an enemy and thereby distract attention from internal, domestic conflicts.

### A Meaning in War

While it is often assumed that contexts of conflict and war, which are often attended by deadly violence, are repugnant to all human beings, it must be remembered that for some individuals and groups, such contexts are psychologically functional; i.e., they serve to give meaning and employment to their lives. The fact that economies often boom and levels of depression often decrease in situations of conflict demonstrates that war can be perceived as functional to at least some human beings. Additionally, there is a need to understand that the very act of killing, or attempting to kill, can, in itself, provide a "high" of meaning in the lives of many perpetrators as Fitzduff (1989) found in her study of paramilitaries in Northern Ireland. Almost all of the paramilitaries that she interviewed said that they had never felt more "alive" than while out on their killing missions.

In her chapter on perpetration-induced traumatic stress, MacNair (Vol. 2, chap. 10), who researched the reactions of veterans to killing, echoes this concern.

> Much research still needs to be done, but it does appear from much clinical observation that killing can at the same time be traumatic in its long-term effects on the mind and yet still have the immediate effect of a sensation of exhilaration, a sense of the thrill of the kill, a combat high.

She also points to what Silva, Derecho, Leong, Weinstock, and Ferrari (2001) refer to as an "action-addiction" syndrome on the part of many veterans which they call "a behavioral pattern involving aggression where the affected individual seeks to re-experience thoughts, feelings and actions related to previous combat experiences." These re-enactments are pursued for pleasure, excitement, postaction calmness, or other mental states the veterans regard as positive, and MacNair suggests that this addiction could be even biochemical in nature. She also points to the fact that war often gives men a sense of exhilaration and power, and subsequently many of these veterans "openly regard civilian life with contempt and think of it as being mundane and inconsequential."

Barber, Schluterman, and Denny (Vol. 2, chap. 9), in their study on adolescents and political violence, point to findings that appear to demonstrate "positive functioning" in response to exposure to political violence on the part of adolescents involved in conflict contexts. Barber et al. claim that this forces a re-evaluation of the scope of inquiry away from the simple search for expected individual pathology. They point to the fact that Bosnian adolescents appear to suffer substantially more psychological distress from their exposure to violence conflict than do Palestinian adolescents. They attribute this to the fact that some adolescents may fare differently in the face of conflict, to the extent that they can understand the conflict as logical, legitimate, and potentially fruitful in meeting the shared, fundamental agenda of their society, particularly if they find a role to play in attempting to achieve this objective. According to their research, Bosnian youth

> were surprised by the war, did not understand its political purpose, could not situate it in a coherent history, had no opportunity to resist the enemy, and, otherwise, did not employ either cultural or religious information or experience to explain the violence.

Palestinian adolescents from Gaza, on the other hand, had a wealth of meaning systems available to them. They "understood the conflict to be a logical extension of the existing struggle, believed in its necessity for political change, participated thoroughly in the resistance, and often employed religious and cultural justifications for the goals of their resistance." In short, their experiences "seem to evidence the elements Baumeister and Vohs (2002) have suggested are key for meaning to be vital: providing purpose, values, self-efficacy, and self-worth."

Wessells, too, in his chapter (Vol. 3, chap. 10), points to the fact that the search for prestige, power, and excitement are powerful motives that lead youth to join an armed group. Child soldiers from both Sierra Leone and Liberia, for example, told Wessells that

> they relished the thrill of battle, putting one's life on the line, and experiencing the special bonds and solidarity that develop with one's comrades under combat conditions. Others, who themselves had become commanders before they had reached 16 years of age, said they enjoyed assuming leadership positions, exercising skill in combat, and being respected by their troops.

Conflict thus appears to provide an opportunity for the operationalization of the idealism of youth, particularly on the part of those who feel themselves to be part of an oppressed group. Wessells and Barber point to the cases of South African, Sri Lankan, and Palestinian youth, where a sense of social injustice leads many children to join armed groups. As Wessells says,

> it is not surprising that youth, being idealistic, are particularly drawn to ideologies of liberation struggle since they are defining their identity and searching for meaning. Particularly in a context saturated with injustice, humiliation, and lack of opportunity, many youth become highly politicized, define their identity, and make meaning in liberation struggles that depict violence as an appropriate instrument for achieving social justice.

### Are Wars Caused by Group Needs and Processes?

#### Belonging and Identity

In the 1960s and 1970s, many social psychologists became increasingly critical of intraindividual explanations of the origins of intergroup conflict, and they began to shift their focus from the individual to a group level analysis of intergroup conflict. Their belief was that an understanding of the nature and influence of group identification and belonging could shed more light on issues of conflict and war. A prime instigator of such work was Sherif (1966; Sherif et al., 1988) whose "realistic" group theory of conflict experiments suggested that when groups are involved in competitive or frustrating activities that are perceived to be of a zero sum nature, each group will develop negative stereotypes about each other, often with attendant hostility. The most famous of his experiments was the Robbers Cave Experiment which randomly split a group into two groups that were given competing goals. This process quickly generated intergroup hostility. As N. Ferguson (Vol. 2, chap. 3) notes, "the experiments illustrated how competition among ordinary, nonpathological individuals for real (land) and symbolic (prestige) resources can instigate intergroup conflict and displays of discriminatory behavior, prejudice, hostile stereotyping, and physical aggression." He points to research that shows that increased ethnocentrism (the view that the in-group is the center of everything) brings increased in-group solidarity, an increased preference for all things particular to the in-group such as language, style of speech, dress, customs, a greater awareness of in-group identity, and the scapegoating of nonconforming in-group members.

In later developments, and challenging Sherif's assertion that competition created the negativity of the groups toward each other, several theorists, notably Tajfel (1981) and Billig (1976) deducted from their research that every individual locates himself or herself and others into social categories. Therefore, the simple act of categorizing individuals into groups was in itself sufficient for the emergence of an "us" and "them" division that had an intrinsic tendency to hostility. This theory became known as the Social Identity Theory (Tajfel, 1978). These groups can be based on almost any identification, e.g., gender, race, class, religion, ethnicity, geographic location, or employment. They will often overlap, and their salience will often vary considerably. Such salience will often depend upon the context, and a context of tension may often pressure people to confirm or choose such an identity. In times of conflict, identities often become more simplistic and more fundamental to the individual's concept of himself or herself, and it becomes harder to see one's group identity as negotiable. In conjunction with perceived grievances, such identity salience can easily develop into large-scale group conflict. As Korostelina (Vol. 2, chap. 8) has pointed out, "in numerous studies it appears that salient ethnic identity, ethnocentrism, perceived economic deprivation, and minority position of the in-group have a strong negative impact on ethnic violence in weak states with sizable and aggrieved minorities." Even in the absence of hostile intentions by the other party, the need for identity and intergroup dynamics produces the enemy. Such images "generate behavior that is hostile and confrontational, increasing the likelihood that the other party will respond with hostile action."

What is important to note is that group belonging also provides an important positive function for human beings, as pointed out by Staub (Vol. 2, chap. 1), where he suggests that belonging to groups is of profound significance for human beings.

> It fulfills deep needs and provides satisfactions inherent in connection. It provides a feeling of security. It is essential in defining the self as a member of a family, a profession, a religious group, voluntary associations, and a nation. Individual identity is defined and the self gains value and significance through identification with groups and the connection to others that membership provides.

He points to research that shows that such group support, whether it is a group of fellow concentration camp victims or companions working for a shared cause, contributes to survival even under the worst conditions.

However, in his chapter Waller (Vol. 1, chap. 4) points to the disturbing fact that "as collectives, we engage in acts of extraordinary evil, with apparent moral calm and intensity of supposed purpose, which could be described only as insane were they committed by an individual." He notes that laboratory studies indicate that in groups, people are more antagonistic, competitive, and mutually exploitive than individuals. Moral constraints are less powerful in groups than in individuals, and there is often a diffusion of power within a group that can make it easier for the members to harm another individual or group. In addition, groups have a power to repress dissent and, thus, encourage the abandonment of the individual self. In so doing, groups provide a moral authority that can give individuals sufficient justification to perpetrate "extraordinary evil."

### A Factor of Leadership?

An individual's need to both categorize and belong can easily be harnessed to serve the purposes of leaders. Many of the conflicts since the end of the Cold War have been fomented by leaders serving themselves, their party, or their identity group. It is, in fact, difficult to find leaders who transcend such group responsivity (Gormley, Peake, & Fitzduff, 2005). Individuals and groups are particularly vulnerable to succumbing to such leaders at times of crisis, particularly when they feel under threat. According to Post, "At moments of societal crisis otherwise mature and psychologically healthy individuals may temporarily come to feel overwhelmed and in need of a strong and self-assured leader" (2004, p. 196). Many of these leaders are what Duffield (1998) calls "warlords" or what Post calls "hate mongering" leadership. Many leaders increasingly appear to be the product of greed, involving themselves in developing drug and armaments trade (Collier, 1998) on the part of some conflict leaders. Such greed may emerge as a significant factor in preventing the end of wars as former ideologues continue to fight for personal or group financial gain. Unfortunately, as the Carnegie Commission on Preventing Deadly Conflict says, "war remains primarily an instrument of politics in the hands of willful leaders" (as cited in Hamburg, George, & Ballentine, 1999).

While Ulman and Apse (1983) emphasize that it is the psychological qualities of the followers that render them susceptible to the force of charismatic leaders, in fact, the relationship between the leader and his followers is often complex and changeable. Schiffer (1973) has observed that all leaders, especially charismatic leaders, are at heart the creation of their followers. Whether leaders lead or follow, it is important to understand that dynamic of both leadership and followership; otherwise attempts to address the issue of groups like al Qaeda may be ultimately unsuccessful. As Post (2004, p. 262) has said,

> One cannot understand the attraction of the violent path of terrorism without understanding the psychopolitical context within which these movements flourish. One cannot understand the destructive charismatic leadership of Osama bin Laden without addressing the psychology of the alienated, despairing Islamic youth to whom he appeals.

Unfortunately, many of these leaders—not just Bin Laden—use such devotion, and their power, to foment wars. In his chapter, B. Ferguson (Vol. 1, chap. 2) talks about the negative contribution of leaders who involve themselves in "ethnic outbidding" and who encourage or command atrocities to be committed by their followers. He also notes, however, the enthusiasm with which such leaders are followed, or even how the phenomena of followers who go beyond what is commanded in terms of hostilities by their leaders points to a complementarity of role and need between leaders and followers that should not be ignored. In situations where people have felt humiliated and attacked, as Lindner suggests in her chapter (Vol. 1, chap. 6), feelings of humiliation may lead to rage, which may be turned inward, as in the case of depression and apathy. However, this rage may also turn outward and express itself in violence, even in mass violence, in case leaders are around who forge narratives of humiliation that feed on the feelings of humiliation among the masses.


## Are Wars Caused by Social Contexts?

### *Unequal Societies*

It was Galtung (1969) who most clearly articulated a distinction between direct violence and structural violence. By the latter he meant problems of power and wealth distribution within a society (or increasingly within a globalizing world), which leaves certain groups excluded from economic and social systems. A development on this theme was the work on human needs theory by Burton (1990), who suggests that there are a range of human needs that are vital to human beings that can neither be negotiated nor repressed without causing great frustration and societal conflict. Among these are the need for recognition, valued relations, distributive justice, identity, autonomy, dignity, belonging, security, and physical needs. Deutsch (2004) talks about repeated, widespread, systematic injustice as the cause of many conflicts. Extensive research has confirmed the links between inequitable and exclusionary systems of governance and conflict, which suggests that unless such issues are satisfactorily addressed, conflicts are likely to continue or return (UNU/Wider, 2000). Clare (2002) also points to the fact that natural resource wars and access to such resources, combined with increasing populations, are likely to be factors in igniting further conflicts in the decades ahead.

The necessity, therefore, to address structural needs, as well as what Ross (1993) calls "psycho-cultural" needs, is vital to the prevention and ending of many conflicts. However, as Fitzduff (2002) has suggested in her analysis of approaches to conflict resolution in Northern Ireland and elsewhere, a significant lack of understanding or respect for each other's analyses and practice has traditionally limited cooperation between the two schools of thought in the field, despite suggestions by people such as Bloomfield (1997) that such approaches need to be complementary.

Drawing on her experience in the Middle East, Maoz (Vol. 2, chap. 7) points to the fact that this division has also been a significant problem in work in the Middle East. Her research shows that a major inhibition in utilizing conflict-resolution activities that focus on the changing behaviors or attitudes of individuals or groups within the Israeli and Palestinian communities is that unless such work is related to the structural realities of a perceived unequal distribution of power and resources, its effect will be extremely limited. Stout, too (Vol. 2, chap. 4), points to the research which shows that it is the confluence of situational-circumstantial factors that can ignite a conflict. Such research suggests that war is usually less the result of malevolent dictators or zealotry than of disproportionate and unfair economic or social circumstances. War is therefore more likely to arise where resources are spread unequally or even perceived to be unequal.

### *Arms Availability*

An additional factor in continuing cycles of violence throughout the world is the increasing amount of small armaments available worldwide. Such weapons are increasing dramatically. Since the end of the Cold War in particular, many are falling into the hands of nonstate conflict organizations and actors. Such availability often aggravates tensions between communities by encouraging the use of guns to solve conflicts. It also undermines any existing power of the law and exacerbates the lethality of any conflicts (Saferworld, 2004).

Stout points to the fact that "portable systems" of armaments such as hand guns, rifles, machine guns, grenades, and explosives are the most current tools for today's conflicts. The market has not only been flooded, but such armaments have significantly decreased in price. For example, an AK-47 is available for the price of a goat or a chicken in some countries. Such availability of arms, combined with an availability of ex-soldiers, is what Stout calls a "Petri dish when it comes to serving as a fertile firmament for conflict."

Therefore, unless psychological approaches take into account such factors as inequitable and unjust resource distribution, corrupt and despotic governance, and the increasing availability of arms, they are likely to be limited in the success they can achieve in preventing and resolving the conflicts of today's world.

## Practice

Given the richness of theories outlined above, it is inevitable that their variety should be reflected in the suggestions about practice that have been developing in tandem with the theoretical developments in the field. While such variations can at times be problematic for policy and program makers (Fitzduff, 2000), what the volumes do evidence is a continuing interest by many theorists in issues of practice and the consequences of their theories for actual policy and program decision making.

### Negotiating Beyond Win/Lose

One of the most prominent early developments in the field that was significant in practice terms was that of game theory (Rapoport & Chammah, 1965; Schelling, 1960). Game Theory was useful in helping analysts to think about the implication of strategies chosen by the various conflict parties in a conflict. It was also influential in helping to develop an alternative paradigm through suggesting possible win/win approaches, in particular through the "prisoner's dilemma" experiment, which attempted to understand the best choices available in a negotiating situation. This game challenged the primacy of a zero sum approach to conflict and established the fact that parties in conflict often have interdependent interests. The work on game theory was further developed by Axelrod (1984), who looked in particular at successful tactics of cooperation in conflict situations. According to Deutsch (2002) game theory has been of considerable value to social psychologists because of its "core emphasis that the parties in conflict have interdependent interests, that their fates are woven together." An additional dimension to traditional ideas of victory and power is the work of Boulding (1989), who developed of the idea of "soft power" as opposed to the hard power of force. He defined soft power as either exchange power, which is associated with bargaining and the compromising approach ("do what I want and I will do what you want"), or integrative power, which is the idea of persuasion and transformative long-term problem solving.

A great deal of the work during the 1970s and 1980s focused on the practice of negotiation (Druckman, 1973; Zartman, 1978). Much of the work of the Harvard Negotiation Project is based on a model that focuses on the interests and needs behind the particular positions taken by the parties in the hope that addressing such will give more flexibility to the negotiations to be undertaken by both parties (Fisher & Ury, 1981).

The role of the mediator, a third party who can assist in establishing positive relationships with and between the conflicting parties, and help them to identify, address, and agree about the conflicting issues, also came under particular scrutiny (Kressel & Pruitt, 1989) and that scrutiny continues to develop and expand (Ury, 2000). The use of mediation as a constructive method of helping to resolve conflict has now become so ubiquitous that it is often seen as synonymous with conflict resolution, and the process of understanding how it best works is continuingly being refined. Retzinger and Scheff (Vol. 1, chap. 9), for instance, point to what they see as a necessary but often neglected area of mediation success, and that is the need to much more fully acknowledge the role of emotions such as anger and shame on the part of the parties, on the basis that the denial of such emotions can lead to intractable conflict. Conflict problems often lie in what they call the emotional/relational world, and unless mediators are trained to recognize and deal constructively with such emotions, the mediation is likely to be unsuccessful, or agreements unsustainable.

However, as already pointed out by Maoz (Vol. 2, chap. 7), it should also be recognized that there are limits to the process of mediation and what it can achieve. Where equity and structural needs are significant components that need to be addressed, where there is a real asymmetry of resources that cannot be negotiated for, given the existing structural systems, and where equality and social justice needs are paramount for one side, then only structural change, or promises of structural change—usually obtained only from outside the mediation framework—can suffice to bring about a sustainable agreement.

### Using Optimal Contact Processes

The central premise of the "contact hypothesis," arising originally from the work of Allport (1954), was that the best way to reduce hostility between groups is to bring them into contact with each other, thereby decreasing their negative images of each other and improving understanding and tolerance between them. There appears to be ample evidence that from the hundreds of studies that have been conducted examining this hypothesis that successful contact processes are, indeed, useful in creating more positive intergroup perceptions, attitudes, and emotions. According to Brown (1995, pp. 237–246), there are a number of conditions that can assist such successful contact such as social and institutional support for such contact, equal status between groups, the development of meaningful relationships between members of differing groups, and collaboration on jointly relevant superordinate goals of cooperation. A recent sociological study, looking at contact at the macrolevel by Varshney (2003), has also been positive in validating this hypothesis. Varshney reported that a rich variety of civic contacts between communities within cities in India appear to have been instrumental in promoting relationships that are better able to withstand the conflict and riots of communities that have occurred where such networks appear to be absent.

The use of contact processes has, therefore, been a significant part of the repertoire of approaches that have been used to foster conflict resolution. In their overview of contact work, Tausch, Kenworthy, and Hewstone (Vol. 2, chap. 5) point to research that shows how effective contact work can help increase a group's learning about the out-group. Such work can reduce processes of negative categorization through assisting processes of decategorization and recategorization by individuals and in some cases the development of a common identity, as well as positive affective processes between groups, reduced intergroup anxiety, and an increase in empathy. They also give practical suggestions as to how to ensure the success of contact work. Several chapters in this volume also point to current issues of best practice in the field using contact processes. Fabick (Vol. 3, chap. 7) discusses the practicalities and some of the actual training processes involved in optimally structured group contact to address what he calls "Us and Them" thinking. D'Estrée (Vol. 3, chap. 5) suggests the need to ensure that participants in a conflict have the opportunity to provide what is called "voice" at the societal level, and at the level of direct interaction between representative members. Providing an opportunity for such voice as part of contact processes gives all of the parties the space to express an opinion and indeed assumes their right to do so as a means of validating their identity. D'Estrée's chapter gives a variety of recommendations for intervention designs so as to assist the parties' capacities for voice. Shapiro and Liu (Vol. 1, chap. 12) address the need to create what they call a "transitional environment," characterized by both safety and legitimacy, in which parties can "stimulate positive emotions that move parties toward improved affiliation, trust, and cooperative intent." Korostelina (Vol. 2, chap. 8) investigates the possibility that such work can benefit from the development of a civic, rather than an ethnocentric or multicultural concept of identity, which decreases the impact of salient national identity for both groups, and advocates civic identity-based training. Such identity restructuring workshops decrease decategorization, assist recategorization and mutual differentiation, and create the basis for different and new common identities. She points out, however, that such workshops will succeed only if members of the group do not see a danger or threat to their primary identity and do not contradict the values of such identity.

However, in their overview, Tausch et al. point to the need to ensure that contact processes also address issues of societal change.

> Contact alone is no solution for intergroup conflict. It has to be supplemented by other interventions, supported by policics, and embedded in societal change. Policy developments should include macrolevel changes such as reducing or eliminating social hierarchies via laws, regulations, and norms that affect human interaction ... in sum, policies should address the realistic, tangible bases of social conflict.

## Promoting Constructive Communication

One of the most common forms of optimal contact processes today is small group intervention called interactive problem-solving workshops, or more recently, interactive conflict resolution (Fisher, 1997). These workshops were inspired by Burton's (1968, 1969) search for alternative models of international relations, within the context of the human relations movement. Generally, these groups bring together semi-official representatives of groups, or states, who are engaged in deadly conflict. The assumption behind such work is that these groups can promote an analytic, interactive view of their conflict among the conflicting parties, and a joint, collaborative problem-solving approach that is conducive to the discovery of win/win solutions that would leave both parties better off and satisfy their needs (Kelman, 1991). In its purest form, such work happens under the guidance of a group of social scientists who are also knowledgeable about group processes.

A major hope of such workshops as described by Kelman (Vol. 2, chap. 6) is that they can play a useful role in a process by assisting the development of official peace negotiations. Although often seen as microprocesses, at their most effective they are intended to produce change in the macroprocess, i.e., the larger process of conflict resolution or a peace process. The ultimate hope is that such a workshop can function as a specially constructed arena for developing new insights and shaping new ideas that can be exported into the political processes within each community. Starting from a context that initiates communication and represents a relatively low degree of commitment, the hope is that as the level of mutual reassurance increases, the parties become able to communicate at correspondingly higher levels of commitment and, ultimately, move toward official negotiations, culminating in a binding agreement. The Oslo process that led to the Israeli-Palestinian agreement is seen as representing the potential of such a process. Fisher (Vol. 3, chap. 3) further elaborates on the possibilities for these workshops, as a supplement to official activities.

> As a prenegotiation method, the problem-solving workshop can examine barriers to negotiation, help to create the conditions for negotiation, and develop joint actions that support entering into negotiations. As a paranegotiation intervention, problem-solving workshops can diagnose obstacles that arise in negotiations, analyze particularly difficult issues, and shed light on topics that are a focus of future negotiations. As a postnegotiation supplement, workshops can help parties develop cooperative attitudes and create plans for the implementation of agreements and can engender reconciliation between enemies so that resolution is ultimately achieved.

Fisher also points to a variety of interactive conflict-resolution interventions, covering both interstate and state interventions that are generally regarded as having been
successful in influencing policy making in situations of conflict.

### Recognizing the Needs of the Differing Stages of a Conflict

An issue on which a general consensus has emerged over the past decade in the
conflict-resolution field has been the agreement that there is the need not only to
address ongoing conflicts and the need to achieve sustainable solutions to them,
but also to be alert to the differing stages of a conflict, which will often warrant differing interventions.

Hence *conflict-prevention* work will usually include work on ensuring democratic
and inclusive governance, equitable distribution of resources between differing
groups, and the monitoring of national and local tensions so as to ensure that emerging conflicts are dealt with quickly (Lund, 1996). Konner (Vol. 1, chap. 1) suggests
that we should consider adopting a disease prevention approach to war, perhaps utilizing an institution analogous to the renowned Centers for Disease Control or the
World Health Organization to monitor outbreaks of ethnic violence and to respond
to them before they become widespread. As he points out, "Interventions by the
international community would be less dangerous and costly and more likely to succeed if they could be systematically mobilized before the violence passes a critical
threshold or tipping point."

*Managing and ending conflicts* will often need security measures to control vio-
lence, negotiations to achieve agreed settlements, and work at all levels of society that
can deal with group and community interests in creating such an agreement (Darby
& MacGinty, 2000; Fitzduff, 2002; Hampson, 1996; Kriesberg, 1998; Stedman,
Rothchild, & Cousens, 2002). Bland, Powell, and Ross (Vol. 3, chap. 6) talk about
the requisites for the successful implementation of a peace agreement in the Middle
East which is informed by their experience of their practical dialogue work on the
Northern Ireland process. The issue of implementation is an often neglected issue
but is crucial to maintaining the hope of communities following any agreed accord.
Prime among these requisites for a successful implementation, they claim, are factors
of continuing dialogue at all levels of society, addressing the problem of "spoilers" to
the agreement more openly and effectively, the willingness of each side to admit its
shortcomings and failures, the need for political leaders to abandon tactics that play
well with their own side but forestall the chance for overall peace, and encouraging
external governments and institutions to play a more positive role in assisting the
parties in implementing any agreements that have been made.

*Postconflict work* will usually address issues of postconflict justice and security
needs, as well as issues of disarmament demobilization, and reconciliation between
the communities so as to prevent further cycles of violence (Mani, 2002). The latter
stage, in particular, has come in for considerable reflection in recent years, and such
interest is reflected in the chapters in these volumes. Mocellin (Vol. 3, chap. 9) looks
at a program aimed at reintegrating former combatants in Somalia and suggests that
the legacy of conflict or of famine-related traumatization highlights the need for the

development of work addressing post-traumatic stress disorder (PSTD) in a post-conflict situation. She is concerned that as long as the affected people remain traumatized or mentally disturbed because of war illnesses, their productivity, self-esteem, energy, and commitment to self-help and recovery remain impaired. Consequently, traditional reintegration programming which is normally based on educational opportunities and job creation schemas are likely to achieve poor results. Gutlove and Thompson (Vol. 3, chap. 8), drawing from their work in the former Yugoslavia, also echo this concern. "Rebuilding a society in the aftermath of war requires the rebuilding of physical and political structures. It also requires psychological healing and empowerment of the survivors, and their reconnection within a functional society." In their chapter they suggest practical strategies for this work integrating health, psychosocial healing, and social reconstruction. MacNair (Vol. 2, chap. 10) points to the often overlooked need to include what she calls perpetration induced traumatic stress (PITS), which is stress caused by being active in actually inflicting trauma. Research has shown that PITS can also cause PSTD symptoms, which, if not managed, can include the perpetration of further violence, hence the need for it to be addressed through appropriate treatment.

The authors writing on their experience of developing postconflict programs note several cautions that need to be taken into account when conducting such work. Mocellin points to the need to be sensitive about too easily assuming the existence of PSTD in developing countries. As she points out, the cross-cultural variations in frequency, patterns, and outcomes of PTSD and other disorders, as well as the moderating effect of culture in these disorders, should be clarified before making any generalizations about the occurrence of PTSD in the developing world. Reflecting on his work on the reintegration of child soldiers, Wessells (Vol. 3, chap. 10) also points to the need to be cautious in assuming frameworks for healing that may be dictated more by Western values than by indigenous needs, and he suggests that considerable advantage can be gained by incorporating local resources and practices into programs of rehabilitation and reconciliation.

Theidon (Vol. 2, chap. 11), reflecting upon her work in developing postconflict programs in Peru, is concerned that PTSD "is a diagnostic category that leaves insufficient space for cultural differences, and for the socio-historical production of illness." She argues that psychological suffering should not be medicalized but should always be contextualized within a context of political, economic, and social structures.

> While reconstruction and reconciliation are therapeutic practices, they are also political, legal, economic, and spiritual practices as well. Communities and societies do not have psyches, and they do not "heal." However, they can change. Our role as concerned third parties is to facilitate the changes that may alleviate the heavy weight of the past on individual lives and collective existence in postwar contexts.

In order to ensure this, she believes that local processes are central to the reconstruction of social relationships and coexistence and that mental health should be located squarely within social recovery and the administration of justice.

In her work on postconflict reconciliation needs, Cohen (Vol. 3, chap. 4) suggests the need to move beyond mere cognitive approaches and rational deliberations and to develop approaches that engage more fully on the affective level. She points to the fact that recent studies in cognitive psychology suggest that rational deliberations alone are unlikely to be sufficient to rebuild intercommunal relations in the aftermath of ethnic violence. There is a need to engage with the emotions of the conflicting groups in transforming aggression into empathy and the desire for revenge into the desire for affiliation. She believes such work can often best be undertaken through versions of art and cultural work that she sees as critical to promoting coexistence and reconciliation in the aftermath of a conflict. Cohen details many such programs in previously conflicted societies, which have drawn upon music, drama, sculpture, poetry and fiction, dance, mourning processes, narrative processes, art—folk art in particular—pointing to the viscerally compelling nature of aesthetic engagement. "Artistic processes can be crafted to support communities to develop more complex and nuanced understandings of their narratives, to acknowledge and begin to address injustices, and to imagine and give substance to new and more equitable relationships and institutions."

## Changing the Culture of Violence

An issue identified by several authors is the need to change the unquestioned acceptance within many societies of the need to use war to resolve conflicts. Unfortunately, as Staub (Vol. 2, chap. 1) points out,

> Many have believed that war is glorious both in itself and in its consequences. We continue to glorify past wars: the companionship, the bravery, the worthy cause, and the honor it brings the nation. Great military leaders, such as Alexander, are celebrated, even if conquest was their only purpose.

Recognizing the need to challenge such beliefs, the United Nations Assembly (2000) has been promoting what it calls "cultures of peace" to refer to a set of values, attitudes, and behaviors that reflect and help initiate social interaction based on principles that promote nonviolence and social justice.[6]

Psychologists have been attempting to identify ways in which they can promote such cultures of peace. Foremost among these are the following: the idea of not permitting ideas of biological determinism to dent our determination to create more peaceful societies, reducing the wealth gap between communities and nations, supporting the learning of more constructive ways of dealing with social justice issues, delegitimizing the use of violence in societies, increasing peoples' capacities to change their own and their communities lives, promoting greater gender equality in the hope of increasing women's participation in issues of war and conflict, and better prevention of wars (Anderson & Christie, 2001).

As seen in the chapter by Bonta and Fry, there are already certain societies where violence as a conflict-resolving method is, in fact, already deemed unacceptable. They have pointed out (Vol. 1, chap. 7) that whether or not a society uses totally or mainly nonviolent approaches to solving conflicts is very much determined by the values that they espouse and internalize.

A positive relationship exists between the intensity of belief in peacefulness and the actual lack of violence in societies. People that maintain commitments to nonviolence as core values in their worldviews seem to be, in fact, among the most highly peaceful. Other societies that do not have such a focus, that idealize peacefulness but do not keep it at the center of their beliefs, that restrict beliefs in peacefulness as a more peripheral part of their worldviews, experience or at least tolerate more violence. This is not to argue that the worldviews of the peaceful societies are the only cause of their nonviolence, but the more emphatically a society's belief system focuses on nonviolence, the more peaceful the society appears to be.

Bonta and Fry see the promotion of such values as therefore crucial for the development and maintenance of more peaceable societies. They point to the importance such societies place on inculcating such values in the children of these societies. "The common element for virtually all of the peaceful societies … is that adults consistently apply their non-violent worldviews, and the social control needed to attain them, in their child-raising practices." They conclude their chapter by asking the question,

If attitudes toward peacefulness and strong commitments to it in fact strengthen nonviolence in peaceful societies, could modern societies in general be more peaceful if people were able to develop more nonviolent worldviews? Or, on a more practical level, would modern societies experience a radical drop in their levels of violence if they were to take seriously the peaceful beliefs that already form part of their existing worldviews?

### Adopting a Multilevel Approach

Formal processes of diplomacy and negotiation are often not enough to end a conflict. Informal, civic society dialogue approaches have often, therefore, complemented official approaches, as was the case with the Dartmouth and Pugwash conferences that took place even during the years of U.S.–Soviet détente. Increasingly, in the last decade, nonstate actors have undertaken many of the most successful processes of conflict resolution, very often working in nongovernmental organizations, whose power has increased exponentially (Fitzduff & Church, 2004). These constitute what Montville (1991) calls second track diplomacy or what Diamond and McDonald (1991) call multitrack diplomacy. Track One diplomacy refers to formal attempts made by policy and decision makers of parties in conflict to explore options and advance resolutions of disputed matters. Track Two processes refer to those members of civic society such as nongovernmental organizations (NGOs), businesses, churches, and others who attempt to assist peace processes through nonformal processes of dialogue and leverage. Such groups are often freer than governments and politicians to undertake such dialogue and to help with developing the groundwork or prepolitical work that is often necessary before formalized dialogue processes can become possible. The need to involve all levels of society in assisting with the prevention of war and the development of peace has also been identified by Lederach (1997).

In his chapter, Fisher (Vol. 3, chap. 3) illustrates the usefulness of a Track Two approach in a wide array of interactive conflict-resolution workshops—all of which have utilized the work of a wide array of NGOs. The thinking from many of these workshops has later permeated the thinking of those who have undertaken the process of more formally negotiating agreements and settlements. And, in his chapter reflecting upon his work on moderating group conflict Fabick (Vol. 3, chap. 7) talks about the usefulness of undertaking what he calls Track Four diplomacy, which brings together grassroots community leaders, under optimum group contact conditions, who work to promote mutual understanding. It is his experience that these groups can diffuse existing and latent tensions through fostering public information. They can also use public pressure on governments to restructure their bilateral relations.

As well as working at different levels, an important addition to the field has been the move toward an understanding that conflict-resolution approaches must always be relevant to their context. This means that issues of development, economics, aid, governance and politics, human rights, and the proliferation of arms must also be addressed as part of the necessary conflict-resolution strategies. Several authors in this book, e.g., Stout, Maoz, and Theidon, have pointed to the need for policy makers and practitioners interested in preventing and solving conflicts to ensure that conflict-resolution approaches are developed in tandem with institutions addressing such issues, thus increasing the capacity of such strategies for success.

### If We Have to Go to War, Do It Better

Conflict-resolution analysts and practitioners often differ in their willingness to consider the necessity of using war as a way to conduct and resolve conflicts. Silver (Vol. 3, chap. 12) assumes that war will occur, despite the best of efforts to understand and eliminate its causes. If there is to be war, he therefore suggests it is useful to consider the psychological aspects of conflict with a view toward conducting "successful" war, which he defines as the attainment of the goals of the war with minimum damage to the national society conducting it, and, where appropriate, the enemy's society. He emphasizes the use of psychology in thinking through the long-term political goals of a suggested war, as opposed to the military goals, which should always be secondary, pointing to the fact that a prime focus on the latter can lead to ultimate failure. Psychological approaches can also help decision makers to understand the psychology of the enemy and prevent them from undertaking activities that, instead of weakening resolve, can only strengthen or increase their hostility. Silver also talks about the psychological understandings that are necessary for decision makers in the wake of waging a war:

> Overcoming the resentment and hostility generated by a foe's defeat or gaining trust and confidence in the wake of a foe's victory are major psychological challenges. Meeting

them requires taking into account what may be an alien culture, particularly when the political goals require a fundamental change in the socio-political structure of the defeated nation.

Silver also suggests that the application of psychological approaches is even more important when trying to understand groups who use terrorist tactics, and he points to the need to address the diversity and contextual nature of such groups and the usefulness or otherwise of a primarily military response to such in achieving their containment and elimination. This point is further elaborated by Durodie (Vol. 3, chap. 13) when he points out that objectives sought by nonstate actors who use terrorist tactics differ according to whether or not they come from a context where political debate is available or otherwise. "One that confidently asserts the rights of sovereign states led to terrorists who fought politically based national liberation struggles. On the other hand, a culture where political debate is weak or nonexistent produces terrorists without goals." Addressing such activities without a clear understanding of the contexts from which they spring and labeling them as a single phenomenon decrease our capacity to effectively deal with them. Such stereotyping, along with a refusal to assess legitimate grievances, and the use of technical resources and a fixation on "hard" as opposed to "soft" power processes to address the phenomenon of global nonstate terrorism may increase the very threat factors that we are trying to avoid. Attacks aimed at deterrence must take into account the psychological consequences of such deterrence activities and their power to rebound with multiplied violence.

For his part, Cimbala (Vol. 3, chap. 11) argues for a greater use of what he calls military persuasion, including processes of deterrence, compellence, and coercive diplomacy to precede or complement war. He points to the need to recognize the interdependence of means and ends in war and suggests that the means employed to conduct a war can in the end lose a war. He particularly highlights the need to recognize the limitations of any external interveners, noting, "Stability operations in Bosnia, Kosovo, Haiti, Somalia, and elsewhere demonstrated that the trump cards for success were held by locals, not by outside interveners." He also points to the prime importance that should be accorded by war makers to understanding the enemy:

> Perspective taking is not the same as sympathizing with the enemy. It involves a willingness to understand the cultural, social, and political settings that produce the enemy mindset: understanding is not tantamount to approval. But understanding does connote respect, at least, for the significance of the opponent's worldview, political objectives, and military art.

Cimbala also points to the need to seek to hold the high moral ground with regard to both ensuring that armies adhere to the strict codes governing their behavior and to the usefulness of gaining as much support and cooperation from other nations, if, in the end, war as an option has to be considered.

### Reflecting upon Theories of Practice and Change

Unfortunately, practitioners rarely reflect upon the theories of practice and change that lie behind the programs that they develop in order to effect change. I. Shapiro (Vol. 3, chap. 1) sets out to map the theories of practice and change that are either explicit or implicit in the many programs that abound in the field and makes the case for a better understanding of these theories in conflict-resolution work. If such theories are made explicit by practitioners and academics, they can help reveal weaknesses and gaps in the field and assist in the task of developing and building complementary and coordinated programs that can be more powerful in effecting change and in enabling such programs to be evaluated. As I. Shapiro explains, such mapping "provides a conceptual framework for articulating and mapping programs' theories of practice and change—or the underlying assumptions that guide intervention design and shape expected outcomes."

For his part, Peterson (Vol. 3, chap. 2) points to the need for the practitioner to be humble in recognizing the universality of our human capacity for oppression and violence and to undertake the work with a humility begotten of that understanding.

## Conclusion

These volumes of exploration by psychologists who are working on issues of war and conflict have been compiled in the hope that their reflections can offer some hope about possible processes by decision makers everywhere to better prevent, manage, and solve conflict and war. What they demonstrate is that the field has indeed been extraordinarily busy. From the first explorations of the pioneers of the field in the middle of the last century, conflict resolution as a discipline, and as institutionalized entity in many universities and other organizations around the world, has grown exponentially. As exemplified by the work in this book, psychologists have been very actively trying to increase their understanding of why the world is so beset by war and what can possibly be done about ensuring its diminution. We hope that those of you who are reading these volumes in the hope of finding more successful ways to address violence and war will find the contributions of significant interest to you. There are many practical lessons to be gained from these chapters for decision makers and practitioners in the field, and in the last chapter of these volumes (Conclusion) we point to what we believe to be the main conclusions of the book for those involved in addressing war and wanting to make a difference in achieving a more peaceful world.

## Notes

1. According to the U.S. State Department, 625 people died in terrorist attacks in 2003. http://www.state.gov/s/ct/rls/pgtrpt/2003/33771.htm
2. I have used the term "conflict resolution" to refer to the totality of work within the field, which includes conflict-prevention work, the management of ongoing conflicts and their

resolution, work directed toward postconflict reconciliation, and transformation work to ensure that conflicts do not reoccur.

3. The last decade has seen programs developed in Costa Rica, Sri Lanka, Indonesia, India, Nigeria, and other countries.

4. Primary among these is the Solomon Asch Institute and a postdoctoral program at University of Massachusetts, Amherst.

5. Calls for chapters for these volumes were sent to all national psychology organizations around the world where such existed. In many developing countries the dissemination of the call was limited by a lack of technological resources and research resources.

6. These include the promotion of nonviolence, human rights, tolerance and solidarity, equality between men and women, sustainable development, democracy and the free flow of information, as well as peace education.

## References

Adorno, T. W., Frenkel-Brunswik, E., & Levinson, D. J. (1950). *The authoritarian personality.* Oxford, England: Harpers.

Allport, G. W. (1954). *The nature of prejudice.* Cambridge, MA: Addison-Wesley.

Anderson, A., & Christie, D. J. (2001). Some contributions of psychology to policies promoting cultures of peace. *Peace and Conflict: Journal of Peace Psychology, 6*(2), 173–178.

Axelrod, R. (1984). *The evolution of cooperation.* New York: Basic Books.

Baumeister, R. F., & Vohs, K. D. (2002). The pursuit of meaningfulness in life. In C. R. Snyder & S. J. Lopez (Eds.), *Handbook of positive psychology.* New York: Oxford University Press.

Billig, M. (1976). *Social psychology and intergroup relations.* London: Academic Press.

Bion, W. R. (1961). *Experiences in groups.* London: Tavistock.

Bloomfield, D. (1997). *Peacemaking strategies in Northern Ireland: Building complementarity in conflict management theory.* New York: Palgrave Macmillan.

Boulding, K. (1989). *Three faces of power.* Thousand Oaks, CA: SAGE Publications.

Brown, R. (1995). *Prejudice: Its social psychology.* Cambridge, MA: Blackwell Publishers.

Burton, J. (1968). *Systems, states, diplomacy, and rules.* New York: Cambridge University Press.

Burton, J. (1969). *Conflict and communication: The use of controlled communication in international relations.* New York: Free Press.

Burton, J. (1990). *Conflict: Human needs theory.* New York: St. Martin's Press.

Christie, D. J., & Dawes, A. (2001). Tolerance and solidarity. (Special issue: Millennium Issue II: Psychological contribution to building cultures of peace.) *Peace and Conflict: Journal of Peace Psychology 7*(2), 131–132.

Church, C. (2005). Mind the Gap: Policy development and research on conflict issues. INCORE www.incore.ulst.ac.uk/policy/rip

Clare, Michael. (2002). *Resource wars: The new landscape of global conflict.* New York: Owl Books.

Collier, P. (1998). Economic causes of civil conflict and their implications for policy. In C. A. Crocker, F. O. Hampson, & P. R. Aall (Eds.), *Turbulent peace.* Washington, DC: United States Institute of Peace.

Darby, J., & MacGinty, R. (Eds.). (2000). *The management of peace processes.* New York: St. Martin's Press.

Dawes, A. (Ed.). (1997). Understanding conflict and promoting peace: Contributions from South Africa [Special issue]. *Peace and Conflict 3*(3).

Deutsch, Morton. (2002, October). A personal perspective on the history of the social psychological study of conflict resolution. *Negotiation Journal*.

Deutsch, Morton. (2004). Destructive Conflict and Oppression. Teachers College, Columbia University. www.humiliationstudies.org/documents/DeutschOppression.pdf

Diamond, L., & McDonald, J. (1991). *Multi-track diplomacy: A systems approach to peace*. West Hartford, CT: Kumarian Press.

Druckman, D. (1973). *Human factors in international negotiations*. Beverley Hills, CA: SAGE Publications.

Duffield, M. (1998). Post-modern conflict, warlords, post-adjustment states and private protection. *Journal of Civil Wars 1*(1), 65–102.

Fisher, R. (1997). *Interactive conflict resolution*. Syracuse, NY: Syracuse University Press.

Fisher, R., & Ury, W. (1981). *Getting to YES: Negotiating agreement without giving in*. In B. Patton (Ed.), *Book Title*. Boston: Houghton Mifflin Co.

Fitzduff, M. (1989). *From ritual to consciousness: A study of change in progress in Northern Ireland*. Unpublished doctoral dissertation, University of Ulster, Londonderry.

Fitzduff, M. (2000). From shelf to field: Functional knowledge for conflict management. Paper presented at the 2000 INCORE Conference in Bonn. Facing ethnic conflicts: Perspectives from research and policy making. Retrieved March 17, 2005 from http://www.incore.ulst.ac.uk/publications/pdf/Shelf_to_Field_3.pdf

Fitzduff, M. (2002). *Beyond violence: Conflict resolution process in Northern Ireland*. New York: United Nations University Press.

Fitzduff, M., & Church, C. (Eds). (2004). *NGO's at the table*. Lanham, MD: Rowman and Littlefield.

Galtung, J. (1969). Violence, peace and peace research. *Journal of Peace Research 6*(3), 167–191.

Gladstone, A. I., & Kelman, H. C. (1951). Pacifists vs. psychologists. *American Psychologist, 6*, 127–128.

Goldstein, J. S. (2002). *War and gender: How gender shapes the war system and vice versa*. New York: Cambridge University Press.

Gormley, Heenan, Peake, Gordon, & Fitzduff, Mari (2005). From warlords to peace lords: A study examining political leadership in conflicted societies involving case studies in Afghanistan, Sierre Leone, Lebanon and Kosovo. UNU/INCORE.

Hamburg, D., George, A., & Ballentine, K. (1999). Preventing deadly conflict: The critical role of leadership. *Archives of General Psychiatry, 56*(11), 971–976.

Hampson, F. O. (1996). *Nurturing peace: Why peace settlements succeed or fail*. Washington, DC: United States Institute of Peace Press.

Kaldor, M. (1999). *New and old wars: Organised violence in a global era*. Stanford, CA: Stanford University Press.

Kelman, H. C. (1981, Spring). Reflections on the history and status of peace research. *Conflict Management and Peace Science*.

Kelman, H. C. (1991). A behavioral science perspective on the study of war and peace. In J. Richard (Ed.), *Perspectives on behavioral science: The Colorado lectures* (pp. 245–275). Boulder, CO: Westview Press.

Kressel, K., & Pruitt, D. G. (Eds.). (1989). *Mediation research: The process and effectiveness of third party intervention*. San Francisco: Jossey-Bass.

Kriesberg, L. (1998). *Constructive conflicts—From escalation to resolution*. Lanham, MA: Rowman and Littlefield.

Lederach, J. P. (1997). *Building peace: Sustainable reconciliation in divided societies.* Washington, DC: United States Institute of Peace Press.

Lorenz, K. (1970). *Studies in animal and human behaviour* (R. Martin, Trans.). Oxford, England: Harvard University Press.

Lund, Michael. (1996) *Preventing deadly conflict.* Washington, DC: United States Institute of Peace Press. Available through USIP http://www.usip.org/pubs.html

Mani, Rama. (2002) *Beyond retribution: Seeking justice in the shadows of war.* Cambridge, England: Polity.

Mead, M. (1949). *Male and female: A study of the sexes in a changing world.* Oxford, England: William Morrow.

Montgomery, M. (2003). Working for peace while preparing for war: The creation of the United States Institute for Peace. *Journal of Peace Research, 40*(4), 479–496.

Montville, J. (1991). The arrow and the olive branch: A case for track two diplomacy. In V. Volkan, D. Julius, & J. Montville (Eds.), *The psychodynamics of international relationships* (Vol. II, pp. 161–175). Lexington, MA: Lexington Books.

Post, J. (2004). *Leaders and their followers in a dangerous world: The psychology of political behavior.* Ithaca, NY: Cornell University Press.

Power, S. (2002). *A problem from hell: America and the age of genocide.* New York: Basic Books.

PRIO (2002). International Peace Research Institute, Oslo. www. prio.no

Rapoport, A., & Chammah, A. (1965). *Prisoner's dilemma.* Ann Arbor: University of Michigan Press.

Rokeach, M. (1950). "Narrow-mindedness" and ethnocentrism. *American Psychologist 5,* 308.

Ross, M. H. (1993). *The culture of conflict: Interpretations and interests in comparative perspective.* New Haven: Yale University Press.

Saferworld (2004). http://www.saferworld.org.uk/

Schelling, T. (1960). *The strategy of conflict.* Cambridge, MA: Harvard University Press.

Schiffer, I. (1973). *Charisma: A psychoanalytic look at mass society.* New York: Simon & Schuster.

Sherif, M. (1966). *In common predicament: Social psychology of intergroup conflict and cooperation.* Boston: Houghton Mifflin Co.

Sherif, M., Harvey, O. J., White, B. J., Hood, W. R., Sherif, C. W., & Campbell, D. (1988). *The robbers cave experiment: Intergroup conflict and cooperation.* Middletown, CT: Wesleyan University Press.

Silva, J. A., Derecho, D. V., Leong, G. B., Weinstock, R., & Ferrari, M. M. (2001). A classification of psychological factors leading to violent behavior in posttraumatic stress disorder. *Journal of Forensic Sciences, 46,* 309–316.

SIPRI: Stockholm International Peace Research Institute. (2004). www.sipri.org

Smith, Dan. (2000). Trends and causes of armed conflicts. In Norbert Ropers, Martina Fischer, Alexander Austin, & Claus-Dieter Wild (Eds.), *The Berghof handbook for conflict transformation.* www.berghof-centre.org/

Stedman, S. J., Rothchild, D., & Cousens, E. (Eds.). (2002). *Ending civil wars: The implementation of peace agreements.* Boulder, CO: Lynne Rienner.

Stout, C. (2002). *The psychology of terrorism: A public understanding.* Westport, CT: Praeger.

Tajfel, H. (1978). Social categorization, social identity and social comparison. In H. Tajfel (Ed.), *Differentiation between social groups: Studies in the social psychology of intergroup relations*. London: Academic Press.

Tajfel, H. (1981). *Human groups and social categories*. Cambridge, England: Cambridge University Press.

Ulman, R. B., & Apse, D. W. (1983). The group psychology of mass madness: Jonestown *Political Psychology 4*(4), 637–661.

UNESCO. (1986). *Seville statement on violence*. (Adopted by UNESCO in 1989). Retrieved March 21, 2005 from http://www.unesco.org/cpp/uk/declarations/seville.pdf

United Nations Assembly (2000). www.un.org/millenium /declaration/ares 552e.pdf

UNU/Wider (2002). The wave of emergencies of the last decade. www.wider.unu.edu/pb2pdf

Ury, W. (2000). *The third side: Why we fight and how we can stop*. New York: Penguin Books.

Van Denguen, Peter (2003). Peace history: An introduction. *Journal of Peace Research, 40*(4), 363–375.

Varshney, A. (2003). *Ethnic conflict and civil life: Hindus and Muslims in India* (2nd ed.). New Haven, CT: Yale University Press.

Volkan, V. (1988). *The need to have enemies and allies: From clinical practice to international relationships*. Northvale, NJ: Jason Aronson, Inc.

Wessells, M. G. (1999). Culture, power, and community: Intercultural approaches to psychosocial assistance and healing. In K. Nader, N. Dubrow, & B. Stamm (Eds.), *Honoring differences: Cultural issues in the treatment of trauma and loss* (pp. 267–282). New York: Taylor & Francis.

Wessells, M., Schwebel, M., & Anderson, A. (2001). Psychologists making a difference in the public arena: Building cultures of peace. In D.J. Christie & R.V. Wagner (Eds.), *Peace, conflict, and violence: Peace psychology for the 21st century* (pp. 350–362). Upper Saddle River, NJ: Prentice Hall.

Wynne-Edwards, V. C. (1962). *Animal dispersion in relation to social behaviour*. New York: Hafner.

Zartman, I. W. (Ed.). (1978). *The negotiation process: Theory and applications*. Beverly Hills, CA: SAGE Publications.

# CHAPTER 1

# HUMAN NATURE, ETHNIC VIOLENCE, AND WAR

## Melvin Konner

Is war inherent in human nature? This is not the same as asking whether war is a permanent part of the human condition, but it is similar to asking whether the *risk* of war is permanent, or whether it will be very difficult to prevent future wars. The distinction is that between a natural tendency and an inevitable consequence. Vulnerability to cancer is inherent in the human condition, but we have made great strides against it and we hope that with imagination and effort it will be largely controlled. Yet the vulnerability is in all likelihood permanent because it is inherent in the processes of life.

I will argue that there is in human nature a natural tendency to violence and, additionally, to war, and that the failure to fully recognize this tendency—a common failure in academic circles—increases the risk. I begin with a consideration of the tendency to violence in general, of which war is a special case, sketching the evolutionary causes of violence and its distribution and function in other animals, then considering the evidence for violence during human evolution.

Next I review the range of levels of violence in human groups, considering not only the most but also the least violent cultures. I proceed to outline the machinery or mechanisms of violence in individual biopsychology. This leads inevitably to an emphasis on males, whose propensity for violence, in species like ours, is much greater than that of females.

Recognizing that violence is not the same as war, I proceed to discuss the necessary conditions for producing the latter from the former, allude to the history of war, and review several strong and perhaps universal human tendencies, in addition to the tendency to violence, that add to our predisposition to war. Finally, I present a modest proposal for reducing the risk of war.

## The Evolution of Violence

Beginning in the 1960s, a renaissance of Darwin's theory changed our understanding of evolution. In essence, life consists of strings of nucleic acids that have one or another degree of stability. Whatever the stable strings have or do that makes them last—in the face of entropic forces constantly trying to tear them down—will last along with them. Nucleic acid strings make proteins, and if those proteins add to stability, they too persist. A protective coating, a molecular machine for garnering energy, a structure that senses light—these and countless more consequences of the strings' capacity to make proteins will, if they further stability, persist. These are adaptations. Since they exist only to stabilize the strings, or at least the ordered information in the strings, evolutionary biologists have a favorite saying: "An organism is a gene's way of making another gene."

At any given moment in the history of life, some organisms are better at this than others. They survive and reproduce while the others do not. Thus competition is of the essence of living matter. Since resources are often scarce, this competition will in many species involve adaptations that harm others. Predation is of course an example, but there will also be a need to outcompete, and sometimes harm, other members of the same species. All socially living animal species exhibit violence. Conflicts usually occur over scarce resources such as food, space, or mating opportunity. In most species females invest more in offspring than males do, and this makes them a scarce resource for males, who fight over them. Females, and in many species males as well, guard the young and fight to defend them.

Toward the end of the twentieth century, the natural history of aggression was transformed. The older view was that aggressive behavior functions to space individuals over a territory (Lorenz, 1970). Threats and other aggressive displays were held to reduce actual violence by spacing individuals and arranging them in a stable hierarchy. Animal field studies seemed to support this view (Wynne-Edwards, 1962). Humans were said to be almost unique among animals in that we kill our own kind. Our use of weapons to distance us from our victims was believed to circumvent the natural restraints on violence.

This argument is now unsustainable. Part of the reason it appeared reasonable was the lack of opportunity to observe animal killings. If baboons killed their own kind at the same rate as Americans do, they would have to be watched for hundreds of years before a killing would be seen or even detected (Wilson, 1975, pp. 246–247). As person-years of field observations accumulated, killing was seen in many species and in varied contexts, pointing to the conclusion that "natural" mechanisms restraining violence do not work much better in nonhuman animals than in humans.

One widespread form of killing is competitive infanticide, first systematically observed in the Hanuman langur (Hrdy, 1977, 1979). Langur groups comprise a hierarchy of female relatives with their young. A small number of males may join the group for a year or more, but when new males appear, they may drive out the resident males and take their places. They kill all infants below six months of age in a matter of days. Females resist without success and mate with the new males as they become fertile again.

Competitive infanticide has been seen in chimpanzees, lions, wild dogs, and many other species in varied contexts (Hausfater & Hrdy, 1984). Cooperation too is adaptive, but violence evolved to serve the interests of individuals in obtaining resources, including mates. Dominant males have privileged access to ovulating females in baboons (DeVore, 1965; Hausfater, 1975) and rhesus monkeys (Wallen & Tannenbaum, 1997). Male predominance in physical aggression is mainly due to such competition for fertile females. Another pattern in monkeys and apes is male violence against females, often in the service of sexual coercion (B. Smuts, 1992; B. B. Smuts & Smuts, 1993).

As for violence in human phylogeny, the hypothesis that the emergence of hunting played a key role—the "killer ape" hypothesis (Ardrey, 1963)—is implausible because of the marked physiological and behavioral differences between predatory and within-species violence. Many vegetarian animals exhibit within-species violence, inflicting serious and sometimes deadly wounds with beaks, teeth, hoofs, and antlers. Chimpanzees, for whom meat makes up only a small part of the diet (Stanford, 1999; Teleki, 1973), show severe aggression against other chimpanzees. This includes attacks on females by much larger males, competitive infanticide by females and, most relevant to this chapter, violence between groups at territorial boundaries (J. Goodall, 1977, 1986; J. v. L. Goodall, 1979; Manson & Wrangham, 1991; Wrangham & Peterson, 1996). In the latter pattern, one or two victims temporarily separated from their own group are attacked by several males that beat, stamp, drag, and bite them to death. Victims may be of either sex, but females of reproductive age are often absorbed into the other group instead of being killed. At least twice, whole groups have been shown to be eliminated by systematic, one-at-a-time ambush killings combined with female transfer (J. Goodall, 1986).

In bonobos, however—as close to us genetically as chimpanzees—males fight much less severely and never attack females, perhaps due to female coalitions (Kano, 1992). Although bonobo females change groups at adolescence just as chimpanzees do, they develop close relationships and alliances sealed by food sharing and sex—rubbing their large clitorises together to what looks like orgasm (Kano, 1989; Wrangham, 1993). Female coalitions prevent male abuse(Parish, 1996), although some observers hold that male bonobos would act like chimp males if they were able to (Wrangham & Peterson, 1996). It is worth noting that bonobos are in imminent danger of extinction, but this may have nothing to do with their nonviolent behavior.

By looking at these two species, each of which shares more than 98 percent of its DNA sequences with us, we can make some inferences about the common ancestor of the three, some 6 to 8 million years ago. Certainly aggression was present, but whether the severe aggression of chimpanzees was an original characteristic or derived in their line since, we do not know. Examination of the fossil record provides the next methodological approach to the evolution of human violence.

## Violence among Our Remote Ancestors

Unfortunately, the early part of the fossil record is weak for our purposes. For most of protohuman history there is no evidence of violence, but that is not evidence of the absence of it. There are only a few hundred specimens, mostly small fractions of skeletons, and a significant incidence of violence might be missed because of paucity of data. The first hominids for whom there is a real abundance of specimens are the Neanderthals, now viewed as off the line to modern humans, since their DNA shows little or no genetic mixture with their contemporaries who gave rise to us. Nevertheless, they are our closest hominid relatives, and they share important behavioral characteristics with us.

Neanderthal skeletons show an exceptionally high frequency of injuries, especially at Shanidar in Iraq (Trinkhaus, 1978; Trinkhaus & Howells, 1979), where there are many healed fractures and unhealed broken bones. One adult male at this site has a partially healed scar on the top of his left ninth rib caused by a sharp object thrust into his chest (Trinkhaus, 1995), probably a deliberate spear wound. He may have suffered a collapsed lung and lived no more than a few weeks after the injury. At another Neanderthal site, Skhul, a skeleton shows spear damage in the leg and pelvis (LeBlanc & Register, 2003). These cases date from 40,000 to 50,000 years ago and comprise the clearest evidence of violence in Neanderthals, but along with their high rate of injury they suggest that violence was not uncommon.

Although not evidence of violence, there is clear proof of Neanderthal cannibalism (Culotta, 1999; Defleur, White, Valenzi, Slimak, & Cregut-Bonnoure, 1999). In the cave of Moula-Guercy in France, cut and broken bones dated to 100,000 years were butchered with the same skilled techniques Neanderthals used on deer and goats. Other evidence suggests that cannibalism may be much older, and it has certainly persisted up to recent times (DeGusta, 1999; Sanday, 1986; Villa et al., 1986; Wade, 2000; White, 1992). Scattered evidence of violence also appears in the later fossil record of modern humans prior to the invention of agriculture.

After that, the record leaves no doubt. Archeological evidence has demolished "the myth of the peaceful savage" (Keeley, 1996; LeBlanc & Register, 2003). The tenacity of this myth required a substantial degree of blindness to evidence, in accounts that have been called "interpretive pacifications" (Keeley, 1996, p. 20). The archeological record, equivocal for prehuman species, leaves no doubt that homicidal violence was part of life in our own species beginning at least 27,000 years ago (Keeley, 1996, p. 37).

At Grimaldi, a site in Italy, a child's skeleton was found with a projectile point embedded in the spinal column. Czechoslovakian cemeteries from roughly the same period show substantial evidence of violent death, perhaps on a large scale. A 20,000-year-old male burial in the Nile Valley had stone projectile points in the abdominal section and another embedded in the upper arm. Egyptian Nubia shows many more such cases in a time frame of 14,000 to 12,000 years ago. And European sites before the spread of agriculture to Europe show ample evidence of common violence, including the famed "Iceman" of 5,000 years ago, whose well-preserved body has an arrow embedded in the upper back.

These violent injuries and deaths occurred squarely within the hunter-gatherer phase of human prehistory, up to 20,000 years before the advent of agriculture in the respective regions, and ethnography has shown that homicidal violence occurs in a wide range of hunting and gathering societies, including the !Kung, Eskimo, Mbuti, Hadza, and others (Knauft, 1987, p. 477; Lee, 1979a). It has been commonly claimed that hunter-gatherers did not have organized or group-level violence, but this claim has been seriously challenged in a cross-cultural study showing that 64 percent of such societies had combat between communities or larger entities at least once every two years (C. R. Ember, 1978). While the sample in this study is itself open to challenge—it includes, for example, equestrian hunters of North America who cannot serve as a model for our collective past—it is clear that the peacefulness of hunter-gatherers has been exaggerated (Eibl-Eibesfeldt, 1979, pp. 171–173). Other evidence of warlike behavior among hunter-gatherers appears in the form of rock paintings in southern Africa, clubs and shields among Australian aborigines, and frequent spear wounds in 2,000-year-old skeletons in the American Southwest (LeBlanc & Register, 2003, pp. 100–127).

With the Neolithic revolution and the spread of agriculture, archeological evidence of warfare becomes decisive and appears independently in widely separated parts of the ancient world. Many collections of skeletons show embedded projectile points, left-sided skull fractures (reflecting blows with weapons in the opponent's right hand), and parry fractures of the lower arm sustained while warding off such blows. Burials with weapons and armor are seen in many sites and evidence of fortifications becomes ubiquitous (Keeley, 1996; LeBlanc & Register, 2003). Indeed, the whole of human history since the hunting-gathering era can be largely understood as a process of relentless, expansionist tribal warfare (Keegan, 1993; Schmookler, 1983). The Neolithic revolution, with its need to feed expanding populations on fixed tracts of cultivated land, may have intensified group violence and warfare, but the hunter-gatherer baseline included violence both within and between groups.

## Cross-Cultural Evidence: Small-Scale Societies

We could suggest an innate aggressive tendency in humans by describing the most violent societies (Bohannan & American Museum of Natural History, 1967; Otterbein, 1970): the Yanomamo of highland Venezuela, the Dani or Enga of highland New Guinea, the equestrian Plains Indians of the United States, the Aztec, the Mongols, the Zulu of nineteenth-century southern Africa, or the Germans of the Third Reich. Among the traditional Enga 25 percent of adult male deaths were due to violence, and life was largely organized around it (Meggitt, 1977). The Yanomamo, called "the fierce people" by themselves and others, are comparable (Chagnon, 1968; Chagnon, 1992). Forty percent of men have killed at least one other man, and those who have killed have demonstrably higher reproductive success than those who have not (Chagnon, 1988). Such descriptions of the most violent societies can be multiplied and give the impression that humans are a very bloody species composed of dysfunctional cultures (Edgerton, 1992). Many older ethnographic accounts of warfare in primitive societies, including some thought to be nonviolent by anthropologists, suggest that, as in archeology, violence has often been ignored (Eibl-Eibesfeldt, 1979, pp. 171–187).

But it is more instructive to look at the least violent societies. Differences in the degree of violence among cultures span three orders of magnitude, and understanding those differences should help us reduce violence. But are there truly nonviolent societies? The !Kung San of Botswana are often cited as among the least violent (Marshall, 1976; Thomas, 1959). They were not observed to have organized group conflicts in recent times. Nevertheless, their homicide rate matches or exceeds that for American cities (Lee, 1979b, chap. 13), and there are many nonlethal acts of violence as well (Shostak, 1981; Shostak, 2000). Moreover, their explicit contempt for other ethnic groups and even for !Kung in other villages who are not their relatives suggests that if they had the technological opportunity and the ecological motivation to make war, they would have the psychological capacity. And historical data indicate that they conducted wars or at least intervillage raids in the past (Eibl-Eibesfeldt, 1979, p. 171).

A different kind of test case is presented by the Semai, slash-and-burn gardeners of Malaysia, a small-scale society like that of the !Kung but more sedentary. Violence was said to be abhorrent to them and virtually nonexistent. "Since a census of the Semai was first taken in 1956, not one instance of murder, attempted murder, or maiming has come to the attention of either government or hospital authorities" (Dentan, 1968, p. 58). This low rate of violence was attributed to upbringing and cultural ideology:

> A person should never hit a child because, people say, "How would you feel if it died?" … Similarly, one adult should never hit another because, they say, "Suppose he hit you back?" … [T]he Semai are not great warriors. As long as they have been known to the outside world, they have consistently fled rather than fight, or even than run the risk of fighting. They had never participated in a war or raid until the Communist insurgency of the early 1950's, when the British raised troops among the Semai, mainly in the west. … Many did not realize that soldiers kill people. When I suggested to one Semai recruit that killing was a soldier's job, he laughed at my ignorance and explained, "No, we don't kill people, brother, we just tend weeds and cut grass." (p. 58)

But when the British engaged the Semai in counterinsurgency against Communist rebels in the mid-1950s, they became extremely violent:

> Many people who knew the Semai insisted that such an unwarlike people could never make good soldiers … they were wrong. Communist terrorists had killed the kinsmen of some of the Semai counterinsurgency troops. Taken out of their nonviolent society and ordered to kill, they seem to have been swept up in a sort of insanity which they call "blood drunkenness." … "We killed, killed, killed. The Malays would stop and go through people's pockets and take their watches and money. We did not think of watches or money. We only thought of killing. Wah, truly we were drunk with blood." One man even told how he had drunk the blood of a man he had killed. (pp. 58–59)

This episode was followed by a return to normalcy:

Talking about these experiences, the Semai seem, not displeased that they were such good soldiers, but unable to account for their behavior. It is almost as if they had shut the experience in a separate compartment. ... Back in Semai society they seem as gentle and afraid of violence as anyone else. To them their one burst of violence appears to be as remote as something that happened to someone else, in another country. The nonviolent image remains intact. (p. 59)

It is perhaps not surprising that such a reversal could occur when a group of men are taken completely out of their normal cultural context, and it may be the lack of prior experience with violence that made the reversal so extreme. Still, this case undermines the belief that violence stems solely from childhood experience or that the individual tendency to participate in war can be prevented by nonviolent experience during development.

It is also quite different from the !Kung case, in which violence was found to have occurred at substantial levels in the traditional cultural context. Culture *can* reduce violence, as indeed the Semai culture did in its normal context. In a cross-cultural study using the Human Relations Area Files and designed to sample representatively the ethnographic universe, it was found that after a society has been pacified by external powers, it becomes less interested in training boys to be aggressive (M. Ember & Ember, 1994). Matrilocal societies, where women live with their female relatives, have less warfare than patrilocal ones where men live with their male relatives (Divale, 1974; M. Ember & Ember, 1971).

Another study using a wide cross-cultural sample found that when husband-wife intimacy is high, organized group conflicts are less common (J. W. M. Whiting & B. B. Whiting, 1975). Cultures where husbands and wives eat together, sleep together, and share the child care are among the least violent, while those that have organized themselves around constant or at least intermittent warfare tend to segregate men away from women and children, with separate men's houses for eating and sleeping, and men's societies in which even young boys are severely stressed and actively trained for warfare. This study indirectly supported the hypothesis that the social dynamic of male aggregations fosters violence (Tiger, 1969). It is not well understood, but it is cross-culturally very widespread and has a dramatic parallel in chimpanzees.

Group ambushes and killings in chimpanzees have now been studied in Uganda as well as in the Gombe Stream Reserve of Tanzania, and it has been shown that the best predictor of such an attack is the aggregation of a critical number of adult males. Research by David Watts and John Mitani followed a group of 150 chimpanzees in the Kibale National Park over a five-year period (Gibbons, 2004a). When a critical mass of about 18 males get together, excitement builds until they go out into the forest in a single file, unusually quiet, passing up hunting opportunities along the way until they cross the boundary of their own territory. If they came upon a single male from the adjacent group they ganged up on this victim and, on five separate occasions, killed him.

This pattern contrasts with the dynamic in bonobos, in which the influence of females and their strong alliances helps suppress most male violence. As for the other great apes, gorillas, more distantly related to us, exhibit two different patterns (Bradley, Doran-Sheehy, Lukas, Boesch, & Vigilant, 2004). Western lowland gorillas show no aggression between males of neighboring groups because (as DNA analyses show) they are relatives who have migrated a short distance from their home groups. Mountain gorillas, on the other hand, tend to stay in their home groups and do show aggression against males in neighboring groups. Orangutans, still more distant from us genetically, are mainly solitary animals, but males frequently mate by forcing themselves on females (Rodman & Mitani, 1987).

## The Male Factor in Violence and War

Males predominate very disproportionately in both intragroup and intergroup violence. The past half-century has seen a salutary correction of naive notions of biologically based gender differences in behavior, but we should not replace them with the equally naive notion that there are no such differences. Compared to the received biases of the past, they are few in number, but violence is among them. Margaret Mead played a major role in dispelling the naive notions. By 1949, when her book *Male and Female* was published, she had done ethnographic research in seven traditional, mostly remote, societies and could amply demonstrate the variety of gender roles. Yet at the same time she inadvertently found one behavioral domain in which there is little variation. Sex roles in one group seemed reversed from our expectations:

> The Tchambuli people ... have built their houses along the edge of one of the loveliest of New Guinea lakes, which gleams like polished ebony, with a back-drop of the distant hills behind which the Arapesh live. ... Here the Tchambuli women, brisk, unadorned, managing and industrious, fish and go to market: the men, decorative and adorned, carve and paint and practice dance-steps, their headhunting tradition replaced by the simpler practice of buying victims to validate their manhood. (p. 54)

Among the Mundugumor, river-dwelling cannibals of New Guinea, men and women seemed equally masculine:

> These robust, restive people live on the banks of a swiftly flowing river. ... They trade with and prey upon the miserable, underfed bush-peoples who live on poorer land, devote their time to quarreling and headhunting, and have developed a form of social organization in which every man's hand is against every other man. The women are as assertive and vigorous as the men; they detest bearing and rearing children, and provide most of the food, leaving the men free to plot and fight. (pp. 53–54)

The variety of gender roles was indeed remarkable and surprised many midcentury social scientists. Mead's work undermined many biologically based notions of gender psychology. Yet in all her cultures there was homicidal violence and, in all, that violence was overwhelmingly male. Tchambuli men may have been effeminate by certain Western conventions, but they killed victims and hunted heads. Mundugumor men were unthreatened by having women provide for them, *because* it freed them to plot and fight.

This sex difference can be traced through thousands of cultures. In every culture there is at least some homicide, in the context of war or ritual or in the context of daily life, and in every culture it is mainly men who do it. Among the !Kung, noted for equality between the sexes as well as pacifism, the perpetrators in 22 documented homicides were all men (Lee, 1979b, chap. 13). Fights over adultery or presumed adultery were involved in several cases, and a majority of the others were retaliations for previous homicides. These two themes of jealousy and vendetta pervade the cross-cultural homicide literature (Ghiglieri, 1999; Knauft, 1987).

In fact, every measure devised to reflect physical aggression favors males at every age in every culture studied. In a sample of 122 societies in the ethnographic spectrum, weapons were made by men in all of them (D'Andrade, 1966, p. 178). Psychological measures support the distinction: In 75 tribal societies on all continents, men were more likely to dream of coitus, wife, weapon, animal, death, red, vehicle, hit, ineffectual attempt, and grass, while women were more likely to dream of husband, clothes, mother, father, child, home, female figure, cry, and male figure (D'Andrade, 1966, p. 198). There are many exceptions at the individual level and in rare cases—such as modern Israel and Eritrea or nineteenth century Dahomey in West Africa—partial exceptions at the group level. Indeed, the United States now places some women in combat. It may strictly speaking be a difference in degree, but it is very large.

Recent research has revisited the relationship between gender and early warfare, and has strongly confirmed the distinction (Low, 2000). Men account for the overwhelming majority of warriors in nonindustrial societies (Ghiglieri, 1999; Manson & Wrangham, 1991), and the capture of women is both a cause and a consequence of war in as many as half of such societies (Divale, 1973; White, 1988; White & Burton, 1988). Literary sources including Homer and the Bible confirm the central role of young women as a goal or perquisite of ancient wars (Hartung, 1992), and despotic empires carry this to an extreme in which large numbers of young women end up in the beds of powerful men (Betzig, 1986, 1992, 1997). Men have always made wars, often over women (Tiger, 1984).

In psychological research, the strongest case for gender difference is also in physical aggression (Hyde, 1986; Maccoby & Jacklin, 1974). Of 94 comparisons in 67 different studies, 57 showed statistically significant sex differences, and in only 5 were females more aggressive. The subjects ranged from age two to adulthood and the measures ranged from hitting, kicking, and throwing rocks to scores on a hostility scale, and included fantasy, dream material, verbal aggression, and aggression against dolls. Of 6 different studies in which actual *physical* aggression was measured, five found that boys exceeded girls, the last showing no difference. A study of more than 500 17-month-olds showed that both aggression and a sex difference in aggression have already emerged by that age (Tremblay et al., 1999).

In the Six Cultures study, Beatrice Whiting and others studied children's behavior through direct, detailed observation in naturalistic settings in a New England town and in five farming and herding villages (B. Whiting & Edwards, 1988; B. Whiting & Whiting, 1975; B. B. Whiting & Edwards, 1973). In Mexico (Juxtlahuaca),

Kenya (Nyansongo), India (Khalapur), Japan (Taira), and the Phillipines (Tarong), as well as in New England, hundreds of hours of observations were made on children from age 3 to 11, using uniform methods. Children were scored on 12 small units of behavior, such as "seeks help," "offers support," "touches," "reprimands," and "assaults." Multidimensional scaling revealed two main dimensions: "egoism versus altruism" and "aggressiveness versus nurturance" (B. B. Whiting & J. W. M. Whiting, 1975). In all six cultures, boys showed greater egoism, greater aggressiveness, or (usually) both. The analysis was later extended to five other quantitatively studied cultures—Kien-taa in Liberia, Kokwet, Ngeca, and Kisa-Kariobangi in Kenya, and Bhubaneswar in India—with similar conclusions (B. B. Whiting & Edwards, 1988). Yet another group used similar methods to study children in four more cultures, in Belize, Kenya, Nepal, and American Samoa (Munroe, Hulefeld, Rodgers, Tomeo, & Yamazaki, 2000). Comparing 96 boys to 96 girls, ages 3, 5, 7, and 9, in all four cultures boys' aggression exceeded that of girls, with boys being aggressive in about 10 percent of their interactions, and girls in 6 percent. Boys' aggression occurred especially in predominantly male groups.

In another cross-cultural study 3-to-5-year-old children were observed in social interaction in London and among the !Kung (Blurton Jones & Konner, 1973). Two observers using different techniques—one recording facial expressions, the other physical acts—both found boys to be more aggressive in both cultures. The excess of physical aggression in males is a highly consistent finding (Edwards, 1993).

## General Biological Mechanisms

While aggression is predominantly male, females have the basic aggressive equipment and actions, which they show in maternal aggression, competition, dominance interactions, and other situations (Hrdy, 1981; Preuschoft, Paul, & Kuester, 1998), including self-defense against males (Hrdy, 1977, 1999; B. Smuts, 1992; B. B. Smuts & Smuts, 1993). Both the shared physiological substrates and those that differentiate males from females are increasingly well understood.

In the late 1930s Heinrich Klüver and Paul Bucy did experiments on monkeys in which they removed the end of each temporal lobe (Kluver & Bucy, 1939). This damaged several structures, including the amygdala and hippocampus, and resulted in tameness, rare in rhesus monkeys. This was not because of general debilitation or fear, but was specific to aggression. Later studies showed that tameness results from removal of the amygdala alone (Horel, Keating, & Misantone, 1975) and that stimulation of the ventral (lower) amygdala using the neurotransmitter glutamate produces aggression in cats (Shaikh, Schubert, & Siegel, 1994; Shaikh, Steinberg, & Siegel, 1993; Siegel, Schubert, & Shaikh, 1994). By the 1950s it was clear that damaging parts of the hypothalamus—the hub of the limbic system at the base of the brain—could make rats violent, while other hypothalamic lesions reduced violence (Ingram, 1956; Siegel, Roeling, Gregg, & Kruk, 1999). Likewise, stimulating different parts of an intact hypothalamus with electrodes could either raise or lower aggression, confirming the pivotal role of the hypothalamus in the limbic, or emotional, brain.

Lesions of the septal area caused rage (Brady & Nauta, 1953), and combined with the effects of amygdala damage, this led to a model of aggression in which the hypothalamus was regulated by higher limbic structures (Smythies, 1970). The amygdala could increase aggression by exciting parts of the hypothalamus and the septal area (or other limbic areas) could reduce it through other hypothalamic areas. Some specifics are controversial, and refinements have been added. For example, the central amygdala can inhibit aggression even as the ventral amygdala enhances it. This inhibition seems to use enkephalin, an opiatelike neurotransmitter, to calm the aggressive circuits (Siegel et al., 1994). But the broader idea is accepted: Aggression requires the hypothalamus, which integrates messages from other parts of the limbic system, biasing it toward or away from violence (Siegel et al., 1999).

To trigger muscle action and arouse the circulatory system, the hypothalamus must relay its message to the spinal cord and out to the periphery. It does this through the central gray area of the midbrain (Flynn, Venegas, Foote, & Edwards, 1970). Rage and fighting can be teased apart with selective brain damage. Cats may have real rage as a prelude to attack, as shown by expressions under sympathetic nervous system control—widening of the eyes, growling and hissing, arching the back, and erection of the fur. But after certain brain lesions they will have only "sham rage"—the same expressive signs never followed by attack (Flynn et al., 1970). This distinction has held up in subsequent research (Panksepp, 1971, 1998; Schubert, Shaikh, & Siegel, 1996).

In essence, exciting the medial hypothalamus causes affective, emotional attack, while exciting the lateral hypothalamus causes a cool, calculated attack. The two output circuits traverse different parts of the midbrain (Schubert et al., 1996), which in turn control parts of the brain stem and spinal cord that produce the attack itself as well as the sympathetic nervous system that expresses angry emotions.

People with brain tumors causing damage to the medial hypothalamus or the septal area have trouble controlling aggression, especially if provoked by a real or imagined insult (Albert, Walsh, & Jonik, 1993). This supports the idea that the septal area inhibits rage and the amygdala stimulates it, both perhaps by regulating the medial (middle) hypothalamus. In some cases, a slowly growing tumor in the limbic system causes increasing irrational aggression over a number of years, while removing the tumor reduces aggression. Charles Whitman, a young Texan who killed his mother and his wife, then climbed a university tower and shot 38 people, was found at autopsy to have a rare brain tumor that may have chronically irritated his amygdala (Malamud, 1967; Moyer, 1987, p. 86).

Although epileptics are very rarely violent, a few with seizures in the amygdala have aggressive outbursts. People with records of criminal aggression have more EEG abnormalities than others, even other kinds of criminals (Elst, Woermann, Lemieux, Thompson, & Trimble, 2000; Moyer, 1987, p. 90; Trimble & Tebartz Van Elst, 1999). Finally, a brain basis for human aggression is supported by large studies of Vietnam veterans over two or more decades since sustaining head injuries in that war. Compared to veterans with other brain damage, those with lower frontal lobe damage are more likely to have outbursts of rage at family members, friends, and colleagues (Grafman et al., 1996). These outbursts are fortunately more often verbal than physical, but they are severe and strain relationships and are consistent with the idea that the ventral part of the frontal lobe is the cortex of the limbic system, monitoring and regulating emotional activity.

Brain imaging studies of violent individuals also suggest that lower activity in the left frontal and temporal lobes reduces inhibition, leading to outbursts of physical rage (Niehoff, 1999, p. 110; Volkow & Tancredi, 1987). In an evaluation of 31 murderers, psychiatrist Jonathan Pincus found that frontal lobe damage often contributed to violent tendencies. But in the presence of two other factors—paranoid symptoms and childhood abuse—the chance of violence became very high. Thus a growing appreciation of the role of frontal lobe dysfunction in violence (Hawkins & Trobst, 2000) can now be tempered with an understanding of other psychiatric and experiential factors. Such studies are multiplying rapidly, and with the growing precision of imaging techniques, will soon form the core of our understanding of how the brain generates violence.

The most controversial insights have come from psychosurgery, a treatment with a long, dismal history. Today there are far more subtle forms of brain surgery and a growing acknowledgment that some surgical interventions may be justified in severe psychiatric illness unresponsive to other treatments (Ballantine, 1986; Rodgers, 1992). One type has been found helpful in the treatment of a very rare violent form of epilepsy (Delgado-Escueta, 1981; Pincus, 1981). As noted above, the vast majority of severe epileptics show no violence, but in a few rare cases the seizure is directed outward and can result in violent attacks.

A handful of patients in the United States and more in Japan and in some European and Latin American countries have received surgical treatment for this disorder (Ballantine, Bouckoms, Thomas, & Giriunas, 1987; Rodgers, 1992; Sano, 1962). One approach used in Japan and Argentina in treating extreme and frequent violent fits is destruction of an area 3 to 5 millimeters in diameter in the back of the medial hypothalamus (Sano, 1962). Another approach used in Japan, India, and the United States has been to damage portions of the amygdala (Mark & Ervin, 1970). Such procedures must be viewed skeptically, but they are part of a growing understanding of how violence is instantiated in the brain.

Another approach is neurochemical (Miczek, Weerts, Haney, & Tidey, 1994). Lab animals are given drugs that influence neurons or neurotransmitters in the junctions between them. For example, mice kept in isolation for several weeks have an increased tendency to fight, and they have either different levels or turnover of several neurotransmitters (Cairns, Hood, & Midlam, 1985). Furthermore, drugs directly affecting those neurotransmitters can increase or decrease isolation-induced fighting (Panksepp, 1998; Valzelli, 1973). (Genetic studies, including those involving gene manipulation, must often use isolation to bring out the added aggressiveness, further proof of the power of this experience, Maxson, 2000.)

In many species reduced brain serotoninactivity lowers the threshold for aggressive reactions to frustration. In humans as in other mammals, decreased serotonin processing is reflected in lower levels of the serotonin metabolite 5-HIAA. Impulsively violent and antisocial individuals have low levels (Coccaro, 1995; Coccaro, Kavoussi, & Lesser, 1992; Coccaro et al., 1997), a relationship seen in children as well as adults (van Goozen, Matthys, Cohen-Kettenis, Westenberg, & van Engeland, 1999). Since the old association between aggression and a high rate of norepinephrine activity has also held up in other studies (Eichelman, 1992; Eichelman & Thoa, 1973), serotonin and norepinephrine may balance each other in controlling violent tendencies.

Drugs that raise serotonin levels increase a male monkey's chance of becoming dominant (Raleigh et al., 1995; Raleigh, McGuire, Brammer, Pollack, & Yuwiler, 1991), which seems at first to contradict the studies showing that lower 5-HIAA predicts violence. But *impulsive* aggression does not lead to a stable dominant role. Males must win fights to become dominant, but they must pick them sensibly, which means controlling rage. The same pattern has been found among females in two different macaque species; females with low 5-HIAA levels showed more evidence of high-intensity aggression, escalated aggression, fight wounds requiring medical attention, and lower status in the hierarchy (Westergaard, Suomi, Higley, & Mehlman, 1999).

## Male-Specific Mechanisms

Sex hormones, especially testosterone, have been repeatedly shown to affect aggression in animals. Testosterone promotes and/or facilitates aggression, certainly in males and possibly in females (J. M. Dabbs & Dabbs, 2000; J. M. J. Dabbs, Carr, Frady, & Riad, 1995; J. M. J. Dabbs & Hargrove, 1997). In various species testosterone injections can increase aggression and male castration can decrease it (Niehoff, 1999). Although it is not clear how testosterone affects aggression circuits in the brain, we know that testosterone injection lowers the firing threshhold for fibers in the stria terminalis (Kendrick & Drewitt, 1979), a pathway from the amygdala to the hypothalamus.

Human studies are more complex, but there is ample evidence that normal levels of testosterone at least facilitate aggression (J. M. Dabbs & Dabbs, 2000). Some studies also suggest that steroid treatment, whether of androgen deficient men, normal athletes, or ordinary volunteers, can increase aggressive tendencies (Su et al., 1993). Conversely, aggression can be reduced by antiandrogen treatment or by a drug that blocks the gonadotropin-releasing hormone, the ultimate regulator of testosterone (Loosen, Purdon, & Pavlou, 1994). In James Dabbs's study of 4,000 army veterans, their natural testosterone level predicted their antisocial behavior (J. M. Dabbs & Morris, 1990). Significantly, it did so more strongly among poorer veterans, suggesting that in a worse environment biological differences matter more. In another criminal population, high testosterone level was associated with more violent and aggressive crimes during adolescence (Kreuz & Rose, 1972). Also, a large, long-term study of Norwegian school bullies found testosterone to be a significant predictor of bullying, along with several social and psychological variables (Olweus, 1988; Olweus, Mattson, Schalling, & Low, 1980, 1988). Finally, testosterone level helps predict aggressive behavior in 5-to-11-year-old boys, especially those of lower cognitive ability (Chance, Brown, Dabbs, & Casey, 2000).

There has also been some cross-cultural testing of the testosterone-aggression relationship. A study of !Kung hunter-gatherers showed that hunting changes testosterone levels in a manner suggesting exercise rather than aggression (Worthman & Konner, 1987), but a later study found that more violent !Kung men, many of whom had scars from fights, had androgen levels correlated with their frequency of fighting (Christiansen & Winkler, 1992). This pair of findings suggests that in human hunter-gatherers as in other predators the biology of prey-killing is quite different from that of defensive aggression.

These are *activational effects* of testosterone, so-called because they activate existing neural circuits, but equally important are the *organizational effects* occurring much earlier in life. Aggression in adulthood is influenced by the amount of testosterone circulating very early in development (before birth in monkeys and just after birth in rats), and this effect is almost certainly the result of long-lasting changes in the brain (Collaer & Hines, 1995; Gorski, 1996). We know that preschool-age boys are more aggressive than girls at an age when circulating androgen levels are very low in both sexes. A classic experiment suggests that this difference is not due to differential rearing (Chamove, Harlow, & Mitchell, 1967). Rhesus monkeys were raised in total social isolation with no sex role training and no chance to identify with a parent. At age 3 each monkey was put in a room with an infant monkey of randomly chosen sex. Females cradled and cuddled the infant more while males hit the infant more, and the difference was highly significant.

Growing evidence suggests that structural brain differences help account for this and related findings (Gorski, 1996, 2000). As early as 1973 it was shown that there are structural differences between male and female brains (Raisman & Field, 1973). In the preoptic area of the hypothalamus male and female rats differed in the density of connections among local nerve cells. In addition, castrating males just after birth left them with the female pattern, and injection of testosterone into females just after birth gave them the male pattern (McEwen, 1978; Reinisch, 1974). This discovery helped explain the already established fact that in mice, rats, dogs, monkeys, and other animals testosterone and related male hormones, given to female young at birth or earlier, suppress female sexual postures and in some species abolish sexual cycling. In males, castration or an antitestosterone drug in early development suppresses normal male sexual behavior later in adulthood, despite replacement therapy with testosterone in adulthood. One of the key experiments in monkeys gave male hormones to female fetuses before birth (Goy, 1970). As juveniles, but before puberty initiated the activational effects of testosterone, these females showed a level of aggressive (rough-and-tumble) play between the ordinarily low female level and the much higher male level.

These and many other studies supported the view that preadolescent gender differences in aggressiveness were as biological in origin as the more easily understood postadolescent ones. Over the ensuing decades the mechanism of the early organizational effects became clearer. Application of relevant hormones to slices of the neonatal mouse hypothalamus produced more and faster-growing extensions of neurons (Toran-Allerand, 1976). Later studies showed that the genes turned on by the hormone make proteins for nerve cell growth, which direct the cell in building extensions that will become axons and dendrites (Toran-Allerand, 1996).

Do similar processes take place in humans? Doubts about this were partly dispelled by studying the condition and clinical treatment of people with anomalies of sexual and gender development. In one such condition, the adrenogenital syndrome, a mutation damages one enzyme in the adrenal cortex (Baker, 1980; Collaer & Hines, 1995; Ehrhardt, 1975), and this produces abnormally large quantities of testosterone. For girls with the syndrome, levels of the hormone are high throughout gestation. After birth the condition can be corrected through surgery and medical treatment, so that the hormone's effects are purely prenatal. Yet at age 10 and in adulthood these girls are psychologically different from their sisters and from unrelated controls. By their own and their mothers' reports, they play less with dolls, are more "tomboyish," and express less desire to be married and have children when they grow up. Studies on several samples of girls with adrenal hyperplasia corrected at birth showed similar results on toy preference, rough-and-tumble play, and preference for playing with boys (Hines & Kaufman, 1994).

A careful review of available studies of clinical syndromes and drug effects that could correspond to early masculinization of the brain concluded that "[e]vidence is most consistent for a developmental influence of androgens on sex-typical play. There also is some evidence supporting a role for androgens in the development of tendencies toward aggression ..." (Collaer & Hines, 1995). Combined with increasing animal evidence and direct evidence of sex differences in the human brain, these findings suggested that in humans, too, some psychosexual divergence may be due to masculinizing hormones acting on the brain before birth.

## Genetic Contributions

We have long known that aggression and violence have partly genetic bases in animals. A classic experiment took 14 purebred mouse strains and, after weeks of social isolation, brought 4 males together from each strain and counted the instances of chase, attack, and fight (Southwick, 1970). Scores ranged from less than 10 to 80, an almost tenfold difference. Blending of strains showed that aggressive genes are dominant, with the young resembling the more aggressive parent. In some crosses, unexpected synergistic effects occurred, producing offspring much more aggressive than either parent. Crosses drew either the father or mother from a given strain, so it was possible to take into account parenting or intrauterine effects. Cross-fostering infants of one strain to parents from another supported both possibilities. It was possible for the foster mother to influence the offspring, but some important strain differences in chase, attack, and fight were due to genetic effects alone.

Modern methods of gene technology have pointed to at least 15 genes on two chromosomes that affect aggression in male mice (Maxson, 2000) and additional ones that affect female aggression as well. Aggressiveness genes (Hen, 1996) include one that codes for a receptor for serotonin and another that makes an enzyme that removes norepinephrine and some other neurotransmitters. There are others, however, and they run the gamut of mechanisms for how genes influence behavior (Maxson, 2000). Take another example: a gene on the X chromosome codes for an androgen receptor. In wild mice the receptor combines with androgens, and the resulting molecule switches on several other genes in certain brain cells. But mutations prevent the combination of androgen and receptor and consequently produce peaceful male mice, even after social isolation. Chromosome 10 carries an estrogen receptor that works similarly, but in this case the mutant females are more aggressive than the wild ones—the opposite of the impact of the same mutation in males. Another way to increase aggression is by knocking out or inserting genes for the neurotransmitter enzyme monoamine oxidase A and the 1B subtype of the serotonin receptor. Knocking out an enzyme that makes nitric oxide yields a mouse that attacks more often and more lethally, by directing its bites more precisely at the opponent's neck instead of occasionally drifting down his back. Knocking out one of the histamine receptors, in contrast, decreases aggression.

Molecular genetic studies are also proceeding in humans. In a large extended family in the Netherlands, a new form of mild mental retardation was found to be X-linked, thus far more common in males (Brunner, 1993). It is also associated with attempted murder, rape, arson, and other acts of impulsive aggression that were not attributable to low intelligence alone. The syndrome was traced to a flawed enzyme, a type of monoamine oxidase that helps remove the neurotransmitters serotonin, norepinephrine, and dopamine. In a separate study, knockout mice were created with a defective gene for the same enzyme (Cases et al., 1995). Their brains had up to nine times the normal level of serotonin and twice the normal level of norepinephrine. The defect produced adult male mice that fought more with each other and were more likely to force their attentions on unwilling females—two symptoms shown by men in the Dutch kindred. And in another study of genetically engineered mice with this enzyme defect, drugs antagonistic to serotonin abolished their exaggerated aggressiveness (Shih et al., 1999).

Most recently the variants of this gene have been studied in many primate species, and it was shown that the human variants are present in all apes and Old World monkeys, but not in New World monkeys. This suggests that the mutation appeared after the split between Old World and New World monkeys but before the split between Old World monkeys and apes, around 25 million years ago. It has been suggested that this very old mutation is maintained at some level in the populations of Old World primates (including humans) because while some aggression is adaptive, impulsive or exaggerated aggression is not, maintaining the gene while limiting its spread (Gibbons, 2004b). This finding strengthens the research strategy of using monkeys and apes as models of aggression in humans.

In addition, a different study showed that mice lacking one serotonin receptor, the 1B, are very aggressive (Saudou et al., 1994). This subtype is abundant in the central gray of the midbrain—just the region that processes aggressive signals from the hypothalamus. Of course, the genetic change is only the first step in a developmental process. The Dutch men were mildly retarded and isolative, with occasional outbursts of very serious aggression. Their self-imposed isolation may have gradually increased their tendency to aggression, as it does in males of many other species. All genetics is developmental genetics and therefore assumes environmental influences in the growing fetus, infant, and child. But that does not make it meaningless to assert genetic influence. In normal human beings, traditional studies leave little doubt as to the power of genes in aggression, almost certainly many different ones (Gottesman, Goldsmith, & Carey, 1997). Some of these affect general traits that may influence the growth of aggression, such as pain sensitivity, impulse control, sensation seeking, and frustration tolerance. Such traits in a toddler could interact with environmental stress or cultural shaping to produce a variety of violent patterns, even without any dedicated brain circuitry for violence.

## How Does Aggression Become War?

It has been aptly said that in considering the nature of organized violence, "organized" is more important than "violence." Actually both words denote necessary contributions. It has also been said that war is only remotely related to individual violence, because it rests on discipline, planning, and rational strategy rather than on emotions such as anger and rage. This section will argue that the latter claim is wrong, although the emotional basis of war goes far beyond anger.

Groups in conflict are collections of individuals who feel that they have more to gain than to lose by fighting (Bueno de Mesquita, 1981; Low, 1993). In cultures of anthropological interest, by far the best predictor of war is the threat of natural disasters (e.g., weather or pests) that destroy food supplies (C. R. Ember & Ember, 1992), although this does not explain war in all settings (Wiessner & Tumu, 1998). But there does not need to be a conscious awareness of the role played by scarcity. In addition, a large proportion of societies that make war take women as captives, and these women often become wives or concubines (Divale, 1973; White, 1988).

Consider a foot soldier. Going to war, he runs the risk of being maimed or killed, but against the background risks of life throughout most of history this may not have been excessive. He also stands to gain the material and sexual spoils of war, together with other rewards at home, and may be punished if he refuses or fails to perform well. This evolutionary risk-benefit analysis leads to and helps explain the subtler psychological gains. The soldier gets to turn his back on the thousand frustrations of home life, while elevating his importance in the eyes of his family; to commit for a time to a purpose that seems pure and clear; to experience the unique excitement of martial adventure; to express and assuage deep-seated frustration and grief; and to achieve the enduring satisfaction and respect for having faced and triumphed over fear and having been willing to risk his life, which may become a lasting source of strength.

Others in the military hierarchy, including the leaders at the top, have purposes of their own, and how these articulate with those of the foot soldier is of the essence of the difference between individual and group conflict. All societies have individual violence, but some small-scale societies appear to have no organized violence in traditional settings. As noted, this is due to lack of organization, not lack of violence. Nor do they lack a propensity for hostility toward identified enemies. Throughout the world, from hunter-gatherer societies through nation-states, people show fear and contempt for neighboring peoples who are culturally or racially different, forming a nested hierarchy of tribal animosities. Karl von Clausewitz said that war is the continuation of political activity by other means, but even modern political conflict in many parts of the world conceals tribal or ethnic conflict that is older and more deeply felt (Ferguson & Whitehead, 1992/1999).

### *Pseudospeciation*: Dichotomizing the Social World

The psychoanalyst Erik Erikson called the process of dichotomizing the social world *pseudospeciation*. The Greeks had their barbarians, the Jews their Gentiles, the Christians their heathen. Ilongot headhunters feud murderously and enduringly with neighboring groups, while traditional highland New Guinea is a patchwork of homicidal enmities (Wiessner & Tumu, 1998). Even the !Kung refer to themselves as "the true people" and others as "strange" or "different." Violent tribal standoffs have occurred recently or are occurring throughout the world: Bosnians, Serbs, and Croats in the former Yugoslavia; Azerbaijanis and Armenians in Georgia; Sikh, Moslem, and Hindu in India and Pakistan; Sinhalese and Tamil in Sri Lanka; Sunni and Shi'a in the Islamic world; Jews and Arabs in Israel; Arabs and Black Africans in the Sudan; Catholics and Protestants in Northern Ireland. Many of these cases are the vestiges of conflicts that were even worse in the past and have the potential to flare up fully again. There is no people in the world that is free of such dichotomies, and they have roots in very basic types of societies. Among the Nuer, Nilotic cattle-herders of the Sudan, "either a man is a kinsman ... or he is a person to whom you have no reciprocal obligations and whom you treat as a potential enemy" (Evans-Pritchard, 1940, p. 183).

Chimpanzees' incipient level of organized violence is a rudimentary version of what is observed in many small-scale societies (Johnson & Earle, 1987; Knauft, 1987). The transition from small to larger chiefdoms appears to be associated with the emergence of full-scale warfare, and this development may have led to the emergence of the state (Earle, 1991). Societies become more complex as their population increases, with such features as social stratification, division of labor, and taxation playing increasing roles. Closely allied military and religious hierarchies form the core of these societies, which continue to grow by conquest, but this process did not require the state. The Nuer, with their clear concept of who is an enemy and with certain advances in military recruitment, became an effective organization for predatory expansion at the expense of their Dinka neighbors, despite having a relatively modest level of social complexity (Kelly, 1985; Sahlins, 1961).

With the advent of true religious and military hierarchies, this pattern becomes much clearer: Although cross-cultural studies show that military prowess leads to expanding boundaries whether the expansionist group is decentralized like the Nuer or centralized like the Aztec, it is also clear that more centralized political systems tend to have greater military sophistication (Otterbein, 1970). The hierarchical society involved in predatory expansion comes increasingly to resemble a state rather than a tribe or chiefdom. At this point we have the level of social organization exhibited by the great antagonists of the Bronze Age, and from there it is a small step—mainly technological—to the antagonisms of modern states (Cook, 2003; Schmookler, 1983). Nationalism, Toynbee said, is new wine in the old bottles of tribalism (Toynbee, 1972).

These antagonisms reflect another basic human tendency already alluded to: the inclination to dichotomize the social world—actually just a special case of dualistic thought (Douglas, 1966; Levi-Strauss, 1962; Maybury-Lewis & Almagor, 1989). Night and day, human and animal, village and "bush," tame and wild, good and evil, male and female, right and left—these are but a few of the dichotomies that have not just been recognized but institutionalized and invested with emotion in a wide range of human cultures. What is often perceptually a weak dichotomy or even a continuum is exaggerated by cognitive processes that make it seem to be two irreconcilable principles divided by an unbridgeable gulf.

It is not clear why the human mind has this propensity, but it may have to do with our low tolerance for ambiguity and for what psychologists call cognitive dissonance (Festinger, 1957). In phonetics, dichotomization is necessary for meaning; there may be a physical continuum between $p$ and $b$, but we must make up our minds which one we are hearing in order to have a language that works (Jakobson & Halle, 1956/1971). Something similar may be true in other areas of cognition. In many situations during our evolution it must have been desirable to make decisions quickly, no doubt facilitated by an algorithm with two clear choices. Confronted with a stimulus, we have first to classify it as familiar or strange and then decide between approach and avoidance. Discrimination, desirable in matters of taste, becomes unfortunate, even tragic, in social classification. Yet such dichotomies as kin and nonkin, us and them, real people versus barbarians or strangers are almost universal tendencies.

Of course, these dichotomies are not merely cognitive, they have an emotional valence. Fear, and fear of the strange in particular, is a basic characteristic of nervous systems. Many studies, from those of how infants respond to novelty to those using brain stimulation in cats, have revealed a continuum from attention through arousal to fear. Mild stimulation of the amygdala can produce alertness while stronger stimulation in the same brain region can produce fear (Ursin & Kaada, 1960). Novelty, depending on the context, can produce attention or fear in infants.

It may be that our basic stance toward the world—mild arousal and attentiveness to every new stimulus we experience, in order to process it and react to it—is on a physiological continuum with a flight from danger. For infants, the second half of the first year is dominated by new distinctions in the social world, as a previously generalized responsiveness to people is reshaped by wariness toward or fear of strangers and by attachment to a primary caregiver (Bowlby, 1969–1977; Lewis & Rosenblum, 1973). The tendency to flee to a protector is bound up with the tendency to fear, and since the world contains many surprises, we probably all have some of both in our everyday lives. If the infant's fear of strangers is transformed in adulthood into something like contempt, then the flight to a protector may take the form of obedience, conformity, chauvinism, or loyalty.

### Group Psychology, Mass Psychology

Because of this inclination, people may submerge their independence in the purposes of a higher authority, a collective will, or both. The fear and anxiety we feel even in everyday life, exacerbated by the impact of a complex world on our relatively simple minds, may be assuaged by unburdening ourselves of responsibility for our actions. We reduce this sense of responsibility and its concomitant anxiety by hewing to a set of rules, participating in collective action, or following a leader. Rules, although they can become rigid, are the most benign of the three options.

More ominous by far is the mass or mob psychology that can sometimes emerge from group loyalty and collective action. Charles Mackay, in his nineteenth century classic *Extraordinary Popular Delusions and the Madness of Crowds*, describes it:

> In reading the history of nations, we find that whole communities suddenly fix their minds upon one object, and go mad in its pursuit; that millions of people become simultaneously impressed with one delusion, and run after it, till their attention is caught by some new folly more captivating than the first. We see one nation suddenly seized, from its highest to its lowest members, with a fierce desire of military glory; another as suddenly becoming crazed upon a religious scruple; and neither of them recovering its senses until it has shed rivers of blood and sowed a harvest of groans and tears, to be reaped by its posterity. ... Men, it has been well said, think in herds; it will be seen that they go mad in herds, while they only recover their senses slowly, and one by one. (1841/1980, pp. xix–xx)

This passage was gravely prophetic of the calamitous twentieth century.

Mackay treats an impressive variety of social phenomena, in itself instructive: lynch mobs and witch hunts; reckless investment schemes such as the South Sea Bubble and the Tulip mania; fads, pilgrimages, revolutions, and wars; all these and more are grist for an analytic mill concerned with the muting of individual will. The mass hysteria of collective violence is what concerns us here, but we should view it in the context of a general human susceptibility to psychological and behavioral contagion, now well demonstrated by psychologists (Hatfield, Cacioppo, & Rapson, 1994). That is, the idea that one should bathe in certain holy waters, wear a bustle or miniskirt, or hate and persecute a particular group of people can take hold of a person for no greater reason than that it has already taken hold of so many others. The fear of ostracism, of being left behind—in effect, the fear of being different and incurring the same wrath—must play a role.

Humans are not really herding animals but (by evolutionary history) members of small groups with complex social dynamics. In our original small groups the rudiments of these processes were no doubt present. A classic experiment in social psychology showed that a subject will predictably deny the evidence of his or her perception of even something as simple as the relative length of lines if a small group of others (confederates of the experimenter) make clear their own denial (Asch, 1951). This repeatedly proven tendency to conform is close to the heart of group psychology. But the "crazed" mass psychology described by Mackay may result in part from population densities that violate the small-group dynamics we evolved with.

Whether in large or small groups, a common manifestation of mass psychology is the identification and destruction of enemies. This contagious enmity takes two forms. The first identifies weak internal enemies, isolates them, and destroys them. Lynch mobs, witch hunts, inquisitions, and genocide are examples. The enemies are viewed as strange, confusing, evil, and dangerous to the spiritual and physical life of the larger group. Their elimination becomes a ritual of purification and is seen as an absolute good (Burkert, Smith, Hamerton-Kelly, & Girard, 1987; Girard, 1979). The second form identifies external enemies, similarly viewed but more capable of defending themselves. The concept of holy war is related to traditions of animal and human sacrifice in ancient societies, partaking of a widespread human attitude that bloodshed is sacred. In a strange reversal, a war *becomes* sacred because of the sacrifice of lives.

Biblical and many other sacrifices attempt to purify the community by exporting sins to the victim. Ilongot headhunting occupies an intermediate position between sacrifice and war, because it is directed against external enemies, yet "it involves the taking of a human life with a view toward cleansing the participants of the contaminating burdens of their own lives" (Rosaldo, 1980, p. 140). Through a process of *mimesis* (Girard, 1979), the collective emotions of two groups exchanging reciprocal contagious enmity eventually justify each other: that is, what may have begun as an irrational fear becomes a rational one as each side contemplates the threat that stems from the growing fear and hatred in the other.

Experiments in social psychology have illuminated the process of group formation and of the emergence and consequences of the us-them distinction. One, known as the Robbers Cave Experiment, addressed questions of group identity and competition through research on young boys (Sherif, Harvey, White, Hood, & Sherif, 1961). Muzafer Sherif led a group that studied 22 average, normal 11-year-old boys, all middle-class Protestants with similar educational backgrounds. During the summer between the fifth and sixth grades, the boys were taken to a 200-acre camp in the Robbers Cave State Park, a densely wooded section of the San Bois Mountains of southeastern Oklahoma.

In Stage 1 of the study, which lasted a week, the boys were randomly divided into two matched groups that differed in no measurable way. Competition was discouraged and there were joint activities, but the groups nevertheless began to show signs of competitive attitudes—they named themselves Eagles and Rattlers, spoke disparagingly of each other, and began to react territorially to each other's "incursions."

In Stage 2, a tournament of planned contests was set up between the two groups—baseball, tug-of-war, tent-pitching, skits, treasure hunts, and cabin inspections. Trophies, medals, and four-bladed knives were offered as prizes.

> After the second day of the tournament, the "good sportsmanship" stated in specific words during the initial period and exhibited after the first contests ... gave way, as event followed event, to increased name-calling, hurling invectives, and derogation of the out-group to the point that the groups became more and more reluctant to have anything to do with one another. (p. 101)

In time, "derogatory stereotypes and negative attitudes toward the out-group were crystallized" (p. 208). Again, there were no differences between these groups, yet bigotry was easily created by arbitrarily assigning and labeling matched boys.

But in Stage 3, the two groups were reblended and given important goals to reach together—such as fixing the water tank that had supposedly been damaged by vandals, so that all the boys would have water to drink. This third stage greatly reduced prejudice and conflict in just a few days; while at the end of Stage 2 there was practically no crossover between the two groups in the question of whom the boys considered their friends, there was considerable healing of this split by the end of Stage 3.

Similar findings have been repeated many times with adults and under a variety of more controlled conditions (Robinson & Tajfel, 1997; Tajfel, 1982). They strongly confirm the ease with which prejudice against arbitrarily formed out-groups emerges, the relative ease with which the prejudice can be reversed if and when in-group and out-group members are brought together again, and the exacerbation of the prejudice by giving the in-group members frustrating experiences or experimentally lowering their self-esteem (Robinson & Tajfel, 1997; Tajfel, 1982).

### The Role of Leaders and Authority

Mackay's observations on mass or crowd psychology have been confirmed and extended (Canetti, 1981; Hatfield et al., 1994), and it is reasonable to think of an army at war as a kind of controlled mass psychology. Yet a human group, however large, is not a herd and may not be merely a mob if it has a leader. Freud's monograph, *Group Psychology and the Analysis of the Ego* ("group psychology" being a questionable translation of the German word, *Massenpsychologie*) takes the view that mass psychology operates fundamentally in relation to a leader (Freud, 1922/1949). Still, the submerging of individual will is similar:

> The lack of independence and initiative in their members, the similarity in the reactions of all of them ... the weakness of intellectual ability, the lack of emotional restraint, the inclination to exceed every limit in the expression of emotion and to work it off completely in the form of action ... . (pp. 81–82)

Freud does not, however, limit his analysis to extraordinary popular contagions:

We are reminded of how many of these phenomena of dependence are part of the normal constitution of human society, of how little originality and courage are to be found in it, of how much every individual is ruled by those attitudes of the group mind which exhibit themselves in such forms as racial characteristics, class prejudices, public opinion, etc. (p. 82)

He views group psychology as a type of hypnosis:

Hypnosis is not a good object for comparison with a group formation, because it is truer to say that it is identical with it. Out of the complicated fabric of the group it isolates one element for us—the behavior of the individual to the leader. (p. 78)

He also emphasizes that the hypnotic power of suggestion is exercised not only by the leader but mutually by rank-and-file group members. Thus the flight to a protector —what Erich Fromm called the "escape from freedom" (Fromm, 1994)—is a flight to the certainty of leader and group alike. Freud's two main illustrations are not mobs but armies and churches, both of which have an us-them distinction as a core feature. Groups and leaders hypnotize their followers, sometimes in isolation but often in relation to an enemy.

Nowhere in the psychological literature is the submerging of individual will to authority clearer than in Stanley Milgram's experiments in which naive subjects were ordered to give presumed electric shocks to an unseen person they thought was another subject but was really a confederate of the experimenter (Milgram, 1963; Milgram, 1974). Most people studied gave what they believed were very dangerous shocks simply because they were ordered to do so by an authority figure. "What is the limit of such obedience?" the experimenter later asked (p. 188).

At many points we attempted to establish a boundary. Cries from the victim were inserted; they were not good enough. The victim claimed heart trouble; subjects still shocked him on command. The victim pleaded to be let free, and his answers no longer registered on the signal box; subjects continued to shock him. (p. 188)

Adding the encouragement of peers to the orders of the experimenter made the obedience even more reflexive. "And what is it we have seen?" Milgram asks:

Not aggression, for there is no anger, vindictiveness, or hatred in those who shocked the victim. Men do become angry; they do act hatefully and explode in rage against others. But not here. Something far more dangerous is revealed: the capacity for man to abandon his humanity, indeed, the inevitability that he does so, as he merges his unique personality into larger institutional structures.

This is a fatal flaw nature has designed into us, and which in the long run gives our species only a modest chance for survival. (p. 188)

Freud the psychoanalyst and Milgram the social psychologist both write of the way nature or evolution has designed us, and their assessment does not contradict current views in evolutionary psychology. In modern terms, certain special individuals, with personalities unrepresentative of their populations but with views that tap into the worst in human nature, can sway large groups of people in unfortunate directions.

## Does Competition for Resources Lead to War?

As previously noted, cross-cultural analysis of hundreds of societies of anthropological interest shows that scarcity resulting from natural disasters, and the fear of such scarcity, form the single best predictor of the frequency of war, explaining fully 50 percent of the variance (C. R. Ember & Ember, 1992). In the long archeological record of violence, it appears to some authorities that "ecological imbalance ... is the fundamental cause of warfare" (LeBlanc & Register, 2003, p. 69).

This idea is not new. In 1798 Thomas Malthus published an essay on population based on two facts: that we need food, and that "the passion between the sexes is necessary and will remain" (Malthus, 1798, p. 14). He predicted a *geometric* progression of human numbers against an *arithmetic* increase in food, with eventual catastrophic results. Today many believe that Malthus has been proved wrong. The population has increased geometrically since he wrote, but so has the food supply, and the projected disaster has therefore not occurred. Worldwide breeding has slowed, and the population "bomb" will be defused during this century.

This view is naive and dangerous. It misses three key points. First, as archeologists have definitively shown since Malthus's *Essay*, the catastrophe of overpopulation, diminishing agricultural returns, ecological destruction, and population crash through war, disease, and famine has happened repeatedly in human history. Sites of great civilizations remind us that the process Malthus described is old, reliable, and real. The disasters that doomed such civilizations, belying their arrogance, were species-wide, but they were continual and predictable according to Malthus's reasoning (Ayres, 1999, pp. 125–131). The species persisted, but when we think of the enormous suffering of the people in those dead civilizations—the hopes dashed, the fear in their children's faces, the sight of those children succumbing to sword, plague, famine, and flame—or at a minimum, dragged from their homes to become paupers and slaves—we can wish we had done more than survive. The Malthusian cycle was not just a model of future events, it was a summary of what had already happened many times.

Second, since Malthus wrote, the process has widened and intensified. A few years after his book came out, the people of France (as Tolstoy put it) decided to go to Russia, carrying Napoleon like a flag. Europeans and then Asians overflowed into land they conveniently claimed was empty, and since it was not, proceeded to empty it by murdering its inhabitants or infecting them with deadly diseases. The English, French, Germans, Spanish, Portuguese, and Dutch went to Africa, South America, and Australia, always prepared for, and frequently carrying out, ethnic wars. In the nineteenth century the newcomers to North America brutally slaughtered one another in disagreement over the fate of the slaves they had brought from Africa. In the twentieth century, the people of Germany went to Russia twice, and France as well, shouting "Lebensraum!" The second time they murdered 11 million civilians, including 6 million Jews, which did leave them some extra living room.

The Russians built a 70-year empire on a process of *self*-destruction, killing scores of millions of their own people. The Japanese went to the South Pacific, Korea, and

China, and the French and the Americans went to Southeast Asia. From time to time the conquering peoples withdrew from exotic places they had gone to, leaving millions of confused or chaotic lives in their wake for generations. Tens, if not hundreds, of millions of people were starving at any given time. Refugee populations throughout the world swelled to enormous proportions. Genocide or something like it took place, with between hundreds of thousands and millions of civilian deaths, in Turkey, Europe, Indonesia, Uganda, Cambodia, Rwanda, and, on a smaller scale, the former Yugoslavia. In the second half of the twentieth century, an era without a major armed conflict, at least 50 million people died in small wars. The collapse of the Soviet Union and its empire left in its wake many small ethnic conflicts that had been suppressed by its power and by the large confrontational logic of the Cold War. There was no peace dividend because there was no change in the basic processes underlying war. Malthus was right. Because the slowing of human population growth will be accompanied by a proportionally larger increase in the material aspirations of the individuals added, Malthus is likely to continue to be right.

## A Tentative Model of War and Ethnic Violence

Let us pause here to sketch briefly the model of collective violence that has been presented. It holds that

1. competition between individual organisms is an intrinsic feature of animal life
2. individual violence, sometimes fatal, is a general characteristic of animal evolution and is also found in all human societies
3. common emotions including frustration, fear, and grief may predispose an individual to aggression
4. physiological, biochemical, and genetic contributions to the tendency to violence are well established
5. males are more disposed to violence than females, partly for biological reasons
6. groups in conflict are collections of individuals who feel that they have more to gain than to lose by fighting
7. a dualistic tendency in human thought exaggerates observed natural differences, including those in the social world
8. fear is a fundamental characteristic of nervous systems, and fear of the strange can stimulate and exacerbate hatreds
9. individuals readily submerge their independent wills to the will of a collective and/or an authoritative leader, partly because this reduces fear
10. the growth in human numbers, combined with periodic natural disasters, produces scarcity and the fear of scarcity, conditions favorable to war.

## A Modest Proposal

This and other analyses show that war and ethnic violence can be understood in an evolutionary context (Boehm, 2003; Fishbein & Dess, 2003; Low, 1993). It is tempting to conclude from this that war and ethnic violence will be impossible to prevent or stop. So far, they have been. In fact, they will be extremely difficult to prevent or stop, something quite different, and there is no excuse for failing to make the attempt.

Consider again the analogy. Cancer has been a scourge of humankind from time immemorial, although to different degrees in different times and places. It takes many forms, but all have in common uncontrollable growth. It has proven genetic and proven environmental contributions, although their relative importance may differ for different forms. And it has been very difficult to eliminate or even reduce, precisely because its essential processes are so similar to the processes of normal life and growth.

Nevertheless, no one is prepared to give up on the goal of cancer control. Great strides have been made, both in treatment and prevention. The treatments remain ugly and imperfect, but they are effective in some kinds of cancer and partly effective in others. Prevention has accomplished at least as much, increasingly so as we have learned that treatments are extremely difficult to develop. All the strategies and tactics we do have result from research. And part of the message of this research is that the tendency to develop cancer is inherent in human biology, and indeed in a sense it is continually happening and continually but imperfectly held in check by other biological processes. Obviously the recognition of the essential nature of cancer, using all the tools of science, has been crucial to combating it.

No one has any difficulty with this characterization, and no one offering it would ever be accused of taking a fatalistic approach to cancer or implying that nothing can be done about it. On the contrary, we all understand that only the truest possible characterization of it and of the inherent natural tendency we have to develop it can give us any hope of control.

Imagine taking the same approach to violence and war—grant that they are in some sense inherent in human nature, do everything possible to understand the process as a behavioral science problem, and set about to solve the problem based on that understanding. Suppose we were to develop a Centers for Conflict Control (CCC) or, more modestly, Centers for Conflict Intervention (CCI) analogous to the Centers for Disease Control (CDC) or the World Health Organization. The role of the CCI would be to monitor outbreaks of ethnic violence vigilantly and to respond to them before they become large. Interventions by the international community would be less dangerous and costly and more likely to succeed if they could be systematically mobilized before the violence passes a critical threshold or tipping point.

In the realm of disease, this did not happen with HIV-AIDS, but it did happen with SARS. CDC and other international health officials responded promptly to the emergence of an apparently new and deadly virus and implemented effective local, national, and transnational programs using communication, mobilization, education, quarantine, treatment, and containment. What could have been a worldwide epidemic of historic proportions remains an obscure communicable disease of interest mainly to specialists. The public health community has responded to hanta virus, ebola, Legionnaire's disease, and other epidemiological threats with similar effectiveness.

As I write, a genocidal or near-genocidal episode of ethnic violence is unfolding in Darfur, in western Sudan. What response has the world made?—some newspaper and magazine articles, a little discussion about intervention at the United Nations, and the usual hand-wringing by human rights activists and nongovernmental aid organizations. The following are excerpts from a *Washington Post* editorial:

### Crisis in Darfur

Saturday, April 3, 2004; Page A22

ACCORDING TO THE United Nations, one of the world's worst humanitarian crises now afflicts a Muslim people who face a horrific campaign of ethnic cleansing driven by massacre, rape and looting. These horrors are unfolding not, as Arab governments and satellite channels might have it, in Iraq or the Palestinian territories, but in Sudan, a member of the Arab League. Maybe because there are no Westerners or Israelis to be blamed, the crisis in Darfur, in northwestern Sudan, has commanded hardly any international attention. Though it has been going on for 14 months, the U.N. Security Council acted on it for the first time yesterday, and then only by issuing a weak president's statement. More intervention is needed, and urgently.

The victims of the ongoing war crimes are non-Arab African people who have lived in the Darfur region for centuries. In February 2003, as the Sudanese government began to negotiate a peace agreement with rebel movements representing the non-Arab peoples of the south, an insurgent movement appeared ... Early this year, after the breakdown of a cease-fire, it launched a scorched-earth offensive in the region that, according to the United Nations and human rights groups, has taken on the character of an ethnic war.

According to a report issued this week by Human Rights Watch, "the government of Sudan and allied Arab militia, called Janjaweed, are implementing a strategy of ethnic-based murder, rape and forcible displacement of civilians." More than 750,000 people have been forced from their homes, and 100,000 more have fled across the border to neighboring Chad, an area of desperate poverty and little water. The dead number in the tens of thousands. ... Humanitarian aid groups have had almost no access ....

As I write this, in September, little further has been done. On May 4, 2004, while genocide was emerging under the aegis of his government, the Sudanese envoy to the United Nations was elected to a three-year term on the U.N. Human Rights Commission.

This comes almost exactly on the tenth anniversary of the genocide in Rwanda, and as the war crimes tribunal for that massive crime is proceeding. Major General Romeo Dallaire of Canada had commanded a small contingent of 450 peacekeepers after the United Nations—and its member countries—withdrew 2,000 other troops just as the genocide was getting under way. Dallaire testified for seven days in February before the U.N. International Criminal Tribunal for Rwanda, sometimes tearfully, saying that he could have saved hundreds of thousands of people slaughtered in 1994 had he been provided with enough troops and equipment by the United Nations. Kofi Annan, now Secretary General, had been the official in charge who denied Dallaire's request and withdrew the 2,000 troops.

As shown by Samantha Power in her disturbing book on genocide, the Rwanda mass murders fell squarely in the tradition of other twentieth-century genocides—that of the Turks against the Armenians in 1915–1916, of the Germans against the Jews in the 1940s, of the Khmer Rouge against other Cambodians in the late 1970s, of Iraq against the Kurds in 1987–1988, and of the Serbs against the Bosnian Muslims in the early 1990s—in that each was preventable at an early stage *if the international community had acted*, which in each case it did not (Power, 2002).

What prevents the assembly of an apparatus of cooperating governments that could respond to the emerging Darfur genocide the way they responded to SARS? There are political obstacles of course, but those exist in the realm of disease as well —some nations have suppressed evidence of epidemics in their midst. But we have reached the point with infectious disease where globalization has become undeniably real, so we act in spite of the embarrassment and resistance of governments. And there is another reason, more relevant to the subject of this chapter: We understand the biology and epidemiology of infections and we know they are very powerful because they are natural. Perhaps when we concede the same about violence and war, we will have the resolve to respond to them in a similar way.

We can find a closer, encouraging analogy in the International Atomic Energy Agency, a transgovernmental apparatus for limiting nuclear weapons proliferation. While hampered by political factors, it has in the past two years made modest progress in assessing and perhaps limiting proliferation in Iran and Korea and in bringing about an end to Libya's nuclear weapons program. But for the untimely interference of the government the United States, it would have proved beyond reasonable doubt its claim that there were no nuclear weapons in Iraq.

Surely at least this level of success could be achieved in relation to emerging genocides—which, according to Raphael Lemkin, who coined the term, occur with almost "biological regularity" (Power, 2002, p. 22). It seems unlikely that the apparatus of intervention could be the United Nations, which has repeatedly proven itself unwilling and ineffective. Perhaps a broad group of governments of advanced countries could build this apparatus to intervene in emerging genocides, the one-sidedness of which should allow a high degree of agreement. Ethnic war on a larger military scale will be more difficult to address, and international war harder still. It is not easy to imagine an agency that could have intervened to separate Pakistan and India, two nuclear powers, when they were in a precarious confrontation. But the control of ethnic violence has to start somewhere, and a serious effort addressing emerging genocides would be a good first step.

## Conclusion

This chapter has presented a biologically based viewpoint on the human tendency to violence, as well as the more complex tendency to organized violence and specifically ethnic conflict. This viewpoint is not really new; most great religious traditions would find it familiar, since it presents in scientific language and supports with scientific evidence some very old hypotheses about human nature. These religious traditions also advise us, for example, that we should recognize our baser passions, including aggressive ones; that we should strive to subdue those passions; that we should try to love our neighbors as ourselves; and that we should not follow a multitude to do evil. Where the sentiments in the advice originate is a question in itself, but their wide occurrence in religious traditions supports the hypothesis of a violent tendency in human nature. Yet the same traditions provide justifications for sanctioned or sacred violence that give periodic opportunities for the expression of this tendency, sometimes on a very large scale.

In 1932 Albert Einstein wrote to Sigmund Freud to begin an exchange of views on war (Einstein, 1963):

> How is it that these devices succeed so well in rousing men to such wild enthusiasm, even to sacrifice their lives? Only one answer is possible. Because man has within him a lust for hatred and destruction. In normal times this passion exists in a latent state, it emerges only in unusual circumstances, but it is a comparatively easy task to call it into play and raise it to the power of a collective psychosis. (p. 202)

This is a great oversimplification, since the posited "lust for hatred and destruction" exists only under certain circumstances. A more general and easily evoked human emotional state is the anger that arises in response to frustration, fear, and grief. Combined with an easy slide into dichotomous thought that may lead to pseudospeciation, the outcome can be ethnic violence, including war or genocide.

Freud, who believed in a death instinct, expressed "entire agreement" with Einstein about the lust for destruction (Freud, 1932/1959, p. 280). They differed, however, on one important point: Freud claimed that "whatever fosters the growth of culture works at the same time against war" (p. 287). Einstein was skeptical of culture's civilizing power, and an anthropologist has to side with Einstein. Civilization emerged in ecological settings where warlike tribal groups were able to operate as organizations for predatory expansion. Karl Marx famously claimed that capitalism emerged from the mud with blood oozing from every pore. This may not be true of capitalism, but it is literally true of what we call civilization, which emerged from the mud of irrigated agricultural land acquired and protected by much slaughter. Joining military force to religious ideology, the early civilizations suppressed and pacified increasing numbers of people who, through taxation, provided resources for further expansion. Confrontation with another similar entity was the inevitable outcome. This pattern has changed little in the thousands of years leading up to the nuclear age. We flatter ourselves that we control the process, but human weakness, human nature, and human biology loom large in the risk of ethnic violence and war.

We say that we need water, food, sex, exercise, sleep, love, peace of mind, even entertainment, but we never say that we need enemies, or even that we like to have them, that they make us feel alive and give us meaning, by setting in motion certain biological processes that we do not understand but that operate deep within us, stimulating and shaping our will. We freely acknowledge that all those other needs are ones we share with other animals. But the thought that the murderous gang ambushes of chimpanzees could have anything to do with the things we think, feel, and do as we carry out ethnic violence is abhorrent to us. If we could end this denial and attain this bit of self-knowledge—accept at last, in the service of a higher good, this affront to human dignity—perhaps it would help us move toward a world where, if we could not embrace our enemies, we could at least leave them alone.

# References

Albert, D. J., Walsh, M. L., & Jonik, R. H. (1993). Aggression in humans: What is its biological foundation? *Neuroscience and Biobehavioral Reviews, 17*, 405–425.

Ardrey, R. (1963). *African genesis: A personal investigation into the animal origins and nature of man*. New York: Dell Publishing Company.

Asch, S. E. (1951). Effects of group pressure upon the modification and distortion of judgments. In H. Guetzkow (Ed.), *Groups, leadership and men* (pp. 177–190). Pittsburgh, PA: Carnegie Press.

Ayres, E. (1999). *God's last offer: Negotiating for a sustainable future*. New York/London: Four Walls Eight Windows.

Baker, S. W. (1980). Psychosexual differentiation in the human. *Biology of Reproduction, 22*, 61–72.

Ballantine, H. T. J. (1986). A critical assessment of psychiatric surgery: Past, present, and future. In P. A. Berger & K. H. Brodie (Eds.), *American handbook of psychiatry* (Vol. 8, pp. 1029–1047). New York: Basic Books.

Ballantine, H. T. J., Bouckoms, A. J., Thomas, E. K., & Giriunas, I. E. (1987). Treatment of psychiatric illness by stereotactic cingulotomy. *Biological Psychiatry, 22*, 807–819.

Betzig, L. (1992). Roman polygyny. *Ethology and Sociobiology, 13*, 309–349.

Betzig, L. (1997). Why a despot? In L. Betzig (Ed.), *Human nature: A critical reader* (pp. 399–401). New York: Oxford University Press.

Betzig, L. L. (1986). *Despotism and differential reproduction: A Darwinian view of history*. New York: Aldine.

Blurton Jones, N. G., & Konner, M. J. (1973). Sex differences in behavior of two-to-five-year-olds in London and amongst the Kalahari Desert Bushmen. In R. P. Michael & J. H. Crook (Eds.), *Comparative ecology and behavior of primates*. London: Academic Press.

Boehm, C. (2003). Global conflict resolution: An anthropological diagnosis of problems with world governance. In R. W. Bloom & N. Dess (Eds.), *Evolutionary psychology and violence: A primer for policy makers and public policy advocates* (pp. 203–237). Westport, CT: Praeger.

Bohannan, P., & American Museum of Natural History. (1967). *Law and warfare; studies in the anthropology of conflict* (1st ed.). Garden City, NY: Published for the American Museum of Natural History New York by the Natural History Press.

Bowlby, J. (1969–1977). *Attachment and loss (3 vols)* (Vol. 1). London: Hogarth Press.

Bradley, B. J., Doran-Sheehy, D. M., Lukas, D., Boesch, C., & Vigilant, L. (2004). Dispersed male networks in western gorillas. *Current Biology, 14*, 510–513.

Brady, J. V., & Nauta, W. (1953). Subcortical mechanisms in emotional behavior: Affective changes following septal forebrain lesions in the albino rat. *Journal of Comparative and Physiological Psychology, 46*, 339–346.

Brunner, H. G. (1993). Abnormal behavior associated with a point mutation in the structural gene for monoamine oxidase A. *Science, 262*, 578–580.

Bueno de Mesquita, B. (1981). *The war trap*. New Haven, CT: Yale University Press.

Burkert, W., Smith, J. Z., Hamerton-Kelly, R., & Girard, R. (1987). *Violent origins*. Stanford, CA: Stanford University Press.

Cairns, R. B., Hood, K. E., & Midlam, J. (1985). On fighting in mice: Is there a sensitive period for isolation effects? *Animal Behavior, 33*, 166–180.

Canetti, E. (1981). *Crowds and power*. New York: Continuum.

Cases, O., Seif, I., Grimsby, J., Gaspar, P., Chen, K., Pournin, S., et al. (1995). Aggressive behavior and altered amounts of brain serotonin and norepinephrine in mice lacking MAOA. *Science, 268*, 1763–1766.

Chagnon, N. A. (1968). *Yanomamo: The fierce people*. New York: Holt, Rinehart and Winston.

Chagnon, N. A. (1988). Life histories, blood revenge, and warfare in a tribal population. *Science, 239*, 985–992.

Chagnon, N. A. (1992). *Yanomamö: The last days of Eden*. San Diego, CA: Harcourt Brace.

Chamove, A., Harlow, H., & Mitchell, G. (1967). Sex differences in the infant-directed behavior of preadolescent rhesus monkeys. *Child Development, 38*, 329–335.

Chance, S. E., Brown, R. T., Dabbs, J. M., Jr., & Casey, R. (2000). Testosterone, intelligence and behavior disorders in young boys. *Personality & Individual Differences, 28*(3), 437–445.

Christiansen, K., & Winkler, E.-M. (1992). Hormonal, anthropometrical, and behavioral correlates of physical aggression in !Kung San men of Namibia. *Aggressive Behavior, 18*, 271–280.

Coccaro, E. F. (1995, January–February). The biology of aggression. *Scientific American Medicine*, 38–47.

Coccaro, E. F., Kavoussi, R. J., & Lesser, J. C. (1992). Self- and other-directed human aggression: The role of the central serotonergic system. *International Clinical Psychopharmacology, 6* (Suppl. 6), 70–83.

Coccaro, E. F., Kavoussi, R. J., Trestman, R. L., Gabriel, S. M., Cooper, T. B., & Siever, L. J. (1997). Serotonin function in human subjects: Intercorrelations among central 5-HT indices and aggressiveness. *Psychiatry Res, 73*(1–2), 1–14.

Collaer, M. L., & Hines, M. (1995). Human behavioral sex differences: A role for gonadal hormones during early development? *Psychological Bulletin, 118*(1), 55–107.

Cook, M. (2003). *A brief history of the human race*. London: Granta.

Culotta, E. (1999). Neanderthals were cannibals, bones show. *Science, 286*, 18–19.

Dabbs, J. M., & Dabbs, M. G. (2000). *Heroes, rogues, and lovers: Testosterone and behavior*. New York: McGraw Hill.

Dabbs, J. M., & Morris, R. (1990, May). Testosterone, social class, and antisocial behavior in a sample of 4,462 men. *Psychological Science, 1*(3), 209–211.

Dabbs, J. M. J., Carr, T. S., Frady, R. L., & Riad, J. K. (1995). Testosterone, crime, and misbehavior among 692 male prison inmates. *Personality and Individual Differences, 18*, 627–633.

Dabbs, J. M. J., & Hargrove, M. F. (1997). Age, testosterone, and behavior among female prison inmates. *Psychosomatic Medicine, 59*, 477–480.

D'Andrade, R. (1966). Sex differences and cultural institutions. In E. E. Maccoby (Ed.), *The development of sex differences* (pp. 178, 179, 198). Stanford, CA: Stanford University Press.

Defleur, A., White, T., Valenzi, P., Slimak, L., & Cregut-Bonnoure, E. (1999). Neanderthal cannibalism. *Science, 286*, 128–131.

DeGusta, D. (1999, October). Fijian cannibalism: Evidence from Navatu. *American Journal of Physical Anthropology, 110*, 215–241.

Delgado-Escueta, A. V. (1981). The nature of aggression during epileptic seizures. *New Eng-land Journal of Medicine, 305*, 711–716.

Dentan, R. K. (1968). *The Semai: A nonviolent people of Malaysia.* New York: Holt, Rinehart and Winston.

DeVore, I. (1965). Male dominance and mating behavior in baboons. In F. Beach (Ed.), *Sexual behavior.* New York: John Wiley.

Divale, W. (1973). *Warfare in primitive societies: A bibliography.* Santa Barbara, CA: American Bibliographic Center Clio.

Divale, W. T. (1974). Migration, external warfare, and matrilocal residence. *Behavioral Science Research, 9*, 75–133.

Douglas, M. (1966). *Purity and danger: An analysis of concepts of pollution and taboo.* New York: Praeger.

Earle, T. (Ed.). (1991). *Chiefdoms: Power, economy, and ideology.* Cambridge, England: Cambridge University Press.

Edgerton, R. B. (1992). *Sick societies: Challenging the myth of primitive harmony.* New York, Toronto: Free Press; Maxwell Macmillan Canada; Maxwell Macmillan International.

Edwards, C. P. (1993). Behavioral sex differences in children of diverse cultures: The case of nurturance to infants. In M. E. Pereira & L. A. Fairbanks (Eds.), *Juvenile primates: Life history, development, and behavior* (pp. 327–338). New York: Oxford.

Ehrhardt, A. A. (1975). Prenatal hornomal exposure and psychosexual differentiation. In E. J. Sachar (Ed.), *Topics in psychoendocrinology* (pp. 67–82). New York: Grune & Stratton.

Eibl-Eibesfeldt, I. (1979). *The biology of peace and war: Men, animals, and aggression* (E. Mosbacher, Trans.). London, England: Thames and Hudson.

Eichelman, B. (1992). Aggressive behavior: From laboratory to clinic: Quo vadit? *Archives of General Psychiatry, 49*, 488–492.

Eichelman, B., & Thoa, N. B. (1973). The aggressive monoamines. *Biological Psychiatry, 6*, 143–164.

Einstein, A. (1963). Why war? Letter to Sigmund Freud. In O. Nathan & H. Nordan (Eds.), *Einstein on peace* (pp. 186–203). London: Methuen.

Elst, L. T. v., Woermann, F. G., Lemieux, L., Thompson, P. J., & Trimble, M. R. (2000). Affective aggression in patients with temporal lobe epilepsy: A quantitative MRI study of the amygdala. *Brain, 123*(2), 234–243.

Ember, C. R. (1978). Myths about hunter-gatherers. *Ethnology, 17*(4), 439–448.

Ember, C. R., & Ember, M. (1992). Resource unpredictability, mistrust, and war: A cross-cultural study. *Journal of Conflict Resolution, 36*(2), 242–262.

Ember, M., & Ember, C. R. (1971). The conditions favoring matrilocal versus patrilocal residence. *American Anthropologist, 73*, 571–594.

Ember, M., & Ember, C. R. (1994, November). Prescriptions for peace: policy implications of cross-cultural research on war and interpersonal violence. *Cross-Cultural Research, 28*(4), 343–350.

Evans-Pritchard, E. E. (1940). *The Nuer.* New York: Oxford University Press.

Ferguson, R. B., & Whitehead, N. L. (1999). *War in the tribal zone: Expanding states and indigenous warfare.* Santa Fe, NM: School of American Research Press. (Original work published 1992)

Festinger, L. (1957). *A theory of cognitive dissonance.* Evanston, IL: Row, Peterson.

Fishbein, H. D., & Dess, N. (2003). An evolutionary perspective on intercultural conflict. In R. W. Bloom & N. Dess (Eds.), *Evolutionary psychology and violence: A primer for policy makers and public policy advocates* (pp. 157–202). Westport, CT: Praeger.

Flynn, J., Venegas, H., Foote, W., & Edwards, S. (1970). Neural mechanisms involved in a cat's attack on a rat. In R. F. Whalen, M. Thompson, M. Verzeano, & N. Weinberger (Eds.), *The neural control of behavior.* New York: Academic Press.

Freud, S. (1949). *Group psychology and the analysis of the ego* (J. Strachey, Trans.). London, England: The Hogarth Press. (Original work published 1922)

Freud, S. (1959). Why war? Letter to Albert Einstein. In J. Strachey (Ed.), *Collected papers, Vol. 5: Miscellaneous papers, 1888–1938* (pp. 273–287). New York: Basic Books. (Original work published 1932)

Fromm, E. (1994). *Escape from freedom* (1st Owl book ed.). New York: H. Holt.

Ghiglieri, M. P. (1999). *The dark side of man: Tracing the origins of male violence.* Reading, MA: Perseus Books.

Gibbons, A. (2004a). Chimpanzee gang warfare. *Science, 304,* 818–819.

Gibbons, A. (2004b). Tracking the evolutionary history of a "warrior" gene. *Science, 304,* 818.

Girard, R. (1979). *Violence and the sacred* (P. Gregory, Trans. Johns Hopkins paperbacks ed.). Baltimore: Johns Hopkins University Press.

Goodall, J. (1977). Infant killing and cannibalism in free-living chimpanzees. *Folia Primatologica 28,* 259–282.

Goodall, J. (1986). *The chimpanzees of Gombe: Patterns of behavior.* Cambridge, MA: Harvard University Press.

Goodall, J. v. L. (1979). Life and death at Gombe. *National Geographic Magazine, 155,* 592–621.

Gorski, R. A. (1996). Gonadal hormones and the organization of brain structure and function. In D. Magnusson (Ed.), *The lifespan development of individuals: Behavioral, neurobiological, and psychosocial perspectives* (pp. 315–340). New York: Cambridge University Press.

Gorski, R. A. (2000). Sexual differentiation of the nervous system. In E. R. Kandel, J. H. Schwartz, & T. M. Jessell (Eds.), *Principles of neural science* (4th ed., p. 1131). New York: McGraw-Hill.

Gottesman, I. I., Goldsmith, H. H., & Carey, G. (1997). A developmental *and* a genetic perspective on aggression. In N. L. Segal, G. E. Weisfeld, & C. C. Weisfeld (Eds.), *Uniting psychology and biology: Integrative perspectives on human development* (pp. 107–130). Washington, DC: American Psychological Association.

Goy, R. W. (1970). Experimental control of psychosexuality. *Philosophical Transactions of the Royal Society of London B, 259,* 149–162.

Grafman, J., Schwab, K., Warden, D., Pridgen, A., Brown, H. R., & Salazar, A. M. (1996). Frontal lobe injuries, violence, and aggression: A report of the Vietnam Head Injury Study. *Neurology, 46,* 1231–1238.

Hartung, J. (1992). Getting real about rape. *Behavioral and Brain Sciences, 15*(2), 390–392.

Hatfield, E., Cacioppo, J. T., & Rapson, R. L. (1994). *Emotional contagion.* Cambridge, England: Cambridge University Press.

Hausfater, G. (1975). *Dominance and reproduction in baboons (Papio cynocephalus)* (Vol. 7). Basel, Switzerland: S. Karger.

Hausfater, G., & Hrdy, S. B. (Eds.). (1984). *Infanticide: Comparative and evolutionary perspectives.* New York: Aldine-de Gruyter.

Hawkins, K. A., & Trobst, K. K. (2000). Frontal lobe dysfunction and aggression: Conceptual issues and research findings. *Aggression & Violent Behavior, 5*(2), 147–157.

Hen, R. (1996, January). Mean genes. *Neuron, 16*, 17–21.

Hines, M., & Kaufman, F. R. (1994). Androgen and the development of human sex-typical behavior: Rough-and-tumble play and sex of preferred playmates in children with congenital adrenal hyperplasia (CAH). *Child Development, 65*, 1042–1053.

Horel, J. A., Keating, E. G., & Misantone, L. J. (1975). Partial Klüver-Bucy syndrome produced by destroying temporal neocortex or amygdala. *Brain Research, 94*, 347–359.

Hrdy, S. B. (1977). *The langurs of Abu: Female and male strategies of reproduction.* Cambridge, MA: Harvard University Press.

Hrdy, S. B. (1979). Infanticide among animals: A review, classification, and examination of the implications for the reproductive strategies of females. *Ethology and Sociobiology, 1*, 13–40.

Hrdy, S. B. (1981). *The woman that never evolved.* Cambridge, MA: Harvard University Press.

Hrdy, S. B. (1999). *Mother nature: A history of mothers, infants, and natural selection.* New York: Pantheon.

Hyde, J. S. (1986). Gender differences in aggression. In J. S. Hyde & M. Linn (Eds.), *The psychology of gender* (pp. 51–66). Baltimore: The Johns Hopkins University Press.

Ingram, W. R. (1956). The hypothalamus. *Clinical Symposia, 8*, 117–156.

Jakobson, R., & Halle, M. (1971). *Fundamentals of language* (2nd ed.). The Hague: Mouton & Co. (Original work published 1956)

Johnson, A. W., & Earle, T. (1987). *The evolution of human societies: From foraging group to agrarian state.* Stanford, CA: Stanford University Press.

Kano, T. (1989). The sexual behavior of pygmy chimpanzees. In P. G. Heltne & L. A. Marquardt (Eds.), *Understanding chimpanzees* (pp. 176–183). Cambridge, MA: Harvard University Press/Chicago Academy of Sciences.

Kano, T. (1992). *The last ape: Pygmy chimpanzee behavior and ecology.* Stanford, CA: Stanford University Press.

Keegan, J. (1993). *A history of warfare.* New York: Vintage Books.

Keeley, L. H. (1996). *War before civilization: The myth of the peaceful savage.* New York: Oxford University Press.

Kelly, R. C. (1985). *The Nuer conquest: The structure and development of an expansionist system.* Ann Arbor: University of Michigan Press.

Kendrick, K. M., & Drewitt, R. F. (1979). Testosterone reduces refractory period of stria terminalis neurons in the rat brain. *Science, 204*, 877–879.

Kluver, H., & Bucy, P. C. (1939). Preliminary analysis of the temporal lobes in monkeys. *Archives of Neurological Psychiatry, 42*, 1979–2000.

Knauft, B. (1987). Reconsidering violence in simple human societies: Homicide among the Gebusi of New Guinea. *Current Anthropology, 28*, 457–500.

Kreuz, L. E., & Rose, R. M. (1972). Assessment of aggressive behavior and plasma testosterone in a young criminal population. *Psychosomatic Medicine, 34*(4), 321–332.

LeBlanc, S., & Register, K. E. (2003). *Constant battles: The myth of the peaceful, noble savage.* New York: St. Martin's Press.

Lee, R. B. (1979a). *The !Kung San. Men, women and work in a foraging society.* Cambridge, England: Cambridge University Press.

Lee, R. B. (1979b). *The !Kung San. Men, women and work in a foraging society.* Cambridge, England: Cambridge University Press.

Levi-Strauss, C. (1962). *The savage mind*. London: Weidenfeld and Nicholson.

Lewis, M., & Rosenblum, L. (1973). *The origins of fear*. New York: Wiley.

Loosen, P. T., Purdon, S. E., & Pavlou, S. N. (1994, February). Effects on behavior of modulation of gonadal function in men with gonadotropin-releasing hormone antagonists. *American Journal of Psychiatry, 151*, 271–273.

Lorenz, K. (1970). What aggression is good for. In C. H. Southwick (Ed.), *Animal aggression: Selected readings*. New York: Van Nostrand Reinhold.

Low, B. S. (1993). An evolutionary perspective on war. In W. Zimmerman & H. K. Jacobson (Eds.), *Behavior, culture, and conflict in world politics*. Ann Arbor, MI: University of Michigan Press.

Low, B. S. (2000). *Why sex matters: A Darwinian look at human behavior*. Princeton, NJ: Princeton University Press.

Maccoby, E. E., & Jacklin, C. N. (1974). *The psychology of sex differences*. Stanford, CA: Stanford University Press.

Mackay, C. (1980). *Extraordinary popular delusions and the madness of crowds*. New York: Harmony Books. (Original work published 1841)

Malamud, N. (1967). Psychiatric disorders with intracranial tumors of the limbic system. *Archives of Neurology, 17*, 113–123.

Malthus, T. (1798). *An essay on the principle of population* (1st ed.). London: J. Johnson.

Manson, J. H., & Wrangham, R. W. (1991, August–October). Intergroup aggression in chimpanzees and humans. *Current Anthropology, 32*(4), 369–390.

Mark, V. H., & Ervin, F. R. (1970). *Violence and the brain*. Hagerstown, MD: Medical Dept., Harper & Row.

Marshall, L. (1976). Sharing, talking, and giving: Relief of social tensions among the !Kung. In R. B. Lee & I. DeVore (Eds.), *Kalahari hunter-gatherers: Studies of the !Kung San and their neighbors* (pp. 349–371). Cambridge, MA: Harvard University Press.

Maxson, S. C. (2000). Genetic influences on aggressive behavior. In D. W. Pfaff, W. H. Berrettini, T. H. Joh, & S. C. Maxson (Eds.), *Genetic influences on neural and behavioral functions* (pp. 405–416). New York: CRC Press.

Maybury-Lewis, D., & Almagor, U. (1989). *The attraction of opposites: Thought and society in the dualistic mode*. Ann Arbor: University of Michigan Press.

McEwen, B. (1978). Sexual maturation and differentiation: The role of the gonadal steroids. In M. A. Corner (Ed.), *Progress in brain research* (Vol. 48). North Holland: Elsevier.

Mead, M. (1949). *Male and female*. New York: Morrow.

Meggitt, M. J. (1977). *Blood is their argument: Warfare among the Mae Enga tribesmen of the New Guinea highlands* (1st ed.). Palo Alto, CA: Mayfield Pub. Co.

Miczek, K. A., Weerts, E., Haney, M., & Tidey, J. (1994). Neurobiological mechanisms controlling aggression: Preclinical developments for pharmacotherapeutic interventions. *Neuroscience and Biohavioral Reviews, 18*(1), 97–110.

Milgram, S. (1963). Behavioral study of obedience. *Journal of Abnormal and Social Psychology, 67*, 371–378.

Milgram, S. (1974). *Obedience to authority: An experimental view*. London: Tavistock.

Moyer, K. E. (1987). *Violence and aggression: A physiological perspective*. New York: Paragon House.

Munroe, R. L., Hulefeld, R., Rodgers, J. M., Tomeo, D. L., & Yamazaki, S. K. (2000). Aggression among children in four cultures. *Cross-Cultural Research: The Journal of Comparative Social Science, 34*(1), 3–25.

Niehoff, D. (1999). *The biology of violence: How understanding the brain, behavior, and environment can break the vicious cycle of aggression.* New York: The Free Press.

Olweus, D. (1988). *Aggression in the schools: Bullies and whipping boys.* New York: John Wiley and Sons.

Olweus, D., Mattson, A., Schalling, D., & Low, H. (1980). Testosterone, aggression, physical, and personality dimensions in normal adolescent males. *Psychosomatic Medicine, 42*, 253–269.

Olweus, D., Mattsson, A., Schalling, D., & Low, H. (1988). Circulating testosterone levels and aggression in adolescent males: A causal analysis. *Psychosomatic Medicine, 50*, 261–272.

Otterbein, K. F. (1970). *The evolution of war; A cross-cultural study.* New Haven, CT: HRAF (Human Relations Area Files) Press.

Panksepp, J. (1971). Aggression elicited by electrical stimulation of the hypothalamus in albino rats. *Physiology and Behavior, 6*, 321–329.

Panksepp, J. (1998). *Affective neuroscience: The foundations of human and animal emotions.* New York: Oxford University Press.

Parish, A. R. (1996). Female relationships in Bonobos (Pan Paniscus): Evidence for bonding, cooperation, and female dominance in a male-philopatric species. *Human Nature, 7*(1), 61–96.

Pincus, J. (1981). Violence and epilepsy. *New England Journal of Medicine, 305*, 696–698.

Power, S. (2002). *"A problem from hell": America and the age of genocide.* New York: Perennial/HarperCollins.

Preuschoft, S., Paul, A., & Kuester, J. (1998). Dominance styles of female and male Barbary macaques (Macaca sylvanus). *Behaviour, 135*, 731–755.

Raisman, G., & Field, P. M. (1973). Sexual dimorphism in the neuropil of the preoptic area of the rat and its dependence on neonatal androgen. *Brain Research, 54*, 1–29.

Raleigh, M., McGuire, M., Melega, W., Cherry, S., Huang, S.-C., & Phelps, M. (1995). Neural mechanisms supporting successful social decisions in simians. In A. Damasio, H. Damasiom & Y. Christen (Eds.), *Neurobiology of decision-making* (pp. 63–82). New York: Springer-Verlag.

Raleigh, M. J., McGuire, M. T., Brammer, G. L., Pollack, D. B., & Yuwiler, A. (1991, September 20). Serotonergic mechanisms promote dominance acquisition in adult male vervet monkeys. *Brain Research, 559*, 181–190.

Reinisch, J. M. (1974). Fetal hormones, the brain, and sex differences: A heuristic integrative review of the literature. *Archives of Sexual Behavior, 3*, 51–90.

Robinson, P., & Tajfel, H. (Eds.). (1997). *Social groups and identities: Developing the legacy of Henri Tajfel.* London: Butterworth-Heinemann.

Rodgers, J. E. (1992). *Psychosurgery: Damaging the brain to save the mind.* New York: Harper Collins.

Rodman, P. S., & Mitani, J. C. (1987). Orangutans: Sexual dimorphism in a solitary species. In B. B. Smuts, D. L. Cheney, R. M. Seyfarth, R. W. Wrangham, & T. T. Struhsaker (Eds.), *Primate societies* (pp. 146–154). Chicago: University of Chicago Press.

Rosaldo, R. (1980). *Ilongot headhunting 1883–1974: A study in society and history.* Stanford, CA: Stanford University Press.

Sahlins, M. D. (1961). The segmentary lineage: An organization of predatory expansion. *American Anthropologist, 63*, 322–345.

Sanday, P. R. (1986). *Divine hunger: Cannibalism as a cultural system.* Cambridge, England: Cambridge University Press.

Sano, K. (1962). Sedative neurosurgery: With special reference to posteromedial hypothalamotomy. *Neurologia Medico-Chirurgica, 4,* 112–142.

Saudou, F., Amara, D. A., Dierich, A., LeMeur, M., Segu, L., Buhot, M.-C., & Hen, R. (1994, September 23). Enhanced aggressive behavior in mice lacking 5-HT $_{1B}$ receptor. *Science, 265,* 1875–1878.

Schmookler, A. B. (1983). *The parable of the tribes: The problem of power in social evolution.* Berkeley: University of California Press.

Schubert, K., Shaikh, M. B., & Siegel, A. (1996). NMDA receptors in the midbrain mediate hypothalamically evoked hissing behavior in the cat. *Brain Research, 726,* 80–90.

Shaikh, M. B., Schubert, K., & Siegel, A. (1994). Basal amygdaloid facilitation of midbrain periaqueductal gray elicited defensive rage behavior in the cat is mediated through NMDA receptors. *Brain Research, 635,* 187–195.

Shaikh, M. B., Steinberg, A., & Siegel, A. (1993). Evidence that substance P is utilized in medial amygdaloid facilitation of defensive rage behavior in the cat. *Brain Research, 625,* 283–294.

Sherif, M., Harvey, O. J., White, B. J., Hood, W. R., & Sherif, C. W. (1961). *Intergroup conflict and cooperation: The Robbers Cave experiment.* Norman, OK: Institute of Group Relations.

Shih, J. C., Ridd, M. J., Chen, K., Meehan, W. P., Kung, M.-P., Seif, I., & De Maeyer, E. (1999). Ketanserin and tetrabenazine abolish aggression in mice lacking monoamine oxidase A. *Brain Research, 835*(2), 104–112.

Shostak, M. (1981). *Nisa: The life and words of a !Kung woman.* Cambridge, MA: Harvard University Press.

Shostak, M. (2000). *Return to Nisa.* Cambridge, MA: Harvard University Press.

Siegel, A., Roeling, T. A. P., Gregg, T. R., & Kruk, M. R. (1999). Neuropharmacology of brain-stimulation-evoked aggression. *Neuroscience & Biobehavioral Reviews, 23*(3), 359–389.

Siegel, A., Schubert, K., & Shaikh, M. B. (1994). Neurochemical mechanisms underlying amygdaloid modulation of aggressive behavior in the cat. *Aggressive Behavior, 21,* 49–62.

Smuts, B. (1992). Male aggression against women: An evolutionary perspective. *Human Nature, 3*(1), 1–44.

Smuts, B. B., & Smuts, R. W. (1993). Male-aggression and sexual coercion of females in non-human-primates and other mammals: Evidence and theoretical implications. *Advances in the Study of Behavior, 22,* 1–63.

Smythies, J. R. (1970). *Brain mechanisms and behavior.* New York: Academic Press.

Southwick, C. H. (1970). Genetic and environmental variables influencing animal aggression. In C. H. Southwick (Ed.), *Animal aggression: Selected readings.* New York: Van Nostrand Reinhold.

Stanford, C. B. (1999). *The hunting apes: Meat eating and the origins of human behavior.* Princeton, NJ: Princeton University Press.

Su, T.-P., Pagliaro, M., Schmidt, P. J., Pickar, D., Wolkowitz, O., & Rubinow, D. R. (1993). Neuropsychiatric effects of anabolic steroids in male normal volunteers. *Journal of the American Medical Association, 269,* 2760–2764.

Tajfel, H. (1982). *Social identity and intergroup relations.* New York: Cambridge University Press.

Teleki, G. (1973). *The predatory behavior of wild chimpanzees.* Lewisburg, PA: Bucknell University.

Thomas, E. M. (1959). *The harmless people*. New York: Vintage Books.

Tiger, L. (1969). *Men in groups*. New York: Random House.

Tiger, L. (1984). *Men in groups*. New York: Marion Boyars.

Toran-Allerand, C. D. (1976). Sex steroids and the development of the newborn mouse hypothalamus and preoptic area in vitro: implications for sexual differentiation. *Brain Research, 106*, 407–412.

Toran-Allerand, C. D. (1996). Mechanisims of estrogen action during neural development: mediation by interactions with the neurotrophins and their receptors? *The Journal of Steroid Biochemistry & Molecular Biology, 56*(1–6), 169–178.

Toynbee, A. (1972). *A study of history*. New York: Oxford University Press.

Tremblay, R. E., Japel, C., Perusse, D., McDuff, P., Boivin, M., Zoccolillo, M., & Montplaisir, J. (1999). The search for the age of 'onset' of physical aggression: Rousseau and Bandura revisited. *Criminal Behaviour & Mental Health, 9*(1), 8–23.

Trimble, M. R., & Tebartz Van Elst, L. (1999). On some clinical implications of the ventral striatum and the extended amygdala: Investigations of aggression. In J. F. McGinty (Ed.), *Advancing from the ventral striatum to the extended amygdala: Implications for neuropsychiatry and drug use: In honor of Lennart Heimer. Annals of the New York Academy of Sciences* (Vol. 877, pp. 638–644). New York: New York Academy of Sciences.

Trinkhaus, E. (1978). Hard times among the neanderthals. *Natural History, 87*, 58–63.

Trinkhaus, E. (1995). *The Shanidar Neandertals*. New York: Academic Press.

Trinkhaus, E., & Howells, W. W. (1979). The Neanderthals. *Scientific American, 241*(6), 118–133.

Ursin, H., & Kaada, B. R. (1960). Functional localization with the amygdaloid complex in the cat. *Electroencephalography and Clinical Neurology, 12*, 1–20.

Valzelli, L. (1973). *Psychopharmacology: An introduction to experimental and clinical principles*. Flushing: Spectrum.

van Goozen, S. H. M., Matthys, W., Cohen-Kettenis, P. T., Westenberg, H., & van Engeland, H. (1999). Plasma monoamine metabolites and aggression: Two studies of normal and oppositional defiant disorder children. *European Neuropsychopharmacology, 9*(1–2), 141–147.

Villa, P., et al. (1986). Cannibalism in the Neolithic. *Science, 233*, 431–437.

Volkow, N. D., & Tancredi, L. (1987). Neural substrates of violent behavior: A preliminary study with positron emission tomography. *British Journal of Psychiatry, 151*, 673–688.

Wade, N. (2000, February 2). If you are what you eat, mind if I move to another table?: Reconsidering cannibalism. *The New York Times*, Section 4, p. 3.

Wallen, K., & Tannenbaum, P. L. (1997). Hormonal modulation of sexual behavior and affiliation in rhesus monkeys. *Annals of the New York Academy of Sciences, 807*, 185–202.

Westergaard, G. C., Suomi, S. J., Higley, J. D., & Mehlman, P. T. (1999). CSF 5-HIAA and aggression in female macaque monkeys: Species and interindividual differences. *Psychopharmacology, 146*(4), 440–446.

White, D. R. (1988). Rethinking polygyny: Co-wives, codes, and cultural systems. *Current Anthropology, 29*(4), 529–558.

White, D. R., & Burton, M. L. (1988). Causes of polygyny: Ecology, economy, kinship, and warfare. *American Anthropologist, 90*(4), 871–887.

White, T. D. (1992). *Prehistoric cannibalism at Mancos 5Mtumr-2346*. Princeton, NJ: Princeton University Press.

Whiting, B., & Edwards, C. P. (1988). *Children of different worlds: The formation of social behavior*. Cambridge, MA: Harvard University Press.

Whiting, B., & Whiting, J. (1975). *Children of six cultures*. Cambridge, MA: Harvard University Press.

Whiting, B. B., & Edwards, C. P. (1973). A cross-cultural analysis of sex differences in the behavior of children aged three through eleven. *Journal of Social Psychology, 91*, 171–188.

Whiting, B. B., & Edwards, C. P. (1988). *Children of different worlds: the formation of social behavior*. Cambridge, MA: Harvard University Press.

Whiting, B. B., & Whiting, J. W. M. (1975). *Children of six cultures: a psychocultural analysis*. Cambridge, MA: Harvard University Press.

Whiting, J. W. M., & Whiting, B. B. (1975). Aloofness and intimacy between husbands and wives. *Ethos, 3*, 183–207.

Wiessner, P., & Tumu, A. (1998). *Historical vines: Enga networks of exchange, ritual, and warfare in Papua New Guinea*. Washington, DC: Smithsonian Institution Press.

Wilson, E. O. (1975). *Sociobiology: The new synthesis*. Cambridge, MA: Harvard University Press.

Worthman, C. M., & Konner, M. J. (1987). Testosterone levels change with subsistence hunting in !Kung San men. *Psychoneuroendocrinology, 12*, 449–458.

Wrangham, R. (1993). The evolution of sexuality in chimpanzees and bonobos. *Human Nature, 4*, 47.

Wrangham, R. W., & Peterson, D. (1996). *Demonic males: Apes and the origins of human violence*. Boston: Houghton Mifflin.

Wynne-Edwards, V. C. (1962). *Animal dispersion in relation to social behaviour*. New York: Hafner.

CHAPTER 2

# TRIBAL, "ETHNIC," AND GLOBAL WARS

## R. Brian Ferguson

Anthropologists define war very broadly. With small but sometimes significant variations, the basic idea is that war is organized, purposeful, lethal combat between different communities (Ferguson, 1984a, p. 3). Why do people do this? Why do people
get together, make a decision, and go out to kill members of a different group—and
think that it is legitimate, even commendable to do so? This chapter presents one
cultural anthropological answer to that question. After briefly considering a major
alternative—the idea that our evolved mind biologically predisposes us to war—I
will sketch out a general approach to why wars happen and apply that perspective
to our contemporary world. I will start by going through a theoretical perspective
with a focus on relatively egalitarian societies, such as the Yanomami. Then I will
apply that perspective to the topic of large-scale political violence within contemporary states, what is often though inaccurately called "ethnic violence," and I call
"identerest violence." Finally, I will make a tentative extension of these ideas to the
issues that preoccupy us today: terrorism and the war in Iraq.

Anthropologists devoted little attention to war prior to the 1960s, but since then
the anthropology of war has grown into a very large and diverse field. The number
of findings and hypotheses on its causes, correlates, and consequences has become
enormous (Ferguson 1984a, 1999; Otterbein 1973, 1977). Only a small part of that
work directly addresses the broad question of why humans make war. Most research
focuses on other issues: How are specific features of social organization related to specific patterns of warring? Does peace need a separate explanation from war? Does war
promote political centralization and hierarchy? Is Western contact responsible for
much of what we formerly assumed was purely "indigenous" warfare? How does
war reflect the values and beliefs of particular cultures? Looking over all the posited
connections between war and society makes it clear that war is an extremely complex

institution. Far more than mere combat, it is an institution that can dramatically affect every aspect of social life. And it hammers home the idea that to understand war in any specific sense, it has to be firmly situated in the total cultural and historical context in which it occurs. But beyond all these specifics, the general question remains: Why do people make war?

There have been three basic kinds of answers to that question: biological, symbolic or cultural, and materialist (Ferguson, 2001). Certainly the theoretical pie could be sliced in other ways. Institutional approaches of varying sorts are probably the most common explanations of war, but these rarely articulate questions about "human nature"—other than that it is social. Biological approaches, I will argue, are poorly substantiated and less than illuminating. The cultural anthropological approach I will present and apply here is based on materialist premises, but in recent work, I have been trying to build a rigorous connection with symbolic or cultural approaches. But first, I will take a look at the competition: biology.

## Biological Approaches to War

Biological theories range from simple invocations of aggressive instincts to sophisticated theories of inborn computational modules. Earlier theories of aggressive drives or killer instincts have been so long and thoroughly discredited that there is no need to rehash them here (Ferguson, 1984a; Klama, 1988). The concept of "human aggression" itself has been challenged as a misleadingly vague label muddying critical distinctions between very different kinds of behaviors (Fried, 1973; H. Van der Dennen, 1986). Since the time of anthropological pioneer Bronislaw Malinowski (1941), anthropologists have recognized the fundamental point that individual aggression is quite distinct from the social process that is war, much as individual athletic ability is quite distinct from organized sports. Humans have always had the potential for lethal violence since, or even before, they became human. But individual homicide is no more war in tribal societies than it is in our own. In tribal societies, rather than an impulsive outburst of aggression, decisions that lead to wars are typically long-considered and debated collective decisions. Still, individual or collective propensities for violent action against others can indeed play a significant role in such discussions, so aggressiveness cannot be ruled out of consideration.

Is aggressiveness biological? In some sense, of course. Neural structures, neurotransmitters, hormones, and genes have all been shown to be somehow involved with different measures of aggression. But involved how, and how much? More to the point, do these vast areas of research indicate that (nonpathological) humans, or maybe just men, have some kind of inborn propensity to do violence to others? These are reasonable questions, but answers are almost always highly debatable. Comparison of aggressiveness in young boys and girls in Western societies (e.g., Maccoby & Jacklin, 1974) inevitably incorporate critical, early periods of socialization, and these can encourage gender differences. In one experiment, adults that were told an unknown infant was a boy gave the child a toy football, but gave a "girl" a doll (Sidorowicz & Lunney, 1980). In another, adults who were shown the same film of a baby crying at a jack-in-the-box, when told it was a boy concluded that he was angry, but when told it was a girl concluded she was frightened (Condry & Condry, 1976).

Cross-cultural comparison does show men to be more aggressive. For instance, Kelly's (2000, pp. 31–32) detailed examination of five egalitarian band peoples found male-on-female (usually spousal) violence to be the most common, although male-male violence only slightly exceeded female-female violence. But there are solid theories explaining such regular gender difference as culturally elaborated outgrowths of social task segregation, based on physical factors such as strength, pregnancy, and requirements of infant care (Divale & Harris, 1976; Eagly & Wood, 2003). Much has been written about testosterone and aggression, but results are often contradictory or noncomparable (Archer, Birring, & Wu, 1998; Baron & Richardson, 1994); the whole subject is immeasurably complicated by the fact that testosterone levels are socially mediated. They rise and fall with personal events and may be as much effect as cause of aggressive interactions (Kemper, 1990; Sapolsky, 1997). In Western societies, whether and how much males or females score higher on aggression depends greatly on the kind of measures that are used, although a meta-analysis of many studies with different measures concluded that male-female differences accounted for about 5 percent of the variance (Hyde, 1984). A notable illustration of this variability by measure is domestic violence. Very large data sets from developed English-speaking nations show that females are slightly *more* likely to use physical force against their partners, but men are far more likely to cause serious physical harm (Archer, 2000).

In sum, we are nowhere near being able to distinguish, much less quantify, how much human or male aggressiveness can be attributed to "nature" rather than "nurture." Of course, many would say that is a false dichotomy: All behavior is the result of both. But that dodges the critical question: Is an evolved male tendency toward aggression an important factor in explaining war? Yet even if we cannot separate out the biological contribution, we can understand the limits of its possible significance: Maleness is one part of biology, biology is one part of aggressiveness, aggressiveness is one part of combat, and combat is one part of war. A part of a part of a part of a part cannot explain a whole.

Leaving aggressiveness itself, what about male reproductive competition? Is war a way individuals maximize the genes they pass along, an expression of male reproductive striving? The critical case is Chagnon's (1988) study showing that *unokais*—males who have undergone a ritual purification loosely associated with a killing—have more children than non-unokais. This study is cited time and again (see Ferguson, 2001, p. 108) by advocates who rarely, if ever, acknowledge the well-known critiques of that study: that *unokai* status is not a valid marker of a "killer" (Albert, 1990; Lizot, 1989); that the standard claim that *unokais* have three times as many children as non-*unokais* of the same age is in fact the figure for all adult men uncontrolled for age, and that age accounts for well over three-quarters of that difference (older men are more likely to have more children and more likely to be *unokai*); that much of the remaining difference can be accounted for by the fact that all headmen are *unokai*, and headmen tend to be more polygynous; and that Chagnon's data exclude consideration of men who have died in war, whose lifetime reproductive success was decidedly lowered by being dead (Ferguson, 1989; 2001, p. 108).

What about the flip side, war as a result of men fighting over women, or raiding to capture them? This is a commonly reported fact of war, even built into theories which make no invocation of reproductive concerns (Siskind, 1973; Harris, 1984). But closer study shows its importance to be highly variable. Kelly's (2000, p. 33) examination of five egalitarian band peoples found that "adultery, sexual rivalry, and jealousy" are relatively infrequent causes of male-male fighting and homicide. Cross-Amazonia comparison of the political significance of fighting over women, and the practice of capturing women, shows that both range from none to a lot, depending on a series of social institutions and practices (Ferguson, 1988). Among the Yanomami, once again the archetypal case (e.g., Chagnon, 1968), woman-capture is not a goal that starts wars—as Chagnon (1996, p. 222) himself makes clear. Fighting over women certainly does occur among Yanomami, but it is entirely unpredictive of war (Ferguson, 1995a, pp. 32, 357–358).

Another argument for war being "in our blood" comes from reported observations of African chimpanzees. It has been claimed in very prominent publications (Ghiglieri, 1999; Wrangham & Peterson, 1996) that human males share with chimpanzees the inclination to kill males of other groups when they can do so with impunity, because in our common evolutionary past this led to reproductive benefits. But this argument is open to major question and criticism. First, the incidence of intergroup killings has been significantly exaggerated beyond actual observation. For instance, it is commonly reported that at two sites (Gombe and Mahale), one group of chimpanzees was wiped out by another (Ghiglieri, 1999, p. 173; Wade, 2003). However, killings at Mahale are entirely inferential, reinterpretations of disappearances in light of Gombe findings (Nishida, 1980). In fact, only one small incident of intergroup violence was reported between the two groups (Nishida, 1979).

Second, the confirmed instances of intergroup killings are almost all in situations where there has been major disturbance of chimpanzee communities by humans, in ways that can plausibly account for the increased competition and violence. For instance, there were three adult killings at Kibale National Park in 2002 (Wilson & Wrangham, 2003). At that same time, Kibale chimpanzees were coming out of the park, raiding crops and even attacking, killing, and eating a few human infants. Why? Kibale is an island surrounded by farmers, with a very dense chimpanzee population. "Squeezed into this diminishing forest resource, chimps are finding it increasingly difficult to locate ample food" (Gavin, 2004, p. 2; Wakabi, 2004). This is hardly a "natural" situation.

Third, any evolutionary continuity of violent behavior from the last common ancestor of humans and chimpanzees is extremely doubtful, given huge divergences and uncertainties in the evolutionary lines. For instance, the hominid line shows a marked reduction in sexual dimorphism beginning about a million and a half years ago, which Wrangham and Pilbeam (2001) agree suggests a selective process *against* intermale physical contests. Many other objections to the "demonic males" perspective could be raised (see Ferguson, n.d.), but instead, this brief discussion will turn to a parallel line of argument: that a human propensity to war is evidenced by archaeological findings showing war throughout our prehistoric past.

To argue that war is a result of some sort of innate predisposition to wage it requires that war be practiced throughout our prehistoric past. Those who make that argument, from various angles, cite Keeley's (1996) *War before Civilization* in support of that point (see Ferguson, in press). Now Keeley has been joined by LeBlanc (2003), who refers back to Wrangham and Peterson (1996) in support of the antiquity of war. Both Keeley and LeBlanc portray war as appearing throughout the archaeological record. Yet several others (including myself) who have searched through that record conclude that the advent of war is a later development, although still very ancient (Ferguson, 1997; Haas, 1999; O'Connell, 1995; Roper, 1969, 1975; J. M. G. Van der Dennen, 1995, pp. 197–214; Vencl, 1984). What is the basis of this difference?

It is not, for the most part, about differences in the interpretation of material evidence, though there is some of that—most significantly about Czech Republic sites that Keeley (1996) and LeBlanc (2003) claim decisively establish warfare in the Paleolithic period, and which I argue does no such thing (Ferguson, in press, footnote 1). Primarily, it is about the basis of generalization. Keeley (1996) and LeBlanc (2003) note those cases where war is indicated in recovered remains and generalize from those cases to all areas. Those who see war starting later and varying dramatically across time and space also take into account the very numerous early sites, where we have good recovery of relevant physical evidence which *should* show war, but where there are no signs whatever of collective violent conflict. Haas (2000) details this difference in approach in regard to LeBlanc's earlier work (1999). In some of the best studied regions of the world, including the ancient Middle East, China, and Europe, signs of war are slim to none in the early record. (Australia is a contrary case, with very early war among simple hunter-gatherers. North America is complicated, with some very early signs of war in some areas but not others) (Ferguson, 2003; in press). Then, in all areas, war becomes very apparent and never goes away. Keep in mind that this still means war is very ancient, beginning perhaps 10,000 years ago in what is now northern Iraq. By roughly 6,000 years ago, war seems omnipresent throughout most of central Europe (Ferguson, in press).

What led to the advent of war? In my (far from finished) research on global origins of war, I identify six preconditions, which in combination make the onset of war more likely. Somewhat oversimplified, they are as follows: a more sedentary existence, growing population, social segmentation (clans or lineages), increasing status hierarchy, increased trade (especially in elite goods), and climatic disturbance. Significance varies considerably by area. For instance, war seems to antedate hierarchy and elite trade in much of North America, though their development later intensified it.

Why then did war become so common over time, found widely even among simple, mobile hunter-gathers? Four trends are suggested: war originated in more places in the world, from those places war spread outward, the rise of ancient states contributed to and extended militarism on their peripheries and trade routes, and European expansionism after 1500 added many new war-inducing transformations, often well in front of the expanding range of contact direct contacts (tribal zones) (Ferguson, 2003a, p. 33; in press). In sum, the archaeological record contradicts the proposition that war has been a timeless expression of reproductive competition and indicates that war was a response to identifiable material, demographic, social, and historical conditions.

The last biological explanation of war I will consider is an inborn tendency to and xenophobia (Ghiglieri, 1999, pp. 211–212; Shaw & Wong, 1989). The idea of a natural tendency of in-group amity/out-group enmity goes back to Social Darwinists, especially Sumner (1906), but the premise was accepted even by those never associated with that orientation, such as Boas (1912). Ethnocentrism is an especially vague term, ranging from a mild sense of superiority to genocidal violence. But valuing one's own ways more than others' is elemental to culture: the norms one learns are those one should live by. Regarding war, however, the relevant notion of ethnocentrism is more specific. It is the idea that humans naturally form bounded social groups, with intense hostility to those beyond.

Anthropological evidence contradicts the idea that this is a basic human pattern. Australian aborigines in some ways provide the best case for biological explanations of war (see Gat, 2000). They are divided into recognized tribes consisting of numerous local bands. Yet the boundaries between these tribes are highly variable. Between some, the difference is a gradual transition rather than a recognized border; between some there is a border, but amicable casual relations across it; between some there is chronic hostility (Meggitt, 1965, pp. 37–43, 324–326; Spencer & Gillen, 1904/ 1969, p. 31; Warner, 1958, pp. 17, 35, 144–145). A detailed survey of intergroup attitudes in East Africa by one of the leading scholars of ethnocentrism found that "ethnocentrism as conceived by Sumner represents an extreme variation in the pattern of intergroup relations," linked to specific distancing and conflict-generating conditions (Brewer & Campbell, 1976, p. 144). Anthropologists have long known that ethnic identification is an often fluid and shifting categorization (Barth, 1969). Of course, hard boundaries with lethal hatreds exist in many wars, but they are a symptom, not the cause of conflicts.

This is consistent with findings of social psychology (e.g., Tajfel and Turner, 1986). Experiments—although almost all in Western societies, where competition is part of the ethos—show that in even the most arbitrarily defined groups, there is a clear bias in favor of members, and against members of some similarly defined out-group. However, these same authors stress such bias is *not* explanatory of intergroup conflict. Research on that specific topic affirms that such conflicts are "realistic"; they come into existence when there is real competition for some scarce, needed good. So "ethnocentrism" cannot explain "ethnic" strife. What can explain it will be suggested below.

This does not exhaust all current biological explanations of war, nor does it deny in principle that evolved predispositions may be relevant for understanding some aspects of war (see Ferguson, 2000). However, the marginal utility of such insights is likely to remain quite limited, while the sweeping claims often made for biology have the effect of distracting the attention of the public and policy makers away from sociocultural explanations. Fukuyama's (1998, p. 33) observations in *Foreign Affairs* illustrate this danger.

> Once one views international relations through the lens of sex and biology, it never again looks the same. It is very difficult to watch Muslims and Serbs in Bosnia, Hutus and Tutsis in Rwanda, or militias from Liberia and Sierra Leone to Georgia and Afghanistan divide themselves up into what seem like indistinguishable male-bonded groups in order to systematically slaughter one another, and not think of the chimps at Gombe.

## An Anthropological Alternative on Tribal War

The main anthropological alternatives to a biological explanation are symbolic or cultural, and materialist. Symbolic/cultural approaches attribute war to the system of norms, values, beliefs, and symbols particular to a given culture. They come in many forms. In terms of simple descriptions, this is the oldest and most widespread anthropological approach to war. Countless ethnographers have told us that the so-and-so go to war to avenge the ghosts of the dead, to gather supernatural power from killing, to capture women, etc. More recently, studies of the cultural psychology of war have grown much more sophisticated and complex. So war to take heads is seen as acting out a prescribed cultural drama in which shame is erased and parity with other men is achieved (Rosaldo, 1983), or war leading to cannibalism expresses cosmological ideas by internalizing that which is exterior (Viveiros de Castro, 1992), or a particularly gruesome sort of shamanic assassination emerges as both a military technique and a deeply meaningful assertion of cultural autonomy in the face of Western influences (Whitehead, 2002). Implicit in all these approaches is the belief that as our ancestral species evolved into culture as the key to adaptive success, behavioral repertoires were shaped, above all, by the shared, culturally constructed *meanings* within local groups (Robarchek, 1990; Sahlins, 1987).

The cultural/symbolic approach to war has been reinforced by a parallel stream of studies, "the anthropology of violence" (Scheper-Hughes & Bourgois, 2004; Schmidt & Schroeder, 2001; Stewart & Strathern, 2002). In this field, war is just one form of violence among many to be studied. These studies focus on meanings of violence, which is often seen as entirely legitimate, at least by one side (Riches, 1986). Researchers see violent acts as *performances* communicating deep messages involving actors, victims, and broader audiences. Many, but not all, of these approaches downplay material goals, seeing them as important only as perceived through particular cultural lenses.

Materialist approaches, in contrast, have tried to understand war as practical struggles over materially important goods or conditions. In simpler societies—that is, those without a pronounced political hierarchy—wars are seen as being over basic needs of the entire war-making group. This most definitely includes the need to protect oneself from the threats of others. In the 1960s and 1970s, materialism was associated with cultural ecology, in which war was argued to be a method of adapting populations to scarce natural resources (Rappaport, 1985; Vayda, 1968). However, critiques developed both within and outside cultural ecology undercut this perspective. Instead of populations adapting in some unconscious manner, actions came to be seen as the outcomes of strategizing actors. Ecological conditions were only one set of factors possibly involved in war, and war was only one possible response to material scarcities (Ferguson, 1984b; Vayda, 1976). Even from the start, however, it was emphasized (e.g., Divale & Harris, 1976; Harris, 1977) that ecological adaptationist models did not apply to war by societies with a pronounced political hierarchy.

My own approach (1990, 1999) is based in a reformulation of cultural materialism (Ferguson, 1995b; Harris, 1979). In a sentence, I argue that wars occur when those who make the decision to fight believe it is in their practical self-interest to do so (although I will be qualifying this view in the next section). This immediately calls attention to the social and political structure of decision making—who calls the shots. And it calls attention to *internal* as well as external interests. In ancient chiefdoms and states, political rule is closely associated with a legitimating ideology of leadership to victory in war, which shows clearly even in archaeological remains (Arkush & Allen, in press). But even among tribal peoples with very limited development of leadership, the internal position of leaders is often a critical issue in those decisions (Maybury-Lewis, 1974; Sillitoe, 1978). I will illustrate this general approach with reference to the Yanomami, the subject of my book *Yanomami Warfare* (Ferguson, 1995a). Source citations for ethnographic claims can be found there.

The Yanomami are an ethnolinguistic group of Native Americans who live in the highlands on the Venezuela-Brazil border. Their remote location has made them, until recently, much less accessible to outsiders than the vast majority of Amazonian peoples, and for this reason they remain unusually populous, with recent estimates putting their total number at something around 29,000 people (Bruce Albert, personal communication). Yanomami warfare became famous within anthropology through the publications of Napoleon Chagnon (1968, 1974). More recently Chagnon has argued that Yanomami wars are struggles for reproductive success. He claims that they typically begin in disputes between men over women and then are carried on for revenge (1988). In this, he portrays the Yanomami as undisturbed by the outside world and as representative of the ancient condition of war for human beings. They are, "our contemporary ancestors" (Chagnon 1983, p. 214).

I have never lived among the Yanomami. My work was historical, combing through the many theses and publications of anthropologists who did do fieldwork among them, as well as historical documents which show, contrary to previous opinion, that Yanomami had been significantly impacted by the European expansion from the middle 1700s or even earlier. Doing this, I strove for a complete record of all wars reported for all Yanomami from all times. Information about these wars is, of course, highly variable, often just a mere mention. But available information clearly demonstrates that most fights over women do not lead to war, and few wars are preceded by any reported disputes over women. Vengeance, though a powerful personal motivator, is politically malleable. It is directed toward those who are "enemies" for other reasons, as are suspicions of witchcraft.

My argument is that the Yanomami wars that we know about (their prehistory is entirely unknown) occur for reasons related to an expanding Western presence. Mapping known Yanomami wars against a reconstruction of their contacts with outsiders shows that the wars occur at moments of major change in the outside presence and activities. That destabilizing changes can foster outbreaks of war between Yanomami groups is an obvious fact, in otherwise hotly disputed accounts of the Mavaca and Siapa River areas from the middle 1980s onward (Chagnon, 1992, pp. 219–221; Tierney, 2000, pp. 181–194). My point is that the critically shaping social, economic, political, and military impacts of Western contact are clear—if one looks for them —in those times and places previously portrayed as pristine, largely unaffected by the outside world.

Not all changes lead to wars however. Those that do are situations where the instability is marked by sharp antagonisms over the Western goods that the outsiders bring, in particular steel cutting tools which almost instantly became necessities for Yanomami garden-makers. Guns and ammunition also add to the brew of war. These goods became available only at specific points of contact, and those Yanomami groups who could monopolize access to the foreigners reaped great benefits, not only in having tools themselves, but in the women and the labor (in labor-intensive local manufactures and bride service) they obtained from more remote Yanomami groups that did not have direct access. Differential access to these trade sources is what generated the antagonisms that led to war. People with good access fiercely protected their position as monopolists, when necessary, with violence. They became first in a line of trade middlemen radiating outward from contact points. Those without good access tried to drive away, or replace, those who came between. In some areas, where an intensifying Western presence was accompanied by new epidemics and other social disruptions, the threshold for violence was lowered, so it took relatively little to start the arrows flying. These are the basic structural patterns that predict periods of war and peace, who attacks, and who is attacked.

Since my book was published, others who have worked with the Yanomami, some of whom endorse aspects of my reconstruction of their history (see Ferguson, 2001, pp. 104–105), have argued that the structured incentives and antagonism I invoke are simply not the way Yanomami themselves conceptualize war. Yanomami think in terms of personal grudges, of violence as an integral part of a broader schema of reciprocity, or more basically of a need for revenge, of suspicions of witchcraft which themselves are part of a broad cognitive complex, and of bravery and cowardice. These ideational factors, my critics contend, are themselves powerful motivations for violence.

I agree that all these are motivating factors in many cases, but in most instances, they provide only individual motivations. Among the relatively egalitarian Yanomami, where no man can order another to go to war, where each warrior makes up his own mind to fight, these alone do not provide the incentive for a *group* to raid. That incentive is provided, however, by the structured inequalities between villages, and even village factions, regarding access to Western goods. Yet these particular values systems truly are integral to the Yanomami war complex. Wars, in general, may be fought over things, but they are fought against other people. Underlying antagonisms will always be translated into interpersonal values, in terms meaningful for a particular culture. My model addresses that fact.

When a group of Yanomami have a common interest in obtaining or controlling Western goods, they all know about this. It is a daily fact of life. When they begin to discuss the possibility of war, there are differences of opinion. There are serious potential costs to be weighed against prospective gains. There are alternative courses of action. Headmen—noncoercive leaders of particular groups or factions—have their own distinct interests, relating to their position within the ever-changing political alignments of village life and alliances. In the public discussions leading up to war, its advocates will use the highest applicable moral standard to make their cases, claiming, "Those people over there are doing witchcraft against us, we have not avenged a death from several years ago, who among you is brave and who is a coward," etc.

I refer to this as the "moral conversion" of self-interests. In some particularly detailed situations, we can see that this is pure manipulation, as when one man exhorted warriors to go raid so he could sneak off to do something else. But in others instances, war advocates truly seem to believe in the moral reasons they invoke. It seems to be a regularity across war-making peoples, that those who start the shooting always say, and commonly believe, that the other side is somehow to blame—"they started it," or at least, "they deserve it." Further, when a situation already teeters on the brink of war, any trivial incident can stand for the whole conflicted relationship and trigger the fighting—thus seeming to be its cause. But it is the underlying structure of material interests and antagonisms that explain why wars happen when and where they do.

That is my position in *Yanomami Warfare*, argued in hard form because it went against established arguments from biological or cultural/symbolic perspectives that material interests *could not* explain their fighting. And these interests *do* explain the occurrence of the great majority of their wars, particularly so when there is more information available. But since then, I have wondered if this view of values as constructed rationalizations of underlying material interests gives sufficient attention to cultural/symbolic aspects. Responding to critiques by Yanomami scholars, I have acknowledged (Ferguson, 2001, p. 106) that the materialist model I develop would be strengthened if it gave more detailed attention to Yanomami beliefs and psychology. Other readings, as for instance about war in highland New Guinea (e.g., Trompf, 1994; Stewart & Strathern, 2002), make me suspect that I need to give more general attention to suspicions of witchcraft, imperatives for revenge, and other more particular cognitive orientations in their own right. The problem in anthropology for many years has been that advocates of cultural/symbolic or materialist approaches, including myself, give a ritual bow toward the other—"of course such factors are involved"—before going on their own way. Yet we know the practical and general, and the symbolic and particular are joined in practice. Cross-cultural studies of reactions to Western contact (see Ferguson & Whitehead, 2000) exhibit great similarities across extremely diverse peoples, while ethnographies of violence unambiguously demonstrate particular local conceptions that clearly shape behavior. But there has been little effort at rigorous integration, something beyond "a little of this, and little of that," or "sometimes this, sometimes that."

And what about situations where tribal peoples make more long-distance warfare, against people of different cultures? Do those cultural differences play an important role? Most Yanomami war involves kin and neighbors, people who have shared food and intermarried. But Yanomami have made war against neighboring Yecuana people and others. In general, antagonisms in those wars follow the structure of conflicts found internally among Yanomami. But the ethnic difference does seem to be a clearly recognized divide shaping cooperation and hostility. The next section describes an effort to expand a materialist approach to more fully integrate symbolic/cultural factors, especially across cultural divides.

## From Tribal Conflict to "Identerest" Violence

The issue of cultural values, and cultural differences, as important causal factors is addressed directly in my Introduction to a recent volume (Ferguson, 2003b) *The State, Identity, and Violence*. That book is concerned with the kind of intrastate, large scale political violence that came to the foreground after the end of the Cold War, although really it was nothing new. In all these crises, combatants included nonstate irregular forces, who often deliberately targeted civilians, often with extreme brutality. Specific cases ranged through religious riots, ethnic cleansing, guerilla war, civil war, and even genocide. An important commonality in all of these very diverse situations is that political violence is somehow linked to personal identities, to different kinds or categories of people. These identities mark off both perpetrators and targets of lethal violence.

In that Introduction, I (2003c) discuss the scope of factors that can be found across different cases, factors running from the most global to the most local. All of these must be brought in to adequately explain a given case of large-scale political violence. I will briefly summarize the most important considerations before zeroing in on some of the cultural-psychological aspects, the nexus where all vectors come together to produce the killing. As with discussions drawn from my book on the Yanomami, details and supporting citations can be found in that Introduction.

Globally, critical factors include an international system that has enshrined *states*, with clear capitals and borders, as the only acceptable form of political organization; legacies of colonialism that created artificial countries without workable systems of governance; the Cold War, which aggravated many local conflicts, spread powerful weapons, and then collapsed leaving clients with sharply reduced support; global economic processes such as the precipitous decline of many primary product markets, which devastated many countries; the growing importance of humanitarian aid, which can be diverted and controlled by local agents; new and often illegal forms of transnational trade, from blood diamonds to narcotics; and regulation of local government policies by international agencies—all of which undermined the control of many governments. While political violence is indeed the creation of local actors, the larger global system plays many critical roles in structuring the field of play.

At the level of the state or government—not the same things but close enough for this discussion—there are patrimonial systems that have lost the ability to dispense sufficient patronage; armies that could not be adequately financed; a governmental class of educated, typically urban people dependent on the state for their livelihood; shadow networks of personal connections that make the key decisions that ostensibly are the domain of formal officials; nationalist ideologies which claim to be all-inclusive, but in practice serve some particular political divisions; and government polices that favor some social categories or identities and penalize or attack others. This mix is a recipe for increasing intergroup suspicion and antagonism, for fostering "ethnic violence."

A big casualty of these developments was the long cherished trinity of economic development, socio-cultural modernization, and a mildly patriotic secular national-ism. For decades, even across the political chasms of the Cold War, global and national leaders had seen that combination as the wave of the future, eroding the more particular identifications and loyalties that led to trouble in the past. Where that trinity was actually delivered, the dream often seemed to be coming true. The problem was that in many countries, or for particular areas or groups within a country, all that was experienced was immiseration, political oppres-sion, and a growing realization that they were simply superfluous in the grand schemes of power.

Locally, there are regional differences in the benefits or costs of government poli-cies and differential recruitment or access to seats of state power; literally grounded agricultural and other production systems, and the social, economic, and political structures that rose on top of them; political elites with their own interests; ethnic, linguistic, religious, tribal, clan, and other divisions; and along with all that, local symbols, values, and a sense of history that affect how people perceive the world around them. Combinations of these local factors provide a basis of political and military mobilization that can be directed against the central government and against world forces and powers above them. That fact is key to understanding the violence which often ensues, and it brings us back to the issue of materialist vs. cultural explanations of war, previously discussed.

There is a debate in the international relations literature as to whether these con-flicts should be understood as the result of "greed" or "grievance" (see Berdal & Malone, 2000). Do they happen because people in power are pursuing their own very selfish material interests, making hay out of chaos and war? Or are they the result of perceived injuries and threat to those who see violence as the only recourse? I see this as a mistaken, and misleading, opposition. Given the social and spatial character of the costs and benefits of state rule and its opposition—"political topog-raphies" one recent book (Boone, 2003) calls them: *who* you are, what kind of per-son, your identity—typically is tightly linked to *how* you are doing, whether you have been a winner or a loser in recent developments.

There are many dimensions to identity. Some are given by birth, some accrue with experience, and some are deliberately chosen. Cultural difference or ethnicity is only one kind of identity. Others include geographic region within a country, position in the continuum from urban capitol to country village, political and/or economic position (or class), religion, language, caste, race, tribe, clan, gender, and age. Some of these, such as ethnicity, language, or religion provide a ready-made category, replete with its own potent symbols, for group mobilization. Others, such as clan, gender, and age, may heavily impact on how particular individuals experience the world and thus make them more or less receptive to pitches at higher levels of identification. This highly variable basis of identity makes the frequently used catchall —"ethnic conflict"—inappropriate. Ethnic identity—recognized cultural distinctiveness—is only one variation. And to focus on ethnicity makes it seem that cultural difference is itself the cause of conflicts.

My point is that ethnic or other identities are not separable from more tangible, material concerns. Identity and interest are commonly *fused* into one. So, with due reluctance, I have proposed a new, hopefully more precise term: *identerest*. To speak of identerest groups and identerest conflicts does not presuppose any one universal basis of antagonism or mobilization. Rather it calls for those bases to be specified. And it calls attention to how material situation and a variety of symbolic understandings come together in groups heading toward lethal struggle, thus joining materialist and cultural/symbolic approaches.

The need for a new term is shown by the evident difficulties involved in existing terms. For illustration, take Ted Robert Gurr (2000), whose long-term work in this area is state of the art. Gurr writes,

> ethnic groups are people who share a distinctive and enduring collective identity based on a belief in common descent and on shared experiences and cultural traits. They are also referred to here as communal and identity groups. Ethnopolitical groups are identity groups whose ethnicity has political consequences, resulting either in differential treatment of group members or in political action on behalf of group interests. (p. 5)

The latter are what I call "identerest groups," because even the prefix "ethno" encourages misunderstandings. As Gurr elaborates,

> Ethnopolitical groups are not necessarily "ethnic" in the narrow sense. Many shared attributes can contribute to the sentiments and interests that lead to joint action ... the salient bases of collective identity include a common language, religion, or national or racial origin, shared cultural practices, and attachment to a particular territory. Most ethnopolitical groups also have a common history or myths of shared experience. (p. 8)

But all these diagnostics can vary independently of each other, and from the critical markers associated with ethnicity—common culture and sense of common ancestry. People of one religion may share a believed history but have radically different cultures and no shared ancestry. People of two large clans at each others' throats may be of identical culture and, at a higher level, acknowledge common ancestors. Submerging all these differences under ethnic or ethno only muddies the water. Alternatives are not better. "Communal groups" suggests an integration which may not exist

prior to conflict, and "identity groups" puts too much stress on one side of the equation (as would going in the other direction with "interest groups"). And Gurr is
among the best. Most people just handle this linguistic stumbling block with something along the lines of "ethnic or whatever-you-want-to-call-them conflicts." I submit that we would be better served by calling them identerest.

In discussions of identerest violence around the world, we hear a lot about weak
states, or even failed states. At one level, this diagnosis is accurate. For reasons noted
above, central governments often are debilitated, unable to maintain order or
respond to violent challenge. But this focus also obscures another critical fact: that
the fighting we see is almost always all about who controls the state and what the
state controls. The contenders seek to hold on to state power, to replace those in
power, to redirect state-controlled resources, or to escape from existing centers of
state power and set up new ones. As Reyna (2003, p. 272) found regarding Chad,
but applicable much more widely, political violence is led by officials, former officials, and would-be officials.

The wars of recent years are often more extreme than normal political struggles.
Some involve a project to replace one regime with another of a radically different
type. Some involve breaking up an existing state into new smaller states. Others
involve pushing the central government back from peripheral areas and replacing it
with local structures of rule. But in one way or another, they are about the government. So there is a real double bind. Strong states are seen as the solution, but simply
increasing the economic, political, or military power of the state makes the struggle
over rule all the more important. The difficult lesson for diplomacy is that some kind
of balance is necessary, increasing central authority, but in a way that does not generate even more opposition (and see Sharani, 2002).

My general theory of war stresses the need to focus on the self-interest of the leaders who call the shots on war. The respective roles of leaders and followers in identerest conflicts have been a big topic of research. Right after the Cold War ended, as new
violent conflicts exploded and suddenly moved to center stage in our attention, many
people argued that the violence was the result of "ancient antagonisms" and "primor-
dial loyalties." Increased scrutiny quickly disposed of that perspective. The issues and
groups involved were, on examination, very contemporary, not continuations of
ancient struggles. By and large, a consensus emerged: the problem was not "the people," but "bad leaders"—leaders who manipulated identities for their own purposes
and created situations of violence. This consensus is accurate, as far as it goes. Yes,
there are leaders who manipulate, exploit, and compel others to kill. Focus on them
is essential. But this view does not go far enough. Clearly, the leaders' charted course
is often accepted with enthusiasm by people on the ground.

A common process in these conflicts is called "outbidding." In a field of potential
leaders, those who rise to the top may be those who offer the most extreme views, the
red meat, to their audience. Leaders often encourage or command atrocities to be
committed, but we also see some followers jump to the opportunity, going beyond
what is commanded. Certainly individual personalities play a big role here—the long
disturbed, who suddenly find themselves with powerful backers and automatic

weapons. But so do local cultural symbols and scripts—as Lan (1985) demonstrates for Zimbabwe, Richards (1996) for Sierra Leone, Taylor (1999) for Rwanda, and Hinton (2004) for Cambodia. Deep themes shape the killings. So it is not *just* bad leaders. We also need to understand what motivates those who follow, including the actual perpetrators. We need to have an idea of how these violent identerest groups form in the interaction of leaders and followers, and in the interaction of practical interests and particular cultural understandings.

Continuing to draw from the introduction to *The State, Identity, and Violence*, I argue that there are four abstractly identifiable general stages in identerest conflicts. Real situations are considerably more diverse, of course. There are major pattern variations, such as whether group formation is one-sided or two-sided (i.e., the targeted people may not be organized), or whether one side is controlled by an existing government. Phases can be collapsed. Beyond that, every situation is unique. But comparison of cases in that book suggests that a broadly similar progression can be discerned even in radically different situations.

Phase one is the development of an active core of identerest entrepeneurs. This is usually some combination of politicians, businessmen, scholars, and clerics, who have convergent interests in promoting a conflict. They forge and widely disseminate a charged political ideology, thoroughly immersed in local cultural understandings, which identifies "our common enemy." They usually seem to believe in this ideology themselves. Remember my point about tribal warfare: self-serving material interests are couched and discussed in terms of cultural values, but the leaders also seem convinced that their proposed course of war is *right*.

Still, the propaganda aspect, the deliberate manipulation of messages to rouse an audience, comes through loud and clear. Blame for a poor life is cast on "them," and better times are pledged if "they" are defeated. "Justice" is invoked, and past grudges are diligently revived and dwelled upon. Violence is used against those who somehow stand against the leaders' definition of "us," sending a warning to others. Potent symbols are manipulated to drum up enthusiastic support. Leaders make a direct pitch to their self-serving construction of a salient identity—be it ethnic, religious, or whatever—and shore that up with self-serving constructions of that identity's history. History is the most potent symbol of all—who "we" are, how we came to be, and above all, how others tried to destroy us in the past, even centuries ago.

But even though their message will be framed in terms of some broad category of people, it typically is received very differently by different kinds of people within that category. So a message that is said to apply to all "Bikar"—to make up a group of some type—will be immediately taken up especially by the "Lokar" subdivision of Bikar, by Bikar in the south, by Bikar working in the mining district, and by young Bikar men in the city. That same message will be doubted or resisted by most Bikar who are urban professionals, or educated women, or Bikar farmers in the northwestern region. Many of these resistors may have active, good, even familial relations with members of the designated enemy. Again and again we have heard that those who slaughter today had lived as peaceful neighbors quite recently. So, to go from message to violent action, the identerest group has to be broadened, lines have to be drawn, and dissent or passivity sanctioned. That brings us to phase two, fostering fear, or as international relations scholars put it, the internal security dilemma.

Again and again we have seen that the perception of threat, of danger, is key to mobilization of followers. The constructed threat is physical, to life and well being —the most material interest of all. But at the same time it is against identity. "You are an 'x,' I am an 'x,' and all those 'y's want to get rid of us because they hate what we are." Leaders actively cultivate these fears, but their success depends in part on how realistic those fears appear to potential targets. The fears draw strength by their plausible correspondence to local histories and current circumstances.

When a perceived threat is directed at a person's sense of self, at the very conception of who he or she is, and at all those who are like him or her, the elicited response is felt not as calculated, rational self-interest, but as bubbling hot passion, beyond or even against rational self-interest. In such situations, the old "prisoner's dilemma" may rule. Both sides would do better by not attacking, but if one is convinced the other will try to get them if they do not protect themselves, attacking first may seem like the only way to go. And usually the message is, "Do not count on the government to protect us—we are on our own." So as larger guarantors of security are seen as impotent, people fall back on loyalties of kin and kind. Who else is there?

By now the conflict is into phase three—guided polarization and projection. The classical dynamics of that well-known process apply. Efforts are made to eliminate the middle ground and make people choose sides. Whatever we do is right; whatever they do is wrong. Trust is said to be impossible with those who come to embody the negative image of whatever we stand for. Alternative narratives of cooperation and coexistence are banished as deluded at best, traitorous at worst. Since we have to defend ourselves, hard-core fighters and enforcers are recruited and organized, and broader sorts of people join in. At this phase, a dense mix of symbols, understandings, values, fears, and staged performances come into play among the hard core, the masses who follow, and even those who sit on the fence. Within the hard core, organizational structures, social pressures, and controlled information create a new reality, channeling them toward new potentialities of violence.

But how widely and deeply these divisive perceptions actually penetrate is variable. A constructed ethnic or tribal polarization used in fighting may be so superficial that it fades almost immediately when fighting stops, as Brown (2003) found in Liberia. The hard core is always a small minority, and as Nordstrom (1998) witnessed on several battlegrounds, the great majority of people, including members of martial forces, are not active killers, but merely want to survive. Misperceiving enemies as of uniform militancy is a deadly trap which precludes negotiation and compromise. Unless those less than committed to violence are recognized and actively engaged against it, a growing minority of committed partisans can easily brush past widespread nonengagement. Unorganized nonpartisans do not count. As partisan bands mobilize, leaders may be pushed into more aggressive postures from below, fueling outbidding.

Phase four is calculated violence, initiated by leaders, which comes in different forms. It may be members of a militia who are sent in to rape and kill, or it may be political mobs of urban youth who attack "enemy" centers, homes, and just people on the street. It must be recognized that this highly visible violence is a performance. Perpetrators communicate deep messages to both supporting and targeted groups (see Riches, 1986; Schmidt & Schroder, 2001). To supporters, the message is, "Look how we stand up for you; this is what needs to be done." To the enemy the message is, "Whatever else you may be as a person, your life and death depend solely on the identity label we attach to you." That is how, as Ignatieff (1977, p. 38) describes for one Croatian village, a man exchanging shots with his former friends and neighbors, had become "only a Serb."

When these identerest group divisions become drenched in blood and atrocity, it is very difficult to turn back. Large-scale fighting is almost inevitable. Unless it is suppressed by some overwhelming external military force, people may keep on killing until they finally get sick of it all. War-exhaustion can be a potent force for ultimately negotiating a peace—but at what a cost. The big lesson of identerest violence over recent decades is that it really must be stopped *before* it starts. It is necessary to work against polarization, by supporting narratives and values and people and reforms that work against further separation, to find ways of peeling off those who start out as being less attracted to militant ideologies, and to somehow engage the political will of outside powers and institutions toward providing the necessary support for local peacemakers.

It is easier said than done. It is anything but easy to mobilize a major international effort to prevent violence in some faraway place that few in politics or the public know or care about, to deal with seemingly intractable problems, where success means the situation remains calm, and CNN viewers never hear about it. Nevertheless, that is where the effort is needed, because an early change of course is the best way to prevent more humanitarian tragedies. And while many today would say, in the middle of a global "war on terrorism," that we cannot afford to be distracted by such humanitarian concerns, situations of violent breakdown of government and civil society can provide an ideal place for global terrorists to operate and grow (Lyman & Morrison, 2004). The issues are strongly connected.

## Terrorism and the War in Iraq

The next-to-last section of this chapter deals with terrorism and the wars in Afghanistan and Iraq. Some of my points concerning tribal warfare and identerest violence do seem applicable to the crisis we face today.

First, I discuss "terrorism." Labeling someone as a terrorist is a process in political symbolism (see Atran, 2003; Byford, 2002). *Enemies* are terrorists. Few who are called terrorists think of themselves in that way. They see themselves as freedom fighters, or religious warriors—and the defenders of those who have been victimized. The label as it is commonly used is the modern equivalent of the ancient label "barbarian," those outside of and endangering self-proclaimed civilization—and indeed the term barbarian was invoked in the last U.S. presidential campaign. It is very difficult to do a sober analysis of a conflict when one defines a situation in such polarized, political terms. So here is how I define things. When nonconventional fighters attack military targets, by whatever means, they are guerrillas. When they deliberately target civilians, they are terrorists. Of course, this conceptual distinction may be very blurry in practice, and fighters may be both at once.

Unfortunately, targeting civilians is how identerest violence usually works. In internal wars during the 1980s, the best estimate is about three-quarters of all deaths were civilian (Ahlstrom, 1991, pp. 9, 17). Why? Because it is "that kind of person" who, somehow, endangers us. And it is common because terror works. U.S. forces were withdrawn from Lebanon after a suicide truck bomber killed 241 servicemen in 1983. It is a cheap and effective tactic against an enemy, who may possess clear superiority in regular military forces. It can disrupt the plans of the powerful and may undercut their bases of support. It shapes the actions of other civilians. That is the world in which we live.

If terrorists resemble identerest fighters in their targeting of civilians, so do they in their form. News reports from Afghanistan and Iraq regularly implicate particular local religious affiliations, regional differences, ethnic identities, tribes, and clans as bases of recruitment. These, and other localized identities around the world, are connected in a loose global network of cell phones and computers, of diasporas and money flows. Their particular cases are disparate, but they are unified by similar radical interpretations of Islam, and linked to that, the perception of a common enemy, who is portrayed as the cause of "our" miseries and dedicated to the destruction of our identity. Be the focus America or Israel, Christianity or the West, there is enough conceptual overlap to foster cooperation. But to focus exclusively on the unifying beliefs, and lose sight of the local structures and processes that generate the fighters, is dangerously myopic. Much of the power in this global struggle comes from very local social identities, interests, and enemies (regarding Afghanistan, see Canfield, 1986, 1988; Sharani, 2002). Thus, Western states at war in Iraq and Afghanistan have become militarily engaged in an array of local identerest struggles.

Among the forces arrayed against the United States and its military allies, there are clearly leaders, and there are followers. Leaders have their own practical interests. Some seek governmental power, some push to increase the reach and influence of the institutions they control; many are well funded. Anti-Americanism has been "a useful tool for radical rulers, revolutionary movements, and even moderate regimes to build domestic support and pursue regional goals with no significant costs ... [It] is equally useful to oppressive Arab regimes, since it allows them to deflect attention from their own many failings" (Rubin, 2002, p. 80). Yet there is no reason to doubt that most believe in their ideologies of division, threat, and struggle. Many are extremely effective at communicating their visions. Those whom they recruit respond not just because the messages are laden with the most potent symbols of self-identity, but also because they are consistent with how some people see the world around them, with their perceived interests and lived experience, especially when that experience includes politically targeted violence. They hear an emotionally powerful message that makes sense. It becomes a cause.

Commonly in localized conflicts, the majority of willing killers are the disenfranchised, frequently young men from camps or slums, young men with no future. But we know that this is not universal. Many with privilege and prospects join up—that has made the news. As the struggle intensifies, the manipulations of symbols and situations, and the growing perception of threat, push more and more into the polarized extremes. In the second Palestinian Intifada, which has provided time and opportunity for research, young supporters of extreme actions seem somewhat more prosperous and educated than average (Atran, 2003, pp. 1536–1537). I believe this is where trends are heading in the global war on terrorism.

The current situation is well illustrated by one *New York Times* (Sachs, 2004) story, the account of a Turkish journalist, a relatively secular Muslim woman, who was taken hostage in northern Iraq, and then, inexplicably freed. She describes being handed off from one distinct group of captors to another, of clearly different ethnicity and language. Her tormentors worked together because of their common opposition to "infidels." "For them, there's no difference between a Christian and a Jew, and Canadian and an American," she said. "These are people who think they are living in the time of the Crusades. They say they are fighting for Islam first and Iraq second. They think their religion is being attacked" (p. A12). She saw how this message is spreading.

> I saw that around Mosul, everybody is the resistance—not terrorists, but not civilians really either. They used the small kids to bring them water, and nobody treated them like children. They'd be talking about cutting heads, and kids would be standing guard, like little men, so you become afraid of the children too.

Child soldiers are another characteristic of modern identerest violence (UNICEF, 1996).

U.S. military and political strategists have been bewildered by this diversity of enemies. In May 2005, the *New York Times* (Bennet, 2005) published an analysis under the heading of "The Mystery of the Insurgency." The general point was that no one could make sense of our opponents, that there was no coherence, no clear ideology, no general plan. That is exactly what is to be expected when the fight involves a variety of identerest groups and subdivisions. There is no one group to lead, but a spectrum of identities and divisions that become more or less salient as political entrepreneurs size up situations and play their cards.

That our adversaries are acting as I have described for identerest leaders is clearly shown in the famous captured letter attributed to Abu Musab al-Zarqawi from February 2004 (Coalition Provisional Authority, 2004). Complaining that their enemies were increasing control throughout Iraq, he worried about having to "pack our bags and search for another land" (p. 8). But he had a clear plan. And the plan shows how the United States and its allies have become ensnared in an exceedingly complex local struggle for power. For al-Zarqawi in early 2004, the allies are just a sideshow. The true adversary are the Shi'a.

[They are] the unsurmountable obstacle, the lurking snake, the crafty and malicious scorpion, the spying enemy, and the penetrating venom. ... The American army has begun to disappear from some cities, and its presence is rare. An Iraqi army has begun to take its place, and this is the real problem that we face, since our combat against the American is something easy. The enemy is apparent, his back is exposed, and he does not know the land or the current situation of the mujahadin because his intelligence information is weak. We know for certain that these Crusader forces will disappear tomorrow or the day after. ... I believe, and God knows best, that the worst will not come to pass until most of the American army is in the rear lines and the secret Shi'a army and its military brigades are fighting as its proxy. They are infiltrating like snakes to reign over the army and police apparatus, which is the strike force and iron fist in our Third World, and to take complete control over the economy like their tutors the jews ... . (p. 3)

In classic identerest style, al-Zarqawi provides a long historical tirade on what he portrays as the evil greed of the Shi'a, how this has long been directed against Sunnis, and how their campaign of killing their religious enemies is already in high gear. Yet the Sunni remain docile. What is to be done?

The Shi'a. These in our opinion are the key to change. I mean that targeting and hitting them in [their] religious, political, and military depth will provoke them to show the Sunnis their rabies. ... If we succeed in dragging them into the arena of sectarian war, it will become possible to awaken the inattentive Sunnis as they feel imminent danger and annihilating death at the hands of these Sabbeans. ... Someone may say that, in this matter, we are being hasty and rash and leading the [Islamic nation] into a battle for which it is not ready, [a battle] that will be revolting and in which blood will be spilled. This is exactly what we want, since right and wrong no longer have any place in our current situation. (pp. 7–8, all brackets in original)

This strategy of al-Zarqawi and other identerest entrepreneurs in Iraq is working. In December 2004, one *New York Times* article (Wong, 2004) was headlined "Mayhem in Iraq Is Starting to Look Like a Civil War." Fighting had already begun along ethnic and religious lines, and leaders were organizing an increasing number of young men into "Anger Brigades" to attack other Iraqis. In July 2005, the *Times* ran an evaluation of Iraq, with two headlines: "If It's Civil War, Do We Know It?" and "Maybe the Nightmare Has Arrived." It is the first time I have seen the idea attributed to U.S. officials that we might have to withdraw in the middle of a civil war and let the Iraqis fight or settle by themselves. One week after that, an Op-Ed piece by Steven Vincent (2005) described the operations of death squads within the Basra police, targeting Sunnis, even as the police were being trained by the British. Two days later Vincent was kidnaped and killed by two men in Iraqi police uniforms, driving an Iraqi police car (Wong, 2005). Perhaps this was just a coincidence.

What can people like al-Zarqawi gain by encouraging such attacks? As he states, violence will rouse the Sunnis, marginalize those among them who wish to cooperate, and put terrorists like himself in the leadership of a much broader political force. By actions and constructed history, he would create a new identerest conflict of broader scope than all the many factions now fighting. If enough Sunnis and Shiites kill each other just because of that identity, the two will polarize along that divide. In recent discussions leading up to the drafting of an Iraqi constitution, the possibility of national partition was repeatedly raised. A few years of forced displacements and mass killing along these constructed divides, and partition may well become unstoppable. The Shiites and Kurds would go their own ways—with whatever that brings. The Allies would be left holding the Triangle of Death bag—which we surely cannot hold for long.

In Iraq, terror and identerest conflict have become one. Without intending to do so, the Allies have followed the playbook for creating civil war. These divisions have been encouraged by the U.S. policy of excluding Sunnis from government while favoring Shiites and Kurds and using the latter two in military and police operations against Sunnis. It seemed necessary for security—but such steps are always taken for the security of a regime. Policies that favor certain categories of people, penalize others, and encourage violence by the most loyal against the more suspect are the tried and true way to shatter a coexisting mosaic and transform it into warring groups.

How did we get into this situation? Our war in Afghanistanhad global support. We were attacked, and—in my view—had to go to the seat of our attackers. The war in Iraq, obviously, is another story. Can the ideas I have presented from anthropology be applied to why the Iraq war happened? I think so. Iraq and the United States are certainly not identerest groups, but the broader theory of practical interests shaping perceptions and being reinforced by identities and values of those who start wars—at least arguably—fits. While there is no comparison of the tyrannical Iraqi regime, all but isolated in the world, with the U.S. governmental system, the "Coalition of the Willing," and its partial reliance on the U.N., nevertheless there are significant parallels on the two sides. (The following points about Iraq are drawn from Davis, 1992; Lewis & Johnston, 2004; Johnston, 2004; Special Advisor, 2004, pp. 21–34, 61–62).

In this case it is unusually clear who were the decision makers on both sides—one top man, and a very small circle of close advisers (though Hussein's advisers were indisputably subservient compared to the ideologically driven American conservatives). On both sides, the path toward war was a path of internal political advantage. For the decade after the first Gulf War, even into early 2003, Hussein was making calculated decisions to ward off what he saw as the greatest threats to his number one priority: regime (and personal) survival. The greatest perceived dangers were Iran, which is what led Hussein to promote the idea that Iraq had weapons of mass destruction (WMD) long after the program had been scrapped, and threats from within his own regime, including restive army officers, whom he felt had to be kept busy. (That was a major reason for invading Kuwait.) External enemies were necessary for Hussein to consolidate a nationalist vision that enshrined and protected him at the pinnacle. The United States, in contrast, was not seen as a military threat, and even into late 2002 Hussein was convinced that the United Nations and other powers would prevent an actual invasion. In the United States, after Republican victories in the 2002 Congressional elections, it was an openly stated strategy to campaign for Bush's re-election on his actions as commander-in-chief. A victorious cakewalk in Iraq followed by joyous democratization would have been a surefire winner. But even the tragic miscalculation and carnage in Iraq could be, and indeed was, turned to electoral advantage—in times of danger, what is needed is a strong leader, a point with which Hussein would undoubtedly concur.

Yet on both sides, the aggressive stance was fueled by deeply held convictions about the moral value of their actions. Hussein was utterly convinced that he was the restorer of Iraq's historical glory and a stalwart defender of Arab dignity against Western pressures. The inner circle of the Bush regime was divided between neoimperialists and assertive nationalists, but both saw aggressive, preemptive use of military power as righteous and necessary for the United States and the way to spread our values through the world (Hirsh, 2002; Ikenberry, 2004; Simes, 2003). Both sides acted on erroneous information: Hussein on the ability of his armies to inflict such casualties that a U.S. invasion would not reach Baghdad, Bush on WMD existing and posing a potential threat, in each case shaped by the willingness of subordinates to tailor information to suit already fixed conclusions. Both sides made enormous miscalculations about things that seemed self-evident to those outside the inner circles: Hussein on his ability to prevail, Bush on the ability to establish order after Hussein had been defeated. Both sides saw the other as morally corrupt by association, with Israel or with al Qaeda. Both sides saw the other as the aggressor.

What I am saying is that the Iraq war is like many wars: the result of a complex dialectic between two sides whose leaders make decisions based on an amalgam of political self-interest, self-identities, and self-serving values and perceptions. The dialectic continues. Iraq has become the recruiting poster for terrorist leaders around the world, the rallying cry of those who benefit from anti-Americanism. Here at home, in American political culture, terrorism has become the new communism. Antiterrorism has expanded into almost every political niche once occupied by anticommunism. For the foreseeable future, how external threats are conceptualized, and what actions will be taken, will respond to the incessant struggle for domestic political advantage. Nothing matters more in American politics than who wins. Terrorists and antiterrorists are feeding off each other.

It is extremely difficult to stop a war once it gets started, especially when identities and interests are as fully engaged as they are in this conflict. It is difficult to see a silver lining, and I have no plausible suggestions to make things better. The way to stop conflicts like these is to keep them from developing in the first place. It is too late for that now. But there certainly is time to avert large-scale identerest violence in many potential crisis areas around the world. What is needed is a better understanding of how wars happen and the political will to prevent them.

## Conclusion

This chapter has covered a lot of ground, from tribal war, through identerest conflicts, to terrorism and the war in Iraq. The first section on biological approaches to war concluded with a quote from Fukuyama (1998, pp. 36–37). We can return to that in closing. Fukuyama's main point was that feminine leadership could be a threat to national security, because "the broader world scene will still be populated by states led by the occasional Mobutu, Milosevic, or Saddam," and "masculine policies" will be needed to deal with them. I would not deny that the tight circle of Washington decision makers exuded machismo. But there were men and women all over the world on both sides of the issue of whether to invade, and would anyone care to argue that the reason we went to war in Iraq is that the two governments were led by macho, macho men?

Cultural anthropology offers a way to approach war that is applicable to both research and preventative action. Understanding war means first identifying and focusing on the key decision makers who take the leading steps down the road to war. What are their practical interests in the dialectic between external and internal political oppositions? What are the identities, moral values, symbols, constructed histories, and perceptions that relate to these interests? How do those two realms come together either as psychologically fused beliefs and/or as deliberate manipulation of others? How are these views conveyed to and/or imposed upon those who follow into war? For followers, what are their interests and understandings, and how do they interact with the promulgations of the political elites?

Disrupting a march toward war involves countering all those connections. It involves exposing, first of all, the interests of leaders, and second, how identities, values, symbols, histories, and perceptions are selectively constructed and used. It involves helping to promote local counterinterpretations and constructions, by supporting people and organizations who work against polarization and violence. It involves working internationally to build together sources of influence and finance to support those efforts. Success will be extremely difficult, because local problems are typically complex and seemingly intractable, and because those who are pushing for war have power behind them. They will typically attempt to marginalize (or worse) their opponents by characterizing them as partisans pursuing their own agendas.

Fighting against war, like any other curse of humankind, will always be frustrating and be doomed to many more failures than successes. Social science is a feeble antidote to the interests of power. But exposing the interests, misconceptions, and manipulations of the masters of war can provide some guidance and encouragement to its opponents. It is a positive contribution. What alternative is there?

## Note

An earlier version of this chapter was presented as a Visiting Scholar lecture at the Department of Anthropology, University of Tennessee, Knoxville, in September 2004. The ideas sharpened through discussion with students in my Fall 2004 course "War" at Rutgers University–Newark and with colleagues at a conference on war at the University of Durham, United Kingdom, in July 2005. Thanks to all.

# References

Ahlstrom, Christer. (1991). *Casualties of conflict: Report for the world campaign for the protection of victims of war.* Department of Peace and Conflict Research, Uppsala University, Sweden. Distributed by the World Campaign for the Protection of Victims of War, Geneva, Switzerland.

Albert, Bruce. (1990). On Yanomami warfare: A rejoinder. *Current Anthropology 31,* 558–563

Archer, John. (2000). Sex differences in aggression between heterosexual partners: A meta-analytic review. *Psychological Bulletin 126,* 651–680.

Archer, John, Birring, Surinder S., & Wu, Frederick C. W. (1998). The association between testosterone and aggression among young men: Empirical findings and a meta-analysis. *Aggressive Behavior 24,* 411–420.

Arkush, Elizabeth, & Allen, Mark (Eds.). (in press) *Violent transformations: The archaeology of warfare and long-term social change.* Gainesville: University of Florida.

Atran, Scott. (2003). Genesis of suicide terrorism. *Science 299,* 1534–1539.

Baron, Robert A., & Richardson, Deborah R. (1994). *Human aggression* (2nd ed.). New York: Plenum Press.

Barth, Frederik (Ed.). (1969). *Ethnic groups and boundaries: The social organization of culture difference.* Boston: Little, Brown and Co.

Bennett, James. (2005, May 15). The Mystery of the Insurgency. *The New York Times,* p. 4:1.

Berdal, Mats, & Malone, David M. (Eds.). (2000). *Greed and grievance: Economic agendas in civil wars.* Boulder: Lynne Rienner.

Boas, Franz. (1912). An anthropologist's view of war. Pamphlet No. 52. New York: American Association for International Conciliation.

Boone, Catherine. (2003). *Political topographies of the African state: Territorial authority and institutional choice.* Cambridge, England: Cambridge University Press.

Brewer, Marilyn B., & Campbell, Donald T. (1976). *Ethnocentrism and intergroup attitudes: The East African evidence.* New York: John Wiley.

Brown, Diana DeG. (2003). Civil war and the "collapse" of the settler state. In R. Brian Ferguson (Ed.), *The state, identity, and violence: Political disintegration in the post-Cold War world* (pp. 217–242). New York: Routledge.

Byford, Grenville. (2002, July/August). The wrong war. *Foreign Affairs 81*(4), 34–43.

Canfield, Robert L. (1986). Ethnic, regional, and sectarian alignments in Afghanistan. In A. Banuazizi & M. Weiner (Eds.), *The state, religion, and ethnic politics: Afghanistan, Iran, and Pakistan* (pp. 75–103). Syracuse, NY: Syracuse University.

Canfield, Robert L. (1988). Afghanistan's social identities in crisis. In J. P. Digard (Ed.), *Le fait ethnique en Iran et en Afghanistan* (pp. 185–199). Paris: Editions du CNRS.

Chagnon, Napoleon. (1968). *Yanomamo: The fierce people.* New York: Holt, Rinehart, and Winston.

Chagnon, Napoleon. (1974). *Studying the Yanomamo.* New York: Holt, Rinehart, and Winston.

Chagnon, Napoleon. (1983). *Yanomamo: The fierce people* (3rd ed.). New York: Holt, Rinehart, and Winston.

Chagnon, Napoleon. (1988). Life histories, blood revenge, and warfare in a tribal population. *Science 239,* 985–992.

Chagnon, Napoleon. (1992). *Yanomamo* (4th ed.). Harcourt Brace Jovanovich College Publishers.

Chagnon, Napoleon. (1996). Chronic problems in understanding tribal violence and warfare. In Gregory R. Bock & Jamie A. Goode (Eds.), *Genetics of criminal and antisocial behavior* (pp. 202–236). Ciba Foundation Symposium 194. New York: John Wiley and Sons.

Coalition Provisional Authority. (2004). Text from Abu Mus'ab al-Zarqawi Letter. Retrieved August 2, 2005, from www.globalsecurity.org/wmd/library/news/iraq/2004/02/040212-al-zarqawi.htm

Condry, J., & Condry, S. (1976). Sex differences: A study in the eye of the beholder. *Child Development 47*, 812–819.

Davis, Eric. (1992). State-building in Iraq during the Iran-Iraq War and the Gulf Crisis. In Manus Midlarsky (Ed.), *The internationalization of communal strife* (pp. 69–92). New York: Routledge.

Divale, William, & Harris, Marvin. (1976). Population, warfare, and the male supremacist complex. *American Anthropologist 78*, 521–538.

Eagly, Alice H., & Wood, Wendy. (2003). The origins of sex differences in human behavior: Evolved dispositions versus social roles. In Cheryl Brown Travis (Ed.), *Evolution, gender, and rape* (pp. 265–304). Cambridge, MA: MIT Press.

Ferguson, R. Brian. (1984a). Introduction: Studying war. In R. Brian Ferguson (Ed.), *Warfare, culture, and environment* (pp. 1–81). Orlando, FL: Academic Press.

Ferguson, R. Brian. (Ed.). (1984b). *Warfare, culture, and environment*. Orlando, FL: Academic Press.

Ferguson, R. Brian. (1988). War and the sexes in Amazonia. In Richard Randolph, David Schneider, & May Diaz (Eds.), *Dialectics and gender: Anthropological approaches* (pp. 136–154). Boulder, CO: Westview.

Ferguson, R. Brian. (1989). Do Yanomamo killers have more kids? *American Ethnologist 16*, 564–565.

Ferguson, R. Brian. (1990). Explaining war. In Jonathan Hass (Ed.), *The anthropology of war* (pp. 26–55). Cambridge, England: Cambridge University Press.

Ferguson, R. Brian. (1995a). *Yanomami warfare: A political history*. Santa Fe, NM: School of American Research.

Ferguson, R. Brian. (1995b). Infrastructural determinism. In Martin F. Murphy & Maxine L. Margolis (Eds.), *Science, materialism, and the study of culture* (pp. 21–38). Gainesville: University of Florida.

Ferguson, R. Brian. (1997). Violence and war in prehistory. In Debra Martin & Paul Frayer (Eds.), *Troubled times: Violence and warfare in the past* (pp. 321–355). Langhorne, PA: Gordon and Breach.

Ferguson, R. Brian. (1999). A paradigm for the study of war and society. In Kurt Raaflaub & Nathan Rosenstein (Eds.), *War and society in the ancient and medieval worlds: Asia, the Mediterranean, Europe, and Mesoamerica* (pp. 389–437). Center for Hellenic Studies, distributed by Cambridge, MA: Harvard University.

Ferguson, R. Brian. (2000). On evolved motivations for war. *Anthropological Quarterly 73*, 159–164.

Ferguson, R. Brian. (2001). Materialist, cultural and biological theories on why Yanomami make war. *Anthropological Theory 1*, 99–116.

Ferguson, R. Brian. (2003a, July/August). The birth of war. *Natural History*, 28–35.

Ferguson, R. Brian. (2003b). *The state, identity and violence: Political disintegration in the post-Cold War world*. New York: Routledge.

Ferguson, R. Brian. (2003c). Introduction: Violent conflict and control of the state. In R. Brian Ferguson (Ed.), *The state, identity and violence: Political disintegration in the post-Cold War world* (pp. 1–58). New York: Routledge.

Ferguson, R. Brian. (n.d.). *Chimpanzees, men, and war*. Book in preparation.

Ferguson, R. Brian. (in press). Archaeology, cultural anthropology, and the origins and intensifications of war. In Elizabeth Arkush & Mark Allen (Eds.), *Violent transformations: The archaeology of warfare and long-term social change*. Gainesville: University of Florida.

Ferguson, R. Brian, & Whitehead, Neil L. (Eds.). (2000). *War in the tribal zone: Expanding Sstates and indigenous warfare* (2nd printing). Santa Fe, NM: School of American Research Press.

Fried, Morton. (1973). On human aggression. In Charlotte Otten (Ed.), *Aggression and evolution* (pp. 355–362). Lexington, MA: Xerox College Publishing.

Fukuyama, Frances. (1998, September/October). Women and the evolution of world politics. *Foreign Affairs*, pp. 24–40.

Gat, Azar. (2000). The human motivational complex: Evolutionary theory and the causes of hunter-gatherer fighting. Part I. Primary somatic and reproductive causes. *Anthropological Quarterly 73*(1), 20–34.

Gavin, Michael. (2004). Chimps and humans in conflict. BBC Science and Nature. Retrieved May 25, 2004, from www.bbc.co.uk/nature/animals/features/325feature2.shtml

Ghiglieri, Michael. (1999). *The dark side of man: Tracing the origins of male violence*. Reading, MA: Perseus Books.

Gurr, Ted Robert. (2000). *People versus states: Minorities at risk in the new century*. Washington: United States Institute of Peace.

Haas, Jonathan. (1999). The origins of war and ethnic violence. In John Carman & Anthony Harding (Eds.), *Ancient warfare: Archaeological perspectives* (pp. 11–24). Phoenix Mill, England: Sutton.

Haas, Jonathan. (2000). Review of the book *Prehistoric warfare in the American Southwest. Journal of Field Archaeology 27*, 483–485.

Harris, Marvin. (1977). *Cannibals and kings: The origins of cultures*. New York: Random House.

Harris, Marvin. (1979). *Cultural materialism: The struggle for a science of culture*. New York: Random House.

Harris, Marvin. (1984). A cultural materialist theory of band and village warfare: The Yanomamo test. In R. Brian Ferguson (Ed.), *Warfare, culture, and environment* (pp. 111–140). Orlando, FL: Academic Press.

Hinton, Alexander Laban. (2004). *Why did they kill? Cambodia in the shadow of genocide*. Berkeley: University of California.

Hirsh, Michael. (2002, September/October). Bush and the world. *Foreign Affairs 81*(5), 18–43.

Hyde, Janet Shibley. (1984). How large are gender differences in aggression? A developmental meta-analysis. *Developmental Psychology 20*, 722–736.

Ignatieff, Michael. (1997). *The warrior's honor: Ethnic war and the modern conscience*. New York: Henry Holt.

Ikenberry, G. John. (2004, March/April). Illusions of empire. *Foreign Affairs 83*, 144–154.

Johnston, David. (2004, October 7). Saddam Hussein sowed confusion about Iraq's arsenal as a tactic of war. *The New York Times*, p. A28.

Keeley, Lawrence H. (1996). *War before civilization: The myth of the peaceful savage.* New York: Oxford.

Kelly, Raymond C. (2000). *Warless societies and the origin of war.* Ann Arbor: University of Michigan.

Kemper, Theodore D. (1990). *Social structure and testosterone: Explorations of the socio-bio-social chain.* New Brunswick, NJ: Rutgers University Press.

Klama, John. (1988). *Aggression: The myth of the beast within.* New York: John Wiley and Sons.

Lan, David. (1985). *Guns and rain: Guerrillas and spirit mediums in Zimbabwe.* Berkeley: University of California.

LeBlanc, Steven. (1999). *Prehistoric warfare in the American Southwest.* Salt Lake City: University of Utah Press.

LeBlanc, Steven. (with Register, Katherine). (2003). *Constant battles: The myth of the peaceful, noble savage.* New York: St. Martin's Press.

Lewis, Neil A., & Johnston, David. (2004, July 2). Hussein in jail, reportedly said little of value. *The New York Times,* pp. A1, A7.

Lizot, Jacques. (1989). Sobre la guerra: Una respuesta a N.A. Chagnon (Science 1988). *La Iglesia en Amazonas 44* (April) 23–44.

Lyman, Princeton N., & Morrison, J. Stephen. (2004). The terrorist threat in Africa. *Foreign Affairs 83*(1), 75–86.

Maccoby, Eleanor E., & Jacklin, Carol N. (1974). *The psychology of sex differences.* Stanford, CA: Stanford University.

Malinowski, Bronislaw. (1941). An anthropological analysis of war. *American Journal of Sociology 46,* 521–550.

Maybury-Lewis, David. (1974). *Akwe-Shavante Society.* New York: Oxford University.

Meggitt, Mervyn. (1965). *Desert people: A study of the Walbiri Aborigines of Central Australia.* Chicago: The University of Chicago.

Nishida, Toshisada. (1979). The social structure of chimpanzees of the Mahale Mountains. In David A. Hamburg & Elizabeth R. McCown (Eds.), *The Great Apes* (pp. 73–121). Reading, MA: Benjamin/Cummings Publishing.

Nishida, Toshisada. (1980). On inter-unit-group aggression and intra-group cannibalism among wild chimpanzees. *Human Ethology Newsletter 31,* 21–24.

Nordstrom, Carolyn. (1998). Deadly myths of aggression. *Aggressive Behavior 24,* 147–159.

O'Connell, Robert L. (1995). *Ride of the second horseman: The birth and death of war.* New York: Oxford University.

Otterbein, Keith. (1973). The Aanthropology of war. In John Honigmann (Ed.), *Handbook of social and cultural anthopology* (pp. 923–959). Chicago: Rand McNally.

Otterbein, Keith. (1977). Warfare: A hitherto unrecognized critical variable. *American Behavioral Scientist 20,* 693–710.

Rappaport, Roy. (1985). *Pigs for the ancestors: Ritual in the ecology of a New Guinea people* (Rev. ed.). New Haven, CT: Yale University.

Reyna, Stephen P. (2003). A Cold War story: The barbarization of Chad (1966-91). In R. Brian Ferguson (Ed.), *The state, identity and violence: Political disintegration in the post-Cold War world* (pp. 261–284). New York: Routledge.

Richards, Paul. (1996). *Fighting for the rain forest: War, youth, and resources in Sierra Leone.* Portsmouth, NH: Heinemann.

Riches, David (Ed.). (1986). *The anthropology of violence.* Oxford, England: Basil Blackwell.

Robarchek, Clayton. (1990). Motivations and material causes: On the explanation of conflict and war. In Jonathan Haas (Ed.), *The anthropology of war* (pp. 56–76). Cambridge, England: Cambridge University Press.

Roper, Marilyn. (1969). A survey of the evidence for intrahuman killing in the Pleistocene. *Current Anthropology 10*, 410–459.

Roper, Marilyn. (1975). Evidence of warfare in the Near East from 10,000–4,300 B.C. In Martin A. Nettleship, R. Dale Givens, & Anderson Nettleship (Eds.), *War: Its causes and correlates* (pp. 299–344). The Hague: Mouton.

Rosaldo, Michelle. (1983). The shame of headhunters and the autonomy of self. *Ethos 11*(3), 135–151.

Rubin, Barry. (2002, November/December). The Real Roots of Arab Anti-Americanism. *Foreign Affairs 81*(6), 73–85.

Sachs, Susan. (2004, September 24). Captive Turk in Iraq tells of fearful struggle to live. *The New York Times*, p. A12.

Sahlins, Marshall. (1987). *Islands of history.* Chicago: University of Illinois.

Sapolsky, Robert M. (1997). *The trouble with testosterone.* New York: Scribner.

Scheper-Hughes, Nancy, & Bourgois, Philippe (Eds.). (2004). *Violence in war and peace: An anthology.* Oxford, England: Blackwell.

Schmidt, Bettina E., & Schroder, Ingo W. (Eds.). (2001). *Anthropology of violence and conflict.* New York: Routledge.

Sharani, Nazif M. (2002). War, factionalism, and the state in Afghanistan. *American Anthropologist 104*, 715–722.

Shaw, R. Paul, & Wong, Yuwa. (1989). *Genetic seeds of warfare: Evolution, nationalism, and patriotism.* Boston: Unwin Hyman.

Sidorowicz, Laura S., & Lunney, G. Sparks. (1980). Baby X revisited. *Sex Roles 6*, 67–73.

Sillitoe, Paul. (1978). Big men and war in New Guinea. *Man 13*, 252–271.

Simes, Dimitri K. (2003, November/December). America's imperial dilemma. *Foreign Affairs 82*(6), 91–102.

Siskind, Janet. (1973). Tropical forest hunters and the economy of sex. In Daniel Gross (Ed.), *Peoples and cultures of native South America* (pp. 226–240). Garden City, NY: Doubleday.

Special Advisor. (2004). *Comprehensive report of the special advisor to the DCI on Iraq's WMD: Regime strategic intent.* Washington, DC: The Central Intelligence Agency.

Spencer, Baldwin, & Gillin, F. J. (1969). *The northern tribes of Central Australia.* Oosterhout, the Netherlands: Anthropological Publications. (Original work published 1904)

Stewart, Pamela J., & Strathern, Andrew. (2002). *Violence: Theory and ethnography.* New York: Continuum.

Sumner, William Graham. (1906). *Folkways.* New York: Mentor Books.

Tafjel, Henri, & Turner, John C. (1986). The social identity theory of intergroup behavior. In Stephen Worchel & William G. Austin (Eds.), *Pyschology of intergroup relations* (2nd ed., pp. 7–24). Chicago: Nelson-Hall.

Taylor, Christopher. (1999). *Sacrifice as terror: The Rwandan genocide of 1994.* New York: Oxford.

Tierney, Patrick. (2000). *Darkness in El Dorado: How scientists and journalists devastated the Amazon.* New York: Norton.

Trompf, G.W. (1994). *Payback: The logic of retribution in Melanesian religions.* Cambridge, England: Cambridge University Press.

UNICEF. (1996). The state of the world's children 1996. Oxford, England: Oxford University Press.

Van der Dennen, Hans. (1986). Four fatal fallacies in defense of a myth: The aggression-warfare linkage. In J. Winde & V. Falger (Eds.), *Essays in human sociobiology*, vol. 2 (pp. 43–67). Brussels: V.U.B. Study Series No.

Van der Dennen, J. M. G. (1995). *The origin of war* (2 vols.). Groningen, the Netherlands: Origin Press.

Vayda, Andrew Peter. (1968) Hypotheses about functions of war. In Morton Fried, Marvin Harris, & Robert Murphy (Eds.), *War: The anthropology of armed conflict and aggression* (pp. 85–91). Garden City, NY: The Natural History Press.

Vayda, Andrew Peter. (1976). *War in ecological perspective: Persistence, change and adaptive process in three oceanian societies*. New York: Plenum

Vencl, Slavomil. (1984). War and warfare in archaeology. *Journal of Anthropological Archaeology 3*, 116–132.

Vincent, Steven. (2005, July 31). Switched off in Basra. *The New York Times*, p. 4:12.

Vivciros de Castro, Eduardo. (1992). *From the enemy's point of view: Humanity and divinity in an Amazonian society*. Chicago: University of Chicago.

Wade, Nicholas. (2003, November 25). A course in evolution taught by chimps. *The New York Times*, pp. F1, F4.

Wakabi, Wairagala. (2004, February 2004). "Drunk and disorderly" chimps attacking Ugandan children. *EastAfrican*. Retrieved May 23, 2004, from www.primates.com/chimps/drunk-n-disorderly.html

Warner, W. Lloyd. (1958). *A black civilization: A study of an Australian tribe*. New York: Harper Torchbooks.

Whitehead, Neil L. (2002). *Dark Shamans: Kanaima and the poetics of violent death*. Durham: Duke University.

Wilson, Michael L., & Wrangham, Richard W. (2003). Intergroup relations in chimpanzees. *Annual Review of Anthropology 32*, 363 392.

Wong, Edward. (2004, December 5). Mayhem in Iraq is starting to look like a civil war. *The New York Times*, pp.A 4–A5.

Wong, Edward. (2005, August 3). American journalist is shot to death in Iraq. *The New York Times*, p. A9.

Wrangham, Richard, & Peterson, Dale. (1996). *Demonic males: Apes and the origins of human violence*. Boston: Houghton Mifflin.

Wrangham, Richard, & Pilbeam, David (2001). African apes as time machines. In Birute M. F. Galdikas, Nancy Erickson Briggs, Lori K. Sheeran, Gary L. Shapiro, & Jane Goodall (Eds.), *All apes great and small, Vol. 1: African apes* (pp. 5–17). New York: Kluwer Academic/Plenum.

CHAPTER 3

# NEUROPSYCHOLOGY OF CONFLICT: IMPLICATIONS FOR PEACEMAKING

## Douglas E. Noll

Recent advances in the neurosciences have established an irrefutable fact: Human beings are far more emotional than rational. Nevertheless, on the strength of Descartes's rationalist philosophy, the Enlightenment opened the doors to modern empiricism and led humanity into the Scientific Revolution. No one doubted the power of rational thinking to solve problems and unravel the mysteries of the observable universe. From these observations came the belief that humans were distinguished from all other creatures because of their rationality. To be irrational was to be something less than human.

This belief deeply influenced English and American law, foreign policy, and economics. Legal standards were set by comparison to a prototypical rational person. Foreign policy was based on the assumption that rational beings could sit together and work through international disputes and conflicts. Economists built an entire field of study on the assumption that consumers acted "rationally" in maximizing their utility. People engaged in peacemaking, from the interpersonal to the international level, assumed that despite the emotions of conflict, people fundamentally were rational.

The truth is that human beings are 98 percent emotional and about 2 percent rational. Thus, the assumptions underlying many disciplines and practices, especially peacemaking, need significant revisions. This chapter explores what neuroscience has discovered about emotions and how that knowledge is relevant to human conflict and peacemaking. Much remains unknown, but the implications of the research so far demonstrate that peacemakers must be far more aware of neuropsychological factors of human conflict. These factors explain much about conflict behaviors. They also provide insights about new interventions in serious and intractable conflicts.

Neuroscience is a highly technical, rapidly developing, and growing area of research. Consequently, for a lay person to distill the basic concepts of emotion is fraught with the peril of oversimplification and generalization. Nevertheless, an understanding of the big picture provides a deeper insight into conflict behaviors and the interventions useful to create positive peace. Consequently, the risk of academic imprecision seems outweighed by the benefit of practical knowledge gained from a broad understanding of the concepts.

All human psychological experience depends on brain activity, making temperament and behavior biologically based (Gray, 1991; Strelau, 1994). Thus, theoretical speculation about the causes of peaceful and conflictual behaviors must be consistent with neurological functioning (Beatty & McCroskey, 1997). If we assume the existence of cognitive processes (e.g., attributing, appraising, construing, etc.), we are obligated to specify the neurological activity responsible for those processes. If we are goal oriented, we must tackle the question of first cause: Where do our intentions, motives, and goals originate if not within the neurobiological structures of our brains? If we can control our cognitive processes or make choices, where does the control originate if not in brain structures? More generally, credible explanations of why and how people engage in peaceful or conflictual behaviors require adequate attention to the neurosciuence of peace and conflict.


## Conflict Behaviors and Emotions

### Conflict Behaviors

The fields of conflict theory and negotiation theory have generally settled on a typology of five conflict behaviors or conflict management styles. These are competing, accommodating, compromising, avoiding, and problem solving. There are variations and subsets within each of these behaviors, but these are primary.

#### *Competing*

Competing is satisfying one's own concerns while disregarding the other's concerns. This is usually a preconscious reaction based on how a schema cluster filters a situation. Parties often make their own demands apparent, then hide their true motives and any other information that might weaken their position. Competing people are quite active in conflict and aggressively pursue personal goals. A competing style is typically not very flexible as people avoid sacrificing any goals (Rubin, Pruitt, & Kim, 1994). Competing is typically seen in two strategies. The first, forcing, occurs when one party simply coerces others to go along. There is neither concern nor understanding for the others' positions nor any attempt to build a future relationship.

The second form of competing is contending. Contending is softer than forcing because it has an element of flexibility. Typically, a contender will be flexible as long as flexibility does not block his or her goals. A contender may also express understanding and sympathy for others' feelings. Unlike forcing, contending shows concern for future relationships.

### Accommodating

Accommodators give in to others to preserve a bad relationship or improve a good relationship (Rubin et al., 1994). Accommodators are highly flexible, as they will accede to the others' demands. They tend to empower others while suspending personal control. Again, this is usually the result of preconscious schema clusters being triggered by some aspect of the current situation.

Accommodation is a useful strategy when relationships are more important than the issues underlying the current conflict. Skillfully employed, accommodation can convey an understanding of the others' needs to improve the relationship. On the downside, accommodation may be viewed by the others as a sign of weakness and encourage a more competitive approach. Accommodation is also a poor style when it results from the fear of facing difficult conflict issues.

### Avoiding

Parties who avoid conflict do not demonstrate concern for their own or others' interests. Avoiding prevents these interests from being aired and addressed. Of course, if one expects to lose a conflict, avoidance is not a bad choice. Even in this circumstance, however, issues will remain unresolved and latent conflict will boil beneath the surface. Avoiding disputes disempowers others by denying the possibility of dealing with the conflict. Thus, avoidant behavior can escalate a conflict because it can be so frustrating for others to deal with.

Sometimes parties avoid conflicts because they have the power to ignore issues. In these cases, the other party is forced to escalate, oftentimes to violence, to provoke a response. In such cases, avoiders become indignant and quite often turn into competitors.

### Compromising

Compromising requires both parties to give up some of their needs to fulfill others. The compromiser looks for an intermediate position in which some important goals can be reached in exchange for trading off others. Compromisers show moderate flexibility as they do relent on some of their demands. They empower themselves and others because shared control is necessary to the give and take necessary for compromise.

Compromising is often confused with problem solving because trade-offs and exchanges seem like integrative behavior. Compromising is advantageous when there are two equally strong parties locked in impasse. However, compromise often results in a low commitment to agreements because parties must give up something they value.

## *Problem Solving*

Problem solving has received attention because its goal is to meet all the important needs of both parties. Successful problem solving does not have any significant disadvantages. Nevertheless, problem solving is difficult to maintain during a conflict because the emotions of the situation trigger other schema strategies. Nevertheless, parties are generally pleased after successful problem-solving sessions, and this satisfaction promotes a high commitment to keep agreements.

Problem solvers are highly concerned with both their own and the others' needs. They are involved in the conflict, seeking understanding of every issue and exploring all possible integrative solutions. They are flexible because they do not rigidly adhere to positions. However, they are also committed to achieving their goals and will not sacrifice them. Problem solving works best when parties have high aspirations for the outcome of the conflict, insist that their goals and needs be satisfied, and are flexible about how this is done (Rubin et al., 1994).

Problem solving requires a high degree of information about issues, needs, and interests. Thus, problem solving requires an open, safe, and secure communication climate. Problem solving also requires mutual empowerment without sacrificing individual power bases. This is most easily accomplished when both parties have common power resources.

## Emotions, Emotional Awareness, and Language

Emotions are information about how well we have achieved our goals in our environment. These goals do not have to be and usually are not consciously selected. Rather, they are part of our scripts and automatic behaviors learned to minimize cognitive processing power. Consequently, emotions may be experienced for no apparent reason, or we may be able to causally link our emotions to some event or memory.

We experience emotions on five levels:

1. Physical sensation
2. Action tendencies
3. Simple emotions
4. Blends of emotions
5. Blends of blends of emotion experiences.

At the fifth level, we appreciate the complexity of our experience and the experiences of others. Our ability to be aware of and express our emotional experience is a significant indication of our ability to be empathic. Language promotes our development of emotional information processing (Lane, 2000). Thus poor language skills, cultural norms inhibiting expression of emotional experience, and education are constraints on emotional awareness. The more we are emotionally aware, the greater our potential to use emotional information for adaptational success. In other words, people with refined emotional awareness are more likely to be successful in unusual or challenging social environments.

### The Emotions of Peace and Conflict

Emotions are associated with the five conflict behaviors. These emotions can be divided into conflict affects and peace affects. Conflict affects and peace affects are described by a continuum of selfish to selfless behaviors. Selfish behaviors are individualistic, competitive, and dichotomous (I win–You lose). These selfish behaviors require no object for expression; instead, it is always meaningful to ask how hungry, cold, happy, aroused, or angry a person feels. Selfless behaviors are communal, social, and inclusive (I gain only if you gain as well). Selfless behaviors always require an object. Thus, it is only meaningful to ask how loving, attached, or compassionate one feels toward someone else. Selfish and individualistic behaviors are always turned on, although they are often manifested at very low levels. In contrast, cooperative behaviors are accessible only when a relationship with another person is salient.

Conflict affects include anxiety, fear, anger, hatred, distrust, sadness, guilt, shame, disgust, and despair. Peace affects include happiness, compassion, contentment, loving kindness, and the will to do good. These affects can be associated with conflict behaviors and fundamental brain functions as follows.

| Conflict Behavior | Associated Affects | Selfish-Selfless | Brain Function |
|---|---|---|---|
| Contending | Fear, anger, hatred, distrust | Selfish | Withdraw (fight) |
| Accommodating | Compassion, contentment, loving kindness | Selfless | Approach |
| Compromising | Anxiety, fear, and distrust<br>Or<br>Happiness, compassion, contentment, loving kindness, and the will to do good | Selfish<br><br>Selfless | Withdraw (flee)<br><br>Approach |
| Collaborating | Happiness, compassion, contentment, loving kindness, and the will to do good | Selfless | Approach |
| Avoiding | Anxiety, fear, anger, hatred, distrust, sadness, guilt, shame, disgust, and despair | Selfish | Withdraw (flee or freeze) |

## The Neuropsychology of Conflict and Peaceful Behaviors

At the risk of oversimplifying a very complex subject, our brains are composed of two distinct emotional systems relevant to conflict and peacemaking. Consistent with identified conflict behaviors, the first system is *selfish* and directed toward self-preservation. This part of the brain contains, among many other systems, the fear response system responsible for the freeze, flee, or fight response to threats. The fear response system can further be separated into a hyperarousal system manifesting in fight or flight behavior and a dissociative system manifesting in freezing and avoidance behavior. Each system is composed of neural networks and is controlled by neurotransmitters and neurohormones.

The second system, consistent with descriptions of peaceful behaviors, is *selfless* and directed toward attachment, social bonding, and cooperation. This system is not as well understood as the fear response system, but it provides the foundation for the mother-infant attachment, sexual pair bonding, group attachment, and social cooperation. Similar to the selfish system, the selfless system is composed of distinct neural networks controlled by neurotransmitters and neurohormones.

### Behavioral Processing Systems

#### The Role of Neurochemicals

The physical structure of the brain operates in large part through a complex neurochemical messaging system. These neurochemical systems act by altering the response properties of transmission and receptor sites (Buck, 1999). Neurohormones may be released by sensory input (day-night cycles, display of other creatures, and presence of food) and internal input, reflecting needs and desires (hunger, thirst, and sex). They either sensitize or desensitize receptor sites and thus excite or inhibit brain cell activity.

#### The Amine Neurotransmitters

The amines are divided into two broad categories: the catecholamines, including dopamine, norepinephrine, and epinephrine, and the indole amines, including serotonin and histamine. The amines function as neurotransmitters, carrying stimulating or inhibiting influences from the presynaptic cell to the postsynaptic cell. The amine neurotransmitters are manufactured in the presynaptic cell, within which they are broken down by the enzyme monoamine oxidase. Once released into the synapse, they are absorbed back into the presynaptic cell in a re-uptake process.

Dopamine and norepinephrine are associated with reward because they cause intense pleasure. Dopamine is involved in the brain's pleasure pathways, some of which run from the hypothalamus, gateway to the endocrine glands, through the emotional areas of the limbic system to the planning and working memory areas of the frontal lobes (Ashby, Turken, & Isen, 1999; J. Brown, Bullock, & Grossberg, 1999; Schultz, Tremblay, & Hollerman, 2000). Dopamine inputs are important for the proper development of frontal lobe circuits in young children. This has been proposed as the mechanism by which proper caregiving, including pleasurable emotional experiences with parents or other caregivers, contributes to the growth of a child's mental capacities (Schore, 1994). Dopamine also probably plays a role in surges of both generosity and creativity in adults brought on by good moods (Ashby et al., 1999).

Serotonin is an indole amine neurotransmitter and appears to counterbalance the catecholaminergic systems. Thus, serotonin promotes sleep, parasympathetic activation, and the antistress relaxation response (Buck, 1999). Drugs that bind to specific serotonin receptor sites include the selective serotonin re-uptake inhibitors that are used in the treatment of major depression. One of these, fluoxetine, is widely known by its brand name Prozac (Buck, 1999). The effect of these re-uptake inhibitors is to allow serotonin to linger long in the synaptic space and thus increase its influence on the postsynaptic neuron.

Serotonin is intimately linked to social status in primates. In experiments changing the level of serotonin in monkeys, monkeys with low levels of serotonin had low status (Brammer, Raleigh, & McGuire, 1994; McGuire & Raleigh, 1986; Raleigh, McGuire, Brammer, & Yuwiler, 1984). When the concentration of serotonin was manipulated, the monkeys' social standing was influenced. Thus serotonin levels directly affect social status. By contrast, higher status was not related to obvious physical features such as larger body size or canine teeth. During the course of the experiments, which lasted several weeks, social status changes were always preceded by changes in affiliative behavior with females. Male monkeys given drugs that increased serotonin engaged in more frequent grooming interactions with females. Increased grooming behavior was followed by female support in dominance interactions, which increased the male's social status.

Conversely, male monkeys given drugs that decreased serotonin had less frequent grooming interactions with females, and female support in dominance interactions diminished, resulting in decreased status for the male. The dominant monkeys were more relaxed and confident; the subordinate monkeys were more likely to be irritable and to lash out at other animals. The experimenters also found that the amount of serotonin was positively related to the frequency of prosocial behavior, such as grooming, and negatively related to antisocial behavior, such as fighting. Thus, serotonin seems to stabilize the relationships between the individual and other members of its social group. In addition, low levels of serotonin are linked to high levels of aggression in men (Asberg, 1994; S. L. Brown, Botsis, & van Praag, 1994; Coccaro, 1993).

### The Peptide Neurohormones

The second kind of neurochemical system involves peptide neurohormones, with particular attention to those that seem to have important emotional properties: the endorphins, cholecystokinin, oxytocin and vasopressin, gonadotropin-releasing hormone, and corticotrophin releasing factor.

The neuropeptides have been characterized as information substances. Each neuropeptide may bias information processing in a unique way when occupying a given receptor site. Pert (1997) noted that these substances are distributed in the mood-regulating areas of the brain.

Endorphin, a contraction for endogeneous morphine, is a morphine produced by the body. Pain is regulated by the endorphins in the spinal cord, which inhibit the release of the peptide neurotransmitter substance P, which carries pain messages. Panksepp (1986) suggested that endorphins are associated with social attachment and that attachment is associated with increased levels of endorphins. The endorphins are associated with subjectively experienced euphoria and inhibit breathing. This suggests, in turn, that strong social attachments increase endorphin levels.

Oxytocin and vasopressin are pituitary peptide hormones derived from an evolutionary divergence of an ancestral hormone, vasotocin (Buck, 1999). Oxytocin and vasopressin appear to act in behavioral opposition to each other.

Oxytocin is important for positive emotions relating to social and family connections. This hormone, found only in mammals, was discovered to be essential for maternal behaviors such as uterine contraction and milk ejection. Thomas Insel, James Winslow, and their colleagues discovered that oxytocin has broader importance for bonding, in male as well as in female animals (Insel, 1992; Insel & Winslow, 1998; Winslow, Shapiro, Carter, & Insel, 1993).

Oxytocin also appears to inhibit the fear responses of flight, flight, or freezing. Oxytocin promotes a positive stress response by seeking positive social interactions and sensory stimulation. Taylor, Klein, Lewis, Grunewald, Gurung, & Updegraff (2000) termed a subclass of these responses "tend-and-befriend." Thus, oxytocin promotes peaceful responses to stress, as opposed to flight, fight, or flee responses.

Uvnäs-Moberg (1997; 1998) found that administering oxytocin to male and female rats counteracted many of the typical physiological and behavioral effects of stress. For example, oxytocin lowered blood pressure and lowered cortisol levels. Cortisol is a hormone typically released in stressful situations. More generally, oxytocin reduced activity in the sympathetic part of the autonomic nervous system, which is activated in the fight-or-flight response. Oxytocin delayed the onset of withdrawal to heat and mechanical stimuli, and to increase the healing rate of wounds, possibly through a shift in the allocation of energy in the body. The physiological antistress effects of oxytocin also occur with both lactation and sexual intercourse. Thus, breast feeding and sex release oxytocin, create pleasure, and reduce stress. Oxytocin may also be released by other forms of pleasurable social contact, such as mutual grooming in animals and supportive friendship in humans. Turner, Altemus, Enos, Cooper, & McGuinness (1999) found that oxytocin levels increased in the blood of women who had never been pregnant in response to relaxation massage. They also found that oxytocin sometimes decreased in response to sad emotions, mainly in women who were insecure in their interpersonal relationships.

**The Fear Response System**

One emotion that has been clearly linked to specific brain structures is fear, which is generated in a brain substructure called the amygdala (LeDoux, 1996). The amygdala is an almond-shaped structure deep inside the temporal lobe. It connects to the hippocampus, the septal nuclei, the prefrontal cortex, and the medial septal nucleus of the thalamus. These connections make it possible for the amygdala to play its important role on the mediation and control of the expression of fear.

The amygdala is like the hub of a wheel in that it receives inputs from a wide range of levels of cognitive processing. These inputs include stimulus features from the sensory thalamus, perception of objects from the sensory cortex, and memories and contexts from the rhinal cortex and the hippocampus. Through these connections, the amygdala is able to appraise emotional meaning and initiate reactions consistent with its appraisal.

The fear reaction system involves a parallel transmission to the amygdala from the sensory thalamus and the sensory cortex. The first information about external stimuli reaches the amygdala by a direct path from the thalamus. This path, being shorter, is much faster than the parallel pathway from the thalamus to the cortex to the amygdala. The downside of the shortcut is that the amygdala does not benefit from cortical processing. Thus, the amygdala is provided with a crude representation of the stimulus and appraises it as either "good" or "bad." The advantage of this down and dirty pathway is speed—we can react to potentially dangerous stimuli before we fully know what the stimulus is. Eventually the cortex processes the stimulus input and sends its information on the parallel, but longer, path to the amygdala. Based on this information, the amygdala may modify its appraisal of the stimulus.

The process can be illustrated as follows: A hiker encounters a snake coiled behind a log. His eyes send the visual information to the thalamus for initial processing. The thalamus sends part of the information to the amygdala and part of the information to the cortex. The path to the amygdala being shorter allows a fast, unconscious response to begin. Right now the hiker does not know if the object is a stick or a snake, but it registers as potentially bad, and the amygdala sends signals to the hypothalamus to arouse the organism for action. Meanwhile, the thalamus feeds information to the visual cortex, which assembles a more detailed representation of the snake. This outcome is sent back to amygdala about a half second after the amygdala received the first inputs from the thalamus. If the thin curved object was a stick, well, better to be safe than sorry. If it was a snake, the earlier, faster response could mean the difference between life and death. Hence, the down and dirty pathway has a powerful survival value.

The amygdala appears capable of not only triggering and steering responses to danger but also of acting on higher-level neocortical processes. First, the amygdala arouses the organism early. Cortical arousal, once established, makes concentration on anything else very difficult. The working memory execution function becomes actively focused on the emotionally arousing situation as it tries to figure out what is going on and what should be done about it. All other inputs are blocked out, resulting in impaired reasoning, decision making, and other higher cortical processes. If you have experienced a feeling of tunnel vision when emotionally engaged, your working memory is shutting out all other inputs as it tries to deal with the source of arousal.

The reason for this is strictly biological. The connections from the amygdala to the cortex are much richer than the connections from the cortex to the amygdala. This allows the amygdala to literally overwhelm the cortex, which in turn feeds the arousal back to the amygdala. A vicious cycle of emotional reactivity results. Thus, arousal tends to lock people into an emotional state. Once the fear system is turned on, it is difficult to turn off unless something else occurs that significant enough and arousing enough to shift the focus off arousal. Worse, stress, as a form of arousal, facilitates amydalic functioning. Thus, stress shifts us even deeper into a mode where we react to danger rather than think about it.

Thus, the amygdala is able to overwhelm the neocortex and the rest of the brain so that a person not only forms emotional ideas but also responds to them. A famous example of this is Charles Whitman, who in 1966 climbed a tower at the University of Texas and indiscriminately killed people with a rifle. Whitman had initially consulted a psychiatrist about his periodic and uncontrollable violent impulses but was unable to obtain relief. Postmortem autopsy of his brain revealed a tumor the size of a walnut compressing the amygdaloid nucleus.

### The Attachment, Bonding, and Cooperation System

During the process of the brain's evolution from reptiles to nonprimate mammals to humans, most of the structural and functional systems found in earlier species were preserved. At the same time, additional mental capacities developed with the massive growth of the cerebral cortex (MacClean, 1989; Pribram, 1981). Specifically, in humans the subcortical system of socially based emotional regulation interacts with the prefrontal cortex. This gives us the ability to process complex social stimuli, rewards, rules, and customs. The prefrontal cortex controls complex emotional responses including social responses. This region is connected to high-order sensory and association areas of the cortex and to emotion-related areas below the cortex (hypothalamus, limbic system, and basal ganglia with extensive autonomic and visceral projections).

The orbitomedial prefrontal cortex links specific sensory events in the environment—for example, particular people or family and social structures—and positive or negative emotional states. This is accomplished through the neural connections of the prefrontal cortex with sensory areas of the cerebral cortex, on the one hand, and with the hypothalamus and autonomic nervous system, on the other hand. In short, the orbitomedial prefrontal cortex has evolved in humans to enable behavioral choices in an increasingly complex social environment (Damasio, 1994).

When a person makes a conscious choice to engage in more caring behavior, the orbitomedial prefrontal cortex releases caring capacities and prevents those capacities from being inhibited by stressful stimuli and beliefs. The prefrontal cortex modulates signals to the parts of the brain that contain oxytocin or the cortisol precursor. Thus, the prefrontal cortex influences the relative likelihood of oxytocin-mediated (tend-and-befriend) versus cortisol-mediated (fight, flight, or freeze) responses. Since the orbitomedial prefrontal cortex seems to store the emotions of social memories, life experience affects its function. Future behavior is therefore strongly influenced by past experience.

A second response selection pathway is probably the loops between cortex, thalamus, and basal ganglia. These loops are a basis for reward-based behavioral regulation (Eisler & Levine, 2002). These same pathways are also believed to be repetitively activated as part of the disrupted regulation caused by drug addiction (Koob & LeMoal, 2001). The strong connections between the prefrontal cortex and the nucleus accumbens (a primary area for both natural and drug-related dopamine rewards) are likely to be important for both tend-and-befriend and dissociative responses.

Finally, this part of the prefrontal cortex has strong reciprocal connections with areas of the limbic system involved in emotional evaluation. These include two parts of the amygdala (central and basolateral) that are also part of a positive feedback loop that mediates stress-related responses (Koob, 1999). Thus it is a third pathway by which the orbitomedial prefrontal cortex might influence response to a social situation.

Specifically, the orbitomedial area is roughly divided into two parts: an orbital part that receives inputs from sensory association areas of the cortex that reflect effects of experiences and a medial part that receives inputs from areas of the hypothalamus that reflect effects of emotional states (Price, 1999). Connections to this prefrontal region from other parts of the cortex and limbic system, representing social stimuli, are strengthened or weakened with experience, including the severity of previous stresses and the person's previous responses. This in turn influences the tendency toward fear response or approach in a given social context.

## Implications for Peacemaking

Eisler (1987, 1995, 2002) argues that throughout history conflict has existed between those who promote mutually respectful and caring relations and those who inhibit peaceful behavior to protect social hierarchies. Rigid hierarchies—whether man over woman, man over man, race over race, religion over religion, or nation over nation—require caring and empathy to be suppressed. Today, beliefs, institutions, and behaviors required of hierarchies of control are often seen as normal—from violence in child rearing and male-female relations to socially and environmentally unsound business practices and the idealization, and even religious incitement, of violence in intranational and international relations.

From a neuroscientific perspective, such beliefs are the result of disrupted prefrontal-subcortical loops. According to Eisler (1987, 1995, 2000), this disruption occurs from the stresses inherent in social structures and hierarchies maintained by fear and force. If the orbitoprefontal cortex contains emotional memories of stress and fear, it will not properly activate the oxytocin system of the brain. Instead, cortisol will be released. Additionally, the orbitoprefrontal cortex will have less control over the amygdala and the fear response system. In optimal contexts, the orbitoprefontal cortex takes over amygdalic functions to coordinate information and correct responses as conditions change. When the orbitoprefontal cortex has not developed this capacity, the fear response system will dominate behavior.

Thus, when we are enmeshed in intractable conflict, we may simply be trapped in a compulsive pattern or not know of alternatives. Peace can lead to a prefrontally regulated readjustment of the set points for reward that the conflict behavior disrupted. What this suggests is that conflict behavior is reversible with sufficient outside support.

## Mediation

Mediation encompasses a broad array of interventions and strategies designed to help parties find peace when they are incapable of doing so on their own. When a conflict is mediated, a third party comes into the conflict to assist the conflict parties. The third party, called a mediator, may assume a wide variety of roles and functions, depending upon the needs of the parties, the nature of the conflict, the geopolitical realities, and the professional judgment of the mediator.

In conflict theory, two paradigms of mediation predominate, the structuralist paradigm and the socio-psychological paradigm. The structuralist paradigm is based on a belief that through the use of persuasion, incentives, and disincentives (i.e., a cost-benefit process), parties in a conflict can be led to and through a negotiated settlement. This paradigm is anchored in a rational choice view of the world and treats the causes of conflict as objective issues that can yield to negotiation. This approach generally ignores the subjectivity of experience and is based on the assumption that humans are essentially rational, not emotional, beings. This paradigm dominates diplomatic mediation.

The socio-psychological paradigm focuses on communication and exchange as a way to change perception and attitudes. This mediation approach provides a forum in which parties can explore options and develop solutions, often outside the highly charged arena of a formal negotiating structure. The approach appeals to superordinate goals and values. Because much of human conflict is anchored in conflicting perception and misperception, the mediator concentrates on changing the perceptions, attitudes, values, and behaviors of the parties to a conflict.

### Limitations of the Mediation Paradigms

The rational choice assumption is not warranted by our current understanding of brain function. As discussed above, we are 98 percent emotional and 2 percent rational. We have all experienced the emotionality of conflict. Despite this experience, we persist in believing that we can reason our way out of disputes. However, people in conflict are emotionally enmeshed at different levels, making rational processing difficult. The higher the conflict is escalated, the more behavior is emotional and the less it is rational. We understand this to be caused by the brain's fear response system and the degree to which life experience has conditioned reactivity over empathy. Furthermore, a mediation process based on competitive negotiation plays to the selfish, individualistic part of the brain, rather than the selfless, cooperative part of the brain. In the long run, agreements will be weaker because they are not supported by the attachment systems of the brain.

The socio-psychological view of mediation is closer to current neuropsychological understanding, but it is likewise based on assumptions that are not supported by neuroscience.

The first assumption is that good communication is a key to peace. Many times, people in conflict are excellent communicators. They are very good at communicating positions, arguments, and defenses. At a deeper level, escalated conflict compels emotionally charged communication that can be perceived as aggressive and threatening. To the extent that the parties lack emotional awareness, they will be unable to communicate their feelings effectively. This can lead to frustration, a sense of disrespect, and stimulation of the fear response system.

The second assumption is that conflict is often based on cultural differences. Cultural differences can seem profound, but culture is merely a technology for achieving attachment, group identity, efficient group coordination, and reduction of uncertainty and anxiety. Focusing on underlying needs, goals, interests, and desires play to the shared attributes of our brains rather than on the relatively superficial differences presented by cultures.

The third assumption is that an understanding and acceptance of value differences can lead conflict parties to common ground. The unstated requirement of this assumption is that brains are in a state to be empathic rather than defended. Value differences may preconsciously trigger fear reactivity, making an empathic connection difficult to achieve.

### Peacemaking

Peacemaking is a form of mediation that seeks a reconciliation between parties. Peacemaking creates relational and structural justice that allows for social and personal well-being. This is an ideal objective, perhaps not attainable in many conflicts. Nevertheless, peacemaking implies the use of cooperative, constructive processes to resolve human conflicts, while restoring relationships.

Peacemaking is a complicated concept because peace can be defined in so many different ways. When we speak of peace, we understand it in two ways. First, there is negative peace. Negative peace means the absence of violence, typically through coercion rather than cooperation. When Mom tells Sally to stop beating up on Sarah, she is imposing a negative peace in the household. Sally's conflict with Sarah is not resolved, but merely suppressed. The concept of negative peace extends not only from our mundane example in the home, but also to international peace. International peace is said to exist at a cessation of violence and hostility. This form of peace is often imposed by U.N. peacekeepers. Again, peace is defined as an absence of war and is imposed coercively or through balances of power or terror as in the Cold War.

The second way of understanding peace is as positive peace. Positive peace implies reconciliation and restoration through creative transformation of conflict. In positive peace, Mom sits Sally and Sarah down and invites them to exchange stories about what led to the fight. Mom and Sarah learn for the first time that Sally feels angry at the way Sarah ignores her. In five minutes, they work out a plan that allows Sally the safety and security to speak out about what she is feeling. Sarah promises to listen more carefully to Sally. Sally promises not to hit Sarah when she, Sally, becomes frustrated. The fighting has stopped, but, more importantly, the relationship has been reconciled and restored. In the process, Sally and Sarah have grown morally just a little. In the same way, a peacemaker looks at conflict not just as an abstract, intellectual exercise in analysis and persuasion, but as an opportunity to help people reconcile. When reconciliation is not possible, separation and resolution is possible with a minimum of hostility and acrimony.

Positive peace is supported by the attachment systems of the brain. Negative peace, especially if imposed through coercion, activates the fear response systems of the brain. Ultimately, if negative peace is not transformed to positive peace, negative peace will dissolve into further conflict. At a neuroscientific level, this is because negative peace does not support the attachment systems of the brain.

## Practice Implications

### Process

The fundamental principle of process should be to encourage attachment and approach. In highly escalated and intractable conflicts, this is challenging. Convening people in the same room without them resorting to violence begs the use of coercion, threats, and promises. Sometimes, coercive measures are required. However, decision makers should be mindful that coercion will disrupt the normal functioning of the loops between the prefrontal cortex and the subcortical parts of the brain.

Peacemaking and negotiation processes, if seeking peace, should take into account how best to stimulate oxytocin, endorphins, and serotonin within the participants' brains. Likewise, process design should consider how to reduce the stimulation of vasopressin, norepinehprine, and cortisol, which are associated with aggression, fear response, and stress. Viewed through the lens of neuroscience, every detail and nuance of process design should be reconsidered for possible inhibitory and stimulating effects on brain systems.

People negotiating conflict should be in a very relaxing, safe, secure environment. As much as possible, the surroundings should evoke feelings of attachment, not fear. Conversations should help the parties relate to those aspects of their lives that give contentment, happiness, and allow for compassion. People will naturally feel angry, hostile, and violent toward their opponents. Rather than deny or suppress these emotions, they should be permitted and perhaps explored. As parties develop emotional awareness, they can make better choices about whether to approach or defend. Assessing fear reaction behaviors therefore becomes an important tool. On the fly judgments about the parties' emotionality, reactivity, empathic openness, and ability to form social bonds profoundly influence process choices. Mediator training should include basic neuropsychology and skills development in nonverbal observation, emotional interpretation, and empathic intervention.

### De-Escalation

From a neuropsychological perspective, de-escalation of conflict requires two steps. The first step requires inhibition of the fear response system. Ritual, dialogue, and empathy all seem to have larger roles in inhibiting the fear response system. Ritual gives the parties a different context in which to process the conflict. It redefines the relationship within a larger community and gives meaning to the peacemaking process. The Native American tradition of the peace feather is a simple but effective ritual to slow down conversations. Only the person holding the feather may speak and has the right to speak without challenge or interruption. More formal rituals opening plenary sessions of negotiations, with the presence of influential outsiders, can impart significance and meaning to the process. The neuropsychological effect is to encourage the attachment systems of the brain to activate such that each person feels a part of the process.

Controlled dialogue requires the presence of a sensitive mediator. The mediator slows the conversation down, acts as a buffer, and allows the parties to take their time forming attachments in place of fear responses. Sometimes, the dialogue does not progress the substantive conflict as fast as some might like. However, the mere fact of face to face civil discourse appeals to the brain's innate attachment mechanisms.

Empathic communication is, of course, a powerful means of attachment because it represents the first experience of relationship for every human—the mother-infant relationship. Empathic communication, properly and sensitively performed, is a powerful de-escalation process.

The second step in de-escalation, which is probably more challenging, is to support the conflict parties as they walk the path toward peace. Walking this path with a history of hostility and violence takes faith and courage. Moving from initial anxiety and insecurity to essential peace seems to require a traverse of intense feelings of inadequacy, incompetency, and increased anxiety. The desire to revert to the fear response can be overwhelming because the fear response system provides immediate, although short-term, relief from anxiety. Finding essential peace seems to require a profound emotional growth in humans that is achieved only through single-minded desire. Choosing the path of peace and rejecting the default fear response should be recognized as a great act of personal courage because it requires moving away from a comfortable, reliable way of being.

### Importance of Trust, Compassion, Patience

One of the most significant aspects of neuropsychology to peacemaking is the discovery that humans are far more alike than they are different. As Pinker (2003) points out, universal mental mechanisms underlie superficial variations across cultures. While familiar categories of behavior vary across cultures, such as marriage, customs, folk traditions, and food taboos, the deeper mechanisms within the human brain that generate them appear to be innate and universal. People may dress differently, but they may do so to show their status through their appearance. People may respect the rights of their family, clan, or tribe, or respect the rights of all human beings, but they all divide the world into an in-group and an out-group.

This commonality is lost in conflict as people exaggerate their differences and minimize their similarities. For peacemakers to grasp that each person has the innate ability to love and be loved, to cherish family, to seek peace significantly reduces judgment and faulty assumptions. Furthermore, understanding that humans invest every perception and thought with emotional content allows peacemakers the ability to see anger, hatred, violence, and hostility with far greater compassion than might be the case if the rationalist philosophy predominated. This understanding also changes how we go about peacemaking. Instead of basing process on negotiation, which may be easily side railed by emotionality, the peace process can be created to account for the need to acknowledge emotion and create empathic connections. Until this work is complete, holding rational negotiations will be limited.

Finally, peacemakers and peace negotiators must develop trust with the parties, exhibit deep compassion, and be supremely patient. Understanding the deep emotionality of conflict and its roots in neurophysiology is a great help because attributions of intention are no longer as relevant. Instead of thinking about how irrational or illogical parties might be, peacemakers can, from a neuropsychological perspective, understand that parties are emotional, not irrational. Emotional is normal, necessary, and therefore an expected component of conflict and of peacemaking. From this perspective, peacemakers should find compassion and patience easier to achieve as they walk with the parties through the darkness to essential peace.

## Conclusion

Rationalist orientations predominate and, in many cases, trivialize the emotion of conflict. Our expanding knowledge of the neuropsychological bases of emotion suggests that a broader, humanistic orientation to peace negotiations be required. Negotiators and mediators should examine their fundamental assumptions about human nature, rationalist philosophy, and human behavior in the context of neuroscience. Perhaps the common assumptions are now outdated and dangerously narrow. Recognizing that the brain operates on at least two emotional systems, assumptions based on power domination and hierarchy might be revised. Power and domination assumptions seem to play to the fear response systems, thereby furthering and reinforcing conflict behavior. Perhaps positive peace can be found only through partnerships that support and encourage the selfless, attachment, and reward systems of the brain.

The fear response system has been a successful evolutionary adaptation to a dangerous, uncertain environment. The selfless social attachment system has also been successful in creating pair bonds, families, and larger communities. The peacemaker's challenge is to encourage the choice of peace rather than conflict. In a larger sense, this may be the next evolutionary step for Homo sapiens. By learning to abandon the fear response system as a default and learning to choose peace, humans will be developing a higher consciousness of relationship. Interestingly, spiritual teachers have advocated this way of being for thousands of years. Only with advances in neuroscience can we see how prescient they were. The problem with peace therefore lies in the emotional brain. How we understand, utilize, and train our emotional brains will determine the course of human conflict.

# References

Asberg, M. (1994). Monoamine transmitters in human aggressiveness and violence: A selected review. *Criminal Behavior and Mental Health, 4,* 303–327.

Ashby, F. G., Turken, A. U., & Isen, A. M. (1999). A neuropsychological theory of positive affect and its influences on cognition. *Psychological Review, 106,* 526–550.

Beatty, M. J., & McCroskey, J. C. (1997). It's in our nature: Verbal aggressiveness as temperamental expression. *Communication Quarterly, 45*(4), 446.

Brammer, G. L., Raleigh, M. J., & McGuire, M. T. (1994). Neurotransmitters and social status. In L. Ellis (Ed.), *Social stratification and socioeconomic inequality* (pp. 75–91). Westport, CT: Praeger.

Brown, J., Bullock, D., and Grossberg, S. (1999). How the basal ganglia use parallel excitatory and inhibitory learning pathways to selectively respond to unexpected rewarding cues, *Journal of Neuroscience 19,* 10,502–10,511.

Brown, S. L., Botsis, A., & van Praag, H. M. (1994). Serotonin and aggression. *Journal of Offender Rehabilitation 21,* 27–39.

Buck, R. (1999). The biological affects: A typology. *Psychological Review, 106*(2), 301–336.

Coccaro, E. F. (1993). Impulsive aggression and central serotonergic function in humans: An example of a dimensional brain-behavior relationship. *International Clinical Psychopharmacology 7,* 3–12.

Damasio, A. (1994). *Descartes' error: Emotion research and the human brain.* New York: Grosset/Putnam.

Eisler, R. (1987). *The chalice and the blade.* San Francisco: Harper.

Eisler, R. (1995). *Sacred pleasure.* San Francisco: Harper.

Eisler, R. (2000). *Tomorrow's children.* Boulder, CO: Westview.

Eisler, R. (2002) *The power of partnership.* Novato, CA: New World Library.

Eisler, R., & Levine, D. S. (2002). Nurture, nature, and caring: We are not prisoners of our genes. *Brain and Mind 3,* 9–52.

Gray, J. A. (1991). The neuropsychology of temperament. In J. Strelau & A. Angleitner (Eds.), *Explorations in temperament* (pp. 105–128). New York: Plenum.

Insel, T. R. (1992). Oxytocin: a neuropeptide for affiliation—evidence from behavioral, receptor autoradiographci, and comparative studies, *Psychoneuroendocrinology 17,* 3–33.

Insel, T. R., & Winslow, J. T. (1998). Serotonin and neuropeptides in affiliative behaviors. *Biological Psychiatry 44,* 207–219.

Koob, G. F. (1999). Corticotropin-releasing factor, norepinephrine, and stress, *Biological Psychiatry, 46,* 1167–1180.

Koob, G. F., & LeMoal, M. (2001). Drug addiction, dysregulation of reward, and allostasis, *Neuropsycho-pharmacology 24,* 97–129

Lane, R. D. (2000). Neural correlates of conscious emotional experience. In R.D. Lane & Lynn Nadel (Eds.), *Cognitive neuroscience of emotion* (p. 345 ). New York: Oxford Unversity Press.

LeDoux, J. (1996). *The emotional brain: The mysterious underpinnings of emotional life*. New York: Simon & Schuster.

MacClean, P. (1989). *The triune brain in evolution in paleocerebral functions*. New York: Plenum Press.

McGuire, M. T., & Raleigh, M. J. (1986). Behavioral and physiological consequences of ostracism. *Ethology and Sociobiology 7*(3–4), 187–200.

Panksepp, J. (1986). The anatomy of emotions. In R. Plutchik & H. Kellerman (Eds.), *Emotion: Theory research and experience: Biological foundations of emotions* (Vol. 3, pp. 91–124). San Diego, CA: Academic Press.

Pert, C.B. (1997). *Molecules of emotion*. New York: Touchstone.

Pinker, S. (2003). *The blank slate: The modern denial of human nature*. New York: Viking/Penguin.

Pribram, K. (1981). Emotions. In S. B. Fiskov & T. J. Boll (Eds.), *Handbook of clinical neuropsychology* (pp. 102–134). New York: Wiley.

Price, J. L. (1999). Prefrontal cortical networks related to visceral function and mood. *Annals of the New York Academy of Sciences 877*, 383–396.

Raleigh, M. J., McGuire, M. T., Brammer, G. L., & Yuwiler, A. (1984). Social and environmental influences on blood serotonin concentrations in monkeys. *Archives of General Psychiatry 41*, 405–410.

Rubin, J., Pruitt, D., & Kim, S. (1994). *Social conflict: Escalation, stalemate and settlement* (2nd ed.). New York: McGraw-Hill.

Schore, A. (1994). *Affect regulation and the origin of the self*. Hillsdale, NJ: Erlbaum.

Schultz, W., Tremblay, L., & Hollerman, J. R. (2000). Reward processing in primate orbitofrontal cortex and basal ganglia, *Cerebral Cortex Special Issue: The Mysterious Orbitofrontal Cortex 10*, 272–283.

Strelau, J. (1994). The concepts of arousal and arousability as used in temperament studies. In J.E. Bates & T. D. Wachs (Eds.), *Temperament: Individual differences at the interface with biology and behavior* (pp. 117–141). Washington, DC: American Psychological Association.

Taylor, S. E., Klein, L. C., Lewis, B. P., Gruenewald, T. L., Gurung, R. A. R., & Updegraff, J.A. (2000). Biobehavioral responses to stress in females: Tend-and-befriend, not fight-or-flight. *Psychological Review 107*, 411–429.

Turner, R. A., Altemus, M., Enos, T., Cooper, B., & McGuinness, T. (1999). Preliminary research on plasma oxytocin in healthy, normal cycling women investigating emotion and interpersonal distress. *Psychiatry 62*, 97–113.

Uvnäs-Moberg, K. (1997). Oxytocin linked antistress effects—the relaxation and grow response, *Acta Physiologica Scandinavica 640 (Suppl.)* 38–42.

Uvnäs-Moberg, K. (1998). Oxytocin may mediate the benefits of positive social interaction and emotion, *Psychoneuroendocrinology 23*, 819–835

Winslow, J. T., Shapiro, L., Carter, C. S., & Insel, T. R. (1993). Oxytocin and complex social behavior: Species comparison. *Psychopharmacology Bulletin 29*, 403–414.

# CHAPTER 4

# BECOMING EVIL: HOW ORDINARY PEOPLE COMMIT GENOCIDE AND MASS KILLING

## *James Waller*

According to Jewish-Christian tradition, the first time that death appeared in the world, it was murder. Cain slew Abel. "Two men," says Elie Wiesel, "and one of them became a killer" (Morrow, 1991, p. 52). Throughout human history, social conflict is ubiquitous. Wars erupt naturally everywhere humans are present. Since the Napoleonic Wars, we have fought an average of six international wars and six civil wars per *decade*. An average of three high-fatality struggles have been in action somewhere in the world at any moment since 1900. The four decades after the end of World War II saw 150 wars and only 26 days of world peace—and that does not even include the innumerable internal wars and police actions. Buried in the midst of all of our progress in the twentieth century were well over a hundred million persons who met a violent death at the hands of their fellow human beings. That is over five times the number from the nineteenth century and more than ten times the number from the eighteenth century (Eckhardt, 1996).

Anthropologist Michael Ghiglieri even contends that war vies with sex for the distinction of being the most significant process in human evolution. "Not only have wars shaped geopolitical boundaries and spread national ideologies," he writes, "but they also have carved the distributions of humanity's religions, cultures, diseases, technologies, and even genetic populations" (1999, p. 162).

There is no sign that we are on an ascendant trajectory out of the shadow of our work of de-creation. At the close of the twentieth century, a third of the world's 193 nations were embroiled in conflict—nearly twice the Cold War level. The bipolar Cold War system has disintegrated into a system of "Warm Wars," with randomized conflicts popping up in all corners of an interdependent world. Retired Army Major Andy Messing Jr., executive director of the conservative-oriented National Defense Council Foundation, warns that the growing proliferation of weapons of mass destruction and an increasing world population only add to the danger. In his words, "It's going to be a very tough next 20 years" (Third of Nations Mired in Conflict, 1999). Even more liberal-leaning voices recognize that present-day population growth, land resources, energy consumption, and per capita consumption cannot be sustained without leading to even more catastrophic human conflict.

The persistence of inhumanity in human affairs is incontrovertible. The greatest catastrophes occur when the distinctions between war and crime fade; when there is dissolution of the boundary between military and criminal conduct, between civility and barbarity; when political, social, or religious groups embrace mass killing and genocide as warfare. I am not speaking here of isolated executions, but of wholesale slaughters. As collectives, we engage in acts of extraordinary evil, with apparent moral calm and intensity of supposed purpose, which could be described only as insane were they committed by an individual.

Aptly dubbed the "Age of Genocide," the past century saw a massive scale of systematic and intentional mass murder coupled with an unprecedented efficiency of the mechanisms and techniques of mass destruction. On the historical heels of the physical and cultural genocide of American Indians during the nineteenth century, the twentieth century writhed from the near-complete annihilation of the Hereros by the Germans in Southwest Africa in 1904; to the brutal assault of the Armenian population by the Turks between 1915 and 1923; to the implementation of a Soviet man-made famine in the Ukraine in 1932–1933 that left several million peasants starving to death; to the extermination of two-thirds of Europe's Jews during the Holocaust of 1939–1945; to the massacre of approximately half a million people in Indonesia during 1965–1966; to mass killings and genocide in Bangladesh (1971), Burundi (1972), Cambodia (1975–1979), East Timor (1975–1979), and Rwanda (1994); and, finally, to the conflict that continues to plague the former Yugoslavia. All told, it is estimated that 60 million men, women, and children were victims of mass killing and genocide in the last century alone (Smith, 2000).

There is one unassailable fact behind this ignoble litany of human conflict and suffering. Political, social, or religious groups wanting to commit mass murder do. Though there may be other obstacles, they are never hindered by a lack of willing executioners. That is the one constant upon which they can count. They can always find individual human beings who will kill other human beings in large numbers and over an extended period of time. In short, people are the weapons by which genocide occurs. How are people enlisted to perpetrate such extraordinary evil?

Unlike much of the research in perpetrator behavior, I am not interested in the higher echelons of leadership who structured the ideology, policy, and initiatives behind a particular genocide or mass killing. Nor am I interested in the middle-echelon perpetrators, the faceless bureaucrats who made implementation of those initiatives possible. Rather, I am interested in the rank-and-file killers—the ordinary men and women at the bottom of the hierarchy who personally carried out the millions of executions. These people were so ordinary that, with few exceptions, they were readily absorbed into civil society after the killings and peacefully lived out their unremarkable lives—attesting to the unsettling reality that genocide overwhelms justice. One point stands clear: to understand the fundamental reality of mass murder we need to shift our focus from impersonal institutions and abstract structures to the actors, the men and women who actually carried out the atrocities.

*The goal of this chapter is to offer a psychological explanation of how ordinary people commit extraordinary evil.* It is an attempt to go beyond the minutiae of thick description ("who," "what," "when," and "where") and look at the bigger questions of explanation and understanding: to know a little less and understand a little more.

The chapter is divided into four parts. First, I will briefly review the work of those who argue that the origins of extraordinary human evil lie not in ordinary individuals but in extraordinary groups, ideologies, psychopathologies, or personalities. Second, I will counter these positions with my central argument that it is ordinary individuals, like you and me, who commit extraordinary evil. Third, I will outline an original theoretical model of extraordinary human evil that considers the wide range of factors involved in the process of ordinary people committing extraordinary evil. Finally, I will conclude the chapter with a discussion of how the model can help us cultivate the moral sensibilities that can curb our capacity for extraordinary evil and, ultimately, help prevent genocide and mass killing.

## Extraordinary Origins of Extraordinary Human Evil

### The Extraordinary Nature of the Collective

One of the ways in which we explain extraordinary evil is to focus on the means by which groups make that evil possible. Intuitively, many of us recognize that we are vulnerable to losing ourselves in a group. There seems to be something about the nature of the collective—a small band of marauders, an army battalion, a mob, a social, political or religious organization, an office staff, a nation—that brings out our worst tendencies. Advocates of this position argue that the inherent nature of a group is to be immature, selfish, uncaring, and even brutal (Niebuhr, 1932; Peck, 1983).

The voluminous literature on group dynamics certainly affirms that groups can develop characteristics that create a potential for extraordinary evil. Laboratory studies indicate that, in groups, we become more aroused, more stressed, and more error-prone on complex tasks. Groups tend to be more antagonistic, competitive, and mutually exploitive than individuals. Moral constraints are less powerful in groups than in individuals. There is a diffusion of responsibility within groups that can make evildoing a relatively simple matter. In addition, groups have a power to repress dissent and, thus, encourage the abandonment of the individual self. In so doing, groups provide a moral authority that can give individuals sufficient justification to perpetrate extraordinary evil. As Israel Charny writes: "It is a human being who operates through the mechanisms of group behavior to do what he does to fellow human beings, but it is the mechanism of group experience that potentiates, legitimates, operationalizes, and narcotizes the emergence of man's various and often unsavory selves" (Charny, 1982, p. 160).

On the other hand, groups also can develop values, institutions, and practices that promote caring and connection. Groups are not inherently selfish and uncaring; they do not always behave at a level that is more primitive and immature than the individuals that comprise the group. Groups can, for instance, help people strengthen their resolve to stop drinking, lose weight, study harder, and expand their spiritual consciousness. At times, groups can even provide the security to *oppose* potentially destructive ideas and practices. Groups brought democracy to Czechoslovakia and Serbia and confronted oppressive governments in China and South Africa.

In short, all collectives are not all bad all of the time. Group processes, like individual processes, are dynamic, not static—changing, not changeless. It seems most true to state that being in a group *reveals* whom individuals are just as much, if not more, than being in a group alters whom they are. In other words, the dynamics of a collective are best understood by the wills and ideologies of the individuals within it. Group interaction then becomes a social amplifier that strengthens the pre-existing signals of the individuals in the group—whether evil or good. So, when our individual tendencies are negative, groups have the capacity to unleash our worst impulses. However, when our individual tendencies are positive, groups accentuate the best of what we are. In short, it is *not* the nature of the collective that limits our possibility for cooperative, caring, nonviolent relations; it is the nature of the individuals that make up the collective.

### The Influence of an Extraordinary Ideology

Could it be possible that an extraordinary ideology provides the soil for an extraordinary national character that predisposes people in that culture to extraordinary evil? Most relevant here, and a perfect case study for the general argument, is the work of Daniel Jonah Goldhagen (1996). In response to the enduring question of how the German people could do the things they did to Jews in the Holocaust, Goldhagen gave a simple and straightforward answer. Because they wanted to. Why did they want to? Because they grew up in an extraordinary culture where an unusually virulent form of anti-Semitismwas commonplace. They were heirs to a set of shared beliefs that included a deep-rooted, pathological anti-Semitism that simply awaited the ascendancy of Hitler and the opportunity of war for its lethal expression.

Following this logic, Goldhagen maintains that ordinary Germans were not forced into performing executions. Rather, they were willing participants in the whole process. These Germans did not view their actions as criminal, nor did they shrink from opportunities to inflict suffering, humiliation, and death—openly, knowingly, and zealously—on their victims. Moreover, many of them were not part of an elite group like the SS. Most were ordinary Germans; Goldhagen posits a minimum figure of 100,000 and says, "it would not be surprising if the number turned out to be five hundred thousand or more" (p. 167) who willingly took part in the Final Solution. They were, in his opinion, killers of conviction.

Ultimately, as several critics have pointed out, Goldhagen's argument is untenable; for example, see Shandley (1998). There is little evidence that the anti-Semitism of

Germans was "eliminationist" aside from the outcome. Germans were not so fundamentally different that it is plausible to attribute to them a single cognitive outlook in stark contrast to the diversity found in the rest of the contemporaneous human community. We will not benefit from an approach that emphasizes uniformity among one particular culture and a sharp difference between "them" and other peoples. We need not invoke a "demonological" hatred of others to explain the commission of extraordinary evil. The existence of widespread negative racial stereotyping in a society—in no way unique to Nazi Germany—can provide fanatical regimes not only the freedom of action to pursue genocide but also an ample supply of executioners.

It is too easy to say that *only* an extraordinary culture, like Germany, and *only* an allegedly extraordinary ideology, like eliminationist anti-Semitism, could produce thousands of willing executioners. We want to assume that mass killing and genocide are simply inherited from cultures and ideologies that preceded a regime's rise to power because then we can believe that extraordinary human evil is curable. Simply change the culture or ideology and you can change the mind-set that leads to something like the Holocaust. Admitting that culture or ideology may simply be the pretext by which we rationalize a more general wish to dominate and destroy is much more discomforting.

Moreover, by ascribing the crimes and their perpetrators to a particular culture or ideology, *their* behavior becomes "unfathomable" and outside of "our" world. Only the Germans could have behaved the way they did; nobody else could have. As a consequence, it cannot be repeated by someone else. Unfortunately, it has been, is being, and will be repeated by many other people. As a result, we must recognize that we are dealing not with "ordinary Germans" but rather with "ordinary people." As Christopher Browning writes,

> if ordinary Serbs, Croats, Hutus, Turks, Cambodians and Chinese can be the perpetrators of mass murder and genocide, implemented with terrible cruelty, then we do indeed need to look at those universal aspects of human nature that transcend the cognition and culture of ordinary Germans. (1996)

## Psychopathology

Clearly there are some perpetrators involved in atrocities who are deranged psychopaths or otherwise psychologically disturbed. Are there enough, though, to responsibly consider psychopathology as a predominant cause of participation in extraordinary evil?

In the most recent and comprehensive reanalysis of the Rorschach tests administered to the Nazi defendants at Nuremberg, psychologist Eric Zillmer and colleagues concluded that the leaders of Nazi Germany were anything but "Mad Nazis." They were, for the most part, extremely able, intelligent, high-functioning people. They were average German citizens—products of a rigid, paternalistic, male-dominated society. There was no evidence of thought disorder or psychiatric conditions in most of these men. In the authors' concluding words,

> High-ranking Nazi war criminals ... participated in atrocities without having diagnosable impairments that would account for their actions. In this sense, the origins of Nazi Germany should be sought for primarily in the context of social, cultural, political and personality, rather than clinical psychological factors. (Zillmer, Harrower, Ritzler, & Archer, 1995, p. 194)

But did the Nuremberg defendants accurately reflect the entire culture of cruelty they created? In other words, how far can we generalize the conclusions drawn from the Nazi elite? Can they be extended to the psychological functioning of the broader population of Nazis? If the "Mad Nazi" thesis did not hold true for the Nazi elite at Nuremberg, does that necessarily mean that it also would not hold true for the rank-and-file killers?

To answer these questions, Zillmer et al. (1995) examined another large bank of nearly 200 Rorschach records of rank-and-file Nazis. These records came from tests administered at the war crimes trials in Copenhagen in 1946. The Rorschach records were those of Danish citizens convicted of collaborating with the Nazi occupation and German military personnel who were sentenced for war crimes committed in Denmark. Their conclusions suggest that these rank-and-file Nazis showed some unusual thought patterns (for example, rigid and pessimistic thinking), but not enough to indicate grossly disturbed thinking. Neither did the perpetrators' responses demonstrate any particular inclination toward violence. Consistent with the Nuremberg Rorschachs, there was a lack of evidence for obvious and severe psychopathology in the Copenhagen Rorschachs. The Mad Nazi thesis applied no better to the rank-and-file Nazi than it did to the Nazi elite.

Not only does the claim of widespread psychopathology among perpetrators contradict available evidence, but it also contradicts all diagnostic and statistical logic. Of the ten Personality Disorder categories in the *Diagnostic and Statistical Manual of Mental Disorders* (*DSM-IV-TR*), the most applicable psychopathology for perpetrators of extraordinary evil is Antisocial Personality Disorder (APD). A pervasive pattern of disregard for, and violation of, the wishes, rights, or feelings of others characterizes this disorder. Individuals with this disorder show little remorse for the consequences of their acts. The incidence of APD among the general population of American males is approximately 3 percent. If we begin with the assumption that military personnel are a fairly representative smaller sample of the larger general population, we can hypothesize that approximately 3 percent of the perpetrators might be classified as APDs.

By their very nature, however, APDs are not easily used in military and paramilitary organizations. Such people rebel against authority, are consistently and extremely irresponsible, and, according to the *DSM-IV-TR*, "may receive dishonorable discharges from the armed services" (American Psychiatric Association, 2000, p. 703). Thus, there is no reason to expect that the distribution of APD among perpetrators of genocide is any greater than that of the general population; there are actually very good reasons to expect that the distribution is *less* than that of the general population. In other words, we could expect that less than three out of 100 perpetrators of extraordinary evil would be diagnosable APDs.

In short, where they exist, perpetrators characterized by extraordinary psychopathology are far too few to account for the litany of atrocities that occur in genocide and mass killing. As much as we may wish it to be true, perpetrators cannot so easily be explained away as disturbed, highly abnormal individuals. Indeed, few psychologists today would argue for the existence of a psychopathic personality in understanding the origins of extraordinary human evil.

### Specific Personality Types

Even if perpetrators are not similar in psychopathology, this argument contends, then certainly they must have a similar, homogenous, nonpathological personality structure that explains their participation in evildoing. Shortly after the Nuremberg trials, Theodor Adorno headed a team of researchers at the University of California at Berkeley—two of whom had fled Nazi Germany—who were drawn to uncovering the psychological roots of an anti-Semitism so poisonous that it led to the Holocaust. The resulting book, *The Authoritarian Personality* (*TAP*) (Adorno, Frankel-Brunswick, Levinson, & Sanford, 1950), suggested the presence of a fascist personality structure that included, among other characteristics, an exploitative power orientation, rigid thinking, and a preoccupation with toughness. Over five years in the making, and nearly 1,000 pages in length, *TAP* became an instant landmark in the field of social psychology.

Over time, however, in the midst of jarring theoretical and methodological critiques, the concept of the authoritarian personality was discredited. Today, the search for a specific, homogeneous personality type that is predisposed to participation in extraordinary evil remains elusive. While there may be certain broad personality differences that relate to the commission of extraordinary evil, there is not a single personality pattern that is inevitably expressed among all, or most, perpetrators.

As affirmed by the historical analyses of Christopher Browning (1992) and George Browder (1996), to bluntly suggest that all Nazis had a common, homogenous extraordinary personality that predisposed them to the commission of extraordinary evil is an obvious oversimplification. Just because they shared, to some degree, a common pattern of behavior does not mean that they also shared a common underlying personality organization. Similarly, our search for a homogeneous personality that characterizes perpetrators of genocide in Armenia, Germany, East Timor, Cambodia, Guatemala, Rwanda, the former Yugoslavia, and Sierra Leone has revealed more variability than consistency; more heterogeneity than homogeneity. All told, we cannot justifiably speak of a psychological coherence or homogeneity among perpetrators as a group. They are not a homogenous group of individuals who have more in common with each other than with any other group of people. Perpetrators are, quite simply, a representative cross section of the normal distribution of humans.

Even where there is a glimpse of homogeneity of personality characteristics, we are still faced with another, equally important, question. Are these commonalties in psychological functioning *unique* to the perpetrators as a group, or do we also find these characteristics in nonperpetrator groups (for example, high-level, successful business executives and bureaucrats, nonkilling military personnel, lawyers, teachers, psychiatrists, etc.)? In other words, do these characteristics discriminate, or differentiate, perpetrators of extraordinary evil from groups of nonperpetrators? Clearly, the answer is no. The few personality structures that describe the psychological organization of a majority of the perpetrators are also common to millions of other individuals who may have done nothing more criminal in their lives than commit a parking meter violation.

## Ordinary Origins of Extraordinary Human Evil

We have seen that the origins of extraordinary evil cannot be isolated in the extraordinary nature of the collective; the influence of an extraordinary ideology; psychopathology; or a common, homogeneous, extraordinary personality type. Perpetrators of extraordinary evil are extraordinary only by what they have done, not by whom they are. They cannot be identified, a priori, as having the personalities of killers. Most are not mentally impaired. Nor are they identified as sadists at home or in their social environment. Nor are they victims of an abusive background. They defy easy demographic categorization. Among them, we find educated and well-to-do people, as well as simple and impoverished people. We find church-affiliated people, as well as agnostics and atheists. We find people who are loving parents, as well as people who have difficulty initiating and sustaining satisfying personal relationships. We find young people and old people. We find people who are not actively involved in the political or social groups responsible for institutionalizing the process of destruction, as well as those who are. We find ordinary people who went to school, fought with siblings, celebrated birthdays, listened to music, and played with friends. In short, the majority of perpetrators of extraordinary evil are not distinguished by background, personality, or previous political affiliation or behavior as being men or women unusually likely or fit to be genocidal executioners.

We are then left with the most discomforting of all realities—ordinary, "normal" people committing acts of extraordinary evil. This reality is difficult to admit, to understand, to absorb. We would rather know Extraordinary Evil as an extrahuman capitalization. This reality is unsettling because it counters our general mental tendency to relate extraordinary acts to correspondingly extraordinary people. But we cannot evade this discomforting reality. We are forced to confront the ordinariness of most perpetrators of mass killing and genocide. Recognizing their ordinariness does not diminish the horror of their actions. It increases it.

Understanding that ordinary people commit extraordinary evil still begs an explanation. *How*, exactly, do ordinary people come to commit extraordinary evil? This question remains a matter of contentious debate within the academic community. There are, for instance, those who argue that extraordinary evil is done by ordinary individuals who have created or activated a second self to commit that evil. I call these "divided self" theories of extraordinary human evil.

Most relevant here is the famous series of studies on obedience to authority conducted in the early 1960s by Stanley Milgram (1974) (also see Waller, 2002). Milgram's experiments posted a simple but intriguing question: How far would ordinary Americans go in inflicting serious harm on a perfectly innocent stranger if they were told to do so by an authority figure? In his initial experiment, of a sample of average Americans, nearly two-thirds were willing to administer what they believed to be life-threatening shocks to an innocent victim, well after he lapsed into a perhaps unconscious silence, at the command of a single experimenter with no apparent means of enforcing his orders. These basic findings have been replicated at least 40 times and have held, without regard to age, gender, or level of education of the subjects, in a range of obedience conditions that tested more than 1000 individuals at several universities. (For an overview of the legacy of the Milgram experiments, see Miller, Collins, and Brief, 1995, and Blass, 2000.)

How, and why, did the subjects so readily delegate their moral decision making, and behavior, to an authority? Milgram postulated a discontinuous, altered state—the "agentic" state—was responsible for the behavior of his subjects. The agentic state, activated by one's integration into a hierarchy, occurs when one "sees himself as an agent for carrying out another person's wishes" (Milgram, 1974, p. 111). In the agentic state one is in a state of openness to regulation by an authority; it is the opposite of the state of autonomy. It is a change in one's self-perception, a cognitive reorientation induced when a person occupies a subordinate position in a hierarchical system.

In the agentic state, inner conflict is reduced through the abrogation of personal responsibility. Unable to defy the authority of the experimenter in Milgram's study, subjects attributed all responsibility to him. In Milgram's words, "The most far-reaching consequence of the agentic shift is that a man feels responsible *to* the authority directing him but feels no responsibility *for* the content of the actions that the authority prescribes" (italics in original) (pp. 145–146). In the agentic state, Milgram argued, we are not governed by the operations of our own conscience; instead, our conscience has been momentarily switched off or given over to the "substitute" conscience of the authority.

Overtly adopting a divided self approach, Milgram argues, "Moved into the agentic state, the person becomes something different from his former self, with new properties not easily traced to his usual personality" (p. 143). It is a dichotomous and all-or-nothing proposition—we are either in one state or another at any given time. Milgram's notion of an "on-off" switch reflects the acutely abrupt nature of the agentic shift—a necessary conceptualization given that Milgram's subjects began and completed their task of administering what they regarded as life-threatening shocks to an innocent victim within the window of one laboratory hour.

Although logically compelling, the empirical evidence supporting the agentic shift is, in fact, weak or contradictory. Mantell and Panzarella (1976), for instance, found that there was *no* relationship between the degree of obedience exhibited by subjects and the subjects' assignment of responsibility. In their research, there were both obedient and defiant subjects who accepted 100 percent of the responsibility, and there were those who accepted none at all. In their words,

> Although the majority of subjects in a command situation like the baseline condition administer all of the shocks, they have not surrendered personal responsibility in becoming agents of the experimenter. Some have. But others continue to hold themselves responsible. A monolithic view of the obedient person as a purely passive agent who invariable relinquishes personal responsibility is a false view. (p. 242)

Despite the lack of empirical evidence for "something different" from a former self in explaining Milgram's results, both scholars and laypeople have continued to hold on to the notion that there is a mystical shift from one self to another that enables a person to commit extraordinary evil. There is something emotionally compelling about the idea that extraordinary evil is committed by a "double" of some sorts— ourselves become not ourselves. Our fascination with the notion of a divided self, or two selves occupying the same person, is reflected in impressive mythological and literary roots. Throughout history, the divided self has appeared via the human imagination as a monster, a dragon, a white whale, an extraterrestrial, or a man or woman so evil that we cannot see ourselves in him or her.

We see this line of thinking yet again in the oft-cited work of Robert Jay Lifton (1986). Drawing on extensive, face-to-face interviews with 29 medical professionals involved at high levels in Nazi medicine, 12 former Nazi nonmedical professionals of some prominence (lawyers, judges, economists, teachers, architects, administrators, and Nazi Party officials), and 80 former Auschwitz prisoners who had worked on medical blocks (more than half of them doctors), Lifton advances the explanatory concept of "doubling" to answer the question of how ordinary people come to commit extraordinary evil (1986). Doubling maintains that the doctors created a second dissociated self to do evil, related to, but more or less autonomous from, the prior self. The two selves are encapsulated, walled off from each other to avoid internal conflict. The second self is a complete functioning self that has its own psychological framework (divided from the prior self), within which ordinary intellectual and moral standards are annulled.

While doubling may be an initial tool of adaptation to evildoing, it offers little in terms of an explanatory principle for understanding how ordinary people commit extraordinary evil (see Waller, 2002, pp. 116–123 for a more detailed critique). Most social scientists today maintain a firm belief in the existence of a coherent, authentic, integrated self that is essential to normal psychological functioning. This self may have a fluid, evolving character that is in a continual process of becoming. Along the way, this self may play different roles in different settings—but it is one unitary self nonetheless. As Berel Lang puts it, "It is more plausible to infer a single moral agent—one that granted greater conviction to evil than to good—than two independent moral domains that were constantly being traversed" (1990, p. 53). There is no credible reason to believe that we *temporarily* become wholly different people, with different ways of thinking, feeling, and behaving, when we commit extraordinary evil.

## Explanatory Model of Extraordinary Human Evil

Each of the arguments for the extraordinary origins of extraordinary human evil, as well as the more ordinary origins of the divided self, contains a grain of truth that helps advance our understanding of perpetrators of mass killing and genocide. In other words, it is not that any one of them is completely *wrong*; rather, each of them is completely *incomplete*. It is in looking at their incompleteness that we most clearly see the need for a new understanding of how ordinary individuals come to commit extraordinary human evil. We need a unified theory in which all of us, "normal human beings," must confront our universal potential for extraordinary evil.

I offer a theoretical model that considers the wide range of factors involved in the process that transforms ordinary people into perpetrators of extraordinary evil (for more detail, see chaps. 5–8 of Waller, 2002). This four-component explanatory model—drawing on existing literature, eyewitness accounts of extraordinary evil by killers and victims of a wide range of genocides and mass killings in the twentieth century, and classic and contemporary research in social psychology—is not an invocation of a single broad-brush psychological state or *event* to explain extraordinary human evil. Rather, it is a detailed analysis of a *process* through which the perpetrators themselves—either in committing atrocities or in order to commit atrocities—are changed. The model (see Figure 4.1) specifically explicates the forces that shape our responses to authority. It does so by looking at whom the perpetrators are (actor), the situational framework they are in (context of the action), and how they see the "other" (definition of the target).

### Our Ancestral Shadow

Is there a basic inborn proclivity or tendency of human nature that limits, or enables, the possibility of cooperative, caring, nonviolent relations between social groups? The subfield of psychology that was most responsible for bringing us back to rethinking the issue of human nature is evolutionary psychology (EP). EP is a multidisciplinary approach within the Darwinian paradigm that seeks to apply theories of evolutionary biology in order to understand human psychology. The specific goal of EP is to discover and understand the design of the human mind in terms of Darwinian evolution. EP is really engineering in reverse. In forward engineering, we design a machine to do something. In reverse engineering, we figure out what a machine—in this case, the human mind—was designed to do. EPs central premise is that there is a universal, evolved psychological architecture that we all share by virtue of being humans—*a* universal human nature. It has reminded us that we are part of the natural world and, like other animals, we have our own particular psychological tendencies or instincts. (For an accessible introduction to evolutionary psychology, see Cosmides and Tooby, 1997).

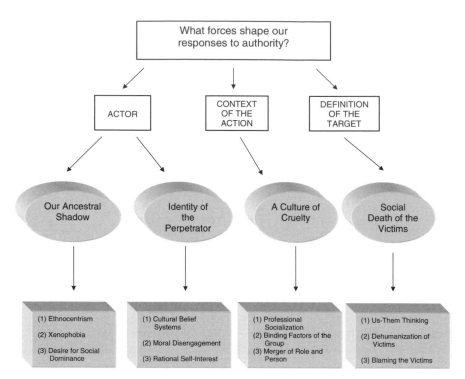

**Figure 4.1**
**A Model of Extraordinary Human Evil**

I focus on three such tendencies of human nature that are particularly relevant in shaping our responses to authority. Studies worldwide show not only that these tendencies are universal in people, but also that they start in infancy.

1. *Ethnocentrism*, the tendency to focus on one's own group as the "right" one.

2. *Xenophobia*, the tendency to fear outsiders or strangers. In some important ways, xenophobia complements ethnocentrism. There is no "us" without a corresponding "them" to oppose.

3. The *desire for social dominance*. Occasionally, our desire for social dominance has prosocial consequences as we realize that helping others creates friendships and coalitions that are useful in our struggle for power. At other times, however, our evolved desire for social dominance means that we have a predisposition to respond to certain kinds of situations aggressively (sometimes even violently) to get our way.

These are some of the powerful, innate, "animal" influences on human behavior that represent evolved social capacities lying at the core of human nature. They are the underlying, distant capacities that, in concert with other immediate and proximal influences, help us understand our capacity for our extraordinary evil to one another.

In short, natural selection has left deep traces of design in our minds and at least some of those designs leave us evolutionarily primed with the capacity to perpetrate extraordinary evil against each other.

### Identities of the Perpetrators

Building on our universal human nature, we must also recognize that the *particular* dispositions and personalities of perpetrators also matter. There is certainly something about *whom* the perpetrators are that must be taken into account in understanding how ordinary people commit extraordinary evil. What are the dispositional influences in responding to authority that are most relevant to understanding perpetrators of extraordinary evil?

In that vein, this component of the model explores the impact of three specific factors that shape the particular identities of the perpetrators.

1. *Cultural belief systems* about external, controlling influences on one's life; authority orientation; and ideological commitment.
2. *Moral disengagement* of the perpetrator from the victim—facilitated by the practices of moral justification, euphemistic labeling of evil actions, and exonerating comparisons.
3. One's *rational self-interest*, both professional and personal. These levels of rational self-interest can help explain both the initial willingness of perpetrators to participate in extraordinary evil as well as the enormous vested interest that promotes their sustained involvement.

We must recognize that these dispositional influences are by no means confined to extraordinary circumstances. From early on in our lives, these influences operate in everyday situations in which we routinely do things that bring us gains at the sake of costs to others.

### A Culture of Cruelty

Perpetrators create, and are created by, an immediate social context—a culture of cruelty—that helps them initiate, sustain, and cope with their extraordinary evil. Such a culture (by "culture," I am not referring to the macrolevel of societies but rather to the microlevel of groups within societies) makes each perpetrator believe that all men are capable of doing what he does. There are three momentum-inducing features of a culture of cruelty that are most relevant to understanding how ordinary people commit extraordinary evil.

1. The role of *professional socialization*, often institutionalized in military and paramilitary organizations and built on escalating commitments, ritual conduct, and the repression of conscience.

2. The *binding factors of the group* that cement one's adherence to the group and its activities—including diffusion of responsibility, de-individuation, and conformity to peer pressure.

3. The *merger of role and person* that helps us understand how evildoing organizations change the people within them. As we work our way into a culture of cruelty, the culture of cruelty also works its way into us.

The huge predominance of extraordinary evil committed in the world is, in some sense, a societal product in which a complex and sustained series of social forces enable ordinary people to commit extraordinary evil. In that process, the perpetrators are themselves fundamentally changed and become capable of autonomously and knowledgably committing extraordinary evil.

### Social Death of the Victims

This brings us to the fourth, and final, component of our explanatory model of how ordinary people commit extraordinary evil: perpetrators' definition of the target of their atrocities, or whom the victims have been made out to be in the eyes of the perpetrators. Often, the common ground between perpetrators and victims in a mass killing or genocide is obliterated by social and legal sanctions. It is the development of moral sanctions, or exclusions, however, that result in the social death of the victims. There are three mechanisms central to understand the social death of the victims, or the legitimization of the "other" as the enemy, in cases of mass killing and genocide.

1. *Us-them thinking* as the basis for how we so quickly and easily form groups, differentiate our group from others, favor those in our own group, and even swiftly mobilize to aggress against those in another group.

2. The various processes involved in the *dehumanization of victims* (for example, the use of language, actions, and propaganda that define the victims as less than human).

3. *Blaming the victims*, a legitimization of the victim as the enemy and, thus, deserving of their victimization.

The social death of victims may come after the extraordinary evil, or it may lead to it. Most times, it makes sense to argue that the social death of victims precedes their physical death. At times, though, one could argue that the social death of victims is a *consequence* of their physical death. In such cases, the social death of victims—as a justification mechanism—comes quickly after the killings begin.

## Conclusion

I developed this explanatory model so that we will have a clearer understanding of how extraordinary evil is produced and, thus, be in a better position to cut off that evil. Education has substantial humanizing effects and, when applied, can be an effective antidote to our collective inhumanity. Ultimately, being aware of our own capacity for extraordinary evil—and the dispositional, situational, and social influences that foster it—is the best safeguard we can have against future genocide.

Now that we have outlined the disease, is there a remedy? What have we learned about how ordinary people commit extraordinary evil that we can then apply to the prevention of mass killing and genocide? The explanatory model, which uses the three components *actor*, *context of the action*, and *definition of the target*, can sensitize us to the forces that shape our responses to authority and, in so doing, help us cultivate the moral sensibilities that can check the forces that may lead us to the commission of extraordinary evil.

### Actor

The model outlined two sets of dispositional influences most relevant to understanding perpetrators of extraordinary evil. First, in examining the universal dispositional nature of human nature—*our ancestral shadow*—we recognized that we cannot underestimate the impact of *what* we are upon *whom* we are. While it is not reasonable to hope for dramatic or quick evolution of whom we are, we should remember that the dark side of our human nature is not inevitable. We can, and should, identify those elements of our human nature that can most usefully serve cooperative and peaceful goals and build on them. There are certainly innate tendencies for cooperative, caring, nonviolent relations that enhanced our ancestors' survival and reproductive success in a world of limited resources. Such prosocial tendencies would have been favored by natural selection and would still be retained, at some level, as long-term adaptations. We can foster cultural practices and resources that activate these adaptations and produce mutually beneficial outcomes for formerly antagonistic groups. As Lyall Watson concludes, "The roots of war lie deep in nature, it seems, but then so too do the roots of peace" (1995, p. 140).

Understanding the universal dispositional nature of human nature, however, tells us only that we all are *capable* of extraordinary evil. It does not explain why only *some* of us actually perpetrate extraordinary evil and, in fact, why the great majority of us never do. To explain why some do perpetrate extraordinary evil but most do not requires sharpening our focus to the more particular dispositional influences that mold the *identities of the perpetrators*—cultural belief systems, moral disengagement, and rational self-interest.

These influences remind us that all cultures, communities, and family systems leave their fingerprints on the members within them. The belief systems in which we have been marinated, and to which we adhere, impact our moral engagement, or disengagement, with the "other." While respecting the diversity of belief systems through the world, we can—and should—identify the socialization practices that transfer control and responsibility from the individual to an external influence or authority, particularly those practices that facilitate a moral disengagement from a specified target group. While cultures and social institutions may not be themselves evil, we must acknowledge that they can—in myriad ways—create the preconditions or enhance the potential for the generation of extraordinary evil. German political philosopher Eric Voegelin (1999) reminds us of the importance of the restraining effects of society when he writes of

> the simple man, who is a decent man as long as the society as a whole is in order but who then goes wild, without knowing what he is doing, when disorder arises somewhere and the society is no longer holding together. (p. 105)

Certain socialization practices also influence how each of us defines rational self-interest. On a professional level, we must recognize that the choices and compromises we make in our own self-interest, though often small and localized, may have dangerous cumulative consequences we cannot predict. On a personal level, some socialization practices can encourage a restricted understanding that defines self-interest only in terms of myself and the people closest to me. Others can encourage a broader understanding that defines self-interest in a more global way—recognizing that evil perpetrated against anyone is evil perpetrated against everyone.

## Context of the Action

The universal and particular dispositional influences that mold the actors do not occur in a vacuum. Their influence must be considered relative to the immediate social context of the actor's action—*a culture of cruelty*. If, as I argued, extraordinary evil is facilitated by a culture of cruelty, then the diminution of extraordinary evil may be partially done at the organizational level. We have created an understanding of how cultures of cruelty can purposively move—or even accidentally lurch— toward causing extraordinary evil. We now need to develop a set of interventions designed to prevent the development of a culture of cruelty in military and paramilitary organizations. These should include a review of the professional socialization involved in such organizations (with particular focus on the role of ritual conduct in the repression of conscience), suggestions to moderate the binding factors of the group that obscure and minimize the agentive role in extraordinary evil, and a renewed understanding of the ways in which evildoing organizations transform the people within them.

## Definition of the Target

Finally, I argued that the *social death of the victims* involves an exclusion that removes them from the perpetrators' universe of moral obligation. This ostracism is built on the backs of three cognitive mechanisms—us-them thinking, dehumanization of the victims, and blaming the victims.

Fortunately, social psychologists have developed specific strategies to combat intergroup biases stemming from these cognitive mechanisms. These can involve structuring intergroup contact to produce more individualized perceptions of the members of the other group, fostering personalized interactions between members of the different groups, engaging in activities to achieve common goals, or redefining group boundaries to create more inclusive, superordinate representations of the groups. Anytime we can alter who is a "we" and who is a "they," we can undermine a contributing force to the social death of victims. Humanizing, decategorizing, or personalizing others all create a powerful self-restraining effect. It is difficult to mistreat a person who has an actual identity, with flesh and blood and family, without suffering a significant level of personal distress and self-condemnation.

Central to this pursuit are educational and societal programs that broaden our boundaries and experiences of the "other." As Maxine Greene writes,

> It is through and by means of education ... that individuals can be provoked to reach beyond themselves ... . It is through and by means of education that they may become empowered to think about what they are doing, to become mindful, to share meanings, to conceptualize, to make varied sense of their lived worlds. It is through education that preferences may be released, languages learned, intelligences developed, perspectives opened, possibilities disclosed. (as cited in Parsons & Totten, 1991, p. 85)

In conclusion, the lesson that ordinary people commit extraordinary evil should not be compartmentalized only as "bad news"—a disturbing, unsettling, disquieting truth about the human condition. The lesson does contain potentially "good news" as well: the commission of extraordinary evil is no longer a mystery. By understanding how ordinary people commit extraordinary evil, we gain insight into how such evil can be lessened. When we understand the ordinariness of extraordinary evil, we will be less surprised by evil, be less likely to be unwitting contributors to evil, and be better equipped to forestall evil. It is important to understand the conditions under which we can be transformed into killing machines. The more we know, and the more open we are to seeing ourselves as we are, the better we can control ourselves. If we can understand more accurately how ordinary people come to commit extraordinary evil, there is at least a faint glimmer of hope that we all may, ultimately, be delivered from extraordinary evil.

## Note

This chapter is based on, and extends research from, James Waller's recent book, *Becoming Evil: How Ordinary People Commit Genocide and Mass Killing* (New York, NY: Oxford University Press, 2002).

## References

Adorno, Theodor W., Frankel-Brunswick, E., Levinson, D. J., & Sanford, R. N. (1950). *The Authoritarian Personality*. New York: Harper.

American Psychiatric Association. (2000). *Diagnostic and statistical manual of mental disorders* (4th ed., text revision). Washington, DC: American Psychiatric Association.

Blass, Thomas (Ed.). (2000). *Obedience to authority: Current perspectives on the Milgram paradigm.* Mahweh, NJ: Lawrence Erlbaum.

Browder, George C. (1996). *Hitler's enforcers: The Gestapo and the SS Security Service in the Nazi revolution.* New York: Oxford University Press.

Browning, Christopher R. (1992). *Ordinary men: Reserve police battalion 101 and the Final Solution in Poland.* New York: HarperCollins.

Browning, Christopher. (1996, April 8). From a presentation given at the United States Holocaust Research Institute at the United States Holocaust Memorial Museum, Washington, DC.

Charny, Israel. (1982). *How can we commit the unthinkable?: Genocide, the human cancer* (p. 160). Boulder, CO: Westview Press.

Cosmides, Leda, & Tooby, John. (1997). *Evolutionary psychology: A primer.* Available at http://www.psych.ucsb.edu/research/cep/primer.html

Eckhardt, William. (1991, December). War-related deaths since 3000 BC. *Bulletin of Peace Proposals.*

Ghiglieri, Michael P. (1999). *The dark side of man: Tracing the origins of male violence.* Reading, MA: Perseus Books.

Goldhagen, Daniel Jonah. (1996). *Hitler's willing executioners: Ordinary Germans and the Holocaust.* New York: Alfred A. Knopf.

Lang, Berel. (1990). *Act and idea in the Nazi genocide* (p. 53). Chicago: University of Chicago Press.

Lifton, Robert Jay. (1986). *The Nazi doctors: Medical killing and the psychology of genocide.* New York: Basic Books.

Mantell, David Mark, & Panzarella, R. (1976). Obedience and responsibility. *British Journal of Social and Clinical Psychology, 15,* 242.

Milgram, Stanley. (1974). *Obedience to authority: An experimental view.* New York: Harper & Row.

Miller, Arthur G., Collins, Barry E., & Brief, Diana E. (1995, Fall). Perspectives on obedience to authority: The legacy of the Milgram experiments. *Journal of Social Issues, 51*(3), 1–19.

Morrow, Lance. (1991, June 10). Evil *Time,* 52.

Niebuhr, Reinhold. (1932). *Moral man and immoral society: A study in ethics and politics.* New York: Charles Scribner's Sons.

Parsons, William S., & Totten, Samuel. (1991, February). Teaching and learning about genocide: Questions of content, rationale, and methodology. *Social Education,* p. 85.

Peck, M. Scott. (1983). *People of the lie: The hope for healing human evil.* New York: Simon & Schuster.

Shandley, Robert R. (1998). *Unwilling Germans?: The Goldhagen debate.* Minneapolis: University of Minnesota Press.

Sivard, Ruth Leger. (1996). *World Military and Social Expenditures.* Ann Arbor, MI: Inter-university Consortium for Political and Social Research.

Smith, Roger W. (2000). Human destructiveness and politics: The twentieth century as an age of genocide. In Isidor Wallimann & Michael N. Dobkowski (Eds.), *Genocide and the modern age: Etiology and case studies of mass death* (p. 21). Syracuse, NY: Syracuse University Press.

Third of Nations Mired in Conflict. (1999, December 30). Associated Press Report.

Voegelin, Eric. (1999). *Hitler and the Germans* (p. 105). Columbia: University of Missouri Press.

Waller, James E. (2002). *Becoming evil: How ordinary people commit genocide and mass killing* (pp. 102–111). New York: Oxford University Press.

Watson, Lyall. (1995). *Dark nature: A natural history of evil* (p. 140). New York: HarperPerennial.

Zillmer, Eric A., Harrower, Molly, Ritzler, Barry A., & Archer, Robert P. (1995). *The quest for the Nazi personality: A psychological investigation of Nazi war criminals* (p. 194). Hillsdale, NJ: Lawrence Erlbaum Associates.

# CHAPTER 5

# FUNDAMENTALISM, VIOLENCE, AND WAR

### J. Harold Ellens

Fundamentalism is more a state of mind than a form of religion, more a psychological than a spiritual matter. As a psychological state of mind, Fundamentalism is always pathological. Wherever it appears and in whatever form or context, it is psychopathology. It is destructive of the health and function of the Fundamentalist and dangerous to those around him or her.

Fundamentalism appears with surprising frequency in every form of religion, profession, and facet of human society. Throughout their history, it has been a prominent characteristic of Judaism, Christianity, Islam, Hinduism, Shintoism, and other types of religion. Engineers can be fundamentalistic about engineering, attorneys about the interpretations and practice of law, and politicians about their views of statesmanship. It surfaces in every worldview and social system, every profession and every human form of operational practice; in ethical, theological, political, and social systems; in scientific perspectives, and in the manner in which a significant percentage of persons in every type of human community carry out their life and craft.

Fundamentalism is a psychological outlook in which rigid adherence to regulation, strict constructionist interpretation of principles and standards, and stringent methods of control of function and behavior take priority over freedom, flexibility, and creative imagination.

The emphasis is upon maintaining a static and orthodox system, rather than upon growth and the risks of change. This approach to life may evidence itself in the practice of medicine, dentistry, surgery, or psychology. Philosophers may be fundamentalistic in their quest for truth and in their crafting of the formulas or constructs in which truth must be expressed. There are physicists, astronomers, surgeons, and rhetoricians who are inflexible in theory and method, producing systems and procedures that ultimately prove counterproductive.

Fundamentalism is a mode of operation which is driven and shaped by obsessive-compulsive forces in the human psyche, insists upon predictable structures, and affords people who manifest it or adhere to it little capacity for coping with ambiguity. Since the ability to deal with ambiguity with a reasonable degree of comfort and efficiency is crucial to healthy life, the psychopathology of Fundamentalism is particularly evident in this obsessive characteristic. Perhaps there is a certain degree of advantage in this obsessive-compulsive rigidity for brain surgeons, dentists, and certified public accountants (CPAs), but I know of few other settings in which it is a virtue. Even though it may work for brain surgeons, dentists, and CPAs, it is still a pathology.

This dysfunctional characteristic is further evidenced in the virtually inevitable tendency of any Fundamentalism to produce an Orthodoxy in whatever field it arises, since Orthodoxies of any sort paint a static and ossified picture of reality, a picture which does not give room for the dynamism of growth and change or critique and response (Ellens, 2004b, pp. 119–142). The system inevitably becomes delusional. It manufactures an altered state of mind and sense of reality out of the rigid ideology of that particular form of Fundamentalism at play in any given situation or system of thought or practice. Since it is, therefore, untrue to reality, Fundamentalism is always and inherently a heresy.

Orthodoxy, which claims to be orthodox precisely because it dogmatically insists that it is the one and only possible formulation of the truth, is always, therefore, exactly the opposite of what it claims.[1] It is fundamentally unorthodox, that is, untrue! It is always an erroneous formulation of purported truth and can never be anything other than that because it refuses to be open to any new insight that might be generated by the ongoing open-ended human quest for understanding.

## Exposition

The pathology of orthodoxy-producing Fundamentalisms arises from the wellspring of prejudice, an insidious part of the unconscious strategies for survival and meaning, inherent in every human psyche. Prejudice has a bad reputation. It should have. It is everywhere and always destructive. Prejudice prevents an objective and sympathetic view of, or address to, anything. It is uniformly and consistently uncongenial with the best interests and quality of human life. Most human beings, I am quite sure, find prejudice reprehensible, but all of us are afflicted by it. We disapprove it, but we do it nonetheless. Pogo was right, "We have met the enemy and it is us!" (as cited in Ellens, 2004a, p. 85).

Prejudice afflicts us in two ways. We are all prejudiced about something and that obstructs our ability to deal with that specific matter, or the persons to which it applies, in the best possible way. Moreover, we are all recipients of the damage other persons' prejudices inflict upon us. I am 73 years old. It was a shock to me to notice that as I passed the age of about 60, at which time I suffered some heart trouble and aged rather more than I had before then, the young clerks in the drugstore or hardware store clearly distanced themselves from me. Whereas the former attendants had been rather congenial, the new and younger ones now treated me as an object. Of course, they had no way of knowing that I was a retired U.S. Army Colonel, an internationally known scholar, a noted lecturer, and a rather nice guy. They could see only that I was an old man who had not had the good sense to die and stop cluttering up their lives.

I notice that whether it is a matter of courtesy in driving on the highway, caring for my interests at a department store, or responding to my requests at a restaurant, airline counter, or other service settings, I am no longer seen by young adults as a *person*; unless they know me, need something from me, or are under my authority as in the case of my students, for example. Instead of being a person I am now an object, often made to feel that I am an inconvenience to those folks. I notice that I am not alone. I watch this happening as well to my friends and colleagues. It always makes me chuckle to see the reaction when I am with one of my elderly friends and we are treated like objects until I introduce him as the Federal Judge, or the U.S. Senator whom they obviously have not recognized, or a General Officer from my army days. Suddenly the prejudice that we are simply a couple of old guys who are a drag upon the U.S. economy evaporates and for a little while we are seen as persons—even larger than life, perhaps.

I am certain that if one asked these young folks whether they were prejudiced against old people, they would stand aghast at the suggestion. I am sure they are not at all aware of their internal image of gray-haired and wrinkled persons as irrelevant, burdensome, and undesirable. That is the nature of prejudice, theirs and mine. It usually operates quite destructively at the unconscious level, and for that very reason is so abusive and does so much damage to the personhood and circumstances of real live human beings. Moreover, young folk have no special mortgage on prejudice nor a special predilection toward it. As I write these paragraphs I am very much aware of my need to reflect upon my own temptation to paint all young adults with this same tar brush, when in fact my own adult children and young people I work with everyday are ample evidence that most young adults are sensitive and generous, perhaps less dogmatic and judgmental than I.

The sensitivity of a senior scholar or an old soldier and the insensitivity toward an old man by young people are painful, of course, but they are relatively trivial forms of prejudice, if one compares them with the biases which have wreaked upon humanity the destruction of racism, genocide, exploitive warfare, economic manipulation, or class and caste distinctions and elitism. These forms of institutionalized prejudice have formed the underpinnings of the abuses of power and have written the subtext of human history from its earliest recording until now. Moreover, the tragedy of it is in the fact that the pain and abuse of prejudicial behavior falls upon real, live, and lively human persons of flesh and blood, mind, and spirit. This violence is tangible, not theoretical; palpable, not abstract. "If you prick us, do we not bleed? If you tickle us, do we not laugh? If you poison us, do we not die?" (Shakespeare, *The Merchant of Venice*, Act III, Scene 1).

In his *Notes on Prejudice*, Henry Hardy quoted at length Isaiah Berlin's "hurried notes … for a friend" (as cited in Hardy, 2001, p. 12). Hardy described Berlin's intense observations as "somewhat breathless and telegraphic" (p. 12) conveying "with great immediacy Berlin's opposition to intolerance and prejudice, especially … stereotypes, and aggressive nationalism" (p. 12). The wisdom of Hardy's selection of this material for *The New York Review of Books* is obvious when we note that its date is just one month after the World Trade Center (WTC) tragedy. There venomous religious and cultural prejudice wreaked havoc on our entire nation—indeed upon the entire world. One might summarize Berlin's passionate expression in one sentence.

> Few things have done more harm than the belief on the part of individuals or groups (or tribes or states or nations or churches) that he or she or they are in the *sole* possession of the truth: especially about how to live, what to be and do—and that those who differ from them are not merely mistaken, but wicked or mad: and need restraining or suppressing. It is a terrible and dangerous arrogance to believe that you alone are right: have a magical eye which sees the truth: and that others cannot be right if they disagree. (p. 12)

Fundamentalisms have reared their ugly heads in every field of human endeavor throughout history and have been particularly noticeable in the fields of religion and ethics. One might cite the history of the Spanish monks who mounted the Inquisition of the late Middle Ages, some of the Gnostic forms of early Christianity that sought to suppress all other forms of Christianity, the Hassidim in Israelite religion, and the framers of the doctrines shaping al Qaeda today. In Christianity, the prominent forms of American Fundamentalism arose out of the Great Awakening and the frontier revivals and their psychology, which characterized the eighteenth and nineteenth centuries in the United States. This mind-set has now been exported everywhere in the world. The late Henry Stob, a wise and very generative Christian philosopher and theologian, of hallowed memory, who taught for an entire career on the faculty of Calvin College and Seminary, often referred to American Fundamentalism as the most dangerous heresy extant in modern history. Today we would certainly be forced to include in that category of most dangerous movements both Islamic religious Fundamentalism and fundamentalistic Israeli politics. All three of the great Western religions, which derive from the ancient Israelite religion of the Hebrew Bible, are plagued by the presence of this sick psychology and its prejudiced heretical products.

Moreover, no one in our world today, except apparently the Fundamentalists, needs much persuasion to agree that the rigorist mind-sets of the orthodoxies that have taken the world by storm in our time are productive of immense real and potential violence. Whether they are the orthodoxies of the American Christian religious right that supports Zionism for the purpose of hurrying the cataclysm of Armegeddon, of the Islamic terrorists whose dogmatism breeds suicide bombings and WTC assaults, or of the Israeli framers of preemptive defense who do not desire to negotiate for peace, the sick psychology is in every case the same. The prejudices and delusions that substitute for truth are very much the same. All are caught up in the ridiculous apocalyptic notions of cosmic conflict and the fight against cosmic forces of evil, none of which are real.

The product of such worldviews is always violence. Whether it is violation of the truth or of persons, property, and appropriate procedures for social and juridical order, it is violence. Whether it destroys persons, the necessary conditions of healthy human existence, or useful understandings of the real world, it is violence. Whether it corrupts freedom, constrains legitimate liberty, or fouls the human nest with mayhem and bestiality, it is violence. Whether it oppresses persons or peoples with the force and power of empire building, represses hope and the resilience of the human spirit with mass casualty fear and intimidation, or terrorizes the tranquility of children with media reports of those kinds of mayhem, it is phenomenally destructive violence.


## Psychobiology and Fundamentalism

Who generates these Fundamentalisms and Orthodoxies that are so destructive for the human spirit, for the conditions of healthy human life, and for the viability of truth and reality? Recently John Medina (2002) published an article entitled *Molecules of the Mind: The MAO A Gene and Exposure to Violent Behavior in Childhood.* In it he presented some very enlightening data regarding violence. The article reported research on the nurture *versus* nature debate regarding the sources of aggressive human behavior. Acknowledging that genetic research has swung the pendulum from environmental models to biochemical models of the origins of human violence, Medina insists that the real data show the importance of both. However, in discussing violent behavior in a specific set of human situations, he was forced to report the incredible influence of genetics.

The familiar enzyme, monoamine oxidase, is important to the "active concentration of neurotransmitters at the synapse" in the brain (p. 10). That is what makes thinking and conscious feeling possible. There are two types of genes that produce the enzyme. They are very similar in structure and very near each other on the X chromosome, shared by males and females. Because of some interesting things that had been seen in animal behavior when one of these MAO genes, designated A, was knocked out, researchers interested in human aggression began to look for "mutations of this gene in human subjects to see if any correlation could be found between aggression and disrupted MAO A chemistry" (p. 12).

Ten years ago a Dutch family was identified in which numerous generations of adult males were prone to extraordinary, sudden, explosive bouts of aggressive behavior. Examination of the data confirmed the inherited nature of the behavior. The cerebral-spinal fluid of all the subjects indicated a complete lack of MAO A. The mutation in this gene had neutralized its function in the neurotransmitter process. Only in early 2002 were new subjects identified so that the research could go forward. The New Zealand Dunedin Multidisciplinary Health and Development research program studied the development of over 1,000 children from their births in 1972.

"Tragically a specific subset of these children were found to be raised in severely abusive home environments" (p. 12).

For study 442 male children were selected, looking for a significant relationship between behavior and genetics. Of those children, 55 who had grown up in violent households had both low MAO A levels and highly violent behavior themselves. Violent behavior in children from violent households but who had high MAO A levels was only about 25 percent of that of children with violent households and low MAO A levels. Children with high or low MAO A levels and stable structured homes all had about 8 percent as much violent behavior as the children with abusive homes and low MAO A levels. These children with 8 percent as much violent behavior were probably reflecting normal levels of aggression.

The import of this research for our concerns here is that, for a proper understanding of the kinds of people that are inclined toward Fundamentalisms and Orthodoxies, genetic studies might prove to be very useful. Fundamentalist psychology is known to produce not only rigid models of thought and worldviews, but also rigidity in other aspects of life, such as regulation of home life and views of professional and personal or family discipline. Fundamentalist Evangelical families produce a higher level of physical and sexual abuse of children than the general population. This phenomenon coincides with specific forms of prejudice among Fundamentalists against ideologies and persons who differ discernibly from them and their thought system. Moreover, Fundamentalisms tend to run in families and in extended family communities. Orthodoxies tend to form specific discreet communities, and these tend to perpetuate themselves throughout generations. It would be of interest to know to what extent this is reflective of a genetic bias that produces at least a proclivity toward such rigid life and thought, toward an inclination to prejudicial attitudes, and toward a pathological lack of openness to more universalizing insights or perspectives on truth and life.

Most of all, it would be of interest to know whether such inflammatory leaders as Osama bin Laden, and many like him, who have created isolationistic groups of followers, with the objective of wreaking violence upon the world or upon others within their own world, may be persons with low MAO A genetics and highly abusive or rigid and oppressive developmental settings. This would be interesting information because it would provide for a rational understanding of the horrid phenomena with which the world is faced in such persons as Joseph Stalin, Adolf Hitler, Osama bin Laden, Ariel Sharon, Yasir Arafat, and the like. These are people for whom early resort to massive violence as the ultimate solution to all major problems seems to have been an addiction. Arafat and Sharon may seem to have been men of different styles, but their methods were the same. Sharon was overtly aggressive in his promotion of massive violence, and Arafat was passive aggressive in his promotion of massive violence, but the outcome is the same. We ought to know why they resort to radical violence as the ultimate solution to every major problem or socio-political impasse, so that we can see these kinds of characters coming on the world scene, but also so that we can anticipate the destructive forces of their Fundamentalist Orthodoxies in politics, ethics, or religion before they have opportunity to wreak

the havoc of slaughter in Palestinian refugee camps in Lebanon (Sharon), or extermi-
nate an entire class of citizens in the farming communities of the Ukraine (Stalin), or
commit genocide in concentration camps (Hitler), or wreak havoc on innocent groups
of persons with suicide bombs (Arafat). Psychobiology may be our hope for the future.

In 1996 Elizabeth Young-Bruehl published a superb analysis of this affliction of
human psychology and society. She called it the *Anatomy of Prejudices*. Her superior
work has not been superceded. Her focus is mainly upon anti-Semitism, racism, sexism, and homophobia. However, her general assessment of the psychodynamics of
this psychosocial malady leads us to an appreciation of the similarities all forms of
prejudice manifest, the distinctive characteristics of each type, and the subtle and bla-
tant forms of their social expression. From the slightest slur to the stupid joke to the
violent act, even war, prejudice functions like the sophisticated computer virus which
adapts its own structure as it goes along eating up all the resources available and using
the wholesome qualities and energies of any system or community, by turning them
on their heads, and redirecting their trajectories to create evil. What were growth-
inducing insights are turned into malevolent analyses and defensive-aggressive reactions, filled with and generating paranoia and hate.

Young-Bruehl observes upon the great difficulty we have in stepping outside our
own prejudices, even in our endeavor to speak or write wisely about prejudice. She
wonders why,

> on this topic of prejudices, so much has been written on such shaky foundations, with
> such a recycling of cliches and unfounded conclusions. I became convinced that the
> way we have learned to speak in ... America about prejudices is a very large part of our
> prejudice problem, a part of which we are, daily, unaware. (p. 2)

She points out that when Gordon Allport (1958) wrote his valuable treatise, *The
Nature of Prejudice*, and surveyed the total scope of the subject in mid-twentieth century America, he announced his objective as seeking out the root of prejudice so as to
understand its nature.

While the course Allport set for the investigation of prejudice was a worthy one,
his model was limited by the implied assumption that "prejudice is something singular with one nature and one root" (Young-Bruehl, 1996, p. 16). However, Allport
actually is at some pains to declare that,

> It is a serious error to ascribe prejudice and discrimination to any single taproot, reaching
> into economic exploitation, social structure, the mores, fear, aggression, sex conflict, or
> any other favored soil. Prejudice and discrimination ... may draw nourishment from
> all these conditions, and many others. (1958, p. xii)

Allport wishes to teach plural causation, but he acknowledges that he is by professional habit disposed to emphasize the role of learning, cognitive processes, and personality formation.

> It is true that I believe it is only within the nexus of the personality that we find the effec-
> tive operation of historical, cultural, and economic factors ... for it is only *individuals*
> who can feel antagonism and practice discrimination ... I place a heavy and convergent
> emphasis upon psychological factors. (pp. xii–xiii)

Allport drew out these psychodynamics of prejudice in a surprisingly creative way for a scholar working on this issue so early in our cultural awareness of the need to study it systematically. He put his finger on the central dynamic of prejudice. His words seem as wise and applicable a half century later as they must have seemed forward looking and wise when he published them a decade after the close of World War II.

> At the time when the world as a whole suffers from panic induced by the rival ideologies of east and west, each corner of the earth has its own special burdens of animosity. Moslems distrust non-Moslems. Jews who escaped extermination in Central Europe find themselves in the new State of Israel surrounded by antisemitism. Refugees roam in inhospitable lands. Many of the colored people of the world suffer indignities at the hands of whites who invent a fanciful racist doctrine to justify their condescension. The checkerboard of prejudice in the United States is perhaps the most intricate of all. … some of the endless antagonism seems based upon a realistic conflict of interests, most of it, we suspect, is a product of fears of the imagination. Yet imaginary fears can cause real suffering. Rivalries and hatreds between groups are nothing new. What is new is the fact that technology has brought these groups too close together for comfort. (p. ix)

Allport did not develop his psychological perceptions very extensively because his approach was, in the end, primarily sociological. However, one experiences throughout his work that he kept his eye open to the inner psychodynamics of the individual. He would, I think, have agreed with the perception that prejudice is primarily a defensive aggressive psychological phenomenon, that it is rooted in ignorance or bad information about the person or community against which the prejudice is directed, that it is generated by the primal human urge for survival combined with the paranoia which lack of accurate information produces, and that it expresses itself as an intention to devalue, disarm, and extinguish the relevance of the object of the prejudice. This psychological process may take the form of slights and verbal disrespect, intimidations and social degrading, physical deprivations and assaults, catastrophic violence and war, or extermination of the object of the discrimination and hatred.

Fundamentalism and its orthodoxies, in whatever field they appear, focused as they are by prejudice, are inherently violent. The reasons are few, consistently the same in all Fundamentalisms, and straightforward. Fundamentalism is a psychology which insists addictively that its view of reality and truth is the only authentic one and is the whole truth. Therefore, any other perspective is willfully false, ignorant, and dangerous to the truth. In this logic, it is for the good of the non-Fundamentalists that the Fundamentalist's truth be imposed upon them.

In religious Fundamentalism it is thought to be the will of God and a favor to all humankind to bring humanity under the umbrella of Fundamentalism. So, it is the imperative of Fundamentalists to impose their model of the truth upon all non-Fundamentalists, by force if they have the predominating power, or by seduction that is usually called evangelism if they do not have the dominant power. Therefore, those who resist such inclusion in Fundamentalism or who threaten it with repression or opposition must be neutralized, either by isolating, demeaning, or destroying them.

This pattern may readily be seen in the history of religions in the violent imposition of Nicean Orthodoxy upon almost all Christian movements in the fourth century and following, with the great destruction of many of the persons and movements that represented Christian alternatives. It is also illustrated by the Inquisition, the Christian Crusades, the witch trials of the American Puritans, the frequent Islamic Fundamentalist crusades against other Muslims throughout history, and now al Qaeda terrorism against Muslims who disagree with them and against the non-Muslim world.

Stirling (2004) and McGuire (2004) explicate the model of René Girard for explaining how specific persons or groups become identified in or by a society as the object of prejudice and its social consequences. They develop Girard's essentially psychoanalytic understanding of these forms of isolation, alienation, devaluation, and extermination, pointing out particularly his metaphor of the scapegoat. This is, of course, an old metaphor, already prominent in ancient Israelite religion and in the Hebrew Bible, which that religion produced. It is carried over in formative ways into the Christian Scriptures of the New Testament and into Islam's sacred scriptures, the Qur'an.

Girard's point comes down to the psychoanalytic insight that the scapegoat, whether it is an individual or another society, becomes a projection of the shadow side of the source or enactor of the prejudice. Prejudice always generates and is generated by an "us *versus* them" mind-set. The circumstances of life often produce realistic situations in which there arises a real-life "us and them" setting. My family and I live in North America. There are many other humans who do not, including a number of my relatives for whom I have great affection. They live in Germany. Whether we discuss the geography of Greenland or the current perspectives on American policy toward the Near Eastern nations and cultures, it is inevitable that their perspective will be that of those who must look westward toward Greenland and ours that of those who must look eastward. That may seem irrelevant, but psychoanalytic psychologists know that the simple difference makes a discernible psychological difference in the way we and they think of Greenland.

On the infinitely more complex and serious matter of Near East policy, the differences in perspective will inevitably be much more remarkable. We may even have the same basic facts and principles in mind, but we will see the implications of them differently if our primary unconscious interest is American and theirs is German. With some significant conscious and rational thoughtfulness we may be able to place ourselves in each other's shoes and gain more global views that might be almost identical, but even then certain flavors and tastes, so to speak, will still make our feelings about the matter distinctive to each of us.

We can, of course, have important differences without resorting to prejudice. We may take a gracious, thoughtful attitude which empowers us to understand a wide range of views on a matter, without feeling less passionate about the one we support. We may be able to allow the others to have their point of view as a legitimate alternative way of looking at things. Or we may feel strongly that the facts are such that they really have no moral right or rational justification to hold to such an ill-

informed outlook. However, even then, it is not necessary for us to resort to prejudice, which is a need to devalue or damage the other person or community because
of the positions they take, the attitudes they evince, or the behavior they act out.

Prejudice is the irrational, unconscious, devaluation of another for no other reason
than that the "other" is different. Prejudice increases with ignorance and the paranoia
ignorance generates. Prejudice identifies, isolates, and alienates its object. The further
this process progresses the easier it is to project upon that other those things we hate
in ourselves. We always hate most in others what we cannot stand in ourselves. Our
own flaws, distortions, inequities, self-defeating habits, and failures we see readily in
others, or believe we do, and unconsciously we attack those in them that we know we
should extinguish from ourselves. Therefore, those things that we cannot face in ourselves, for which we cannot forgive ourselves, we make into the reasons for devaluing
or destroying them.

If those dysfunctions in ourselves which we cannot stand, cannot deal with, cannot
correct, or cannot forgive, happen to be religiously and morally laden with some
kind of divine censure, in our perception, we will see our attack upon those very
things in others as divinely sanctioned, justified by God, even the imperatives of
his own will and mandate for us. We may feel called by God, in such instances, to
wreak havoc upon those others who are the "legitimate" objects of our prejudice.
This surely was the motive and the mind-set of the terrorists of the 9/11 tragedy. It
is the outlook of Christian pro-lifers, whose disgust with abortion on demand may
be appropriate, but who are intent upon killing doctors and nurses who service abortion clinics. The same motive seems to have been clearly that of the ancient biblical
Israelites who confused their own acquisitive prejudices with the divine will when
it came to extermination of the Canaanites, "because the cup of their iniquity was
filled." Few readers notice that the Canaanite cup was filled with exactly the idola-
trous and abusive behavior to which the Israelites were forever inclined themselves,
given half a chance to diverge from the "call of Yahweh" to be a distinctive people
of grace. That prejudicial motive is surely also the disposition and dynamics of the
modern Palestinians and Israelis who seem forever ready to destroy their own world
in order to save it.

Allport had an interesting way of getting at the underpinnings of these psychological dynamics of prejudice. He thought that our negative prejudices are the obverse of
those things that we love and cherish and that the most important categories we have
in terms of which to think and feel about things are our personal values. We live by
and for them, without consciously needing to think about them or evaluate them.
We defend them in terms of the intensity of our feelings about them and we compel
our reason and assessment of evidence to fit in with them.

> As partisans for our own way of life we cannot help thinking in a partisan manner. Only
> a small portion of our reasoning is ... "directed thinking" ... controlled exclusively by
> outer evidence and focused upon the solution of objective problems. ... Such partisan
> thinking is entirely natural, for our job in this world is to live in an integrated way as
> value-seekers. Prejudgments stemming from these values enable us to do so. (1958,
> p. 24)

Unfortunately, prejudgments can easily slide into prejudice. Allport was aware of the fact that affirming our way of life may lead to the "brink of prejudice" (p. 24). He cites Spinoza's notion of "love-prejudice," namely, having more love feelings for someone or something than is appropriate to that object. We "overgeneralize" the virtues of such objects, whether a lover, a doctrine, a church, a nation, or a cause.

> This love-prejudice is far more basic to human life than is its opposite, hate-prejudice (which Spinoza says "consists in feeling about anyone through hate less than is right"). One must first overestimate the things one loves before one can underestimate their contraries. ... Positive attachments are essential to life. ... Why is it that we hear so little about love-prejudice—the tendency to overgeneralize our categories of attachment and affection? One reason is that prejudices of this sort create no social problem. ... When a person is defending a categorical value of his own, he may do so at the expense of other people's interests or safety. If so, then we note his hate-prejudice, not realizing that it springs from a reciprocal love-prejudice underneath. ... negative prejudice is a reflex of one's own system of values. We prize our own mode of existence and correspondingly underprize (or actively attack) what seems to us to threaten it. The thought has been expressed by Sigmund Freud: "In the undisguised antipathies and aversions which people feel towards strangers with whom they have to do, we recognize the expression of self-love, of narcissism. (pp. 24–26)

Particularly relevant to our present moment in history and the international circumstances in the Western World is Allport's next paragraph.

> The process is especially clear in time of war. When an enemy threatens all or nearly all of our positive values we stiffen our resistance and exaggerate the merits of our cause. We feel—and this is an instance of overgeneralization—that we are wholly right. (If we did not believe this we could not marshal all our energies for our defense.) And if we are wholly right then the enemy must be wholly wrong. Since he is wholly wrong, we should not hesitate to exterminate him. But even in this wartime example it is clear that our basic love-prejudice is primary and that the hate-prejudice is a derivative phenomenon. (p. 26)

Isaiah Berlin thought that under these circumstances of significant conflict of values we tend to operate from the certainty that there is only one worthy goal for one's self, church, nation, or humanity; "only one true answer to the central questions which have agonized mankind" (as cited in Hardy, 2001, p. 12); and that it is worth risking all for that final solution, no matter how costly. We tend to be particularly willing to accept exorbitant costs in loss and suffering, particularly if it is mainly the enemy's loss and suffering. He cited Robespierre as saying, "through an ocean of blood to the Kingdom of Love" (p. 12).[2]

Berlin grieved that if we have not learned from history the foolishness and self-defeat in this outlook, "we are incurable" (p. 12). That may be so. It is almost certainly so if we cannot rid ourselves of the West's endemic tendency to assume that human conflicts, like God's conflicts in the Hebrew Bible, are ultimately best resolved by precipitating catastrophe. This leads us to delay earlier, safer, and saner resolutions of misunderstandings and collision courses of policy or ambition, trusting that if all else fails, which it surely will in such an irresponsible model, we can always resort to the ultimate violence. We are inherently addicted to cataclysm, so we do not fear our prejudices as much as we fear the loss of what we "love more than is right" (Allport, 1958, p. 24).

During the last decade of the twentieth century Robert M. Baird and Stuart E. Rosenbaum (1992) edited a series of psychosocial studies entitled *Contemporary Issues*. These amounted to a series of handbooks on various topics related mainly to legal and ethical issues in social management. One useful monograph in the series was entitled *Bigotry, Prejudice, and Hatred; Definitions, Causes, and Solutions*. Two chapters in this volume proved to be particularly helpful. Chapter 10 by Elliot Aronson (1992) investigated the causes of prejudice. Pierre L. van den Berghe (1992) wrote the following chapter on the biology of nepotism. Both of these relate directly to this particular phase of our discussion here, in that they address the underside of our love-prejudice and paint a picture of a Girardian take on our hate-prejudice. Aronson led off with the following paragraph:

> one determinant of prejudice in a person is a need for self-justification ... if we have done something cruel to a person or a group of people, we derogate that person or group in order to justify our cruelty. If we can convince ourselves that a group is unworthy, sub-human, stupid, or immoral, it helps us to keep from feeling immoral if we enslave members of that group, deprive them of a decent education, or murder them. We can then continue to go to church (or Synagogue or Mosque, I would add) and feel ... good ... because it isn't a fellow human we've hurt. Indeed, if we're skillful enough, we can even convince ourselves that the barbaric slaying of old men, women, and children is a ... virtue—as the crusaders did when, on their way to the holy land, they butchered European Jews in the name of the Prince of Peace. ... this form of self-justification serves to intensify subsequent brutality. (p. 111)

Sociological studies tend to suggest that the more the security of one's status and power is jeopardized, the more prejudiced one tends to be and behave. Van den Berghe (1987) makes a cogent argument for finding the roots of prejudice in nepotism. His basic argument is that

> ethnic and racial sentiments are extensions of kinship sentiments. Ethnocentrism and racism are thus extended forms of nepotism—the propensity to favor kin over non-kin. There exists a general behavioral predisposition, in our species as in many others, to react favorably toward other organisms to the extent that these organisms are biologically related to the actor. The closer the relationship is, the stronger the preferential behavior. (p. 125)

Blood is still thicker than water, apparently!

It is interesting, of course, that humans are seldom cannibals, and if they are it is generally with great revulsion and in extremity. Most humans are willing to consume other mammals, birds, and creatures lower on the evolutionary tree such as fish. Even many of those who argue for being vegetarian on the grounds that one ought not to eat "meat" will, nonetheless, eat chicken and fish. Chicken is presumably from the dinosaur line and fish more closely related to reptiles, both a long way from our human branch of the evolutionary tree. Those vegetarians who also avoid chicken, fish, and dairy, Vegans, who wish only a strictly vegetarian diet, are usually mystified when I ask them how they can possibly tolerate killing these living things they eat, the poor lettuce leaf, celery stalks, beautiful carrots, and the like. They tend to respond that these are short-lived forms of life anyway, are planted for harvesting, and have no consciousness or feelings. Well, that is a very relative and imperialistic statement. I doubt the lettuce leaf would agree, should he or she or it be honestly "inquired of."

Of course, there is a significant debate about whether the implied claim is true, i.e., that plants have no consciousness or feelings. There seems to be adequate evidence that plants respond to what seems comparable to our central nervous system stimulation. However, when all is said and done, the argument boils down to the fact that plants are so far down the evolutionary tree as to be not worth considering as a life-form in the sense that humans are life-forms. Van den Berghe's claim is vindicated by this rather simple human proclivity to argue for the privilege of those most like us and against the privileged status of those most unlike us. Thus blacks can more easily feel and act out prejudice against whites than against other blacks, and whites have demonstrated the same thing on their side of the equation, in monstrous ways, throughout history.

However, Young-Bruehl is less certain than van den Berghe that the familial connections in the dynamics of prejudice are biological or grounded in kinship issues. She wonders, with Erich Fromm, whether the familial influence is not rather psychosocial, particularly the sociological side of that. She investigated (1996, pp. 64–65) the extent to which it is the family power structure and the values related to it that sets the course for prejudicial patterns and dispositions. Adorno and Horkheimer (1950) were sure that the patriarchal family is the nexus of prejudice by reason of its authoritarian socialization of the family members. This is basically the "frustration-aggression" model for explaining prejudice as rage displaced upon a scapegoat and forming the foundation for such models as that of Girard.

In the end Young-Bruehl (1996, pp. 64–65) concludes in her study that the sources and dynamics of prejudice are so complex that one must avoid above all the temptation to generalizations, normally the objective of all science. Instead, she urges, we must address the operational issues of prejudicial behavior in specific situations: specific categories such as racism, sexism, homophobia, and anti-Semitism; and specific incidences such as this lynching, that genocide, this caste system, that slavery, this riot, that family feud. I agree, but it is clear that there are generalizing similarities at work in the tragedies of prejudice. They include the following list of factors. First, the difficulty humans have in living with the unknown and the very different. Second, the human tendency to make dogmatic claims that differences of values and styles means the moral inferiority of the other. Third, the human inclination to fear the unknown or different and react to or act out that fear in defensive aggressive strategies. Fourth, the human need to justify those feelings and that behavior by demonizing the object of the prejudice. Fifth, the corollary behavior of isolating, alienating, devaluing, degrading, disempowering, and if necessary exterminating that object whether a person or a community. Sixth, the human inclination to believe there is a single and final solution to the impasse of difference and conflict. Seventh, the willingness to pay any price for the ultimate cataclysm that will resolve the tension, stress, and burden of that impasse, particularly if that cost is mainly at the expense of the object of the prejudice, the enemy.

### Religious Fundamentalism Worldwide

Christian Fundamentalism is a uniquely American heresy. Unfortunately, it has been exported worldwide by industrious mission efforts. Its central objective is the promotion of a strange kind of Orthodoxy. Its components are mainly the following five. It holds to a theology of sacred scripture which claims that the Bible is verbally inspired by God in such a way that it is totally inerrant in every word and detail of content, and, therefore, is to be taken literally as the authoritative foundation of all truth. Second, Fundamentalism subscribes to the apocalyptic worldview that a cosmic conflict between God and the Devil, between cosmic forces of good and evil, rages everywhere and at all times on the battlefields of history and the human heart. Third, it claims that the communities of humans and of transcendental beings such as angels and demons are divided into two camps, namely, the righteous and the unrighteous, and that the temporal blessing and the eternal destiny of each community, and the individuals within it, depends upon the degree to which those beings conform to the law of God. Fourth, Fundamentalism professes that there is a mechanism for escape from the eternal judgment of God upon those who fail to keep his law, namely, confession of sins and correction of behavior. In this case, the justice of God which has been breached by misbehavior is satisfied because the implorations of confession and reformation access the merits of the sacrifice of Jesus for human sin in his crucifixion and that merit balances the scales of divine justice. Fifth, Fundamentalism expects that ultimately God will win the cosmic conflict and subdue what amounts to the evil god, the Devil, and terminate history in a cataclysm that will damn the unrighteous to eternal hellfire and embrace the righteous into a blissful heaven.

Martin E. Marty and R. Scott Appleby (1991) have done us a great favor in helping us understand religious Fundamentalism worldwide, by the publication of their immense and immensely important volume, *Fundamentalism Observed*. It is the first of five volumes in *The Fundamentalism Project* (1991–1995). It offers a survey of Fundamentalism in all major religious traditions. Sixteen scholars have joined them in trying to achieve both an appreciation and an assessment of Fundamentalisms in North American Protestantism, Roman Catholic Tradition, Protestant Fundamentalism in Latin America, The Jewish Fundamentalism of the *Haredim*, Jewish Zionist Fundamentalism, Sunni and Shiite Muslim Fundamentalisms, Asian Islamic Fundamentalism, Hindu Fundamentalism, Sikh Fundamentalism, Theravada Buddhist Fundamentalism, Confucian Fundamentalism in East Asia, and Political and Religious Fundamentalism in Japan. Marty and Appleby call all this the hypothetical family of Fundamentalism, implying the universal underlying psychospiritual commonality that reigns in all of these otherwise quite disparate movements.

> The premise ... is that religious fundamentalism, a term historically associated with versions of American Protestantism and more recently employed to describe certain expressions of Islam, exhibits generic characteristics which apply to various religious settings. Hence, not only Christianity and Islam but also Hinduism, Buddhism, Judaism, and other religions may be found to have fundamentalist variants. Moreover, an understanding of each of these versions of fundamentalism, ... will shed light on the phenomenon as a whole. (p. 197)

This encyclopedic work takes as its theme the proposition that Fundamentalism of every kind is a dogmatically asserted and defended ideological system that is, therefore, not open to either review or critique. It is inflexibly closed to any continued acquisition of truth or insight, modification or expansion. North American Protestant Fundamentalism expresses itself in a non-negotiable creedal posture and has radicalized both ethics and politics in terms of that ideology. Its aggression has been channeled into an effort to shape national politics through infiltrating the historic system of the American political process in efforts to elect Fundamentalists. It is also aggressively saturating the populace with mass media of all types and focusing upon specific local socio-political and ethical battles such as assaults upon abortion clinics. This strategy for getting Fundamentalist ideology into the forefront of national life and significantly increasing its influence upon the mind-set of the populace has been surprisingly successful. Moreover, no effective critique has been offered to counter it since the typical liberal approach has been, "The less said the better. Maybe it will go away." Of course, it will not. Only the open arena of dialogue, informed with good ideas founded in truth and reality, will maintain a decent balance and ward off the very real dangers that attend any significant rise of Fundamentalism anywhere.

A Fundamentalist fringe group of one sort or another has existed in Roman Catholicism since the beginning of its long history. Some of those groups became orders of monks or nuns within the church, eventually received papal consecration, and were domesticated into fairly mainline enterprises. Largely in response to the *aggiornamento* (updating) that Pope John XXIII brought into the Roman Catholic communion by convening the Second Vatican Council in 1962–1965 and shepherding it through its aggressively innovating agenda, a countermovement of Fundamentalism resurged in the church. Archbishop Marcel Lefebvre claimed the church had lost its moorings in its creeds and traditions by the liberalizing openness of Vatican II, so he ordained three bishops into a new movement to re-establish the historic traditions of the church. This was an act that violated the order of the church, so he, his bishops, and their followers were excommunicated.

> The emergence of a "traditionalist" ... movement spearheaded by a "rebel" archbishop indicates the scope of the conflict that has divided Catholics ... of hierarchical leadership ... who claim the high ground of Catholic orthodoxy. The rise of the traditionalist movement also illustrates how Catholicism's troubled encounter with modernity has spawned movements and ideological orientations closely paralleling those associated with Protestantism's own fundamentalist reactions to the modern world. ... Lefebvre's

brand of Roman Catholic traditionalism is a militant and organized reaction against the intellectual and cultural inroads of modernism … to arrest and reverse religious change … and to preserve the ideological, organizational, and cultic patterns altered, abandoned, or discredited …, a protest against the blurring of Catholic identity and the loss of Catholic hegemony. (p. 67)

This Catholic traditionalist movement is worldwide today and at least loosely organized as a fraternity. The church's response to this kind of dissent over the centuries has generally been surprisingly wise. It has tended to move with extreme patience, giving some room for the dissent to work itself out without enough pressure on it to produce overt violence or ruptured relationships, and then eventually it has tended to co-opt the unconventional movement. Frequently this very process has energized the inner spiritual drivers of the whole church. Particularly in the United States, such an approach has worked rather well for the last 40 years with regard to the absorption of this traditionalist movement back into the mainstream of the church.

In Latin American, on the other hand, the Roman Catholic Church, traditionally the dominant religious force in culture, politics, society, and liturgy, has lost a great deal of ground to Protestant Fundamentalism, exported from North America by Evangelical Fundamentalist missions. This is thought by some to be the result of a rather arid formalism having permeated the Roman Catholic Church in Latin America from the sixteenth century to the mid-twentieth century, together with the rather unsuccessful strategies of Liberation Theologies in all of the mainline denominations in South America. With the demise of the USSR the Marxist Liberation Theologies have lost much of their impetus. The vacuum has been filled in Latin America with Fundamentalism in the Christian traditions but also Fundamentalist mystery religions with quasi-African roots, instead of Christian foundations.

Within Judaism, worldwide, an ultraorthodox scion has grown up called the *Haredim*. Fundamentalist Orthodoxy has always been a significant presence in Judaism, as well as in ancient Israelite religion. These Jews hold to the ideology that *their* religious truths, precepts, and formulations have been and must be an unbroken tradition from Abraham to the present moment and on through the future until the Messiah arrives. "To these Jews the past is the great teacher: today is never as great as yesterday, and the best that tomorrow can promise is a return to the great days of yesteryear" (p. 197). The name by which they are called means, "Those who tremble at the word of the Lord." They are sure that they are the only ones to whom God pays attention.

Historically, the term *Haredim* referred to those who were scrupulous or obsessive about religious punctiliousness. It is interesting that one of the sins that the Roman Catholic Church named in the Middle Ages was scrupulosity. To call it a sin and require confession for it was a hedge against the psychological illness that is manifested in or incited by obsessive religiosity or self-discipline. In this is the typical rigidity of Fundamentalism evident in the *Haredim*. It is true of their approach to theology, biblical study, ethics, social controls, and personal habits. Judaism worldwide has been radicalized to a significant degree by the forces of this movement. This is particularly true in Israel itself where the ultraorthodox have managed to achieve significant political power by manipulating the various coalition governments, made necessary by the increasingly divided society.

Historically, Zionism was a relatively general term referring to the Israelite longing for a homeland in Palestine. In the late 1960s it was radicalized by a small group of people who, armed with military weapons, militantly began to force the occupation of Palestinian territories by Jewish settlers, at the same time wreaking havoc upon the persons and property of Palestinians. The current memory is that this movement arose in response to a sermon by Rabbi Kook, the Younger, on the 19th anniversary of Israeli independence. In the sermon at a Jerusalem religious academy, Merkaz Harav Yeshiva, Kook emphasized passionately several messianic tenets of his mystical system that he claimed would constitute the spiritual base of the revolutionary Jewish-Zionist movement.

Kook claimed that divine redemption of Israel was in process at that very moment, nationally and politically, since Israel had been established and successfully maintained as a nation for nearly two decades; but that what was lacking was a corollary religious and ethical redemption. Most Israelis were secular and the moral and ethical codes of the society were not those of the Torah or Talmudim, but were merely utilitarian ethics of secular Western society. Kook launched the course that the Israeli nation has come to follow into the tragic mayhem of perpetual violence and mutual destruction of Palestinians and itself. Moreover, this form of violent Jewish Fundamentalism has produced the current general world crisis in and regarding the Near East.

According to the Jewish scholar, Gideon Aran, at the outset few people in Israel took the Jewish-Zionist drive seriously and most Israelis were greatly offended by its violence, injustice, and ideological dogmatism (see Marty & Appleby, 1991). This movement promoted the illegal establishment of Israeli settlements in the land properly belonging, by treaty and title, to the Palestinians. Moreover, it claimed that the territories from the Tigris to the Nile properly belonged to Israel, as in the golden age of David's and Solomon's Kingdoms. This bizarre ideology became a driving undercurrent in Israeli politics and social ferment until an increasing number of Israelis began to endorse the vision. General Sharon and the Israeli Defense Force took advantage of this perspective in support of the invasion of Lebanon, and progressively the movement gained political power until it can now essentially manipulate the government. It is of some considerable help to the movement that now General Ariel Sharon is Prime Minister Ariel Sharon. It is largely in response to this abusive form of Jewish Fundamentalism that the Islamic Fundamentalism of al Qaeda and of the militant Palestinians has become increasingly focused, unified, and aggressive against the United States, the primary ally of Israel. It is not yet clear that Sharon's withdrawal from Gaza will be adequately persuasive to dissuade the Palestinians from violence.

As a result of Anwar Sadat's rapprochement with Israel, Sunni Egyptian Fundamentalists shot and killed their president on October 6, 1981. They were carrying out a jihad that they believed was mandated by God. That was, for many of us, the opening gun of the militancy of Islamic Fundamentalism and its worldwide battle against all those who do not agree with its religious ideology. The spirit is the same sick psychology as that of the Israeli Zionists who provoked the evil these evil Fundamentalist Muslims oppose. The momentum of this violently destructive Islamic religious movement has increased weekly since that day two and a half decades ago when Sadat fell victim to the supposed divine mandate. Its victims now number in the tens of thousands and are fast moving to the hundreds of thousands, in Europe, Asia, India, Africa, Israel, Kurdic Iraq, the Mediterranean basin, and the Americas. Their violent guerrilla-type warfare has been carried out on land, in the air, and on the sea. It been targeted mainly against civilian noncombatants, demonstrating the inherently unethical barbarism and cowardly abusiveness of these psychopathic Fundamentalists.

Their movement is referred to as Islamic Fundamentalism because it is their attempt to reaffirm the foundational principles that they think shaped original Islam and should shape the structures and laws of Muslim society, religion, and ethics everywhere today. Just like the Jewish-Zionist movement, these Sunni Muslims wish to recall fellow Muslims to the correct path of their religion, which they, of course, feel divinely appointed to define. All Muslims hold to the authority and life-shaping claims of their sacred scriptures, but the Fundamentalists have an exclusivist and literalist interpretation of the message, mandates, and moral program of the Qur'an, from which they derive a rigorist pattern for social and political regulation of life in Islamic nations. "Islamic fundamentalism is ... a distinctive mode of response to major social and cultural change introduced either by exogenous or indigenous forces and perceived as threatening to dilute or dissolve the clear lines of Islamic identity, or to overwhelm that identity in a synthesis of many different elements" (p. 346). Like their Jewish counterparts these Fundamentalists are eager to resort to armed violence and open assault upon civilian or military targets to gain their vicious and lawless objectives.

The Ayatollah Ruholla Mussaui Khomeini represented, in his lifetime and his days of power in Iran, the other branch of Islamic Fundamentalism, that of the Shiites. He came to power on February 1, 1979, after being befriended and promoted by France for 15 years, contrary to Western political policy and, as it turned out, contrary to the best interests of the people of Iran. Saddam Hussein, a secular Arab described by Osama bin Laden, together with Hussein's fellow Iraqi leaders, as a nest of infidels, made war upon Khomeini and his Fundamentalist regime in Iran. It was, as we remember, a phenomenally destructive war for both nations. Hundreds of thousands of citizens died on both sides. Hussein's opposition to Islamic Fundamentalism was illustrated at that time by his execution of the noted Shiite leader in Iraq, Ayatollah Muhammad Baquir al-Sadr, on April 9, 1980. Subsequently, Hussein supported the Taliban and al Qaeda in Afghanistan against the USSR, as did the United States, and subsequently Hussein seemed to be willing to work with al Qaeda, if it paid off for him in his war with the United States.

One form of Fundamentalism is difficult to distinguish from another, and their willingness to resort to unlawful and barbarous forms of violence together to gain their short-term objectives, with little good vision for the long term consequences, makes strange bedfellows out of a great variety of Fundamentalists in specific *ad hoc* situations. One gets the distinct impression that American Fundamentalists, who are bent upon attacking and violently closing abortion clinics, however constructive their objective of decreasing abortions on demand, would welcome an al Qaeda terrorist to assist them by bombing a few such clinics. None of us would be at all surprised if CNN Headline News reported tomorrow that American Fundamentalists in Atlanta hired a Palestinian suicide bomber to go into an abortionist clinic and set himself off, with the promise that the suicide bomber's family in Hebron would get a check for $25,000 (U.S.). They all smell the same, look the same, act the same, resort to the same abusive aggression, and invoke the same nonexistent god, namely, the ridiculous barbarous god of Fundamentalist dogmatic heresy.

Of course it must be remembered that from the inside of the system, for the religious Fundamentalist personally, the intention is to establish a structured and secure society, blessed by the order and discipline that Fundamentalists believe God's will and law should impose upon all society, religion, ethical systems, intellectual models, and philosophical worldviews. The Fundamentalist is sure that such a world is not only God's imperative but also the best arrangement for humanity; thus the means of attaining it are justified by the ends achieved. The vicious and barbarous violence is not the legal pattern for the lawful world order to come, but merely the expedient to which one must resort to achieve God's ends and purposes here and now. This is thought by the religious Fundamentalist to be not only justified but required by the rubrics of sacred scriptures, whether those are the examples of Jesus's violence in the New Testament, the model of Muhammed's military jihad in the Qur'an, or the narrative of the divinely ordered extermination of the Canaanites by the ancient Israelites in the Hebrew Bible.

The Fundamentalist character of a special kind of Hinduism that has arisen with strength in the last quarter century is becoming increasingly evident. This sect is particularly evident in northern India and Kashmir, where it arose in the early 1980s as a response to the Islamic Fundamentalism progressively causing socio-political and religious turbulence in that region. Initially it was militant and has subsequently turned murderous. The influence of this barbarously violent Hinduism is now seeding itself throughout India, giving traditional Hinduism generally a new quality and a rigid, sharp edge. This could easily turn to generalized violence throughout India, particularly where it can be aimed at Islam. It has unified Hindus of a rigid conservative mind-set and given a new and violent revolutionary tone to the religion and its culture throughout the country. The movement now dominates the leadership of the religion virtually everywhere in India, creating a tinderbox of volatility that could easily move the entire nation into an irrational and destructive revolutionary mood.

The more rational and traditional forces of Hinduism have always been rather low-key, disparate, and scattered in focus. It has tended to be a religion of the individual rather than of communities. This has begun to change under the instigation of what is now called the Arya Samaj, a movement that arose in Mumbai in 1875 as a religious reform, and appealed largely to the educated classes. It supported the nationalism movements in the early twentieth century that led to the demise of the British Raj. While quite different from the Arya Samaj, a second movement has had a similar effect upon Hindu India. It is the Rashtriya Svayamsevak Sangh or RSS, which styles itself as a movement for the reform and renewal of Hindu culture and society, secular in its identity and character. The effect of these two forces, particularly in northern India where the clash with Islamic religion and culture is a prominent issue, is a reinforcement of destabilizing and frequently violent actions of local communities. Both of these Hindu organizations worked unsuccessfully for caste reform in India. They were effective in creation of a network of schools for raising the education level of the citizenry, but the effort has proved to be vastly inadequate for the needs of the whole country.

These Hindu Fundamentalisms continue to flourish in modern India and are "an increasingly growing force in cultural as well as political life" (p. 575). It is an important question as to what forces perpetuate Fundamentalist religion among Hindus, particularly its frequent recent resort to mob violence. The original energy of these Fundamentalisms was generated by their resistance to colonialism. Now the movements seem to be stimulated and energized by the combination of hostility toward Islam, the rise of a new tribalism within Hindu culture, and a reaction to the disillusionment of ineffective social, political, and economic structures in Indian society. These movements have acquired the use of contemporary weapons, and this has enhanced the lethality of their historical militancy. Daily reports of vicious and horrible abuse, exterminating human life, are increasingly the way of Indian life.

There are numerous other manifestations of Fundamentalist psychology in the religions and politics of India. The most prominent is probably that of the Sikh religious tradition. To a lesser degree Theravada Buddhism may be encountered in that subcontinent. India is organized as a secular constitutional democracy, but the Sikh religion, while operating within that setting, does not concede any separation between politics and religion. While its local worshiping groups are comparable to the Christian churches of the Western World, the faith communities consciously claim that no dualistic categories or idolatry of either images or creeds is tolerable. Life is a unity: a spiritual, social, religious, political, military, and economic unity.

Sikhism was founded upon the precepts of the Adi Granth, also referred to as the Granth Sahib, the sacred scriptures of this faith group. The Golden Temple at the center of Sikh worship and consciousness was built by Guru Arjan, the fifth of ten Sikh leaders. He lived from 1563 to 1606. The temple is called Harmandir, the temple of god. Arjan's son, Guru Hargobind (1595–1644) built a second temple the year his father died. It is known as Akal Takht, the throne of the immortal god, and it faces Harmandir. The religious perspective of these gurus was universalistic. Harmandir has four doors, one toward each of the points of the compass. Guru Arjan said, "My faith is for the people of all castes and creeds from which ever direction they come and to which ever direction they bow" (as cited in Madan, 1991, p. 595).[3] The Golden Temple was built for the singing of hymns of peace, reflections upon the sacred scriptures, and listening to the teaching of the gurus regarding life, god, and godliness. The Akal Takht, however, became the site for celebration, in song and lecture, of heroism, military exploits, conquest, and religious instruction that promoted those perspectives.

A persuasive guru named Bhindranwale led an armed militant movement beginning in the early 1980s to give concrete and operational expression to Sikh "assertion of the political and economic rights and religious prerogatives of the Sikhs," which were thought to be under threat (p. 596). He is generally viewed in India as a Fundamentalist, namely, a leader who has selected a few militant aspects of Sikhism in order to motivate his fellow Sikhs to action. His intended action was purportedly for protecting the rights and interests of Sikhs and to promote freely his notion of what Sikhism ought to be. He and his armed band are considered, even by most Sikhs, to be extremists. He created a bizarre Orthodoxy that would be considered by most Sikhs to be unorthodox in terms of the historic principles of their faith. True Sikh Orthodoxy, it is generally understood, would work against this Fundamentalism, since historic Sikhism was oriented upon peace, ecumenism, universalistic openness to a great variety of people and ideas, and advocated "catholicity and not narrowness of the mind" (p. 596).

In 1983 this band of Fundamentalists barricaded themselves in the temple complex, increasingly reinforcing it militarily over time. They conducted a terrorist campaign in which they murdered and pillaged at will, killing hundreds of innocent Hindus. In 1984 the Indian armed forces, under the command of two Sikh generals and one Hindu general directed an assault upon the temple complex, killing Bhindranwale and many of his associates. This was the source of great sadness to Hindus and Sikhs alike, throughout India, since such violence is contrary to the ethics of both communities, but particularly that of the Sikhs. Moreover, the temple complex was badly damaged by this Operation Blue Star, as it was officially called. While these Fundamentalists considered themselves to be the authentic Sikhs, "defenders of the 'basic teachings' of the Sikh gurus ... and of the economic interests of the Sikh community ..." (p. 597), the government could see them only as terrorists, judged by their behavior and their publicly announced creeds and objectives.

The 1984 Fundamentalist crisis took place against the background of numerous preceding violent sectarian clashes within the Sikh community and between Sikhs and Hindus. In 1978 a particularly bloody riot killed members of two battling conservative sects fighting over political party issues. This conflict brought Bhindranwale into prominence as a religious and political leader and led to the later violence. The difference between the two sects was their view of their sacred scriptures. One held that nothing could be added to the sacred scriptures and that they constitute the "written guru" from which all truth and authority is derived. The other claimed that only living gurus have authority and each can add to the sacred scriptures as he is led to understand new insight or revelation. Each claimed, with a Fundamentalist militant rigidity, that its Orthodoxy was the true historic Sikh Orthodoxy. They resorted readily to murderous terrorism, and that tradition continues. This has regularly resulted in destructive clashes between Fundamentalist Sikhs and the Hindu majority of India.

Like all other Fundamentalisms, the Sikh variety depends upon a radical notion of the authority of their sacred scriptures, selective emphasis upon elements of the historic faith that promote current militancy and terrorism, charismatic leaders who are willing to inflame the community with paranoia and violence, commemoration of past events which can be made to seem like abuse of Sikh Fundamentalists by other groups, a cultivated and manipulated sense of isolation, and aggressive reaction to any perception of constraint upon Sikh Fundamentalist rights by outside powers. Madan is quite sure that there is no good sign that Sikh Fundamentalism will abate in the near run. The fundamental difference between the definition of the relationship between the state and religion in the secular Indian constitution, on the one hand, and in the mind of the Sikh Fundamentalists, on the other, is so radical and persistent that it will continue to stoke the fires of dissent, isolation, hostility, paranoia, and aggressive behavior. This psychology, and the aggression it incites, is always just a hairbreadth from terrorism in India. It tends to bleed into other partisan conflicts present in that very complex society and inflame them further with Sikh Fundamentalist energy.

Two additional Fundamentalist movements complete this cursory survey of the phenomenon of Fundamentalism in our modern world: Theravada Buddhism and Confucianism. Buddha died in 544 BCE, and his influence throughout the world has competed aggressively with that of Jesus of Nazareth for the last two millennia. Theravada Buddhism, a product of the original Hinayana Buddhism, is a Fundamentalist form of conservative Buddhism. It arose early in the history of this faith tradition. It is not quite clear why one should call Buddhism a religion or faith tradition, since it is really a form of nontheistic ethical philosophy. However, it is regularly listed as one of the great religions of the world, probably because it takes the form of a humanist spirituality and has a transcendental dimension, the achievement of Nirvana.

Buddhism sprang up quickly and spread widely from the moment of Gautama Buddha's original enlightenment. Nearly simultaneous with the rise of Theravada Buddhism, two other mainstreams of the tradition developed, Mahayana and Vajrayana Buddhism. These are complex philosophical systems in the tradition, which have become widely syncretistic and eclectic, and emphasize the importance of social responsibility and cultural development for the improvement of the quality of human life, as well as the encouragement of all humans to practice Buddhist philosophy and ethics. This is a type of Buddhism that has appealed rather intensely to the Western World. Theravada Buddhism tends to be oriented toward escape from mundane material desire and emphasizes and practices meditation that enhances self-transcendence and access to Nirvana. It functions in intense tension, therefore, with its social environment and earthly existence.

The Fundamentalism of Theravada Buddhism is expressed in a claim that its roots are in the original true traditions of Hinayana Buddhism of Buddha himself and that it has preserved the true form of these traditions. It is rigoristic and rigid in its prescriptions for spiritual and social function, it is militant in whichever culture it finds itself, and it aggressively promotes itself worldwide. It has been very influential throughout history in providing the partisan energy for consolidating the sense of identity and, hence, the unification of nationalism in many countries such as Thailand, Burma, Laos, Cambodia, and Sri Lanka.

In these processes Theravada Buddhism has tended to be terroristic and violent to achieve its ends. It is difficult to discern how this comports with the transcendental orientation of Theravada Buddhism, but it is easy to see its sense of social tension reflected in this aggressive behavior. In Sri Lanka, for example, the Sinhalese are Theravada Buddhists, for the most part, and the Tamil are Hindus. The violent and destructive repression of the Tamils by the Sinhalese has been a virtually uncritical process of the Buddhists for generations. It is quite surprising how terroristic these policies have been. Only in recent years, as a result of the militant rise of the Tamil themselves, has any significant constraint been imposed upon these vicious practices of the Buddhist Fundamentalists.

A great variety of Theravada Buddhisms has developed in the numerous nations in which Buddhism has had significant presence and influence over the centuries. However, this is particularly true in the postcolonialist and now in the postmodern era. Some of these have taken the form of rigorously disciplined, conservative ethical systems, focused upon the eradication of social evils and the demeanment of human life and equality. In his Fundamentalistic Movements in Theravada Buddhism, in *Fundamentalism Observed*, Donald K. Swearer (1991) summarizes the entire matter crisply:

> Fundamentalistic movements ... (are) frequently led by strong, often militantly aggressive, charismatic leaders whose followers ..., perceive themselves to be variously threatened as individuals, communally, or as a nation. The ideologies embraced by such movements tend to rest upon simplistic, dualistic, and absolutistic worldviews. Often exclusivistic (although ... evangelistic), the movements reject competing groups ... as morally evil, spiritually confused, and/or intellectually misguided. Possessed of an almost obsessive sense of their unique role ... these movements may be quasi-messianic or explicitly millenarian in nature ... anti-rationalist, anti-intellectual, ... anti-ritualist ... open to the criticism that it ... lacks the depth of its classical predecessors. (p. 678)

In China things took a slightly different turn, but with similar consequences. Confucius was certain when he died that he had thoroughly failed. Subsequently, and rather quickly after his fifth century BCE pilgrimage, his philosophy spread throughout East Asia, permanently shaping China and heavily influencing Korea, Mongolia, Japan, and most of the rest of East Asia. Particularly in the last century Confucianism experienced a vigorous revival throughout that area. Confucianism is an ethical philosophy with neither a theistic nor a transcendental orientation. From its beginning in the life and teaching of Confucius it was oriented upon the enhancement of the education, social order, economic development, and the quality and equality of life for all humans.

The recent revival of Confucianism has taken the form of a quest for the roots and specific precepts of the teaching of Confucius. As a result it has tended toward a Fundamentalist character and psychology. This has driven the quest back to the Analects of Confucius himself. In the nineteenth century Japan chose a Westernization process rather than a Fundamentalist resurgence of Confucianism. In China and Korea, the attempts to strengthen Confucianism largely failed to produce workable political and social structures. Thus it was largely in the pre-Maoist government in China, carried over in 1950 to Taiwan by the evacuation from mainland China of the Kuomintang Forces under Chiang Kai-shek, that the resurgence of Confucianism was seeded. So it is in Taiwan that the Fundamentalist revival has borne the most fruit.

The contest between Maoist Marxism in China and Confucianism in Taiwan has been carried out primarily as an ideological contest. However, it has regularly degraded into actual military conflict. Mainly, it has persisted in the form of political barrages, regularly exchanged. Over the last half century, however, with the modernization and capitalization of China, Confucianism has resurged within Maoist Marxism in China itself. Meanwhile, moderation of Taiwan policies and political rhetoric has resulted in the Fundamentalist Confucians in Taiwan being increasingly forced into a defensive posture, marginalized, and isolated within their own society. This has increased their militancy and their calls for radical opposition to any rapprochement with China.

Thus, the potential for violent conflict between the Fundamentalist Confucians in Taiwan, and in a larger sense throughout industrialized East Asia, and the forces in power there, is ideologically increased, while at the same time politically and militarily less likely of success. The Confucian resurgence has been, in part, a response to Westernizing influences everywhere in the world today, a quest for a more idealistic homegrown ethic and social code. It is an attempt to hold in check the Western type of modernization in the hopes of preserving more traditional or historic ideologies and codes, indigenous to East Asia itself. Moreover, the appeal for the Fundamentalist mind-set of this Confucian revival lies in the general dissatisfaction with Western moral and ethical values, as well as with what is perceived to be trivial and trivializing Western philosophy and cultural models. It is not surprising that this is so, considering that so much of what is purveyed to the world in general as Western culture has taken the form of rather risqué Hollywood movies, rather cacophonous American music, rather violent videos from many sources but most surprisingly even from Disney productions, remarkably cynical Western philosophies, and weapons-oriented U.S. industrial products.

Tu Wei-ming (1991) reminds us of the 1958 manifesto that was prepared by a number of Chinese scholars as their proposal for Chinese understanding of how Confucian tradition may be made relevant to the future development of a holistic model of psychosocial idealism for their nation.

> A faith in the efficaciousness of the Confucian core curriculum and an assumption of the authentic transmission of the Confucian heritage throughout history are implicit in the manifesto, but the main thrust of the argument is to present a Confucian perspective on the human condition defined in terms of modern Western categories … a denunciation of the sterility of modern commercial culture and the New Confucians' reconstruction of the meaning of the human "life world." (pp. 773–774)

This Confucian revival is widespread and diverse in East Asia. It is a search for cultural roots as an "integral part of modern consciousness and ... persistent universal human concern" (p. 774). Confucian Fundamentalism seems to have been the least violent form of Fundamentalism so far in history. That may be a derivative of a non-paranoid Chinese communal personality or the lack of need for violent aggression to achieve the goals of this conservative philosophical reawakening. It may be a characteristic inherent to Confucian principles themselves.

## Conclusion

Fundamentalism was once thought to be merely a special type of rather obsessive and rigoristic Protestant Christian heresy, championed by people who had a psychological need for high levels of spiritual and socio-theological control, who tended to be rather esoteric in their belief system, passionate in their certainty that they alone possessed God's truth, and aggressive in their compulsion to impose it and its implications upon others. Now we understand that Fundamentalism is a psychological pathology that can shape and take possession of the framework of thought and action in any arena of life, and particularly any ideology. This makes religion particularly vulnerable to the pathology of Fundamentalism, a dangerous heresy almost anywhere we find it.

The danger in Fundamentalism takes the shape of false Orthodoxies. They are dangerous in many ways, but at least in the ways in which they corrupt the truth, disrupt community, violate personal and communal prerogatives, and promote socio-political and physico-material strategies of destruction. We have been made profoundly aware in recent years of the intimate links between religious Fundamentalism and worldwide terrorism. This is associated in our minds at this time primarily with Islamic Fundamentalism. However, what we need to discern is the manner and degree to which every form of Fundamentalism has the potential for teroristic tactics to achieve its "divincly appointed" ends, and most Fundamentalisms have resorted to gross violence at some point in their histories.

It is imperative, therefore, that we identify Fundamentalism wherever it may be found, define and name it as the psychopathology that it is, engage it, contain its violent potentials, and reduce its influence as much as possible. As with countering all strategies of organized violence, the greatest challenge is to defeat it without resorting to its own tactics and thus being dragged down to its own subhuman moral level. In America's leadership in the elimination of the Fundamentalist violence of worldwide terrorism today, it is crucial that we find our way without triumphalism or a resort to the arrogance of power. Power properly and humanely applied is one thing. Arrogant power is quite another. Ignorant arrogance is the worst of all.

The incredibly grace-filled late medieval or early modern philosopher, Baruch Spinoza, in his tract on politics, said that in his quest for understanding the facts, foibles, and fruits of human life and thought he tried to be very careful not to laugh, cry, or denounce humans in their very human pilgrimage, but instead he always tried simply and gently to understand.[4] It reminded me of the noted acerbic cartoon editor of the

*Kansas City Star,* who upon retirement was asked to say what he really thought of the human race, after his years of rather vicious caricatures of it. He rose and said, "I think we should be kind to it. It is the only one we've got." So, in the spirit of Spinoza and the cartoonist, I hope we can learn something crucial from the pathological experiments of the Fundamentalisms of the world and history and shepherd ourselves to greater gracefulness and mutual goodwill.

It is clear that prejudice is a devastating force in our political and social order and that it arises in a very sick psychology at the center of our souls and imposes a large toll upon our spirituality. It is the shadow side of our inherent need to survive, grow, develop, and achieve freedom and stasis. It may be considered to have a positive side, in Spinoza's sense of "love-prejudice." Humans are capable of imagining a virtually perfect world and are able to create only a flawed one. The distance that our real world falls short of our idealized imagination we identify as failure and pain. We internalize that pain as guilt rather than simply being able to accept it as a function of our limited humanness. That guilt prompts us to self-justification and defensive aggressive behavior, setting in motion the strategies of prejudice discussed above.

The general claim of this chapter is that some of our ancient religious metaphors create the kind of negative psychological archetypes at the center of our selves, that inflame our prejudices and the psychodynamics behind them. At the center this is a spiritual problem and there is no fixing it except a spiritual renewal which is framed and shaped and driven by a theology of grace, a religion of grace, a sociology of grace, and a self-psychology of grace. Divine grace! Human grace! Grace is unconditional positive regard for the other. Judaism hatched this idea of unconditional grace as the redemptive dynamic of true religion and healthy psychology. As I argued previously, all three Western religions, Judaism, Christianity, and Islam have, as their mainstream, this notion of grace inherited from the precursors of Judaism, namely, ancient Israelite religion, the religion of the Hebrew Bible.

For 3,000 years, however, this mainstream has been muddied, distorted, and obscured by a completely erroneous religious metaphor also derived from ancient Israelite religion and the Hebrew Bible: the notion that this world is the arena of an apocalyptic cosmic conflict between good and evil. This useless and psychotic metaphor seems to justify our worst prejudices and our most destructive behavior. Yet it has no ground under it. There is no evidence for ontic evil. However, in all three of these major religions, our sacred scriptures lock us into this notion. That defines us. Unless we radically revise our theology of sacred scriptures, in all three religions, we cannot escape this prison house of prejudice. We cannot transcend the built-in bigotry. We cannot become fully human. We cannot escape the tragedy of terroristic Fundamentalisms, which lead to spiritual devolution, social violence, and war. We cannot achieve a communal life of grace.

## Notes

An earlier form of various parts of this chapter appeared in J. Harold Ellens (Ed.). (2004). *The Destructive Power of Religion: Violence in Judaism, Christianity, and Islam,* Vols. 1–4, Westport,

CT: Praeger. See, for example, the following chapters by J. Harold Ellens in that work: Vol. 2, *Religion, Psychology, and Violence*, Chap. 4, The Dynamics of Prejudice (pp. 85–98); and Vol. 4, *Contemporary Views of Spirituality and Violence*, Chap. 7, Fundamentalism, Orthodoxy, and Violence (pp. 119–142). This modification of that material is published here with permission.

1. The use of the term "Orthodox" as it appears in the name of various Christian denominations, such as Greek or Russian Orthodox Churches, is a different phenomenon. That use of the term is in proper nouns which are official historic names of communities of faith, and so they derive from special historical origins. Fundamentalisms and pathological orthodoxies may exist in such denominations, but that is not inherently implied by their official names.

2. Hardy thinks this may be a reference Berlin makes "off the top of his head," so to speak, to Robespierre's sentence, "en scellant notre ouvrage de notre sang, nous puissons voir au moins briller l'aurore de la felicite universelle" ("by sealing our work with our blood, we may see at least the bright dawn of universal happiness"), in *Rapport sur les principes de morale politique que doivent guider la Convention nationale dans l'administration interieure de la Republique*, Paris, 1794, p. 4.

3. Madan cites the work of Gopal Singh (1988, p. 177) as the source of his information about this story. He adds the note that according "to Sikh tradition, unsupported by historical evidence, the foundation stone of the Golden Temple was laid by a Muslim Sufi, Mian Mir. It bears testimony to the traditional Sikh approach to religious differences that such a story should be believed" (p. 623).

4. I was reminded of this wonderful sentiment of Spinoza by Martin E. Marty's observation upon it (Marty, 1992, p. 15).

# References

Adorno, Theodor, & Horkheimer, Max. (1950). *The authoritarian personality.* New York: Harper.

Allport, Gordon. (1958). *The nature of prejudice.* Garden City, NY: Doubleday Anchor.

Aronson, Elliot. (1992). Causes of prejudice. In Robert M. Baird & Stuart E. Rosenbaum (Eds.), *Bigotry, prejudice, and hatred; definitions, causes, and solutions: Vol. X. Contemporary issues* (pp. 111–124). New York: Prometheus Books.

Baird, Robert M., & Rosenbaum, Stuart E. (Eds.). (1992). *Bigotry, prejudice, and hatred; definitions, causes, and solutions: Vol. X. Contemporary issues.* New York: Prometheus Books.

Ellens, J. Harold. (2004a). The dynamics of prejudice. In J. Harold Ellens (Ed.), *The destructive power of religion, violence in Judaism, Christianity, and Islam: Vol. 2. Religion, psychology, and violence* (pp. 85–98). Westport, CT: Praeger.

Ellens, J. Harold. (2004b). Fundamentalism, orthodoxy, and violence. In J. Harold Ellens (Ed.), *The destructive power of religion, violence in Judaism, Christianity, and Islam: Vol. 4. Contemporary views on spirituality and violence* (pp. 119–142). Westport, CT: Praeger.

Hardy, Henry. (2001, October 18). The New York Review of Books, Vol. 18, No. 16, p. 12.

Madan, T. N. (1991). Fundamentalism and the Sikh religious tradition. In Martin E. Marty & R. Scott Appleby (Eds.), *Fundamentalism observed.* Chicago: University of Chicago Press.

Marty, Martin E., & Appleby, R. Scott (Eds.). (1991). Fundamentalism observed. *The fundamentalist project* (5 vols. 1991–1995). Chicago: University of Chicago Press.

Marty, Martin E., & Appleby, R. Scott (Eds.). (1993). Jewish Zionist Fundamentalism: The bloc of the faithful in Israel (Gush Emunim). *The fundamentalist project* (5 vols. 1991–1995). Chicago: University of Chicago Press.

Marty, Martin E. (1992). Fundamentals of fundamentalism. In Lawrence Kaplan (Ed.), *Fundamentalism in comparative perspective* (p. 15). Amherst: University of Massachusetts Press.

McGuire, Cheryl. (2004). Judaism, Christianity, and Girard: The violent messiahs. In J. Harold Ellens (Ed.), *The destructive power of religion, violence in Judaism, Christianity, and Islam: Vol. 2. Religion, psychology, and violence* (pp. 51–84). Westport. CT: Praeger.

Medina, John. (2002, December). Molecules of the mind: The MAO A gene and exposure to violent behavior in childhood. *Psychiatric Times, XIX*(12), 10–15.

Singh, Gopal. (1988). *A history of the Sikh people.* New Delhi: World Book Centre.

Stirling, Mack. (2004). Violent religion: René Girard's theory of culture. In J. Harold Ellens (Ed.), *The destructive power of religion, violence in Judaism, Christianity, and Islam: Vol. 2. Religion, psychology, and violence* (pp. 11–50). Westport, CT: Praeger.

Swearer, Donald K. (1991). Fundamentalistic movements in Theravada Buddhism. In Martin E. Marty & R. Scott Appleby (Eds.), *Fundamentalism observed.* Chicago: University of Chicago Press.

Van den Berghe, Pierre. (1987). *The ethnic phenomenon.* Westport, CT: Greenwood Press.

Van den Berghe, Pierre. (1992). The biology of nepotism. In Robert M. Baird and Stuart E. Rosenbaum (Eds.), *Bigotry, prejudice, and hatred; definitions, causes, and solutions: Vol. X. Contemporary issues* (pp. 125–138). New York: Prometheus Books.

Wei-ming, Tu. (1991). The search for roots in industrial East Asia: The case of the Confucian revival. In Martin E. Marty & R. Scott Appleby (Eds.), *Fundamentalism observed* (pp. 740–781). Chicago: University of Chicago Press.

Young-Bruehl, Elizabeth. (1996). *Anatomy of prejudices.* Cambridge, MA: Harvard University Press.

# CHAPTER 6

# HUMILIATION, KILLING, WAR, AND GENDER

## *Evelin Gerda Lindner*

## Humiliation, War, and Gender

This chapter represents a psychological device, namely persuasion, with the aim to mobilize you, the reader, to *get up* instead of *standing by* on the global arena. This chapter tries to entice you to use a psychological mind-set for the maintenance of our *global village* that you might have observed in some of your female family members (not exclusively of course), namely, the art of how to focus on relationships and their sustainable maintenance.

January 11, 1998, in Nairobi, I met with Asha Ahmed. She is a young Somali woman and was at that time Information/Dissemination Officer at the Somalia Delegation of the International Committee of the Red Cross (ICRC). She and her colleague described to me how they, over years, had struggled to explain the Geneva Convention and the concept of human rights to fellow Somalis. However, so she recounted, to their surprise all such difficulties went away in 1997. "How?" I asked. The explanation was interesting. The ICRC had invited historians from all Somali clans to do research and come up with what eventually became the *Spared from the Spear* booklet by the International Committee of the Red Cross Somalia Delegation (1997).

This booklet shows something remarkable, namely, that women and children traditionally were "spared from the spear." It documents that traditional Somali war code explicitly protects civilians against warrior onslaughts. Women were not to be touched. Women represented potential bridges between families and clans, precisely because they could move freely, even in wartime. Asha pointed out: "When you look at this booklet, the Geneva Convention is all in there! At first the Geneva Convention was like Latin to the Somalis!"

In my doctoral dissertation— Lindner (2001f, pp. 342–343)— I give Ambassador Dualeh the word. I interviewed him on January 9, 1999, in Nairobi. He backs up what I learned from Asha; see also Lindner (2000a):

> There is one thing which never was part of traditional quarrelling between clans, and this is rape, especially mass rape in front of the family. This is new. It happened for the first time when Siad Barre's dictatorial regime sent soldiers to annihilate us. Soldiers would rape our women in front of their husbands and families.
>
>     …
>
> It is somehow a "tradition" that young men of one clan steal camels from another clan, and sometimes a man gets killed. But women were never touched, never. There might have been the rare case when a girl was alone in the desert guarding her animals, and a young man having spent a long time in the desert lost control and tried to rape her. She would resist violently, and at the end the solution would perhaps be that he had to marry her. But mass rape, especially rape in front of the family, this never happened before, this is new.
>
>     …
>
> Have you noticed how many Somali families live apart? Have you ever thought about the reason why so many Somali women with their children live apart from their husbands? It is because the men cannot live with the humiliation caused by the fact that they were not able to defend their women against the soldiers who raped them. The husband cannot live together with his wife, because he cannot bear to be reminded of his inability to protect her. The perpetrators intended to humiliate their enemies and they succeeded thoroughly. Rape creates social destruction more "effectively" than any other weapon.
>
>     …
>
> This is the reason why today Somalia is so divided. We Somalis are united through our common ethnic background, we speak one language, and are all Muslims. Why are we divided today? Humiliation through rape and its consequences divides us. The traditional methods of reconciliation are too weak for this. It will take at least one generation to digest these humiliations sufficiently to be able to sit together again.

At the end of our conversation, Ambassador Dualeh sighed: "Evelin, believe me, humiliation, as I told you before, was not known to the Somali before Siad Barre came to power!"

Scandinavia houses a large Somali diaspora community. The divorce rate is very high. I remember one Somali woman angrily contesting Ambassador Dualeh's framing; it was in an informal setting in 2001 in Norway. She called out,

> It is us, the Somali women, who leave our husbands! Particularly in the diaspora! Because here we receive support for our quest to be treated like human beings! Do you know the saying that a Somali husband will fetch the doctor when his camels are sick, but not for his wives? How come that our husbands shun us after we were raped? Are we not human beings who need more support after being victimized, and not less? How come that these men are so consumed by their own pride and honor—and how it has been humiliated— that they do not see that we suffer and need help? Instead of helping us they sulk and nurture their feelings of humiliation and their hurt pride!

So far, my aim was to whet the "appetite" of the reader of this chapter and create question marks. Let me continue: On December 3, 1998, I was a guest in a *khat* chewing "focus group" session in Hargeisa, capital of Somaliland. Such sessions typically last for many hours, starting in the afternoon and running through half of the night (typically, such meetings are not attended by "respectable" women; I tried therefore to keep "decent" by at least not chewing *khat* myself ...). I asked the men in the round about humiliation or *quudhsiga* (belittling = humiliation). The hours were well invested and yielded many proverbs, such as the following: "Hadellca xun ayaa ka xanuun kulul xabada," meaning "Humiliation is worse than killing; in times of war words of humiliation hurt more than bullets," or "Rag waxaaa ku maamula agaan ama ku maamuusi," meaning "I can only be with people who are equal," or "Masse inaanu nahay oo tollim meerto no tahay," meaning "A man deserves to be killed and not to be humiliated."

At this point, I would like to end my introductory vignettes. I hope that they have elicited the reader's interest for the topic of humiliation, war, and gender. As you understand, for some, humiliation overrides fear of death—indeed, a formidable phenomenon. And as you also see, in much of traditional warfare—and incidentally also in blood feud—women go free; they are, ideally, spared selectively while men are targeted selectively.[1] And in case such rules are violated or neglected, stark feelings of humiliation may be rendered or maintained in the hearts and minds of those who identify with these codes of behavior.

However, and this I also found out, the fact that women are spared in certain settings does not necessarily signify that women are too valuable to lose or that women stand for more "peaceful" attitudes than their fellow males. Sometimes, I was told in Somalia, it was the women who drove their men into tribal war to address their grievances.[2] And, furthermore, women were not spared under all circumstances. In different situations, women were—and in numerous cultural contexts still are—the ones to be killed selectively, for example, in cases of so-called honor killings. When family honor is perceived to be soiled and humiliated through the rape of a daughter, for example, it is first and foremost the raped daughter who is killed, and rarely also the rapist (Nadera Shalhoub-Kevorkian, a criminologist of the Hebrew University in Jerusalem, feels uneasy with the term "honor killings" and prefers to use the term "femicide," personal communication, November 2003, Jerusalem[3]).[4]

Thus, women and men—in what I, in the spirit of Weber's *ideal-type* approach, call *traditional hierarchical honor-based societies*—are either selectively identified as persons to be spared or selectively identified as persons to be killed, according to certain rules.[5] And the violation of such rules carries the potential to elicit or maintain feelings of humiliation. In all these cases humiliation and gender—or, more precisely, humiliation and the gender-selective taking or sparing of lives—are interlinked in very precisely defined ways.

Apart from such cases, clearly, in the course of human history, killing and dying also occurred with no gender selection involved and no humiliation being invoked. History offers ample examples. Often men, women, and children died from the ravages of war, indiscriminately. Wars destroyed whole regions so that their inhabitants withered away from famine and lack of resources. In pre-human-rights times, the latter case typically was not regarded as any violation or humiliation; it was rather seen as "fate" or "God's will" or "natural disaster."

In contrast, nowadays, wherever human rights ideals are guiding moral deliberations, the killing of people is deplored and seen as illegitimate, under whatever circumstances (except in clear cases of self-defense, for military personnel in wars that are perceived to be legitimately waged, or for those waiting in the death row in countries that legitimize capital punishment). In present times, predominantly in the West, but also in many non-Western cultural spheres, the overall ethical framework is in the process of changing. Human rights ideals stipulate that people ought to be offered so-called "enabling environments" that give them the chance to build dignified lives. People should not be victimized by warlords who render their homes unsafe and bring famine upon them. And the killing of raped girls in order to redress humiliated family honor is not condoned by human rights either. On the contrary, a human rights promoter may claim that the act of killing a girl—who has been victimized through being raped—victimizes her doubly and thus compounds humiliation instead of redressing it. Incidentally, as is widely known, rape has lately increasingly been used as a "weapon" in war, thus intensifying the moral dilemma entailed in such cases.

In the following, I will briefly describe how I researched the notion of humiliation that formed the starting point for my subsequent theoretical work on humiliation. I am currently building a *theory of humiliation* that is transdisciplinary and entails elements from anthropology, history, social philosophy, social psychology, sociology, and political science.[6] After laying out my research, I will explain the current state of the art of related research carried out by other scholars. Thereafter I will discuss how the phenomenon of humiliation is embedded into a larger historical timeline. I will describe in what way I see globalization at work. At the end I will address what can be done about the destructive effects of humiliation.

Before proceeding further, let me make a little note. In everyday language, the word "humiliation" is used at least threefold. First, the word *humiliation* points at an *act*, second, at a *feeling*, and third, at a *process*: "I humiliate you, you feel humiliated, and the entire process is one of humiliation." In this text the reader is expected to understand from the context which alternative is referred to, because otherwise language would become too convoluted.

Let me give you, furthermore, the definition of humiliation that I use in my work:

> Humiliation means the enforced lowering of a person or group, a process of subjugation that damages or strips away their pride, honor or dignity. To be humiliated is to be placed, against your will (or in some cases with your consent, for example in cases of religious self-humiliation or in sado-masochism) and often in a deeply hurtful way, in a situation that is greatly inferior to what you feel you should expect. Humiliation entails demeaning treatment that transgresses established expectations. It may involve acts of force, including violent force. At its heart is the idea of pinning down, putting down or holding to the ground. Indeed, one of the defining characteristics of humiliation as a process is that the victim is forced into passivity, acted upon, made helpless.

People react in different ways when they feel that they were unduly humiliated: some just become depressed—anger turns against oneself—others get openly enraged, and yet others hide their anger and carefully plan for revenge. The person who plans for revenge may become the leader of a movement. ... Thus, feelings of humiliation may lead to rage, that may be turned inwards, as in the case of depression and apathy. However, this rage may also turn outwards and express itself in violence, even in mass violence, in case leaders are around who forge narratives of humiliation that feed on the feelings of humiliation among masses.

There are many points that would merit closer attention and that are not discussed here, out of lack of space. For example, what is the difference between humiliation that is felt genuinely and feelings of humiliation that are instigated by propaganda or prescribed culturally? Or, if feelings of humiliation are felt by individuals, how are they elevated to group levels, if at all? Or, what about people who are resilient to feeling humiliated even in the face of serious attempts to humiliate them? Why did Nelson Mandela find a constructive way out of humiliation, and Hitler unleashed a world war? Why did Mandela not instigate genocide on the white elite in South Africa? All these questions and many more are attended to elsewhere in Lindner's writing as previously cited.

Furthermore, what should be discussed in more length is my personal stance in relation to human rights. I promote human rights ideals, where human worthiness and dignity are regarded to be equal for every human being. However, I stand in for human rights not because I enjoy presenting myself as an arrogant Westerner who humiliates the non-West by denigrating their honor codes of ranked human worthiness. On the contrary, in my view, people who endorse honor codes may not be looked down upon; my conceptualization is that honor codes had their respected place in a world that did not yet experience the coming together of humankind into *one single* family. However, we live in a new reality, the vision and emerging reality of a *global village*, and this new reality can, according to my view, best be tackled with human rights norms. I believe that human rights represent a normative framework that is better adapted to an emerging *global village*. Thus, I wish to encourage every inhabitant of the globe to abandon "we" and "them" differentiations and define herself or himself as "we," and "we humanity," who *together* search for the best ways to provide our children with a livable world.

## My Research and the Current State of the Art

In 1994, after many years of international experience—as a medical student and a psychology student in Asia, Africa, Middle East, America, and Europe, and later seven years as a psychological counselor and clinical psychologist in Cairo, Egypt—I asked myself: "What is the most significant obstacle to peace and social cohesion?" My hunch was that dynamics of humiliation may be central. This hunch was based not only on my clinical experience but also on other evidence. There is a widely shared notion that Germany was humiliated through the Versailles Accords and that this gave Hitler the necessary platform to unleash World War II and the Holocaust. Marshal Foch of France said in 1919 about the Versailles Treaties, "This is not a peace treaty—it will be a cease-fire for 20 years" (as cited in R. Fuller, 2005).

In 1996, I began to examine the available literature and was surprised that humiliation had not received much academic attention. Search terms such as "shame" or "trauma" would render innumerable hits, however, not "humiliation." I was astonished, because, if humiliation indeed can trigger war, there must be a large body of research to be found. However, this was not the case. I thus designed a doctoral research project on humiliation (for a doctorate in psychology).

I conducted a four-year doctoral research project at the University of Oslo (1997–2001). It was entitled *The Feeling of Being Humiliated: A Central Theme in Armed Conflicts. A Study of the Role of Humiliation in Somalia, and Rwanda/Burundi, Between the Warring Parties, and in Relation to Third Intervening Parties*. I carried out 216 qualitative interviews addressing Somalia, Rwanda, and Burundi and their history of genocidal killings. From 1998 to 1999 the interviews were carried out in Africa (in Hargeisa, capital of Somaliland, in Kigali and other places in Rwanda, in Bujumbura, capital of Burundi, in Nairobi in Kenya, and in Cairo in Egypt), and from 1997 to 2001 also in Europe (in Norway, Germany, Switzerland, France, and Belgium).

As the title of the project indicates, three groups had to be interviewed, namely, both the conflict parties in Somalia and Rwanda/Burundi, and representatives of third parties who intervene. These three groups stand in a set of triangular relationships (at least this is the minimum version—where there are more than two opponents, as is the case in most conflicts, the pattern, obviously, has more than three corners). Both in Somalia and Rwanda/Burundi, representatives of the "opponents" and the "third party" were approached. The following people were included in the "network of conversations" that was created in the course of the research:

- Survivors of genocides were interviewed, that is, people belonging to the groups that were targeted for genocidal killing. In Somalia this included, among others, the Isaaq tribe, in Rwanda the Tutsi, in Burundi the Hutu and the Tutsi. The group of survivors is typically divided into two parts, namely, those who survived because they were not in the country when the genocide happened—some of them returned after the genocide—and those who survived the onslaught inside the country. The German background of this fieldwork consists of the network of contacts that I have established, over some decades, with survivors from the Holocaust and, especially, their children.

- Freedom fighters were included into the "network of conversation." In Somalia, interviews were conducted with SNM (Somali National Movement) fighters in the North of Somalia, who fought the troops sent by the central government in Mogadishu in the South; in Rwanda the interviewees were the former Tutsi refugees who formed an army, the RFP (Rwandese Patriotic Front), and attacked Rwanda from the North in order to oust the extremist Hutu government that carried out the genocide in Rwanda in 1994; in Burundi there were also Hutu rebels. In Germany, the equivalent of these contacts was exchanges with those aristocratic circles in Germany that fed opposition against Hitler, but also with those, especially from the researcher's family, who advocated human rights in the middle of

World War II and paid a high price for their human compassion. Furthermore, the researcher's contacts with people from the occupied countries who tried to sabotage German oppression, for example, the Norwegian resistance movement, belong in this group, as well as representatives of the allies who finally put an end to German atrocities.

- Some Somali warlords who have their places of retreat in Kenya were interviewed.
- Politicians were included, among them people who were in power before the genocide and whom survivors secretly suspected of having been collaborators or at least silent supporters of those who perpetrated the genocide. The equivalent in Germany is the atmosphere of underlying suspicion in which I grew up, generally a mistrust toward everybody of a certain age, but, in particular, suspicion toward the past of those people in power, a suspicion that diminishes only as the years pass and people die.
- Somali and Rwandan/Burundian academicians who study the situation of their countries were interviewed. For Germany the last striking manifestation in this field, and a focal point for discussions, has been Daniel Jonah Goldhagen's book on *Hitler's Willing Executioners*.
- Representatives of national nongovernmental organizations who work locally for development, peace, and reconciliation were included. In Germany, the response to the atrocities of World War II permeates everybody's life—even the generation born after the war—and the researcher's intimate knowledge of a culture of German self-criticism may stand as an equivalent to the preoccupation with past, present, and future anticipated bloodshed that characterizes people's lives in Somalia, Rwanda, and Burundi.
- Third parties were interviewed, namely, representatives of U.N. organizations and international nongovernmental organizations who work on emergency relief, long-term development, peace, and reconciliation in all parts of the world.
- Egyptian diplomats in the foreign ministry in Egypt who deal with Somalia were visited; Egypt is a heavyweight in the Organization of African Unity.
- African psychiatrists in Kenya who deal with trauma and forensic psychiatry were asked about their experience with victims and perpetrators from Rwanda/Burundi and Somalia. In Kenya many nationals from Somalia and Rwanda/Burundi have sought refuge, some in refugee camps, others through various private arrangements. Some, both victims and perpetrators, seek psychiatric help. The equivalents in Germany are those researchers who focus on the effects of the German Holocaust and other World War II atrocities.
- Those who have not yet been interviewed are the masterminds of genocide in Rwanda, those who have planned the genocide and organized it meticulously. Some of them are said to be in hiding in Kenya and other parts of Africa, or in French-speaking parts of Europe, or in the United States and Canada. Some are in prisons in Rwanda and in Arusha, Tanzania. However, accounts of people who were close to Somali dictator Siad Barre have successfully been collected. In the case of Hitler and those who supported him, a culture of openness and frank discussion is currently unfolding in Germany—the whole country has entered into a phase of "working through" these past experiences, and people who never talked before, do so now, more than 50 years after World War II.
- The topic has also been discussed with more than 500 researchers working in related fields. The current state of the art has been mapped, showing that few researchers have turned their attention to this field. A theory of humiliation is currently being developed by the author, and a larger book project is envisaged (in cooperation with Dennis Smith, professor of sociology).

Some of the interview conversations were filmed (altogether the author produced 10 hours of film, comprising many interviews, but also images of Somaliland and Rwanda), other interviews were taped on minidiscs (altogether more than 100 hours of audiotape), and in situations where this seemed inappropriate the researcher made notes. The interviews and conversations were conducted in different languages; most of them in English (Somalia) and French (Great Lakes), many in German, and in Norwegian.

Few researchers have studied humiliation explicitly. In many cases the term "humiliation" is not differentiated from other concepts; humiliation and shame, for example, are often used exchangeably, among others by Silvan S. Tomkins (1962–1992) whose work is carried further by Donald L. Nathanson. Nathanson describes humiliation as a combination of three innate affects out of altogether nine affects, namely, as a combination of shame, disgust, and dis-smell (personal communication, October 1, 1999).[7]

In Lindner's work, humiliation is distinctly addressed on its own account and differentiated from other concepts. Humiliation is, for example, not regarded simply as a variant of shame. Dennis Smith, professor of sociology at Loughborough University, United Kingdom, and founder of LOGIN, has been introduced to the notion of humiliation through Lindner's research and has since incorporated the notion actively into his work in a fascinating way; see, for example, D. Smith (2002).

The view that humiliation may be a particularly forceful phenomenon is supported by the research of, for example, Suzanne M. Retzinger (1991) and Thomas J. Scheff and Retzinger (1991), who studied shame and humiliation in marital quarrels. They show that the suffering caused by humiliation is highly significant and that the bitterest divisions have their roots in shame and humiliation. Also Vogel and Lazare (1990) document *unforgivable humiliation* as a very serious obstacle in couples' treatment. Robert L. Hale (1994) addressed "the role of humiliation and embarrassment in serial murder." Humiliation has also been studied in such fields as love, sex and social attractiveness, depression, society and identity formation, sports, history, literature, and film.

Donald Klein (1991) carried out very insightful work on humiliation in, for example, the *Journal of Primary Prevention* that devoted a special issue to the topic of humiliation in 1991, in 1992, and in 1999. Hartling and Luchetta (1999) pioneered a quantitative questionnaire on humiliation (Humiliation Inventory) where a rating from 1 to 5 is employed for questions measuring *being teased, bullied, scorned, excluded, laughed at, put down, ridiculed, harassed, discounted, embarrassed, cruelly criticized, treated as invisible, discounted as a person, made to feel small or insignificant, unfairly denied access to some activity, opportunity, or service, called names or referred to in derogatory terms*, or viewed by others as *inadequate*, or *incompetent*. The questions probe the extent to which respondents had felt harmed by such incidents throughout life and how much they feared such incidents.

Scheff and Retzinger extended their work on violence and the Holocaust and studied the part played by *humiliated fury* in escalating conflict between individuals and nations—see Scheff (1997, p. 11); the term *humiliated fury* was coined by Helen Block Lewis (1971). Consider Masson (1996), Scheff (1988, 1990a, 1990b, 1997), Vachon (1993), Znakov (1990), and see, furthermore, Charny (1997) for his analysis of excessive power strivings. Psychiatrist James Gilligan (1996), as well, focuses on humiliation as a cause for violence, in his book *Violence: Our Deadly Epidemic and How to Treat It*.

Vamik D. Volkan and Joseph Montville carried out important work on psychopolitical analysis of intergroup conflict and its traumatic effects. See Montville (1990, 1993), Volkan (1988, 1992, 1994, 1997), Volkan and Harris (1995), and Volkan, Demetrios, and Montville (1990). See also Blema S. Steinberg (1996). Furthermore, Ervin Staub's work is highly significant; see Staub (1989, 1990, 1993, 1996). See also the journal *Social Research* in 1997, whose special issue was stimulated by the *Decent Society* by Avishai Margalit (1996).

Nisbett and Cohen (1996) examined an honor-based notion of humiliation. The honor to which Cohen and Nisbett refer is the kind that operates in the more traditional branches of the Mafia or, more generally, in blood feuds. William Ian Miller (1993) wrote a book entitled *Humiliation and Other Essays on Honor, Social Discomfort, and Violence*, where he links humiliation to honor as understood in *The Iliad* or Icelandic sagas, namely, humiliation as violation of honor.

There is a significant literature in philosophy on *the politics of recognition*, claiming that people who are not recognized suffer humiliation and that this leads to violence; see also Honneth (1997), on related themes. Max Scheler (1912) set out these issues in his classic book *Über Ressentiment und moralisches Werturteil*. In his first period of work, for example, in his *The Nature of Sympathy*, Scheler (1954) focuses on human feelings, love, and the nature of the person. He states that the human person is at bottom a loving being, *ens amans*, who may feel *ressentiment*.

This overview does not exhaust the contributions to be found in the literature on the topic of humiliation—or rather on related issues—since, to my awareness, only Miller, Hartling and Luchetta, and the two above-mentioned journals explicitly put the word and concept of *humiliation* at the center of their attention. Later in this chapter other authors will also be introduced and cited.

However, as soon as we turn to issues that are related to humiliation, then a wide field of research opens up: Research on mobbing and bullying touches upon the phenomenon of humiliation and should therefore be included.[8] Research on mobbing and bullying leads over to the field of prejudice and stigmatization,[9] which in turn draws on research on trauma and post-traumatic stress disorder (PTSD),[10] aggression (see further down), power and conflict,[11] stress,[12] and last, but not least, emotions.[13]

Conflict and peace are topics that have been widely studied; thousands of publications are to be found that cover a wide range of conflicts, from interpersonal to intergroup and international conflict. The search word *terrorism* renders thousands of hits in databases. Instead of presenting large lists of publications at this point, I would like to mention some of those that had particular significance for this research project on humiliation. A pioneer of conflict studies in social psychology was Morton Deutsch, the founder of the International Center for Cooperation and Conflict

Resolution (ICCCR) at Teachers College, Columbia University, New York; see, for example, Deutsch and Coleman (2000).

Also Herbert C. Kelman was among the first to work in this field; see, for example, Kelman (1999) and Kelman and Society for the Psychological Study of Social Issues (1965). David A. Hamburg's work for prevention, as President of the Carnegie Corporation, has been crucial; see, for example, Hamburg (2002).

Lee D. Ross, principal investigator and co-founder of the Stanford Center on Conflict and Negotiation (SCCN), addresses psychological barriers to conflict resolution; see, for example, Ross and Ward (1995). William Ury, Director of the Project on Preventing War at Harvard University, co-author of *Getting to YES. Negotiating Agreement without Giving In* (Fisher, Ury, & Patton, 1991), and author of *Getting to Peace. Transforming Conflict at Home, at Work, and in the World* (Ury, 1999) focuses in his anthropological work on conflict. Monty Marshall (1999), founding director of the Integrated Network for Societal Conflict Research (INSCR) program at the Center for International Development and Conflict Management (CIDCM), University of Maryland, wrote a seminal book on protracted conflict and the hypothesis of *diffusion of insecurity*. Bar-On & Nadler (1999) call for more attention to be given to conflicts in contexts of power asymmetry.

In cases where humiliation shall be studied in cross-cultural settings, cross-cultural psychology has to be included,[14] and the anthropological, sociological, and philosophical embeddedness of processes of humiliation in different cultural contexts has to be addressed. If humiliation between groups or even nations is to be studied, then history and political science play a central role.

## Women Are *In* and *Down* and Men Are *Out* and *Up*

The questions that formed the starting point for my research in 1996 were the following:[15] What is experienced as humiliation? What happens when people feel humiliated? When is humiliation established as a feeling? What does humiliation lead to? Which experiences of justice, honor, dignity, respect, and self-respect are connected with the feeling of being humiliated? What role do globalization and human rights play for humiliation? How is humiliation perceived and responded to in different cultures? What role does humiliation play for aggression? What can be done to overcome violent effects of humiliation?

How can these questions be addressed? How can the gender dimension be included? A family in Norway, for example, whose daughter was raped, might send its child into trauma therapy and not want to kill her in order to remedy humiliation. This stark and brutal example shows that what is experienced as humiliation and what it leads to, together with experiences of justice, honor, dignity, respect and self-respect, deeply varies depending on the overall cultural context. Even the use of the honor-killing example itself in this text, employed by me, a Western author with the best intentions, elicits angry protests, for example, among Palestinian female students, who claim that it exposes humiliating arrogance on behalf of the author (personal communication, March 2004, Jerusalem).

How are we to understand this confusing situation, and how are we to tackle it? In the following I will make the argument that globalization (or better, the *ingathering* of humankind) is central to the transition toward a new paradigm of dignity that is characterized by human rights ideals. Later, I will address the last question, namely, what can be done to overcome the violent effects of humiliation.

Let me first explain why I believe that the coming into being of the term and the reality of a "global village" is crucial. Please bear with me for a journey. As mentioned earlier, I have spent the past thirty years practicing being a global citizen, living, studying, and working in different parts of the world and in various cultural spheres. Wherever I spent time, I observed women predominately inhabiting the private sphere. I call this the *inside* sphere. Men, in contrast, moved around in what the respective community defined as *outside* sphere—or they straddled the border between both spheres.[16] Let me give you some examples.

### Women Are *In* and Men Are *Out*

In Cairo, traditional urban houses had a segregated space for women, the so-called *harem*, which was not to be visited by males who were not part of the family. Today these houses can still be seen in Cairo; they are now museums. An old saying, not only in Egypt, prescribes that a "good" woman ought to leave the house only twice in her lifetime: first, when she gets married and moves from the house of her father to the house of her husband, and second, when her dead body is carried to the cemetery. Even though houses with harems are not anymore built today in Egypt, still daily life is reminiscent of this segregation. For example, I have Egyptian friends where the woman inhabits the master bedroom and her husband is only a guest— he usually sleeps with the boys; or, in other families, only the women use the bathroom inside the house, while the men go out and relieve themselves in the fields; or, women receive their female friends inside the house, while men meet their male friends outside, in the tea house. The different versions of body cover that are used in many traditional communities, including Muslim, Christian, and others—*burka, burkha, bourka, hijab*, headscarf, etc.—could be interpreted as "portable inside spheres," making it possible for a woman to stay *inside* while actually venturing *out*. There is an Egyptian proverb saying that "the woman is the neck and the man the head," and the explanation I received was that the woman is in control of the position of the "head" *inside* the home—by telling the husband what to represent *outside*. The list of examples highlighting an *inside/outside* dichotomy that is linked to gender could be prolonged almost indefinitely.

One may expect that such customs and traditions are restricted to non-Western parts of the world. Clearly, as compared to earlier historic times, women are welcomed into the public sphere more than ever before. However, the transition is far from complete, even in the West. In Germany, there is a proverb saying "Der Mann geht hinaus in das feindliche Leben" or "the man goes out into the hostile world" while the woman stays home; indeed, Germany, still today, ranks on a comparatively meager place 17 (in 2001) on the Gender-related Development Index (GDI).[17] Not only in the non-West but also in the West are women typically still the homemakers, not men. Even in the most egalitarian family, where women have top jobs, the women are the ones to remember the birthdays of family members, friends, and neighbors; they are the ones to buy the gifts; they are the ones to maintain emotional and social life *inside* their families; they attempt to create harmony and console the distressed, and they heal and repair social cohesion.

I would like to insert a clarifying note at this point. I am not an advocate of the view that women and men are irreconcilably different by nature, even though there are undoubtedly hormonal differences between the two sexes.[18] I believe that a woman can step into a male role and vice versa. When I talk about female or male roles, I refer to them as a set of culturally determined "recipes," "prescriptions," "templates," or "scripts."[19] I see those scripts as a set of "how to do" and "how to be," which are assimilated through socialization by every individual.[20] I value the following formulations: "Femininity is neither a natural nor an innate entity, but rather a condition brought about by society, on the basis of certain physiological characteristics" (Simone de Beauvoir, 1962, p. 291). "The feminine character, and the ideal of femininity of which it is modelled, are products of masculine society" (Theodor Adorno, 2005, para. 59).

### Women Are *Down* and Men Are *Up*

To continue my previous thought, even though in many parts of the world, for example, in modern Western societies, men are increasingly expected to take over some of the competence for "inside matters" that originally were the reserve of female socialization, this still frequently ends in bitter disappointment. Instead of bringing joy and mutual understanding, this expectation shift often merely opens up a painful expectation gap. As a clinical psychologist, I frequently witnessed women struggling to communicate with their spouses, expecting to be able to attain a relationship of "mutual understanding on an equal footing" with their men. After years of attempting to build what she would call a "real" relationship with her husband, the wife would give up and file for divorce. He, on his side, would be flabbergasted. To his view, everything was fine, apart from her sometimes being a little "difficult," something he prided himself of generously overlooking. It escaped him that her "hysteria" indicated that she painfully realized that her expectations had never made it into his heart and mind, namely, her hope that her husband would become part of the female world of relationship building on one side, and she would be allowed into his world on the other side. See also Lindner (1999).

The last example not only gives a feel for the *inside* sphere where women are "responsible," as compared to *outside* spheres where men roam, but also for its ranking. Female *inside* maintenance tasks enjoy a lower prestige and status than male control of *outside* spheres. In other words, what we can observe is not only an *inside/outside* dichotomy, it is furthermore a dichotomy that is ranked and not deemed to be equally worthy. This state of affairs has been labeled by a number of terminologies, such as that of patriarchy or male chauvinism.[21] Even though the earlier quoted Egyptian proverb of women being in control of men shows that the situation is not completely clear-cut—women do indeed carry power—altogether we may conclude that men are not only *outside*, but also *up*, while women are *inside*, and *down*. And the current historic transition that our generations witness and forge sees women attempting to come *out* and rise *up*, while inviting men *in* and *down*.

Interestingly, not only men, also women struggle with the current transition, not least with regard to their own selves. Admittedly, women no longer cripple themselves by binding their feet so as to become humble eligible brides who thus make themselves stay *inside* and *down*, as they did for a millennium in China. Yet, just listen to Jane Fonda and her speech at the National Women's Leadership Summit in Washington, D.C. on December 2, 2003[22]:

> Before I turned sixty I thought I was a feminist. I was in a way, I worked to register women to vote, I supported women getting elected. I brought gender issues into my movie roles, I encouraged women to get strong and healthy, I read the books we've all read. I had it in my head and partly in my heart, yet I didn't fully get it. See, although I've always been financially independent, and professionally and socially successful, behind the closed doors of my personal life I was still turning myself in a pretzel so I'd be loved by an alpha male. I thought if I didn't become whatever he wanted me to be, I'd be alone, and then, I wouldn't exist.

I hope I have by now given you some interesting perspectives on the interlinked dichotomies of *inside/down/female* and *outside/up/male* and how they currently are in the process of shifting. We currently observe historic transitions that deeply affect male and female role descriptions, a process that is evolving daily and that is far from finalized. *Outside/up/male* and *inside/down/female* linkages are on the move. Women attempt to rise *up* and go *out*, while men are invited *in* into relationships characterized by equal dignity. Concepts of humiliation, honor, war, and violence are profoundly linked to these transitions and are equally on the move.

I would like to continue this chapter by offering you, in the next section, my conceptualization of the underlying conditions that, according to my analysis, might guide the historic transition in which we find ourselves. I will start the following section by pointing out that my conceptualization not only offers a historical contextualization, but also an answer to pressing questions such as, "Why were women *inside* and *down* and not 'worth' being warriors?"

## Why Were Women *In* and *Down* before and Now Want to Get *Out* and *Up*?

In my analysis I give attention to globalization and its effect on gender. I believe that gender role differentiations are weakened in the course of globalization (I define the term globalization in a very specific way, namely, as the coming together of humankind). I have coined the word *egalization* to match the word *globalization*, in order to preserve the coming together aspect in *globalization* that concerns *inside* and *outside* demarcations. I place the currently growing level of global injustice (concerning the question of who is *up* and who is *down*) in a different term, namely, *egalization*. Thus, through the conceptualization of the *inside/outside* and the *up/down* dichotomies and linking them with global historical developments such as globalization, I contextualize the current historic shift that relates to gender, humiliation, and war in a specific way. Let me explain more in the following sections.

### Times of Transition: Before, "Many Villages" and Hierarchical Ranking of Worthiness

Prior to the emergence of the imagery and terminology of the *global village*, which clearly signifies *one single* village covering the entire globe, the world consisted, if we follow the logic of the term, of *one* village, of *many* villages. And indeed, historically this is what we observe. More so, these *villages* were often pitted against each other; between the sovereigns of *villages*—heads of tribes, fiefdoms, nations—wars were frequently waged. People drew clear boundaries between in- and out-group, "we" and "them," "friends" and "enemies." There was little doubt about where *inside* and *outside* spheres were to be defined. *Inside* was *inside* the house, or at best *within* city walls or village demarcations. *Outside* was beyond city walls, at best beyond the frontiers of one's *in*-group's territory.

International relations theory ascribes to this state of affairs the term "security dilemma." Security dilemma is a term that encapsulates a dilemma that each sovereign found himself facing. No sovereign could risk not amassing weapons, lest the neighbors were to attack. However, amassing weapons typically has a counterproductive effect. Bulging weapon arsenals, apart from soothing one's own people's fears, make the neighbors grow more fearful and make them respond with amassing even more weapons on their part. In short, one's own people's decrease of fear is paid for with increasing fear among neighbors. Thus, arms races and ultimately wars were almost inevitable. Fear of attack was bound to dominate the emotional arsenal of both sovereigns and underlings. Being prepared for the emergency of war was of eminent importance.

I suggest that the fear of imminent war, the necessity to continuously staying prepared for the emergency of sudden attack from *outside*, may in many cases have been overwhelming and all defining. And, I furthermore propose that this state of continuous fear and emergency alert, combined with the particularities of human reproduction features, may be taken to present a push toward the dominance of men. As widely accepted, Jeanne d'Arc was an exception; typically men—and not women—were the ones to be sent *out* to defend the borders of the *village*.[23] I do not wish to enter here into the discussion of whether this *division of labor* was a functional adaptation to biological differences or not.[24] Perhaps it was. Men are expandable, women much less, considering that women can never be procreators of as many children in their lifetimes as men.

As soon as a *division of labor* is in place that puts men at the task of dealing with the continuously reigning fear and the tackling of emergencies emanating from attacks threatening from *outside*, while women are to take care of maintenance *inside*, men enjoy a certain kind of definitorial priority. This is because emergencies typically trump maintenance. Not least our bodies demonstrate this; stress hormones take over in case of emergency, while maintenance— digestion, restitution, repair—are secondary and have to wait. Emergency comes first, maintenance second (a state that, if continued for too long, leads to grave neglect of maintenance and eventually to collapse; the human body, for example, might react with a heart attack, or, for societies, the underuse of human potential for social cohesion may be the result).

In other words, prior to the emergence of the idea and reality of *one global village*, humankind lived in *many villages*, and these *villages* were usually hierarchically organized. Elites, mostly males, were meant to tackle fear of attack by guarding the borders toward the *outside*, while underlings, among them almost all women, inhabited secondary and lowly positions *inside*. This state of affairs was regarded as God's will or nature's order, starting about 10,000 years ago and slowly encompassing almost the entire globe, while hunting-gathering societies (which were rather egalitarian) were pushed aside.[25] During the past millennia, usually, neither elites nor underlings in hierarchical cultural contexts questioned this order. If underlings rose, they typically replaced the master and kept hierarchy as it was. Honor was the concept that was used to describe and encapsulate everybody's position in the hierarchical ranking order.

How is honor structured? And how are gender, humiliation, and war linked to it? I propose to merge the two elements already discussed, namely, the *inside/outside* dichotomy (women *inside*, men *outside*), and the *top*dog/*under*dog dichotomy (women *down*, men *up*) into one single image, an image that is often alluded to, not least in the above-mentioned Egyptian proverb and in cases of honor killings, namely, the image of the *body* for a group. In other words, I suggest analyzing the world of honor and humiliation in traditional societies by taking the body as a guiding image. In that image, the man represents the *head* that thinks, steers, strategizes, and decides, and the woman represents both the *substrate* of the body and its *caring hands*, with which to extend maintenance and continuous renewal. Men are conceptualized as the rationally and responsibly thinking *heads* of social entities conceptualized as bodies —families, tribes, nations, or what I earlier called *villages*—being in control of *outside* matters, while the *caring hands* of the women are to maintain, so to speak, harmony *inside* these social entities.

In such contexts, men represent the outer shield, the armor covering *inside* spheres; they defend family honor against humiliation by going to duel with other men who attack from *outside*. Free will, independent deliberation, rational evaluation of risks, autonomous decision, all this is the world of honorable men, particularly those in ruling elites, who move *outside*, where Hobbsian anarchy reigns between *villages*.[26] Women, on the other hand, not only are meant to be *caring hands*, they also represent the *fabric* of the inside sphere. In such framings, women do not *act*, they *are*; they *are* either *pure* or *rotten*. Men are seen as *actors*, women are *substrate*. In cases of honor killings the raped girl is killed because she resembles a rotten limb that has to be cut out of the body, lest the entire body should begin to rot. I was frequently confronted with this framing and explanation.[27]

As long as honor codes are strongly anchored in a given community, both men and women are caught in their respective role descriptions as parts of a larger *body*. A man, for example, cannot avoid "being a man," even if he wishes to. Many men were killed in duels that they would have avoided if they had a personal choice. I had a client in Egypt who ridiculed the blood-feud practices of his native village; he did not identify with those "anachronistic traditions" as he called them. He was the next in line to be killed in a blood feud of his village. He stopped mocking his fellow villagers after narrowly escaping the first attempt to kill him. Also women are caught in this social system. A raped girl is a "living dead" person, if not physically dead, then at least socially dead, reports Victoria Firmo-Fontan (2004) from her fieldwork in Iraq. A raped girl cannot escape her fate of being killed by her family, and even if she were to avoid death, she would never be able to be part of her social home again. Firmo-Fontan quotes from Khayyat (1990), who explains that in Iraq a raped woman is considered to be dead to society for having enticed males to abuse her.

To summarize, in what I call *traditional societies*—societies based on honor codes that rank humans as *lesser* and *higher* beings, including gender ranking—humiliation is linked in very specific ways to the selective killing or sparing of men and women. See Table 6.1. In blood feuds, humiliated family honor is redressed by the selective killing of men, while women are not regarded to be "worthy" of being killed. In duels as well, men are killed so as to redress humiliated honor; women are not entitled to defend their honor with the sword in duels. Men of battle age are never regarded as civilians but rather as continuously representing potential enemies "worthy to be

**Table 6.1**
**Humiliation and the Selective Killing of Men and Women in Honor-Based Social Contexts**

| *Humiliation and the selective killing of men in honor-based social contexts* | | |
|---|---|---|
| Blood feud | $\Rightarrow$ | Redress of humiliation of family honor |
| Duels | $\Rightarrow$ | Redress of humiliation of family honor |
| Propensity to kill males in battle age among enemy groups independently of them being civilians or not, because all males are regarded as potential warriors/soldiers | $\Rightarrow$ | Prevention/redress of potential future humiliation of family/clan/tribal/ national honor |
| *Humiliation and the selective killing of women in honor-based social contexts* | | |
| Honor killings | $\Rightarrow$ | Redress of humiliation of family honor |

killed." National honor in many countries, still today, resembles male honor, and its humiliation is redressed by duel-like wars.

### Times of Transition: Today, Globalization and Egalization

We live in times of transition. And these transitions are marked not least by a shift in the meaning of the word humiliation. In the English language, the verbs *to humiliate* and *to humble* parted around 250 years ago. Their meanings and connotations went into diametrically opposite directions. Up to 1757 the verb *to humiliate* did not signify the violation of dignity. *To humiliate* meant merely *to lower* or *to humble*. I quote from Miller, who informs us that "the earliest recorded use of *to humiliate* meaning to mortify or to lower or to depress the dignity or self-respect of someone does not occur until 1757" (1993, p. 175, italics in original).

Thus, the old meaning of the word *to humiliate* (1757) lasted almost until the American Declaration of Independence (July 4, 1776) and the French Revolution (August 4, 1789), both important starting points for the subsequent rise and canonization of human rights ideals. Undoubtedly, the ideas that feed into today's human rights ideas predate 1757. Not least important religions such as Christianity and Islam entail significant ideals of equality. However, these ideals seem to have gathered pace only about 250 years ago.

Historians are the ones to describe the transition that acquired significance around 250 years ago; this text is not the place. However, I believe that we live in the middle of a transition from old honor codes in traditional hierarchical settings to new human rights based on equal dignity norms. Clearly, we are far from having arrived "on the other side" yet. Old honor norms and related feelings of humiliation are still alive and well—alongside new equal dignity norms and their respective emotional expressions. Therefore it is important to understand both.

What is important for the topic of humiliation is, I believe, that with the advent of human rights ideals, the notion of humiliation changes its attachment point. It moves from the top to the bottom of pyramids of power, from the privileged to the disadvantaged. In the new human rights framework, the downtrodden underling is given the right to feel humiliated. The master, on the other side, is called upon to humble himself, and he is no longer given permission to resist this call by labeling it as humiliating. Elites who arrogate superiority lose their age-old right to cry "humiliation!" when they are asked to descend and humble themselves.

The human rights revolution could be described as an attempt to collapse the master-slave gradient to the line of equal dignity and humility. The practice of masters arrogating superiority and subjugating underlings is now regarded as illicit and obscene, and human rights advocates invite both, masters and underlings, to join in shared humility at the line of equal dignity.

It is important to note that I speak about the *vertical ranking of human worth and value,* and less about *inequality, hierarchy,* or *stratification.* This is because the significant point for my discussion is not the absence or presence of hierarchy, inequality, or stratification, but whether human worthiness is ranked or not. The horizontal line is meant to represent the line of equal dignity and humility. This line does not signify that all human beings are equal, or should be equal, or ever were or will be equal, or identical, or all the same. This horizontal line is to represent a worldview that does not permit the hierarchical ranking of existing differences of human worth and value. Masters are invited to step down from arrogating *more* worthiness, and underlings are encouraged to rise up from humiliation, up from being humiliated down to *lower* value. Masters are humbled and underlings empowered. See Figure 6.1.

As mentioned above, I believe that what anthropologists call the *ingathering* of the human family is a central force in the current historic shift. Ury (1999) states

> Over the last ten thousand years, there has been one fairly steady trend in our history: the ingathering of the tribes of the earth, their incorporation into larger and larger groups, the gradual unification of humanity into a single interacting and interdependent community. For the first time since the origin of our species, humanity is in touch with itself. (p. XVII)

In my theory of humiliation, I base myself on the work of William Ury (1999). I recently detected that also Carol Lee Flinders (2002) conceptualizes human history in similar ways. I suggest that we can describe a historical development from hunting-gathering to complex agriculturalism and finally to the global information and

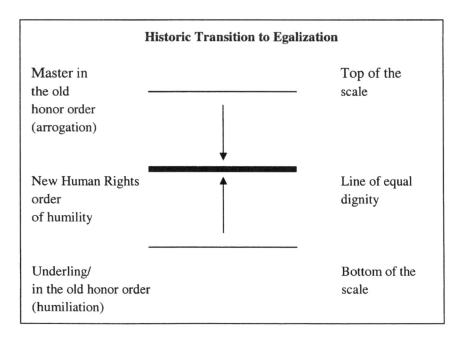

**Figure 6.1**
**The Historic Transition to Egalization**

knowledge society. Thus, I propose that globalization is significant for the current human rights call for collapsing the master-slave gradient, and for related changes in the humiliation dynamic that in turn have deep effects on concepts of gender and war.

I propose that "globalization critics" do not oppose all aspects of *globalization*— global civil society, for example, benefits from the coming together of humankind —however, that they are uneasy about what I call *egalization*.

Lindner (2003a, p. 9) defines egalization as follows:

> The word *egalization* has been coined by the author in order to match the word *globalization* and at the same time differentiate it from words such as equality, because the main point is not equality. The point is rather equal dignity, even though there is a connection between equality and equal dignity. (The connection is "hidden" in the Human Rights stipulation that equal chances and enabling environments for all are necessary to protect human dignity.)
>
> The term egalization is meant to avoid claiming that everybody should become equal and that there should be no differences between people. Egality can coexist with functional hierarchy that regards all participants as possessing equal dignity; egality can not coexist, though, with hierarchy that defines some people as lesser beings and others as more valuable.
>
> If we imagine the world as a container with a height and a width, *globalization* addresses the horizontal dimension, the shrinking width. *Egalization* concerns the vertical dimension, reminiscent of Hofstede's power distance. Egalization is a process away from a very high container of masters at the top and underlings at the bottom, towards a flat container with everybody enjoying equal dignity.
>
> Egalization is a process that elicits hot feelings of humiliation when it is promised but fails. The lack of egalization is thus the element that is heating up feelings among so-called "globalization-critics." Their disquiet stems from lack of egalization and not from an overdose of globalization. What they call for is that *globalization* ought to marry *egalization*.

To conclude, we find ourselves in times of transition, a transition from hierarchical rankings of human worthiness to equal dignity as stipulated in human rights ideals. Globalization critics, according to my view, burn for globalization that is infused with egalization and oppose globalization that lacks egalization. They do not oppose globalization as I define it. The transition that causes hot feelings is the transition toward egalization—and among the hottest feelings are feelings of humiliation that are felt by those who perceive themselves or identify with the downtrodden.

The vision of a new world of equal dignity calls for individuals to represent whole and dignified entities in themselves. Nobody shall be regarded as a subservient part of the larger "body" of a group. Killing women or men is not anymore legitimate. Particularly using human lives as means of sending "messages" of honor between groups is not anymore condoned. See Table 6.2.

The vision of the *global village* signifies nothing but the vision of *one single in-group*, namely, of all humankind, and the retreat of the notion of *out*-groups. Together with the weakening of *out*-group conceptualizations, all former *out*-group

**Table 6.2**
**Humiliation and Killing of People in Human Rights Based Social Contexts**

| *Humiliation and killing of people in human rights based social contexts* | | |
| --- | --- | --- |
| The killing of people is deplored and seen as illegitimate, under whatever circumstances (except in clear cases of self-defense, for military personnel in wars that are perceived to be legitimately waged, or for those waiting in the death row in countries that legitimize capital punishment) | $\Rightarrow$ | Killing people is not regarded as a means for redressing humiliation |

concepts are weakened. No longer are men those to guard the frontiers of the *inside* against aggression from *outside*, no longer are *out*-groups being called "enemies." Instead, good and bad neighbors share *one village, one in-group, one single inside* sphere. In this new *inside* sphere that covers the entire globe, traditional *inside* conflict management methods such as, for example mediation, gain importance. Women and men share this common *inside* sphere and all engage in cooperative communication patterns that formerly were rather specific for the socialization of females. This is no dream or idealized world vision, it is an emerging reality that is driven by the *ingathering* of humankind and is currently conquering the hearts and minds of an ever-increasing number of earth dwellers.

## What Can Be Done?

What can be done to overcome the violent effects of humiliation? The following paragraph outlines the background of UNESCO's (United Nations Educational, Scientific and Cultural Organization's) Culture of Peace Programme: "The end of the Cold War has enabled the United Nations to begin realizing the potential for which it was created nearly fifty years ago, that is, to save succeeding generations from the scourge of war" (UNESCO, 1994, p. 1).

So, how are we to "save succeeding generations from the scourge of war" and how is humiliation and gender relevant to that? In *An Agenda for Peace*, published in 1994, the UNESCO Secretary-General outlines the areas where the United Nations and its Specialized Agencies face challenges: "preventive diplomacy, which seeks to resolve disputes before violence breaks out; peacemaking and peace-keeping, which are required to halt conflicts and preserve peace once it is attained, and postconflict peace-building—to strengthen and solidify peace in order to avoid a relapse into conflict" (UNESCO, 1994, p. 1).

In short, what we need, worldwide, is nothing else but *global social control*. I think the term *social control* is useful in this context because it combines psychological tools and aspects of strategies that formerly were allotted to the female versus male role description. Please read Lindner (1999, p. 94):

> The term "social control" expresses the combination of both aspects. On the national level, police and prisons represent some of the coercive aspects (more effective if the average citizen does not carry weapons), while institutions like lawyers, courts and rehabilitation programmes have the potential to fulfill the role of social caring and healing. The culture of peace is a multifaceted, creative combination of certain aspects of traditional "male" and "female" role strategies. At this historical point of an emerging, increasingly interdependent "global village", traditionally "female" strategies of caring and healing are more needed and must be integrated on the international level. As mentioned above, the notion of a "culture of peace" advocates on the social level what "sustainable development" promotes on the ecological level. In both cases, the aim is to achieve a better quality of life and the challenge is the long-term maintenance of interdependent systems. In order to tackle this challenge traditional female role descriptions concerning maintenance must be elevated from the private to the public sphere and used there by both men and women.

Please read more in Lindner (1999) on female role characteristics for keeping *inside* harmony and how they currently emerge on the new world stage of an *ingathering* humankind. The following paragraph is adapted from Lindner (1999, p. 94):

UNESCO's Culture of Peace Programme urges precisely the strengthening of the "female" aspect in conflict-resolution efforts. Space does not allow me to give a detailed description of every facet of this female contribution. The list is a long one: using multitrack, "track II" and citizen-based diplomacy[28]; installing early warning institutions; rethinking the notion of state sovereignty; setting up projects to better study and understand the history of potential conflict areas, collecting this information, and making it available to decision makers; using psychology not only on a microlevel, but also on a macrolevel, taking identity as a bridge[29]; keeping communication going with warring parties; talking behind the scenes; including more than just the warlords in peace negotiations; developing conflict-resolution teams with less hierarchy and more creativity; setting up mediation teams; installing "truth commissions[30];" allowing warring parties to feel the world community's care, respect, and concern; taking opponents in a conflict out of their usual environment[31]; taking the adversaries' personal feelings and emotions seriously; recognizing the importance of human dignity[32]; introducing sustainable long-term approaches on the social and ecological level[33]; progressing from spending aid money after a disaster to allocating resources to prevent it; and so on. All these rather "female" efforts must be combined with a certain amount of "male" coercion if necessary.

May I conclude this section by quoting George Monbiot (2003, p. 23, italics in original),

> Globalization is not the problem. The problem is in fact the *release* from globalization which both economic agents and nations states have been able to negotiate. They have been able to operate so freely because the people of the world have no global means of

restraining them. Our task is surely not to overthrow globalizing, but to capture it, and to use it as a vehicle for humanity's first global democratic revolution.


## Concluding Remarks

Globalization—here defined as the coming together of humankind in *one single in*-group, namely, *one single global village*—weakens gender segregation. This is one of the central propositions in this chapter. Men and women are not anymore pressed into strict gender templates but can develop more flexible and interchangeable gender identities. The backdrop for this process is, I suggest, that the reality and the perception of *outside* spheres disappear in tact with the emergence of the reality and perception of *one in*-group, *one* humanity, or *one* global village. No longer is it "we" against "them," but "we," humanity, together. What is left in a *global village* is *one single inside* sphere, a sphere that, incidentally, traditionally is the sphere of women. This sphere is now jointly inhabited by men and women.

Clearly, this process is not finalized yet; humankind currently finds itself in the middle of a transition; I use the above introduced Weberian *ideal-type* approach. My point is that the imagery, framing, and emerging reality of the *global village*, or *one* single *in*-group or *one single inside* sphere is bound to impact upon segregational gender definitions that reserve *inside* spheres for woman and *outside* spheres for men. The disappearance of *outside* spheres cannot but weaken gender segregation. We currently observe how the *outside/male* sphere increasingly disappears, both in reality and in our cultural production of imagery and framings, and women and men now have to learn to cohabit in *one single inside* sphere.

More so, globalization must be expected to not only weaken gender *segregation* but also gender *ranking*. This is my second proposition. Men no longer are worth more than women. This, I suggest, is brought about by that fact that the fear of being attacked from *outside* subsides together with the disappearance of the perception of *outside* spheres. What we have *inside* a village—and a global village is no exception —is criminality, or terrorism, or civil war at best. Classical imperial war *between villages* becomes irrelevant in tact with these *villages* merging into *one single global village*. As a consequence, traditional male prowess, male preparedness for *outside* attack, loses its former anchoring in reality and imagery.

As discussed above, males traditionally were assigned to guard *outside* borders and be prepared for the emergency case of attack. Since emergency trumps maintenance, this arrangement gave men a definitional precedence over women, who were assigned to maintain the *inside* sphere. Consequently, as soon as *one global village* emerges and preparedness for emergency attacks from *outside* loses its urgency, male predominance loses its definitional foothold. Women and men, together, now police and maintain the global village. Not anymore are men soldiers and women homemakers, but both are maintainers of the social cohesion of the *one single inside* sphere that is about to be left, namely, the *global village*.

One other effect of these transitions is that the notion of humiliation changes its relationship with respect to gender, killing, and war. In former times women were "spared from the spear" and were not to be killed or molested in war. Only battle-aged men were "worthy" enemies, worthy to defend humiliated male honor with the sword, and worthy of being killed in honorable battles or duels. Women were not worthy of being killed in such ways or invoke humiliation. There was no "female honor" similar to "male honor," except that women were expected to accept lowliness and subjugation with deference and display chastity. Men represented the "head" of the "body" of the family, tribe, or village—men were the ones entitled to thinking, strategizing, leading, steering, showing the direction, and enjoying privileges in return. Women represented the less important "limbs" of the body. Women's worth lie primarily in embodying the proof that their men could protect them against hostile male intruders—for example, by displaying an intact hymen—as well as in maintaining the *inside* sphere and therein create the next generation. Women were not regarded as actors, but as "substrate" and were supposed to be killed when they were "rotten." As mentioned above, the current explanation for honor killings—and I have received such explanations—is that a raped daughter represents "a rotten part of the body" that has to be "cut out."

As soon as a sense of *one single human family* emerges, what I call "*inside* ethics" expand to the entirety of the human family. The reach of morals is called the *scope of justice*. Coleman (2000) expresses this as follows: "Individuals or groups within our moral boundaries are seen as deserving of the same fair, moral treatment as we deserve. Individuals or groups outside these boundaries are seen as undeserving of this same treatment" (p. 118). Human rights, according to my understanding, represent, at least partly, *inside* ethics, or how groups typically organize their *inside* dealings, only that human rights no longer address one in-group among surrounding out-groups, but the *one single in*-group that is left: all of humanity inhabiting *one single global village*.

Furthermore, my understanding is that human rights ideals not only represent traditional *inside* ethics expanded onto all humanity, but also what I call the first continuous revolution in human history. What made globalization possible—technology that brings us closer together—makes also a permanent uprising of underlings possible; this is my conceptualization. In former times, revolutionaries, those coming *up* from *below*, when successful, typically replaced the master and preserved the hierarchical structures. Nowadays, a continuous push from *below* does not permit masters to settle in their privileged seats; this push calls for the dismantling—not only of the tyrant or the master—but of the very hierarchical social and societal structures. Those coming *up* from *below* are women, blacks, the poor, in other words, all those who formerly were assigned *lowly* places. Human rights bestow equal dignity on all and call for the *global villagers* to work for enabling environments for all, including men and women.

The new situation entails that new Realpolitik no longer is the same as old Realpolitik. New Realpolitik is bound to attend to what women always were socialized to attend to, namely, to relationships *inside* an *in*-group. Women and men are not anymore relegated to be either the "heads" or the "caring hands" of larger social bodies. Men and women are encouraged to learn to construct themselves as individual entities or "bodies" and to contribute to society as individuals in egalitarian ways. In earlier times, society was like a ship with a captain (male) and subordinate crew (lower males and women); increasingly, today, every individual represents his or her own ship. Women learn how to be heads and lead, while at the same time continuing to be carers, and men learn how to be caring hands that nurture and maintain, while still continuing to be good leaders. Both caring and leading activities merge and both activities evolve in new ways; modern teamwork is far removed from former autocratic ways of organizing groups.

Today, we find ourselves in a world that is characterized by a transition that pits representatives of the old honor order against those who promote a new dignity order. In that context complicated dilemmas emerge. Women may acquire a new "worthiness" to be killed as actors, and not merely as substrates: while formerly women were "spared from the spear," they may now be found "worthy of the spear." Thus, acquiring a more egalitarian status may lead to more victimization of women in war. Or, on the other side, the killing of battle-aged men no longer is accepted as the worthy and honorable fate for any male, but as deplorable gendercide; see, for example, A. Jones (1994).

Avishai Margalit (1996)[34] wrote a book entitled *The Decent Society*, in which he calls for institutions that do not anymore humiliate citizens. Decency reigns when humiliation is being minimized, humiliation in relationships, but also humiliation inflicted by institutions. Decency rules when dignity for all is made possible. Decency does not mean that everybody should like everybody; decency is the minimum that is necessary to keep a neighborhood functioning—coexisting without mayhem—even when neighbors dislike each other.

I wish to extend the call for decency from national to global levels. The vision of a *decent global village* is spelled out in detail in the *United Nations Millennium Declaration* of September 2000. Another relevant key term is *sustainability*. What we need is sustainability for our planet, ecological and social sustainability. However, on the way to a *decent and sustainable global village*, we have to be alert to dynamics of humiliation and heal and prevent them (Lindner, 2002b). Particularly the danger emanating from the current lack of egalization must be taken seriously. Lagging egalization threatens to fuel feelings of humiliation, and feelings of humiliation in turn entail the potential to lead to violence. This danger has to be heeded, since feelings of humiliation represent the "nuclear bomb of the emotions" (term coined by Lindner). Former masters must learn new humility and former underlings must develop new self-empowerment so that all can cooperate as equally dignified players of a global team.

All the international community, its men and its women, carry a particular responsibility in the current transition period. People who are caught in cycles of humiliation may not be able to exit from them on their own; they need the support and sometimes even pressure from outside. The international community, if it wishes to extinguish local fires that might inflame the globe, needs to take up this responsibility. The international community has to stand up and not stand by (see Staub, 1989).

Incidentally, safeguarding social cohesion in the emerging *global village* is a task that entails many psychological tools and elements that traditionally were primarily part of female socialization. Not allowing the globe to descend into warring neighborhoods but into a *decent global village* is a task that can be greatly enhanced by the psychological "tool kit" for which formerly particularly females were trained. I call for a worldwide *Moratorium on Humiliation* in order to facilitate the building of a *decent global village*.

## Notes

1. Blood feud has become rampant in Albania since Hodscha's downfall. Today, around 10,000 men sit in their homes and cannot go out, because they fear blood revenge. At the same time, their women can go around freely; thus they have to shoulder all family responsibilities and tasks alone. See other evidence relating to blood feuds in Boehm (1984), Malcolm (1998), and Rodina (1999).

2. Militarism has been examined from a feminist point of view in, for example, *Women and War* by Elshtain (1995). Jean Elshtain examines how the myths of *man* as *just warrior* and *woman* as *beautiful soul* are undermined by the reality of female bellicosity and sacrificial male love, as well as the moral imperatives of just wars. Cynthia Enloe (1990) investigates international politics and reveals the crucial role of women in implementing governmental foreign policies; see also Enloe (2000). International relations as a mirror to masculinity have been discussed, for example, by J. Ann Tickner (1992). She examines the meaning of global security through a gender-sensitive lens. V. Spike Peterson and Anne Sisson Runyan describe both women's roles in world politics and the impact of world politics on women's roles; see Peterson (1992a, 1992b) and Peterson and Runyan (1993).

3. See, for example, Shalhoub-Kevorkian (2000), and literature she uses, such as Abu-Odeh (2000), Al-Khayyat (1990), Baker, Gregware, and Cassidy (1999), Polk (1994), Radford and Russel (1992), Hanmer, Hester, Kelly, and Radford (1996), and Stout (1992).

4. The phenomenon of "honor killings" is to be found in many parts of the world, even though they occur most in Muslim countries, despite the fact that Islamic religion and law do not sanction it. According to Stephanie Nebehay (2000), honor killings "have been reported in Bangladesh, Britain, Brazil, Ecuador, Egypt, India, Israel, Italy, Jordan, Pakistan, Morocco, Sweden, Turkey and Uganda." Afghanistan, where the practice is condoned under the rule of the fundamentalist Taliban movement, can be added to the list, along with Iraq and Iran (Nebehay, 2000).

5. Please read in Coser (1977),

Weber's three kinds of *ideal types* are distinguished by their levels of abstraction. First are the *ideal types* rooted in historical particularities, such as the "western city," "the Protestant Ethic," or "modern capitalism," which refer to phenomena that appear only in specific historical periods and in particular cultural areas. A second kind involves abstract elements of social reality—such concepts as "bureaucracy" or "feudalism"— that may be found in a variety of historical and cultural contexts. Finally, there is a third kind of *ideal type*, which Raymond Aron calls "rationalizing reconstructions of a particular kind of behavior." According to Weber, all propositions in economic theory, for example, fall

into this category. They all refer to the ways in which men would behave were they actu-
ated by purely economic motives, were they purely economic men. (p. 224)

6. See, for example, Lindner (1999, 2000b, 2000c, 2001a, 2001b, 2001c, 2001d, 2001f,
2002a, 2002b, 2002c, 2003b, 2003c). The concept of humiliation may be deconstructed
into at least seven layers (Lindner, 2001e), each requiring a different mix of interdisciplinary research and analysis. The seven layers include (a) a core that expresses the universal
idea of "putting down," (b) a middle layer that contains two opposed orientations towards
putting down, treating it as, respectively, legitimate and routine, or illegitimate and
traumatizing, and (c) a periphery whose distinctive layers include one pertaining to cultural differences between groups and another four peripheral layers that relate to differences in individual personalities and variations in patterns of individual experience of
humiliation.

7. See also Nathanson (1992).

8. See especially Heinz Leymann for work on mobbing, Leymann (1990, 1996), Leymann
& Gustafsson (1996), as well as Dan Åke Olweus on mobbing and bullying at school
(1993, 1997). The confusion around the use of the terms "mobbing" and "bullying"
stems from the fact that these phenomena are addressed differently in different countries.
Leymann suggests keeping the word "bullying" for activities between children and teenagers at school and reserving the word "mobbing" for adult behavior at workplaces.

9. Edvard E. Jones (1984), *Social Stigma—The Psychology of Marked Relationships*, is a central book on stigmatization.

10. There exists a huge body of research and literature; see, for example, Bremner, Southwick,
Brett, Fontana, Rosenheck, and Charney (1992), Eitinger (1990), Everly (1993), Figley
(1989), Gerbode (2000), Havermans (1998), Horowitz, Weine, and Jekel (1995),
Kardiner (1941), Lavik, Laake, Hauff, and Solberg (1999), McCann and Pearlman
(1992), Nadler and Shushan (1989), Pearlman (1994, 1998), Perry (1994), van der Kolk,
Bessel, Blitz, Burr, and Hartmann (1984), van der Kolk (1994), van der Kolk and van der
Hart (1989, 1991), and van der Kolk and Kadish (1987).

11. Political scientists Bachrach and Baratz (1962) were among the first to address power and
conflict in their article "The Two Faces of Power" that is placed within the context of the
civil rights movement in the United States of the 1960s. See also Tedeschi, Schlenker, and
Bonoma's (1973) *Conflict, Power, and Games: The Experimental Study of Interpersonal
Relations*.

12. Standard reading on stress psychology is Richard S. Lazarus's (1966) *Psychological Stress
and the Coping Process* and Lazarus and Folkman's (1984) *Stress, Appraisal and Coping*.
Stress is not necessarily negative; it may also be a stimulating challenge—and there are
individual differences why some people thrive under stress and others break. See, for
example, *Resilience and Thriving: Issues, Models, and Linkages* by Carver (1998), *Embodying Psychological Thriving: Physical Thriving in Response to Stress* by Epel, McEwen, and
Ickovics (1998), *Quantitative Assessment of Thriving* by Cohen, Cimbolic, Armeli, and
Hettler (1998), *Beyond Recovery From Trauma: Implications for Clinical Practice and
Research* by Calhoun and Tedeschi (1998), and *Exploring Thriving in the Context of Clin-
ical Trauma Theory: Constructivist Self Development Theory* by Saakvitne, Tennen, and
Affleck (1998).

13. Antonio R. Damasio (1994), with his book *Descartes' Error. Emotion, Reason and the
Human Brain*, provides a perspective on the important "constructive" role that emotions
play for the process of our decision making; it shows how the traditional view of "heart"

versus "head" is obsolete. Daniel Goleman (1996), in his more widely known book *Emotional Intelligence—Why It Can Matter More than IQ* relies heavily on Damasio. Goleman gives, among others, a description of the brain activities that lead to post-traumatic stress disorder. *The Handbook of Emotion and Memory: Research and Theory* by Christianson (1992) addresses the important interplay between emotions and memory. Humiliation is a process that is deeply embedded in the individual's interdependence with his or her environment, and therefore relational concepts of mind such as Gibson's ecological psychology of "affordance" are relevant. Gibson "includes environmental considerations in psychological taxonomies" writes de Jong (1997) (Abstract). M. A. Forrester (1999) presents a related approach, which he defines as "discursive ethnomethodology," that focuses on "narrativization" as the process of bringing together Foucault's (1972) discourse theory, Gibson's (1979) affordance metaphor and conversation analysis. I thank Reidar Ommundsen and Finn Tschudi for kindly helping me to get access to psychological theories on emotion, especially as developed by Tomkins and Nathanson. Silvan S. Tomkins (1962) developed one of the most interesting theories of the human being and emotions; see his four volumes of *Affect Imagery and Consciousness*. See also Virginia Demos (1995), editor of *Exploring Affect. Selected Writings of S. S. Tomkins*, a book that eases the otherwise difficult access to Tomkins's thinking. Donald L. Nathanson (1996) builds on Tomkins's work; he writes on script, shame, and pride. Nathanson describes humiliation as a combination of three innate affects out of nine, namely, a combination of shame, disgust, and dis-smell (personal communication, October 1, 1999 in Oslo). Abelson (1976) addresses the issue from the cognitive perspective, compared to Tomkins's personality-psychological perspective. Also the sociology of emotions is relevant; see especially the work of Thomas J. Scheff (1988, 1990a, 1990b, 1997) on violence and emotions, such as shame.

14. See, for example, the work of Michael Harris Bond. I can present only a small selection of important books and some articles: Bond (1997), Bond (1998), Bond, Leung, and Schwartz (1992), and P. B. Smith and Bond (1999). Harry Charalambos Triandis is an important name as well; see, for example, Triandis (1980), Triandis (1990), Triandis (1995), Triandis (1997), and Schwartz (1994). Richard W. Brislin is another very relevant name; see, for example, Brislin (1993), Cushner and Brislin (1996), and Landis and Brislin (1983).

15. I thank Dagfinn Føllesdal for his support in formulating these questions.

16. Read on *gender and space*; see, for example, Massey (1994), Rose (1993), and Spain (1992). I thank Nick Prior for making me aware of this literature.

17. United Nations Development Programme (UNDP) (2002) explains,

The human development index (HDI) is a simple summary measure of three dimensions of the human development concept: living a long and healthy life, being educated and having a decent standard of living. … Thus it combines measures of life expectancy, school enrolment, literacy and income to allow a broader view of a country's development than using income alone, which is too often equated with well-being. Since the creation of the HDI in 1990 three supplementary indices have been developed to highlight particular aspects of human development: the human poverty index (HPI), gender-related development index (GDI) and gender empowerment measure (GEM). (p. 34)

18. On *genes, hormones*, and *violence*, see, for example, Bernhardt (1997), Caspi et al. (2002), Clark and Grunstein (2000), J. L. Fuller and Thompson (2003), and Hamer and Copeland (2000).

19. Donald L. Nathanson builds on Tomkins's work; he writes on *script*, shame, and pride (Nathanson, 1987, 1992, 1996). Scripts are "the structures within which we store scenes;" they are "sets of rules for the ordering of information about SARS" (Stimulus-Affect-Response Sequences) (Nathanson, 1996). See for work on scripts also Eric Berne (1972), with his book *What Do You Say After You Say Hello?* that illuminates script theory from the clinical perspective.

20. Henri Tajfel (1984) wrote, "it is not the difference which matters, but the distinction." Larrow and Wiener (1992) contribute to the same subject:

> There has been much controversy over the use of the terms *stereotype* and *prejudice*. … We would distinguish three terms: categorization, stereotypes, and prejudice. *Categorization* will be used when classification of a person into a category is based on the necessary defining attributes of class membership. *Stereotype* is the classification based on non-definitional attributes. Finally, *prejudice* is classified when social evaluation is explicitly included with the stereotype. In the field of sex/gender research, we would like to make a distinction between using the term sex to refer to categorization of males and females based on biological attributes, such as chromosomes, genitals, reproductive functions, and so on, and *gender* to refer to stereotypes of women and men based on non-biological attributes such as clothes, hairstyle, behaviours, and the like. Most of our beliefs about men and women are based on gender stereotypes. (p. 239)

> Unger and Crawford (1992) formulate it succinctly: "When sex is not present, people need to invent it. They use sex as a cue even when more useful sources of information are available" (p. 619). The authors look for alternative explanations and name inequality through power difference as often explaining more of observable differences than sex or gender differences. I would agree concerning the necessity of alternative explanations but would be careful with the power argument, as long as the power argument is simply used as men having the power and women being the suppressed ones. I would take into account the distribution of tasks of different urgency leading to a power difference.

21. Clearly, the intertwined relationship between social construction and biological facts (and their construction) requires a more thorough discussion. Yet, it would take too much space here. See for masculine domination as patriarchy and male power, for example, *Men in the Public Eye: The Construction and Deconstruction of Public Men and Public Patriarchies* (Hearn, 1992).

22. See http://www.trans4mind.com/healing/fonda.html or http://www.awakenedwoman .com/jane_fonda_talk.htm. I thank Linda Hartling for making me aware of Fonda's speech.

23. Read on *masculinity, violence,* and *war*; see, for example, Breines, Connell, and Eide (2000), Brittan (1989), Brod (1987), Connell (1995), Connell (1996), Connell (1997), Hanmer, Hester, Kelly, and Radford (1996), Hooper (2001), Kimmel (1996), Kimmel (1997), Kimmel (2000), Messner (1997), Morgan (1992), Walby (1990), Whitehead (2002), Wrangham and Peterson (1996), Zalewski and Parpat (1998). See also *The Men's Studies Bibliography* at http://www.xyonline.net/mensbiblio/

24. Read, for example, Durkheim (1993).

25. See Ury (1999) for a very accessible presentation of the historical and anthropological background of the transition from hunting-gathering to agriculture and from there to today's global knowledge society.

26. Life is "nasty, brutish and short," according to Hobbes (1651, p. 91). "Anarchy" is what Hobbes calls this abominable experience.

27. See interesting related work, for example, by Mary Douglas (1984) on purity and taboo.

28. See the efforts of individuals such as the former American President Jimmy Carter, or the Norwegians helping behind the scene in the Israel-Palestine peace process.

29. The Peace Research Institute in Oslo (PRIO), for example, has taken up national identity as a major new field of interest, thereby incorporating social psychology into peace research (source: Dan Smith, director of the institute).

30. See, for example, Ethiopia, where reconciliation within a society can be reached through "truth commissions" if other ways, such as tribunals, would be too disrupting.

31 See the Norwegian approach in the Israel-Palestine Oslo agreement.

32. Whatever has been learned on a microlevel in therapeutic contexts about conflict and conflict resolution, from confession to forgiveness, also applies to the community level.

33. Brundtland (1992), a woman and a very active Scandinavian politician, writes (p. 17): "We must not be blinded by the immediate. We must all take a longer-term view. We need to expand and share knowledge and we must get many more people engaged in the overriding issues of our time. We will have to rely on the gift of information technology for spreading knowledge and for developing those common perspectives and attitudes which our human predicament now requires." This is a woman advocating a combination of traditionally "female" long-term thinking being promoted by "male" technology.

34. See also Frankfurt (1997), Honneth (1997), Lukes (1997), Mack (1997), Margalit (1997), Oksenberg Rorty (1997), Pettit (1997), Quinton (1997), Ripstein (1997), and Schick (1997).

# References

Abelson, Robert P. (1976). Script processing in attitude formation and decision making. In John S. Carroll & John W. Payne (Eds.), *Cognition and social behavior*. Hillsdale, NJ: Lawrence Erlbaum.

Abu-Odeh, Lama. (2000). Crimes of honor and the construction of gender in Arab society. In Pinar Ilkkaracan (Ed.), *Women and sexuality in Muslim society* (pp. 363–380). Istanbul: Women for Women's Human Rights.

Adorno, Theodor W. (2005). *Minima Moralia* (Dennis Redmond, Trans.). Retrieved August 31, 2005, from http://www.efn.org/~dredmond/MM2.html. Original German text available from Suhrkamp Verlag as Theodor W. Adorno. *Collected Works*. Suhrkamp Verlag, Vol. 4.

Al-Khayyat, Sana'a. (1990). *Honour and shame: Women in modern Iraq*. London: Saqi.

Bachrach, Peter, & Baratz, Morton S. (1962). The two faces of power. *American Political Science Review, 56*, 947–952.

Baker, Nancy, Gregware, Peter, & Cassidy, Margery. (1999). Family killing fields: Honor rationales in the murder of women. *Violence Against Women, 5*(2), 164–184.

Bar-On, Daniel, & Nadler, Arie. (1999). *From peace making and conflict resolution to conciliation and peace building*. Beer-Sheva, Israel: Proposal for the International Award of the State of Nordrhine-Westfalia for Research in the Humanities and Social Sciences.

Berne, Eric. (1972). *What do you say after you say hello?* New York: Bantam.

Bernhardt, Paul C. (1997, April 2). Influences of serotonin and testosterone in aggression and dominance: Convergence with social psychology. *Current Directions in Psychological Science, 66*, 44–48.

Boehm, Christopher. (1984). *Blood revenge: The anthropology of feuding in Montenegro and other tribal societies.* Lawrence: University Press of Kansas.

Bond, Michael Harris. (1997). *Working at the interface of cultures: Eighteen lives in social science.* London: Routledge.

Bond, Michael Harris. (1998). Unity in diversity: Orientations and strategies for building a harmonious, multicultural society. *Trames, A Journal of the Humanities and Social Sciences,* 234–263.

Bond, Michael Harris, Leung, Kwok, & Schwartz, Shalom H. (1992). Explaining choices in procedural and distributive justice across cultures. *International Journal of Psychology, 27,* 211–225.

Breines, Ingeborg, Connell, Robert W., & Eide, Ingrid (Eds.). (2000). *Males roles, masculinities and violence. A culture of peace perspective.* Paris: UNESCO.

Bremner, J. Douglas, Southwick, Stephen M., Brett, Elizabeth A., Fontana, Alan, Rosenheck, Robert, & Charney, Dennis S. (1992). Dissociation and posttraumatic stress disorder in Vietnam combat veterans. *American Journal of Psychiatry, 149,* 328–332.

Brislin, Richard W. (1993). *Understanding culture's influence.* Fort Worth, TX: Harcourt Brace Jovanovich.

Brittan, Arthur. (1989). *Masculinity and power.* Oxford, England: Blackwell.

Brod, Harry (Ed.). (1987). *The making of masculinities: The new men's studies.* Winchester, MA: Allen and Unwin.

Brundtland, Gro Harlem (1992). From the global jungle to the global village. In *Socialist Affairs, 4,* 14–17.

Calhoun, Lawrence G., & Tedeschi, Richard G. (1998). Beyond recovery from trauma: Implications for clinical practice and research. *Journal of Social Issues, 54*(2), 357–371.

Carver, Charles S. (1998). Resilience and thriving: Issues, models, and linkages. *Journal of Social Issues, 54*(2), 245–266.

Caspi, Avshalom, Moffitt, Terri E., Mill, Jonathan, Martin, Judy, Craig, Ian W., Taylor, Alan, & Poulton, Richie (2002, August). Role of genotype in the cycle of violence in maltreated children. *Science, 297,* 851–854.

Charny, Israel W. (1997). A personality disorder of excessive power strivings. *Israel Journal of Psychiatry, 34*(1), 3–17.

Christianson, Sven-Åke (Ed.). (1992). *The handbook of emotion and memory: Research and theory.* Hillsdale, NJ: Lawrence Erlbaum.

Clark, William R., & Grunstein, Michael (2000). *Are we hardwired?* New York: Oxford University Press.

Cohen, Lawrence H., Cimbolic, Kathleen, Armeli, Stephen R., & Hettler, Tanya R. (1998). Quantitative assessment of thriving. *Journal of Social Issues, 54*(2), 323–335.

Coleman, Peter T. (2000). Power and conflict. In Morton Deutsch & Peter T. Coleman (Eds.), *The handbook of conflict resolution: Theory and practice.* San Francisco: Jossey-Bass.

Connell, Robert W. (1995). *Masculinities.* Cambridge, England: Polity Press.

Connell, Robert W. (1996). Teaching boys: New research on masculinity, and gender strategies for schools. *Teachers College Record, 98*(2), pp. 206–235.

Connell, Robert W. (1997). *Arms and the man: Using the new research on masculinity to understand violence and promote peace in the contemporary world.* Oslo: Paper presented at the expert group meeting on "Male Roles and Masculinities in the Perspective of a Culture of Peace", Oslo, Norway, 24-28 September 1997.

Coser, Lewis A. (1977). *Masters of sociological thought: Ideas in historical and social context* (2nd ed.). Fort Worth, TX: Harcourt Brace Jovanovich.

Cushner, Kenneth, & Brislin, Richard W. (1996). *Intercultural interactions: A practical guide* (2nd ed.). Thousand Oaks, CA: SAGE.

Damasio, Antonio R. (1994). *Descartes' error. Emotion, reason and the human brain.* New York: Avon Books.

de Beauvoir, Simone. (1962). *The prime of life [La forcede l'âge I–II, 1960].* Cleveland, OH: World Publishing.

de Jong, H. Looren (1997). Some remarks on a relational concept of mind. *Theory & Psychology, 7*(2), 147–172.

Demos, Virginia (Ed.) (1995). *Exploring affect. Selected writings of S. S. Tomkins.* Oxford, England: Oxford University Press.

Deutsch, Morton, & Coleman, Peter T. (Eds.). (2000). *The handbook of conflict resolution: Theory and practice.* San Francisco: Jossey-Bass.

Douglas, Mary (1984). *Purity and danger: An analysis of the concepts of pollution and taboo.* London: Ark Paperbacks.

Durkheim, Emile (1993). *The division of labor in society.* New York: Macmillan.

Eitinger, L. (1990). Imprisonment in a concentration-camp and psychic traumatization. *Psyche-Zeitschrift Für Psychoanalyse Und Ihre Anwendungen, 44*(2), 118–132.

Elshtain, Jean Bethke (1995). *Women and war.* Chicago: University of Chicago Press.

Enloe, Cynthia (1990). *Bananas, beaches and bases: Making feminist sense of international politics.* Berkeley: University of California Press.

Enloe, Cynthia (2000). *Maneuvers: The international politics of militarizing women's lives.* Berkeley: University of California Press.

Epel, Elissa S., McEwen, Bruce S., & Ickovics, Jeannette R. (1998). Embodying psychological thriving: Physical thriving in response to stress. *Journal of Social Issues, 54*(2), 301–322.

Everly, George S. (1993). Psychotraumatology—a 2-factor formulation of posttraumatic stress. *Integrative Physiological and Behavioral Science, 28*(3), 270–278.

Figley, Charles R. (1989). *Helping traumatized families.* San Francisco: Jossey-Bass.

Firmo-Fontan, Victoria (2004). Polarization between occupier and occupied in post-Saddam Iraq: Humiliation and the formation of political violence. In *Terrorism and Political Violence.* Unpublished manuscript.

Fisher, Roger, Ury, William, & Patton, Bruce (1991). *Getting to YES. Negotiating agreement without giving in.* New York: Houghton Mifflin.

Flinders, Carol Lee. (2002). *Rebalancing the world: Why women belong and men compete and how to restore the ancient equilibrium.* San Francisco: HarperSanFrancisco.

Forrester, Michael A. (1999). Reflections and projections of the developing self. *Theory & Psychology, 9*(1), 29–46.

Foucault, Michel. (1972). *The Archaeology of Knowledge.* London: Tavistock.

Frankfurt, Harry G. (1997). Equality and respect. *Social Research, 64*(1), 3–15.

Fuller, John L., & Thompson, William R. (2003). *Foundations of behavior genetics.* St. Louis, MS: C. V. Mosby Company.

Fuller, Richard. (2005). *The Treaty of Versailles—28th June 1919.* Retrieved August 31, 2005, from http://www.rpfuller.com.gcse/history/2.html

Gerbode, Frank A. (2000). *Critical issues in trauma resolution.* Retrieved March 15, 2000, from http://www.healing-arts.org/tir/issues.htm

Gibson, James J. (1979). *The ecological approach to visual perception*. Boston: Houghton-Mifflin.

Gilligan, James (1996). *Violence: Our deadly epidemic and how to treat it.* New York: Putnam.

Goleman, Daniel (1996). *Emotional intelligence—Why it can matter more than IQ*. London: Bloomsbury.

Hale, Robert L. (1994). The role of humiliation and embarrassment in serial murder. In *Psychology. A Journal of Human Behaviour, 31*(2), 17–23.

Hamburg, David A. (2002). *No more killing fields: Preventing deadly conflict.* Lanham, MD: Rowman and Littlefield.

Hamer, Dean, & Copeland, Peter. (2000). *Living with our genes: Why they matter more than you think.*London: Pan Books.

Hanmer, Jalna, Hester, Marianne, Kelly, Liz, & Radford, Jill (Eds.). (1996). *Women, violence and male power: Feminist activism, research and practice.* Buckingham, England: Open University Press.

Hartling, Linda M., & Luchetta, Tracy. (1999). Humiliation: Assessing the impact of derision, degradation, and debasement. *Journal of Primary Prevention, 19*(5), 259–278.

Havermans, Jos. (1998). Many people feel burned out: Great Lakes Traumas Puzzle NGOs. *Conflict Prevention Newsletter, 1*(1), 2–3.

Hearn, Jeff. (1992). *Men in the public eye: The construction and deconstruction of public men and public patriarchies.* London: Unwin Hyman/Routledge.

Hobbes, Thomas. (1651). *Leviathan.* The APHIL Library, retrieved November 9, 2000, from http://coombs.anu.edu.au/Depts/RSSS/Philosophy/Texts/LeviathanTOC.html

Honneth, Axel (1997). Recognition and moral obligation. *Social Research, 64*(1), 16–35.

Hooper, Charlotte (2001). *Manly states: Masculinities, international relations and gender politics.* New York: Columbia University Press.

Horowitz, Karyn, Weine, Stevan M., & Jekel, James. (1995). PTSD symptoms in urban adolescent girls: Compounded community trauma. *Journal of the American Academy of Child and Adolescent Psychiatry, 34*(10), 1353–1361.

International Committee of the Red Cross Somalia Delegation. (1997). *Spared from the spear: Traditional Somali behaviour in warfare.* Nairobi: International Committee of the Red Cross.

Jones, Adam. (1994). Gender and ethnic conflict in ex-Yugoslavia. *Ethnic and Racial Studies, 17*(1), 115–134.

Jones, Edvard E. (1984). *Social stigma—The psychology of marked relationships.* New York, NY: W. H. Freeman.

Kardiner, Abraham. (1941). *The traumatic neuroses of war.* New York: Hoeber.

Kelman, Herbert C. (1999). The interdependence of Israeli and Palestinian national identities: The role of the Other in existential conflicts. *Journal of Social Issues, 55,* 581–600.

Kelman, Herbert C., & Society for the Psychological Study of Social Issues (1965). *International behavior: A social-psychological analysis.* New York: Holt, Rinehart and Winston.

Khayyat, Sana. (1990). *Honour and shame: Women in modern Iraq.* London: Saqi Books.

Kimmel, Michael. (1996). *The politics of manhood.* Philadelphia: Temple University Press.

Kimmel, Michael. (1997). *Reducing men's violence: The personal meets the political.* Paper presented at the expert group meeting on "Male Roles and Masculinities in the Perspective of a Culture of Peace," Oslo, Norway, 24–28 September 1997.

Kimmel, Michael. (2000). *The gendered society.* Oxford, England: Oxford University Press.

Klein, Donald C. (1991). The humiliation dynamic: An overview. The humiliation dynamic: Viewing the task of prevention from a new perspective I (Special Issue, Section 1). *Journal of Primary Prevention, 12*(2), 93–121.

Landis, Dan, & Brislin, Richard W. (1983). *Handbook of intercultural training.* New York: Pergamon Press.

Larrow, M. F., & Wiener, M. (1992). Stereotypes and desirability ratings for female and male roles. In Joan C. Chrisler & Doris Howard (Eds.), *New directions in feminist psychology: Practice, theory, and research.* New York: Springer.

Lavik, Nils Johan, Laake, P., Hauff, Edvard, & Solberg, Øivind (1999). The use of self-reports in psychiatric studies of traumatized refugees: Validation and analysis of HSCL-25. *Nordic Journal of Psychiatry, 53*(1), 17–20.

Lazarus, Richard S. (1966). *Psychological stress and the coping process.* New York: McGraw-Hill.

Lazarus, Richard S., & Folkman, Susan (1984). *Stress, appraisal and coping.* New York: Springer.

Lewis, Helen Block. (1971). *Shame and guilt in neurosis.* New York: International Universities Press.

Leymann, Heinz. (1990). Mobbing and psychological terror at workplaces. *Violence and Victims, 5*(2) 119–126.

Leymann, Heinz. (1996). The content and development of mobbing at work. In Dieter Zapf & Heinz Leymann (Eds.), *Mobbing and victimization at work. A special issue of the European Journal of Work and Organizational Psychology.* Hove, UK: Psychology Press.

Leymann, Heinz, & Gustafsson, Anneli. (1996). How ill does one become of victimization at work? In Dieter Zapf & Heinz Leymann (Eds.), *Mobbing and victimization at work. A special issue of the European Journal of Work and Organizational Psychology.* Hove, UK: Psychology Press.

Lindner, Evelin Gerda. (1999). Women in the global village: Increasing demand for traditional communication patterns. In Ingeborg Breines, Dorota Gierycz, & Betty Reardon (Eds.), *Towards a women's agenda for a culture of peace* (pp. 89–98). Paris: UNESCO.

Lindner, Evelin Gerda. (2000a). *Humiliation, rape and love: Force and fraud in the erogenous zones.* Oslo: University of Oslo. Manuscript submitted for publication.

Lindner, Evelin Gerda. (2000b). Were ordinary Germans Hitler's "willing executioners"? Or were they victims of humiliating seduction and abandonment? The case of Germany and Somalia. *IDEA: A Journal of Social Issues, 5*(1); see http://www.ideajournal.com/lindner-willing-executioners.html

Lindner, Evelin Gerda. (2000c). *What every negotiator ought to know: Understanding humiliation.* Oslo and Coalition for Global Solidarity and Social Development. Peace and Conflicts: http://www.globalsolidarity.org/articles/what.pdf

Lindner, Evelin Gerda. (2001a). How research can humiliate: Critical reflections on method. *Journal for the Study of Peace and Conflict,* Annual Edition 2001–2002, 16–36; see also on http://jspc.library.wisc.edu/

Lindner, Evelin Gerda. (2001b). Humiliation—Trauma that has been overlooked: An analysis based on fieldwork in Germany, Rwanda/Burundi, and Somalia. In *TRAUMATOLOGYe, 7* (1) Article 3 (32 pages); see http://www.fsu.edu/%7Etrauma/v7/Humiliation.pdf

Lindner, Evelin Gerda. (2001c). Humiliation and the human condition: Mapping a minefield. *Human Rights Review, 2*(2), 46–63.

Lindner, Evelin Gerda. (2001d). Humiliation as the source of terrorism: A new paradigm. *Peace Research, 33*(2), 59–68.

Lindner, Evelin Gerda. (2001e). *The concept of humiliation: Its universal core and culture-dependent periphery.* Unpublished manuscript, Oslo: University of Oslo.

Lindner, Evelin Gerda. (2001f). *The psychology of humiliation: Somalia, Rwanda/Burundi, and Hitler's Germany.* Oslo: University of Oslo, Department of Psychology, doctoral dissertation.

Lindner, Evelin Gerda. (2002a, March 1). Gendercide and humiliation in honor and human rights societies. *Journal of Genocide Research, 44,* 137–155; see also http://www.gendercide.org/affiliates.html

Lindner, Evelin Gerda. (2002b). Healing the cycles of humiliation: How to attend to the emotional aspects of "unsolvable" conflicts and the use of "humiliation entrepreneurship". *Peace and Conflict: Journal of Peace Psychology, 8*(2), 125–138.

Lindner, Evelin Gerda. (2002c). Mujeres en la aldea global: Creciente exigencia de los patrones tradicionales de comunicación. In Ingeborg Breines, Dorota Gierycz, & Betty Reardon (Eds.), *Mujeres a favor de la paz: Hacia un programa de acción* (pp. 117–129). Paris and Madrid: Ediciones UNESCO, NARCEA Ediciones.

Lindner, Evelin Gerda. (2003a). *Definitions of terms as they are used in Lindner's writing.* Unpublished manuscript, Oslo: University of Oslo.

Lindner, Evelin Gerda. (2003b, January 1). Humiliation or dignity: Regional conflicts in the *Global Village. The International Journal of Mental Health, Psychosocial Work and Counselling in Areas of Armed Conflict, 1,* 48–63; see also http://www.transnational.org/forum/meet/2002/Lindner_RegionalConflicts.html

Lindner, Evelin Gerda. (2003c). *Humiliation: A new basis for understanding, preventing, and defusing conflict and violence in the world and our lives.* Unpublished book manuscript, Oslo: University of Oslo.

Lukes, Steven. (1997). Humiliation and the politics of identity. *Social Research, 64*(1), 36–51.

Mack, Arien. (1997). The decent society—Editor's introduction. *Social Research, 64*(1), 1-1.

Malcolm, Noel. (1998). *Kosovo: A short history.* London: Papermac.

Margalit, Avishai. (1996). *The decent society.* Cambridge, MA: Harvard University Press.

Margalit, Avishai. (1997). Decent equality and freedom: A postscript. *Social Research, 64*(1), 147–160.

Marshall, Monty G. (1999). *Third World War: System, process, and conflict dynamics.* Lanham, MD, and London: Rowman and Littlefield; see also on http://members.aol.com/cspassoc/tww/index.html

Massey, Doreen. (1994). *Space, place and gender.* Cambridge, UK: Polity Press.

Masson, Philippe. (1996). When soldiers prefer death to humiliation. *Historia* (596), 54–56.

McCann, I. L., & Pearlman, Laurie Anne. (1992). Constructivist self development theory: A theoretical model of psychological adaptation to severe trauma. In D. K. Sakheim & S. E. Devine (Eds.), *Out of darkness: Exploring satanism and ritual abuse* (pp. 185–206). New York: Lexington Books.

Messner, Michael A. (1997). *Politics of masculinities: Men in movements.* Thousand Oaks, CA: SAGE.

Miller, William Ian. (1993). *Humiliation and other essays on honor, social discomfort, and violence.* Ithaca, NY: Cornell University Press.

Monbiot, George. (2003). *The age of consent: A manifesto for a new world order.* Hammersmith, UK: Flamingo.

Montville, Joseph V. (1990). The psychological roots of ethnic and sectarian terrorism. In Vamik D. Volkan, Demetrios A. Julius, & Joseph V. Montvill (Eds.), *The psychodynamics of international relationships: Vol I. Concepts and theories* (pp. 161–176). Lexington, MA: Lexington Books.

Montville, Joseph V. (1993). The healing function in political conflict resolution. In Dennis Sandole & Hugo van der Merwe (Eds.), *Conflict resolution theory and practice: integration and application* (pp. 112–127). Manchester, UK: Manchester University Press.

Morgan, David I I. J. (1992). *Discovering men: Sociology and masculinities.* London: Routledge.

Nadler, Arie, & Ben Shushan, D. (1989). 40 years later—Long-term consequences of massive traumatization as manifested by Holocaust survivors from the city and the Kibbutz. *Journal of Consulting and Clinical Psychology, 57*(2), 287–293.

Nathanson, Donald L. (1987). *The many faces of shame.* New York: Guilford.

Nathanson, Donald L. (1992). *Shame and pride: Affect sex and the birth of the self.* New York: Norton.

Nathanson, Donald L. (1996, Spring/Summer). What's a Script? *Bulletin of The Tomkins Institute, 3,* 1–4.

Nebehay, Stephanie (2000, April 7). "Honor Killings" of women said on rise worldwide. *Reuters Dispatch.*

Nisbett, Richard E., & Cohen, Dov. (1996). *Culture of honor: The psychology of violence in the south.* Boulder, CO: Westview Press.

Oksenberg Rorty, Amélie. (1997). From decency to civility by way of economics: "First let's eat and then talk of right and wrong." *Social Research, 64*(1), 112–130.

Olweus, Dan Åke. (1993). *Bullying at school. What we know and what we can do.* Oxford: Blackwell.

Olweus, Dan Åke. (1997). Bully/victim problems in school: Knowledge base and an effective intervention program. *Irish Journal of Psychology, 18*(2), 170–190.

Pearlman, Laurie Anne. (1994). *Vicarious traumatization: The impact of helping victims of genocide or group violence.* Santiago de Compostela, Spain: Paper presented at the Annual Meeting of the International Society of Political Psychology, July 12–15.

Pearlman, Laurie Anne. (1998). Trauma and the self: A theoretical and clinical perspective. *Journal of Emotional Abuse, 1,* 7–25.

Perry, Bruce D. (1994). Neurobiological sequelae of childhood trauma: Post-traumatic stress disorders in children. In M. Murberg (Ed.), *Catecholamines in post-traumatic stress disorder: Emerging concepts* (pp. 253–276). Washington, DC: American Psychiatric Press.

Peterson, V. Spike. (1992a). *Gendered states: Feminist (re)visions of international relations theory.* Boulder, CO: Lynne Rienner.

Peterson, V. Spike. (1992b). Transgressing boundaries: Theories of knowledge, gender and international relations. *Millennium—Journal of International Studies, 21*(2), 183–206.

Peterson, V. Spike, & Runyan, Anne Sisson. (1993). *Global gender issues.* Boulder, CO: Westview.

Pettit, P. (1997). Freedom with honor: A republican ideal. *Social Research, 64*(1), 52–76.

Polk, Kenneth. (1994). Masculinity, honour, and confrontational homicide? In Tim Newburn & Elizabeth Stanko (Eds.), *Just boys doing business? Men, masculinities and crime.* London/New York: Routledge and Kegan Paul.

Quinton, Anthony. (1997). Humiliation. *Social Research, 64*(1), 77–89.

Radford, Jill, & Russel, Diana (Eds.). (1992). *Femicide: The politics of woman killing.* Buckingham, England, UK: Open University Press.

Retzinger, Suzanne M. (1991). *Violent emotions: Shame and rage in marital quarrels.* Newbury Park, CA: SAGE.

Ripstein, Arthur. (1997). Responses to humiliation. *Social Research, 64*(1), 90–111.

Rodina, Mihaela. (1999, June 30). *Blood code rules in northern Albania.* Paris: Agence France-Presse dispatch.

Rose, Gillian (1993). *Feminism and geography: The limits of geographical knowledge.* Minneapolis: University of Minnesota Press.

Ross, Lee D., & Ward, Andrew. (1995). Psychological barriers to dispute resolution. *Advances in Experimental Social Psychology, 27*, 255–304.

Saakvitne, Karen W., Tennen, Howard, & Affleck, Glenn. (1998). Exploring thriving in the context of clinical trauma theory: Constructivist self development theory. *Journal of Social Issues, 54*(2), 279–299.

Scheff, Thomas J. (1988). Shame and conformity: The deference-emotion system. *American Sociological Review, 53*(3), 395–406.

Scheff, Thomas J. (1990a). *Bloody revenge: Emotions, nationalism and war.* Chicago: University of Chicago Press.

Scheff, Thomas J. (1990b). Socialization of emotions—Pride and shame as casual agents. In Theodore D. Kemper (Ed.), *Research agendas in the sociology of emotions* (pp. 281–304). Albany: State University of New York Press.

Scheff, Thomas J. (1997). *Emotions, the social bond and human reality. Part/whole analysis.* Cambridge, England: Cambridge University Press.

Scheff, Thomas J., & Retzinger, Suzanne M. (1991). *Emotions and violence: Shame and rage in destructive conflicts.* Lexington, MA: Lexington Books.

Scheler, Max. (1912). *Über Ressentiment und moralisches Werturteil.* Leipzig: Engelmann.

Scheler, Max. (1954). *The nature of sympathy.* London: Routledge and Kegan Paul.

Schick, Frederic. (1997). On humiliation. *Social Research, 64*(1), 131–146.

Schwartz, Shalom H. (1994). Beyond individualism/collectivism. New cultural dimensions of values. In U. Kim, Harry Charalambos Triandis, C. Kagitcibasi, S. C. Choi, & G. Yoon (Eds.), *Individualism and collectivism: Theory, method, and applications* (pp. 85–119). Newbury Park, CA: SAGE.

Shalhoub-Kevorkian, Nadera (2000). *Mapping and analyzing the landscape of femicide in Palestine.* Research report submitted by the Women's Center for Legal Aid and Counseling (WCLAC) to UNIFEM.

Smith, Dennis. (2002). The humiliating organisation: The functions and disfunctions of degradation. In Ad van Iterson, Willem Mastenbroek, Tim Newton, & Dennis Smith (Eds.), *The civilized organisation.* Amsterdam: Benjamin.

Smith, Peter Bevington, & Bond, Michael Harris (1999). *Social psychology across cultures: Analysis and perspectives.* (2nd ed.). Boston: Allyn and Bacon.

Spain, Daphne. (1992). *Gendered spaces.* Chapel Hill, NC: University of North Carolina Press.

Staub, Ervin. (1989). *The roots of evil: The origins of genocide and other group violence.* Cambridge: Cambridge University Press.

Staub, Ervin. (1990). Moral exclusion, personal goal theory, and extreme destructiveness. *Journal of Social Issues, 46*, 47–64.

Staub, Ervin. (1993). The psychology of bystanders, perpetrators, and heroic helpers. *International Journal of Intercultural Relations, 17*, 315–341.

Staub, Ervin (1996). Cultural societal roots of violence—The examples of genocidal violence and of contemporary youth violence in the United States. In *American Psychologist, 51*(2), 117–132.

Steinberg, Blema S. (1996). *Shame and humiliation: Presidential decision making on Vietnam.* Montreal/UK: McGill-Queen's.

Stout, Karen. (1992). "Intimate femicide": Effect of legislation and social services. In Jill Radford & Diana Russel (Eds.), *Femicide: The politics of woman killing.* Buckingham, England, UK: Open University Press.

Tajfel, Henri. (1984). Intergroup relations, social myths, and social justice in social psychology. In Henri Tajfel (Ed.), *The social dimension.* Cambridge, England: Cambridge University Press.

Tedeschi, James T., Schlenker, Barry R., & Bonoma, Thomas V. (1973). *Conflict, power, and games: The experimental study of interpersonal relations.* Chicago: Aldine.

Tickner, J. Ann (1992). *Gender in international relations: Feminist perspectives on achieving global security.* New York: Columbia University Press.

Tomkins, Silvan S. (1962–1992). *Affect imagery and consciousness* (Vols. I–IV). New York: Springer.

Triandis, Harry Charalambos. (1980). *Handbook of cross-cultural psychology.* Boston: Allyn and Bacon.

Triandis, Harry Charalambos. (1990). Theoretical concepts that are applicable to the analysis of ethnocentrism. In Richard W. Brislin (Ed.), *Applied cross-cultural psychology* (pp. 34–55). London: SAGE.

Triandis, Harry Charalambos. (1995). *Individualism-collectivism.* Boulder, CO: West.

Triandis, Harry Charalambos. (1997). *Culture and social behavior.* New York: McGraw-Hill.

UNESCO. (1994, September 27–29). *Final report over the first consultative meeting of the Culture of Peace Programme.* Paris: UNESCO.

Unger, Rhoda Kesler, & Crawford, Mary. (1992). *Women and gender: A feminist psychology.* New York: McGraw-Hill.

United Nations Development Programme (UNDP). (2002). *Human development report 2002: Deepening democracy in a fragmented world.* New York: Published for the United Nations Development Programme (UNDP), Oxford University Press. Retrieved November 2002, from http://www.undp.org/hdr2002/complete.pdf

Ury, William. (1999). *Getting to peace. Transforming conflict at home, at work, and in the world.* New York: Viking.

Vachon, Stéphane. (1993). Passer de l'appauvrissement à la pauvreté comme on va de l'humiliation à l'humilité. *Voix Et Images, 18*(2), 382–387.

van der Kolk, Bessel A. (1994). The body keeps the score: Memory and the evolving psychobiology of posttraumatic stress. *Harvard Review Psychiatry, 1*(5), 253–265.

van der Kolk, Bessel A., Blitz, R., Burr, W. A., & Hartmann, E. (1984). Nightmares and trauma: Life-long and traumatic nightmares in veterans. *American Journal of Psychiatry, 141,* 187–190.

van der Kolk, Bessel A., & Kadish, W. (1987). Amnesia, dissociation, and the return of the repressed. In Bessel A. van der Kolk (Ed.), *Psychological trauma.* Washington, DC: American Psychiatric Press.

van der Kolk, Bessel A., & van der Hart, O. (1989). Pierre Janet and the breakdown of adaptation in psychological trauma. *American Journal of Psychiatry, 146,* 1530–1540.

van der Kolk, Bessel A., & van der Hart, O. (1991). The intrusive past: The flexibility of memory and the engraving of trauma. *American Imago, 48*(4), 425–454.

Vogel, William, & Lazare, Aaron. (1990). The unforgivable humiliation: A dilemma in couples' treatment. *Contemporary Family Therapy, 12*(2), 139–151.

Volkan, Vamik D. (1988). *The need to have enemies and allies: From clinical practice to international relations.* Northvale, NJ: Jason Aronson.

Volkan, Vamik D. (1992). Ethnonationalistic rituals: An introduction. *Mind and Human Interaction, 4*, 3–19.

Volkan, Vamik D. (1994). *Turks and Greeks: Neighbours in conflict.* Huntingdon, UK: Eothen Press.

Volkan, Vamik D. (1997). *Bloodlines: From ethnic pride to ethnic terrorism.* New York: Farrar, Straus and Giroux.

Volkan, Vamik D., Demetrios, Julius A., & Montville, Joseph V. (Eds.) (1990). *The psychodynamics of international relationships.* Lexington, MA: Lexington Books.

Volkan, Vamik D., & Harris, Max (1995). Negotiating a peaceful separation: A psychopolitical analysis of current relationships between Russia and the Baltic Republics. In Mark F. Ettin, J. F. Fidler, & Bertram D. Cohen (Eds.), *Group process and political dynamics* (pp. 303–334). Madison, CT: International University Press.

Walby, Sylvia (1990). *Theorizing patriarchy.* Oxford, England: Blackwell.

Whitehead, Stephen M. (2002). *Men and masculinities: Key themes and new directions.* Cambridge, England: Polity Press.

Wrangham, Richard, & Peterson, Dale. (1996). *Demonic males.* New York: Houghton Mifflin.

Zalewski, Marysia, & Parpat, Jane (Eds.) (1998). *The "man question" in international relations.* Boulder, CO: Westview.

Znakov, Viktor V. (1990, January/February). The comprehension of violence and humiliation situations by aggressive adolescents. *Voprosy-Psikhologii*, 20–27.

CHAPTER 7

# LESSONS FOR THE REST OF US: LEARNING FROM PEACEFUL SOCIETIES

## Bruce D. Bonta and Douglas P. Fry

The Batek abhor interpersonal violence and have generally fled from their enemies rather than fighting back. I once asked a Batek man why their ancestors had not shot the Malay slave-raiders, who plagued them until the 1920s ... with poisoned blowpipe darts. His shocked answer was: "Because it would kill them!" (Kirk Endicott, 1988, p. 122)

Anthropologist Edwin Burrows (1963) comments on a tendency for people to assume that certain characteristics from their own culture can be found everywhere: "We generally assume that we know ... what is universally human. But a little scrutiny will show that such conclusions are based only on experience with one culture, our own. We assume that what is familiar, unless obviously shaped by special conditions, is universal" (p. 421). Thus the potency of Batek nonviolence, as illustrated in the above epigraph, may catch Western readers by surprise, for it dramatizes the possibility that common presumptions about violence may be false. The quotation suggests, for instance, that not all societies view responding to violence with counter-violence as being culturally appropriate. As we shall soon see, societies have very different beliefs about the appropriateness and inappropriateness of expressing violence. Some people have reacted to information about nonviolent cultures, such as the Batek, that contradicts their own beliefs about the universality of violence by simply dismissing peaceful societies as fantasy or exaggeration (e.g., Wrangham & Peterson, 1996). After all, much of what we see in the media corresponds with the proposition that humanity is basically violent. Another way to deal with this literature is to temporize, to make the peaceful societies seem irrelevant to the rest of us, to claim that these cultures can exist only in "special circumstances," so their relevance is limited at best. However, as we will consider in this chapter, the evidence for the existence of peaceful societies is incontrovertible. And rather than debunking or temporizing peaceful societies because they do not match certain preconceptions, it might be useful to ask instead, What might we learn about creating and maintaining peace from societies that are highly successful in handling conflicts nonviolently?

The first, basic lesson that peaceful societies hold is that *human beings clearly are capable of creating and living in societies with very little violence and dealing with conflicts in ways that do not involve physical force.* A second point, which forms the backbone of this chapter, is that *peaceful societies might hold some valuable insights for the rest of us about ways to reduce violence.* Therefore, we propose that examining societies that already have in place effective ways of keeping the peace can prove beneficial. Of course, no existing peaceful society can serve as a sole, perfect model for creating peacefulness in another social context. Each society has a unique history, experience, worldview, culture, social structure, geographical setting, and so forth. The one commonality with peaceful societies is that they are just that: quite peaceful. The goal of this chapter, then, is a hopeful one: to examine peaceful societies, to look at the welter of their complexities, and to explore several common features that may provide insights for replacing violence and war with less destructive ways of dealing with conflict in other cultural settings. The fact that scores of societies have already achieved high levels of peacefulness is surely important. In a sense, the peaceful societies have paved the way, unintentionally of course, and it is up to the rest of the world to see how they might be able to follow their paths. The various paradigms that undergird the peaceful societies, that provide the foundations for their social, psychological, and cultural structures of peacefulness, suggest that we could implement new approaches for dealing with conflict in the rest of the world.

## Conceptual Issues

Before considering several specific areas in which peaceful societies might hold practical lessons for reducing violence, it may be useful to examine several conceptual issues. A cross-cultural perspective reveals that the amount of physical aggression manifested within societies is highly variable. Each society can be viewed as occupying a position on a spectrum that ranges between high amounts of violence at one end and the virtual absence of physical aggression at the other, with most societies falling somewhere between the extremes (Fry, 2006). Visualizing a cross-cultural continuum of peaceful to violent is useful for several reasons. It suggests that dichotomizing between *peaceful* and *aggressive* cultures is an oversimplified distortion. Where should one make such a split between peaceful and aggressive anyhow? Any decision is arbitrary and thus open to debate. At the same time it is clear that relative to the vast majority of the cultures in the middle range of the continuum, at one end of the spectrum some societies are very peaceful, and at the other end of the spectrum some societies have much higher levels of aggression.

Viewing societies on a cross-cultural continuum also helps to emphasize that peacefulness is relative, not absolute (Gregor, 1996). In talking about peaceful societies, we do not propose that societies exist that are completely and totally devoid of all types of physical aggression. Rather, peaceful societies are those wherein acts of physical aggression are extremely rare. Furthermore, Ross (1993a) found, based on a cross-cultural sample of 90 societies, that internal conflict and external conflict are correlated. Ross's findings bear out the impression that there is a tendency for internally peaceful societies also to avoid engaging in war. There are exceptions to this pattern, however.

Another point to consider is that the peacefulness/aggressiveness of a given society is not immutably fixed through time. Shifts toward violence and shifts toward peacefulness occur over years, generations, and centuries. The fact that a culture has a high level of physical aggression today does not preclude a shift toward peacefulness in the future. For example, the Fipa, an agricultural society of 100,000 people in Tanzania, radically transformed their society in the nineteenth century, before European contact, from an aggressive, warlike culture to a highly peaceful one in which acts of violence are rare anomalies (Willis, 1989b). The Waorani of Ecuador provide another example of a transformation toward peacefulness as they managed to decrease their initially very high rate of homicide by over 90 percent in just a few years (Robarchek & Robarchek 1996a, 1998).

The creation of peace is a dynamic, ongoing process (Kemp, 2004; Nordstrom, 1997a, 1997b). Consequently, the amount of violence manifested within a society, whether high or low, should not be viewed as static and immutable. Shifts can and do occur (Dentan, 1992). Viewing the maintenance of peace as a dynamic process raises key questions: How can peaceful behavior be actively promoted within and among societies? How can violence actively be prevented and minimized? Shortly we will turn to existing peaceful societies for some insights.

Peaceful societies are not devoid of conflict. Individuals in any social group will have periodic differences in needs, desires, and interests—experience conflict, in other words. However, in most—perhaps all—societies, only a minority of conflicts actually lead to any form of physical aggression. A culturally comparative perspective shows that people deal with conflict in numerous nonviolent ways such as by avoiding each other, simply putting up with a difficult situation, talking it out, negotiation solutions, going to court, and so forth. There is also plenty of conflict in peaceful societies, but nearly all of it is handled without any violence.

Gregor (1996) points out that peace can by created and maintained in at least three spheres. *Sociative peace* entails the values, attitudes, and institutions that interconnect people via shared interests and sentiments—the basic fabric of social life—features that are antithetical to the expression of violence. Sociative peace is reflected in the attitude of a Ladakhi man, who when asked why he simply ignored an annoyance caused by a neighbor, responded, "We have to live together" (Norberg-Hodge, 1991, p. 46). Second, the concept of *restorative peace* applies to the ways in which conflict is handled so as to prevent or minimize violence. For instance, attitudes, practices, institutions, rituals that resolve grievances, prevent the escalation of conflict, and reconcile disputants constitute restorative peace. The *becharaa'* dispute resolution assemblies of the Semai, the *tultulan* collective discussions of the Buid, and the conflict-resolution meetings of Birhor elders are examples of restorative peace processes (Gibson, 1989; Robarchek, 1979, 1997; Sinha, 1972). Third, *separative peace* involves the prevention of violence through avoidance and deterrence. Gregor (1996, p. xx) refers to it as "the peace of nonrelationship." Nomadic hunter-gatherers, for example, are renowned for "voting with their feet" as disputants simply separate and join other bands Overall, the nomadic egalitarian type of hunter-gatherer social organization tends to be relatively peaceful compared to more complex forms of social organization (Fry, 2006; Kelly, 1995; Reyna, 1994; Service, 1966). In short, there are many ways to create and maintain peace and different societies adopt different approaches, some more effectively than others.

## Ethnographic Data on Peaceful Societies

Much anthropological information on peaceful cultures exists. In recent years the interest in this topic has proliferated (Bonta, 1993, 1996, 1997; Fabbro, 1978; Fry, 1999, 2001, 2006; Gregor, 1996; Gregor & Sponsel, 1994; Howell & Willis, 1989; Kemp & Fry, 2004; Levinson, 1994; Montagu, 1978; Ross, 1993a, 1993b; Sponsel, 1996a, 1996b; van der Dennen, 1995, Chapter 7). In preparing this chapter, we reviewed the anthropological and sociological literature to compile a list of societies that are *both internally peaceful and nonwarring*. This list of internally peaceful and nonwarring societies appears in the Appendix and includes over 40 cases. *Internally peaceful societies* tend to have values, attitudes, enculturation practices, and conflict-resolution procedures that emphasize nonviolent approaches to resolving social tensions and disputes (Bonta, 1996; Sponsel, 1996a). Internally peaceful societies—cultures with extremely low levels of physical aggression and corresponding beliefs that favor nonviolence—can be found in various parts of the world. In compiling this list of *nonwarring societies*, we differentiate warfare from feuding (see Otterbein, 1968, 1970). *War* is defined as "armed combat between political communities" (Otterbein, 1968, p. 279), whereas *feuding* is "blood revenge following a homicide" (Otterbein & Otterbein 1965, p. 1470). Boehm (1987, p. 221) points out, "Feuding is quite different from all-out warfare for several reasons: feuding is limited to one or two killings at a time; only one side takes the offensive at a time; and there is no necessary political objective beyond the maintenance of honor."

A few of the societies listed in the Appendix do engage in limited amounts of feuding, but all are nonwarring. We suspect that additional nonwarring, internally peaceful societies can be located in the literature, and thus we view this list as provisional. The list includes societies with various types of subsistence patterns. Some are hunter-gatherers (foragers), others are shifting cultivators, and still others are agriculturalists. They range from societies that live on the fringes of national economies to peoples who are integrated—economically—into modern industrial societies. Some of the peaceful societies number only a few hundred people, while others number in the tens of thousands. Peaceful societies can be found on all continents and come from many different ethnic backgrounds. As Sponsel (1994, p. 18) comments, "Nonviolent and peaceful societies appear to be rare—not because they are, in fact, rare, but because nonviolence and peace are so rarely considered in research, the media, and other arenas."

In this chapter, we present only a sampling from the anthropological and sociological data on peaceful societies. These data illustrate that peaceful social life is possible. We also address the practical question: What insights do peaceful societies offer for reducing violence and war in other social settings? In addressing this question, rather than giving light treatment to many ideas, instead we focus on three typical features of peaceful societies: nonviolent worldviews, core values such as respect that are antithetical to violence, and socialization processes.

## The Importance of Worldview for Creating Peace

[The] Semai ... have an image of themselves, developed during enculturation as nurturant, dependent, affiliative, and non-aggressive ... . It is regularly expressed in statements such as "The Malays and Chinese are always fighting, but we sit [quietly]." (Robarchek, 1980, p. 113)

One of the best ways to understand the behaviors of societies is to examine their religions, cosmologies, beliefs, and value systems—their so-called *worldviews*. Human behaviors are often based on the perceptions people make, their logical structures, and their assumptions. When outsiders ignore the ways other societies view their own experiences, when they try to define their realities for them, they may end up denying them rationality, or even worse, imposing their own worldviews on others (Silberbauer, 1994). Some anthropologists focus directly on the beliefs of the people they study. Spradley (1979, p. 3) points out, for instance, that Bronislaw Malinowski saw as the goal of ethnography "to grasp the native's point of view, his relation to life, to realize *his* vision of *his* world." This perspective offers a significant avenue for understanding social phenomena, such as the amount of violence or peacefulness in different societies.

Numerous ethnographies have been written about the worldviews of individual peaceful societies (Adhikary, 1984; Kirk Endicott, 1979; S. Howell, 1984; Robarchek, 1980). The worldview concept allows anthropologists to understand the societies they study and to explain their social conditions. Howell and Willis (1989) argue that violence can be viewed as the result of people acting on their values. By similar reasoning, peacefulness results as people, for the most part, behave in accordance with their nonviolent social beliefs and ideals. While the worldviews of the nonviolent societies certainly do not explain all of their actions, anymore than they would for any other society, the actions of most people in the peaceful societies do appear to be guided by their belief systems.

Is it possible to synthesize, at least to some extent, the worldviews of a number of similar societies? If successful, such a synthesis should provide insights into the common traits of those societies. If it is valid to compare the worldviews of different societies, and if we can accept the proposition that some societies are far less violent than others, then it ought to be reasonable to examine a group of peaceful societies to determine how their worldviews influence their actions. Do their beliefs in peacefulness translate into the absence of violence in their lives? Are the societies which focus their worldviews most strongly on peace the ones with the least violence? Do the societies which view nonviolence as more peripheral, in fact, have more incidents of violence?

To judge by the literature, the answers to these questions appear to be affirmative. For people in the most peaceful societies, avoiding violence—at least, thinking and feeling that they must avoid it—is not only real to many of them, it is defining for them. Individuals in some peaceful societies see themselves *as* peaceful, and they clearly take pride in that peacefulness, a striking contrast, in their minds, to other, manifestly less peaceful societies with which they come in contact. For some of these societies, particularly the most highly peaceful ones, this very sense of definition of themselves as nonviolent is the most critical aspect of their worldviews.

A few examples from highly peaceful societies illustrate this point. The Semai, Chewong, and Batek peoples who live in the mountains of Peninsular Malaysia clearly cherish and are committed to their own peacefulness. Peace is central to their beliefs. The Semai consider the peaceful unity of their group to be their highest ideal (Robarchek, 1979). They emphasize and re-emphasize the importance of resolving their disagreements nonviolently whenever they have meetings. The Chewong do not even have words for fighting, war, aggression, or crime, and their typical response to aggressive actions by outsiders is to flee immediately (S. Howell, 1984). An example illustrating the extent of nonviolent thinking among the Batek was presented in the chapter epigraph—it was unthinkable even to have harmed slave raiders. Similarly, the worldviews of the Piaroa, Ifaluk, Amish, Hutterites, Ladakhis, and Tristan Islanders, while very different from one another, all maintain their ideals of peacefulness at the heart of their systems of beliefs. These societies have a strong commitment to nonviolence and define themselves as peaceful. And, in fact, in these societies, as among the Semai, Chewong, and Batek, actual violent incidents of any kind are extremely rare to nonexistent.

Lighting up the differences in their beliefs throws the one similarity—the commitment to peacefulness—into sharper relief. Ifaluk is a fishing and gardening society on a small atoll in Micronesia. Spiro (1952, p. 497) writes that "this culture is particularly notable for its ethic of non-aggression, and its emphasis on helpfulness, sharing, and cooperation." Burrows (1952, p. 25) elaborates: "It was almost impossible to convey to the people the concept of murder, the thought of wantonly killing another person is so completely alien to their thinking." The people of Ifaluk link peacefulness to physical and emotional well-being. Good health, they believe, depends on effectively following the precepts of their worldview, which include their beliefs in *maluwelu, fago, mweol,* and *song,* among others. To the Ifaluk, *maluwelu* means calmness, either for a person or for the lagoon when the wind dies. In their understanding of the word, the *maluwelu* person is a giving person. *Maluwelu* is reciprocated, as much as is needed, with *fago,* a word that combines both love and compassion. The Ifaluk word *mweol,* generous, friendly, and obedient, suggests one of their idealized traits—reciprocal sharing. They view food, tobacco, and other goods as "our" food, "our" cigarettes, and so forth. *Song,* justifiable anger, will be provoked most strongly if people fail to share as they should. The positive traits which the Ifaluk so highly value—reciprocal sharing, nonaggression, cooperation, and calmness—are expressed by their trait words which describe the ideal person. For them, peacefulness is the central value of their beliefs (Lutz, 1985b; 1988). In practice, Lutz (1982, p. 114) tells us, "Murder is unknown; the most serious incident of aggression in a year involved the touching of one man's shoulder by another, a violation that resulted in the immediate payment of a severe fine."

The Amish worldview focuses on nonresistance, one of the central messages, they believe, that Christ delivered in the Sermon on the Mount. They see themselves as a separate society, a people who live in a broader society but are not part of it. They do not marry non-Amish, form business partnerships with them, or hold intimate social relations with them. The key to understanding the Amish worldview is the German word *Gelassenheit*, submission, a concept which includes simplicity, humility, thrift, and accepting the will of higher authorities. The Amish person yields to the will of God, serves others, is guided by the will of the group, and talks, acts, and dresses modestly. *Gelassenheit* implies abandoning one's will in favor of following divine will, as the Amish perceive Christ to have done. It suggests loving one's enemies, praying for them, and never taking revenge—as Christ commanded. To the Amish, their nonresistance prevents employing force in any human relationship: they cannot defend themselves if attacked, file law suits, serve on a police force or a jury, hold a political office, or engage in competition. If faced with hostile neighbors or governments they would simply sell or abandon their farms and move. They believe they are forbidden by Christ from becoming involved in any warfare or violence. They handle conflicts with silence and avoidance. There are almost no instances of violence or crime among the Amish (Kraybill, 1989).

On the opposite side of the earth, and radically different from the Amish, the Buddhist people of Ladakh, who farm and herd animals in the high Himalayan valleys of northern India, believe that the person who seriously wants to help others must be just as serious about trying to cleanse his own mind and heart, for only when the mind is clear of falseness, greed, and possessiveness can it guide one's actions. Such a pure spirit of inner strength and peace is essential, in their belief system, in order for one's love to have effect, in order to bring peace and strength to others. The individual who is in the world but not part of it, not stained by it, can be the most helpful. The lotus flower rises from the mud, but it is not composed of mud and has no mud on its petals. The perfection that should be sought is not only the perfection of mind and intelligence, it is also a perfection of the heart and of love. Both aspects are linked together in Buddhist thinking (Harvey, 1983). One observer, who lived among the Buddhist Ladakhis for 16 years, described arguments and aggression as "exceptionally rare;" villagers told her that "there has been no fighting in the village in living memory" (Norberg-Hodge, 1991, p. 46).

The Piaroa subsist in the forest along tributaries of the Orinoco River in "a place almost totally free of all forms of physical violence, where children, teenagers, and adults alike never express their anger through physical means" (Overing, 1986, p. 88). Their worldview focuses on mythological beliefs that support their fervent rejection of competition—it is equivalent to cannibalism—and of the ownership or control of resources. They are in constant danger from the violence of their mythic past, in which Wahari the Tapir constantly battled with his father-in-law Kuemoi the Anaconda. The Piaroa depict Kuemoi through slapstick comedy that illustrates their association of evil with excess and the lack of mastery over knowledge. Kuemoi lurks rather than hides, he laughs raucously, his evil deeds rebound on him, his plots are ridiculous. But part of the reason for the strife in the mythic past is the fact that Wahari did not reciprocate the relationship with Kuemoi, from whom he got his wife; he gave nothing in return, not even a child. Today the wild, dangerous, poisonous powers that could destroy human society are controlled by the celestial gods, secured by them in crystal boxes. They release the powers only cautiously so that the Piaroa experience peace, not violence. To assist this process, the shamans chant every night and blow the words of their chants into water and honey which, consumed the next morning by adults and children, will keep them safe for another day (Overing, 1985; 1986; Overing Kaplan, 1984).

The differences in beliefs between the Ifaluk, Amish, Ladakhis, and Piaroa are stark. But the concepts of peacefulness—*maluwelu, Gelassenheit,* inner peace, and nonviolence—are at the center of their widely differing belief systems. The reasons they so highly value nonviolence, and of course the ways peacefulness relate to other aspects of their beliefs, are unique to each society. The only common issue, the one point that can be generalized, is that *peacefulness is at the heart of each worldview.* This contrasts with other societies where peacefulness is fairly important, but it is not as central to them. One good example is the Zapotec village of "La Paz." The people of La Paz do not place nonviolence at the heart of their belief system: their primary values are cooperation, respect, and responsibility which, to some extent, achieve the same thing (O'Nell, 1981, 1986). Since those values are firmly accepted and acted upon by the people of La Paz, they do achieve some measure of peacefulness, in contrast to some neighboring Zapotec communities, where people do not effectively internalize those values and they are, as a result, fairly violent (Fry, 1992, 1994). But the modest occurrence of violence in La Paz highlights the fact that an ironclad commitment to nonviolence does not exist in the town.

This brief discussion of the relative importance of peacefulness within the worldviews of different societies suggests that a positive relationship exists between the intensity of belief in peacefulness and the actual lack of violence in societies. *People that maintain commitments to nonviolence as core values in their worldviews seem to be, in fact, among the most highly peaceful.* Other societies that do not have such a focus, that idealize peacefulness but do not keep it at the center of their beliefs, that restrict beliefs in peacefulness as a more peripheral part of their worldviews, experience, or at least tolerate, more violence. This is not to argue that the worldviews of the peaceful societies are the only cause of their nonviolence, but the more emphatically a society's belief system focuses on nonviolence, the more peaceful the society appears to be. It is not even clear from the literature if causation exists. Does a firmly held belief in peacefulness cause a society to be nonviolent, or is it possible that the reverse is true: the absence of violence causes the belief? Or do both feed on each other? All this review suggests is that while there are no simple relationships—human societies are too complex for that—there clearly appears to be a correlation between the degree of peacefulness in a society and how strong a commitment it makes to nonviolence. Other factors outside the scope of this chapter also help develop peacefulness in these societies, such as psychological structures which build and reinforce commitments to nonviolence (e.g., Lutz, 1985b), geographic isolation, economic structures, histories, and so on.

## Promoting Core Values That Are Incompatible with Violence: The Example of Respect

> Kindness, considerateness, and respect for another person's individual integrity are outstanding traits ... of the Tristan community ... . As one islander expressed it, "The worst thing you can do on Tristan is to be unkind to someone." (Munch & Marske, 1981, p. 165)

The morning after the September 11 terrorist attacks, Bonta had to go shopping at a small Amish farm stand in a nearby Pennsylvania valley. The proprietor had already heard about the events of the previous day from other customers, but since Bonta is a long-time customer she asked his opinions of the news while he looked over the vegetables. At first the conversation went well, but soon he started expressing his opinions in fairly forceful terms. As his condemnation of the senseless tragedy became more emphatic, the Amish proprietor became increasingly uncomfortable. Even though she doubtless agreed with his sentiments about violence, she evidently could not handle his forceful expressions. She grew silent and simply waited for him to take his tomatoes and leave.

The Amish—and most of the other peaceful societies as well—negatively value forcefulness, assertiveness, anger, and vehemence, along with such other egocentric character traits as boastfulness, self-assertion, and leadership. In one way or another, people in those societies feel that strong assertions of the self may undermine the values they place on respect for others, a key element in their social systems. The peaceful societies have different ways of handling respect, of course, different approaches to the issue. For the Amish, respect is engrained within their beliefs in submission and humility. Their gentleness and interpersonal deference help build very strong feelings of respect between one another and between their community and the rest of us. The first definition of respect in the dictionary is that it is the act of showing or feeling deferential regard and esteem for others. Respect suggests valuing other people as much as oneself or perhaps even slightly more so. Respect is certainly a virtue that Americans in general believe in and practice, but it has rarely been as deeply felt in the mainstream society of the United States as it is in the peaceful societies. For them, it is an all pervasive element, a virtue, a commitment that, to our American way of thinking, they seem to exaggerate.

Respect is normally felt and expressed in a reciprocal manner in peaceful societies. The farming people of rural Thailand respect people who have higher social status simply because of their positions, but the people in the superior positions almost always respect those with less status because their society requires it, because they believe in respecting the essential dignity of all people. Thai children are socialized with this firm belief in respect. They are raised to accept their position in the authority structure of the family and society, but Thai adults respect the essential dignity of their children, even of babies. Parents will try to inculcate good habits in children by example and coaxing, but if they are not able to persuade, or get their way through a withdrawal of affection, the adults will simply give up and admit that the children have the right to decide what they will do. Their will must be respected. In rural Thailand, adults maintain respect for others through avoidance and indirection. They try to avoid face-to-face conflict through constant good humor, affability, friendliness, conviviality, and gentleness with one another. Their conversations are marked by nervous giggling and discussions of inoffensive or inconsequential topics, as people strive to find out what the others are thinking in order to maintain a minimal amount of interpersonal contact. While those characteristics are not unique to the Thai villagers, they emphasize them with a ritualized, stylized mode of behavior. As a result, there is little overt interpersonal aggressiveness. If two people in rural Thailand so much as feel that there might be the possibility of a quarrel, they will separate to avoid it (Phillips, 1965). Similarly, feelings of respect are reciprocated regardless of status or social position among other peaceful societies, such as the Tristan Islanders (Munch, 1945), the Fipa (Willis, 1989b), the Ifaluk Islanders (Lutz, 1985a), and the Zapotec of La Paz village (O'Nell 1986, 1989).

Respect permeates almost all levels of the peaceful societies—it is especially pervasive among peoples who want to avoid trouble with anyone. Respect for neighboring peoples is an important strategy that some of the peaceful societies realize will help to maintain external peace (Bennett, 1967), an idea that appears to be largely ignored in the contemporary American approach to strategic international thinking. Within each peaceful society, respect permeates human relationships, no matter how closely people are related. Among married couples in most of the peaceful societies, men have a very high degree of respect for their wives. Some of the societies are highly egalitarian (Morris, 1982); in others the men have a clearly higher status than their wives (Mann, 1972). But we emphasize, a strong sense of respect for women prevails throughout the literature on peaceful societies (e.g., Willis, 1989a). Spouses are not necessarily close in all of these societies (though they are very close in many), and of course many families in less peaceful societies are close as well. But family respect seems to be one of the most critical foundations for the all-pervasive nonviolence in the peaceful societies.

Respect is not only deeply felt by people in the peaceful societies, it is emphasized, exaggerated, in our terms carried to an extreme. It is essential, they appear to feel, for the success of their peacefulness. The most vivid, perhaps the most extreme form of showing respect for others may be practiced by the Buid, a society of shifting cultivators in the mountains of Mindoro Island in the Philippines. One of the ways the Buid show their respect for others is to avoid, as much as possible, any possibility of stressful, dyadic interpersonal relationships. When two individuals converse, they do not face one another or address comments or questions directly to the other person; instead, they often sit facing the same direction, or even back-to-back, making comments that the other person may or may not respond to, depending on whether he or she agrees. Rather than contradicting the speaker, the listener may make his or her own comments on a different subject, to which the first speaker may respond or not, or change the subject again. When the Buid are preparing to engage in cooperative agricultural tasks such as clearing, planting, or harvesting, the community will get together, everyone squatting and facing in the same direction, perhaps concentrating on a distant mountain. Each person will address the group and indicate his need for assistance; if conflicts are perceived, the parties will talk them out. In no case, though, do two individuals address each other: instead, individual comments are made to the group as a whole. Since the speaker is an individual and the listener a group, clashes of wills are avoided. Avoiding social interaction between symmetrical units such as individuals minimizes confrontations, competition, and the possibility of conflict among people who consistently condemn any acts of boastfulness, aggression, or violence, and who place no value on the concepts of courage or braver (Gibson, 1986, 1988).

Sometimes when peaceful hunter-gatherers have given up their nomadic ways, rates of violence seem to have increased (Kent, 1989). However, in other cases, nonviolent nomadic societies in which respect is highly valued seem to lose very little of their peacefulness when they settle into stable, permanent communities. Inuit people who have moved into a town in the Canadian Arctic have adapted their traditional means of communicating strong feelings, tensions, and hostilities into modern forms that preserve their traditions of mutual respect. Traditionally they cleared the air with song duels, stylized encounters where individuals competed with one another to display their tensions through elaborate narrative songs that allowed people to resume reasonable personal contacts (Eckert & Newmark, 1980). Now they convey their feelings on call-in talk radio programs, on which vaguely worded, sometimes very practical personal messages convey many levels of meaning but preserve face and a sense of mutual respect (Briggs, 2000). Similarly, the Paliyan people who have settled into a stable village in the plains of South India try very hard to preserve everyone's sense of respect, the same as the more nomadic Paliyans who still subsist in the forested mountains nearby. Almost all Paliyans are highly uncomfortable with behavior that suggests that some people might be more capable or in any way above others. In both the Paliyan village in the plains and the more nomadic settlements in the forest, the strong ethic of respect fosters forbearance instead of conflict after most insensitive incidents. Aggressive incidents may occur slightly more often among the settled Paliyans, but those incidents of aggression recorded by one anthropologist in the village were nonetheless really very mild. They were shocking to the Paliyans, but they actually consisted of just a few light slaps, a brief swat on the buttocks of a disobedient child, and so on (Gardner, 2000a, 2000b, 2004).

A high level of respect and deference for others is not just endemic within peaceful nomadic or recently settled hunter-gatherer societies. The literature on peaceful societies reveals strong manifestations of respect in various social contexts. An atmosphere of respect, for instance, suffuses the sociological literature on the farming and fishing people of Tristan da Cunha, a small island in the South Atlantic that was settled by Europeans, Americans, and Africans nearly 200 years ago. As in almost all activities of the islanders, leadership exists only in a very discrete fashion, if at all, a characteristic that is common to most of the peaceful societies. Commands are rarely, if ever, given, even in the operation of landing the longboat, which requires exacting precision, skill, and coordination if everyone is to make it safely back through the surf to shore. The helmsman scarcely gives any commands or directions; he may make quiet suggestions in a soft voice, in the same tone as other quiet conversation, that imply another man might want to do something a little bit differently and it might make the course of the boat improve a little. In their gentle working relations they are humble, yet dignified and poised with one another (Munch, 1971). But it may not be appropriate to label the social practices on Tristan as an extreme example of practicing respect. It might be better to label the Tristan Islanders as people who passionately believe in their ideal of peacefulness and who realize that a fervent commitment to respecting others is an essential ingredient of that belief. It is important to add that a fight has not occurred on Tristan in living memory, and quarrels are very rare. Even personal disagreements that prompt individuals to avoid speaking with one another cause a lot of stress, so the Islanders do not allow even mild tensions to last very long (Munch, 1945).

There are a number of ramifications of this strong sense of respect that prevails in these societies. For one thing, there are few winners and losers, and very few instances of competition—perhaps they feel that respect for someone might be compromised if people had to admit that one individual was less capable than others. The young people in the peaceful societies play many games, but they are almost always noncompetitive in nature (Bennett, 1967; Dentan, 1968; Draper, 1976; Ehrenfels, 1952; Kirk Endicott, 1979; Hostetler & Huntington, 1971; Howell, 1988; Overing, 1989; Silberbauer, 1981). Avoiding winners or losers and maintaining everyone's respect may be part of the reason these societies tend not to make decisions by voting. In peaceful societies, including those that subsist on hunting and gathering, those that have stable agricultural systems, and those that are more or less integrated within modern industrial societies, the recurring pattern is for people to resolve issues by consensus—avoiding confrontations that produce clear winners and loosers—and thereby preserve their strong sense of mutual respect.

## The Next Generation: Socialization and Internalization Processes

The Waura [believe] that selfish or violent behavior, and especially cruelty to children is ... shameful: "The whiteman ... beats and kicks his own children; this too I have seen. This is not the way human beings behave. This is why the whiteman is so angry and brutal. He mistreats and abuses his children when they are small, and so they grow up filled with the anger their parents have put into them, and do not know how to be men." (Ireland, 1988, pp. 160–161)

In this section, we will contrast the United States, as an example of a society in which a substantial amount of violence is tolerated and the statistics on child abuse are disturbing, to what children typically experience in peaceful societies. According to a 1989 estimate, between 1,200 and 5,000 children die in the United States each year from abusive treatment, and more than 160,000 suffer from serious physical harm. Using a broader concept of maltreatment, which includes neglect as well as abuse, in 1988 about 2.4 million American children were maltreated to the extent that the problems were reported to state, county, or municipal protection and social service agencies (Reiss & Roth, 1993). If the definition of severe violence includes hitting the child with an object such as a strap or paddle, over 11 percent of American children were abused in 1985 (Straus, 1991).

The difficulty with including strapping or paddling in the calculation of violence is the fact that most Americans insist on exempting corporal punishment from definitions of child abuse. Cultural norms in the United States that favor corporal punishment of children are widely accepted. Research on the acceptability of punishment has produced varying results. One study showed that the percentage of parents and other primary caregivers who believe in punishment had dropped from 94 percent in 1968 to 68 percent in 1994, although belief in it remains very strong. However, another survey of American attitudes revealed that in 1970, 77 percent of Americans felt that corporal punishment of children was necessary, and in 1993 the number had grown very slightly to 80 percent (Tedeschi & Felson, 1994). Whichever may be the case, when a wave of American states passed laws designed to prevent child abuse, they were written so that continuing physical punishment by parents was not affected. Corporal punishment has been outlawed in some American schools, but it has not been curtailed in the homes; a backlash in some states has sought to protect potentially abusive parents from interference by child protective agencies (Straus & Mathur, 1996). Social scientists might not be so concerned if there were no connection between violent treatment of children and family violence in general—but that is not the case.

A number of studies have indicated that corporal punishment and violent treatment in general have harmful effects on children: a higher percentage of children who are abused go on to become criminals compared to children who are not abused, people who are convicted of assaults are very likely to have parents that punished them harshly, children who are punished physically are likely to respond with violence toward their parents and siblings, and aggressive, antisocial boys are much more likely than other boys to respond aggressively to punishment by their parents (Berkowitz, 1993; Gelles & Cornell, 1990; Straus, 1995; Wauchope & Straus, 1995; Widom, 1989). The National Family Violence Survey showed that there is a positive relationship between physical punishment received during childhood and assault of spouses later in life. The reason is that *corporal punishment teaches children that violence is to be expected, particularly between family members who may otherwise love one another.* To express this another way, corporal punishment shows that it is all right to hit people you love. This lesson is especially clear if the parent who administers the punishment is caring and loving (Straus, 1991).

One of the reasons Americans may be so supportive of corporal punishment is that part of their worldview—control, order, and stability—appears to demand it. The American emphasis on punishment is particularly strong among conservative Protestants, whose views influence the rest of the country (Ellison & Barthowski, 1997). Ellison and Barthowski (1997) suggest that conservative Protestants believe that punishment is an appropriate and necessary aspect of a hierarchical, authoritarian society that is prescribed by the Bible and is exemplified by the shepherd/flock relationships of God to his people, the minister to his congregation, and the parent to his or her children. The biblically ordained punishing of children conveys the conservative view of God as the giver of love and the punisher of sin. The parent acts in the place of God, to teach the child His ways, by serving as an example of God's love and divine authority, neither of which is complete without the other. This worldview, based on biblical inerrancy, includes clear lines that prohibit child abuse and yet require punishment for children, especially for willful disobedience. The important issue is for children to be obedient to their parents, as adults must be obedient to the will of God. Protestant leaders are often aware that this sacralized commandment to perform corporal punishment might lead to a predisposition to increased aggressiveness and violence (Ellison & Barthowski, 1997). Other Americans may not have as strong a religious basis for their belief in corporal punishment, but it is a practice that is deeply rooted in American thinking and culture history (Barnett, Miller-Perrin, & Perrin, 1997; Walters, 1975). "It goes without saying that spanking children is about as common, and viewed as equally normal, as Pampers. Parents have told us again and again that their kids 'need to be hit' or 'deserve to be hit' " (Gelles & Straus, 1988, p. 53).

In contrast to all of this, the beliefs of the people in most peaceful societies focus on raising their children to perpetuate their nonviolence. As their worldviews differ radically from those of most Americans, and to some extent from each other, so also do many aspects of their child-raising strategies differ radically from those employed in the United States. Typically, for people raised in peaceful societies the idea that an adult would physically abuse a child is inconceivable. The types of physical punishment observed by anthropologists in peaceful societies tend to be infrequent and very mild—by no stretch of the imagination do they constitute child abuse. Among the La Paz Zapotec, the typical punishment episode consisted of only one contact behavior—one pull on a child's arm, a rap with the knuckles to the child's forehead, or one slap, for instance (Fry, 1993). More serious forms of punishment were never witnessed in La Paz. Among the Paliyans, Gardner (2000a, 2000b, 2004) reports comparably mild and infrequent use of punishments by parents. Observing only 10 punishment incidences in 202 days, Gardner (2004, p. 62) describes a typical episode as "a mother scurrying after a child, usually a four- to seven-year-old, protesting its behavior in a relatively normal-level voice, and perhaps swatting toward it with her hand, a piece of grass, or a flaccid frond of greenery—very mild acts by most cultural standards." Among the Semai, physical punishment usually entails only the pinching of the child's cheek or the patting of the child's hands (Dentan, 1968).

The literature on peaceful societies suggests that child abuse is so rare as to be virtually nonexistent. Consequently, the issues that call for consideration relate not to child abuse but rather to understanding positive strategies for raising nonviolent children. Is punishment, in fact, an important aspect of their child-raising beliefs? How do they discipline their children? How do they handle instances of children's aggressions? Most important of all, how do they raise their children to believe in nonviolence and to internalize the value of practicing it with others?

In the nonviolent societies, parents seem to recognize the importance of their own peaceful behaviors in setting favorable examples for their children. Some of the societies favor talking with children who misbehave in order to correct and educate them, since they feel that talking with children, explaining correct patterns of behavior, and other nonviolent strategies are the most effective ways of getting youngsters to internalize patterns of nonviolence (Fry, 1992, 1993, 1994). Many of these societies do not place much faith in physical punishment of children because they feel it might produce adults who are not able to control their tempers, who may become aggressive when they grow up (Lutz, 1985b). The Batek, for example, are highly opposed to physically punishing their children, and in fact to any interpersonal violence—they flee from enemies instead of fighting. Neither Batek fathers nor mothers will assume authoritarian relationships with their children. What little authority they feel they have over their children is shared equally. Parents may tell their children they are irritated with their behavior, but children are free to ignore them. Parents rarely if ever strike a child: their word *sakel* means both "to hit" and "to kill," abhorrent concepts to them. They do threaten children with punishment by their thunder god if they misbehave, but neither parent is seen as a punishing figure. In fact, Batek fathers tend to be as close to their children as are the mothers—they sleep with them, cook for them, and keep them clean and safe. The children are raised to devalue, in fact, not even to consider, violence as a reaction to threats or aggressiveness (Kirk Endicott, 1988; Karen Lampell Endicott, 1992).

Some of the peaceful societies are so highly indulgent that children are not taught any belief in the higher authority of parents. Children are free to obey their parents or not, as they wish—and they are free to suffer the consequences of ignoring the recommendations of adults. They are rarely ordered to do things and are rarely if ever physically punished, as among the Buid, for example (Gibson, 1986). In one traditional Ju/'hoansi camp, for instance, a father who was engaged in a conversation with an older man called repeatedly to his son to bring him his tobacco. The boy ignored him and finally yelled back that he should get it himself. The father got up and fetched the tobacco without any recriminations toward his son (Draper, 1975). If the parent or older sibling is not able to convince a child to do something, or not to do something, he or she will simply give up and admit that the child has the right to decide what to do, which must be respected (Dentan, 1968; Phillips, 1965).

However, punishment is used quite strenuously by a few of the nonviolent societies, especially the societies based on European cultural roots: the Amish, Hutterites, and Tristan Islanders. Sociologists who have investigated these three Western-based societies have reported how important strong male authority is to them. To the Hutterites, an unquestioning obedience to authority is essential for raising children properly, though they do not teach children to feel guilty about their behavior since they believe that by teaching them to accept higher authority, children will learn correctly to direct their own actions. Adults mete out physical punishment quickly whenever infractions of the rules are discovered (Hostetler, 1974; Hostetler & Huntington, 1996). Amish children similarly learn when they are quite young that they must obey their parents or they will receive a sound physical punishment. Obedience to higher authority is one of the foremost principles of their society and is instilled quite effectively by parents (Hostetler, 1980; Hostetler & Huntington, 1971). The Tristan Island family is also strongly patriarchal—children are expected to obey their parents' directives and are subject to stern corporal punishment if they do not (Loudon, 1970; Munch, 1945). Despite their authoritarian family styles, these societies are quite successful in maintaining a high degree of nonviolence. Their basic strategy is to quickly make the children compliant, docile, and quietly accepting of the rules of the society.

The common element for virtually all of the peaceful societies, both those that punish and those that do not, is that adults consistently apply their nonviolent worldviews, and the social control needed to attain them, in their child-raising practices. Raising children to be nonviolent requires more than just an intense commitment to peacefulness at the center of the societies' beliefs, and a consistent approach to child raising that socializes children into accepting that worldview. The peaceful societies also train their children using a variety of psychological approaches to reinforce their nonviolent beliefs. The ways they socialize their children vary from one society to the next, so generalizations are difficult and tentative. But it can be argued that their peacefulness is as much based on the effectiveness of their socializing styles and the psychological conditioning they use on their children as it is on their beliefs in nonviolence.

While only a minority of the peaceful societies use any corporal punishment at all, quite a number socialize their children to be fearful. They are taught to fear a variety of possible events, such as hostile spirits, dangerous animals, strange people, exclusion from the group, and potential natural disasters (Hostetler & Huntington, 1996; Levy, 1969; O'Nell, 1979; Robarchek, 1977). The literature on a sizable group of the peaceful peoples indicates that they inculcate fear into their children in order to make them more docile and more fearful of anger or other strong emotions. Their strategy produces adults who will be hesitant to aggressively forward their own interests, since that might provoke others. They try to emphasize uncertainty about the intentions of others, so that even though children are raised in environments where everyone talks about the importance of nonviolence, and of course acts peacefully, one cannot be absolutely sure of the love and continuing goodwill of others. Children in these societies internalize the belief that they must constantly be alert to danger signals of possible conflicts, even with the closest family members, and to adjust their actions accordingly. Several of the societies scare their children by telling them that bogeys of various descriptions will get them if they do not act properly. Ifaluk adults teach children that a special kind of ghost will get them if they wander away from the house or misbehave, and they will go so far as to have one of the women dress up in a costume and impersonate the ghost, which appears menacingly at the edge of the compound and threatens to kidnap and eat the wayward child. When the child reacts in terror, the protective adult will tell the ghost that the child will no longer misbehave any more and tells the ghost to go away (Lutz, 1983).

A number of the peaceful societies rely on more positive strategies to correct their children's misbehaviors, approaches which Americans might view more approvingly than fear-inducing techniques, such as the use of bogeys. Perhaps the most important one is the power of adult example—nonviolent, supportive, socially correct, behavior. In some cases, adults seem to realize that since they rarely display aggression, their children will have little opportunity to emulate aggressive behaviors (Briggs, 1970; Draper, 1978; Norberg-Hodge, 1991). The fact of growing up in a society where violence is rare to nonexistent is supplemented, reinforced, and cemented by constant adult repetition of their worldview of nonviolence. This is as critical as the example of peacefulness that the children witness. For instance, children raised in the relatively nonviolent Zapotec community of La Paz not only are rarely exposed to violence on the part of their parents, they also hear adults constantly expressing the opinion that they have a peaceful community. Parents reiterate that people do not fight in this town, we are always respectful of others, we do not get jealous, and we always act in a cooperative fashion with others. Ideals and behavior patterns of adults mesh in patterns that convince the children to diffuse their own aggressive feelings and grow up to be as nonviolent as their parents (Fry, 1992). As a father from La Paz expressed,

> If my boy sees that I also do not have respect for other persons, well ... he thus acquires the same sentiment. But if I have respect for others, well he imitates me. It is done like this. Above all, the father must make himself an example, by showing how to respect. (1993, p. 183)

A number of other societies have similar approaches: children have few opportunities to learn aggressive behaviors since they rarely see their parents or other adults fighting, and they are not, themselves, objects of aggression or corporal punishment. The worldview of these societies is presented to children devoid of the contradictions of aggression or violence (Robarchek, 1980).

Several of the peaceful societies—for example, the Ju/'hoansi, G/wi, Kadar, and Paliyan—are also notable for employing a strategy that should be known as "affectionate distraction," a very positive, peaceful way of helping children learn not to solve problems through violence or aggression. Whenever small children exhibit signs of aggression, adults quickly intervene to diffuse their hostilities. When children try to abuse their own parents or other adults, or start acting aggressively toward their peers, adults will carry them off and distract them into other activities. This distraction is often done with a lot of laughter or other behavior that will excite the child's interest in something different from what they were just doing. When they are distracting children in this fashion, adults do not punish them for their truculent behaviors (Draper, 1978; Ehrenfels, 1952; Gardner, 1966; Silberbauer, 1972; D. J. Thomas, 1994).

The important issue for these parents and for other adults is to prevent and prohibit aggression whenever children shows signs of it. In the nonviolent societies, not surprisingly, adults have an intolerance for fighting or any other displays of aggression; in many they will actively tell their children to not fight (Dentan, 1968; Draper, 1976; Hold, 1980). The Ifaluk Islanders constantly remind their children of their concept of love, which to them includes the idea of compassion. If a toddler picks up an object and starts to make a threatening gesture toward another, nearby adults will immediately remind the youngster to remember the need to love/have compassion on the other (Lutz, 1988). Even in the societies that do not limit a child's autonomy, the only limit that adults place on the freedom of their children is to actively prevent them from expressing physical aggressiveness to others. The relatively less violent and more violent Zapotec communities—La Paz and neighboring San Andrés—illustrate the different ways of viewing children between people who emphasize violence and people who emphasize peacefulness. The people in the more violent town see children as naturally unruly and mischievous: they expect and even condone fighting among their children so they punish them severely. Adults in the nearby more peaceful town view their children as respectful, good, and responsible; they actively discourage fighting, and, as indicated previously, they rarely punish them (Fry, 1988).

## Conclusion: Insights from Peaceful Societies

> Respect for the rights of others is peace. (Benito Juárez, Zapotec leader and former President of Mexico, as cited in Fry, 1992, pp. 621, 636)

Clearly, peaceful societies provide insights relevant for reducing violence (Fry, 2004). In this brief chapter, we can only begin to examine the implications that peaceful societies hold for creating and maintaining peace. We have chosen to emphasize three areas that recur across otherwise diverse peaceful societies: nonviolent worldviews, core values that are incompatible with violence, respect being a recurring example, and socialization processes that entail the minimal use of physical force by adults coupled with the discouragement of physical aggression by children and youth.

The mere existence of a substantial number of internally peaceful and nonwarring societies is important, because it challenges a set of assumptions about the naturalness of violence and the inevitability of war. Such assumptions have a long history in Western thought and are reflected in a batch of recent books (e.g., Ghiglieri, 1999, Keeley, 1996, Wrangham & Peterson, 1996), which place great emphasis on the human capacity for violence, sometimes in melodramatic terms: "We live in a world in which cheaters, robbers, rapists, murderers, and warmongers lurk in every human landscape" (Ghiglieri, 1999, p. 246). With some variation from author to author, humanity is once again portrayed as basically violent and warlike.

Humans are capable of engaging in many forms of interpersonal and group violence from murder to war. Nonetheless, the painting of all humanity as natural-born killers, a characterization so stridently advocated in some recent writing, goes far beyond the facts, as is clear from the data presented in this chapter (Fry, 2001). Furthermore, exaggerating the human capacity for violence while dismissing the human capacities for creating and maintaining peace can contribute to detrimental consequences in the real world. The message that humans are naturally warlike can lead to a self-fulfilling prophecy that justifies the use of violence and military force as simply inevitable. It is a parallel situation to how slavery was justified in past centuries by citing as a self-evident "fact" that people of European descent were naturally superior to other peoples (e.g., Gould, 1978). In a parallel way, some people today evoke the self-evident fact that humans are naturally warlike as a rationale or justification for warfare. Barash (1991, p. 22) elaborates:

> If war is considered inevitable, and societies therefore prepare to fight—for example, by drafting an army, procuring weapons that threaten their neighbors, following a bellicose foreign policy—war may well result. And that fact will then be cited as proof that the war was inevitable from the start; moreover, it will be used to justify similar behavior in the future.

In sum, an important insight from peaceful societies that is directly relevant to creating a more peaceful world is that their very existence demonstrates that humans have a substantial capability to prevent, limit, and handle conflicts nonviolently. The existence of peaceful societies shows that violence and warfare are not inevitable. This insight offers hope for breaking away from a long-standing self-fulfilling prophecy.

The observation that peaceful societies have nonviolent worldviews and core values that are incompatible with the expression of violence raises some challenging questions. If attitudes toward peacefulness and strong commitments to it in fact strengthen nonviolence in peaceful societies, could modern societies in general be more peaceful if people were able to develop more nonviolent worldviews? Or, on a more practical level, would modern societies experience a radical drop in their levels of violence if they were to take seriously the peaceful beliefs that already form part of their existing worldviews? Conversely, do worldviews that accept violence, or that are at least willing to allow for various forms of antisocial human behavior, lead to higher rates of violence? A preliminary comparison of the nonviolent worldviews in peaceful societies with those in more violent societies suggests that this, in fact, may be the case. Can people, through the process of reviewing, challenging, and changing their ideologies, beliefs, and attitudes take an active role in modifying the worldviews of their societies, perhaps from tacitly accepting violence into unconditionally rejecting it? Is a commitment to a worldview of nonviolence perhaps one of the essential elements, one of the cornerstones, of creating peace? The peaceful societies provide examples of the challenges that face modern societies that want to do more than just study and talk about peace.

People tend to take the worldview of their native culture for granted, learning and accepting its features without much question. Over centuries, a shared worldview has emerged within and among nations that accepts the institution of warfare. The majority of leaders and people on the planet, although certainly not favoring war, simply accept the validity of this social institution that has recurred throughout history. The idea that war should be abolished is not new and continues to be raised, but it is rarely taken seriously by most people, let alone national leaders. There are, of course, many reasons for this: Nations are perceived as having the right to defend themselves, nations also have national interests to safeguard, dangerous power mongers may initiate or provoke conflict that necessitates defensive actions, and so on. Basically, the prevailing worldview, shared in the world community, is that the abolition of war is simply impractical, unrealistic, and, paradoxically, dangerous.

A study of worldviews in peaceful societies, however, may broaden our perspective on the assumed necessity of approaching international conflicts through military options. For peaceful peoples, it is warfare itself, not its abolition, that is impractical, unrealistic, and dangerous, if not immoral under the tenets of their nonviolent belief systems. In other words, accepting the legitimacy of warfare, something many other societies simply take for granted, is incompatible with the worldviews of peaceful societies. Thus awareness of the worldviews in peaceful societies may help to open for re-evaluation the unquestioning acceptance of warfare.

Bearing in mind the fate of slavery in the West may also be instructive. Historically, slavery was widely accepted, then progressively challenged, and ultimately abolished. This historical example shows that even widely held beliefs and solidly entrenched social institutions can change. But the change must start with the questioning of assumptions. As we have seen, peaceful societies rarely resort to force when dealing with conflicts. This observation raises the question: Why could we not set up new regional and global social institutions to deal effectively with conflict without military force? If we remain locked within the traditional worldview, the dominant paradigm that accepts the legitimacy and necessity of war as a social institution, we can in all likelihood come up with a long list of reasons why alternatives to military action would never work to ensure peace and security. By contrast, we could undertake the challenging task of thinking afresh about how to create new institutions that would provide security and resolve international conflicts without recourse to war. As former U.S. President Harry Truman once envisioned:

> When Kansas and Colorado have a quarrel over the water in the Arkansas River, they don't call out the National Guard in each state and go to war over it. They bring suit in the Supreme Court of the United States and abide by the decision. There isn't a reason in the world why we cannot do that internationally. (as cited in Hudgens, 1986, p. 12)

The literature on peaceful societies (see the Appendix) leads to a host of questions. How do peaceful societies remain peaceful? Why do our own societies have so much more violence and accept the practice of warfare? What values, what fundamental parts of our belief systems, would we need to modify if we became really serious about enhancing peace? Or the complement to that question, what values and beliefs within our own traditions could we emphasize to enhance our peacefulness? Is peacefulness *really* a top priority in our societies—more so than other values such as personal advancement, competition, or attaining material wealth? Or, conversely, do we just pay lip service to peace, more often than not?

This brief description of peaceful societies suggests that many of the dominant Western paradigms—capitalism, democracy, competition, rationalism—may be unacceptable to the peaceful peoples. Most of those societies are strongly opposed to competition (Bonta, 1997), they reach decisions through indirection and consensus rather than the divisiveness of win-lose contests, and they avoid leadership, individual recognition, and so on. Readers who wish to really contemplate the creation of peace may recognize that the peaceful societies are clearly based on paradigms that vary widely from the ones that dominate most modern societies.

Perhaps the most concrete implications for reducing violence in this chapter stem from the discussion of childhood socialization. We have seen that peaceful societies are highly successful at instilling in children peaceful beliefs and behaviors. Children in peaceful societies internalize nonviolence as a way of thinking and acting. As a group, peaceful societies do not favor the regular or frequent application of physical punishment to children. The obvious policy implication from these observations is that shifting away from the use of physical punishment in other social contexts could also help to reduce violence overall. In fact, research on family violence leads to the same conclusion (Straus, 2001; for further discussion, see Fry, 1993, 2004). Studies of peaceful societies additionally lead to the recommendation that children be taught beliefs and attitudes favoring nonviolence over violence. Specific training programs in nonviolent conflict resolution, offered in schools or community organizations, for example, could augment a corresponding shift away from beliefs and attitudes that condone or favor the use of physical force in interpersonal or international contexts. Such programs have had success in reducing youth aggression in countries such as Norway (see, e.g., Dobinson, 2004; Olweus, 1997).

If we take the lessons from peaceful societies seriously, if we really desire to flesh out and build a more peaceful world, then we have to advocate new paradigms that devalue power, abolish gender privileges, and cherish and centralize the peaceful elements in our existing worldviews. Until people in very large-scale societies such as the United States engage in really thorough criticism of the dominant paradigms that are conducive to and accepting of physical force, it is doubtful that a great deal of progress will be made. The United Nations recently adopted an outline for creating a *culture of peace*. It is up to the rest of us to develop our visions of peacefulness for our own societies and to effectively evaluate them in truly peaceful fashions. The peaceful societies provide inspiration for these tasks.

## Appendix: Peaceful Societies

The following societies are described as nonwarring *and* as having very low levels of internal violence. The societies are geographically diverse and range in size from small communities (e.g., the La Paz Zapotec) to populations in the thousands or tens of thousands (e.g., the Semai or the Fipa). Primary sources are followed in some cases by reliable secondary sources. Undoubtedly additional nonwarring, internally peaceful societies could be located through further checking of the anthropological literature.

| Society | Region | Source of Information |
|---|---|---|
| Amish | North America | Hostetler, 1980; Hostetler & Huntington, 1971; Kraybill, 1989 |
| Batek | Southeast Asia | Kirk Endicott 1979, 1988, 1993, p. 235 |
| Birhor | South Asia | Adhikary, 1984; Sinha 1972, pp. 390, 392–393 |
| Buid | Philippines | Gibson 1986, 1989, 1990, pp. 130–133 |
| Canadian Inuit [Utkuhikhalkik & Qipisa] | North America | Briggs 1970, 1978, 1994, 2000; see also Irwin, 1990 |
| Cayapa | South America | Barrett, 1925; Murra, 1948, p. 282; Altschuler, 1964, 1967, 1970 |
| Chewong | Southeast Asia | S. Howell, 1984, 1988, p. 150, 1989 |
| Fipa | Africa | Willis, 1989a, 1989b |
| Greenland Inuit [East & West] | Greenland | Nansen, 1893; Kleivan, 1991 |
| G/wi | Africa | Silberbauer, 1972, 1981, 1982 |
| Hanunóo Agta | Philippines | Conklin, 1954; LeBar, 1975, p. 76; Hockings, 1993, p. 91 |
| Hill Pandaram (see Malapandaram) | | |
| Hutterites | North America | Bennett, 1967; Hostetler, 1974; Hostetler & Huntington, 1996 |
| Ifaluk | Micronesia | Lutz, 1982, 1983, 1988 esp. pp. 136–138, 174–182, 184–185; Spiro, 1952; Burrows 1952, p. 23; also see Betzig & Wichimai, 1991 |
| Inuit (see Canadian Inuit, Greenland Inuit, and Polar Eskimo) | | |

| Society | Region | Source of Information |
|---|---|---|
| Irula | South Asia | Nobel & Jebadhas, 1992, p. 107; Zvelebil, 1988; Murdock, 1934, p. 110; also see Hockings, 1992, pp. 15, 17; Wolf, 1992, p. 137 |
| Jahai | Southeast Asia | van der Sluys, 1999, pp. 307, 310; see also Kirk Endicott, 1993 |
| Ju/'hoansi/ Ju/wasi (!Kung) | Africa | Lee, 1979, esp. Chap. 13, 1993, esp. Chap. 7; Draper, 1978; Marshall, 1976; E. Thomas, 1959, pp. 21–24; 1994; N. Howell, 1979; also cf. Knauft, 1987 for discussion |
| Kadar | South Asia | Ehrenfels, 1952 |
| !Kung (see Ju/'hoansi) | | |
| Ladakhi/Ladaki | South Asia | Mann, 1986; Norberg-Hodge, 1991 |
| Lapps (see Saami) | | |
| Lepchas | South Asia | Gorer, 1967; DiMaggio, 1992, p. 149 |
| Malapandaram | South Asia | Morris, 1977, esp. pp. 230, 237–238, 1982, 1992, p. 100; see also Gardner, 1966, p. 402 |
| Mbuti | Africa | Turnbull, 1965a, 1965b, 1968, p. 341, 1978 |
| Nubians | Africa | R. A. Fernea, 1973, 2004; see also E. W. Fernea & R. A. Fernea, 1991 |
| Paliyans | South Asia | Gardner, 1966, 402, 1972, e.g., p. 425, 1985, pp. 413–416, 421, 1995, 1999, p. 263; 2000a, 2000b, esp. Chaps. 5 & 6, 2004 |
| Panare | South America | Henley, 1982, p. 153, 1994, p. 266 |
| Pemon | South America | D. Thomas, 1982, 1994, pp. 272–273 |
| Piaroa | South America | Overing, 1986, 1989, Zent, 1994 |

| Society | Region | Source of Information |
|---|---|---|
| Polar Eskimo [Inughuit] | Greenland | Gilberg, 1984, 1991; Murdock, 1934; also see Irwin, 1990, pp. 194–196; NB: Polar Eskimos, or Inughuit, are culturally distinct from other Greenland Eskimos |
| Punan/Penan [esp. eastern group] | Southeast Asia | Needham, 1972, p. 180; Hose, 1894, pp. 157–158; Holsti, 1913, p. 71 |
| Rural Thai | Southeast Asia | Phillips, 1965; Martin & Levinson, 1993, p. 71 |
| Saami | Europe | Anderson & Beach, 1992, p. 222; Davie, 1929, p. 49; Holsti, 1913; Montagu, 1976, pp. 187, 270 |
| Sanpoil | North America | Ray, 1980; Ruby & Brown, 1989 |
| Saulteaux | North America | Hallowell, 1974, esp. p. 278; see also Holsti, 1913 |
| Semai | Southeast Asia | Dentan, 1968, 1978, 1988, 1992, 1993, 1995, 1999, pp. 419, 420, 2000, 2004; Dentan & Williams-Hunt, 1999; Gregor & Robarchek, 1996; Robarchek, 1979, 1980, 1986, 1989, 1990, 1997; Robarchek & Robarchek, 1992, 1996a, 1996b; Robarchek & Dentan, 1987 |
| Semang | Southeast Asia | LeBar, Hickey, & Musgrave, 1964, p. 185; Kirk Endicott, 1993; Schebesta, 1929, p. 280; see also Holsti, 1913 |
| Sherpa | South Asia | Paul, 1977, p. 176, 1992, p. 259; Ortner, 1978, 1989; Fürer- Haimendorf, 1984 |
| Siriono | South America | Holmberg, 1969; see also Morey & Marwitt, 1975, p. 447 |
| Tahitians | Polynesia | Levy, 1969, 1973, 1978 |
| Thai (see Rural Thai) | | |

| Society | Region | Source of Information |
|---------|--------|-----------------------|
| Toda | South Asia | Rivers, 1986; Walker, 1986, cf. pp. 91–96; 1992, p. 297 |
| Tristan Islanders | South Atlantic | Loudon, 1970; Munch, 1945, 1971; Munch & Marske, 1981 |
| Ufipa (see Fipa) | | |
| Veddahs/Vedda | South Asia | Seligmann & Seligmann, 1969, p. 34; Stegeborn, 1999, p. 271; Montagu, 1978, p. 5; Davie, 1929, pp. 50–51; Hobhouse, 1956, p. 105; Lesser, 1967, pp. 94; Levinson, 1994, pp. 122, Holsti, 1913, p. 71 |
| Wauja (Waura) | South America | Ireland, 1988, 1991 |
| Yanadi | South Asia | Raghaviah, 1962; see also Gardner, 1966, p. 403 |
| Zapotec of "La Paz" | North America | Fry, 1988, 1992, 1993, 1994, 2006; O'Nell, 1979, 1981, 1986, 1989 |

# References

Adhikary, Ashim Kumar. (1984). *Society and world view of the Birhor: A nomadic hunting and gathering community of Orissa.* Calcutta: Anthropological Survey of India.

Altschuler, Milton. (1964). *The Cayapa: A study in legal behavior.* Ph.D. Dissertation, University of Minnesota.

Altschuler, Milton. (1967). The sacred and profane realms of Cayapa law. *International Journal of Comparative Sociology 8*, 44–54.

Altschuler, Milton. (1970). Cayapa personality and sexual motivation. In Donald S. Marshall & Robert C. Suggs (Eds.), *Human sexual behavior* (pp. 38–58). New York: Basic Books.

Anderson, Myrdene, & Beach, Hugh. (1992). Saami. In Linda A. Bennett (Ed.), *Encyclopedia of world cultures, volume IV, Europe* (pp. 220–223). Boston: G. K. Hall.

Barash, David P. (1991). *Introduction to peace studies.* Belmont, CA: Wadsworth.

Barnett, Ola W., Miller-Perrin, Cindy L., & Perrin, Robin D. (1997). *Family violence across the lifespan: An introduction.* Thousand Oaks, CA: SAGE.

Barrett, S. A. (1925). *The Cayapa Indians of Ecuador, Parts I and II.* New York: Museum of the American Indian, Heye Foundation.

Bennett, John W. (1967). *Hutterian Brethren: The agricultural economy and social organization of a communal people.* Stanford, CA: Stanford University Press.

Berkowitz, Leonard. (1993). *Aggression: Its causes, consequences, and control.* Philadelphia: Temple University Press.

Betzig, Laura, & Wichimai, Santus. (1991). A not so perfect peace: A history of conflict on Ifaluk. *Oceania 61*, 240–256.

Boehm, Christopher. (1987). *Blood revenge: The enactment and management of conflict in Montenegro and other tribal societies.* Philadelphia: University of Pennsylvania Press.

Bonta, Bruce D. (1993). *Peaceful peoples: An annotated bibliography.* Metuchen, NJ: The Scarecrow Press.

Bonta, Bruce D. (1996). Conflict resolution among peaceful societies: The culture of peacefulness. *Journal of Peace Research 33,* 403–420.

Bonta, Bruce D. (1997). Cooperation and competition in peaceful societies. *Psychological Bulletin 121,* 299–320.

Briggs, Jean L. (1970). *Never in anger: Portrait of an Eskimo family.* Cambridge, MA: Harvard University Press.

Briggs, Jean L. (1978). The origins of nonviolence: Inuit management of aggression. In Ashley Montagu (Ed.), *Learning non-aggression: The experience of non-literate societies* (pp. 54–93). New York: Oxford University Press.

Briggs, Jean L. (1994). "Why don't you kill your baby brother?" the dynamics of peace in Canadian Inuit camps. In Leslie E. Sponsel & Thomas Gregor (Eds.), *The anthropology of peace and nonviolence* (pp. 155–181). Boulder, CO: Lynne Rienner.

Briggs, Jean L. (2000). Conflict management in a modern Inuit community. In Peter P. Schweitzer, Megan Biesele, & Robert K. Hitchcock (Eds.), *Hunters and gatherers in the modern world: Conflict, resistance, and self-determination* (pp. 110–124). New York: Berghahn.

Burrows, Edwin G. (1952). From Value to Ethos on Ifaluk Atoll. *Southwestern Journal of Anthropology 8,* 13–35.

Burrows, Edwin G. (1963). *Flower in my ear: Arts and ethos on Ifaluk Atoll.* Seattle: University of Washington Press.

Conklin, Harold C. (1954). *The relation of Hanunóo culture to the plant world.* New Haven, CT, Ph.D. Dissertation, Yale University.

Davie, Maurice R. (1929). *The evolution of war: A study of its role in early societies.* New Haven, CT: Yale University Press.

Dentan, Robert Knox. (1968). *The Semai: A nonviolent people of Malaya.* New York: Holt, Rinehart and Winston.

Dentan, Robert Knox. (1978). Notes on childhood in a nonviolent context: The Semai case (Malaysia). In Ashley Montagu (Ed.), *Learning non-aggression: The experience of non-literate societies* (pp. 94–143). New York: Oxford University Press.

Dentan, Robert Knox. (1988). On reconsidering violence in simple human societies. *Current Anthropology 29,* 625–629.

Dentan, Robert Knox. (1992). The rise, maintenance and destruction of peaceable polity; A preliminary essay in political ecology. In James Silverberg & J. Patrick Gray (Eds.), *Aggression and peacefulness in humans and other primates* (pp. 214–270). New York: Oxford University Press.

Dentan, Robert Knox. (1993). Senoi. In Paul Hockings (Ed.), *Encyclopedia of world cultures: Vol. V. South and Southeast Asia.* (236–239). Boston: G. K. Hall.

Dentan, Robert Knox. (1995). Bad day at Bukit Pekan. *American Anthropologist 97,* 225–250.

Dentan, Robert Knox. (1999). Spotted doves at war: The *Praak Sangkiil. Asian Folklore Studies 58,* 397–434.

Dentan, Robert Knox. (2000). Ceremonies of innocence and the lineaments of ungratified desire: An analysis of a syncretic Southeast Asian taboo complex. *Bijdragen tot de Taal-, Land- en Volkenkunde (Journal of the Humanities and Social Sciences of Southeast Asia and Oceania) 156,* 193–232.

Dentan, Robert Knox. (2004). Cautious, alert, polite, and elusive: The Semai of Central Peninsular Malaysia. In Graham Kemp & Douglas P. Fry, *Keeping the peace: Conflict resolution and peaceful societies around the world* (pp. 167–184). New York: Routledge.

Dentan, Robert Knox, & Williams-Hunt, Bah Tony (Anthony). (1999). Untransfiguring death: A case study of rape, drunkenness, development and homicide in an apprehensive void. *Review of Indonesian and Malaysian Affairs 33*, 17–65.

DiMaggio, Jay. (1992). Lepcha. In Paul Hockings (Ed.), *Encyclopedia of world cultures: Vol. III. South Asia* (pp. 148–149). Boston: G. K. Hall.

Dobinson, Kristin (2004). A model of peacefulness: Rethinking peace and conflict in Norway. In Graham Kemp and Douglas P. Fry (Eds.), *Keeping the peace: Conflict resolution and peaceful societies around the world* (pp. 149–166). New York: Routledge.

Draper, Patricia. (1975). !Kung women: Contrasts in sexual egalitarianism in foraging and sedentary contexts. In Rayna R. Reiter (Ed.), *Toward an anthropology of women* (pp. 77–109). New York: Monthly Review Press.

Draper, Patricia. (1976). Social and economic constraints on child life among the !Kung. In Richard B. Lee & Irven DeVore (Eds.), *Kalahari hunter-gatherers: Studies of the !Kung San and their neighbors* (pp. 199–217). Cambridge, MA: Harvard University Press.

Draper, Patricia. (1978). The learning environment for aggression and anti-social behavior among the !Kung. In Ashley Montagu (Ed.), *Learning non-aggression: The experience of non-literate societies* (pp. 31–53). New York: Oxford University Press.

Eckert, Penelope, & Newmark, Russell. (1980). Central Eskimo song duels: A contextual analysis of ritual ambiguity. *Ethnology: An International Journal of Cultural and Social Anthropology 19*, 191–211.

Ehrenfels, U. R. (1952). *Kadar of Cochin.* Madras: University of Madras.

Ellison, Christopher G., & Bartkowski, John P. (1997). Religion and the legitimation of violence: Conservative Protestantism and corporal punishment. In Jennifer Turpin & Lester R. Kurtz (Eds.), *The web of violence, from interpersonal to global* (pp. 45–67). Urbana: University of Illinois Press.

Endicott, Karen Lampell. (1992). Fathering in an egalitarian society. In Barry S. Hewlett (Ed.), *Father-child relations, cultural and biosocial contexts* (pp. 281–295). New York: deGruyter.

Endicott, Kirk. (1979). *Batek Negrito religion: The world-view and rituals of a hunting and gathering people of Peninsular Malaysia.* Oxford, England: Clarendon Press.

Endicott, Kirk. (1988). Property, power and conflict among the Batek of Malaysia. In Tim Ingold, David Riches, & James Woodburn (Eds.), *Hunters and gatherers 2: Property, power and ideology* (pp. 110–127). Oxford, England: Berg.

Endicott, Kirk. (1993). Semang. In Paul Hockings (Ed.), *Encyclopedia of world cultures, volume V, South and Southeast Asia* (pp. 233–236). Boston: G. K. Hall.

Fabbro, David. (1978). Peaceful societies: An introduction. *Journal of Peace Research 15*(1), 67–83.

Fernea, Elizabeth Warnock, & Fernea, Robert A. 1991. *Nubian ethnographies.* Prospect Heights, IL: Waveland Press.

Fernea, Robert A. (1973). *Nubians in Egypt: Peaceful people.* Austin: University of Texas Press.

Fernea, Robert A. (2004). Putting a stone in the middle: The Nubians of Northern Africa. In Graham Kemp & Douglas P. Fry (Eds.), *Keeping the peace: Conflict resolution and peaceful societies around the world* (pp. 105–121). New York: Routledge.

Fry, Douglas P. (1988). Intercommunity differences in aggression among Zapotec children. *Child Development 59*, 1008–1019.

Fry, Douglas P. (1992). Respect for the rights of others is peace: Learning aggression versus nonaggression among the Zapotec. *American Anthropologist 94*, 621–639.

Fry, Douglas P. (1993). The intergenerational transmission of disciplinary practices and approaches to conflict. *Human Organization 52*, 176–185.

Fry, Douglas P. (1994). Maintaining social tranquility: Internal and external loci of aggression control. In Leslie E. Sponsel & Thomas Gregor (Eds.), *The anthropology of peace and nonviolence* (pp. 133–154). Boulder, CO: Lynne Rienner.

Fry, Douglas P. (1999). Peaceful Societies. In Lester R. Kurtz (Ed.), *Encyclopedia of violence, peace, and conflict* (pp. 719–733). San Diego, CA: Academic Press.

Fry, Douglas P. (2001). Is violence getting too much attention? Cross-cultural findings on the ways people deal with conflict. In J. Martin Ramirez & Deborah S. Richardson (Eds.), *Cross-cultural approaches to research on aggression and reconciliation* (pp. 123–148). Huntington, NY: Nova Science.

Fry, Douglas P. (2004). Conclusion: Learning from peaceful societies. In Graham Kemp & Douglas P. Fry (Eds.), *Keeping the peace: Conflict resolution and peaceful societies around the world* (pp. 185–204). New York: Routledge.

Fry, Douglas P. (2006). *The human potential for peace: An anthropological challenge to assumptions about war and violence.* New York: Oxford University Press.

Fürer-Haimendorf, Christoph von. (1984). *The Sherpas transformed: Social change in a Buddhist society of Nepal.* New Delhi: Sterling.

Gardner, Peter M. (1966). Symmetric respect and memorate knowledge: The structure and ecology of individualistic culture. *Southwestern Journal of Anthropology 22*, 389–415.

Gardner, Peter M. (1972). The Paliyans. In M. G. Bicchieri (Ed.), *Hunters and gatherers today: A socioeconomic study of eleven such cultures in the twentieth century* (pp. 404–447). New York: Holt, Rinehart and Winston.

Gardner, Peter M. (1985). Bicultural oscillation as a long-term adaptation to cultural frontiers: Cases and questions. *Human Ecology 13*, 411–432.

Gardner, Peter M. (1995). Escalation avoidance and persistent Paliyan nonviolence. Paper presented at the meetings of the American Anthropological Association, Washington, DC, 15–19 November.

Gardner, Peter M. (1999). The Paliyan. In Richard B. Lee & Richard Daly (Eds.), *The Cambridge encyclopedia of hunters and gatherers* (pp. 261–264). Cambridge, England: Cambridge University Press.

Gardner, Peter M. (2000a). Respect and nonviolence among recently sedentary Paliyan foragers. *Journal of the Royal Anthropological Institute 6*, 215–236.

Gardner, Peter M. (2000b). *Bicultural versatility as a frontier adaptation among Paliyan foragers of South India.* Lewiston, NY: Edwin Mellen.

Gardner, Peter M. (2004). Respect for all: The Paliyans of South India. In Graham Kemp & Douglas P. Fry (Eds.), *Keeping the peace: Conflict resolution and peaceful societies around the world* (pp. 53–71). New York: Routledge.

Gelles, Richard J., & Cornell, Claire Pedrick. (1990). *Intimate violence in families* (2nd ed.). Newbury Park, CA: SAGE.

Gelles, Richard J., & Straus, Murray A. (1988). *Intimate violence.* New York: Simon and Schuster.

Ghiglieri, Michael P. (1999). *The dark side of man: Tracing the origins of male violence*. Reading, MA: Perseus.

Gibson, Thomas. (1986). *Sacrifice and sharing in the Philippine highlands: Religion and society among the Buid of Mindoro*. London: Athlone Press.

Gibson, Thomas. (1988). Meat sharing as a political ritual: Forms of transaction versus modes of subsistence. In Tim Ingold, David Riches, & James Woodburn (Eds.), *Hunters and gatherers 2: Property, power and ideology* (pp. 165–17). Oxford, England: Berg.

Gibson, Thomas. (1989). Symbolic representations of tranquility and aggression among the Buid. In Signe Howell & Roy Willis (Eds.), *Societies at peace: Anthropological perspectives* (pp. 60–78). London: Routledge.

Gibson, Thomas. (1990). Raiding, trading and tribal autonomy in Insular Southeast Asia. In Jonathan Haas (Ed.), *The anthropology of war* (pp. 125–145). Cambridge, England: Cambridge University Press.

Gilberg, Rolf. (1984). Polar Eskimo. In David Damas (Ed.), *Handbook of North American Indians: Vol, 5. Arctic* (pp. 577–594). Washington, DC: Smithsonian Institution.

Gilberg, Rolf. (1991). Inughuit. In Timothy J. O'Leary & David Levinson (Eds.), *Encyclopedia of world cultures: Vol. I. North America* (pp. 159–161). Boston: G. K. Hall

Gorer, Geoffrey. (1967). *Himalayan village: An account of the Lepchas of Sikkim*. New York: Basic Books.

Gould, Stephen Jay. (1978). Morton's ranking of races by cranial capacity. *Science 200*, 503–509.

Gregor, Thomas. (1996). Introduction. In Thomas Gregor, *A natural history of peace* (pp. ix–xxiii). Nashville, TN: Vanderbilt University Press.

Gregor, Thomas, & Robarchek, Clayton A. (1996). Two paths to peace: Semai and Mehinaku nonviolence. In Thomas Gregor (Ed.), *A natural history of peace* (pp. 159–188). Nashville, TN: Vanderbilt University Press.

Gregor, Thomas, & Sponsel, Leslie E. (1994). Preface. In Leslie E. Sponsel & Thomas Gregor (Eds.), *The anthropology of peace and nonviolence* (pp. xv–xviii). Boulder: Lynne Rienner.

Hallowell, A. Irving. (1974). Aggression in Saulteaux society. In A. Irving Hallowell (Ed.), *Culture and experience* (pp. 277–290). Philadelphia: University of Pennsylvania Press.

Harvey, Andrew. (1983). *A journey in Ladakh*. Boston: Houghton Mifflin.

Henley, Paul. (1982). *The Panare: Tradition and change on the Amazonian frontier*. New Haven, CT: Yale University Press.

Henley, Paul. (1994). Panare. In Johannes Wilbert (Ed.), *Encyclopedia of world cultures: Vol. VII. South America* (pp. 264–267). Boston: G. K. Hall.

Hobhouse, L. T. (1956). Part II. Peace and order among the simplest peoples. *British Journal of Sociology 7*, 96–119.

Hockings, Paul. (1992). Badaga. In Paul Hockings (Ed.), *Encyclopedia of world cultures: Vol. III. South Asia* (pp. 14–18). Boston: G. K. Hall.

Hockings, Paul. (1993). Hanunóo. In Paul Hockings (Ed.), *Encyclopedia of world cultures: Vol. V. South and Southeast Asia* (pp. 90–91). Boston: G. K. Hall.

Hold, Barbara C. L. (1980). Attention-structure and behavior in G/wi San children. *Ethology and Sociobiology 1*, 275–290.

Holmberg, A. R. (1969). *Nomads of the long bow: The Siriono of Eastern Bolivia*. New York: American Museum Science Books.

Holsti, Rudolf. (1913). *The relation of war to the origin of the state*. Helsinki: Annales, Academiae Scientiarum Fennicae.

Hose, C. (1894). The natives of Borneo. *Journal of the Anthropological Institute of Great Britain and Ireland 23*, 156–172.

Hostetler, John A. (1974). *Hutterite society.* Baltimore: Johns Hopkins University Press.

Hostetler, John A. (1980). *Amish society* (3rd ed.). Baltimore: Johns Hopkins University Press.

Hostetler, John A., & Huntington, Gertrude Enders. (1996). *The Hutterites in North America.* New York: Harcourt Brace.

Hostetler, John A., & Huntington, Gertrude Enders. (1971). *Children in Amish society: Socialization and community education.* New York: Holt, Rinehart and Winston.

Howell, Nancy. (1979). *Demography of the Dobe !Kung.* New York: Academic.

Howell, Signe. (1984). *Society and cosmos: Chewong of Peninsular Malaysia.* Singapore: Oxford University Press.

Howell, Signe. (1988). From Child to human: Chewong concepts of self. In Gustav Jahoda & I. M. Lewis (Eds.), *Acquiring culture: Cross cultural studies in child development* (pp. 147–168). London: Croom Helm.

Howell, Signe. (1989). 'To be angry is not to be human, but to be fearful is': Chewong concepts of human nature. In Signe Howell & Roy Willis (Eds.), *Societies at peace: Anthropological perspectives* (pp. 45–59). London: Routledge.

Howell, Signe, & Willis, Roy (Eds). (1989). *Societies at peace: Anthropological perspectives.* New York: Routledge.

Hudgens, Tom A. (1986). *We need law: Let's abolish war.* Denver, CO: BILC Corporation.

Ireland, Emilienne. (1988). Cerebral savage: The Whiteman as symbol of cleverness and savagery in Waura myth. In Jonathan D. Hill (Ed.), *Rethinking history and myth: Indigenous South American perspectives on the past* (pp. 157–173). Urbana: University of Illinois Press.

Ireland, Emilienne. (1991). Neither warriors nor victims: The Wauja peacefully organize to defend their land. *Cultural Survival Quarterly 15*, 54–60.

Irwin, C. (1990). The Inuit and the evolution of limited group conflict. In J. van der Dennen & V. Falger (Eds.), *Sociobiology and conflict: Evolutionary perspectives on competition, cooperation, violence and warfare* (pp. 189–226). London: Chapman and Hall.

Keeley, Lawrence H. (1996). *War before civilization: The myth of the peaceful savage.* New York: Oxford University Press.

Kelly, Robert L. (1995). *The foraging spectrum: Diversity in hunter-gatherer lifeways.* Washington, DC: Smithsonian Institution Press.

Kemp, Graham. (2004). The concept of peaceful societies. In Graham Kemp & Douglas P. Fry (Eds.), *Keeping the peace: Conflict resolution and peaceful societies around the world* (pp. 1–10). New York: Routledge.

Kemp, Graham, & Fry, Douglas P. (2004). *Keeping the peace: Conflict resolution and peaceful societies around the world.* New York: Routledge.

Kent, Susan. (1989). And justice for all: The development of political centralization among newly sedentary foragers. *American Anthropologist 91*, 703–712.

Kleivan, Inge. (1991). West Greenland Inuit. In Timothy J. O'Leary & David Levinson (Eds.), *Encyclopedia of world cultures: Vol. I. North America* (pp. 376–379). Boston: G. K. Hall.

Knauft, Bruce M. (1987). Reconsidering violence in simple human societies: Homicide among the Gebusi of New Guinea. *Current Anthropology 28*, 457–500.

Kraybill, Donald B. (1989). *The riddle of Amish culture.* Baltimore: Johns Hopkins University Press.

LeBar, Frank M. (1975). Hanunóo. In Frank M. LeBar (Ed.), *Ethnic groups of insular Southeast Asia: Vol. 2. Philippines and Formosa* (pp. 74–76). New Haven, CT: Human Relations Area Files Press.

LeBar, Frank M., Gerald C. Hickey, & John K. Musgrave. (1964). Semang. In Frank M. LeBar, Gerald C. Hickey, & John K. Musgrave (Eds.), *Ethnic groups of mainland Southeast Asia* (pp. 181–186). New Haven, CT: Human Relations Area Files Press.

Lee, Richard Borshay. (1979). *The !Kung San: Men, women, and work in a foraging society.* Cambridge, England: Cambridge University Press.

Lee, Richard Borshay. (1993). *The Dobe Ju/'hoansi* (2nd ed.). Fort Worth: Harcourt Brace College Publishers.

Lesser, Alexander. (1967). War and the state. In Morton Fried, Marvin Harris, & Robert Murphy (Eds.), *War: The anthropology of armed conflict and aggression* (pp. 92–96). Garden City, NY: Natural History Press.

Levinson, David. (1994). *Aggression and conflict: A cross-cultural encyclopedia.* Santa Barbara, CA: ABC-CLIO.

Levy, Robert I. (1969). On getting angry in the Society Islands. In William Caudill & Tsung-Yi Lin (Eds.), *Mental health research in Asia and the Pacific* (pp. 358–380). Honolulu: East-West Center Press.

Levy, Robert I. (1973). *Tahitians: Mind and experience in the Society Islands.* Chicago: University of Chicago Press.

Levy, Robert I. (1978). Tahitian gentleness and redundant controls. In Ashley Montagu (Ed.), *Learning non-aggression: The experience of non-literate societies* (pp. 222–235). New York: Oxford University Press.

Loudon, J. B. (1970). Teasing and socialization on Tristan da Cunha. In Philip Mayer (Ed.), *Socialization: The approach from social anthropology* (pp. 193–332). A.S.A Monographs No. 8. London: Tavistock.

Lutz, Catherine. (1982). The Domain of Emotion Words on Ifaluk. *American Ethnologist 9*, 113–128.

Lutz, Catherine. (1983). Parental goals, ethnopsychology, and the development of emotional meaning. *Ethos: Journal of the Society for Psychological Anthropology 11*, 246–262.

Lutz, Catherine. (1985a). Depression and the translation of emotional worlds. In Arthur Kleinman and Byron Good (Eds.), *Culture and depression: Studies in the anthropology and cross-cultural psychiatry of affect and disorder* (pp. 63–100). Berkeley: University of California Press.

Lutz, Catherine. (1985b). Ethnopsychology compared to what? Explaining behavior and consciousness among the Ifaluk. In Geoffrey M. White & John Kirkpatrick (Eds.), *Person, self, and experience: Exploring pacific ethnopsychologies* (pp. 35–79). Berkeley: University of California Press.

Lutz, Catherine. (1988). *Unnatural emotions: Everyday sentiments on a Micronesian atoll & their challenge to Western theory.* Chicago: University of Chicago Press.

Mann, R. S. (1972). Intra and inter family relations among the Ladakhis of Ladakh. *Bulletin of the Anthropological Survey of India 21*, 88–106.

Mann, R. S. (1986). *The Ladakhi: A study in ethnography and change.* Calcutta: Anthropological Survey of India.

Marshall, Lorna. (1976). *The !Kung of Nyae Nyae.* Cambridge, MA: Harvard University Press.

Martin, M. Marlene, & Levinson, David. (1993). Central Thai. In Paul Hockings (Ed.), *Encyclopedia of world cultures: Vol. V. East and Southeast Asia* (pp. 69–72). Boston: G. K. Hall.

Montagu, Ashley. (1976). *The nature of human aggression.* New York: Oxford University Press.

Montagu, Ashley (Ed.). (1978). *Learning non-aggression: The experience of non-literate societies.* New York: Oxford University Press.

Morey, Robert V., Jr., & Marwitt, John P. (1975). Ecology, economy, and warfare in Lowland South America. In Martin A. Nettleship, R. Dale Givens, & Anderson Nettleship (Eds.), *War, its causes and correlates* (pp. 439–450). The Hague: Mouton.

Morris, Brian. (1977). Tappers, Trappers and the Hill Pandaram (South India). *Anthropos 72,* 225–241.

Morris, Brian. (1982). *Forest traders: A socio-economic study of the Hill Pandaram.* London: Athlone.

Morris, Brian. (1992). Hill Pandaram. In Paul Hockings (Ed.), *Encyclopedia of world cultures, Vol. III, South Asia* (pp. 98–101). Boston: G. K. Hall.

Munch, Peter A. (1945). *Sociology of Tristan da Cunha.* Oslo: Det Norske Videnskaps-Akademi.

Munch, Peter A. (1971). *Crisis in utopia: The ordeal of Tristan da Cunha.* New York: Crowell.

Munch, Peter A., & Marske, Charles E. (1981). Atomism and Social Integration. *Journal of Anthropological Research 37,* 158–171.

Murdock, George Peter. (1934). *Our primitive contemporaries.* New York: MacMillan.

Murra, J. (1948). The Cayapa and Colorado. In Julian H. Steward (Ed.), *Handbook of South American Indians Volume 4, The Circum-Caribbean Tribes* (pp. 277–291). Washington, DC: United States Government Printing Office.

Nansen, Fredtjof. (1893). *Eskimo life.* (William Archer, Trans.). London: Longman, Green.

Needham, Rodney. (1972). Penan. In Frank M. LeBar (Ed.)., *Ethnic groups of insular Southeast Asia: Vol. 1. Indonesia, Andaman Islands, and Madagascar* (pp. 176–180). New Haven, CT: Human Relations Area Files Press.

Nobel, William A., & Jebadhas, A. William. (1992). Irula. In Paul Hockings (Ed.), *Encyclopedia of world cultures: Vol. III. South Asia* (pp. 104–109). Boston: G. K. Hall.

Norberg-Hodge, Helena. (1991). *Ancient futures: Learning from Ladakh.* San Francisco: Sierra Club Books.

Nordstrom, Carolyn. (1997a). The eye of the storm: From war to peace—Examples from Sri Lanka and Mozambique. In Douglas P. Fry and Kaj Björkqvist (Eds.), *Cultural variation in conflict resolution: Alternatives to violence* (pp. 91–103). Mahwah, NJ: Lawrence Erlbaum.

Nordstrom, Carolyn. (1997b). *A different kind of war story.* Philadelphia: University of Pennsylvania Press.

O'Nell, Carl W. (1979). Nonviolence and personality disposition among the Zapotec: Paradox and enigma. *Journal of Psychological Anthropology 2,* 301–322.

O'Nell, Carl W. (1981). Hostility management and the control of aggression in a Zapotec community. *Aggressive Behavior 7,* 351–366.

O'Nell, Carl W. (1986). Primary and secondary effects of violence control among the nonviolent Zapotec. *Anthropological Quarterly 59,* 184–190.

O'Nell, Carl W. (1989). The non-violent Zapotec. In Signe Howell and Roy Willis (Eds.), *Societies at peace: Anthropological perspectives* (pp. 117–132). London: Routledge.

Olweus, Dan. (1997). Tackling peer victimization with a school-based intervention program, in D. P. Fry and K. Björkqvist (Eds.), *Cultural variation in conflict resolution: Alternatives to violence* (pp. 215–231). Mahwah, NJ: Lawrence Erlbaum.

Ortner, Sherry. (1989). *High religion: A cultural and political history of Sherpa Buddhism.* Princeton, NJ: Princeton University Press.

Ortner, Sherry B. (1978). *Sherpas through their rituals*. Cambridge, England: Cambridge University Press.

Otterbein, Keith F. (1968). Internal war: A cross-cultural study. *American Anthropologist 70*, 277–289.

Otterbein, Keith F. (1970). *The evolution of war: A cross-cultural study*. New Haven, CT: HRAF Press.

Otterbein, Keith F., & Otterbein, Charlotte S. (1965). An eye for an eye, a tooth for a tooth: A cross-cultural study of feuding. *American Anthropologist 67*, 1470–1482.

Overing, Joanna. (1985). There is no end of evil: The guilty innocents and their fallible God. In David Parkin (Ed.), *The anthropology of evil* (pp. 244–278). Oxford, England: Blackwell.

Overing, Joanna. (1986). Images of cannibalism, death and domination in a "non-violent" society. In David Riches (Ed.), *The anthropology of violence* (pp. 86–101). Oxford, England: Blackwell.

Overing, Joanna. (1989). Styles of manhood: An Amazonian contrast in tranquillity and violence. In Signe Howell and Roy Willis (Eds.), *Societies at peace: Anthropological perspectives*. London: Routledge.

Overing Kaplan, Joanna. (1984). Dualisms as an expression of difference and danger: Marriage exchange and reciprocity among the Piaroa of Venezuela. In Kenneth M. Kensinger, *Marriage practices in lowland South America* (pp. 127–155). Urbana: University of Illinois Press.

Paul, Robert A. (1977). The place of truth in Sherpa law and religion. *Journal of Anthropological Research 33*, 167–184.

Paul, Robert A. (1992). Sherpa. In Paul Hockings (Ed.), *Encyclopedia of world cultures: Vol. III. South Asia* (pp. 257–260). Boston: G. K. Hall.

Phillips, Herbert P. (1965). *Thai peasant personality: The patterning of interpersonal behavior in the village of Bang Chan*. Berkeley: University of California Press.

Raghaviah, V. (1962). *The Yanadis*. New Delhi: Bharatiya Adimjati Sevak Sangh.

Ray, Verne F. (1980). *The Sanpoil and Nespelem: Salishan peoples of Northeastern Washington*. New York: AMS Press.

Reiss, Albert J., Jr., & Roth, Jeffrey A. (Eds.). (1993). *Understanding and preventing violence*, Vol. 1. Washington, DC: National Academy Press.

Reyna, S. P., (1994). A mode of domination approach to organized violence. In S. P. Reyna and R. E. Downs (Eds.), *Studying war: Anthropological perspectives* (pp. 29–65). Langhorne, PA: Gordon and Breach.

Rivers, W. H. R. (1986). *The Todas*. Jaipur: Rawat.

Robarchek, Clayton A. (1977). *Semai nonviolence: A systems approach to understanding*. Riverside, CA: Ph.D. Dissertation, University of California, Riverside.

Robarchek, Clayton A. (1979). Conflict, emotion, and abreaction: Resolution of conflict among the Semai Senoi. *Ethos 7*, 104–123.

Robarchek, Clayton A. (1980). The image of nonviolence: World view of the Semai Senoi. *Federation Museums Journal 25*, 103–117.

Robarchek, Clayton A. (1986). Helplessness, fearfulness and peacefulness: The emotional and motivational context of Semai social relations. *Anthropological Quarterly 59*, 177–183.

Robarchek, Clayton A. (1989). Hobbesian and Rousseauan images of man: Autonomy and individualism in a peaceful society. In Signe Howell and Roy Willis (Eds.), *Societies at peace: Anthropological perspectives* (pp. 31–44). London: Routledge.

Robarchek, Clayton A. (1990). Motivations and material causes: On the explanation of conflict and war. In Jonathan Haas (Ed.), *The anthropology of war* (pp. 56–76). Cambridge, England: Cambridge University Press.

Robarchek, Clayton A. (1997). A community of interests: Semai conflict resolution. In Douglas P. Fry & Kaj Björkqvist (Eds.), *Cultural variation in conflict resolution: Alternatives to violence* (pp. 51–58). Mahwah, NJ: Lawrence Erlbaum.

Robarchek, Clayton A., & Robarchek, Carole J. (1992). Cultures of war and peace: A comparative study of Waorani and Semai. In James Silverberg and J. Patrick Gray (Eds.), *Aggression and peacefulness in humans and other primates* (pp. 189–213). New York: Oxford University Press.

Robarchek, Clayton A., & Robarchek, Carole J. (1996a). Waging peace: The psychological and sociocultural dynamics of positive peace. In Alvin W. Wolfe & Honggang Yang (Eds.), *Anthropological contributions to conflict resolution* (pp. 64–80). Athens: University of Georgia Press.

Robarchek, Clayton A., & Robarchek, Carole J. (1996b). The Aucas, the cannibals, and the missionaries: From warfare to peacefulness among the Waorani. In Thomas Gregor (Ed.), *A Natural History of Peace* (pp. 189–212). Nashville, TN: Vanderbilt University Press.

Robarchek, Clayton A., & Robarchek, Carole. (1998). *Waorani: The contexts of violence and war.* Fort Worth: Harcourt Brace College Publishers.

Robarchek, Clayton A., & Dentan, Robert Knox. (1987). Blood drunkenness and the bloodthirsty Semai: Unmaking another anthropological myth. *American Anthropologist 89*, 356–365.

Ross, Marc Howard. (1993a). *The culture of conflict.* New Haven, CT: Yale University Press.

Ross, Marc Howard. (1993b). *The management of conflict.* New Haven, CT: Yale University Press.

Ruby, Robert H., & Brown, John A. (1989). *Dreamer-prophets of the Columbia Plateau: Smohalla and Skolaskin.* Norman: University of Oklahoma Press.

Schebesta, Paul. (1929). *Among the forest dwarfs of Malaya.* (Arthur Chambers, Trans.). London: Hutchinson.

Seligmann, C. G., & Seligmann, Brenda Z. (1969). *The Veddas.* Oosterhout, the Netherlands: Anthropological Publications.

Service, Elman R. (1966). *The hunters.* Englewood Cliffs, NJ: Prentice-Hall.

Silberbauer, George B. (1972). The G/wi Bushmen. In M. G. Bicchieri (Ed.), *Hunters and gatherers today: A socioeconomic study of eleven such cultures in the twentieth century* (pp. 271–326). New York: Holt, Rinehart and Winston.

Silberbauer, George B. (1981). *Hunter and habitat in the central Kalahari Desert.* New York: Cambridge University Press.

Silberbauer, George B. (1982). Political process in G/wi bands. In Eleanor Leacock & Richard Lee (Eds.), *Politics and history in band societies* (pp. 23–35). New York: Cambridge University Press.

Silberbauer, George B. (1994). A sense of place. In Ernest S. Burch, Jr., and Linda J. Ellanna (Eds.), *Key issues in hunter-gatherer research* (pp. 119–143). Oxford, England: Berg.

Sinha, D. P. (1972). The Birhors. In M. G. Bicchieri (Ed.), *Hunters and gatherers today: A socioeconomic study of eleven such cultures in the twentieth century* (pp. 371–403). New York: Holt, Rinehart and Winston.

Spiro, Melford E. (1952). Ghosts, Ifaluk, and teleological functionalism. *American Anthropologist 54*, 497–503.

Sponsel, Leslie E. (1994). The mutual relevance of anthropology and peace studies. In Leslie E. Sponsel & Thomas Gregor (Eds.), *The anthropology of peace and nonviolence* (pp. 1–36). Boulder: Lynne Rienner.

Sponsel, Leslie E. (1996a). Peace and nonviolence. In David Levinson and Melvin Ember (Eds.), *Encyclopedia of cultural anthropology* (Vol. 3, pp. 908–912). New York: Henry Holt.

Sponsel, Leslie E. (1996b). The natural history of peace: A positive view of human nature and its potential. In Thomas Gregor (Ed.), *A natural history of peace* (pp. 95–125). Nashville, TN: Vanderbilt University Press.

Sponsel, Leslie E., & Gregor, Thomas (Eds.). (1994). *The anthropology of peace and nonviolence.* Boulder: Lynne Rienner.

Spradley, James P. (1979). *The ethnographic interview.* New York: Holt, Rinehart and Winston.

Stegeborn, Wiveca (1999). The Wanniyala-aetto (Veddahs) of Sri Lanka. In Richard B. Lee and Richard Daly (Eds.), *The Cambridge encyclopedia of hunters and gatherers* (pp. 269–273). Cambridge, England: Cambridge University Press.

Straus, Murray A. (1991). Physical violence in American families: Incidence rates, causes, and trends. In Dean D. Knudsen and JoAnn L. Miller (Eds.), *Abused and battered: Social and legal responses to family violence* (pp. 17–34). New York: deGruyter.

Straus, Murray A. (1995). Ordinary violence, child abuse, and wife beating: What do they have in common? In Murray A. Straus and Richard J. Gelles (Eds.), *Physical violence in American families: Risk factors and adaptations to violence in 8,145 families* (pp. 403–424). New Brunswick, NJ: Transaction Publishers.

Straus, Murray A. (2001). Physical aggression in the family: Prevalence rates, links to non-family violence, and implications for primary prevention of societal violence. In M. Martinez (Ed.), *Prevention and control of aggression and the impact on its victims* (pp. 181–200). New York: Kluwer Academic/Plenum.

Straus, Murray A., & Mathur, Anita K. (1996). Social change and the trends in approval of corporal punishment by parents from 1968 to 1994. In Detlef Frehsee, Wiebke Horn, & Kai D. Bussmann (Eds.), *Family violence against children: A challenge for society* (pp. 91–105). New York: deGruyter.

Tedeschi, James T., & Felson, Richard B. (1994). *Violence, aggression and coercive action.* Washington: American Psychological Association.

Thomas, David John. (1982). *Order without government: The society of the Pemon Indians of Venezuela.* Urbana: University of Illinois Press.

Thomas, David John. (1994). Pemon. In Johannes Wilbert (Ed.), *Encyclopedia of world cultures: Vol. VII. South America* (pp. 271–273). Boston: G. K. Hall.

Thomas, Elizabeth Marshall. (1959). *The harmless people.* New York: Knopf.

Thomas, Elizabeth Marshall. (1994). Management of violence among the Ju/wasi of Nyae Nyae: The old way and a new way. In S. P. Reyna and R. E. Downs (Eds.), *Studying war: Anthropological perspectives* (pp. 69–84). Langhorne, PA: Gordon and Breach.

Turnbull, Colin M. (1965a). *Wayward servants: The two worlds of the African pygmies.* Garden City, NY: Natural History Press.

Turnbull, Colin M. (1965b). The Mbuti pygmies of the Congo. In James L. Gibbs, Jr. (Ed.), *Peoples of Africa* ( pp. 279–317). New York: Holt, Rinehart, and Winston.

Turnbull, Colin M. (1968). Discussion: Primate behavior and the evolution of aggression. In Richard B. Lee & Irven DeVore (Eds.), *Man the hunter* (pp. 339–344). Chicago: Aldine.

Turnbull, Colin M. (1978). The politics of non-aggression. In Ashley Montagu (Ed.), *Learning non-aggression: The experience of non-literate societies* (pp. 161–221). New York: Oxford University Press.

Van der Dennen, Johan M. G. (1995). *The origin of war, volumes 1 & 2*. Gronginen, Netherlands: Origin Press.

Van der Sluys, Cornelia M. I. (1999). The Jahai of Northern Peninsular Malaysia. In Richard B. Lee & Richard Daly (Eds.), *The Cambridge encyclopedia of hunters and gatherers* (pp. 307–311). Cambridge, England: Cambridge University Press.

Walker, Anthony R. (1986). *The Toda of South India: A new look*. Delhi, India: Hindustan.

Walker, Anthony R. (1992). Toda. In Paul Hockings (Ed.), *Encyclopedia of world cultures: Vol. III. South Asia* (pp. 294–298). Boston: G. K. Hall.

Walters, David R. (1975). *Physical and sexual abuse of children: Causes and treatment*. Bloomington: Indiana University Press.

Wauchope, Barbara A., & Straus, Murray A. (1995). Physical punishment and physical abuse of American children: Incidence rates by age, gender, and occupational class. In Murray A. Straus & Richard J. Gelles (Eds.), *Physical violence in American families: Risk factors and adaptations to violence in 8,145 families* (pp. 133–148). New Brunswick, NJ: Transaction Publishers.

Widom, Cathy S. (1989). The cycle of violence. *Science 244*, 160–166.

Willis, Roy. (1989a). Power begins at home: The symbolism of male-female commensality in Ufipa. In W. Arens & Ivan Karp (Eds.), *Creativity of power: cosmology and action in African societies* (pp. 113–128). Washington, DC: Smithsonian Institution Press.

Willis, Roy. (1989b). The "peace puzzle" in Ufipa. In Signe Howell & Roy Willis (Eds.), *Societies at peace: Anthropological perspectives* (pp. 133–145). London: Routledge.

Wolf, Richard Kent. (1992). Kota. In Paul Hockings (Ed.), *Encyclopedia of world cultures: Vol. III. South Asia* (pp. 134–138). Boston: G. K. Hall.

Wrangham, Richard, & Peterson, Dale. (1996). *Demonic males: Apes and the origins of human violence*. Boston: Houghton Mifflin.

Zent, Stanford. (1994). Piaroa. In Johannes Wilbert (Ed.), *Encyclopedia of world cultures: Vol. VII. South America* (pp. 275–278). Boston: G. K. Hall.

Zvelebil, Kamil V. (1988). *The Irulas of the Blue Mountains*. Syracuse, NY: Syracuse University.

# CHAPTER 8

# INTEGRATIVE COMPLEXITY AND COGNITIVE MANAGEMENT IN INTERNATIONAL CONFRONTATIONS: RESEARCH AND POTENTIAL APPLICATIONS

## Peter Suedfeld, Dana C. Leighton, and Lucian Gideon Conway III

The beliefs, attitudes, and cognitive processes that underlie political decision making have long been among the major concerns of political psychologists. Shortly after World War II, there was a burgeoning interest about personality factors that might be related to the heinous genocidal actions that had been carried out by the Axis countries before and during the war. Research focused on finding some aspect of the personality that would predispose individuals to participate in, or at least not to oppose, policies that led to such actions.

## Early Cognitive Styles Research

The seminal text in the field was, and perhaps still is, *The Authoritarian Personality* (Adorno, Frenkel-Brunswik, Levinson, & Sanford, 1950). The book applied attitude measurement and psychoanalytic theory to explain anti-Semitic, ethnocentric, and antidemocratic beliefs. One of the products of *The Authoritarian Personality* was the F (Fascism) Scale, widely used (and misused) in research since that time (R. Christie, 1991). Although the F Scale was demonstrated to be useful in measuring "antidemocratic and fascist tendencies" (Meloen, 1993), it also became a springboard for researchers who proposed that there are pervasive individual differences in information processing that characterize a person's cognitive approach regardless of the content or topic of thought.

### Cognitive Complexity

Such differences, soon to be known as *cognitive styles*, include a wide variety of constructs. A significant proportion of theory and research addresses *cognitive complexity*, which refers to how predisposed the individual is to process or avoid new information and novel ideas, flexible thinking, and cognitive nuance (Goldstein & Blackman, 1978; Schroder & Suedfeld, 1971).

Working from the personality structure research of George Kelly (1955), cognitive complexity researchers recognized that authoritarianism is not just an aspect of political preference but has broad implications for information processing regardless of the topic of the information. New theories and scales minimized the role of specific attitudes or ideologies in favor of concentrating on the structure of thought. These have included dogmatism and rigidity (Rokeach, 1947, 1956, 1960), need for closure (nClos, Kruglanski & Webster, 1996), and need for cognition (nCog, Cacioppo & Petty, 1982). Dogmatism and rigidity refer to resistance to new information and attitude change; the nClos measure evaluates people's preference for goal direction, planning, and avoidance of arousal; and high nCog indicates a preference for gathering new, sometimes contradictory, information (Suedfeld, 2000).

### Conceptual (Trait) Complexity

One version of the cognitive complexity approach to information processing styles is *conceptual complexity* theory. Unlike adherents of some other approaches to cognitive styles, conceptual complexity theorists argued that highly complex cognition involves not only the recognition of alternatives, nuances, and new information (*differentiation*); it also involves the recognition of relationships among these and the ability to view them in various combinatorial ways (*integration*) (Gardiner & Schroder, 1972; Streufert & Schroder, 1965; Suedfeld, Tetlock, & Streufert, 1992; Tetlock, 1993; Tetlock & Suedfeld, 1988). Perhaps as a consequence, the association between conceptual complexity and other cognitive complexity constructs tends to be in the low to moderate range.

Schroder, Driver, and Streufert's semistructured instrument, the Paragraph Completion Test or PCT (1967), eventually became the most widely used method for measuring conceptual complexity. The PCT was used successfully in many simulation studies with laboratory subjects (Schroder et al., 1967) and was shown to have high face and predictive validity. PCT scores, ranging from 1 at the lowest level of complexity to 7 at the highest, are assigned by trained scorers to paragraphs written by subjects completing stems related to major socio-psychological variables such as relations to authority and peers, conflict, and uncertainty. Later, a highly sophisticated simulation was developed and applied to the study of decision making by corporate and public-sector managers (Streufert & Swezey, 1986).

# The Emergence of Integrative Complexity Research

The *integrative complexity* approach emerged about a decade after the beginning of conceptual complexity research. The focus expanded to include studies of actual (rather than simulated) high level decision making. Two innovations made this possible. One is the measurement of complexity from archival materials rather than by the PCT, enabling researchers to assess complexity in individuals and groups who are not available for direct research participation due to distance, chronology, and/ or position. The other is an emphasis on level of complexity as a functional as opposed to a personality variable (Suedfeld & Rank, 1976). Information processing complexity as demonstrated in writing and speech is conceived to be a joint function of a stable personality disposition (conceptual, or trait, complexity) interacting with internal and external situational variables that affect the actual level of complexity at which the individual is then operating (integrative, or state, complexity) (cf. Streufert & Nogami, 1989; Streufert & Schroder, 1965; Streufert & Streufert, 1978; Suedfeld & Tetlock, 2001; Tetlock, Peterson, & Berry, 1993). This approach takes integrative complexity (IC) out of the category of cognitive styles, as a more broadly behavioral variable that incorporates, but is not totally determined by, the personality aspect of cognition. In the pages that follow, we shall consider how both the stable, trait component and the changing, state component of complexity are related to political decision making, problem solving, and negotiations.

Measuring the IC of political leaders at a distance involves examining archival textual samples (speeches, diaries, and letters) and coding them on the 1–7 scale used to score the PCT. Normally, passages to be scored are drawn only from complete transcripts or documents. Excerpts are subject to the bias of the person who chooses them and therefore may not be representative of the IC of the source. Careful procedures ensure that the paragraphs are sampled randomly from all available paragraphs. Details of the scoring procedure are available elsewhere (e.g., Baker-Brown et al., 1992; Suedfeld, Guttieri, & Tetlock, 2003). The scoring manual, and training materials to become an independent scorer, can also be obtained on the Internet at http:// www.psych.ubc.ca/~psuedfeld/RESTlab/Complexity.

To summarize the scoring scheme, a paragraph that shows unidimensional, dichotomous categorization is given the lowest score, 1. As the material exhibits degrees of differentiation, the level rises to 3; when both differentiation and integration are evident, a score of 5 is assigned. When multiple, interrelated schemata are evidenced in a dynamic, interrelated relationship, then the highest score is given a score of 7. Scores of 2, 4, or 6 are assigned when the passage shows some indications of the next higher level, but not clearly enough for the higher score.

When complexity of materials from political decision makers is measured, some interesting characteristics appear. Ideological "true believers" are more dogmatic, intolerant of ambiguity, and less integratively complex than ideological moderates. Isolationists exhibit lower integrative complexity than nonisolationists. Conservative U.S. Senators show less integrative complexity than moderates or liberals. Confidential interviews with members of the British Parliament showed that moderate socialists were more complex than both extreme socialists and either extreme or moderate conservatives (Tetlock, 1993). On a less exalted political level, Suedfeld, Bluck, Loewen, and Elkins (1994) found that members of Canadian campus political groups differed in IC: those belonging to ideologically based parties, whether on the left or on the right, were less complex than members of pragmatic, centrist parties.

### International Politics and Integrative Complexity

In the realm of international politics, several relevant findings point toward the predictive utility of IC scoring. An individual who is thinking at a low level of IC will prefer certainty and rules, tend to see the world as dichotomous, and make rapid judgments about the world. Lowered IC may be a prerequisite for the initiation of violence.

Major outbreaks of violence in the Middle East region were predictably preceded by a reduction of integrative complexity on both sides (Suedfeld, Tetlock, & Ramirez, 1977). Iraq's surprise invasion of Kuwait was preceded by lowered complexity of communications from the Iraqi government and higher complexity from Kuwait. Immediately after the attack, the complexity of Kuwait's leaders declined precipitously to match their attacker's level. Thereafter, complexity changes mirrored each other (Suedfeld, Wallace, & Thachuk, 1993). This pattern of complexity change was consistent with changes preceding other surprise attacks that occurred in the twentieth century (Suedfeld & Bluck, 1988). Similar patterns of results were found in a recent analysis of the integrative complexity of British, American, and terrorist leaders before and after the September 11, 2001, attacks on the United States by the al Qaeda terrorist network (Suedfeld & Leighton, 2002).

Lower integrative complexity is sometimes associated with reduced effectiveness of conflict resolution, increased other-directed attributions of blame in conflicts (Sillars & Parry, 1982), and with more extreme views on capital punishment (de Vries & Walker, 1987). People exhibiting lower IC are more likely to endorse violence. The cognitive load associated with environmental stressors results in people thinking less complexly, more concretely, and in black-and-white terms (Schroder et al., 1967). For example, violence initiated by the other side generally evokes low-IC responses from the victim (Driver, 1962; Suedfeld & Bluck, 1988), and a recent analysis of political speeches across time periods and cultures found a reduced level of integrative complexity in speeches delivered in times leading to the initiation of violent conflict (Conway, Suedfeld, & Tetlock, 2001).

We emphasize, however, that although a low level and/or reduction of IC is frequently a precursor of violence, it is not an infallible index. Just as low trait complexity may be associated with either chronic bellicosity or rigid pacifism, so it is possible for a highly stressed individual or leadership group to resolve problems other than by attacking (e.g., by withdrawing or surrendering). Still, on the whole, individuals low in integrative or conceptual complexity are relatively likely to resort to competitive actions in negotiations and to turn to violence or other drastic complexity-reducing responses when frustrated (Conway et al., 2001).

A person using higher IC, on the other hand, will tend to find richness in ambiguity and see a multidimensional array of stimuli in the world (Tetlock, 1993). Higher IC might therefore enhance the chances for successful negotiation and nonviolent conflict resolution.

Given the relationship between integrative complexity and competitive or violent behavior and its effects on interpersonal conflict communication, it becomes apparent that it is likely to play a role in negotiation as well as in decision making and strategy development. Since negotiation and peaceful conflict resolution are highly dependent on effective problem solving and communication between participants, the IC of both parties may ultimately influence the effectiveness of negotiation and thus the likelihood of war. Supporting this hypothesis are studies looking specifically at complexity's effect on negotiation outcomes. All factors being equal, negotiations are more likely to result in mutually beneficial outcomes when the negotiators are both high in IC (Pruitt & Lewis, 1975). But, as we show later, high—especially unilaterally high—integrative complexity may also lead to suboptimal, and perhaps disastrous, results.

## Complexity in Cognitive Processing: Trait and State

From a theoretical standpoint, the differing characteristics of simple and complex information processing lead to predictable differences in strategies and outcomes.

Despite the multiplicity of the variables that have an impact on IC, we can make some statements about general aspects of three important questions:

- How do people who differ in trait complexity differ in their decision making and information-processing behavior?
- When other people interact with individuals who differ in trait complexity, what differences do they perceive?
- How does the course of decision making and information processing actually differ as a function of the level of state complexity at which the individual decision maker is operating?

We now pursue each of these three questions in turn.

### Trait Complexity and Information Processing

One issue in looking at complexity in the political setting is the separation of conceptual (trait) from integrative (state) complexity. There are individuals whose conceptual complexity is more or less stable at some given level. That base level may be high, leading to complex information processing across situations, with the recognition of alternatives and the ability to put them together into a coherent *Gestalt*. Such individuals may be quite flexible in adapting to widely differing situations, a characteristic of at least some highly successful diplomats (Wallace & Suedfeld, 1988). It may be moderate—manifested, for example, in the person's ability to see both (or all) sides of every question or both the positive and negative sides of any course of action, but without being able to see how these interact, how they may all fit into a larger overall picture, or how to balance the trade-offs among them. Alternatively, it may be simple, the individual perceiving only one legitimate viewpoint or only one appropriate strategy and either ignoring or rejecting all alternatives. Fanatics and ideologues may be characterized in this way (Suedfeld, 2003).

In brief, the research relevant to this cognitive style suggests that decision makers who are low in trait complexity

- are less responsive to new or changed information from the environment;
- persist longer in pursuing strategies that they had selected earlier in the process;
- when new information is so convincing that they do change their decision, they abandon it in a wholesale manner rather than by trying to identify and modify only those aspects that the new information shows to be erroneous;
- over time and with a variety of issues to be considered, tend to make decisions that are less connected to others either horizontally (across time periods) or vertically (across decision domains) than those made by high-complexity individuals.

In addition to being adept cognitive processors, high-complexity persons also tend to possess other traits that may enhance the negotiation process. For example, highly complex persons tend to be more assertive in complex (but not simple) situations, have more self-confidence, are more socially adept, have better performance in academic contexts, and have moderately high "everyday," as well as componential, intelligence (Bruch, Heisler, & Conroy, 1981; Coren & Suedfeld, 1995; Gottfredson, 1997; McDaniel & Lawrence, 1990; Suedfeld & Coren, 1992).

However, these characteristics do not necessarily lead to complex information processors being liked or admired by their peers or superiors. Research on the perceived characteristics of people varying in conceptual complexity, or messages varying in integrative complexity, has been quite scarce. However, one major study by Tetlock, Peterson, and Berry (1993) used MBA students as the people being rated and their peers and instructors as the raters. Tetlock et al. found that while more complex persons described themselves as open-minded and creative, expert judges viewed them as narcissistic and antagonistic. Thus, despite possessing numerous qualities generally viewed as positive, leaders or group members who are high in complexity may come across to others as arrogant.

### Trait Complexity within Groups

When the members of a group function at a similar level of conceptual complexity, the group's information processing resembles that of an individual at that level. For example, more complex groups use more dimensions to judge other groups, track more information that is not easily available, look for a variety of information sources, and base decisions on a relatively even weighting of all information. Their decisions are also more interconnected over time and across decision domains. When group members are stressed by failure or by information overload or underload, less complex groups lose the ability to generate connected strategic decisions (Schroder et al., 1967).

In an interesting variation, Santmire et al. (1998) varied the homogeneity, rather than the level, of conceptual complexity in their groups of participants. The context was a simulated hostage negotiation. The task for each group was to negotiate a resolution to the hypothetical hijacking of an Indian airliner to Pakistan. Each group consisted of three participants, representing India, Pakistan, and the Sikh separatist hijackers. The groups were heterogeneous (very dissimilar), homogeneous (similar), or "ultrahomogeneous" (virtually identical) in trait complexity as measured on a pretest. The level of complexity of individual negotiators had less to do with the negotiation outcomes than did the degree of homogeneity within the group. Homogeneous groups achieved mutually beneficial agreements 75 percent of the time, as opposed to 50 percent for ultrahomogeneous negotiators, and 35 percent when the negotiators' complexity was heterogeneous. The ultrahomogeneous groups, although reaching fewer mutually beneficial agreements, were the fastest in negotiation. Heterogeneous groups were fastest to cease negotiations and opt out, with an unsatisfactory outcome. They were also slower at reaching mutually beneficial outcomes. The implication is that there needs to be moderate variety in complexity to produce a range of approaches, leading to optimal negotiation outcomes.

## Beyond Trait Complexity: Situational Influences

Recent research has concentrated on comparing decision makers and negotiators operating at either high or low levels of IC, and on the implications of a change in IC level on the part of one or both sides. Whatever trans-situational trait tendencies exist with regard to complexity of information processing, the actual level of complexity at which the individual operates is also affected by other variables. Among these are external environmental factors, such as information load, time pressure, recent and long-term history of successes and failures, the likelihood of serious future gain or loss, and the existence and severity of concurrent problems.

Studies have shown stress to be one of the factors that can reduce the IC exhibited by people in conditions such as information overload or underload, illness, fatigue, political crisis, accountability, time pressure, significant gain or loss contingent on making the right decision, the number and seriousness of other concurrent problems, and social stressors. The extensive simulation research of Streufert and his colleagues has shown a variety of physiological influences on IC. Such influences may be related to personality (e.g., Type A) or to caffeine (either overdose or deprivation) or alcohol (Streufert & Pogash, 1994; Streufert et al., 1994).

According to the *cognitive manager model* (Suedfeld, 1992), the relationship between challenge (which subsumes stress) and IC follows a curvilinear pattern (Selye, 1987; Yerkes & Dodson, 1908). Very low and very high levels of challenge are both associated with low IC (Schroder et al., 1967). If challenge is low, the cognitive manager may see no need to expend the time, effort, and resources required by complex thinking. Up to a certain point, growing challenge leads to higher IC as the individual musters cognitive resources to deal with the problem—as in Selye's resistance phase (if we consider the problem-solving situation to be the stressor). The effective cognitive manager applies complex thinking as needed to deal with the particular problem. Beyond an optimal level of arousal and resource availability, IC decreases as stress increases and cognitive coping ability is depleted. In the IC literature, this phenomenon—which is the counterpart of Selye's phase of exhaustion —is known as *disruptive stress* (e.g., Suedfeld & Granatstein, 1995).

As predicted, high stress levels have been shown to reduce levels of IC, supporting the disruptive stress hypothesis (e.g., Porter & Suedfeld, 1981; Schroder et al., 1967; Suedfeld, 1992; Suedfeld & Granatstein, 1995). For example, the complexity of writings and speeches by American political leaders during the Cuban Missile Crisis decreased as the crisis wore on (Guttieri, Wallace, & Suedfeld, 1995). Analyses of the written records of Confederate General Robert E. Lee and of Canadian World War II General E. L. M. Burns similarly found decreases in IC with the stresses of war and higher complexity when these stressors ended (Suedfeld, Corteen, & McCormick, 1986; Suedfeld & Granatstein, 1995). Not surprisingly, communication effectiveness deteriorates during stressful interpersonal conflict situations (cf. Sillars & Parry, 1982).

### Group Factors in Integrative Complexity

Although we emphasize the importance of individual factors in political decision making, clearly there are aspects of group dynamics that also influence the behavior of policy makers. One such influence, groupthink (Janis, 1972, 1982), is hypothesized to be a factor in suboptimal decision making. According to the groupthink model, some decisions are reached through a behavioral and attitudinal complex that favors the decisions that the group already prefers, at the expense of exploring alternative decisions that may require critical analysis of the issues and consultations with external sources. The group identifies with a charismatic leader, is imbued with a sense of its own moral righteousness and the infallibility of its plans, devalues dissenters, and is both rigid and closed-minded in its information processing. High stress is among the factors that can evoke groupthink decision strategies from a susceptible group. According to Janis, groupthink decisions tend to be failures. Some of his examples are the escalation of American involvement in the Vietnam War and the mishandling of the USS *Pueblo* incident. Janis compares the decisions that led to these failures to decisions he considers successful, such as the peaceful resolution of the 1962 Cuban Missile Crisis.

The conceptual connection between groupthink and IC theory is obvious. Janis's characterization of groupthink decisions resembles the common description of low-complexity strategies, and increasing stress is posited as one causal factor in both. Among other critical works, Tetlock's (1979) experimental analysis of historical documents in some of the decisions discussed by Janis offers only partial support for groupthink theory. Janis's categorization of some of the decisions as being or not being based on groupthink was arguable, and decisions made under groupthink conditions were not always worse than those where groupthink was not evident. However, groupthink was generally associated with lower levels of IC.

Depending on the nature of the conflict situation, efforts to reduce stress for political leaders, policy makers, and negotiators prior to and during conflict situations could help increase IC, perhaps leading to more effective communication and conflict resolution. It is important to add a *caveat* here, though: higher IC is not always associated with optimal decisions. We will make frequent discriminations in this chapter between situations that required higher or lower complexity for more beneficial outcomes. It will also become clear that the complexity of any one party in a negotiation does not necessarily determine the outcome; often, the critical factor is the interaction of complexity levels among and within the parties. Thus, effective negotiations may require that one accurately evaluate the complexity of the other protagonists.

### State Complexity and International Relations

It should be amply evident at this point that a wide range of variables influences a person's cognitive complexity. Although people have chronic differences in cognitive style, factors closely related to the immediate environment and organismic condition also influence the operating level of complexity. Whether deriving from chronic cognitive styles or from temporary influences, however, the level of integrative complexity that a leader or official maintains during difficult international relations is likely to have an impact on the outcome of the situation.

Our repeated references to the role of IC in the context of negotiations are not meant to minimize its importance in other information processing and decision-making domains: leaders, leadership groups, and advisors functioning at particular levels of IC exhibit the same cognitive tendencies as negotiators. Nor does our emphasis imply that the principles apply only to face-to-face negotiating sessions; we subsume the kinds of official and unofficial exchanges of communications (memoranda, white papers, and public speeches in a variety of fora) through which governmental leaders, diplomats, and other high-ranking officials attempt to present and defend their positions in political (especially international) disagreements. Although most of the relevant research has been conducted on political communications, the principles may also operate in other interactions: legal disputes, business deals, union-management negotiations, and perhaps even personal arguments.

What kind of behavior might one expect from political leaders or negotiators who are either at a particular stable level of conceptual complexity or are temporarily operating at a particular level of integrative complexity? Extrapolating from existing data, we hypothesize that as the functioning level of IC rises, the negotiator will become

- more capable of recognizing the mutual advantages of trade-offs and more likely to accept them;
- more likely to generate, and more open to considering, novel analyses of problems and solutions (which may make trade-offs unnecessary);
- less likely to view issues as "non-negotiable";
- more able to perceive links among issues and decisions;
- more likely to pursue several goals or values simultaneously and to understand the difficulty of maximizing *all* of them;
- able to understand the other side's point of view, and to accept that it is legitimate, without necessarily agreeing with it;
- less prone to viewing opponents as evil, implacable, or not worthy of consideration;
- less able to make clear-cut decisions without qualifications;
- more likely to ask for or impose delays in the process of reaching decisions;
- more vulnerable to information overload, to the point of being distracted or diverted from major points by considering too many minor, tangential, or irrelevant issues.

Negotiators need to be alert in monitoring possible changes in the IC level of their counterparts. For example, if a previously low-IC negotiator begins to show an increase, it may be that the situation has changed (e.g., new instructions from the home organization or a reduction in stress) so that more concessions could be in the offing. Contrarily, a drop in IC may indicate a hardening of the negotiator's (or his bosses') position.

To sum up, despite many undeniable virtues, high IC in a leader, advisor, or negotiator is not entirely a good thing. It may unduly prolong negotiations, stall progress or the emergence of an actual decision, frustrate the other side (or even one's own side), and lead to dangerous optimism about the other side's willingness to compromise. It may also divert the individual's attention from critical to trivial issues (the dilution effect, Tetlock, Lerner, & Boettger, 1996). The high-IC negotiator may also be seen as condescending and antagonistic (e.g., Tetlock et al., 1993), not a good image to be projecting.

Given the potential trade-offs between thinking simply and thinking complexly, which is better? Practically speaking, what should international leaders and diplomats actually *do* during negotiations? Should they be integratively complex or integratively simple? Our response is that this is the wrong question. The right question is, *When* is complex (versus simple) thinking more effective in negotiations? In the remainder of this chapter, we discuss the practical implications for decision makers and negotiators of considering this complex issue.

## Implications for Policy Makers, Advisors, and Negotiators

International relations is a complex business. People who formulate, recommend, or implement foreign policy have to seek solutions that at least appear to accommodate the (generally divergent) needs of different factions and nations (Sanson & Bretherton, 2001); understand and interpret intelligence—military, diplomatic, political, and economic—that may be shifting, contradictory, vague, or of unknown reliability (Langholtz & Leentjes, 2001); comprehend the real, sometimes concealed, goals of the other parties (Galtung & Tschudi, 2001); and do all this (and more) working with or against others who have extremely different cultural expectations and norms (Pederson, 2001). Navigating one's way through such a maze of different expectations, values, hopes, and goals is almost inherently complex. As Galtung and Tschudi note,

> Obviously, this work is difficult, requiring experience, and the capacity to internalize vast amounts of emotional/cognitive material from which to make that quantum jump to a new image/perspective with sufficient clarity, combined with the wordsmith's ability to find the right words. (p. 214)

### The Structure of Persuasive Arguments

Political decision makers do not operate in a social vacuum, free from the influence of superiors and constituents. They must sometimes persuade those audiences, and others, that their view of the situation is correct. How best to do this? Knowledge of one's target audience is crucial for an argument's persuasiveness, which has been shown to be affected by the initial position, previous exposure to relevant information, and educational level of the target audience. A one-sided message is more persuasive among those who are less educated, unfamiliar with the relevant arguments, and already favorable to the argument being presented. Two-sided messages are more effective among more educated and better-informed persons, regardless of the initial views they hold, and among individuals who are initially neutral or opposed to the message. Audiences that are convinced by a two-sided message are also more resistant to subsequent counterpersuasion by contradictory messages (Hovland, Janis, & Kelley, 1953; McGuire & Papageorgis, 1961).

Unless they are merely a rhetorical ploy to weaken the opposing position by setting it up as a straw man, two-sided arguments are by definition at least differentiated. If the two positions are presented as irreconcilable, they will reach only that level; if interactive or synthesizing solutions are noted, the argument may rise to the level of integration.

### *Accountability*

A crucial aspect of the political, including international, process is that decisions are made in a social environment that usually includes *accountability*, an interpersonal process that helps to enforce social norms and rules, connects a thinker to social forces, and affects both the content and the structure of the thoughts that are generated (Tetlock, Skitka, & Boettger, 1989). Leaders and representatives who will be judged by their citizens and audiences, under conditions where those judgments will affect what happens next, are likely to process information differently from those who are not subject to such judgments, either because no one will know who is responsible for what is being said or done or because their judgments are not subject to outside review.

Accountability is affected by prior public commitment and one's knowledge of the audience to which he or she is accountable. It is lower when the speaker is anonymous, is transmitting someone else's decisions, or merely represents a group in which responsibility for the decision is diffused. High accountability can reduce a leader's or negotiator's flexibility if his or her constituencies demand a tough stance or adherence to previously stated positions (Pruitt, 1981).

Such rigidity may seem indicative of low IC, but it would be a fallacy to assume that accountability necessarily leads to reductions in complexity. Its relationship to IC is, in fact, variable and is affected by what the speaker (or decision maker, negotiator, etc.) knows about the audience to whom he or she is accountable. According to the social contingency model of judgment and choice (Tetlock, 1992), there are contingencies in being accountable that affect how we think about issues. Tetlock et al. (1989) have shown that people who do not know the views of the audience to which they are accountable for the thoughts they express show higher IC than those who are either unaccountable to anyone or are accountable to an audience that they know to be liberal or conservative (see also Suedfeld & Wallbaum, 1992).

Accountability to an unknown audience increases tolerance of ambiguity and prompts anticipation of arguments likely to be raised by a variety of critics. It may also help to attenuate the effects of heuristics and biases in decision making, perhaps as a result of raised IC. Increasing integrative complexity in situations of accountability may have a cost, though. It can also motivate people to consider irrelevant information in a situation, making spurious inferences that could lead to impaired decision making. In addition, it can also lead to putting off decisions until later (or too late) and to avoiding responsibility for one's decisions (Tetlock, 1992).

It is important that policy makers consider accountability issues when conducting sensitive international negotiations. Political leaders who know the accountability demands experienced by the other protagonist(s) in a negotiation may be able to direct their own negotiating team's strategies more effectively. In turn, knowing how accountability demands are affecting the leader's own thinking can help him or her avoid the tendency to direct negotiations in line with accountability demands when to act in conformity to those demands might lead to poorer decisions or limit one's ability to negotiate.

### High Complexity as an Ideal

In view of all of these factors, it is perhaps no surprise that psychological approaches to international negotiations have focused on how dauntingly complex the relevant factors are or that psychosocial models of negotiations tend to assume and emphasize the need to meet that environmental complexity with psychological complexity.

Further, a preference for complexity is probably a professional bias of social scientists who build such models (Suedfeld & Tetlock, 1992). To illustrate, we counted how many times forms of the words "complexity" and "simplicity" appeared in the "peace-making" section of a recent edited book on the psychology of peace (D. J. Christie, Wagner, & Winter's *Peace, Conflict, and Violence: Peace Psychology for the 21st Century*, 2001). Complexity and its variants were used 25 times; simplicity, and its variants, by contrast, only three times. (In three additional instances, "simple" was used to mean the opposite of its face value—for example, "not simple." Those cases were disregarded.)

The message is clear: It is currently fashionable, when discussing the peace-making process, to emphasize the complexity of both the problems and the solutions. Some of the reasons for this bias include inappropriate transfer of the meaning of the terms from the situational to the cognitive context, the preferences (although not necessarily the functioning) of social scientists, the association between simple information processing and personality traits that are anathema to intellectuals, and the emphasis of much of the psychological literature on the drawbacks of cognitive shortcuts, heuristics, and other simplifying strategies (Suedfeld, 1992; Suedfeld & Tetlock, 1991). We are reminded of President Truman's wish for a one-armed scientific advisor, who would give him clear-cut (i.e., simple) advice rather than constantly (and more complexly) saying "On the one hand this, on the other hand that."

It should be clear that we are not suggesting that the road to a successful political outcome, or to peace, is actually simple or that leaders or negotiators should, as a rule, be simple people. As we have shown, thinking complexly can have multiple benefits when it occurs in appropriate situations. Rather, our goal is to provide some balance to the general modern tenor that psychological complexity in international relations is inherently a good thing. Sometimes, high IC aids international relations; sometimes, it is disastrous. Frequently, the surest road to peace involves psychological complexity; frequently, it involves simplicity. And, despite prevailing dogma, sometimes war is both morally and pragmatically preferable to peace. At Munich, Neville Chamberlain's doomed attempts to ensure "peace in our time" were much higher in complexity than Adolf Hitler's triumphant approach to the negotiation; before the American Civil War, leaders who were willing to compromise on the issue of slavery showed higher IC than either straightforward supporters or abolitionists (the latter of whom, most people would now agree, held the moral high ground; Tetlock, Armor, & Peterson, 1994).

## The Complexity "Match" between Negotiators

We have already discussed at length some of the psychological costs that accompany complex thinking. These costs are not merely psychological, however; a unilateral commitment to complex solutions can have negative consequences for the ultimate goal of peace in international relations. There are some negotiating circumstances where increasing complexity may actually undermine the prospects of international peace. One of the most important aspects of the negotiating context involves the complexity (or simplicity) of the primary political opponents. We consider below how the "match" between opposing negotiators affects the outcome of the negotiation process and use this as a jumping off point to give some practical advice to foreign policy makers.

### Bilateral Low or High Complexity

Often, the complexity of a negotiating party tends to adjust to the level of the other party involved in negotiations (Tetlock, 1985). As a result, many times the complexity levels of negotiating parties will be similar during negotiating phases. When this occurs, the consequences are relatively straightforward. As we have already discussed, history has shown that when both parties are low in complexity (or when both parties drop simultaneously in complexity), aggressive military action frequently follows. Bilateral low complexity in negotiations is a precursor of war, and a drop in IC by one side may precede a surprise strategic attack. Whenever foreign policy makers or negotiators are aware of such a state of things, they should prepare for the worst.

On the other hand, bilateral high complexity in negotiations is a precursor of peace (see, e.g., Conway et al., 2001, for a review). For example, in 1911, competition between France and Germany over spheres of influence in North Africa very nearly led to a general European war. Gunboat diplomacy in the Moroccan port of Agadir could have become a *casus belli*, but with British diplomatic intervention, the Agadir Incident was resolved peacefully, with a negotiated trade. France ceded 100,000 square miles of the French Congo to Germany, which in turn officially recognized France's dominance in Morocco. During this crisis, the IC of the primary leaders of all three key nations (France, Germany, and Great Britain) was consistently in the 5–6 range, showing integration of differentiated perceptions—much higher than it was three years later when another crisis, which could probably also have been contained, instead led to the outbreak of World War I (Suedfeld & Tetlock, 1977). It is important to note that not only the same three Great Powers, but in a number of cases the very same national leaders, were involved in both crises.

Similarly, the Soviet-instituted Berlin Blockade (1948) could have provoked a military response from the Western Allies. The possibility of using armored forces to break through the blockade was rejected in favor of a massive airlift to bring crucial food, fuel, and other goods to surrounded and isolated West Berlin. After close to a year, the USSR called off the blockade. This peaceful outcome was preceded by higher IC on the part of U.S. and Soviet leaders than was found in diplomatic exchanges between the two countries prior to the Korean War two years later (Suedfeld & Tetlock, 1977). Incidentally, the same pattern of continuing relatively high IC around the Berlin Blockade has been replicated and extended to a later Berlin crisis that was also resolved peacefully (Raphael, 1982).

The past few years of the recurrent crisis between India and Pakistan have been marked by an increase in the complexity of leaders on both sides even during major terrorist violence, thus suggesting a resolution without major war—a prediction that, to date anyway, has been fulfilled (Suedfeld, Jhangiani, & Weiszbeck, 2003). The message is clear: When both parties' leaders and negotiators are high in (or show an increase in) complexity, a nonaggressive solution to a problem is the most likely outcome. As our examples demonstrate, high IC does not need to be related to a particular kind of resolution: it led to a trade-off in the Agadir Incident, a creative nonviolent course in Berlin until the other side decided that its tactic was unsuccessful and abandoned it, and acceptance of a tolerable, even if not ideal, long-term balance in South Asia.

It now appears that a similar pattern occurs in ethnopolitical confrontations. In recent peace negotiations between Mayan insurgents (the Zapatista Liberation Army, EZLN) and the Mexican government, complex communications by government negotiators elicited increased complexity from the insurgent representatives. Such occurrences were associated with perceived progress in the negotiation. An interesting sidelight is that the stimulus-response link was asymmetrical: complexity changes in the comments of the insurgents did not affect the IC of the government officials representing the more powerful side.

This was the first study to look at a communication process between rebels and their government and also the first to score IC in face-to-face ongoing negotiations in which communications were oral and followed each other in a matter of minutes, not—as in research on diplomatic communications—days or even weeks (Liht, Suedfeld, & Krawczyk, 2005).

### Mixed Levels of Complexity

Many times, however, negotiators will have very different levels of complexity during the negotiating process. What happens when one side's primary leaders decrease in complexity, while the other side's leaders increase?

The consequences of such mismatched complexity levels can be utterly disastrous to peaceful efforts. Following up an unpredicted finding in their study of the enduring rivalry between Israel and her Arab neighbors (Suedfeld et al., 1977), Suedfeld and Bluck (1988) undertook to study a number of surprise strategic attacks by one nation against another. In every case but one, the eventual attackers' complexity levels decreased during the weeks prior to the attack. However, the complexity levels of the target nations tended to increase prior to the attack. While the attackers were secretly planning their aggressive action, the targets were still trying to negotiate a peaceful outcome. But this strategy obviously did not work. Thus, when your opponent has reached a drastic, low-IC decision, it may be useless to continue approaching the issues with higher levels of complex reasoning.

## Practical Advice for Policy Makers and Negotiators

Although the complexity research reported here was not designed specifically with the goal of changing foreign policy, the reflections of this chapter do have some practical implications for negotiators and foreign-policy makers on handling difficult international relations. The suggestions that follow carry more of a flavor than a specific recipe. They are more about maintaining a particular attitude about complexity rather than concrete advice about saying X when your opponent says Y. The specific ingredients necessary, the concrete tactics themselves, vary greatly from situation to situation. We know something about them, but the data are not extensive enough at this point to support more than tentative advice (cf. Tetlock, 1986).

### Choosing a Negotiation Strategy

The most obvious piece of advice to be drawn from the complexity literature is that negotiators should learn to recognize those contexts where complexity is most likely to be successful and use it only in those situations. For example, a complex negotiating strategy is most likely to be effective when one's opponent is thinking complexly; a simple negotiating strategy is most likely to be effective when one's opponent is thinking simply.

To illustrate, consider an episode described by Follett (1940; cited in Sanson & Bretherton, 2001). Once, she and a friend were debating about a window in the room they were sitting in. She wanted the window open; her friend wanted it shut. Follett points out that a half-and-half compromise would have been futile: Leaving the window half-open would have satisfied neither herself nor her friend. But, rather than using either a power struggle or a straight compromise to solve their problem, both parties were willing to think further to find a mutually satisfying solution. Discussion revealed that Follett wanted the window open to keep the air inside fresh, while her friend wanted the window shut to keep a direct breeze from blowing on her. Given those two needs, a solution was struck that thoroughly satisfied both parties: opening a window in an adjacent room.

Follett uses this example to illustrate what can be done when negotiators are willing to think more deeply about the underlying reasons for the positions taken by each side and then use this information to find a solution that integrates those two needs. But notice, Follett's analogy is dependent upon both sides being willing to think complexly about the situation. To arrive at the acceptable agreement, each side must recognize the legitimacy of the other's needs about the window ("Well, now that I understand that she just does not want the air to get stale, I think maybe we can try to figure out what to do"), and each side must have the motivation and ability to come up with a good solution. In terms of integrative complexity, the agreement they struck was fairly complex: At least a "5" on the 7-point scale, a level that international negotiators are rarely able to maintain consistently. It requires that both parties recognize the legitimacy of both sets of motives (desire for fresh air and desire for protection from wind) and the integration of those motives (opening a window in an adjoining room, thus allowing for fresh air without a draft).

When both sides are willing (and able) to think complexly, we fully endorse the practical advice implied by Follett's example. Everyone stands to gain if all parties approach the issues at a complex level; thus, to the degree that one's counterparts are doing so, negotiators are wise to meet such complexity with complexity themselves. In such a case, high levels of IC maximize the likelihood that a solution will be found that is satisfactory to both sides—and will be found with as little (hopefully no) loss of life as possible. So, in one sense, foreign policy commentators are right to emphasize the necessity of thinking complexly.

It is encouraging to note that, at least under some circumstances, higher IC on the part of one negotiator evokes the same from the other. Tetlock (1985) found such a pattern in his analysis of long-term interactions between Soviet and American representatives, and Liht et al. (in press) confirmed it in the context of negotiations between Mexican government negotiators and a group of rebel leaders. To the extent that mutual high IC is a precursor of peaceful solutions, this pattern implies a strategy worth trying: If your side is truly interested in a mutually satisfactory solution, your operating at a high level of complexity may encourage your counterpart to do likewise. This pattern of emulation may be (and we think it is) unconscious rather than deliberate, which may add to its potency.

## Goals Affect Strategies

However, what if your counterpart window debaters are completely unwilling to consider your point of view? What if they insist that getting fresh air is not a reasonable goal or that it is merely a cover story concocted to disguise your actual wish that they catch a cold from sitting in the blast of the wind? What if they slam the window every time you try to open it and say, "The decision is final—accept the closed window or get out"? If that happens, complex negotiation on your part is a futile enterprise. If someone says, "I do not care what you say; that and all windows will remain shut no matter what," then you have three options. You must stand and fight, leave, or submit to breathing stale air.

But sometimes the world is like that. History is abundantly full of national leaders for whom negotiation is only a tactic, to muster public support, to obtain as much as possible without fighting, or to gain time for preparing their attack. To say otherwise is simply to turn a blind eye to history: a psychological, but not scientific, option. Indeed, one cannot take for granted that in any negotiation setting both parties begin with an underlying desire to reach a peaceful and mutually satisfying agreement. Many international struggles involve clashes of basic principles or conflict over truly needed but truly insufficient resources. Opposing parties in difficult negotiations do not always have a good working relationship and a genuine interest in reaching an agreement that will benefit both sides. We suspect that policy makers and negotiators are often flung against a wall of simplicity that defies a more complex approach. It appears that many times, one of the parties in the negotiation is not actually interested in obtaining an agreement short of total victory. As the columnist George Jonas wrote concerning the Israeli-Palestinian impasse, "It's futile to make concessions to someone who isn't interested in the deal itself" (2003).

Psychological complexity in such situations is futile. It is like throwing pictures of negotiation models (however beautifully complex they may be) at an incoming nuclear missile. The missile can be stopped only with a force simple enough to combat its own simple movement. It does not care how complex your negotiation model is. In fact, the missile (could it think and feel) would be perfectly happy for you to keep trying to stop it with complexity, because it would know that your complex countertactic affords it more time to reach its target. It is a simple, all-out response that the missile would fear.

Consider this: Hitler's negotiating style was defined by extremely low levels of integrative complexity (Satterfield, 1998; Suedfeld, 1992). "Now Poland is in the position I wanted her," Hitler said in August 1939, "I am only afraid that some swine or other will submit to me a plan for mediation" (as cited in Satterfield, p. 680). His mind was uncompromisingly set on world conquest. Yet, time after time Britain's Prime Minister Neville Chamberlain attempted to counter this simplicity with complexity. Although such judgments are often difficult to make (see Suedfeld, 1992), the nearly universal judgment of history is that the results of this mismatch in complexity were nothing short of disastrous. Appeasement flopped, and millions of innocent people likely lost their lives in consequence. Far from preventing human suffering, Chamberlain's complex approach almost certainly guaranteed its increase.

Interestingly, the previously mentioned work on surprise attacks suggests that there is often a tendency for negotiators to futilely throw complex pictures at missiles. Recall that the IC of those who led nonaggressive nations tended to go up shortly before they were attacked. This tendency to counter simplicity with complexity is probably best resisted. It is not only useless; it may be fatal. War is a terrible thing, and averting it is a noble goal. But sometimes war is thrust upon a nation, or it is the only way to preserve its basic principles and integrity. If a drastic, uncompromising outcome is unavoidable, or even highly probable, it is better to meet it head-on, square in the face—to meet it simply. Sometimes, the best way to stop large-scale war from occurring is to use military coercion as soon as possible—as even the United Nations acknowledges (see, e.g., Langholtz & Leentjes, 2001).

In a sense, our recommendation is analogous to research on the Prisoner's Dilemma gamethat suggests the most effective strategy for maximizing a positive outcome is "tit for tat": If your counterpart behaves aggressively, then you should respond in kind. However, if your counterpart learns a lesson from this and begins to behave cooperatively, then you should again respond in kind by cooperating (e.g., Axelrod, 1980; for a pioneering analysis of a similar, but somewhat more patient and lenient version of this strategy in the Cold War, see Osgood, 1962). Persons who do not adapt to their counterparts' moves—who *always* behave competitively or cooperatively, regardless of the context—do not do well. Perennially competitive persons are always incurring the costs of constant competition; perennially cooperative persons are always being taken advantage of. Revolutionary leaders who remained in power after their cause succeeded moved from low IC during the armed struggle to higher IC once in government; those who were too high during the battle or remained low after victory tended to fall out of leadership positions, sometimes "to the wall" (Suedfeld & Rank, 1976). Flexibility seems to be a consistent "good" when looking at IC in political situations.

## Specific Strategy Suggestions

Our recommendation with respect to complexity follows. It applies to interactions where the two sides have approximately equal resources; obviously, if one party is overwhelmingly powerful and is willing to exert that power, the IC of the other side may become irrelevant. However, the resources may not have to be in the same domain. For example, if one party is totally superior in military or economic might but is limited in its potential actions by serious concern about its international reputation or domestic political support, the objectively weaker side may still have the opportunity to use more or less complex strategies to get at least some of what it wants. Note also that our suggestions do not address the content of negotiations, but only their structure.

1. Negotiators should start out by outlining their perception of the situation at a high level of IC; this gives the opponent notice that compromise or some other mutually acceptable solution is possible.

2a. If the opponent responds with increased complexity, then negotiators should respond in kind.

2b. However, if the opponent responds to initial complexity with simple, uncompromising demands, then we advise the negotiators to lower their complexity as well.

3a. If the opponent continues its low-complex aggressive stance, then aggression may be inevitable.

3b. If the opponent becomes more complex, then (once again) negotiators should become complex with them.

We recognize that this strategy may well lead to aggressive actions on both sides. We recognize, too, that (as a result) this advice will be largely unpopular. Our defense rests on two premises: (a) Although political psychology is not primarily about moral principles (see, e.g., Conway et al., 2001; Suedfeld, 1992), we assume that (given no greater moral principle is violated) the principle "peace is preferable to wide-scale war" is or should be shared by most foreign policy makers; and (b) sometimes, the only way to prevent war or surrender is by being ready (or seem to be ready) to stand firm in the face of aggressive signals. If (b) is false, then attempting to maintain chronically high IC would almost certainly be the best way to accomplish the goal stated in (a), and suggestions about shifting between complex and simple strategies would be meaningless.

We need to address two problems underlying one's ability to tailor our IC strategy to a counterpart's complexity level. First, it is imperative that we know exactly what that level is. This is not always an easy task. It may be that changes in IC during negotiations will be undetectable except by formal coding. Complexity is not necessarily revealed by the content of a message; thus, changes in IC may even be moving in the direction opposite to communication content (e.g., paeans to peace may accompany IC reductions as the speaker's country prepares to go to war—Suedfeld et al., 1977). If leaders cannot detect changes in complexity, then naturally they cannot respond to them.

However, there is reason for optimism. Evidence suggests that one does not necessarily have to be an expert in integrative complexity coding (unlikely among diplomats and politicians) in order to put complexity theory to good use in negotiations. People do not need to be familiar with complexity theory, or even be educated in the social sciences, to intuitively recognize different levels of complexity. Suedfeld, de Vries, Bluck, Wallbaum, and Schmidt (1996) showed that "naive" subjects could accurately identify communications that differed in complexity, specify the direction in which complexity would change under different conditions (e.g., if the communicator was tired, or stressed, or dealing with a crucial problem, etc.), and fairly correctly rate their own level of complexity against a set of templates representing the major nodes (undifferentiated, differentiated but not integrated, and differentiated and integrated). Thus, an experienced and able negotiator may intuitively attend to cues associated with different levels of IC and respond appropriately to them.

The second problem is the manipulation of one's own IC as a deliberate strategy. Whether this is actually possible except in short-term, artificial situations is an open and controversial question in the literature. Tetlock (1981; Tetlock, Hannum, & Micheletti, 1984) has argued that *impression management* is a potent influence on IC levels; Suedfeld and his colleagues (e.g., Conway et al., 2001) maintain that IC is rarely under voluntary control, being determined by personality and situational factors of which the person is usually unaware—and even when aware, unable to overcome. Numerous data analyses have shown leaders to zig when by all rational expectations they should zag: exhibiting lower IC when flexibility and compromise might have averted imminent disaster, or higher IC when standing firm might have cowed an opponent (e.g., Saddam Hussein; cf. Suedfeld, 2003). If, in fact, it is impossible or improbable that one can purposefully alter one's IC as a strategic tool, the advice that we outlined above becomes moot.

Other aspects of the situation, too, can affect when complexity is most likely to aid or hinder international negotiations. For example, increasing psychological complexity is likely to have more impact where the primary problem appears to be one of different cultural norms (see Pederson, 2001; Sanson & Bretherton, 2001).

Making this judgment is difficult, but to the degree that debates center around cultural and individual differences—as opposed to tangible resources such as land and food—complexity is likely to be more effective. If two competing parties both mean something different by the word "land," recognizing this fact may aid the negotiating process. For example, when the Israeli-Egyptian dispute over the Sinai was recognized as Israel's need for land that could provide defense in depth and Egypt's need to recover some of the land lost in the humiliating defeat of 1967, turning the area back to Egyptian sovereignty but keeping it demilitarized (with a U.N. "trip-wire" force in the middle) was acceptable to both sides. This could be seen as an integrative solution similar to the open-or-closed window situation. However, if the two sides both simply want to own the same piece of land (perhaps because it possesses a specific resource that is crucial to both), no level of complexity is likely to solve the problem.

Learning to differentiate between these two kinds of problems is a useful skill for a negotiator. While we offer no direct practical advice as to how to develop it, we emphasize that it is important to acknowledge the existence and relevance of the distinction. An Irish prayer asks for the wisdom to tell the difference between tractable and intractable problems; political leaders must recognize that merely trying harder to find a complex solution cannot solve some situations. Some statesmen came to that recognition in the summer of 1914, as the conflict in Europe spiraled toward war, apparently irresistibly. The drops in IC then presaged their surrender to an unavoidable conclusion.

## Choosing a Negotiating Team

Given the strengths of individuals who are high in conceptual (trait) complexity, it may seem a good idea to choose such people for leadership roles and for the tasks of negotiating with opponents. However, this strategy may appear to be more attractive than it is successful; such a simple decision rule can have disastrous consequences if applied without qualification. Perhaps the *most* important goal is to ensure that the leader and the team possess a high level of metacomplexity: the ability to recognize when the situation calls for a change in IC level and the ability to make that shift. It is important to emphasize that these abilities do not have to involve conscious assessment and change. As we said before, the latter may not even be feasible. Meta-complexity, like both conceptual and integrative complexity, may vary and function quite outside the everyday awareness of the individual.

Theoretically, the establishment of an appropriately metacomplex team could be accomplished in at least two ways. The first is to create the team with a mixture of conceptual complexity levels, so that there are some members who are complex most of the time and others who are simple most of the time. This would be akin to selecting advisory groups whose members are known in advance to possess a mixture of political orientations and areas of expertise; conceptual complexity would be just one more characteristic on which diversity would be sought.

Different individuals could then be moved into the top leadership slot as the situation seemed to favor one or another complexity level. One would assign a low-complexity leader when the team faces a completely determined and uncompromising opponent. One would not assign such a person to lead a team whose opponent is more flexible and willing to consider trade-offs. Thus, Churchill—low in trait complexity—would have been a better British representative than Chamberlain to face Hitler, but the reverse was true in the negotiations with Congress Party leaders during the process of achieving Indian independence. Indeed, history confirms that Churchill's low-IC functioning was more successful in dealing with Hitler than with Gandhi, Nehru, and their Congress Party colleagues (Tetlock & Tyler, 1996).

A different, probably more reliable, but also probably less realistic, strategy is to select all members of the team with an eye to their ability to shift across complexity levels when appropriate. This means that, unlike Churchill or Chamberlain, and regardless of their underlying level of trait complexity, all participants should be responsive and flexible in adapting IC to changing situations.

Whether by constituting teams varying in trait complexity, assigning persons functioning at different levels to different tasks, or picking all members with the capacity for flexible IC functioning, the most important concern from the standpoint of complexity is that some person or persons in the group have the ability to shift between different levels of complexity—and that they have the power to apply the right level of complex strategies to each situation.

## Concluding Thoughts

Although, as we have seen, many studies have addressed the road to war or peace, no research has been directed to the ending of a war once it has begun. Do statesmen recover a high level of IC as they try to negotiate a peace agreement? At what point in a war does that happen? Does a simple, unidimensional "unconditional surrender" strategy gain more concessions than a more complex set of peace terms? What about the situation where the content and the structure of peace demands or offers are dissonant—for example, where an explicit demand for unconditional surrender actually allows for secret concessions (e.g., the American agreement at the end of the war in the Pacific in 1945 that the Emperor of Japan would be permitted to retain his throne)? If we begin to develop answers to some of these questions, the chore of decision makers and negotiators might be made easier.

We are not, despite appearances, recommending that policy makers and negotiators simply learn to think more (or less) simply. We are seeking cognitive managers. Indeed, our approach requires a higher degree of complexity than many political figures and, *a fortiori*, political analysts, may in fact be accustomed to. The belief that complexity is always the best route to peacemaking in international relations is itself a simple thought; and we challenge those persons who influence foreign policy to expand their horizons, consider the appropriateness of simple strategies in various situations, and thus to think more complexly about complexity itself. We hope we have provided some useful suggestions along these lines. In the future, all of us—scholars, practitioners, and commentators—will learn more about the role of complexity in foreign and domestic policy and how to adjust it to maximize the likelihood of achieving the shared goal of international peace.

## References

Adorno, T. W., Frenkel-Brunswik, E., Levinson, D. J., & Sanford, R. N. (1950). *The authoritarian personality.* New York: Harper & Brothers.

Axelrod, R. (1980). More effective choice in the Prisoner's Dilemma. *Journal of Conflict Resolution, 24*, 379–403.

Baker-Brown, G., Ballard, E. J., Bluck, S., de Vries, B., Suedfeld, P., & Tetlock, P. E. (1992). The conceptual/integrative complexity scoring manual. In C.P. Smith (Ed.), *Motivation and personality: Handbook of thematic content analysis* (pp. 401–418). New York: Cambridge University Press.

Bruch, M. A., Heisler, B. D., & Conroy, C. G. (1981). Effects of conceptual complexity on assertive behavior. *Journal of Counseling Psychology, 28*, 377–385.

Cacioppo, J. T., & Petty, R. E. (1982). The need for cognition. *Journal of Personality & Social Psychology, 42*, 116–131.

Christie, D. J., Wagner, R. V., & Winter, D. D. (Eds.). (2001). *Peace, conflict, and violence: Peace psychology for the 21st century.* Englewood Cliffs, NJ: Prentice-Hall.

Christie, R. (1991). Authoritarianism and related constructs. In J. P. Robinson & P. R. Shaver (Eds.), *Measures of personality and social psychological attitudes* (pp. 501–571). San Diego, CA: Academic Press.

Conway, L. G. III, Suedfeld, P., & Tetlock, P. E. (2001). Integrative complexity and political decisions that lead to war or peace. In D. J. Christie, R. V. Wagner, & D. D. Winter (Eds.), *Peace, conflict, and violence: Peace psychology for the 21st century* (pp. 66–75). Englewood Cliffs, NJ: Prentice-Hall.

Coren, S., & Suedfeld, P. (1995). Personality correlates of conceptual complexity. *Journal of Social Behavior and Personality, 10*, 229–242.

de Vries, B., & Walker, L. J. (1987). Conceptual/integrative complexity and attitudes toward capital punishment. *Personality & Social Psychology Bulletin, 13*, 448–457.

Driver, M. J. (1962). Conceptual structure and group processes in an inter-nation simulation. Part One: The perception of simulated nations. *Princeton, NJ: Educational Testing Service Research Bulletin*, RB 62-15.

Follett, M. P. (1940). Constructive conflict. In H. C. Metcalf & I. L. Urwick (Eds.), *Dynamic administration: The collected papers of Mary Parker Follett* (pp. 1–20). New York: Harper.

Galtung, J., & Tschudi, F. (2001). Crafting peace: On the psychology of the TRANSCEND approach. In D. J. Christie, R. V. Wagner, & D. D. Winter (Eds.), *Peace, conflict, and violence: Peace psychology for the 21st century* (pp. 210–222). Englewood Cliffs, NJ: Prentice-Hall.

Gardiner, G. S., & Schroder, H. M. (1972). Reliability and validity of the Paragraph Completion Test: Theoretical and empirical notes. *Psychological Reports, 31*, 959–962.

Goldstein, K. M., & Blackman, S. (1978). *Cognitive style: Five approaches and relevant research.* New York: Wiley.

Gottfredson, L. S. (1997). Why g matters: The complexity of everyday life. *Intelligence, 24*, 79–132.

Guttieri, K., Wallace, M. D., & Suedfeld, P. (1995). The integrative complexity of American decision makers in the Cuban missile crisis. *Journal of Conflict Resolution, 39*, 595–621.

Hovland, C. I., Janis, I. L., & Kelley, H. H. (1953). *Communication and persuasion: Psychological studies of opinion change.* New Haven, CT: Yale University Press.

Janis, I. L. (1972). *Victims of groupthink: A psychological study of foreign-policy decisions and fiascoes.* Boston: Houghton Mifflin.

Janis, I. L. (1982). *Groupthink: Psychological studies of policy decisions and fiascoes* (2nd ed.). Boston: Houghton Mifflin.

Jonas, G. (2003, November 3). Sharon is not fuelling suicide bombers. *National Post*, p. A-11.

Kelly, G. A. (1955). *The psychology of personal constructs.* New York: Norton.

Kruglanski, A. W., & Webster, D. M. (1996). Motivated closing of the mind: "Seizing" and "freezing." *Psychological Review, 103*, 263–283.

Langholtz, H. J., & Leentjes, P. (2001). U.N. peacekeeping: Confronting the psychological environment of war in the twenty-first century. In D. J. Christie, R. V. Wagner, & D. D. Winter (Eds.), *Peace, conflict, and violence: Peace psychology for the 21st century* (pp. 173–182). Englewood Cliffs, NJ: Prentice-Hall.

Liht, J., Suedfeld, P., & Krawczyk, A. (2005). Integrative complexity in face-to-face negotiations between the Chiapas guerrillas and the Mexican government. *Political Psychology, 26*, 543–552.

McDaniel, E., & Lawrence, C. (1990). *Levels of cognitive complexity: An approach to the measurement of thinking.* New York: Springer-Verlag.

McGuire, W. J., & Papageorgis, D. (1961). The relative efficacy of various types of prior belief-defense in producing immunity against persuasion. *Journal of Abnormal & Social Psychology, 62*, 327–337.

Meloen, J. D. (1993). The F scale as a predictor of fascism: An overview of 40 years of authoritarianism research. In W. F. Stone, G. Lederer, & R. Christie (Eds.), *Strength and weakness: The Authoritarian Personality today* (pp. 47–69). New York: Springer-Verlag.

Osgood, C. E. (1962). *An alternative to war or surrender.* Urbana: University of Illinois Press.

Pederson, P. B. (2001). The cultural context of peacemaking. In D. J. Christie, R. V. Wagner, & D. D. Winter (Eds.), *Peace, conflict, and violence: Peace psychology for the 21st century* (pp. 183–192). Englewood Cliffs, NJ: Prentice-Hall.

Porter, C. A., & Suedfeld, P. (1981). Integrative complexity in the correspondence of literary figures: Effects of personal and societal stress. *Journal of Personality & Social Psychology, 40*, 321–330.

Pruitt, D. G. (1981). *Negotiation behavior.* New York: Academic Press.

Pruitt, D. G., & Lewis, S. A. (1975). Development of integrative solutions in bilateral negotiation. *Journal of Personality & Social Psychology, 31*(4), 621–633.

Raphael, T. D. (1982). Integrative complexity theory and forecasting international crises: Berlin, 1946–1962. *Journal of Conflict Resolution, 26*, 423–450.

Rokeach, M. (1947). Ethnocentrism and a general mental rigidity factor—a further experiment. *American Psychologist, 2*, 413–414.

Rokeach, M. (1956). Political and religious dogmatism; an alternative to the authoritarian personality. *Psychological Monographs, 70*(18, Serial No. 425), 43.

Rokeach, M. (1960). *The open and closed mind: Investigations into the nature of belief systems and personality systems.* Oxford, England: Basic Books.

Sanson, A., & Bretherton, D. (2001). Conflict resolution: Theoretical and practical issues. In D. J. Christie, R. V. Wagner, & D. D. Winter (Eds.), *Peace, conflict, and violence: Peace psychology for the 21st century* (pp. 193–209). Englewood Cliffs, NJ: Prentice-Hall.

Santmire, Tara E., Wilkenfeld, J., Kraus, S., Holley, K. M., Santmire, Toni E., & Gleditsch, K. S. (1998). The impact of cognitive diversity on crisis negotiations. *Political Psychology, 19*, 721–748.

Satterfield, J. M. (1998). Cognitive-affective states predict military and political aggression and risk taking. *Journal of Conflict Resolution, 42*, 667–690.

Schroder, H. M., Driver, M. J., & Streufert, S. (1967). *Human information processing; Individuals and groups functioning in complex social situations.* New York: Holt, Rinehart and Winston.

Schroder, H. M., & Suedfeld, P. (Eds.). (1971). *Personality theory and information processing.* New York: Ronald.

Selye, H. (1987). Stress without distress. In L. Levi (Ed.), *Society, stress, and disease, Vol. 5: Old age* (pp. 257–262). London: Oxford University Press.

Sillars, A., & Parry, D. (1982). Stress, cognition, and communication in interpersonal conflicts. *Communication Research, 9,* 201–226.

Streufert, S., & Nogami, G. Y. (1989). Cognitive style and complexity: Implications for I/O psychology. In C. L. Cooper & I. T. Robertson (Eds.), *International review of industrial and organizational psychology 1989* (pp. 93–143). Oxford, England: John Wiley & Sons.

Streufert, S., & Pogash, R. (1994). Another cup of coffee? Caffeine effects upon complex task performance. *MTA Conference Proceedings,* Rotterdam, 436–441.

Streufert, S., Pogash, R., Roache, J., Severs, W., Gingrich, D., Landis, R., et al. (1994). Alcohol and management performance. *Journal of Studies on Alcohol, 55,* 230–238.

Streufert, S., & Schroder, H. M. (1965). Conceptual structure, environmental complexity and task performance. *Journal of Experimental Research in Personality, 1,* 132–137.

Streufert, S., & Streufert, S. C. (1978). *Behavior in the complex environment.* New York: V. H. Winston.

Streufert, S., & Swezey, R. W. (1986). *Complexity, managers, and organizations.* San Diego, CA: Academic Press.

Suedfeld, P. (1992). Cognitive managers and their critics. *Political Psychology 13,* 435–453.

Suedfeld, P. (2000). Cognitive styles: Personality. In A. E. Kazdin (Ed.), *Encyclopedia of psychology* (Vol. 2, pp. 166–169). Oxford, England: Oxford University Press.

Suedfeld, P. (2003). Saddam Hussein's integrative complexity under stress. In J. M. Post (Ed.), *The psychological assessment of political leaders: With profiles of Saddam Hussein and Bill Clinton* (pp. 391–396). Ann Arbor: University of Michigan Press.

Suedfeld, P. (2003). Integrative complexity of Western and terrorist leaders in the war against the Afghan terrorist regime. *Psicología Política* (Seville), No. 27, 79–91 (Special monograph issue, *Psychological responses to the 2001 terrorist attack on the USA,* W. F. Stone, Coordinator).

Suedfeld, P., & Bluck, S. (1988). Changes in integrative complexity prior to surprise attacks. *Journal of Conflict Resolution, 26,* 626–635

Suedfeld, P., Bluck, S., Loewen, L., & Elkins, D. J. (1994). Sociopolitical values and integrative complexity of members of student political groups. *Canadian Journal of Behavioural Science, 26,* 121–141.

Suedfeld, P., & Coren, S. (1992). Cognitive correlates of conceptual complexity. *Personality and Individual Differences, 13,* 1193–1199.

Suedfeld, P., Corteen, R. S., & McCormick, C. (1986). The role of integrative complexity in military leadership: Robert E. Lee and his opponents. *Journal of Applied Social Psychology, 16,* 498–507.

Suedfeld, P., de Vries, B., Bluck, S., Wallbaum, A. B. C., & Schmidt, P. W. (1996). Intuitive perceptions of decision-making strategy: Naive assessors' concepts of integrative complexity. *International Journal of Psychology, 31,* 177–190.

Suedfeld, P., & Granatstein, J. L. (1995). Leader complexity in personal and professional crises: Concurrent and retrospective information processing. *Political Psychology, 16,* 509–544.

Suedfeld, P., Guttieri, K., & Tetlock, P. E. (2003). Assessing integrative complexity at a distance: Archival analyses of thinking and decision making. In J. M. Post (Ed.), *The psychological assessment of political leaders: With profiles of Saddam Hussein and Bill Clinton* (pp. 246–270). Ann Arbor: University of Michigan Press.

Suedfeld, P., Jhangiani, R., & Weiszbeck, T. (2003, July). *Integrative complexity of leaders in the confrontation between India and Pakistan.* Paper presented at the 26th annual meeting of the International Society of Political Psychology, Boston.

Suedfeld, P., & Leighton, D. C. (2002). Early communications in the war against terrorism: An integrative complexity analysis. *Political Psychology, 23,* 585–599.

Suedfeld, P., & Rank, A. D. (1976). Revolutionary leaders: Long-term success as a function of changes in conceptual complexity. *Journal of Personality & Social Psychology, 34,* 169–178.

Suedfeld, P. & Tetlock, P. E. (1977). Integrative complexity of communications in international crises. *Journal of Conflict Resolution, 21,* 169–184.

Suedfeld, P., & Tetlock, P. E. (1992). Psychologists as policy advocates: The roots of controversy. In P. Suedfeld & P. E. Tetlock (Eds.), *Psychology and social policy* (pp. 1–30). Washington, DC: Hemisphere Publishing Corp.

Suedfeld, P., & Tetlock, P. E. (2001). Individual differences in information processing. In A. Tesser & N. Schwarz (Eds.), *Blackwell handbook of social psychology: Intraindividual processes* (pp. 284–304). Malden, MA: Blackwell.

Suedfeld, P., Tetlock, P. E., & Ramirez, C. (1977). War, peace, and integrative complexity: UN speeches on the Middle East problem, 1947–1976. *Journal of Conflict Resolution, 21,* 427–442.

Suedfeld, P., Tetlock, P. E., & Streufert, S. (1992). Conceptual/integrative complexity. In C. P. Smith (Ed.), *Motivation and personality: Handbook of thematic content analysis* (pp. 393–400). New York: Cambridge University Press.

Suedfeld, P., & Wallbaum, A. B. C. (1992). Modifying integrative complexity in political thought: Value conflict and audience disagreement. *Interamerican Journal of Psychology, 26,* 19–36.

Suedfeld, P., Wallace, M. D., & Thachuk, K. L. (1993). Changes in integrative complexity among Middle East leaders during the Persian Gulf crisis. *Journal of Social Issues, 49,* 183–199.

Tetlock, P. E. (1979). Identifying victims of groupthink from public statements of decision makers. *Journal of Personality & Social Psychology, 37,* 1314–1324.

Tetlock, P. E. (1981). Pre- to postelection shifts in presidential rhetoric: Impression management or cognitive adjustment. *Journal of Personality & Social Psychology, 41,* 207–212.

Tetlock, P. E. (1985). Integrative complexity of American and Soviet foreign policy rhetoric: A time-series analysis. *Journal of Personality and Social Psychology, 49,* 1565–1585.

Tetlock, P. E. (1986). Psychological advice on foreign policy: What do we have to contribute? *American Psychologist, 41,* 557–567.

Tetlock, P. E. (1992). The impact of accountability on judgment and choice: Toward a social contingency model. In M. P. Zanna (Ed.), *Advances in experimental social psychology, Vol. 25* (pp. 331–376). San Diego, CA: Academic Press.

Tetlock, P. E. (1993). Cognitive structural analysis of political rhetoric: Methodological and theoretical issues. In S. Iyengar & W. J. McGuire (Eds.), *Explorations in political psychology* (pp. 380–405). Durham, NC: Duke University Press.

Tetlock, P. E., Armor, D., & Peterson, R. S. (1994). The slavery debate in antebellum America: Cognitive style, value conflict, and the limits of compromise. *Journal of Personality & Social Psychology, 66,* 115–126.

Tetlock, P. E., Hannum, K. A., & Micheletti, P. M. (1984). Stability and change in the complexity of senatorial debate: Testing the cognitive versus rhetorical style hypotheses. *Journal of Personality & Social Psychology, 46,* 979–990.

Tetlock, P. E., Lerner, J. S., & Boettger, R. (1996). The dilution effect: Judgmental bias, conversational convention, or a bit of both? *European Journal of Social Psychology, 26*, 915–934.

Tetlock, P. E., Peterson, R. S., & Berry, J. M. (1993). Flattering and unflattering personality portraits of integratively simple and complex managers. *Journal of Personality & Social Psychology, 64*, 500–511.

Tetlock, P. E., Skitka, L., & Boettger, R. (1989). Social and cognitive strategies for coping with accountability: Conformity, complexity, and bolstering. *Journal of Personality & Social Psychology, 57*, 632–640.

Tetlock, P. E., & Suedfeld, P. (1988). Integrative complexity coding of verbal behaviour. In C. Antaki (Ed.), *Analysing everyday explanation: A casebook of methods* (pp. 43–59). Thousand Oaks, CA: SAGE.

Tetlock, P. E., & Tyler, A. (1996). Churchill's cognitive and rhetorical style: The debates over Nazi intentions and self-government for India. *Political Psychology, 17*, 149–170.

Wallace, M. D., & Suedfeld, P. (1988). Leadership performance in crisis: The longevity-complexity link. *International Studies Quarterly, 32*, 439–451.

Yerkes, R. M., & Dodson, J. D. (1908). The relation of strength of stimulus to rapidity of habit formation. *Journal of Comparative Neurology and Psychology 18*, 459–482.

CHAPTER 9

# EMOTION, ALIENATION, AND NARRATIVES IN PROTRACTED CONFLICT

*Suzanne Retzinger and Thomas Scheff*

> If we could read the secret history of our enemies, we would find sorrow and suffering
> enough to dispel all hostility.
>
> —Henry Wadsworth Longfellow (1857)

Most current training for negotiation/mediation hardly mentions feelings and emotions. Much of the literature on mediation states or at least implies that emotions should be ignored, as if both sides of a dispute can be coaxed into behaving rationally. However, Fisher, Ury, and Patton, in *Getting to YES* (1991), the most popular book in this field, suggest that emotions need to be dealt with first, before substance (pp. 29–32). But their discussion is brief. The only emotion that is specifically named is anger. They seem to assume that anger is a simple and unitary emotion and give only brief hints about managing it.[1] We propose that the lack of detailed attention to emotions and relationships is the biggest gap in our understanding of conflict.

Of course there are mediations in which emotions can be safely ignored. In such situations, the parties' concerns over substance can be negotiated directly, and resolution or compromise can be reached quickly. For the average mediator, simple conflicts like these may occur in the majority of cases. There are many cases, however, in which one or both sides seem intractable. In some of these cases, there is flagrant hostility. In others both sides are courteous but remote. In both of these situations progress toward settlement is slow or absent. We propose that in seemingly intractable conflict or impasse, headway can be made if the mediator is skilled enough to help the parties explore not only the substantive issues, but also the emotional/relational side of their conflict.

## Managing Anger

An example of the need for further training in emotions and relationships is provided by the topic of anger management. The advice currently given in the literature is to usually allow venting of anger—"letting off steam" (Fisher et al., 1991, p. 31). Although this advice is right for some cases, for others it is inadequate or even destructive. Just as making distinctions between kinds of snow is important for a skier, distinguishing kinds of anger is essential for a mediator/negotiator.

One should certainly encourage the venting of one kind of anger, pure anger that is unalloyed with other emotions. This kind of anger mobilizes the intellect of both speaker and listener, is not inappropriate or excessive, and does not lead to name-calling or disrespect. The person who expresses anger constructively may provide listeners with a rapid, exact, and comprehensive description of his or her grievances and needs. This kind of anger marshals respect for the speaker and is informative for the listeners.

Unfortunately, this kind of anger is quite rare. Usually anger is not actually expressed but rather acted out. Most anger displays in negotiation and in real life are not pure anger but anger alloyed with other emotions, such as disgust, contempt, or feelings of rejection or humiliation. These alloys seldom lead to constructive responses; indeed they almost always lead to excess and insults that are disruptive. (There is recognition of the mischief caused by shame admixed with anger, but only in passing, in Stone, Patton, and Heen, 1999, p. 96.)

This problem is illustrated by a incident reported by Saposnek (1983), involving the couple "Joan" and "Paul," in mediation of a custody dispute: "in the middle of a heated exchange, a wife said to her ex-husband, 'You never paid any attention to the children, then you left me, and you're NOT getting the children now or ever!' " (p. 185).

Does the mediator intervene or allow the husband to reply? If the mediator does intervene, what would he or she say? We return to this particular question below, after framing the negotiation of conflict within a larger context, the interplay between ideology/narrative, substantive interests, and emotional/relational issues.

### Theory: Ideology/Narratives and Economic/Political Interests in Conflict

Ideology seems to be an important element in intractable conflict. Typically, it provides justification for actions, as is the case when one or both sides vilify the other and idealize themselves. Without fail this process prolongs and intensifies conflict.

Ideology gives rise to (and is generated by) the story that each side tells to itself and others about the conflict. This story contains crucial elements that can either perpetuate or resolve conflict: the identity that each side awards to itself, the history and future of the struggle, both reflects and generates the explosive emotions connected with the conflict. Changes in the ideology and its accompanying narratives can change the nature of the conflict.

But adherents to an entrenched ideology/narrative may resist even verbal changes. Aggressors often feel that being victimized themselves justifies their aggression. Spouses who abuse their partners often argue that their aggression was caused by actions of the partner. Men who beat their wives may claim that the wife was the true culprit, because of her taunts or insults, unfaithfulness, disobedience, or some other action culpable in the husband's eyes.

The victim ideology is a potent force in aggression not only between persons but also between groups. From news reports, it was clear that Serbians thought of themselves as victims, which they used to justify their aggression. And it is true that Serbians have actually been victimized for hundreds of years. What is left out of the Serbian narratives is the fact that as well as being victims, they are also perpetrators. Their ideology/narrative is defensive, in that it distorts their role in generating conflict with other groups.

How can entrenched narratives be changed? Stories that express hidden emotion may be a beginning. An example is provided by the "Speak Bitterness" meetings in the early days of the Chinese Communist Revolution. Before they took power, Chinese communists attempted to liberate the peasants from their history of suffering and despair by social psychological means. They had been victims of oppression for so long that they had lost hope. In the Speak Bitterness meetings, they were allowed to tell their stories of oppression. This process resulted in mass weeping. The meetings seemed to build hope among the peasants and allowed them to mobilize in support of the revolution. After the communists took power, they used similar meetings as means of domination. But earlier they played a part in causing profound changes in narratives and behavior. The "truth-telling" that has recently occurred in South Africa may also have had a similar effect in allowing both black and white citizens to express their suffering.

## Marx's Theory of Conflict

These examples suggest that changing ideology/narrative can be effective in ending conflict but also that ideology/narrative is itself a product of more primitive causes. Theorists have long debated the relative importance of ideology and material interests. In this debate, Marx's ideas were the most powerful, or at least the most widely known. In his theory of conflict, he proposed that ideology was only a superstructure. Location in the means of production is the substructure. That is, Marx thought that ideology was a product of political/economic interests. Later Marxians, especially Communist theoreticians, elevated this crude proposition to the central core of their theory.

However, Marx himself qualified the proposition in several ways. First of all, he allowed that certain middle-class intellectuals, like himself, would forsake their class interests to become the vanguard of the proletariat. What force could bring these intellectuals to forsake their class interests?

Marx's theory of alienation implies such a force. It suggests that in addition to economic and political causes of class conflict, there are relational and emotional ones.

The middle-class intellectuals who formed the vanguard had presumably become alienated from their class. More generally, Marx proposed that persons in capitalist societies become alienated not only from the means of production, but from others and from self. That is, capitalism reflects and generates disturbances in social relationships and in the self. In his review of empirical studies of alienation, Seeman (1975) found evidence of both kinds of alienation, from others and from self (Seeman referred to the latter as "self-estrangement").

Marx went on to implicate the emotions that accompany alienation. He proposed that it gives rise to feelings of "impotence" (shame) and "indignation" (anger) (as cited in Tucker, 1978, pp. 133–134). Marx's theory of alienation proposes that the causes of class conflict are not only political and economic, but also relational and emotional.

Although Marx supplemented his theory of political/economic causes of class conflict with a theory of emotional/relational causes, there is a great disparity in his development of the two theories. The political/economic theory is lavishly elaborated. The bulk of his commentary on alienation takes place in his early work. Even there, as in later works, formulation of theory of alienation is brief and casual. It is easy to understand why Marx's followers have also made it secondary to material interests.

## Preliminaries to a General Theory

Our theory of emotional/relational causes of intractable conflict develops the effects of alienation, particularly disturbances in communication and emotion, beyond Marx's formulation. Like capitalism, the emotional/relational system in modern societies is a partially autonomous system. The two systems interact in complex ways. In intractable conflict, the importance of emotional/relational motives seems to wax in more or less the same degree as material interests wane.

For example, in Northern Ireland, the parties in conflict have acted as if economic incentives were of little concern. There are four parties to the conflict: the Protestant and Catholic factions in Northern Ireland, and England, and the Republic of Ireland. All four parties expended vast amounts on engaging in or defending against aggression. England, the largest group, was expending perhaps $6 billion a year to keep the peace by show of force. The other three groups are expending equivalent amounts, relative to their smaller sizes. They are all risking bankruptcy. Even if a settlement is reached, we still need to know why it has taken so long.

Most of the experts on the conflict in Northern Ireland are of the opinion that the impediments to peace and reconciliation are deep-seated emotions. Here is one example:

> Anyone who studies Northern Ireland must be struck by the intensity of feeling which the conflict evokes. It seems to go beyond what is required by a rational defence of the divergent interests that undoubtedly exist. *There is an emotional element here, a welling-up of deep unconscious forces* [italics added]. It is worth examining what contribution psychology can make to an explanation of the conflict. (Whyte, 1990, p. 14)

Whyte does not indicate, however, what these emotions might be, nor do any of the other experts who hold a similar opinion.

The materialist ("realist") approach to conflict assumes that political/economic forces are the most important causes, with emotional, relational, and symbolic causes subsidiary. This approach may be true in some cases. But in *intractable* conflict, it is probably not. Although variously referred to as status, prestige, honor, glory, etc., intractable conflicts seem to be fueled by nonmaterial as well as material concerns.

Hitler's motivation provides an example. In his writing and speeches, he provided a material motive for German aggression: room for the German people to live (Scheff, 1994/2000). But there is a powerful subtext in the same writing and speeches, revenge for the humiliations that the Germans had suffered, which he thought would restore community and pride to the German nation. Hitler was a master at exploiting emotions to his own ends. He used them to manipulate the German people. Finding internal and external enemies to assure support for the leader's policies is a common strategy, as witnessed by the actions of the present government of the United States.

We propose that ideology and narratives are important elements in all intractability but that they in turn are products of political/economic and emotional/relational interests. It seems to us that most present-day negotiation techniques mostly ignore emotional/relational concerns. Perhaps interventions need to be developed that would acknowledge and change the emotional/relational world of the adversaries.

### Mediating the Emotional/Relational World

One direction for stuck negotiations would be to pay particular attention to emotional/relational issues, negotiating the *relationship* between the adversaries. In relationship mediation, one would appropriately acknowledge the suffering of the parties in such a way that might allow both sides to feel *deeply heard*. This kind of mediation could be a step toward substantial changes in the mood of the negotiation.

Perhaps the biggest block to progress in negotiating stuck conflicts is that one or both parties feel that their stories have not been told, or if told, not heard. When both parties feel deeply heard, the mood may change to the point that actual negotiation can be begun. The mediator's key task, in such cases, would be to help the parties to formulate their stories in a way that does not delete the emotions, and to be sure that when they are told, that they are acknowledged.

At least in most formal, and especially in public, negotiations, the vulnerable emotions that express suffering are completely suppressed. The parties to a conflict usually wish to appear strong, rather than weak. They hide their vulnerable emotions, even from themselves. In the wake of 9/11, it would be hard to imagine Bush opening negotiations with his public with the following apology:

I AM TRULY SORRY THAT THE 9/11 ATTACK OCCURRED. SINCE I WAS IN CHARGE WHEN IT HAPPENED, I FEEL PARTLY RESPONSIBLE FOR ALLOW-ING IT TO OCCUR.

I FEEL VIOLATED, WEAK, HELPLESS, IMPOTENT, HUMILIATED. I AM
ASHAMED OF MY OWN HELPLESSNESS. I AM ASHAMED THAT I CANNOT
PROTECT MY OWN PEOPLE. I AM ASHAMED THAT I LACKED THE FORE-
SIGHT TO SEE THIS COMING.

I AM SAD BEYOND RECKONING AT ALL THE LOSSES THAT WE HAVE
SUFFERED. I NEED TO CRY BITTER TEARS FOREVER.

I AM AFRAID. I AM AFRAID TO DIE. I FEAR FOR MY LOVED ONES AND
THE CITIZENS OF THIS COUNTRY AND THE WORLD.

He attacked Afghanistan and Iraq instead. Men, particularly, have a hard time admitting to painful feelings of weakness, shame, humiliation, grief, and fear (Scheff,
2003). Not just Bush, Cheney, and Rumsfeld, but also Saddam Hussein, Osama
bin Laden, Sharon, Arafat, all act as if they belong to the Crypts or the Bloods.

## Emotions and Alienation in Protracted Conflict

The integration of political/economic, narrative, and emotional/relational interests into a single program of negotiation has yet to be accomplished. This chapter
is only a first step in that direction. We address two kinds of protracted conflict:
(1) *Interminable quarrel*: irrational anger, resentment, or hatred. (2) *Impasse*: Both
parties are more or less polite, but negotiation is stuck. These cases are dominated
by a seemingly impenetrable *mood* of either hostility or remoteness. Can mediators
influence the mood of a negotiation?

### Theory: When a Solution or Compromise Cannot be Reached, the Problem May Lie Hidden in the Emotional/Relational World

1. *Relational* dynamics concern the social *bonds* between and within the disputing
parties. In our theory, bimodal alienation (**isolation** *between* the disputing groups
and **engulfment** (fusion) *within* each group) causes protracted conflict (Scheff,
1994/2000). These dynamics are hidden from the participants, especially the fusion
part. Engulfment means that members give up part of self in order to be loyal to the
group but are unaware of what they have lost (Seeman's self-estrangement). Fanatical
nationalism ("My country (gender, race, ethnicity, family, etc.) is right or wrong.") is
the result. It is much easier to imagine union with the unknown members of one's
sect ("imaginary communities") than to do the demanding work of making relationships in one's real interpersonal network more livable.

2. *Emotion* dynamics: In interminable quarrels, **shame/anger spirals** (humiliated
fury, helpless anger) within and between the disputing parties, with the shame component hidden from self and other, cause intractability (Retzinger, 1991; Scheff,
1994/2000). Both Gaylin (1984) and Gilligan (1996, 2001) have proposed shame
as the cause of rage. In impasse, both shame and anger are hidden.[2] In both cases it
is the *hidden* shame that does the damage, because hidden shame blocks the possibility of repair of damaged bonds. To the extent that shame is hidden from self and
others, one cannot bring one's self to connect with the other side, leading to more

alienation, and so on, around the loop. Hidden shame and alienation are the emotional and relational sides of the same dynamic system, a cycle of violence.

The following example is an episode from an interview with John Silber, as described in Milburn and Conrad (1996). Silber is the ex-president of Boston University, and he is still a powerful conservative force in Massachusetts politics. His approach to political issues is a prime example of the politics of rage in the United States. As Milburn and Conrad (1996) suggest, it was an outburst of rage during a TV broadcast on the eve of the election that seemed to cost him the race when he ran for governor.

In an earlier interview, Silber told the interviewer that his sixth grade teacher laughed at him for wanting to be a veterinarian, since Silber had a withered arm. When the interviewer asked him how he felt about being laughed at, Silber replied that he was not humiliated, it made him stronger. In the framework of our theory, this episode can be interpreted to mean that Silber's rage as a person and as a politician might arise from the denial of shame. It is not alienation or emotion alone that cause protracted conflict, but their denial by the participants. We propose that the *denial of emotion and alienation lead to intractable conflict.*

At first glance this proposition seems counterintuitive. First of all, it violates the realist approach in political thinking that all conflict involves material interests. It also violates the rationalist approach, which considers conflict to be the outcome of conscious intentions. Since rationalism is pervasive in the social sciences, we will consider this issue further.

The therapeutic approach runs counter to rationalism, especially psychodynamic theories of therapy, which posit unconscious motives. This approach has had little impact on theories of conflict, because most social scientists reject therapeutic approaches as irrelevant to collective behavior, and psychodynamic psychologists have shown little concern for large-scale conflict.

But in world literature there is a much broader rejection of rationalism, implied in the quest for self-knowledge. Long before Freud, the Greek philosophers proposed that the goal of philosophical thinking was knowledge of the self, and by implication, that human folly is a result of lack of self-knowledge. This thread forms one of the central concerns in both ancient and modern literature. For at least 3,000 years, stories, myths, fables, satires, and more recently, novels have explored the theme of the dire consequences of lack of self-knowledge.

This theme is epitomized in a line from one of Goethe's plays, *Torquato Tasso* (1789/1985): "God gave me the gift of being able to speak my suffering, when other men would be struck dumb" (p. 22).

Also related to our treatment of intractability is a comment by the late Helen Lewis (1971), who said that most of us, rather than turn ourselves inside out, would rather turn the world upside down. This is the theme of Scheff's (1994/2000) treatment of the Franco-German wars (1870–1945). The French took their defeat at the hands of Prussia in 1871 as a collective humiliation. Rather than acknowledge this feeling, they plotted revenge on the Germans, resulting in their instigation, with Russia, of the First World War. After their defeat in 1918, it was the turn of the

Germans to experience defeat as a collective humiliation. Hitler's appeal to the German people involved exploiting this feeling. Hitler's own biography appears to be a classic example of the need to turn the world upside down rather than discover and acknowledge one's own feelings, since he was extraordinarily shamed and shame-prone from childhood.

Just as lack of knowledge of self lies at the heart of the emotional drive toward intractability, so lack of knowledge of the other is the key to alienation. We learn about self through knowing others, and vice versa. Impairment of knowledge of the other damages knowledge of self, and vice versa. Denial of emotion and of alienation go hand in hand. We propose that intractability arises out of lack of knowledge of the emotional/relational world, i.e., denial of alienation and emotion.

### Practice: The Acknowledgment of Shame and Alienation: Gaining Knowledge of the Emotional/Relational World

Our practice follows from the premise that intractability arises from lack of knowledge of self and other, from denial of suffering. To begin to resolve a stuck conflict, help the clients **acknowledge**, or acknowledge for them, at least a small part of their alienation and/or hidden emotions, in a way that leaves some dignity intact. When this has occurred, real negotiation can begin. (Although Stone et al., 1999, do not develop the idea of acknowledgment of hidden emotions, their discussion of emotional expression implies that it is a key element in dealing with difficult negotiations, pp. 106–107).

Alienation: mediators learn to identify *patterns* of alienation and the ensuing dysfunctional communication between and within the disputing groups.

Emotion: mediators learn to identify *cues* to unacknowledged emotions in the discourse of the disputing parties.

Special training is necessary for detecting shame, because most of it is disguised and/or denied. (See Retzinger's cues to hidden anger and shame, 1991, 1995, and in the Appendix of this chapter). Following Helen Lewis (1971), we find that most shame occurs either in the *overt, undifferentiated* form, or in the *bypassed* form. In the first type, there is intense emotional pain, but it is misnamed or encoded ("I feel miserable, hurt, insulted, inadequate, a failure, foolish, etc.). In bypassed shame, however, there is virtually no emotional pain. Instead, there is obsessive rumination, incessant talk, or hyperactivity. In this latter form, one can be in a state of shame without *feeling* ashamed (see Silber episode above). Bypassing appears to be the primary form that men use for denying shame, fear, and grief. Their arrogance and aggression serve to mask hidden emotions.

Accurately reflecting alienation and unacknowledged emotions back to the disputing parties can help them to feel heard. But the mediator needs great skill to detect the undercurrents of denied emotions and alienation, and tact to reflect them back in a form that will not further embarrass the clients.

This practice is not a form of psychotherapy, but of crisis management. The mediator is quickly in and out, entering the clients' emotional/relational world only long enough to get the negotiation process unstuck. The mediator's accurate reflections of the clients' hidden feelings allows them to **communicate** better and to feel deeply **heard**. We believe that the basic stuckness of protracted conflict is a product of clients not feeling heard by each other, the mediator, and the world at large. This failure is mostly due to the clients: most delete their emotions from the stories they tell. But it is these emotions that are driving their intractability.

Example: The sticking point for the Nationalist Catholics in the North Ireland conflict may have been that after 600 years of humiliation by the English, they still have not found a way of acknowledging their feelings of shame and humiliation. They have been masking their humiliation by anger and aggression for so many generations that they can no longer access it without outside help. Feelings of humiliation were not acknowledged in the Northern Ireland peace negotiations, which have dealt only with substance rather than relationship (Fisher et al., 1991).

Here we take a step toward describing the way shame generates anger, and more generally, identifying and untangling the strands of hidden emotions and alienation in protracted conflict. Our work on the role of hidden emotions in conflict has been extended by Volkan's (2003) analysis of what might be called "the vulnerable emotions," shame, grief, and fear.

Volkan's theory (1988, 1997, 2003) of collective violence begins with *the chosen trauma*. The defeat of Serbs by Turks at the battle of Kosovo in 1396 was the battle cry in the 1990s for ethnic cleansing of the Moslems. Although the defeat occurred over 600 years ago, it lives on in the minds and hearts of Serbians.

The next step is the *failure to mourn* for the losses sustained in the chosen trauma. This is why the trauma lives on. Then comes the feeling of *entitlement to revenge*. Rather than facing the anguish of mourning and self-examination, a group can find distraction in self-righteous hostility and aggression against a purported enemy.

Then there is *collective regression*. Under the pressure of fear/anxiety, a majority regresses to early childhood mentality in which mixtures of good and bad are unknown. One's parents and leaders are good, and one's enemies are bad. This mentality views violence as the only alternative; since we are completely good, the enemy is not just bad, but evil.

These four steps are implied in Dr. Volkan's *The Need for Enemies* (1988), and *Bloodlines* (1997). However, the newer book provides a fifth element not explicit in the previous work. The key to the failure to mourn is that the group has experienced the chosen trauma as a *humiliation*; they are ashamed of their defeat. To avoid feeling shame, an "us-them" world is constructed: we have nothing to be ashamed of; it is those bastards. This path leads precipitously to revenge. Even if no enemy is at hand, one can be fabricated in order to avoid one's true feelings.

The addition of the fifth element, humiliation, is a step toward an integrated theory of emotion dynamics. In Scheff's study (1994/2000) of the origins of the Franco-German wars (1870–1945), he proposed that both sides had suppressed shame by hiding their humiliation behind anger. Volkan's book implies that the earlier study should have also considered unresolved grief and fear as possible causal agents.

Recent studies of "terror management" (Pyszczynski, Solomon, & Greenberg, 2003) imply that fear is an important element in response to violence. Although this work is stated in cognitive terms, it implies fear as a key element. Indeed, Landau et al. (2004), in introducing their study of the terror management underlying support of G. W. Bush, quote Becker (1971): "It is [fear] that makes people so willing to follow brash, strong-looking demagogues with tight jaws and loud voices ..." (p. 161). At the moment, with the exception of Vokan's latest book, work on emotional components in violence is compartmentalized. All of Volkan's earlier studies focused on the failure to mourn (grief) and fear/anxiety. Even in his latest book, the role of anger is only implied (in the hostility toward purported enemies). Beck's (1999) book on hatred focuses largely on anger and anxiety. However, a close reading suggests that his model implies shame/humiliation as well, since he proposes that anger responses almost always involve feeling diminishment before anger (p. 31 and passim).

Our own earlier work (Scheff & Retzinger, 1991/2001) on conflict focused on anger, shame, and humiliation. Lindner's work on violence (2002) has been even more specialized, considering only humiliation. The studies in terror management mentioned above have considered only "mortality salience" (fear) as causal.

Each of these studies makes a plausible case for the particular emotions that they emphasize. But we need to integrate all four emotions into a wider consideration of *emotional/relational worlds*. These worlds, although next to invisible in hypercognizing, individualist, modern societies, seem to play an important part in generating either public support or opposition to collective violence.

A pertinent example of the virtual invisibility of the emotional/relational world occurs within the social and behavioral sciences themselves. Most studies in the various disciplines elide around emotions and relationships in favor of individual cognition and behavior, even though all four areas are equally important. Compared with their precise knowledge of cognition and behavior, neither laypersons nor experts know much about the emotional/relational world.

With integration, it becomes easier to see how social institutions might play a part, as they do in the case of gender. If individuals and/or groups suppress grief, shame, and/or fear (the vulnerable emotions), either violence or silent withdrawal is likely. Boys and men learn that vulnerable feelings are seen as signs of weakness, but anger, even if faked, shows strength.

In Western cultures, at least, boys and men hide vulnerable feelings, either in silence or anger. That is, young boys learn first in their families, and later, in school, to suppress the vulnerable emotions they feel. They either maintain silence or explode in anger.

Since men usually dominate state and ethnic nationalism, the theory predicts a violent future unless something can be done about understanding emotions. It would seem to be necessary to study these four emotions both separately and in interaction. Are there gradations of repression, or is it all or nothing? Can numbing a single emotion, such as fear, lead to silence/violence, or does it take all three? Does repression of one emotion spread to other emotions? None of these questions appear to have been directly addressed in the literature on emotions.

Perhaps the more a person is backed up on one or more of these four emotions, the less he or she will be able to experience any of them. For example, those who are still suffering from their previous losses (perhaps a majority of adults in modern societies) will be unable to mourn and will not tolerate mourning in others. This mechanism would create what Volkan calls the transgenerational transmission of trauma, a key feature of his explanation of continuing enmity between groups.

Collective regression of the kind described by Volkan has a less direct effect on the conduct of one's daily life than it does on large matters at a distance. But with respect to these distant matters, it incapacitates judgment. One is in the grip of a massive delusion. With complete and unwavering confidence, one might as well believe that the earth is flat, or that water flows uphill.

Volkan's theory seems to explain many elements in today's world. For example, the state of Israel has taken the Holocaust as its chosen trauma, and public support for Sharon's destructive policies toward Palestinians is generated by the suppression of grief, shame, and fear. In this country, we have 9/11 as our chosen trauma. The failure to collectively mourn our losses and to face our fear and shame has resulted in support for the completely gratuitous Iraq war. Hidden vulnerable emotions and all too obvious anger may be the matrix from which unnecessary violence arises.

### Identifying Patterns of Alienation and Dysfunctional Communication

1. Topic vs. relational talk (Watslawick, Beavin, & Jackson, 1967; Fisher et al., 1991, make what seems to be the same distinction, calling it substance vs. relationship). The negotiation of most protracted conflict seems to be entrapped in a succession of topics, with little or no attention to the relationship between the disputants, especially the emotional relationship.

2. Respect vs. disrespect. Often respect issues are subtle rather than flagrant. Typically, disputants deny that their verbal and nonverbal communications may be insulting to the other party. Indeed, though each party is supremely sensitive to the disrespect in communications of the other party, they are often mostly or even completely unaware of the disrespect in their own.

3. Triangling (Bowen, 1978). This is a variation on topic vs. relational talk, with the topic being an absent third party. For example, in Northern Ireland negotiations, although there were actually four parties involved in the impasse, all of them are seldom present in a particular meeting. Those present may blame the absent party in order to avoid emotional/relational issues among those present.

Emotions: For many people, their most accessible emotion is anger. But anger is usually a secondary emotion. Underneath the anger, there is usually a primary emotion, commonly referred to as "hurt." *What is the hurt in each instance of anger?* How can the hurt be reflected in a way that will allow the client to feel heard? Emotion analysis is a way of clarifying the hurt and locating it within the relational matrix of conflict. Our findings suggest that the dominant component of hurt, at least the kind of hurt that leads to hatred and aggression, is hidden shame.

Given our emphasis on hidden shame and anger, what advice do we give mediator/negotiators on the venting of anger? Our answer is that clients' anger can be encouraged or tolerated as long as it is not damaging the bond between them. Since most displays of anger and rage are destructive, mediators should be trained to usually interrupt expressions of anger immediately, not even allowing the other party to respond.

The custody dispute between Joan and Paul (Saposnek, 1983), mentioned above, provides an example. The wife has said, "You never paid any attention to the children, then you left me, and you're NOT getting the children now or ever!" (p. 185). Should the mediator intervene at this point or allow the husband to respond? According to our theory, the mediator must intervene, in order to avoid further escalation.

Joan does not discuss her feelings directly, but they are implied. In her one sentence there are three statements that imply perceived insults and humiliations leading to angry revenge[3]. First, Joan complains about and blames Paul, implying that he is an inadequate father; then she reveals a context for intense humiliation, "you left me" (he severed the bond between them). The third breath is a threat of angry revenge—to withhold the children from Paul. All three statements are potentially humiliating for Paul—he is the one at fault with the children, the marriage, and a threat to separate him from his children (as he has separated himself from Joan). There is a mountain of both anger and shame. At this point, the mediator intervened before Paul had a chance to reply, saying,

> The anger and hurt you feel right now is not unusual, and it is very understandable. It is also not unusual for a parent who was not involved with the children before a divorce to decide to become sincerely involved after the divorce. Allowing that opportunity will give your children a chance to get to know their father in the future in a way that you wanted in the past. But give yourself plenty of time to get through these difficult feelings. (pp. 185–186)

This is a crucial moment for intervention: the mediator acknowledges and reframes for both parties in a way that helps them to begin building a new bond—that of co-parents. At the same time the intervention deflects potential humiliation, the mediator interprets vulnerable feelings for both parents, legitimating their anger and hurt (shame).

The mediator interrupted the cycle in which the disputants had been entangled, but in a way that did not further humiliate either party. The intervention was paradigmatic; even though it saved face, it did not endorse the position of either party. The mediator was able to remain neutral; he did not become enmeshed in the family conflict. Saposnek describes the effects of the intervention:

> On hearing this the husband kept quiet, for he knew that the mediator's remark implied support for his continuing relationship with the children, yet presented it in a way that allowed both him and his wife to save face. He then tearfully expressed his sincerity in wanting to become more involved with the children. The wife cried and was able to constructively express her hurt feelings at being left by the husband. Negotiations then became possible. (p. 186)

By interrupting the quarrel cycle, and by expressing shame and hurt for the clients, the mediator appears to have avoided further escalation.

This incident illustrates repair of the relationship in several ways. First, it suggests that in order to build a new bond between the disputants, the mediator must be active rather than passive. Social bonds are at risk in all encounters; if they are not being built, maintained, or repaired, they are being damaged. A fallacious result of "cathartic" theories has been the unfortunate notion that a passive mediator is allowing the parties to "blow off steam." There can be little benefit from contempt, disgust, ridicule, or disrespect of any kind. On the contrary, these types of emotional expressions are harmful, because they further damage bonds, perpetuating the quarrel system.

The mediator's intervention illustrates key components of repair: saving face (avoiding further shaming transactions) and helping clients to acknowledge their hurt. In the case of Joan and Paul, the mediator appears to have detected the potential for humiliation of the husband in the utter rejection implied in the wife's comment: *[4]"You don't count; it doesn't matter to me what you say, think, or feel." The old bond between wife and husband has been broken; if the mediator allowed this comment to pass, it would become more difficult to form a new bond as co-parents.

Most of the components for repairing the bond are present in this single intervention: (1) the source of impasse, seen in the sequences of Joan's first utterance, (2) face-saving (respectful tactics), (3) acknowledgement of feeling and the state of the bond, (4) knowledge of interacting systems, and (5) a secure base is provided by the mediator for exploration.

Although the intervention itself is masterful, the author does not utilize theory in generating or explaining it, nor a method for identifying shame/anger sequences. The intervention was apparently based on the author's intuitive response to the underlying emotions, which was in turn based on years of experience with similar situations. Our theory of conflict offers a way of justifying such interventions and training new mediators/negotiators to have similar intuitions without having extensive experience.

In summary, the mediator's accurate reflections of the state of the bond and emotion can change the mood of a conflict, allowing real negotiation to begin. The basic task is to help the clients formulate their stories so that they do not delete the emotional/relational components and then to be sure that the stories are heard and acknowledged. Even if the clients cannot really hear each other's stories, it is important that the mediator hear them.

## Stages for the Resolution of Protracted Conflict

Our proposal is the opposite of three easy steps in self-help books because it involves three increasingly difficult steps:

1. Training mediators: the mediators learn to identify unacknowledged emotions and patterns of alienation, including their own, as a tool for changing the mood of negotiation.

> The difficulty of this kind of training can be grasped if you think of the task of training someone like John Silber to be this kind of mediator.

2. The actual negotiation: The mediator reflects back on his or her clients' unacknowledged emotions and alienation, allowing resolution.

3. Returning home (in the case of collective conflicts): The clients reflect back on their constituents' unacknowledged emotions and alienation, building support for the mediated solution.

This last step has a utopian ring to it, but it may at least allow us to see the magnitude of the problem. This skill may have been at the heart of Desmond Tutu's management of the ending of apartheid in South Africa, but it is as yet rare among current mediators. Perhaps an emphasis on the relational/emotional world could create a new generation of mediators/negotiators for resolving intractable conflict.

## Appendix

### Verbal Markers

**SHAME:**

*alienated:* rejected, dumped, deserted, rebuffed, abandoned, estranged, deserted, isolated, separated, alone, disconnected, disassociated, detached, withdrawn, inhibited, distant, remote, split, divorced, and polarized.

*confused:* stunned, dazed, blank, empty, hollow, spaced, giddy, lost, vapid, hesitant, and aloof.

*ridiculous:* foolish, silly, funny, absurd, idiotic, asinine, simple-minded, stupid, curious, weird, bizarre, odd peculiar, strange, different, and stupid.

*inadequate:* helpless, powerless, defenseless, weak, insecure, uncertain, shy, deficient, worse off, small, failure, ineffectual, inferior, unworthy, worthless, flawed, trivial, meaningless, insufficient, unsure, dependent, exposed, inadequate, incapable, vulnerable, unable, inept, unfit, impotent, and oppressed.

*uncomfortable:* restless, fidgety, jittery, tense, anxious, nervous, uneasy, antsy, jumpy, and hyperactive.

*hurt:* offended, upset, wounded, injured, tortured, ruined, sensitive, sore spot, buttons pushed, dejected, intimidated, and defeated.

**ANGER:** cranky, cross, hot-tempered, ireful, quick-tempered, short fuse, enraged, fuming, agitated, furious, irritable, incensed, indignant, irate, annoyed, mad, pissed, pissed off, teed-off, upset, furious, aggravated, bothered, resentful, bitter, spiteful, and grudge (the last four words imply shame-rage compounds).

### Other Verbal Markers

**SHAME:** Mitigation (to make appear less severe or painful); oblique, suppressed reference, e.g., "they," "it," "you"; vagueness; denial; defensiveness; verbal withdrawal (lack of response); indifference (acting "cool" in an emotionally arousing context).

**ANGER:** interruption, challenge, sarcasm, and blame

**Shame-rage:** Temporal expansion/condensation or generalization ("you *always* ..."; "you never ..."). Triangulation (bringing up an irrelevant third party or object).

### Paralinguistic Markers

**SHAME:** (vocal withdrawal/hiding behaviors and disorganization of thought): oversoft, rhythm irregular, hesitation, self-interruption (censorship), filled pauses (—uh—), long pauses ( ), silences, stammering, fragmented speech, rapid speech, condensed words, mumbling; breathiness, incoherence (lax articulation), laughed words, and monotone.

**ANGER:** staccato (distinct breaks between successive tones), loud, heavy stress on certain words, sing-song pattern (ridicule), straining, and harsh voice qualifiers.

**Shame-rage:** whine, glottalization (rasp or buzz), choking, tempo up/down, and pitch up/down.

### Visual Markers

**SHAME:** (1) Hiding behavior: (a) the hand covering all or parts of the face and (b) gaze aversion, eyes lowed or averted. (2) Blushing. (3) Control: (a) turning in, biting or licking the lips, and biting the tongue, (b) forehead wrinkled vertically or transversely, and (c) false smiling (Ekman & Freisen, 1982) or other masking behaviors.

**ANGER:** (1) Brows are lowered and drawn together; vertical lines appear between them. (2) The eyelids are narrowed and tense in a hard fixed stare and may have a bulging appearance. (3) Lips are pressed together, the corners straight or down, or open but tense and square. (4) Hard direct glaring. (5) Lean forward toward other in challenging stance. (6) Clenched fists, waved fists, and hitting motions.

These markers are context related; that is, their relevance depends on the relationship between self and other. Constellations in context are more meaningful than isolated single markers.

From Retzinger (1991, 1995).

## Notes

A shorter version of this chapter was published as an article in a mediation journal (Retzinger & Scheff, 2000).

1. Although they reported and tried to deal with rage in their attempts to mediate intense internation conflicts, Rogers and Ryback (1984) had no theory of emotions or relationships and do not mention any emotions other than rage. Irving and Benjamin (1995) consider emotions only in general and abstractly. The present chapter concerns the meaning of empathy in mediation (Bush & Folger, 1994) at the level of specific emotional and relational dynamics.

2. In the 1996 book, Gilligan proposed that shame leads to violence when it is a secret. That is, in our language, when it is not acknowledged to self and others. But this idea is missing from the 2001 volume.
3. The analysis of this episode from Saposnek's book (1983) is based in part on Retzinger (1991, pp. 168–170.)
4. As in linguistics, the asterisk signifies a "counter-factual," a statement that is only implied by what was said.

# References

Beck, A. (1999). *Prisoners of hate: The cognitive basis of anger, hostility, and violence.* New York: HarperCollins.

Becker, Ernest. (1971). The birth and death of meaning. New York: Free Press.

Bowen, Murray. (1978). *Family therapy in clinical practice.* New York: Jason Aaronson.

Bush, Robert, & Folger, Joseph. (1994). *The promise of mediation.* San Francisco: Jossey-Bass.

Ekman, P., & Friesen, W. V. (1982). Felt, false and miserable smiles. *Journal of Nonverbal Behavior, 6*(4), 238–252.

Fisher, Roger, Ury, William, & Patton, Bruce. (1991). *Getting to YES.* New York: Penguin.

Gaylin, Willard. (1984). *The rage within: Anger in modern life.* New York: Simon and Schuster.

Gilligan, James. (1996). *Violence: Reflections on a national epidemic.* New York: Vintage.

Gilligan, James. (2001). *Preventing violence.* New York: Thames and Hudson.

Goethe, Johann Wolfgang. (1985). *Torquato tasso.* London: Angel Books. (Original work published 1789).

Irving, Howard, & Benjamin, Michael. (1995). *Family mediation.* Thousand Oaks, CA: SAGE.

Landau, M., Solomon, S., Greenberg, J., Cohen, F., Pyszczynski, T., Arndt, J., et al. (2004). Deliver us from evil: The effects of mortality salience and reminders of 9/11 on support for President George W. Bush. *Personality and Social Psychology Bulletin, 30*, 1136–1150.

Lewis, Helen. (1971). *Shame and guilt in neurosis.* New York: International Universities Press.

Lindner, E. (2002). Healing the cycles of humiliation: How to attend to the emotional aspects of "unsolvable" conflicts and the use of "humiliation entrepreneurship." *Peace and Conflict: Journal of Peace Psychology, 8*(2), 125–139.

Longfellow, Henry Wadsworth. (1857). *Driftwood.* Boston: Houghton Mifflin.

Milburn, Michael, & Conrad, Sheree. (1996). *The politics of denial.* Cambridge, MA: MIT Press.

Pyszczynski, T., Solomon, S., & Greenberg, J. (2003). *In the wake of 9/11: The psychology of terror.* Washington, DC: American Psychological Association.

Retzinger, Suzanne. (1991). *Violent emotions.* Newbury Park, CA: SAGE.

Retzinger, Suzanne. (1995). Identifying shame and anger in discourse. *American Behavioral Scientist, 38*, 104–113.

Retzinger, S., & Scheff, T. (2000). Emotion, alienation, and narratives: Resolving intractable conflict. *Mediation Quarterly, 7*, 3–19.

Rogers, Carl, & Ryback, David. (1984). One alternative to nuclear planetary suicide. *The Counseling Psychologist, 12*(2), 3–12.

Saposnek, Donald. (1983). *Mediating child custody disputes.* San Francisco: Jossey-Bass.

Scheff, Thomas. (2000). *Bloody revenge.* iUniverse. (Original work published 1994)

Scheff, Thomas. (2003). Male emotions and violence: A case study. *Human relations, 56*, 727–749.

Scheff, Thomas, & Retzinger, S. M. (2001). *Emotions and violence: Shame and rage in destructive conflict*. iUniverse. (Original work published 1991)

Seeman, Melvin. (1975). Alienation studies. *Annual Review of Sociology, 1*, 91–124.

Stone, Douglas, Patton, Bruce, & Heen, Sheila. (1999). *Difficult conversations*. New York: Viking.

Tucker, R. C. (1978). *The Marx-Engels reader*. New York: Norton.

Volkan, V. D. (2003). *Blind trust: Large groups and their leaders in times of crisis and terror*. Charlottesville, VA: Pitchstone Publishing.

Volkan, V. D. (1997). *Bloodlines: from ethnic pride to ethnic terrorism*. New York: Farrar, Straus and Giroux.

Volkan, V. D. (1988). *The need to have enemies and allies: from clinical practice to international relationships*. Northvale, NJ: J. Aronson.

Watzlawick, Paul, Beavin, J., & Jackson, D. (1967). *Pragmatics of human communication*. New York: Norton.

Whyte, John. (1990). *Interpreting Northern Ireland*. Oxford, England: Oxford University Press.

# CHAPTER 10

# The Capacity for Religious Experience Is an Evolutionary Adaptation to Warfare

*Allen D. MacNeill*

If we were forced to say in one word who God is and in another what the Bible is about, the answer would have to be: God is a *warrior*, and the Bible is about *victory*.
— Jack Miles, *God, A Biography* (1995, p. 106)

Recent events have reinforced a pattern observable for at least the past 6 millennia: that religion and warfare are tightly, perhaps inextricably, intertwined. Even a cursory review of the history of wars and warlike conflicts indicates that religion has played a central role in these events. The common use of words and phrases such as "crusade," "holy war," and the now-infamous "jihad" point to the intimate connection between religion and warfare. From the most exalted "god-kings" to the lowliest "grunts" in the foxholes (where, as tradition tells us, there are no atheists), religion has both accompanied and facilitated warfare.

That religion and warfare are at some level related is virtually undeniable. What is less obvious at first glance is the quality of this relationship; is it causal, and if so, in which direction? There are at least three possibilities:

- Religions cause wars,
- Warfare promotes religion, or
- Both religion and warfare are causally linked to other, more general causative factors.

However, a more sophisticated analysis may indicate that religion and warfare are both cause and effect of each other. That is the thesis of this chapter: that the capacity for religious experience exists among humans primarily because it has facilitated warfare, which in turn reinforces the underlying causes of religion. In other words, the human capacities for religious experience and warfare have adapted to each other in a coevolutionary spiral that has made individual and group mass murder and suicide virtually inevitable, given prevailing ecological subsistence patterns.

## The Capacity for Religion Is an Evolutionary Adaptation

In *The Descent of Man*, Darwin argued that humans do not have an innate instinct to believe in God:

> The belief in God has often been advanced as not only the greatest, but the most complete of all the distinctions between man and the lower animals. It is however impossible ... to maintain that this belief is innate or instinctive in man. (1871, p. 612)

He based this conclusion on the widespread observation that many human cultures do not include a belief in a deity that can be interpreted as being in any way conceptually similar to the monotheistic Judeo-Christian God. However, Darwin went on to point out that "a belief in all-pervading spiritual entities seems to be universal; and apparently follows from a considerable advance in man's reason, and from a still greater advance in his faculties of imagination, curiosity and wonder" (p. 612).

Implicit in Darwin's argument is the idea that only species-wide behavior patterns can legitimately be thought of as evolutionary adaptations. This is a common assumption among both ethologists and evolutionary psychologists, and in my opinion is at best misguided. I prefer G. C. Williams's definition of an adaptation: "An adaptation is any trait that enhances fitness and [has been] modified by selection to perform that role" (1966, p. 4). However, even this definition is somewhat muddied by the inclusion of the term "fitness." The working definition for "evolutionary adaptation" that will be used throughout the rest of this chapter is as follows:

- **An evolutionary adaptation** is any heritable phenotypic character whose frequency of appearance in a population is the result of increased reproductive success relative to alternative versions of that heritable phenotypic character.

Let us set aside for the moment the question of how such phenotypic characters are inherited. As we will see, this is not a trivial question, but one that in the long run does not fundamentally alter the argument I am about to make. Given this definition of evolutionary adaptation, it should be immediately clear why pan-specificity alone is a poor criterion for determining whether some character is an adaptation.

Implicit in this definition of evolutionary adaptation is the idea that there is some real (i.e., nontrivial) *variation* in the phenotypic characteristics present among the members of a population. Indeed, it was the recognition of the existence of such variation, and the insistence that this variation is the basis for natural selection, that was perhaps Darwin's most revolutionary discovery. Any trait that is an evolutionary adaptation will show some nontrivial variation in the expression of that trait, from individuals who express it to a very high degree, to individuals in whom its expression is virtually unnoticeable. What appears at first glance to be pan-specificity is actually the numerical preponderance of individuals whose expression of the trait is close to the population mean for that trait.

Is there other evidence that can be used to determine if a particular characteristic is an evolutionary adaptation? In addition to showing that the numerical preponderance of a particular phenotypic trait is the result of differential survival and reproduction, it may also be possible to link the phenotypic trait with an underlying anatomical and/or physiological substrate that is the efficient cause of the trait in question. For example, it is commonly accepted at present that the ability to speak and understand speech is an evolutionary adaptation in humans. This conclusion was originally based primarily on linguistic grounds (cf. Lenneberg, 1964, 1967; Chomsky, 1965) but has more recently been correlated with underlying neurological processes (Pinker & Bloom, 1999).

Another way of determining if a characteristic is an evolutionary adaptation is to correlate the population dynamics of the adaptation with its evolutionary environment of adaptation (Bowlby, 1969):

- **The evolutionary environment of adaptation** (*EEA*) is the ecological milieu under which a particular adaptation has arisen as the result of selection.

The concept of an EEA can be fruitfully employed when trying to determine whether a particular characteristic is an adaptation by attempting to show how the ecological circumstances prevalent in the EEA would have resulted in differential survival and reproduction. However, application of this technique is complicated by the fact that determination of the EEA of a given adaptation can be a somewhat circular process. Ideally, the circumstances of the EEA should be determined by means other than reference to a particular adaptation, followed by an analysis of the effects of the inferred EEA on the survival and reproduction of the organisms inhabiting it.

Final verification that a particular trait is indeed an evolutionary adaptation would require all of the foregoing, plus linking the appearance of the trait to an underlying gene or gene complex and showing that the frequency of the controlling gene(s) in the population in question has indeed been altered as the result of differential survival and reproduction. This is difficult to do even with very simple genetic traits, such as sickle-cell anemia. Furthermore, it may be that the causal connection between the underlying genes and the trait for which they code may be indirect at best. However, rather than abandon the concept of evolutionary adaptation altogether (as some have suggested; cf. Margulis, 1997), it may still be useful to apply Definition 1 (above) with four further qualifications:

- **Qualification 1:** An evolutionary adaptation will be expressed by most of the members of a given population, in a pattern that approximates a *normal distribution*;
- **Qualification 2:** An evolutionary adaptation can be correlated with *underlying anatomical and physiological structures*, which constitute the efficient (or proximate) cause of the evolution of the adaptation;

- **Qualification 3:** An evolutionary adaptation can be correlated with a preexisting *evolutionary environment of adaptation*, the circumstances of which can then be correlated with differential survival and reproduction; and

- **Qualification 4:** An evolutionary adaptation can be correlated with the presence and expression of an *underlying gene or gene complex*, which directly or indirectly causes and influences the expression of the phenotypic trait that constitutes the adaptation.

Given the foregoing, we can reframe Darwin's question thusly: Is *religion* an evolutionary adaptation? This question is similar to the question, "Is speaking English an adaptation?" Clearly, speaking English is not adaptive, any more than is speaking French or Tagalog. Given Definition 1 and the qualifications enumerated above, to assert that speaking English is an evolutionary adaptation would require that one verify that individuals who speak English survive and reproduce more often than individuals who speak some alternative language. Furthermore, their differential survival and reproduction must be shown to be causally related to their speaking English, and not to some other, related characteristic, such as the ability to speak, regardless of what language is spoken.

Here is the essential distinction: the *capacity* to speak English (or any other language, for that matter) is quite clearly an evolutionary adaptation (Pinker, 1994). That it is so is reinforced by the fact that there are specific circuits and regions in the human brain that are dedicated to the production and understanding of speech. Damage to these structures can severely limit or even completely destroy a person's ability to speak or understand spoken language (Penfield & Roberts, 1959). Furthermore, although every neurologically normal person can learn to speak and understand speech, there is the same kind of natural variation in this capacity that Darwin first pointed out as the basis for natural selection. That is, some individuals learn to speak and understand speech with great difficulty, others do so with great facility, while the vast majority of humanity muddles through with one "mother tongue." The point here is that the *capacity* for religious experience appears to have the same characteristics as the capacity for language. While it is pan-specific, there is considerable individual variation in the capacity for religious experience, with some individuals having very high capacity, others very low, and the average person somewhere in the middle (see Qualification 1 above).

Furthermore, there is accumulating evidence that there are underlying neurological structures that facilitate religious experience. The work of d'Aquili and Newberg (1999), Newberg and d'Aquili (2001), Persinger (1987), Ramachandran and Blakeslee (1998), and Saver and Rabin (1997) all purport to find correlates between religious experiences and specific brain structures and neurological processes. The point here is not to argue for the specific neurobiology underlying the particular states described by these researchers nor to argue that the neurological states they have studied comprise the whole of what we mean by the term "religion." Rather, the fact that some psychological states identified with religious experience have been correlated with specific neurological activity in specific structures in the human brain satisfies, at least in part, the criterion enumerated in Qualification 2 (above).

Finally, is there a "religion gene" that can be shown to correlate with the capacity for religious experience and whose frequency can be shown to vary in such a way as to approximate the patterns characteristic of an evolutionary adaptation? No, nor should we expect there to be one. Only in so-called "vulgar socio-biology" are there presumed to be single genes (or even gene complexes) that code for complex human behaviors such as the capacity for speech or religion. Rather, there are genes that code for the assembly, operation, and modification of "mental modules" that bring about these complex behavior patterns.

One way to avoid the whole morass of gene-behavior linkages is to employ what Stephen Emlen has called the "correlation approach" to behavioral ecology (1976). According to this method, one may be able to "interpret and partially predict the social structure of a species on the basis of a limited set of environmental or ecological variables ... [that] impose limits on the range of types of social organization that will be adaptive" (p. 736). According to this viewpoint, "[Species] faced with similar ecological 'problems' exhibit a predictable convergence in their 'solutions,' as shown in their social organizations" (p. 737). Following Emlen's lead, we can compare the types of religious experiences and patterns of religious behaviors exhibited by humans in different ecological subsistence patterns and at different times and places. In so doing, we may find some general patterns that will point to the underlying evolutionary dynamics influencing the development of the biological and cultural mechanisms producing those experiences and behaviors.

Adaptive characteristics do not increase in frequency monotonically in populations, nor are selective pressures usually limited to one or even a few parameters. Following the lead of Sewell Wright (1968–1978), it has been very common for evolutionary biologists to model the *adaptive landscape* for a given population or species (cf. Ridley, 1996, pp. 215–219). However, what is sometimes lost in diagrams such as these is the fact that there are individual organisms represented by nearly every point on the surface illustrated. That is, not all individuals in the population have risen to the adaptive peaks in the population, nor are all of them slipping down into the troughs of maladaptation. Perhaps it would be better to imagine each individual and its descendents as a boatlike cluster of adjacent points on this surface, tossed up and down by the vicissitudes of ecological change.

In this viewpoint, it may be easier to see that some changes in the environment are much less important than others and that some shifts in adaptive character may be much more significant than others. In particular, it is quite possible for a major change in one parameter in the environment to cause a corresponding change in the adaptive characteristics of the population, swamping any effects of smaller changes. In essence, what I am describing here is an evolutionary override of sorts, in which selection for one characteristic swamps selection for most or all other characteristics among the members of a population.

At this point, it appears likely that the capacity for religious experience has many of the characteristics of an evolutionary adaptation:

- the capacity for religious experience is pan-specific in humans, although there is considerable variation in this capacity, both within and between human groups,
- the capacity for religious experience has been correlated with underlying neurological structures and processes,
- the capacity for religious experience can be correlated with a known evolutionary environment of adaptation (i.e., intergroup warfare in agricultural societies, as will be discussed in more detail below), and
- although no underlying genetic mechanisms for the development of the capacity for religious experience are now known, the existence of consistent cross-cultural patterns of religious expression indicates that religious behavior is subject to evolutionary convergence in a manner analogous to other evolutionary adaptations.

## The Capacity for Warfare Is Also an Evolutionary Adaptation

Now it is time to address the other half of the coevolutionary spiral, to wit: Is warfare (or, more precisely, the capacity for warfare) an evolutionary adaptation? Once again, Darwin was unequivocal on this subject. In *The Descent of Man*, he wrote,

> When two tribes of primeval man, living in the same country, came into competition, if (other circumstances being equal) the one tribe included a great number of courageous, sympathetic and faithful members, who were always ready to warn each other of danger, to aid and defend each other, this tribe would succeed better and conquer the other … . Thus the social and moral qualities would tend slowly to advance and be diffused throughout the world. (1871, p. 130)

Two things are immediately noticeable about this description: that Darwin assumes that the ability to be successful in warfare arises from courage, sympathy, and faithfulness within human groups and that the level at which selection is operating in the evolution of such qualities is the group, rather than the individual. As we shall soon see, neither of these assumptions is necessarily in accord with the evidence.

Before we can decide if warfare is adaptive, it is first necessary to define precisely what we mean by warfare. There appear to be at least three intergroup aggressive activities that are often referred to by the same name. It is important to my later argument that these be distinguished, and so here they are:

- **Raiding** (or *rustling*, as in cattle rustling) is an activity in which small groups of humans, virtually always men and almost always close kin groups, spontaneously and with relatively little planning or hierarchical organization, temporarily enter the recognized territory of a nearby group with the intention of forcibly obtaining resources, usually domesticated animals or women, or both. Not all members of a given kin group will necessarily participate in raiding, and all "warlike" activity and organization occurs immediately before, during, and after a raid. At all other times, the participants in such a raid are engaged in other domestic activities, generally unrelated to raiding.
- **Militia Warfare** is an activity in which somewhat larger groups of humans, again almost exclusively male but not necessarily close kin groups, band together periodically with some

planning and hierarchical organization, with the intention of either forcibly entering the recognized territory of a nearby group or defending against the forcible entry by similarly constituted raiding parties or militias from other groups. In militia warfare, most of the able-bodied males in a given social group will participate in some way, either in direct combat or combat support. However, once the immediate warlike activity has ended, the militia disbands and most, if not all, of its members turn to other tasks. An important characteristic that distinguishes raiding from militia warfare is the presence in the latter of generally recognized hierarchical ranks and specialized duties and training, a situation generally lacking in raiding/rustling.

- **Professional Warfare** is an activity in which relatively large groups of humans (i.e., armies), again almost exclusively male but usually not close kin groups (and often including non-combatant female auxiliaries), band together regularly or permanently with considerable planning and hierarchical organization, with the intention of either forcibly commandeering the recognized territory of a nearby group or defending against the forcible entry by similarly constituted armies from other groups. In professional warfare, many of the able-bodied males in a given social group will participate in some way, either in direct combat or combat support. Furthermore, regardless of when or if the immediate warlike activity has ended, the army continues to exist, and its members pursue specialized tasks within the military organization. An important characteristic that distinguishes raiding and militia warfare from professional warfare is the proliferation in the latter of strictly defined hierarchical ranks and specialized duties and the existence of a permanent professional class of warriors which includes almost all officers, but not necessarily all combatants (i.e., the grunts get to go home and take up other occupations after the war ... assuming they survive).

Although there are many variations on these three themes (and an almost infinite gradation of one into the other), there are broad patterns of correlation between these three patterns across most societies. Furthermore, the three types of warlike organizations are generally correlated with ecological subsistence patterns. Raiding is most common among hunter-gatherers and pastoralists (i.e., people who raise domesticated animals as an important part of their subsistence) Militia warfare is more common among simple agriculturalists, especially those who live in widely dispersed villages and who depend primarily on domesticated crop plants for their subsistence. Professional warfare is most common among societies that are characterized by a combination of village agriculture and urban living. In particular, the maintenance of a professional army requires both large populations and a large surplus of food and other resources, as the members of the army themselves are no longer available for food production or distribution and must therefore be supported by the rest of the population.

According to Wallace, "[t]here are few, if any, societies that have not engaged in at least one war in their known history" (1968, p. 173). Indeed, there is reason to believe that warfare (or at least raiding) predates the evolution of the genus *Homo* and may not even be restricted to the order Primates. Jane Goodall (1986) describes behaviors among the chimpanzees (*Pan troglodytes*) of the Gombe preserve that are remarkably similar to the raiding behavior of humans in pastoral societies. Moving beyond the Primates, Hans Kruuk (1972, pp. 253–258) describes behaviors among the spotted hyaenas (*Crocuta crocuta*) of east Africa, which bear some resemblance to the behaviors described by Goodall.

Given that raiding and other forms of social aggression appear to be pan-specific, can they be considered to be adaptations? Or, to be more precise, is the *capacity* for social aggression, either offensive or defensive (or both), an evolutionary adaptation? I believe the answer to this question is yes. Clearly, there are neurological modules for aggressive behavior in humans and related primates. Primatologist Richard Wrangham (1999) has proposed that both chimpanzee and human males have a genetically influenced tendency to raid and kill members of neighboring groups whenever there is a state of intergroup hostility and one group can muster sufficient force to raid the other with relatively little fear of losses (1999, pp. 1–12). Wrangham and Peterson (1996) have pointed out that there are striking similarities between the raiding behavior of wild chimpanzees and the raiding behavior of the Yanomami (pp. 64–72). Chagnon (1990) has taken this argument further; in a discussion of the behavior of Yanomami warriors designated as *unokais* (a designation given to males that have undergone a ritual purification following a killing), Chagnon points out that *unokais* have a significantly higher reproductive success than non-*unokais*, as shown by statistical analysis of reproductive success at different ages. Males with the highest relative reproductive success are middle-aged men with children, a pattern that is repeated in many other societies (1988, pp. 985–992).

Tooby and Cosmides (1988) have argued that the capacity for raiding and warlike behavior shown by humans and other primates is based on an evolutionary "algorithm" in which the costs of warfare are balanced by the corresponding benefits to reproductive success (p. 5). I think we need to be clear that, in this context, "reproductive success" is used in the same sense as it is used by evolutionary biologists: that is, the net number of offspring produced by individuals performing different behaviors. We are not necessarily speaking of a kind of sexual selection for the capacity for warfare. Rather, we are referring simply to the number of offspring that survive in each behavioral cohort, for whatever reason. Ecological factors, such as the availability of food resources (especially proteins), the spatial and temporal distribution of such resources (e.g., dispersed and nondefensible versus clumped and defensible), the availability of specific tools and weapons (such as metal tools), and the number, size, and physical development of potential fighters, all play a part in the calculation of potential costs and benefits of warlike social behavior. In other words, the algorithm postulated by Tooby and Cosmides is a mental means of factoring in all of the various costs and benefits of alternative behaviors to determine which alternative will result in the most positive outcome.

At what level—individual or group—must such outcomes be positive for the capacity for warfare to be adaptive? Sober and Wilson (1998) have argued that cooperative behavior (i.e., "altruism") can evolve as the result of natural selection at the level of groups. Although, at first glance, it may not seem that warfare is altruistic. However, it clearly is, as individual members of a society engaged in warfare risk (and sometimes lose) their lives in defense of the group. Sober and Wilson do not specifically discuss warfare, but clearly it would qualify as a form of cooperative behavior. So, does the capacity for warfare evolve as the result of selection at the level of groups?

In the early 1960s, V. C. Wynne-Edwards used the concept of group selection as the basis for the explanation of nearly all of animal social behavior (1962). It was in response to Wynne-Edwards that G. C. Williams wrote *Adaptation and Natural Selection* (1966) in which he argued forcefully for the primary importance of selection at the level of individuals, rather than groups. Williams pointed out that any group of organisms in which reproductive success has been lowered by group processes (specifically by decreasing the number of offspring per individual by means of various mechanisms) is vulnerable to invasion and ultimate replacement by individuals who are not so constrained. His model for individual selection has been extended to the evolution of social behavior and cooperation by Hamilton (1964), Trivers (1971), Axelrod (1984), and Dawkins (1982).

Warfare is often thought of as an aberration, rather than a central characteristic of human sociality. However, even a brief review of human history should impress upon one that warfare has been a constant, if episodic, aspect of human social behavior. The point here is that, even if it does not happen regularly, warfare can have an effect on natural selection equivalent to—and in some cases greater than—a constant selective pressure. During periods in which warfare is not occurring, selection will result primarily from those sources of mortality and reduced reproductive success characteristic of peacetime society: disease, famine, competition for scarce resources, etc. However, during periods of warfare, these "everyday" forms of selection can be overwhelmed by the effects of warfare-specific changes in mortality and reproductive success. In other words, periods of warfare act like evolutionary "bottlenecks" selecting with greatly increased relative intensity for any physiological or behavioral characteristic that allows for differential survival and reproductive success.

Furthermore, it seems likely that these selective pressures will be exerted primarily at the level of individuals, rather than groups. To understand why, consider Sober and Wilson's definition of a group: "a set of individuals that influence each other's fitness with respect to a certain trait, but not the fitness of those outside the group" (1998, p. 92). To be consistent with standard practice in evolutionary theory, let fitness (symbolized by $\mathbf{w}$) be defined as the average per capita lifetime contribution of an individual of a particular genotype to the population after one or more generations, measured in number of offspring bearing that individual's genotype. If we apply this definition of fitness to Sober and Wilson's definition of a group, then each individual member of a group will have some fitness ($\mathbf{w_i}$), with the group fitness reducing to the sum of the fitnesses of the individuals that make up the group ($\mathbf{w_G} = \mathbf{w_I} + \mathbf{w_j} + \ldots \mathbf{w_n}$). Furthermore, let us assume that fitness is a function of some limited resource. In real terms, this resource might be food, or shelter, or access to mates, or some other factor that contributes directly or indirectly to survival or reproduction. Each individual can exploit some small fraction of the limited resource with the aggregate consumption of resources eventually reaching a maximum value (i.e., when each individual has maximized its fitness via the exploitation of that resource and the resource has been completely subdivided among the individuals in the group). Until that limit has been reached, competition between individuals in the group is relatively unimportant, and so individual fitness of each member of the group will not be limited by group membership.

Under such circumstances, there are at least three different ways in which intra-group cooperation could affect individual fitness:

- The fitness effect of group membership on individual fitness could be **negative**, compared with the fitness of each individual acting alone; that is, being a member of the group **detracts** from each individual's fitness, compared with acting alone; see Figure 10.1.

This is the situation described by Wynne-Edwards (1962) and criticized by G. C. Williams (1966). Under these conditions, the addition of each new member to a group *decreases* the average fitness of each member of the group, with the effect that such a group is constantly vulnerable to invasion and replacement by individuals who act entirely in their own interests. Given the relationship between group size and individual fitness, it is unlikely that this type of group selection would prevail under most natural conditions.

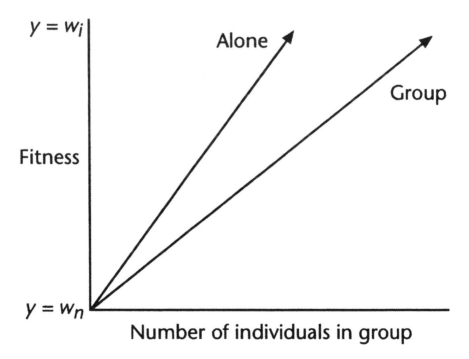

**Figure 10.1**
**Negative Group Selection**

- The fitness effect of group membership on individual fitness could be **positive**, compared with the fitness of each individual acting alone; that is, being a member of the group **adds** to each individual's fitness, compared with acting alone; see Figure 10.2.

This is the essentially the situation proposed by Sober and Wilson (1998). Under these conditions, the addition of each new member to a group *increases* the average fitness of each member of the group, with the overall effect that such a group becomes less vulnerable to invasion and replacement by "selfish" individuals as it grows larger. Unlike the situation with negative group fitness above, this type of group selection could easily evolve, as membership in the group clearly benefits individuals and vice versa.

- The fitness effect of group membership on individual fitness could be **negative** when the group size is below some critical value but could become **positive** as that critical group size is exceeded; see Figure 10.3.

Under such conditions, a group would have to reach a "critical group size" before the fitness benefits of intragroup cooperation would begin to be felt. This would seem to present a barrier to the evolution of such cooperation via group selection. However, the group might reach critical size for reasons unrelated to the activities

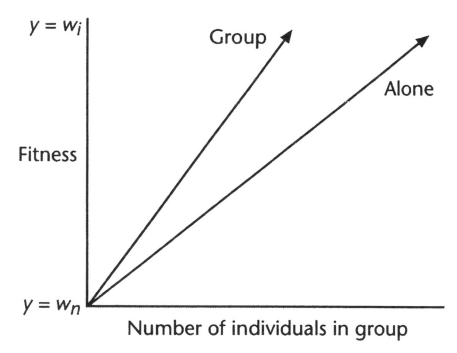

**Figure 10.2**
**Positive Group Selection**

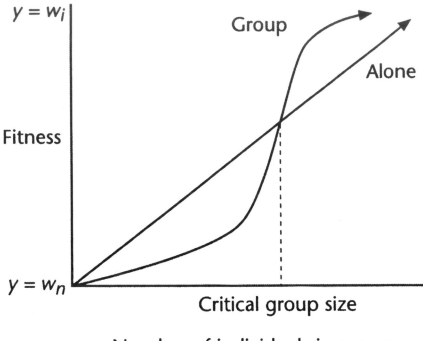

**Figure 10.3**
**Variable Group Selection**

resulting in reduced aggregate fitness. Once above the critical size, adding new members to the group would add to the fitness of each individual.

There are many circumstances in nature in which the kind of variable group fitness described above has been shown to exist. For example, in a study of the hunting behavior of wolves (*Canis lupus*) on Isle Royale, Mech (1970) found that the larger a wolf pack was, the better able it was to exploit larger prey (1970, p. 38). Intragroup cooperation is often essential to the success of hunting forays among social carnivores in general. Teleki (1973) found the same to be true for hunting behavior among wild chimpanzees. Indeed, chimpanzees exhibit unusually cooperative behavior when hunting, especially when their prey is other primates.

It is very likely that human warfare follows the pattern described in Figure 10.3. That is, there is a critical group size above which the effectiveness of warfare increases, as reflected in its effects on fitness. There are two primary reasons for this:

- As virtually any military commander would point out, the larger the military force, the more likely it is to prevail over its opponents. Calculation of the relative sizes and strengths of the opposing sides in any warlike interaction would be of crucial importance to the participants, regardless of rank. Therefore, it is likely that natural selection would have resulted in the evolution of mental algorithms that would facilitate such calculations under conditions of repeated or sustained warfare.

• As the size of a military force increases, the probability of injury or death to each individual member of the group generally decreases. One-on-one violent interactions between individual combatants are most likely to result in the injury or death of one or both combatants. As the number of combatants increases, the number of injuries and deaths per capita generally decreases (except in the case of modern technological warfare, where overwhelmingly powerful weapons can injure or kill huge numbers of combatants and noncombatants). This decrease in probability of injury and death with the size of a military force is another factor in the mental calculations performed by any potential participant in warfare.

Given the foregoing, it should now be clear that participation in warfare can have positive effects on both individual fitness and group fitness, when group fitness is measured as the aggregate fitness of the individuals making up the group. Participants in warfare—combatants and their supporters—can gain access to territory and to resources if they are on the winning side in a conflict. In particular, it is a well-known (but not often discussed) fact that the winners in virtually all warlike conflicts have greatly increased reproductive success compared with both the losers and nonparticipants in their own group. Wars and warlike interactions (including simple raids) are often followed by increases in birth rates among the winners. In particular, soldiers (i.e., combatants) are notorious for the commission of rape during war (Thornhill & Palmer, 2000). That this is the case has been recognized as far back as the founding myths of Western civilization: the legend of the rape of the Sabine women is based on an actual event in the early history of the city of Rome. Many authors have pointed out that access (including, of course, forcible access) to reproductive females is a constant theme in the genesis and prosecution of warfare. The Old Testament contains numerous examples of such forcible reproductive access, including several cases in which God specified which females (young, but not yet pregnant) were to be forcibly taken for reproductive purposes and which females (pregnant, old, or infertile) were to be killed, along with all males (including children).

Rape as a constant in warfare has of course continued to the present day (cf. Beevor, 2002). That rape would result in increased reproductive success on the part of soldiers is fairly obvious. What is not obvious is that this would also result in increased reproductive success on the part of the females being raped. So long as being raped does not result in injury or death, and so long as the person being raped is not subsequently harmed or placed under conditions of increased risk of harm, having been raped by a soldier would result in essentially the same increase in reproductive success as any other form of copulation. That the male Yanomami studied by Chagnon (1988) who participated in raids on neighboring groups in which females were forcibly abducted would have an increased reproductive success as a result has not been seriously questioned (except see Ferguson, 2001). What has not been systematically investigated are the effects of such abduction on the reproductive success of the females so abducted. In the absence of such data, the idea that such victims could indeed benefit (in a purely Darwinian sense) from the affects of warfare remains at present an interesting but untested hypothesis.

Being on the losing side in a warlike conflict need not be entirely negative for males either. From a Darwinian standpoint, what matters is reproductive success, not happiness or freedom from oppression. In ancient Rome, it was quite common for members of the conquered peoples to be pressed into slavery by the Romans. Although being a slave under such conditions might not be what one would have preferred, it was quite common for slaves to be allowed to marry and have children. Indeed, if the children of a slave became the property of the slave's owner, then there would have been a positive incentive for the slave owner to encourage the fecundity of his slaves. The point here is obviously not to endorse slavery but rather to point out that there are conditions under which the losers in a warlike conflict might benefit from participation in such conflict almost as much as the winners.

In sum, then, we may also conclude that the capacity for warfare, like the capacity for religious experience, has many of the characteristics of an evolutionary adaptation:

- the capacity for warfare is pan-specific in humans, although there is considerable variation in this capacity, both within and between human groups,
- although it has not yet been possible to correlate the capacity for warfare with underlying neurological structures and processes, there is ample evidence for a correlation between aggressive and violent behavior and the emotional control centers of the brain,
- the capacity for warfare can be correlated with known evolutionary environments of adaptation (raiding with hunting/gathering and pastoral agriculture, militia warfare with settled agriculture, and professional warfare with large-scale agriculture and urban culture), and
- although no underlying genetic mechanisms for the development of the capacity for warfare are now known, the existence of consistent cross-cultural patterns of group violence and coercion indicates that warlike behavior is subject to evolutionary convergence in a manner analogous to other evolutionary adaptations.

## The Evolution of Religion: The Standard Model

Before turning to the crux of the argument, it is necessary to consider in more detail what the capacity for religious experience consists of. Recent work on the evolutionary dynamics of religion have converged on a "standard model" in which religions are treated as epiphenomena of human cognitive processes dealing with the detection of and reaction to agents, especially human agents, under conditions of stress anxiety and perceived threat. Boyer has proposed a comprehensive theory of the evolution of religion based on an underlying cognitive process whereby "Our minds are prepared [to give] us particular mental predispositions" (2001, p. 3). In particular, "evolution by natural selection gave us a particular kind of mind so that only particular kinds of religious notions can be acquired" (p. 4).

Boyer begins by asserting that "[r]eligion is about the existence and causal powers of nonobservable entities and agencies" (p. 7). He then proceeds to show that the common explanations for the origin of religion—explanations of puzzling physical and mental phenomena, explanations of evil and suffering, provision of comfort in times of adversity, and provision of the moral basis for social order—cannot be reduced to or included in an explanation of the evolutionary origin of the capacity for religious experience (pp. 5–12). Boyer then points out that "there is only a limited catalogue of possible supernatural beliefs" (p. 29). This is because "[t]he religious concepts we observe are relatively successful ones selected among many other variants" (p. 32). Therefore, "religion emerges … in the selection of concepts and the selection of memories" (p. 33).

What are the criteria by which certain concepts are reinforced and others are lost? Following Sperber (1985), Boyer distinguishes between simple concepts and templates. The latter are large-scale concepts that subsume many smaller, simpler concepts, essentially by analogy. For example, the word "animal" designates a template, which is usually applied to any entity that is obviously alive (especially because it moves under its own power and with intentionality), eats things, reproduces, and has a general body plan that conforms to what most people would agree is an animal body plan. According to this model of mental classification, religious concepts are easily transmitted from person to person because they both conform to such templates in most respects but violate them in obvious and memorable ways: they "surprise people by describing things and events they could not possibly encounter in actual experience" (p. 55).

In this way, religious concepts are much more easily remembered and transmitted than nonreligious concepts:

> Some concepts … connect with inference systems in the brain in a way that makes recall and communication very easy. Some concepts … trigger our emotional programs in particular ways. Some concepts … connect to our social mind. Some … are represented in such a way that they soon become plausible and direct behavior. The ones that do *all* this are the religious ones we actually observe in human societies. They are most successful because they combine features relevant to a variety of mental systems. (Boyer, 2001, p. 50)

Central to Boyer's theory on the evolution of the capacity for religious experience is the concept of *agency*:

- **Agency** is that set of characteristics by which we infer the existence and action of an *agent*; that is, a living (or lifelike) entity whose behavior indicates that it has intentions and can act upon them. Agents are purposeful, and purposeful (i.e., teleological) action is the hallmark of agency.

Along with other cognitive and evolutionary psychologists, most notably Barrett (1996), Boyer asserts that the ability to detect agency has high selective value. Barrett points out that humans, like other potential prey animals, should have "hyperactive agency detectors," because any human who did not would be more likely to be injured or killed by a predator. Selection for ultrasensitive agency detectors would result in a tendency for such detectors to produce "false positives," that is, the tendency to infer the existence of agency in an entity in which it is absent.

Although Boyer seems to be on the right track, there is a strong implication throughout his work that the capacity for religious experience is an epiphenomenon that arises secondarily as the result of the action of agency detection and the increased mnemonic transmissability of concepts that violate cognitive templates. J. Donovan (1994, 2002) disagrees: for him, "religion has direct evolutionary advantages that have been directly selected. That benefit relates to the mitigation of existential anxiety with its roots in death awareness" (2002, p. 18). Donovan asserts that religion arises primarily as the result of the selectively positive effect of the reduction of anxiety arising as the result of the awareness of death. Donovan looked at the ability of "spiritual healers" to enter into possession trances, and he concluded that this is arguably a genetically based ability that has been selected as a belief-enhancing mechanism by which the palliative effect of religious participation can be rendered (1994, personal communication, March 19, 2003).

Atran incorporates Boyer's argument from cognitive processes into a more comprehensive selectionist explanation for the evolution of the capacity for religious belief and behavior. Atran agrees with Boyer that there are underlying cognitive (and therefore presumably neurological) processes by which certain types of beliefs can be spread with greatly increased ease and fidelity of transmission. However, he adds a social and political dimension to Boyer's argument, tying religion to the establishment and maintenance of social organization and political power. He quotes Irons (1996) to the effect that "[r]eligions in large-scale societies all show evidence of social dominance" (Atran, 2002, p. 103). Atran goes on to point out that religious rituals usually involve submissive displays, such as kneeling, bowing, prostration, hand spreading, and throat baring, which he likens to the submissive displays of subordinate nonhuman primates (p. 127). Taking this line of reasoning further, Atran points out that "[h]uman worship requires even dominant individuals to willingly submit to a higher moral authority in displays of costly, hard-to-fake commitment or risk losing the allegiance of their subordinates" (p. 127).

This is the heart of Atran's argument: that religion forms a kind of "social glue" that uses ritualized demonstrations of commitment to supernatural authority to encourage and even coerce individual adherence to group norms and goals. Atran's argument is essentially that all members of a society (i.e., a "group," in the parlance of group selection), from the most subordinate to the most dominant, benefit from the social cohesion and singularity of purpose that religion fosters. He states that "[t]he more a ruler sacrifices and suffers, the more the ruler earns respect and devotion" (p. 127). But clearly the same principle would apply to his subordinates, at any level: individual demonstrations of sacrifice and suffering (or at least the willingness to do so) on behalf of the group tend to encourage group solidarity.

There are two problems with this outlook: it assumes that costs and benefits are shared approximately equally throughout such groups, and it implicitly focuses on the group as the primary unit of selection. Atran is clearly aware of the first of these shortcomings. He refers to the classical Marxist "coercion argument" for the origin of religion, by which he means that "religion was [according to Marx] created by and for rulers to materially exploit the ruled, with ... secondary benefits to the oppressed masses of a low but constant level of material security" (as cited in Atran, p. 128). He then goes on to cite Diamond's theory that in large-scale societies (by which he presumably means settled agricultural societies with a mixed village and urban settlement pattern), the members of the ruling hierarchy (or "kleptocracy") gains the support of their subordinates by "constructing an ideology or religion justifying kleptocracy" (Diamond, 1997, p. 277). Diamond asserts that this reification of the supercision of the ruling hierarchy by religion represents a fundamental shift from the situation in bands and tribes (of hunter-gatherers and pastoralists), in which "supernatural beliefs ... did not serve to justify central authority" (p. 277).

Diamond concludes his discussion of the origin of religion by asserting that institutionalized religion confers two important benefits to centralized societies:

- shared ideology or religion helps solve the problem of how (genetically) unrelated individuals can cooperate, by providing a bond not based on (genetic) kinship, and
- religion gives people a motive, rather than genetic self-interest, for sacrificing their lives on the behalf of others (Diamond, p. 278).

I believe that both Atran and Diamond are on the right track, but their arguments are derailed by a common misapplication of selectionist thinking. Atran proposes what appears to be a relatively weak counterargument to the coercion argument, pointing out that religions can be liberating as well as oppressive (Atran, p. 129). While this is true in some cases, I believe it misses the point: if religion (or, more properly, the *capacity* for religious experience) is to evolve by natural selection, it must do so at the level of individuals in the context of specific ecological circumstances.

If Williams is correct about the nonexistence of group selection, then for the capacity for religion to evolve it must somehow increase *individual* reproductive success. In the context of small, relatively nonhierarchic bands or tribes of hunter-gatherers or nomadic pastoralists, it seems most likely that selection at the level of individuals would result in behaviors that would approximate those observed in hunting groups of primates and social carnivores. Although there are clearly recognized dominant individuals in such groups, all of the members of such groups clearly benefit from their membership in them. This is because there are circumstances in which groups of cooperative individuals can obtain resources that would be out of the reach of individuals acting on their own.

This same argument applies at all levels of social organization. For particular social processes to evolve by classical Darwinian selection, there must be some benefit that accrues to individuals from participating in such processes, a benefit that equals if not clearly supercedes the benefit to be gained from acting alone. That such benefits to individuals do result from highly organized social interactions in human and other animal societies is not in question. What is still to be decided here is whether such increases in individual fitness can be observed as the result of the capacity for religious experience, specifically in the context of warfare.

## The Capacity for Religious Experience Has Evolved via Individual Selection Among Humans in the Context of Warfare

Here we come to the crux of my argument: that the capacity for religious experience is an adaptation that facilitates warfare. Let me begin by carefully defining the following terms:

- **The capacity for religious experience** is the capacity to formulate, communicate, and act on beliefs (that is, concepts, memories, and intentions or plans) that include reference to supernatural entities and processes. Like the capacity for language, such a capacity must be based on a corresponding neurological "hard wiring," although the dimensions (and limitations) of such neurological structures and processes await further investigation.

- **Religion** is not the specific content of the beliefs that arise from such a capacity. Rather, religion is the overall pattern of such beliefs, including concepts like omniscience, omnipotence, and omnipresence (on the part of supernatural deities), the existence of a soul that is separable from (and can live on after the death of) a physical body, and the existence of supernatural realms inaccessible to normal senses but accessible to deities and incorporeal entities such as souls.

Note that this definition of religion is not as inclusive as that used by Boyer, who includes not only the concepts and entities noted above, but also virtually all forms of "folk belief" (i.e., superstition) (2001). It seems likely to me that the origin of the capacities for both folk beliefs and religion has its roots in the same neurological substrate: a neurological mechanism that reduces anxiety in the face of stress induced by unknown, unpredictable, and presumably dangerous circumstances However, part of my thesis here is that true *religious* experience is a later development in the evolution of the human mind (and presumably the human nervous system), one that has evolved as the result of individual selection primarily in the context of warfare.

How, precisely, does the capacity for religious experience evolve in the context of warfare? Consider the decision that each potential combatant must make prior to participating in a raid, a battle, or an extended military campaign. This decision will include (but is certainly not limited to) the following:

- The probability that one will be seriously injured or killed in the raid, battle, or campaign,

- The possible consequences of *not* participating (e.g., everything from social disapprobation to summary execution),

- The probability that one will gain something (e.g., resources, social position, access to mates, etc.) as the result of one's participation, and

- The quality of such gains, especially when compared with the costs of nonparticipation.

It is important to note that the calculation of such costs and benefits need not be overtly conscious. Whether conscious or unconscious, the outcome of such a calculation would be either an increased or decreased motivation to participate in the impending conflict.

What happens during war? According to von Clausewitz,

> War is nothing but a duel on an extensive scale. If we would conceive as a unit the countless number of duels which make up a war, we shall do so best by supposing to ourselves two wrestlers. Each strives by physical force to compel the other to submit to his will: his first object is to throw his adversary, and thus to render him incapable of further resistance. (1832, p. 12)

War involves violent force, up to and including killing people. To participate in a war means to participate in an activity in which there is a significant probability that one will either kill other people or will be killed by them.

This means that any participant in warfare is faced with the possibility of painful and violent death as the result of such participation. Given this probability, if natural selection acts at the level of individuals, how can natural selection result in a propensity to participate in warfare? Clearly, either the probability that one will be killed must be perceived as low or the potential payoff from such participation must be perceived as high. If natural selection is to operate at the level of individuals, these two circumstances should ideally be obtained simultaneously,

Here is where the capacity for religious experience is crucial. By making possible the belief that a supernatural entity knows the outcome of all actions and can influence such outcomes, that one's "self" (i.e., "soul") is not tied to one's physical body, and that if one is killed in battle, one's essential self (i.e., soul) will go to a better "place" (e.g., heaven, valhalla, etc.) the capacity for religious experience can tip the balance toward participation in warfare. By doing so, the capacity for religious belief not only makes it possible for individuals to do what they might not otherwise be motivated to do, it also tends to tip the balance toward victory on the part of the religiously devout participant. This is because success in battle, and success in war, hinges on commitment: the more committed a military force is in battle, the more likely it is to win, all other things being equal. When two groups of approximately equal strength meet in battle, it is the group in which the individuals are more committed to victory (and less inhibited by the fear of injury or death) that is more likely to prevail. To give just one example, the battle cry and motto of the clan Neil has always been "*Buaidh na bas!*"—"Victory or death!"

Religions tell people what they most want to hear: that those agents and processes that they most fear have no ultimate power over them or pose no threat to themselves or the people they care about. In particular, by providing an intensely memorable, emotionally satisfying, and tension-releasing solution to the problem of mortality, religions make it possible for warriors to master their anxieties and do battle without emotional inhibitions. This makes them much more effective warriors, especially in the hand-to-hand combat that humans have fought throughout nearly all of our evolutionary history.

Consider the characteristics that are most often cited as central to religious experience. Newberg and d'Aquili have presented an integrated model of the neurobiological underpinnings of religious experience. They have pointed out that central to most religious experience is a sensation of awe, combined with "mildly pleasant sensations to feelings of ecstasy" (2001, p. 89). They have shown that such sensations can be induced by rhythmic chanting and body movements, combined with loud music and colorful visual displays, all of which produce a condition of sensory overload. This process then induces a neurological condition characterized by a sense of depersonalization and ecstatic union with one's surroundings.

This is precisely what happens as the result of military drill and training. It is no accident that humans preparing for war use exactly the same kinds of sensory stimuli described by Newberg and d'Aquili. They have tied such displays to religious activities and shown the deep similarities between religious rituals and secular ones: "patriotic rituals ... emphasize the 'sacredness' of a nation, or a cause, or even a flag ... turn[ing] a meaningful idea into a visceral experience" (p. 90). The two types of activities—religious rituals and patriotic rituals—use the same underlying neurological pathways and chemistry.

Religious experience is often equated with a state of mystical union with the supernatural. But what exactly does this mean, and in the context of this chapter, is there a connection between mystical experience and warfare? The answer is almost certainly yes. That combatants have had experiences that would be classified as mystical before, during, and after battle is a simple historical fact. The Scottish flag is based on just such an experience: the white crossed diagonal bars against a field of azure of the St. Andrew's cross is said to have appeared to King Hungus and his warriors during a battle against in the Saxons. Legend says this so encouraged the Scots and frightened their adversaries that a victory was won (Middlemass, 2000).

A common thread in all mystical experiences is a loss of the sense of self and a union with something larger than oneself (Newberg & d'Aquili, 2001, p. 101) Additionally, there is often a sense of submission to a higher power, in which one's personal desires and fears are subordinated to the purposes of that higher power. If that higher power were identified with the leaders of a military hierarchy, it is easy to see how such experiences could be used to increase one's loyalty and submission to that hierarchy.

It is likely that the same underlying neurological circuits that produce the sensations described by mystics also produce the sensations of fear, awe, and ecstasy that are experienced by combatants during the course of a battle. Like the evolutionary implications of rape, this is a topic that is rarely discussed outside of military circles but is a well-known phenomenon during battle. The noise and movement, the confusion and excitement, intensified tremendously by the imminence of injury and death combine to produce a state of massive arousal in the sympathetic nervous system of the combatant. This state of intense arousal is very similar to the state of arousal felt during copulation; indeed, some soldiers will candidly admit that during the heat of battle, they often experience a kind of sexual arousal, leading in some cases to ejaculation. This fusion of sensory and motor states in a condition of intense arousal, combined with a sensation of depersonalization, can easily produce in susceptible individuals a condition in which a kind of "blood lust" overwhelms most thoughts of self-preservation.

## The Ultimate Sacrifice

Let us return to group selectionist arguments for the evolution of both religion and warfare. D. S. Wilson (2002) has proposed that the capacity for religion has evolved among humans as the result of selection at the level of groups, rather than individuals. Specifically, he argues that benefits that accrue to groups as the result of individual sacrifices can result in increased group fitness, and this can explain what is otherwise difficult to explain: religiously motivated behaviors (such as celibacy and self-sacrifice) that apparently lower individual fitness as they benefit the group.

At first glance, Wilson's argument seems compelling. Consider the most horrific manifestation of religious warfare: the suicide bomber. A person who blows himself or herself up in order to kill his or her opponents has lowered his or her individual fitness. Does this not mean that such behavior must be explainable only at the level of group selection? Not at all: the solution to this conundrum is implicit in the basic principles of population genetics. Recall that one of Darwin's requirements for evolution by natural selection was the existence of variation between the individuals in a population (1859, pp. 7–59). Variation within populations is a universal characteristic of life, an inevitable outcome of the imperfect mechanism of genetic replication. Therefore, it follows that if the capacity for religious experience is an evolutionary adaptation, then there will be variation between individuals in the degree to which they express such a capacity.

Furthermore, it is not necessarily true that when an individual sacrifices his or her life in the context of a struggle, the underlying genotype that induced that sacrifice will be eliminated by that act. Hamilton's principle of kin selection (1964) has already been mentioned as one mechanism, acting at the level of individuals (or, more precisely, at the level of genotypes), by which individual self-sacrifice can result in the increase in frequency of the genotype that facilitated such sacrifice. Trivers (1971) has proposed a mechanism by which apparently altruistic acts on the part of genetically unrelated individuals may evolve by means of reciprocal altruism.

Given these two mechanisms, all that is necessary for the capacity for religious behavior, including extreme forms of self-sacrifice, to evolve is that as the result of such behaviors, the tendency (and ability) to perform them would be propagated throughout a population. The removal of some individuals as the result of suicide would merely lower the frequency of such tendencies and abilities in the population, not eliminate them altogether. If by making the ultimate sacrifice, an individual who shares his or her genotype with those who benefit by that sacrifice will, at the level of his or her genes, become more common over time (E. O. Wilson, 1975, p. 4).

## To the Winner Go the Spoils

Let us now consider the flip side of war: the benefits that accrue to the winners of warlike conflicts. Given the mechanisms of kin selection, one can see how warfare and the religious beliefs that facilitate it might evolve among the closely related kin groups that constitute the raiding parties characteristic of hunting/gathering and pastoral peoples. It is also possible to construct an explanation for militia warfare and professional warfare on the basis of a blend of kin selection and reciprocal altruism. However, a closer examination of the spoils of war make such explanations relatively unnecessary.

Betzig (1986) performed a cross-cultural analysis of the correlation between despotism and reproductive success in 186 different cultures. Her conclusion was that

> [n]ot only are men regularly able to win conflicts of interest more polygynous, but the degree of their polygyny is predictable from the degree of bias with which the conflicts are resolved. Despotism, defined as an exercised right to murder arbitrarily and with impunity, virtually invariably coincides with the greatest degree of polygyny, and presumably, with a correspondingly high degree of differential reproduction. (Betzig, 1986, p. 88)

In other words, males who most successfully use violence and murder as a means of influencing the actions of others have historically had the most offspring. In the context of warfare, this means that the winners of a battle, or even more so, of a war will pass on to their offspring whatever traits facilitated their victory, including the capacity to believe in a supernatural force that guides their destiny and protects them in battle. The effects of such capacities are not trivial; as Betzig points out, the differences between the reproductive success of the winners of violent conflicts and the losers is measured in orders of magnitude. As noted earlier, wars are bottlenecks through which only a relative few may pass, but which reward those who do with immensely increased reproductive success.

Putting all of this together, it appears likely that the capacity for religious experience and the capacity for warfare have constituted a coevolutionary spiral that has intensified with the transitions from a hunting/gathering existence through subsistence agriculture to the evolution of the modern nation-state. As pointed out earlier, there is a correlation between the type of intergroup violence and the ecological context within which that violence occurs. Generally speaking, raiding/rustling is correlated with hunting/gathering and pastoralism, militia warfare with village agriculture, and professional warfare with urban society and the nation-state. There is a corresponding progression in the basic form of religious experience and practice: animism is most common among hunter-gatherers, while polytheism is more common among agriculturalists, and monotheism is most common in societies organized as nation-states. This is not to say there are no exceptions to this correlation. However, the fact that such a correlation can even be made points to the underlying ecological dynamics driving the evolution of subsistence patterns, patterns of warfare, and types of religious experience.

## Genes, Memes, or Both?

It is extremely unlikely that any human behavior (or the behavior of any animal with a nervous system complex enough to allow learning) is the result of the expression of any single gene. On the contrary, it is almost universally accepted among evolutionary psychologists that all behaviors show a blend of innate and learned components. What is interesting to ethologists is not the question of "how much," but rather the much simpler question of "how"?

One answer that has been suggested is that there are two different carriers of information that can be transmitted among humans: genes and memes. According to Dawkins, a meme is "a unit of cultural transmission" corresponding to things like "tunes, ideas, catch-phrases, clothes fashions, ways of making pots or of building arches" (1976, p. 206). Dawkins even addressed the possibility that God Himself might be a meme:

> Consider the idea of God …. What is it about the idea of a god which give it its stability and penetrance in the cultural environment? The survival value of the god meme in the meme pool results from its great psychological appeal. It provides a superficially plausible answer to deep and troubling questions about existence. It suggests that injustices in this world may be rectified in the next …. God exists, if only in the form of a meme with high survival value, or infective power, in the environment provided by human culture. (p. 207)

Is all of religion simply a meme, or more precisely, a "meme complex"? And does the answer to this question tell us anything about the connection between the capacity for religion and warfare? There are at least three hypotheses for the mode of transmission of the capacity for religious experience:

- **Hypothesis 1:** The capacity for religious experience might be almost entirely innate; that is, it arises almost entirely out of "hard-wired" neural circuits in the human brain, which produce the sensations, thoughts, and behaviors that we call religious.

- **Hypothesis 2:** The capacity for religious experience might be almost entirely learned; that is, it arises almost entirely from concepts (i.e., "memes") that are transmitted from person to person via purely linguistic means, and without any underlying neurological predisposition to their acquisition.

- **Hypothesis 3:** The capacity for religious experience might arise from a combination of innate predispositions and learning; that is, like many animal behaviors, the capacity for religious experience might be the result of an innate predisposition to learn particular memes.

Both Boyer's and Atran's theories of the origin of religion are closest to the third hypothesis. From the foregoing analysis, it should also be clear that my own hypothesis for the origin of the capacity for religious experience is closest to hypothesis 3. However, unlike Boyer and Atran, I have proposed that the specific context within which the human nervous system has evolved has been persistent, albeit episodic, warfare.

A common objection to the hypothesis that the capacity for religious experience is an evolutionary adaptation is that there has been insufficient time for natural selection to produce the vast diversity in religious experiences and practices that exists in our species. I think there are two responses to this objection. First, although the diversity of religious beliefs and practices is quite surprising at first glance, this diversity is neither unlimited nor devoid of general trends. For example, virtually all religions include supernatural entities. However, the class of actual supernatural entities is not unlimited. Indeed, most supernatural entities bear a strong resemblance to humans, although with some qualities that humans are not observed to possess, such as the ability to fly, pass through walls, hear other's thoughts, etc. Furthermore, the qualities of most deities are remarkably similar to those attributed to kings, priests, and military leaders, although to a greater extent and with fewer "human" limitations. The global pantheon is overpopulated with warrior gods, and this overpopulation is not accidental.

Furthermore, there are circumstances under which selection can produce a dramatically accelerated rate of evolutionary change. Lumsden and Wilson (1981, 1983) describe this kind of evolutionary change as "autocatalytic gene-culture coevolution" (1981, p. 11) According to their theory, genes prescribe, not specific behaviors, but rather epigenetic rules of development by which minds are assembled (1983, p. 117). The mind then grows by incorporating parts of the culture (i.e., memes) already in existence. Culture, therefore, is created constantly from the combined decisions and innovations of all of the members of society. Most importantly, some individuals possess genetically inherited epigenetic rules that enable them to survive and reproduce better than other individuals. Consequently, the more successful epigenetic rules spread through the population, along with the genes that encode them. In other words, culture is created and shaped by biological processes, while those same biological processes are simultaneously altered in response to further cultural change. Genes and memes coevolve, with each change in one catalyzing a corresponding change in the other (1983, pp. 117–118).

The primary reason for the accelerated rate of evolution that results from gene/meme coevolution is the alternation between the temporal modes of the two types of evolution. If one conceives of time as passing along a vertical axis, then genetic transmission is almost entirely vertical. That is, genes are passed from parents to offspring. Genetic transmission also involves a very low mutation rate, relative to memetic evolution. Memetic transmission, by contrast, is both vertical and horizontal. That is, memes can be transmitted between contemporaries, as well as between parents and offspring. Furthermore, as Boyer has pointed out, the mutation rate of memes is immensely higher than that of genes. "Cultural memes undergo mutation, recombination, and selection inside the individual mind every bit as much and as often (in fact probably more so and more often than) during transmission between minds" (Boyer, 2001, p. 39).

Combining the concept of gene/meme coevolution with the episodic nature of selection during warfare, it appears that the evolution of the capacity for religious experience evolves via a kind of bootstrap effect. Each change in the underlying neurological capacity for religious experience is followed by a corresponding change in the conceptual (i.e., "memetic") structure of the religions that are produced as a result of that capacity. This, in turn, sets the stage for further selection at the level of genes, as individuals with particular religious meme complexes succeed (or fail). Stir warfare into the mix, including the tremendous assymetries in reproductive success described by Betzig (1986), and it appears likely that a substantial fraction of the whole of what we call "religion" is the result of gene/meme coevolution in the context of intergroup warfare.

## New Directions in the Evolution of Religion and Warfare

Given the current state of our knowledge of the underlying neurobiology of religious experience, the foregoing amounts to little more than a tantalizing hypothesis for the evolution of the capacity for religious experience. However, it suggests some avenues of investigation that would help to clarify the relationships between the capacity for religious experience and warfare. For example, it would be very interesting to know whether and to what extent religious experience and concomitant beliefs are reinforced by participation in warfare, and whether there is a positive or negative effect on such experiences and beliefs as the result of being on the winning or losing side in a warlike conflict. Collection of what would essentially be natural history data on the prevalence, spread, or disappearance of religious experiences or beliefs in the context of warfare vs. peacetime would help to determine both rates of change and possible mechanisms of spread or extinction. Empirical studies using controlled test populations could also shed light on the connections between religious experiences and beliefs and stress and perceptions of potential threat. Finally, and most importantly, detailed demographic analysis of reproductive success and religious beliefs, especially as they relate to a history of warfare, might find the kinds of correlations suggested here.

In closing, it seems likely that throughout the history of our species warfare has contributed significantly to the evolution of the capacity for religious experience, which has in turn facilitated warfare. Intergroup warfare can be adaptive whenever resources are concentrated, predictable, and defensible. Agriculture and industrial/urban subsistence patterns have facilitated warfare but have also steadily increased its costs. High technology warfare, especially when waged using weapons of mass destruction, has greatly increased the costs of warfare without appreciably increasing its benefits. In an age when the decisions of a single military leader can unleash nuclear annihilation, warfare is clearly maladaptive. As a consequence, it may be desirable to eliminate, or at least redirect, our capacity for warfare. However, if the deep evolutionary connections between the capacities for religion and warfare that I have proposed do, in fact, exist, this may mean redirecting (or possibly eliminating) the capacity for religious experience. Only time will tell, and only God (if He exists) knows how much time we have left.

## Note

This chapter originally appeared under the same title in *Evolution and Cognition*, volume 10, number 1, 2004, pages 43–60. Used by permission.

## References

Atran, S. (2002). *In gods we trust: The evolutionary landscape of religion.* Oxford, England: Oxford University Press.

Axelrod, R. (1984). *The evolution of cooperation.* New York: Basic Books.

Barrett, J. L. (1996). *Anthropomorphism, intentional agents, and conceptualizing God.* Unpublished Ph.D. dissertation, Cornell University, Ithaca, New York.

Beevor, A. (2002). *The fall of Berlin 1945.* New York: Viking.

Betzig, L. (1986). *Despotism and differential reproduction: A Darwinian view of history.* New York: Aldine.

Bowlby, J. (1969). *Attachment.* New York: Basic Books.

Boyer, P. (2001). *Religion explained: The evolutionary origins of religious thought.* New York: Basic Books.

Chagnon, N. (1988). Life histories, blood revenge, and warfare in a tribal population. *Science, 239,* 985–992.

Chagnon, N. (1990). Reproductive and somatic conflicts of interest in the genesis of violence and warfare among tribesmen. In J. Haas (Ed.), *The anthropology of war* (pp. 77–104). Cambridge, England: Cambridge University Press.

Chomsky, N. (1965). *Aspects of the theory of syntax.* Cambridge, MA: MIT Press.

d'Aquili, E. G., & Newberg, A. B. (1999). *The mystical mind: Probing the biology of religious experience.* Minneapolis, MN: Fortress.

Darwin, C. R. (1859). *On the origin of species by means of natural selection, or the preservation of favoured races in the struggle for life.* London: Murray.

Darwin, C. R. (1871). *The descent of man and selection in relation to sex.* London: Murray.

Dawkins, R. (1976). *The selfish gene.* Oxford, England: Oxford University Press.

Dawkins, R. (1982). *The extended phenotype.* San Francisco: Freeman.

Diamond, J. (1997). *Guns, germs, and steel: The fates of human societies.* New York: W. W. Norton.

Donovan, J. (1994). Multiple personality, hypnosis, and possession trance. *Yearbook of Cross-Cultural Medicine and Psychotherapy,* pp. 99–112.

Donovan, J. (2002). Implicit religion and the curvilinear relationship between religion and death anxiety. *Implicit Religion, 5*(1), 17–28.

Emlen, S. T. (1976). An alternative case for sociobiology. *Science, 192,* 736–738.

Ferguson, B. (2001). Materialist, cultural, and biological theories on why Yanomami make war. *Anthropological Theory, 1*(1), 99–116.

Goodall, J. (1986). *The Chimpanzees of Gombe.* Cambridge, MA: Belknap.

Hamilton, W. D. (1964). The genetical theory of social behavior. *Journal of Theoretical Biology, 12*(1), 1–52.

Irons, W. (1996). Morality, religion, and human nature. In W. M. Richardson and W. Wildman (Eds.), *Religion and science.* New York: Routledge.

Kruuk, H. (1972). *The spotted hyena: A study of predation and social behavior.* Chicago: University of Chicago Press.

Lenneberg, E. H. (1964). A biological perspective on language. In E. H. Lenneberg (Ed.), *New directions in the study of language* (pp. 65–88). New York: Wiley.

Lenneberg, E. H. (1967). *Biological foundations of language.* New York: Wiley.

Lumsden, C. J., & Wilson, E. O. (1981). *Genes, mind, and culture.* Cambridge, MA: Harvard University Press.

Lumsden, C. J., & Wilson, E. O. (1983). *Promethean fire: Reflections on the origin of mind.* Cambridge, MA: Harvard University Press.

Margulis, L. (1997). Big trouble in biology: Physiological autopoiesis versus mechanistic neo-Darwinism. In L. Margulis and D. Sagan (Eds.), *Slanted truth: Essays on Gaia, symbiosis, and evolution* (pp. 265–282). New York: Springer-Verlag.

Mech, L. D. (1970). *The wolf: The ecology and behavior of an endangered species.* Garden City, NY: Natural History Press.

Middlemas, T. (2000). Legendary origin of the [Scottish] flag. [Electronic Version] VisualNet. Retrieved March 30, 2003, from http://www.fotw.ca/flags/gb-scotl.html#leg

Miles, J. (1995). *God, A biography.* New York: Knopf.

Newberg, A. B., & d'Aquili, E. G. (2001). *Why God won't go away: Brain science and the biology of belief.* New York: Ballantine.

Penfield, W., & Roberts, L. (1959). *Speech and brain mechanisms.* Princeton: Princeton University Press.

Persinger, M. A. (1987). *Neuropsychological bases of God beliefs.* New York: Praeger.

Pinker, S. (1994). *The language instinct.* New York: Morrow.

Pinker, S., & Bloom, P. (1999). Natural language and natural selection. In J. H. Barkow, L. Cosmides, & J. Tooby (Eds.), *The adapted mind: Evolutionary psychology and the generation of culture* (pp. 451–493). Oxford, England: Oxford University Press.

Ramachandran, V. S., & Blakeslee, S. (1998). *Phantoms in the brain: Probing the mysteries of the human mind.* New York: Morrow.

Ridley, M. (1996). *Evolution* (2nd ed.). Cambridge, MA: Blackwell Science.

Saver, J. L., & Rabin, J. (1997). The neural substrates of religious experience. *Journal of Neuropsychiatry, 9*(3), 498–510.

Sober, E., & Wilson, D. S. (1998). *Unto others: The evolution and psychology of unselfish behavior.* Cambridge, MA: Harvard University Press.

Sperber, D. (1985). Anthropology and psychology: Towards an epidemiology of representations. *Man, 12,* 73–89.

Teleki, G. (1973). *The predatory behavior of wild chimpanzees.* Lewisburg, PA: Bucknell University Press.

Thornhill, R., & Palmer, C. T. (2000). *A natural history of rape: Biological bases of sexual coercion.* Cambridge, MA: MIT Press.

Tooby, J., & Cosmides, L. (1988). *The evolution of war and its cognitive foundations.* Institute for Evolutionary Studies Technical Report No. 88-1.

Trivers, R. L. (1971). The evolution of reciprocal altruism. *Quarterly Review of Biology, 46*(4), 35–57.

Von Clausewitz, C. (1832). *On war* (J. J. Graham, Trans.) Berlin: Dümmlers Verlag [Electronic version] Retrieved March 28, 2003, from http://www.clausewitz.com/CWZHOME/On_War/ONWARTOC.html

Wallace, A. (1968). Psychological preparations for war. In M. Freud, M. Harris, & R. Murphy (Eds.), *War.* New York: Natural History Press.

Williams, G. C. (1966). *Adaptation and natural selection.* Princeton, NJ: Princeton University Press.

Wilson, D. S. (2002). *Darwin's cathedral: Evolution, religion, and the nature of society.* Chicago: University of Chicago Press.

Wilson, E. O. (1975). *Sociobiology: The new synthesis.* Cambridge, MA: Belknap.

Wrangham, R. (1999). Evolution of coalitionary killing. *Yearbook of Physical Anthropology,* 1–29.

Wrangham, R., & Peterson, D. (1996). *Demonic males: Apes and the origins of human violence.* Boston: Houghton Mifflin.

Wright, S. (1968–1978). *Evolution and genetics of populations* (Vols. I–IV). Chicago: University of Chicago Press.

Wynne-Edwards, V. C. (1962). *Animal dispersion in relation to social behavior.* Edinburgh, Scotland: Oliver and Lloyd.

CHAPTER 11

# CONFLICT TRANSFORMATION: A GROUP RELATIONS PERSPECTIVE

## Tracy Wallach

The only thing we have to fear is fear itself—nameless, unreasoning, unjustified terror which paralyzes needed efforts to convert retreat into advance.
Franklin D. Roosevelt, First Inaugural Address, March 4, 1933

Fear is, I believe, a most effective tool in destroying the soul of an individual—and the soul of a people.
Anwar el-Sadat, "The Second Revolution," *In Search of Identity* (1977)

In the documentary film, *The Fog of War* (Morris, 2003), and in his memoirs, Robert McNamara (1996), former Secretary of Defense under Presidents Kennedy and Johnson, describes the deliberations of the Executive Committee during the Cuban Missile Crisis from October 16–28, 1962. At the height of the Cold War, the USSR introduced missiles into Cuba, though U.S. intelligence reports indicated that warheads had not yet been delivered. In response, 185,000 U.S. troops were mobilized. Having received two conflicting communications from Soviet President Khrushchev, one "soft-" and the other "hard-line," the committee faced a huge dilemma. While major voices in the United States were calling for invasion, one member of the team, Tommy Thompson, had known Khrushchev personally from his years serving as ambassador to Moscow. Given his understanding of President Khrushchev's thinking, Thompson urged President Kennedy to respond to the soft message and to offer Khrushchev a way out of his dilemma without losing face with his people. Ultimately, Kennedy heeded Thompson's advice. In 1992, McNamara learned that at the time of the crisis, there already had been nuclear warheads on the island. A U.S. invasion of Cuba would most probably have provoked nuclear retaliation.

McNamara stated that at that moment, "rational individuals came close to nuclear destruction of their societies," and only "luck prevented nuclear war" (Morris, 2003).

Two years later, on August 2, 1964, the U.S. destroyer *Maddox* was attacked in the Tonkin Gulf off the coast of North Vietnam. At that time, President Johnson decided not to retaliate. On August 4, there were reports of yet another attack on the *Maddox* and on another destroyer. This time, the data were much more confused and conflicted. While one patrol commander aboard the *Maddox* was doubtful as to whether the ship was attacked, since "freak weather effects on radar and overeager sonar men may have accounted for many reports" (McNamara, 1996, p. 133), an admiral reported to the director of the Joint Staff that there was no doubt in his mind that a second attack had occurred (McNamara, 1996). The president authorized a "limited" reprisal attack on North Vietnam's patrol boat bases, and a few days later he asked for and received from Congress the authorization for "U.S. combat operations in Southeast Asia should they prove necessary" (p. 135). Congress passed the Gulf of Tonkin Resolution on August 7, the first step in escalation of the war in Vietnam.

Reflecting on both these incidents many years later, McNamara notes that during the Cuban Missile Crisis, we were able to "put ourselves in the skin" of the Soviets (Morris, 2003), whereas in the case of Vietnam, "we found ourselves setting policy for a region that was terra incognita" (McNamara, 1996, p. 32). He goes on to state, "we failed to analyze our assumptions critically, then or later. The foundations of our decision-making were gravely flawed" (p. 33). He quotes Assistant Secretary of Defense for International Security Affairs William Bundy to say that "rational calculations should have taken account of the irrational ... Washington did not want an incident, and it seems doubtful that Hanoi did either. Yet each misread the other, and the incidents happened" (p. 141). Embedded in aCold War mentality, decision makers were convinced that the North Vietnamese were pawns of the Chinese or the Russians and were aiming to spread communism throughout Southeast Asia. U.S. policy makers were unable to see the North Vietnamese struggle as one for independence. Nor were they able to recognize that U.S. intervention would be perceived as a fight "to enslave us" (Morris, 2003). Says McNamara, "we didn't know them (the North Vietnamese) well enough ... they saw us as using them to advance colonial interests. We saw them as an element of the cold war, and not as they saw it—a civil war" (Morris, 2003).

The U.S. decision to invade Iraq in 2003 was similarly embedded in a fear mentality prevalent in the aftermath of the 9/11 attacks on the World Trade Center in New York. The determination to go to war was predicated on the belief that Iraq posed an imminent threat to the United States and had the capacity to utilize weapons of mass destruction. Nearly one year after the invasion and occupation, David Kay, former chief weapons inspector for the United States, reported that Iraq probably did not have stockpiles of weapons of mass destruction, which had been the justification for preemptive war. Public outcry following this report forced President Bush to form an independent commission to examine the intelligence on Iraq before and after the war (Yaukey, 2004). Similar questions were raised in the United Kingdom.

In February 2004, Lord Hutton released results of his inquiry into the death of David Kelly, a former chief weapons inspector in Iraq with the United Nations Special Commission. The report explored allegations made by the BBC that the British government "sexed up" intelligence reports (see http://www.the-hutton-inquiry.org.uk/content/rulings/statement280104.htm. #12), claiming that Iraq could deploy biological or chemical weapons within 45 minutes of an order to use them. While clearing Tony Blair's government of any deliberate distortion of facts in the decision to go to war with Iraq, Lord Hutton acknowledged that subconscious processes, on the part of intelligence agents, might have contributed to faulty analysis of the intelligence data available; see http://www.the-hutton-inquiry.org.uk/content/rulings/statement280104.htm, #48 (7).

The above examples illustrate the role of irrational processes, based on unconscious beliefs, assumptions, and anxieties, in determinations about managing global conflict. In each, unexamined and unchecked assumptions and anxieties influenced decision makers' perceptions and interpretations of facts on the ground. Nonrational processes thus played an enormous role in the resultant decisions taken. In a world of change, turbulence, and uncertainty, practitioners and policy makers must be able to work with conflict on *both* the rational *and* nonrational/emotional levels in order to deal with it effectively.

My approach to thinking about conflict and its transformation stems from psychoanalytic and open systems theories and the work of Wilfred Bion. These theories have been explored and developed at the Tavistock Institute in London, The A. K. Rice Institute in the United States, and other group relations organizations around the world. In this chapter, I summarize some of the concepts of group relations theory that I believe are relevant to the work of conflict transformation. By introducing concepts from group relations theory to the field of conflict transformation, I hope to shed light on the role of nonrational processes in societal and international conflict. Implications for policy makers and practitioners will be explored.

## The Nature of Conflict

Conflict and aggression are normal aspects and reflections of the human condition. Conflict is neither positive nor negative in and of itself. Rather, it is an outgrowth of the diversity that characterizes our thoughts, attitudes, beliefs, perceptions, and our social systems and structures. Agazarian and Philibossian (1998) contend that living human systems survive, develop, and transform from simple to complex through an ongoing process of recognizing and integrating differences. At the same time, differences and conflict stir up feelings of discomfort, irritation, and anxiety. Because conflict stirs up these difficult feelings, it is often viewed as a problem to be fixed or extruded, rather than an expression of a polarity/paradox that is inherent in group life (Berg & Smith, 1987). Nitsun (1996) states that constructive and destructive processes in groups exist simultaneously, and it is this dialectic that provides the opportunity for transformation. The ability to sit with difference, and the conflict it arouses, offers opportunities for reflection, growth, innovation, and transformation. Transformation is not possible without first bringing to light the difference and conflict that exist within any living human system.

Current theory and practice in conflict resolution tend to be rationally based. A number of authors (Bazerman & Neale, 1982; Carpenter & Kennedy, 1988; Fisher & Ury, 1991; Susskind & Cruikshank, 1987) posit that it is possible to reach win/win agreements if one can create a rational process where the right people are involved, the necessary data are available to fully analyze the conflict/problem, there is a structure, and particular procedures and rules are followed. And, indeed, providing a structure, with procedures and ground rules, can provide a psychological container in which problem solving can occur and agreements can be made. Kelman (1999) demonstrated this in his work when convening problem-solving workshops-with Israelis and Palestinians over the past 30 years. Rational processes are very important in working with conflict. It is also important to be able to connect the rational and conscious process with the extremely powerful (and often unconscious) feelings of anxiety, fear, anger, etc. that are stirred up in conflict situations and that further fuel conflicts. There are some practitioners who do work with conflict on its emotional levels (see, for example, Duek, 2001; Ettin, Fidler, & Cohen, 1995; Mindell, 1995; Montville, 1991; Volkan, 1991). Montville (1991) contends that revealing the "critical psychological tasks" is "the essential business of the prenegotiation stage of any true resolution of a conflict, before formal negotiations focus on the essentials of political institution building" (p. 540). Besod Siach, an Israeli association, specifically works at the unconscious and emotional level in its work facilitating dialogue between conflict groups in Israel (Duek, 2001).


## Levels of Conflict

Conflict occurs on many levels (Deutsch, 1973): within oneself (intrapsychic conflict), between two people (interpersonal conflict), between subgroups within a group (intragroup conflict), between groups (intergroup conflict), organizations, ethnic or religious groups, or nations. At all of these levels, conflict may be either overt and conscious, or covert and unconscious. What happens on one level invariably affects and reflects what happens at the other levels. Individuals are defined by the group contexts in which they live (family, social groups, communities, and nations), while at the same time, these larger groups and systems (family, social groups, communities, and nations) are created by the individuals that make them up (Miller & Rice, 1967/1975; Rice, 1965/1975). A conflict at one level may find its expression on the other levels. Unconscious internal conflicts may get projected onto the other person, group, or nation. Collective narratives and myths of larger groups and nations also find their expression on the individual level. For that reason, awareness of one's own ideas, feelings, assumptions, beliefs, and values, and their inter-relatedness with the larger system, is essential for policy makers and practitioners in the field of conflict transformation.

## Intrapsychic Conflict

Psychoanalytic theory offers a language that helps us think about conflict on an intrapsychic level. Our personalities are defined by our upbringing, our family and cultural background, as well as by our genetic makeup. Our national, ethnic, or religious cultures, as well as our gender, age, and life experiences, contribute to our particular ways of managing our emotions. The experience and expression of particular emotions may be more acceptable in some cultures than in others. We are often not conscious of our individual and culturally conditioned ways of managing emotions, until, that is, we come in contact with difference.

### Defense Mechanisms

We all find that certain emotions are difficult to bear. Psychoanalytic theory posits that we protect ourselves from these difficult or intolerable feelings in various ways, known as *defense mechanisms*.[1] Defense mechanisms offer a way to manage internal conflict and the anxiety it arouses. Just as countries develop various kinds of defenses and weaponry to protect themselves from perceived enemies, so, too, do individuals try to protect themselves from perceived dangers. Below a few of the defense mechanisms that are particularly relevant to conflict transformation are described.

*Splitting* is a defensive process in which we gain relief from internal conflicts by dividing emotions into either "all good" or "all bad" parts. We split our emotions due to our difficulty in holding two paradoxical experiences at the same time. Containing both the good and the bad parts of ourselves and seeing others as containing both good and bad aspects presents an intolerable conflict. We split in order to protect ourselves from the anxiety that the conflict arouses.

*Projection* is a defense in which an individual disowns and then off-loads onto someone else the disowned (split off) feelings he or she is experiencing. Whether the feelings are objectively "good" or "bad," the individual experiences them as intolerable. Projection is often seen in conjunction with splitting, with the split-off aspects of the self then projected onto another party because of the induced anxiety of holding onto the feelings oneself.

Splitting and projective processes allow an internal conflict to be externalized and located outside the self (e.g., *we* are good, *they* are evil; *we* are rational, *they* are emotional; *we* are victims, *they* are perpetrators; *we* are peace loving, *they* are aggressive; *we* are heroes, *they* are cowards, etc.). Thus, the complex and ambiguous is made to seem simple and clear.

### Working with Intrapsychic Conflict

In psychoanalytically informed theory and practice, intrapsychic conflict is brought into the consulting room in the form of transference, in which the patient transfers to the therapist emotions that he or she had toward authority figures in childhood. Healing occurs when unconscious conflicts, as expressed through the transference, can be contained, made conscious, and put into words. This process helps the patient to make meaning of his or her experience (Foulkes, 1965/1980; S. Freud, 1915/1959; Lazar, 2003) and occurs in the context of a therapeutic "holding environment" (Ogden, 1982; Winnicott, 1960/1965).

### Interpersonal Conflict

In analytic terms, intrapsychic conflict may be transformed into interpersonal conflict through the process of *projective identification*. Unlike projection and splitting, which are one-party defenses, projective identification is a collusive process between two or more parties. In this process, once the projector has off-loaded his intolerable feelings onto another, the recipient of the projection identifies with and internalizes the projected feelings as his own. The target of the projection thus changes in response to the projected feeling or impulse. The projector can manipulate or train an individual or group to act according to his projections by himself behaving *as if* those projections are true. The "projector" needs to stay in contact with the recipient in order to maintain a connection to the disowned, projected feelings (Horwitz, 1983).

A typical example of projective identification in interpersonal conflict is offered in the following illustration of a couple relationship:

Person A is emotional and attracted to Person B for B's ability to think and act rationally. B is attracted to A's ability to connect with emotions. Over time, A disowns, that is, splits off and projects onto B and allows B to carry more and more of the rationality that A finds uncomfortable (since B has a valence or predisposition for that), while B disowns and allows A to carry more and more of the emotionality that B finds uncomfortable (since A has a valence for that). As a result, A becomes less adept at thinking rationally, and B becomes less adept at managing emotions. A becomes distressed with B over B's inability to express feelings, while B becomes irritated with A for A's inability to think rationally. The couple becomes polarized.

The above example shows how an initial difference, over time, leads to polarization in a couple relationship. Similar dynamics may play out in other kinds of two-party relationships, such as business partnerships, parent/child relationships, and friendships. While the above illustration demonstrates a particular split, emotionality/rationality, not uncommon in couples, the split may also occur around other emotions and characteristics, such as strength/vulnerability, victim/perpetrator, kind/critical, happy/sad, optimistic/pessimistic, laziness/ambition, etc., depending on the valences of the individuals involved and the context in which they live. The valence or predisposition for a particular emotion is based upon the individual's own psychological makeup or personality.

### Working with Interpersonal Conflict

Splitting and projective identification are unconscious processes. Couples that have become polarized through continual projective identification are often not aware of the aspects of themselves that they have off-loaded onto the other. Healing a conflict in an interpersonal relationship requires recognition of the particular valences of each party. It also requires each party to recognize and own the split-off aspects of themselves that they have projected onto the other. That is, they have to reinternalize the conflict that has been externalized. This presents a dilemma and is an obstacle to resolving interpersonal conflict, since the individual must then face the conflict that has been previously managed through the process of splitting. In the therapeutic dyad, the therapist serves as a container for the patient's projections and can then "return to the patient a modified version of an unconscious defensive aspect of the patient that has been externalized by means of projective identification" (Ogden, 1982, p. 87). By interpreting the defense in a palatable manner, the patient can then reinternalize and integrate that which has been projected. Splitting and projective processes also contribute to conflict within groups and larger systems. These will be discussed in greater detail below, following a brief introduction to some basic concepts of group relations theory.

## Conflict within Groups: Group Relations Theory

### Structural Sources of Conflict in Groups: Task, Role, Boundaries, Leadership

Groups tend to join together based on similarities and in order to pursue a common task. The *primary task* of any group is what it must do in order to survive. To accomplish a group's task, members must differentiate, by taking on different roles in service of the larger group task. Often, differences in skill, viewpoint, or values are also necessary to achieve a group's primary task. Boundaries are formed or created around a group and its subsystems, task, and roles to define what is part of the group and what is to be excluded. Leadership is assigned to those most able to help a group achieve its primary task (Miller, 1989; Miller & Rice, 1967/1975; Zagier Roberts, 1994). Bion (1961/1975) referred to the above described overt and conscious level of group functioning as the *work group*.

The concepts of task, role, boundary, leadership, and authority help us to understand the overt and covert dynamics of groups and systems. When these elements are agreed upon and in alignment with each other, groups and systems may function relatively well. Conflict can arise when there is disagreement, spoken or unspoken, or when task, role, boundaries, and authority are not in alignment. Therefore, when a group is in the throes of a conflict, it is often useful to first look at the group structure. What is its primary task? What roles do members take up? Are these roles clear to everyone? Are they agreed upon? Do group members interpret the primary task and their roles in the same way? How are boundaries managed? How is leadership assigned? How is authority taken up? How are members authorized to do the work of the group?

### Psychological Sources of Conflict

We all belong to many kinds of groups—some of which we consciously choose to join, such as a work group or organization, professional groups or societies, or particular task groups. Other groups, related to identity, offer no choice about membership —the family we are born into, our particular ethnic, racial, gender, or age group. Group membership stirs up conflicting feelings. We long to be a part of something bigger than ourselves, while at the same time, we want to hold on to our individual identity (Bion, 1961/1975; McCollom, 1990). Conflict may signify the normal ambivalences of individual and collective life and may also signify a particular challenge that needs to be faced in the life of a group at a particular time (Berg & Smith, 1987; Heifetz, 1994).

Wilfred Bion (1961/1975), a British psychoanalyst at the Center for Applied Social Research in London's Tavistock Institute of Human Relations, explored the relationship between the individual and the group. He believed that individual members enter groups with their own rational and nonrational aims and needs and employ psychosocial defenses such as splitting, projection, and projective identification in order to tolerate the powerful tensions of group life. The group and its leader serve as a container for the various projections of individual group members, and the group takes on a life of its own as a consequence of these processes. As a result, individual group members act not only on their own behalf, but also on behalf of the larger group or system. These processes make up the unconscious of the group as a whole. The group as a whole becomes an entity much greater than its individual members, with a character of its own. Just as individuals utilize defense mechanisms, such as splitting and projective identification, so do groups, organizations, communities, and nations mobilize social defenses to protect themselves against unbearable feelings and unconscious anxieties (Menzies, 1997). Groups may also avoid anxiety and other difficult feelings and decisions by substituting routines or rituals for direct engagement with the painful problem.

In groups, conflict may manifest between individuals in the group, between subgroups, between the group as a whole and an individual, or between the group as a whole and a particular subgroup. A group that is anxious about confronting a conflict directly may unconsciously find covert ways of containing or managing the conflict. For example, groups may use particular members or subgroups to carry or hold a difficult emotion, thought, or point of view on behalf of the group as a whole. That is, an individual group member, a pair, or a subgroup may be compelled, through the processes of projective identification in a group, to take up a role to meet the unconscious needs of the group. The group as a whole can maintain its equilibrium, as long as it can view "the problem" as located in one individual or subgroup. Groups that operate largely unconsciously, and in seeming opposition to their stated primary task, are said to be operating under *basic assumption* mentality (Banet & Hayden, 1977; Bion, 1961/1975; Hayden & Molenkamp, 2003; Lawrence, Bain, & Gould, 1996; Miller, 1989; Rioch, 1970/1975). Basic assumption groups assign leadership to those most able to help the group meet its unconscious survival needs and contain its anxiety. Basic assumption leaders collude with the group in avoiding reality and may be extruded or replaced if they break this unconscious agreement.

For example, a group with conflicts around dependency issues may find an "identified patient" in the group who it can take care of. By loading the dependency into one person, the group frees itself of the anxiety caused by the intolerable dependency, while at the same time maintaining the connection with those feelings in the person of the identified patient. Conversely, a group with anxieties related to competence may project all of its competence into one member or the leader and then rely on that leader to take care of the group. Bion (1961/1975) referred to this dynamic as basic assumption dependency. The example of Judith and Holophernes in the Apocrypha has been cited in the group relations literature as an example of the dangers of extreme dependency upon a leader. Judith cut off the head of the Assyrian leader, Holophernes, and then displayed it to his army. Without their leader, or "head," the army acted as if they had "all lost their own heads" (Obholzer, 1994, p. 43) and were quickly defeated by the Israelites.

A group that struggles with its own aggression may find a member or subgroup onto whom it may project its own aggressive tendencies (or other characteristic that contradicts the group's perception of itself). The group locates the intolerable characteristic in one individual and can then scapegoat that individual for owning the characteristic. Bion (1961/1975) referred to this dynamic as basic assumption fight/flight. How a group may use an individual member to express a conflicted aspect of itself is described in the example below.

In December 2002, the U.S. Senate was engaged in a debate over the future of Trent Lott who was Senate Majority Leader at the time. In a party honoring Senator Strom Thurmond on his 100th birthday, Senator Lott referred to Thurmond's 1948 presidential campaign and stated that the country "would have been better off had he won" (Hulse, 2002, p. 1). Thurmond had run that campaign on a policy of segregation. Lott was immediately attacked for his comments by both the left and the right wings of both parties. The senators who spoke up most stridently against Lott and pressured him to resign had questionable records in regard to their own stands on civil rights (Gettleman, 2002). The group focused on a particular scapegoat, as a method of avoidance of its own racism, and a way to escape really grappling with the issue. While Senator Lott may have volunteered for the role of scapegoat, he was not the only senator who had made public racist comments or voted against civil rights legislation. The focus on one person as "the racist" or the problem served to distract the rest of the Senate from dealing with the anxiety about race and racism in the United States, engaging in a deeper discussion about the issue, or taking any meaningful action. The senator resigned his leadership role after six weeks of controversy (Hulse, 2002), and the Senate ceased further discussion of racism in the country.

The above example illustrates how a group may use one of its members, through the processes of splitting and projective identification, to manage anxiety around a particular problem or conflict. By locating the intolerable feeling or point of view (in this case, racism) in one person, the rest of the group members may divest themselves of responsibility and thus can continue to deny their own contribution to the problem. By scapegoating a particular individual, the group maintains a connection with the split-off aspects of itself, without having to actually take ownership of those parts or to feel the anxiety that such ownership would involve. "The deviancy is informing the group about aspects of its nature of which it would prefer to remain ignorant" (Berg & Smith, 1987, p. 91). Scapegoating allows a group to manage its anxiety about conflict or a particular challenge it might be facing. Ultimately, it also interferes with a group's ability to effectively face that challenge or conflict or to adapt to its environment. Real change or transformation can thus be avoided. Heifetz (1994) maintains that the role of the leader is to help the group face its adaptive challenges. If the group succeeds in extruding the scapegoat from the group, it is likely that the problem or conflict that the scapegoat represented will surface elsewhere in the system.

A group may also offer up a pair who gives voice to the conflict existing in the group at a particular time. That is, the group may designate two of its members to fight with each other, while the remainder of the group observes passively. Thus, rather than the group as a whole engaging in a dialogue to reflect on the conflict, it may instead be lodged in two individuals who give voice to the conflict on behalf of the larger system. Pairs of members may also be asked to hold a sense of hope for the group. Bion (1961/1975) referred to this dynamic as basic assumption pairing. Basic assumption functioning is also discussed in Rioch (1970/1975), Miller (1989), Lawrence, Bain, and Gould (1996), Banet and Hayden (1977), Hayden and Molenkamp (2003), and Stokes (1994). This may still be problematic, as the group as a whole continues to avoid dealing with reality. This is illustrated in the example below.

In a training program for conflict transformation, with participants from conflict areas around the world, conflict was virtually unspeakable. Pairs of participants from opposing sides of particular conflicts (Israel/Palestine, Bosnia/Serbia, Greek and Turkish Cypriots, etc.) were engaged by the course director and the group to serve as emblems of hope. At the same time, conflict and dialogue within the whole group was discouraged. The course was structured in such a way as to bar real engagement and dialogue. Theater-style seating, minimal time allowed to work in small groups, and avoidance of the feelings generated in the room of 60 participants all contributed to a sense of emotional and intellectual constriction. Conflict went underground in the group and resurfaced in the form of repeated lateness to sessions and several complaints of sexual harassment. Participants who spoke up or complained about the course structure were labeled as "troublemakers" by the course director and were effectively silenced.

Groups can exert enormous pressure, both overt and covert, on an individual member, pair, or subgroup to take up a particular role on behalf of the whole group. Demographic characteristics, such as age, gender, race, ethnicity, socioeconomic status, and physical characteristics, may serve as the basis for which certain members are ascribed particular roles (Berg & Smith, 1987; Horowitz, 1983; Reed & Noumair, 2000). For example, women, based on cultural expectations, may be asked to take on caretaking roles on behalf of the larger group or to give voice to emotions in the group. Members of a particular ethnic group in a society may hold certain characteristics, such as aggression or sexuality, deemed intolerable by another ethnic group. Sometimes, these projections get translated into policy or law. In his book *Enemy Aliens*, Cole (2003) notes that during nearly every national security crisis in the United States, the U.S. government has restricted the rights of immigrant and noncitizens' groups, as if those groups were to blame for the nation's problems. Fears of French and Irish immigrants led Congress to enact the Enemy Alien Act in 1798, authorizing the president to restrict the rights of foreign nationals without regard to evidence of criminal conduct or suspicion of such. During World War I, German immigrants were targeted, and over 110,000 persons of Japanese ancestry were interned during World War II. Fears of anarchist terrorists in the early 1900s led to the first federal laws penalizing radical associations, in which immigrant groups were targeted exclusively. In the aftermath of 9/11, U.S. Attorney General John Ashcroft created a Foreign Terrorist Tracking Force, using immigration law as a pretext for preventive detention of foreign nationals. This focuses almost exclusively on Muslim and Arab immigrant communities. Says Cole (2003, p. 5), "No one has ever been voted out of office for targeting foreign nationals in times of crisis; to the contrary, crises often inspire the demonization of 'aliens' as the nation seeks unity by emphasizing differences between 'us' and 'them.' "

Basic assumption mentality, as described in the examples above, simplifies what is complex and allows a group to manage its anxiety without actually addressing the reality at hand. In her study of religious militants, Stern (2003) notes, "they enter a kind of trance, where the world is divided neatly between good and evil, victim and oppressed. Uncertainty and ambivalence, always painful to experience, are banished" (p. 282). She goes on to note that for some terrorist groups, "survival of the group becomes more important than the grievance it formed to address" (p. 292). Terrorist attacks are aimed at mobilizing support within the group and as a tool to attract more followers, more than they are aimed at the group that is actually attacked. Christian martyrs provoked the Romans to retaliate so as to increase the appeal of Christianity to the greater public, similar to the way in which Hamas provokes Israel to retaliate with violence in order to mobilize support for jihad. Stern (2003) further posits that the 9/11 attacks made bin Laden more appealing to followers. In describing the decision-making process to proceed with sustained bombing attacks on North Vietnam, Robert McNamara notes that General Westmoreland agreed to "Rolling Thunder not because he believed it would significantly affect the North's will or its ability to re-supply the South, but rather because of its expected boost to South Vietnamese morale" (McNamara, 1995, p. 176). Lazar (2003) contends that the U.S.–led war in Iraq serves to deflect attention from internal conflicts in the United States stemming from the economic downturn, such as the national debt, unemployment, the widening gap between rich and poor, and the health-care crisis.

Groups that are invested in maintaining a particular view of themselves (a group identity) and of other groups can exert similar pressure on its members to behave according to group norms/expectations as a way of keeping them "in line." Speaking against predominating group norms may carry the risk of being scapegoated. Evidence of this type of scapegoating can also be found in the second Bush administration's attitudes toward dissent—those in the United States who disagreed with the administration's policies toward Iraq were labeled as "unpatriotic," while the president stated to European allies, "if you're not with us, you're against us" (BBCNews/Europe, 2001). Peace builders, by virtue of their location on the boundary—between their own identity group and that of the other, are subject to particular pressures from within. They may face sanction from their own group if they violate group norms in attempting to reach out to the other. Anwar Sadat and Yitzhak Rabin were assassinated by members of their own constituencies for their attempts to make peace with the other without adequately addressing the profound anxieties in their own groups (Heifetz & Linsky, 2002).

### Working with Conflict within Groups

Working with a group in conflict involves viewing the conflicting individuals and subgroups as part of a larger system. Conflict analysts and practitioners must ask the following questions: What is the meaning of the conflict for the larger system? What is the adaptive challenge that the group needs to face? What is the conversation that the group needs to have as a system? What is being avoided in the group as a whole that is being located in particular individuals or subgroups in the system? In other words, what are the fears, needs, and emotions that are being projected into the conflicting parties? As with interpersonal conflict, transforming conflict on the group level also involves taking back and reowning those projections. The role of the practitioner or leader is to create a containing environment where such emotions can be explored and understood (Lazar, 2003; Ogden, 1982; Winnicott, 1960/1965). In addition to observing the group process, the practitioner must be able to use his or her own emotional experience as data in understanding the underlying dynamics in the group. (The idea that emotions may be viewed and used as "intelligence" is explored in Armstrong, 2000.) For instance, how do the practitioner's emotions mirror the emotional experience of the group or a particular subgroup? What do these emotions suggest about how the group is "using" the practitioner and/or how the group may use particular members to manage its internal conflicts? Would sharing these data with the group help the group face its adaptive challenges? These questions must be examined in order to help a group in conflict move forward.

## Intergroup Conflict

The dynamics that emerge within any particular group are influenced by the larger system and environment within which the group is embedded. For instance, within an organizational context, the process of a particular group tends to reflect the larger organizational culture: its assumptions, values, and beliefs. The organizational culture, in turn, is influenced by the culture of the larger community and nation.

Individuals are members of multiple groups in addition to their work groups. By virtue of their outside identity group memberships, group members import conflicts and ways of looking at conflict from the larger environment (Berg & Smith, 1987). The group then serves as a microcosm of the larger environment. Individual members of the group can then export back into their outside groups new conflicts or new ways of perceiving conflicts.

### Splitting and Projective Identification in an Intergroup Context

Groups may attempt to avoid or deny their own internal conflicts by finding an external group or enemy onto whom it can project its unacceptable, split-off parts. This is the root of stereotyping, sexism, racism, and other "isms." The less personal contact we have with other groups or individuals who represent different group identities, the more they may serve as a blank screen onto which we project our own images, ideas, desires, longings, anxieties, and prejudices. The external groups may have a valence (propensity or predisposition) for the characteristic that is being projected and may also be compelled to take on those characteristics by virtue of the behavior of the projecting group. The more we treat a group as if it has a particular characteristic, the more we actually encourage or even create that behavior.

We can see many examples of splitting and projective processes in the international political arena. Various leaders in many countries (currently and historically) have invoked an external enemy in order to mobilize public sentiment and to distract attention from internal group conflicts. For example, in the 1980s in the United States, Ronald Reagan referred to the former Soviet Union as the "Evil Empire" and gained support for his Strategic Defense ("Star Wars") Initiative (Heifetz, 1994). In the former Yugoslavia, leaders mobilized anxiety and hatred toward "other" ethnic groups (that had previously enjoyed good relations) rather than help the country as a whole face the adaptive challenges of the breakup of the Soviet Bloc. As illustrated in the examples below, the invocation of an external enemy sets into motion a vicious cycle of projective identification, which serves to create internal unity while deflecting attention away from internal conflicts or adaptive challenges that need to be faced.

Right-wing politicians in Israel focus on Palestinian terrorism and thereby distract attention from serious conflict within the Israeli Jewish community. Concomitantly, retaliation for terrorist attacks in the form of targeted assassinations, home demolitions, and incursions into Palestinian territory, for the purpose of arresting reported terrorists, confirm Palestinian perceptions of Israel as a colonialist occupying power. Political leaders in Arab nations in the Middle East target Israel as the problem while ignoring problems and conflicts within their own countries. Verbal attacks on Israel and Arab support for groups such as Hamas and Hezbollah, responsible for suicide attacks on Israeli citizens, play into Israeli anxieties and perceptions that its Arab neighbors have no interest in coexistence and want to destroy the Jewish state.

Another example is the U.S. response to the 9/11 attacks on the New York World Trade Center. The terrorist attacks and the ensuing U.S. retaliation had the effect of creating unity within the American public, evidenced by the widespread display of American flags on homes and on lapels. Bumper stickers reading "united we stand" were ubiquitous. Six weeks after the attacks, in the name of national security, President Bush signed the USA PATRIOT Act, thereby limiting civil liberties for many foreign nationals living in the United States (Cole, 2003). And later, using phrases such as "axis of evil," and "evil doers" to describe Saddam Hussein's regime in Iraq and implicitly linking Iraq to the attacks on the World Trade Center (BBC News/ World Edition, 2003; BBC News/Europe, 2002), the administration convinced Congress to pass a resolution authorizing the use of force in Iraq. In the anxious environment in the United States after 9/11, these actions may have provided temporary comfort to frightened Americans that the government was "doing something" to manage the terrorist threat. However, as Cole (2003) suggests, these actions might not necessarily increase the nation's security.

From the perspective of projective identification, it might be argued that Bush's continued verbal attacks on the Iraqi leader may have further encouraged Hussein's intransigence and that the unilateral invasions of Afghanistan and Iraq played into the view (held by terrorist and other groups) of the United States as imperialistic. Cole (2003) and Stern (2003) suggest that U.S. actions in Afghanistan and Iraq have resulted in increased recruitment and mobilization of support for terrorist organizations in the Arab world and that the arrest of Muslim or Arab suspects without clear evidence of terrorist activity may serve to alienate or even to radicalize the Muslim community in the United States.

In the examples above, each side provokes, through rhetoric and action, a response from the other side that will conform to its projections. With each successive provocation and response, the groups become increasingly polarized, and further removed from reality, as they become more convinced as to the correctness of their assumptions. Volkan (2001) maintains that regression takes place in societies following massive trauma involving dramatic "losses of life, property, or prestige, and/or humiliation by another group" (p. 11) and functions to protect or repair a sense of group identity. Societal regression is characterized by, among other things, the loss of individuality, extensive use of projective mechanisms, leading to a sharp division of "us" and "them," and a sense of entitlement to do anything in order to maintain its shared group identity (Volkan, 2001, p. 11). Prior to and since 9/11, U.S. citizens have lost confidence in many societal institutions stemming from sexual abuse allegations in the Catholic Church and corporate corruption scandals resulting in the loss of jobs, a wildly fluctuating stock market, and a weakened economy. Since 9/11, the military is reportedly one of the few societal institutions in which the American public remains confident.

### Working with Conflict between Groups

As with intragroup conflict, working with conflict between groups involves viewing the conflicting groups or nations as part of a larger (global) system. In the analysis of conflict, policy makers and practitioners must ask the following questions: What is the meaning of the conflict for the larger system? What might two groups or nations be holding on behalf of the larger global community? What internal national conflicts are being projected onto external enemies? How do other nations or groups benefit from the continuation of the conflict? What underlying anxieties/issues/problems are being masked by the conflict? How might nations not involved in the conflict be using (consciously or unconsciously) the groups/nations in conflict for their own benefit?

Members of Besod Siach, the Israeli organization mentioned earlier in this chapter, are themselves players in the larger conflict. Representing the political left and right, secular and religious, Jewish and Arab, Ashkenazi and Mizrachi elements of Israeli society, staff members stay in dialogue among themselves as they consult to groups in conflict. Using group relations theory and innovations of conference methodology, the organization offers public dialogue conferences. The temporary institution of the conference (consisting of 40–60 participants) is viewed as a microcosm of Israeli society and enables participants to learn about the conscious and unconscious motivations for the conflict. The conference provides a containing environment in which participants have the opportunity to examine their assumptions about us and them and to recognize, reinternalize, and integrate that which has been projected outward. Staff members consult to groups of various sizes (representing the street, the neighborhood, and the home) and offer interpretations or hypotheses about the unconscious dynamics in the group as a whole, inviting participants to examine their own roles in creating these dynamics. Conference participants may then export back to their own communities what they have learned in the conference (Duek, 2001; Sarel, Said, Mayer, & Ben-Yosef, 2003).

## Implications for Policy Makers and Practitioners

In order for conflict transformation to occur, systems must be able to discern and integrate differences. The role of leaders, policy makers, and practitioners is to provide the containment in which people can tolerate the level of anxiety necessary to get through to the other side. In analyzing and intervening in conflict situations, policy makers, leaders, and practitioners need to consider both the rational and nonrational sides of human behavior, both in themselves as individuals and in the groups with which they work. Unconscious processes fuel conflict and may also interfere with analysis and problem solving on the decision-making level. Knowledge of the emotional dynamics of conflict and the ways that individuals and groups may defend themselves against the anxieties aroused by conflict will greatly aid policy makers and practitioners in their analysis and decision-making process.

Sound policy decisions are built upon sound analysis and sound process. Sound analysis depends upon good intelligence (data) and the capacity to interpret the data received. Conscious and unconscious assumptions, beliefs, and values provide a lens through which one views information and may also serve to distort how those data are perceived and interpreted. Sound process depends upon the ability of a group to discriminate and integrate different information from dissenting viewpoints.

Nonrational processes and basic assumption activity is most likely to take hold in a closed system, where boundaries do not allow new information or ideas from the outside to penetrate. In his memoir, Robert McNamara (1996) repeatedly emphasizes the lack of debate about escalating the war in Vietnam. This was true at the highest decision-making levels in the executive branch and in Congress, as well as with the American public.

Suskind (2004) describes a similar lack of debate in the second Bush administration. Suskind (2004) suggests that Bush's foreign policy advisors were all part of a neoconservative community. He further states that policy meetings appeared to be "scripted" (p. 148), and there was no room to bring in opposing viewpoints. The ideology of preemptive war on Iraq was, according to former Treasury Secretary Paul O'Neill, "impenetrable by facts" (Suskind, 2004, p. 307). In National Security Council discussions on Iraq,

> "There was never any rigorous talk about this sweeping idea that seemed to be driving all the specific actions," O'Neill said, echoing the comments of several other participants in NSC discussions. "From the start, we were building the case against Hussein and looking at how we could take him out and change Iraq into a new country. And, if we did that, it would solve everything. It was all about finding *a way to do it*. That was the tone of it. The President saying, 'Fine. Go find me a way to do this.' " (p. 86)

The lack of debate/dialogue among different viewpoints can lead to grave distortions in understanding and analysis. Perspectives of multiple stakeholders and practitioners on the front line can provide data that are vital to an understanding of the whole system. Different points of view shed light on the assumptions underlying decision making and offer different choices.

In deciding whether or how to intervene in a conflict situation, policy makers need to reflect upon the meaning of the conflict for the larger system. How might they use or be used by the parties in conflict? They need to consider how the parties in conflict will perceive such interventions and what the long-term impact of such interventions will be. For instance, by using the mujahideen to fight against the Soviet occupation during the Afghan War, the United States (and Saudi Arabia) helped to create what became the biggest threat to its national security (Stern, 2003). Deviant, extremist, or terrorist groups within a society or in the global community may express a concern or adaptive challenge that needs to be addressed on behalf of the larger society. Leaders and policy makers need to understand and address the underlying anxieties that make such groups appealing to their members and supporters. Such was the case with the global terrorist threat posed by the anarchists during the late 1800s and early 1900s (Rauchway, 2003). During that time, the industrial revolution and unrestrained capitalism resulted in societal anxiety stemming from "vast displacements of population, the expansion of the towns, the unrest and discontent of the masses" (Theodore Roosevelt, as cited in Rauchway, 2003). Roosevelt

> diagnosed a growing awareness among Americans of genuine injustice ... Instead of writing off terrorism as the work of foreigners and madmen, Roosevelt turned the problem into a chance for American self-examination and self-improvement. In the wake of a

national trauma, nobody seriously challenged him. His agenda of changing American capitalism, in part so that it would attract less animosity, ruled American politics thereafter. (p. D2)

The change and turbulence of today's world and the loss of confidence in and uncertainty about traditional societal institutions mirror the anxious world that Roosevelt faced. Uncontained anxiety may give rise to basic assumption mentality, and, with that, an inability to think and to face reality. Leadership plays a vital role in helping groups and nations to face their adaptive challenges (Heifetz, 1994). In the following quote, Lazar (2003) emphasizes the importance of the leader in performing a "containing function" if he or she is to help followers to function successfully:

> If anxieties, irrationalities, aggressions, envy and rivalry, disruptive unconscious fantasies and ideas, etc. are not adequately contained, they threaten to paralyze the group or to blow it up … . If this is the case, then the group will be forced to fall back on functioning in a basic assumption mode in order to prevent such threats and disturbances from destroying the group altogether. The price paid for this is the loss of task orientation and with it, the capacity to do work. When, however, the work group leader is capable of offering the group enough containment, these disturbing factors can be "digested," can be better metabolized into the group's dynamic life, and it can then "feed" on this experience, can grow on it, learn from it, and thereby improve its capacity to devote itself to the task at hand and to achieve good results. (p. 7)

This suggests that the leader take an interpretive stance (Shapiro, 2003), "which would both affirm and help them bear their painful experience by placing what they had repressed or dissociated in a larger context" (p. 125).

Practitioners and organizations on the front lines of conflict can further assist with the interpretive process and work with groups in conflict to develop hypotheses about the meaning of the conflict. Organizations that are located in countries where a conflict is ongoing and that are involved in peace building and conflict transformation may mirror internally, through the process of importation (Berg & Smith, 1987), the conflict that is being waged on the outside. Parallel defensive structures and assumptions may operate within the organization as operate within the groups in conflict. If the organization is to be effective in pursuing its primary task, it is vital to have the capacity to reflect, to think, and to dialogue about the parallel organizational experiences. Exploration of the internal processes and conflicts of a group or organization can lead to greater understanding of the larger context and conflict in which the group is embedded. This understanding can then be exported back to the groups with which they work.

Experiential methods, which allow participants to examine their own (conscious and unconscious) assumptions, values, and beliefs in the context of the environment in which they live and work, are essential in the training of conflict transformation practitioners. Organizations such as the Tavistock Institute in the United Kingdom, The A. K. Rice Institute in the United States, and others around the world[2] have been offering such experiential learning conferences for over 50 years. The temporary organization of the conference system provides the opportunity to study authority, leadership, and group dynamics experientially, as they unfold.[3]

In order to get to transformation it is crucial to be able to live with uncertainties, paradoxes, and anxieties of conflict. We leave our assumptions unexamined at our own peril. Policy makers and practitioners are subject to the same unconscious and irrational processes that we see in groups in conflict. Unconscious processes fuel conflicts on the overt level, such as those arising from scarce resources or different values and thus may prevent problem solving and compromise. It is only by sitting with the uncertainties and anxieties of conflict that it is possible to create something new.

## Summary

This chapter has offered a group relations perspective of conflict and conflict transformation. Using concepts from psychoanalytic and open systems theories, I have explored how conflict manifests on various levels and how unconscious processes such as splitting, projection, and projective identification can fuel interpersonal, group, and intergroup conflict. I have given examples of how nonrational processes, based upon unexamined assumptions, values, beliefs, emotions, and fantasies, may also be translated into policy and law.

The rate of change in society and the turbulence it causes creates an atmosphere of tremendous anxiety. Projective processes offer a means of defending against such anxiety by creating enemies who will carry for us those characteristics that are unacceptable: evil, imperialism, fundamentalism, irrationality, vulnerability, etc. Leaders, policy makers, and practitioners of conflict transformation must understand and address these conscious and unconscious anxieties, in themselves and in others, in order to be effective.

## Notes

An earlier version of this chapter was published in the May 2004 issue of the journal *Peace and Conflict Studies*, under the title "Transforming Conflict: A Group Relations Perspective."

1. Defense mechanisms and how they manifest on the individual and group level have been written about extensively in the psychoanalytic and group relations literature (see, for example, Bion, 1961/1975; A. Freud, 1966; S. Freud, 1926/1959; Halton, 1994; Klein, 1959/1984; Obholzer, 1994; Ogden, 1982).
2. A partial listing includes Group Relations Australia in Australia; Fondation Internationale de L'Innovation Sociale in Belgium; Process Aps in Denmark; Forum Internationale de L'Innovation Sociale in France; MundO in Germany; The Grubb Institute in the United Kingdom; The Israel Association for the Study of Group and Organizational Processes, OFEK, and Besod Siach in Israel; ISMO in Italy; Istituto Mexicano de Relaciones Grupales y Organizacionales in Mexico; Group Relations Nederland in the Netherlands; Norstig in Norway; ISLA in South Africa; Associacio per a la Innovacio Organitzativa i Social in Spain; and AGSLO in Sweden.
3. A full description of the conference experience can be found in Rice (1965/1975), Banet and Hayden (1977), Hayden and Molenkamp (2003), and Miller (1989).

# References

Agazarian, Y., & Philibossian, P. (1998). A theory of living human systems as an approach to leadership of the future with examples of how it works. In E. B. Klein, F. Gabelnick, & P. Herr (Eds.), *The psychodynamics of leadership* (pp. 127–160). Madison, CT: Psychosocial Press.

Armstrong, D. (2000). *Emotions in organizations: Disturbance or intelligence?* London: Tavistock Consultancy Service.

Banet, A. G., & Hayden, C. (1977). A Tavistock primer. In J. E. Jones & J. W. Pfeiffer (Eds.), *The 1977 annual handbook for group facilitators.* La Jolla, CA: University Associates, Inc.

Bazerman, M. H., & Neale, M. A. (1992). *Negotiating rationally.* New York: The Free Press.

BBCNews/Europe (2001, November 6). Bush urges anti-terror allies to act. Retrieved March 2004, from http://news.bbc.co.uk/2/hi/europe/1642130.stm

BBCNews/Europe (2002, December 2). Bush's evil axis comment stirs critics. Retrieved March 2004, from http://news.bbc.co.uk/2/hi/americas/1796034.stm

BBCNews/World Edition (2003, January 29). State of the Union address: Full text. Retrieved March 2004, from http://news.bbc.co.uk/2/hi/americas/2704365.stm

BBCNews/World Edition. (2003, March 20). Timeline: Steps to war. Retrieved March 2004, from http://news.bbc.co.uk/2/hi/middle_east/2773213.stm

Berg, D. N., & Smith, K. K. (1987). *Paradoxes of group life.* San Francisco: Jossey-Bass.

Bion, W. R. (1975). Selections from: Experiences in groups. In A. D. Colman & W. H. Bexton (Eds.), *Group relations reader 1* (pp. 11–20). Jupiter, FL: The A. K. Rice Institute. (Original work published 1961)

Bion, W. R. (1952). Group dynamics: a re-view. Reprinted in S. Scheidlinger (Ed.), *Psychoanalytic group dynamics: Basic readings* (pp. 77–109). New York: International Universities Press, 1980.

Carpenter, S. L., & Kennedy, W. J. D. (1988). *Managing Public Disputes.* San Francisco: Jossey-Bass.

Cole, D. (2003). *Enemy aliens.* New York: The New Press.

Deutsch, M. (1973). *The resolution of conflict: Constructive and destructive processes.* New Haven, CT: Yale University Press.

Duek, R. (2001). Dialogue in impossible situations. Keynote address presented at SOCI conference, August 12–16, Stockholm, Sweden.

Ettin, M. F., Fidler, J. W., & Cohen, B. D. (Eds.). (1995). *Group process and political dynamics.* Madison, CN: International Universities Press.

Fisher, R., & Ury. W. (1991). *Getting to YES: Negotiating agreement without giving in.* New York: Penguin Books.

Freud, A. (1966). *The ego and the mechanisms of defense* (Rev. ed.). New York: International Universities Press.

Freud, S. (1959). *Inhibitions, Symptoms and Anxiety* (Revised and edited by J. Strachey). New York: W. W. Norton & Company. (Original work published 1926)

Freud, S. (1959). The unconscious. In J. Riviere (Trans.), *Sigmund Freud collected papers* (Vol. 4, pp. 98–136). New York: Basic Books. (Original work published 1915)

Foulkes, S. H. (1980). Psychodynamic processes in the light of psychoanalysis and group analysis. Reprinted in S. Scheidlinger (Ed.), *Psychoanalytic group dynamics: Basic readings* (pp. 147–162). New York: International Universities Press. (Original work published 1965)

Gettleman, J. (2002, December 22). The nation: Southern liberals had Lott moments too. *The New York Times, Week in Review,* p. 3.

Halton, W. (1994). Some unconscious aspects of organizational life: Contributions from psychoanalysis. In A. Obholzer & V. Zanier Roberts (Eds.), *The Unconscious at work: Individual and organizational stress in the human services* (pp. 11–18). New York: Routledge.

Hayden, C., & Molenkamp, R. (2003). *The Tavistock primer II*. Jupiter, FL: The A. K. Rice Institute.

Heifetz, R. A., & Linsky, M. (2002). *Leadership on the line*. Boston: Harvard Business School Press.

Heifetz, R. A. (1994). *Leadership without easy answers*. Cambridge, MA: The Belknap Press of Harvard University Press.

Horwitz, L. (1983). Projective identification in dyads and groups. In A. D. Colman & M. H. Geller (Eds.), *Group relations reader 2* (pp. 21–36). Jupiter, FL: The A. K. Rice Institute, 1985.

Hulse, C. (2002, December 21). Divisive words: The overview. *The New York Times*, p. 1.

Hutton, B. (2004). *The Hutton Inquiry*. Retrieved March 2004, from http://www.the-hutton-inquiry.org.uk/content/rulings/statement280104.htm

Kelman, H. C. (1999). Experiences from 30 years of action research on the Israeli-Palestinian conflict. In K. P. Spillmann & A. Wenger (Eds.), *Zeitgeschichtliche hintergründe aktueller konflikte VII: Zürcher beiträge zur sicherheitspolitik und konfliktforschung*, No. 54, 173–197.

Klein, M. (1984). Our adult world and its roots in infancy. In Roger Money-Kyrle (Ed.), in collaboration with Betty Joseph, Edna O'Shaughnessy, & Hanna Segal, *Envy and gratitude and other works 1946–1963* (pp. 247–263). New York: Free Press. (Original work published 1959)

Lawrence, W. G., Bain, A., & Gould, L. J. (1996). The fifth basic assumption. *Free associations*, 6, Part 1, (37).

Lazar, R. A. (2003, September 20). *Follow the leader…? Leadership, followership, seduction and persecution in groups and institutions*. Paper presented at the National Scientific Meeting of The A. K. Rice Institute, Boston, MA.

McCollom, M. (1990). Group formation: Boundaries, leadership and culture. In J. Gillette & M. McCollom (Eds.), *Groups in context* (pp. 34–48). Lanham, MD: University Press of America.

McNamara, R. S. (1996). *In retrospect*. New York: Vintage Books.

Menzies Lyth, I. (1997). *Containing anxiety in institutions: Selected essays, Volume I*. London: Free Association Books.

Miller, E. J., and Rice, A.K. (1975). Selections from: Systems of organization. Reprinted in A. D. Colman & W. H. Bexton (Eds.), *Group relations reader 1* (pp. 43–68). Jupiter, FL: The A. K. Rice Institute. (Original work published 1967)

Miller, E. J. (1989). The Leicester Conference. London: Tavistock Institute of Human Relations.

Mindell, A. (1995). *Sitting in the fire: Large group transformation using conflict and diversity*. Portland, OR: Lao Tze Press.

Montville, J. V. (1991). Epilogue. In J. V. Montville (Ed.), *Conflict and peacemaking in multi-ethnic societies* (pp. 535–541). New York: Lexington Books.

Morris, E. (Director). (2003). *The fog of war*. [Motion picture]. United States: Sony Pictures Classics.

Nitsun, M. (1996). *The anti-group*. London and New York: Routledge.

Obholzer, A. (1994). Authority, power, and leadership. In A. Obholzer & V. Zanier Roberts (Eds.), *The unconscious at work: individual and organizational stress in the human services* (pp. 39–47). New York: Routledge.

Ogden, T. H. (1982). *Projective identification and psychotherapeutic technique.* New York: Jason Aronson.

Rauchway, E. (2003, September 7). The president and the assassin, *The Boston Globe,* p. D2.

Reed, G. M., & Noumair, D. A. (2000). The tiller of authority in a sea of diversity: Empowerment, disempowerment and the politics of identity. In E. Klein, F. Gabelnick, & P. Herr (Eds.), *Dynamic consultation in a changing workplace* (pp. 51–80). Madison, CN: Psychosocial Press.

Rice, A. K. (1975). Selections from: Learning for leadership. In A. D. Colman & W. H. Bexton (Eds.), *Group relations reader* (Vol. 1, pp. 71–158). Jupiter, FL: The A. K. Rice Institute. (Original work published 1965)

Rioch, M. (1975). The work of Wilfred Bion on groups. In A. D. Colman & W. H. Bexton (Eds.), *Group relations reader* (Vol. 1, pp. 43–68). Jupiter, FL: The A. K. Rice Institute. (Original work published 1970)

Sarel, A., Said, N., Mayer, A., & Ben-Yosef, S. (2003, September 19). *Dialogue between conflict groups in uncertain times.* Panel presentation at the National Scientific Meeting of The A. K. Rice Institute, Boston, MA.

Shapiro, E. (2003). The maturation of American identity: A study of the elections of 1996 and 2000 and the war against terrorism. *Organisational and Social Dynamics, 3*(1), 121–133.

Stern, J. (2003). *Terror in the name of God: Why religious militants kill.* New York: Harper Collins.

Stokes, J. (1994). The unconscious at work in groups and teams: Contributions from the work of Wilfred Bion. In A. Obholzer & V. Zanier Roberts (Eds.), *The unconscious at work: Individual and organizational stress in the human services* (pp. 19–27). New York: Routledge.

Suskind, R. (2004). *The price of loyalty: George W. Bush, the White House, and the education of Paul O'Neill.* New York: Simon and Schuster.

Susskind, L., & Cruikshank, J. (1987). *Breaking the impasse: Consensual approaches to resolving public disputes.* New York: Basic Books.

Volkan, V. D. (1991). Psychoanalytic aspects of ethnic conflicts. In J. V. Montville (Ed.), *Conflict and peacemaking in multiethnic societies* (pp. 81–92). New York: Lexington Books.

Volkan, V. D. (2003). September 11 and societal regression. *The Austen Riggs Center Review, 16*(1), 10–14. (Reprinted from *Mind & Human Interaction, 12,* No. 3, 2001)

Winnicott, D. W. (1965). The theory of the parent-infant relationship. *The maturational processes and the facilitating environment* (pp. 37–55). New York: International Universities Press. (Original work published 1960)

Yaukey, J. (2004, February 5). Bush picks seven members for study commission on Iraq. *USA Today.* Retrieved March 2004, from http://www.usatoday.com/news/world/iraq/2004-02-05-mccain-iraq_x.htm

Zagier Roberts, V. (1994). The organization of work: Contributions from open systems theory. In A. Obholzer & V. Zanier Roberts (Eds.), *The unconscious at work: Individual and organizational stress in the human services* (pp. 28–38). New York: Routledge.

CHAPTER 12

# Psychology of a Stable Peace

## Daniel Shapiro and Vanessa Liu

## Snapshot 1

1991: Vojislav Seselj, leader of the Serbian Radical party, pledges to "gouge out the eyes of Croats with rusty spoons."

December 28, 2003: The Radicals win the Serbian general elections. Their leader looks on from jail in the Hague while awaiting trial at the Yugoslavian war crimes tribunal. "We won this victory for Vojislav Seselj and other Hague indictees and for Serbia's citizens who had enough of being humiliated," proclaims acting Radical Party Chief Tomislav Nikolic.

The revival of the party advocating a "greater Serbia" has alarmed the international community, still wary of the wars that tore the region apart in the 1990s. Will it be possible for Serbia's feuding reformers to maintain stability in the region?

## Snapshot 2

"We had always lived in peace with the Eritreans in our village," recalls Abeba Gebre Selassie, a former resident of Gerhu Serhnu on the Ethiopian-Eritrean border. "We had been living together—we had always been a community. Our people were in love with each other." (BBC News, 1999)

Belen Telegn describes how the border conflict between Ethiopia and Eritrea transformed her Ethiopian neighborhood: "The coldness of the governments spread throughout the people. The people used to live together for a long time with peace and love, but it seemed like they forgot what they were like yesterday, and friends became enemies." (Tegen, n.d.)

Two years of bloody conflict officially ended with a peace accord in 2000, although relations between Ethiopia and Eritrea remain tenuous.[1] How can Abeba, Belen, and their
neighbors rebuild their communities? At a local level, how can a stable peace be created
that does not get sabotaged by resentment, grudges, and vengeance?

Violent conflicts are likely to occur where violent conflicts have happened. Throughout history, conflicts such as the ones in the Balkans and the Horn of Africa have
repeated themselves over and over again. Plagued by physical, material, and psychological insecurity, postconflict environments are vulnerable to renewed violence.

Rebuilding war-torn environments has become a central focus for many international and nongovernmental organizations. Upon the signing of a peace accord or a
cease-fire by a country struck with violence, the international community tends to
mobilize in an effort to rebuild the physical and material infrastructure. This is true
in present-day Iraq and Afghanistan, where the United States is pushing for a new
constitution, and groups such as the World Bank, International Red Cross, and
USAID have launched transition programs to support the process of economic revi-
talization, reconstruction, and political stabilization. Aid packages focus on essentials
such as revitalizing the economy, rebuilding destroyed homes and buildings, increasing the capacity of the new governments, building citizen confidence, and increasing
the capacity of the media.

Yet emotions do not simply resolve upon the signing of a peace agreement. And
lives are not simply rebuilt upon the reconstruction of one's home. The toxic emotions from violent conflict can leave a deep-seated scar that distances groups from
one another and can become the seed of future violent conflict.

In this chapter, we suggest ways to deal with residual anger, resentment, and other
negative emotions between divided groups who interact with one another postconflict. Macrolevel interventions such as economic realignments to improve equity or
equality are necessary but not sufficient for long-term, stable peace. Negative emotions also need to be transformed, and relationships need to be healed. This process
takes time, but anything short of this process will increase the risk of recidivism to
violence.

This chapter is organized into four main sections. First, we describe ways in which
postconflict "residual emotions" create obstacles to cooperative interactions between
individuals from historically divided groups. Second, we argue that a major "cause"
of those toxic emotions lies in a relational syndrome called "vertigo" (Shapiro,
2004), which diminishes the ability of individuals to see beyond their misery and
anger. Third, we provide strategies to deal with vertigo. We close by illustrating the
utility of these strategies in two real cases of conflict repetition—one which is at
the high levels of government in Serbia, and another which is at the grassroots level
in Eritrea and Ethiopia.

## Role of Emotions in Postconflict Environments

Strong negative emotions pose many obstacles to postconflict peace building in
the short and long run. At an internal level, many survivors of violent conflict have

symptoms of re-experiencing traumatic events afterward as a result of the strong negative emotions that were elicited during the conflict. For most people, these fears tend to fade over time. However, for some, the trauma of violent conflict can take a debilitative form called post-traumatic stress disorder (PTSD), where psychological and biological symptoms including nightmares, difficulty sleeping, feelings of detachment and estrangement, and altered brainwave activity have long-term effects and can impair a person's daily life.

At a relational level, strong negative emotions felt about other people or groups during a violent conflict can lead to a ruptured relationship between the parties. Such relationship damage has immediate effects, such as challenges in working jointly in rebuilding postconflict societies, and long-term effects, including the perpetuation of strong negative emotions and stereotypes of the "evil other" through the generations. Over 40 years after the Holocaust, some Jews in the United States continue to refuse to buy German-made cars. Many children of Nazi perpetrators live with the guilt and shame resulting from the actions enacted by their parents.

The presence of strong, negative residual emotions is dangerous in postconflict societies. These emotions tend to fuel the escalation of conflict even after a society has begun to stabilize economically and politically. Strong emotions of resentment, humiliation, shame, and anger toward the "other" often do not cease once a peace agreement is signed, nor after reconstruction efforts have begun. Consider the present situation in Serbia. Nearly 10 years have passed since the Yugoslavian War ended with the signing of the Dayton Peace Accord. Despite a 4 percent growth in the economy and a revaluation of the dinar, Serbia increasingly suffers from political and social unrest (Wood, 2004). Negative emotions apparently have continued to haunt the region as neighbors and leaders alike suddenly come face to face with the "enemy," whose presence can prime negative emotions.

Strong emotions may maintain themselves over time. In some circumstances, these emotions have an impact on a person's day-to-day emotional experience. Simple tasks such as buying groceries or shopping for clothes become more complicated when the grocer or shopkeeper is a member of the group who tormented your family or threatened the local survival of your ethnic group. In other circumstances, these emotions remain dormant, awaiting some persuasive leader to revive them—and in some cases even to escalate them to the point that violent action becomes a person's inevitable desire.

## Vertigo: A Relational Syndrome Fueled by Strong Emotions

We argue that in a conflict situation, a relational syndrome called *vertigo* can fuel strong negative emotions. Shapiro (2004) conceptualizes vertigo as a polarized perception of one's relationship with another person or group. In vertigo, a person becomes preoccupied with a single relationship, failing to consider alternative or expanded perspectives of the relationship or of other relationships. In its positive form, vertigo occurs when someone falls head over heals in love with someone else; almost nothing can jolt the lover out of the constant thoughts and feelings of that visceral love. In its negative form, vertigo manifests in the form of obsessive anger, resentment, fear, or shame and can lead to microlevel behaviors that invoke or reinvoke violent conflict.

Vertigo is intrinsically a relational experience, and the emotions it generates pertain directly to one's relationship with another individual or group. During vertigo, any of a long list of emotions may be induced—from anger and shame to love or hate. In its extreme, the experience of vertigo may implicate emotions so strong that intrapersonal psychopathology results.[2] This chapter, however, focuses on how negative emotions compel people to view a situation through a limited, black-and-white lens.

## Theoretical Background

Before detailing the characteristics of vertigo and its remedy, we provide background about theory underlying vertigo. Two theories are particularly informative.

*Object relations*, a branch of psychoanalysis, suggests that we mentally internalize images of others and of our selves. These images, known as "objects," are the mental representation of an individual ("my self"), another person ("my mother"), a part of a person ("her funny sense of humor"), a group ("the Jews"), and even an inanimate object ("a teddy bear"). Over time, we internalize a relationship between our selves (i.e., an object of one's "self" in the mind) and the specific object with which we are interacting. This relationship is what is meant by an object relation. Some object relations are associated with positive emotions, others are associated with negative emotions, and ambivalence is common.

The most powerful object relations presumably develop during one's early years as one builds enduring internal models for relating to parents and other important caretakers. A boy with a nurturing mother may grow up to perceive and treat middle-aged women kindly; these women, in turn, are more likely to nurture the male, who thus constructs a living model of his internal relationship.

Most object relations do not remain constant over time. Emotions, memory, and fantasy can change the perception of our relation with an object. By 2004, for example, many Haitian citizens had come to see their long-time president, Jean Aristide, as making empty promises of alleviating poverty; their perception of him shifted from "heroic president" to "despotic ruler." The emotions binding together the relation of objects shifted from positive to negative.

Object relations theory offers useful insights for postconflict transformation. This theory suggests that to reduce relational polarization, members of polarized groups need to change the object relations upon which they draw their understanding of their relationship with the other group. Thus, for groups who may coexist in neighboring villages, each group member does not need to interact with members of the other group in order for relational healing to occur. Actual human interaction is but one way to change the internal representations each group has of its relation to the other. A heart-wrenching autobiography may be written jointly by two mothers —one Serb and one Muslim—who each lost a son in the Yugoslavian war. Bosnian readers of the story—both Serb and Muslim—may come to understand the emotional experience of both sides better, and the object relations of the two groups may change from "enemies" to "fellow Yugoslavians who each have suffered greatly."

Object relations theory is consistent with much of the laboratory-based research conducted in the field of *social cognition*. This branch of social psychology investigates how people make sense of others and themselves. Research in social cognition has shown that people consciously and unconsciously construct their experiences by drawing on mental schemas, organizations of information in their mind.

## Diagnosing Vertigo

Three diagnostic questions can be used to assess the likelihood that individuals of conflicting groups may be experiencing vertigo and therefore at risk of repeating violent activity. Are individuals experiencing the following:

1. Diminished self-reflection?
2. A psychological collapse of time and space?
3. Relational categorization of the "other" as "enemy?"

### *Diminished Self-reflection*

One of the distinctive characteristics of human beings is that we can reflect upon our thoughts, emotions, and actions (Hartley, 1999). After we think a thought, feel a feeling, or act out an action, we usually have the ability to stop and think; we can try to make sense of our experience and to modify future behavior in reaction to current conditions.

Vertigo severely disrupts one's capacity to self-reflect. A dramatic shift in the functioning of one's identity diminishes this capacity. Identity can be separated into two interdependent components: an "I" and a "me" (Mead, 1934; Rogers, 1951, 1961; Rogers & Stevens, 1967; Strauss, 1956). The I is the experiencing self (Epstein, 1990), the present state of consciousness that is forever spontaneous in its experience of the world (Hartley, 1999). Present experience is guided by a rich resource of interwoven memories of the past, including one's relationships with others. The I has no ability to self-reflect (Epstein, 1998); rather, it takes relational schemas and tries to apply them within present situations (Hartley, 1999). The me is the second component of identity. It is the reflective and evaluative component of the self (Hartley, 1999). This part of identity takes one's experiences and turns them into an "objective" understanding of whom that person is (Strauss, 1956).

We cannot consciously stay aware of both the I and the me simultaneously, though both exist. We can focus only on one of these dimensions at any single point in time. The important point is that the me influences the I just as much as the I influences the me (Epstein, 1990). Every modification that the me makes to one's self-conception contributes to a changed data pool from which the I draws guidance for behavior. And every experience initiated by the I becomes data for analysis by the me.

Diminished self-reflection can have a negative impact on a survivor of a violent conflict. During vertigo, the typical functioning of one's identity convolutes. The distinctive function of the me dissolves, and there no longer is a mental structure to objectify one's actions. The self loses its capacity to make meaning of its actions. No room is available for reflection. There is simply reaction to salient stimuli, such as confrontation with the enemy. The self is completely subjective, at the whim of primed, negative memories.

Diminished self-reflection has a second damaging consequence. Those skilled at managing conflict, such as effective negotiators, are able to hold in their mind multiple, conflicting perspectives of an issue (Putnam & Holmer, 1992). They can see their own perspective on a situation while simultaneously understanding the way in which the other party sees things differently. This ability is hampered by the reduced operation of the me.

### Time and Space Collapse

The second characteristic of vertigo is that one's world becomes increasingly inward focused, shifting a party's sense of time and space. One no longer draws one's understanding of time and place from external cues, but from relational memories and experiences in one's head.

This inward focus contributes to a collapse of time and space in two senses of the word. First, the external world collapses in the sense that it no longer is affecting the person's sense of time and place. Second, the internal world collapses in the sense that memories of the past compress with experiences in the present; past memories "reignite" and impact the self as though they were being experienced now, for the first time, with a fullness of emotional consequence. Each of these forms of collapse will now be described more fully.

#### Constricted Emotions about the Here and Now

During vertigo, there is a collapse of a disputant's awareness of his or her present surroundings (his or her "space") and of the regular passage of time. Attention constricts to the person's experiential, I world. The reflective me in effect disappears, and reactions are driven by "mindless," uncalibrated use of internal object relations. Behavior is predominantly a re-enactment of relational scripts in one's head (Greenberg & Mitchell, 1983). The result of subjective domination is that one's surroundings become secondary to this relational filtering of reality, to this interpersonal space and moment in time. In some conflicts, a party feels so aggrieved that he or she can focus on nothing other than seeking vengeance. Neither the consequences of vengeance nor anything else distracts the person from his or her singular focus on revenge.

A corollary consequence of time/place constriction is the reduced ability to experience self-conscious emotions such as guilt, shame, or embarrassment. These emotions result from an appraisal of how we think others think about us and how we want them to evaluate us (Frijda, 1993). A major discrepancy between these two appraisals can trigger self-conscious emotions. Parties immersed in vertigo lack the influence of the me and therefore lose the capacity to monitor the morality of their behavior. They no longer can evaluate the social consequences of their individual behavior. Consequently, they may act in immoral or atypical ways. Once vertigo recedes, parties are left asking themselves, "What came over me? Am I *really* that type of person?"

### Revived Emotions of the Then and There

Time and space also collapse in the sense that memories of the past are re-experienced with a fullness of emotional intensity—as though they happened today. In intergroup conflicts, group members experience "chosen traumas" when events from their history elicit "an event that causes a large group to feel helpless and victimized" (Volkan, 1992). Michael Ignatieff (1997) describes the experience of a time collapse in the Balkans:

> What seems apparent in the former Yugoslavia, in Rwanda and in South Africa is that the past continues to torment because it is not the past. These places are not living in a serial order of time but in a simultaneous one, in which the past and present are a continuous, agglutinated mass of fantasies, distortions, myths, and lies. Reporters in the Balkan wars often observed that when they were told atrocities stories they were occasionally uncertain whether these stories had occurred yesterday or in 1941, or 1841, or 1441. (pp. 16–17)

A collapse of time and space heightens a person's sense of personal vulnerability. Past and present merge, and the survivor of violent conflict experiences relational wounds of the past as visceral threats in the present. Consequently, each survivor dons a cloak of self-protection to defend against the "dangerous" other. In this defensive stance, the ability of survivors to listen well and work jointly is greatly reduced.

## Relational Categorization

The third characteristic of vertigo, relational categorization, involves a schema-driven understanding of the relationship between self and other (Fiske & Taylor, 1991). The complex relationship between self and other reduces to a categorical stereotype such as "ally," "adversary," or the like. Attention drifts from the actual attributes of the relationship to relational fixtures in the mind.

Three significant consequences emerge if those in conflict draw upon a negative relational categorization, viewing one another as adversaries.

### Reduction to a Stereotype of the Full Emotional Experience

As parties rely increasingly on their internal world of object relations, they fail to utilize data from their external interactions as a basis for relational understanding. A party's categorical conception of the relationship with the other as "adversarial" reduces the fullness of the emotional experience between them into a stereotyped set of emotional experiences (Fiske & Neuberg, 1990; Fiske & Taylor, 1991). A person no longer tries to understand the actual intentions or emotions of the other person but instead relies on category-based understandings drawn from relational assumptions—"object relations"—in one's mind.

As parties categorize each other as adversary, parties focus increasingly on their own emotional world. Humanity shrinks to a single dimension, a single self-it continuum. The more pain one party feels, the less he or she considers the pain of the other party. Consequently, a party's heightened sense of subjectivity—whether in the form of pain, hurt, or hope—leads to perceptions of the apparent perpetrator of the pain as an "it," an object with no human value.

This partitioning of self and other has a negative impact on the interaction between parties. The categorical view each party holds of the other can promote a dangerous cycle of mutual objectification. The more a party treats others as objects, the more the others respond in unfriendly ways, reinforcing the party's view of the others as objects (Lewicki, Gray, & Elliot, 2003). For many warring parties, the emotional distance between them increases with every new wave of violence.

### Loss of Hope for a Mutually Positive Relationship

For parties who hold adversarial impressions of the relationship, it tends to be difficult to hold onto the hope that a better relationship might be possible. The relational reality they construct feels "true," because they continuously are able to take ambiguous data from the interaction and to use it to confirm the validity of their categorical construction. Parties construct a relationally hopeless situation, systematically gather evidence that supports their construction, and then make conclusions about the hopelessness of the situation. In this sense, they do not just experience learned helplessness (Peterson, Maier, & Seligman, 1993). They actively construct a hopeless situation.

### Compulsion to Repeat Past Behavior

In a hopeless situation, one's attention turns from the future to the present (Peterson, Maier, & Seligman, 1993). How can I survive this moment—and perhaps a few more moments? During vertigo, the I is in charge, and therefore the information guiding present actions derives from relational scripts in the disputant's head (Kitron, 2003). With a hopeless situation constructed and with an inability to self-reflect, the party is condemned to repeat past behavior (Lazarus, 1991; Russell, 1998). Past behavior may lead to a temporary "resolution" to a situation but will tend not to address the complex emotions involved in the ongoing relationship between parties.

Consequently, long-term, stable peace remains a dream. In the conflict in Yugoslavia, for example, Serbs, Croats, and Muslims fought a terrible war that led to many deaths. The war ended, but to this day resentment continues to foster, and there is a growing movement of local retributive violence (Balderston, 2002).

In the next section of the chapter, we turn to strategies to address each of the elements of vertigo. The goal of the strategies is to help negotiators deal with the impact of vertigo once it is experienced, although certainly the best intervention is prevention.[3]

## Strategy to Deal with Vertigo in Postconflict Environments

In this chapter, we conceptualize three phases for building a stable peace at the microrelational level. People in postconflict societies need to move through these phases in order to transform strong negative emotions into positive (or at least not negative) emotions toward one another. Each phase addresses one of the characteristic problems of vertigo. These phases are by no means linear and sequential in time, though we present them as such for purpose of clarity. It is possible for a person metamorphosing out of vertigo to complete phase one, move to phase two, recede back to phase one, and then to move on again.

The process of recovery can take time—months, years, and even generations. And the final phase toward a stable peace—aligning internal relational schemas with external potentials for cooperation—is never complete. A stable peace is not a passive peace. It is not an emotional massage being given to individuals in society. At the psychological level, a stable peace is active. People must actively work toward improving their relationships with former adversaries.

### Three Phases of Recovery

Because vertigo reduces an individual's ability to reflect upon his or her subjective experience, the fundamental method to deal with vertigo is to revive his or her capacity to objectify subjective experience. Breaking the grip is a three-step process. A person cannot move directly from a state of vertigo to a state of enthusiastic participation in a negotiation. A transition is needed. The following three strategies comprise elements of such a process:

1. *Switch to a metaframe.* This perspective shift helps negotiators to reframe their subjective experience as an object of reflection from which meaning can be constructed.

2. *Create a transitional environment.* A transitional environment provides time and space boundaries in which parties can work through their past issues and toward a better future.

3. *Align internal object relations with external potential for cooperation.* In the transitional environment, parties can realign their internal world with the external potential for cooperation.

Each of these elements of a prescriptive strategy will be discussed in turn. (Refer to Table 12.1 for a summary of each element of vertigo and related strategies.)

### *Diminished Self-Reflection? Switch to a Metaframe*

The tight grip of vertigo can diminish an individual's capacity (1) to reflect on possible courses of action when interacting with a former enemy and (2) to choose carefully from among them (Lovallo & Kahneman, 2003). Behavior is reactive, immediate, and, like the deeds of a drunk, fraught with the risk of regret. As the I overshadows the me, individuals lose the capacity to objectify their emotional experience. They are swallowed in their own subjectivity.

**Table 12.1**
**Diagnostic Elements of Vertigo and Related Prescriptive Strategies**

| Element of Vertigo | Prescriptive Approach |
|---|---|
| 1. Diminished self-reflection | 1. Switch to a metaframe |
| 2. Time-space collapse | 2. Create a transitional environment |
| 3. Relational categorization | 3. Align internal object relations with external potential for cooperation |

Therefore, the first priority is to revive the functioning of the me and the cooperative functioning of the I and me. Survivors of violent conflict need the capacity to make sense of their subjective experience. This is done by having them switch to a metaframe, an expanded perspective from which to understand the conflict and their own place in it. This perspective shift helps individuals to reframe their subjective experience as an object of reflection.

Three methods are particularly helpful to create a metaframe. Each will now be discussed.

*Surprise*

An unexpected event can jolt people out of diminished self-reflection. At the international level, consider the surprise visit of Egyptian President Anwar al-Sadat to Israel in 1977. Until the visit, Israelis had little hope of peace with Egypt. After the surprise visit, Israeli optimism for peace skyrocketed and was a major factor in the eventual peace agreement between the two countries (Ury, 1999). Sadat's visit jolted the Israeli public out of their inability to see past a gloomy status quo.

*Conscious Focus on the Self*

Another technique to establish a metaframe is to focus consciously on the situation and on one's experience in the situation (Grant & Crawley, 2001). This notion is illustrated in the common negotiation advice that a negotiator mentally "step onto the balcony" and see the interaction from that perspective (Heifetz & Linsky, 2002a, 2002b; Ury, 1991). This is a form of switching to a metaframe, of stepping outside of a purely subjective perspective to an objectified understanding of the emotional experience (Lewicki, Gray, & Elliot, 2003).

*Context Change*

A change in context is a third way to foster a metaframe. People who travel to other countries often acquire a metaperspective of their home country's policies and politics. What seemed an obviously good idea while at home may now take on new meaning once distanced from the context in which the idea sprouted.

Context change has been used successfully in resolving international conflicts. Part of the success of the original Camp David accords is likely to be due to the fact that

President Carter suggested Israeli Prime Minister Begin and Egyptian President Sadat meet in rural Maryland, a location far enough away from the Middle East brouhaha that each one of the leaders could begin to see, in a new light, the destructive dynamic between their countries.

### Time and Space Collapse? Create a Transitional Environment

As vertigo strikes, one relies less and less on external cues to guide behavior. Time and space become increasingly understood through the context of relational memories in one's head. This mental reality holds some validity, but there is also a need in a conflict for a place and time to reconcile the demands of the external world with the constraints imposed on oneself by one's internal object relations.

Thus, any strategy to remedy vertigo should include creation of a "transitional environment," a space and time in which to discriminate the inner from the outer world (Giovacchini, 2001). Winnicott stressed the importance of a "transitional space" between the internal world and "reality" (Grant & Crawley, 2001; Winnicott, 1953). This space mediates a person's internal and external world through play and imagination (Phillips, 1988). It is in this sense that a transitional environment is important in dealing with vertigo. A transitional environment is both a space *and* a time in which parties can explore the intersubjective experience between internal reality and external demands, between now and then, between self and other (Phillips, 1988; Pizer, 1998).

Shapiro (2004) calls this bounded time and space a transitional environment rather than a "transitional structure," because the boundaries of an environment, like those of a cloud, are fuzzier than the boundaries of a structure such as a house. No transitional environment is perfectly safe or fully legitimate to everyone.

A transitional environment does more than simply contain toxic emotions (Bion, 1967). The goal of the environment also is to stimulate positive emotions that move parties toward improved affiliation, trust, and cooperative intent.

#### Qualities of a Transitional Environment

Two qualities characterize the essence of a transitional environment. First, parties must feel a sense of physical and emotional *safety*. Fear is the enemy of open disclosure and understanding (Levy & Campbell, 2000). A transitional environment reassures parties that their words and emotional expressions will not come back unexpectedly to haunt them. Second, there needs to be *legitimacy* to the environment. A credible social authority, such as governmental officials or academics, need to sanction the efficacy of the social structure (Gelpi, 2003).

Either party in a conflict, or a third party, can construct a transitional environment. Two models of a transitional environment that have been tried with some success in intergroup conflicts are (1) truth and reconciliation commissions and (2) problem-solving workshops. We will now point out how each meets the criteria of a transitional environment.

**Truth and Reconciliation Commissions.** Perhaps the most well-known truth commission was the Truth and Reconciliation Commission (TRC) developed in

South Africa in response to government-sanctioned apartheid. With the end of apartheid in 1994, South African officials faced the decision of whether to use traditional war trials or reparative reconciliation. They chose the latter to "rehabilitate and affirm the dignity and personhood of those who for so long had been silenced, had been turned into anonymous, marginalized ones" (Tutu, 2000).

There are several ways that the TRC tried to construct a *safe* space and time to deal with the conflict (Friedman, 2000). First, during TRC hearings, victims were able to sit in the same room with perpetrators without fear of physical attack. Many victims would attend the hearings of the perpetrator of their injury. The hearings were in a controlled, safe environment. Martha Minow (1998) describes part of the interaction between a perpetrator and victim at a TRC hearing:

> During the hearing, Mr. Benzien addressed one of his former victims, Tony Yengeni, who appeared in the audience, as "Sir." Yengeni, who now serves as a member of Parliament for the African National Congress, asked, "What kind of man uses a method like his one of the wet bag, on other human beings, repeatedly listening to those moans and cries and groans, and taking each of those people very near to their deaths? Benzien replied, "With hindsight, sir, I realize that it was wrong," but that at the time he thought he was working to rescue South Africa from a communist movement and to fight for his and his family's right to live as they had in their country. After apologizing for his wrong-doing, Benzien concluded that the new regime made him "extremely amazed and very happy to still be in South Africa today—and I am still a patriot of the country." (pp. 130–131)

Second, the explicit structure of the TRC provided victims with expectations about what was going to be revealed. The victim could "emotionally prepare" for the situation. Third, perpetrators who revealed the full activity of their wrongs were, in some cases, granted amnesty. This motivated perpetrators to talk more openly, because disclosure contributed to their safety, not harm.[4]

The TRC tried to construct itself as a *legitimate* institution. In 1995, the Government of National Unity passed a law under the title "Promotion of National Unity and Reconciliation Act." This act set up the Truth and Reconciliation Commission (see the Truth and Reconciliation Commission Web site, http://www.doj.gov.za/trc), providing it with institutional and political legitimacy. Further, the process of reconciliation roots itself in an African concept called *ubuntu* (Tutu, 2000). This concept suggests that all people are interconnected parts of a greater whole. Injury to one is thus injury to all. The indigenous birth of this concept provided the TRC with additional social and historical legitimacy.

**Problem-Solving Workshops.** Problem-solving workshops (R. J. Fisher, 1980, 1993; Kelman & Rouhana, 1994, 1995; Shapiro, 2000) are another example of a transitional environment. In a typical problem-solving workshop, a few members of rival groups are invited to attend a joint meeting—usually two to five days long —to understand and problem solve issues. Participants are guided through a process of understanding one another's interests and needs and brainstorming ways to address them.

These workshops often are conducted in affiliation with universities, thus reinforcing the unofficial nature of the interaction and providing an institutional symbol of legitimacy. The workshops tend to be led by university professors or "conflict-resolution professionals" who have studied the effectiveness of problem-solving workshops, giving the process further legitimacy. Over the years, the Harvard Negotiation Project has led a number of problem-solving workshops for high-level negotiators (Shapiro, 2000; Young, 2003). Most recently, problem-solving workshops were conducted involving Israelis and Palestinians negotiators.

Problem-solving workshops also create an environment that is fairly safe. A key characteristic of problem-solving workshops involves framing the interaction as unofficial, which creates safety. Participants attend in their personal capacity, and no official decisions are made. Moreover, the events are confidential and not public, allowing any party to deny anything attributed to them.

### Relational Categorization? Align Object Relations with External Potential for Cooperation

By necessity, the human mind uses categories to aid in the efficiency and effectiveness of social interaction. Otherwise, the mind could not possibly make meaning from the infinite sources of data to which humans are exposed.

Two goals improve the likelihood of a cooperative interaction in the face of the human tendency to categorize. First, parties want to reduce the negative impact of categorical thinking on cooperative possibilities. Rather than seeing one another as objects that can be mistreated without guilt or shame, parties would be well served to see the richness of human emotions in one another (Fiske & Neuberg, 1990). Second, parties want to increase the usefulness of any categorical thinking that might occur, such as by making salient the relational schema of "colleagues" over that of "adversaries" (Taylor, Kemeny, Reed, Bower, & Gruenewald, 2000).

Three major activities are needed to operationalize the alignment of mental models with external potentials for cooperation.

#### Appreciate the Richness of Their Emotional Experience—and Yours

To move beyond stereotyping, parties want to develop an appreciation of one another's emotional landscape. Appreciation is a three-step process that involves understanding a person's emotional experience, finding merit in it, and communicating that understanding (R. Fisher & Shapiro, 2005).

**Become Aware of Relational Identity Concerns.** Vertigo is commonly triggered when a party's *relational identity concerns* are enhanced or threatened. Relational identity concerns are a class of wants that revolve around our desire to feel valued within a relationship (Shapiro, 2002b, 2005). We want our identity to feel valued within a relationship. And if our concern for a positive relational identity goes unmet, negative emotions often get stirred. Because this class of concerns is relational, they can generate vertigo and stimulate its perpetuation.

Two key relational identity concerns are autonomy and affiliation (Shapiro, 2002b, 2005). *Autonomy* is the freedom to govern one's own actions without the imposition of others. Parties exercise autonomy when they act on the basis of internalized, personally accepted principles rather than on coercion from others (Averill & Nunley, 1992). *Affiliation* is a positive emotional connection that one party feels toward another. Parties who build cooperative relations with others tend to cultivate a sense of affiliation (Shapiro, 2002b).

Vertigo tends to emerge from incongruence between our perceived and desired degree of treatment regarding autonomy or affiliation. A diplomat who brings along a small team of associates without first consulting his or her counterpart may easily stir vertigo in the other, whose autonomy is likely to feel impinged. "Why didn't you consult me about bringing associates? I just sent my two closest associates on another assignment. If I had known about this, I would have asked them to stay." The experience of vertigo may result.

The flames of vertigo often are fueled not by the importance of the issue at stake, but rather by the felt importance of the underlying relational identity concerns that are met or unmet. Thus, road rage ("vehicle vertigo") can be sparked if a driver senses that another driver is disrespecting his or her autonomy. Similarly, a negotiator's emotions may spin into vertigo if his or her autonomy feels inappropriately limited.

**Satisfy Relational Identity Concerns.** To increase emotional understanding, parties can reconstruct their roles to foster cooperation. Such roles tend to be those that give each party a sense of meaning and of status where merited (Shapiro, 2002b). As a practical illustration, two negotiators may transform their roles from adversaries to colleagues working side by side (R. Fisher & Shapiro, 2005).

Once helpful roles are established, parties should try to enhance one another's sense of autonomy and affiliation. Autonomy can be improved in many ways, such as by having each party establish a practice of consulting with the other party before making any important decisions that affect both groups Affiliation can be improved through such activities as sharing personal stories about one's background or asking for the advice of the other party.

### Build a Vision for a Better Future

After parties feel emotionally appreciated, they then are in a place to brainstorm, either jointly or alone, ways to improve their long-term relationship. The goal of such brainstorming is to envision ways each party may enhance a mutual sense of autonomy and affiliation in the relationship.

A 50-year border dispute between Ecuador and Peru was resolved in large part due to the relational vision built and enacted by the key negotiators (Shapiro, 2002a). Ecuadorian President Jamil Mahuad and Peruvian President Alberto Fujimori met 10 times over the course of a few months to negotiate a settlement to their conflict. Before President Mahuad met with President Fujimori, he consulted with negotiation expert Professor Roger Fisher. They brainstormed ways that President Mahuad might build a positive relationship with his counterpart. Professor Fisher suggested that in the initial meeting between the presidents, President Mahuad should ask the advice of Fujimori: "I have been a president for four days. You have negotiated with four of my predecessors. Based upon your experience, how do you think we might deal with this border dispute in a way acceptable for Ecuador and Peru?" This solicitation demonstrated respect for Fujimori's autonomy and signaled an openness to work jointly, as colleagues in affiliation with one another. Ultimately, the conflict was resolved peacefully, with much of the credit due to the joint work of the two presidents.

### Move Forward Jointly

Despite visions of a better future, parties all too easily may repeat past behavior (Russell, 1998). Such repetitive behavior can be helpful if the habits a person re-enacts produce constructive ends. But in a conflict, there is a great risk that the party's past behaviors for dealing with similar conflicts were not very helpful. Otherwise, the party would probably not be in the current situation that he or she *is* in.

Therefore, parties need to make a concerted, conscious, and very deliberate effort *not* to repeat undesirable past behaviors (Kitron, 2003; Russell, 1998). This needs to an explicit act—an activity of the self-reflective "me." Consider two neighbors of different ethnopolitical groups whose families had fought against one another in a war. Small differences over land boundaries, excess noise, or other issues can easily escalate into a serious neighbor conflict. The compulsion to repeat violent intergroup behavior can be reduced if the neighbors make explicit their compulsion to repeat unhelpful behavior patterns. Toward the beginning of their argument, one of the neighbors might say, "Right now, I can sense that we are about to get into our old habit of conflicting over issues rather than trying to work together. Let's choose a different path today? How about we take a break for a moment and each think about possible next steps for jointly working out our situation?"

This advice works in other contexts, too. In the international arena, for example, plenty of conflicts reignite where past conflicts have happened (Rohrbaugh & Shoham, 2001). Parties involved in resolving the conflict might be wise to make explicit note of the allure of the repetition compulsion—and the economic, political, moral, and human risks of taking such a path.[5]

# Illustrative Applications of Our Microlevel Framework

There is no one model for dealing with negative emotions and bringing solace and healing to communities in postconflict environments. Rather, each type of situation requires a custom-built process. However, we suggest that all successful processes embody elements along the three phases of recovery outlined in the previous section. To illustrate how switching to a metaframe, creating a transitional environment, and aligning internal object relations with external potential for cooperation can be applied to postconflict situations, this section revisits the situations in the Balkans and the Horn of Africa and provides recommendations to help reach a long-term, stable peace.

### The Balkans

After the Dayton Peace Accords were signed, the International Criminal Tribunal was chosen as the first step in a process to heal relations between Serbia and its neighbors, as well as the international community. It aimed to create a transitional environment where key leaders that were responsible for the war would be brought to justice and the tarnish of Serbia's "collective guilt" would be wiped away. Yet, years after it first started prosecuting war crime suspects, the court is being criticized for its potential role in fueling the nationalists' revival in Serbia (*The Economist*, 2004). Even ordinary Serbians point to the one-sidedness of the court, where no ethnic Albanians have been indicted over the killings of hundreds of Serb civilians, and other issues such as whether NATO could have prevented killing Serbia civilians in its air war are not being raised. Rather than a source of stability, the tribunal is now at the forefront of Serbia's rising tide of anger.

How can the momentum of Serbia's spiral into instability be stopped? The symptoms of the Serbian situation imply that its citizens are experiencing another time-space collapse and have receded from phase two of vertigo back to phase one. Just as the accumulating years of bloodshed and the need for peace in the region jolted many citizens out of a state of diminished self-reflection in the early 1990s, another metaframe is now required to nudge citizens to develop a metaperspective of current Serbian policies and politics.

A change in context, involving informal, unofficial talks among current senior Serbian leaders and initiated and mediated by officials of other governments, may foster a metaframe. Given the inward focus of the various parties within the Serbian government, an unexpected outside request from a respected third party for informal discussions may create an opportunity for leaders to understand the current situation with an expanded perspective. The involvement of other external participants, such as high-level officials from neighboring Balkan states and NATO countries, would be critical for the discussions, given the focus of Serbian resentment today as well as the roles these other parties have played in Serbian history.

For such a discussion to be successful, the requesting third party should invite leaders in their personal capacities, rather than their official roles, for problem-solving workshops that are aimed at surfacing the issues facing Serbia. The meetings should be framed as opportunities for participants to explore and probe more fully their own and others' ideas and suggestions, with the aim of seeing how these issues might address the discontent that many Serbian citizens are experiencing. Ideally, the *process* of officials working together should be publicized so that the public can benefit from this expanded perspective made legitimate by key leaders. The substantive outcome of such meetings is less important for promoting a metaframe than the fact that leaders from each side are working together.

Compared to the international tribunal, these problem-solving workshops would also serve as safer and more legitimate transitional environments for parties to deal with their differences and strong emotions and also provide opportunities for object relations to be realigned. Rather than augmenting the adversarial position that

Serbians have been labeled with since the start of the war in the Balkans, these problem-solving workshops would provide a safe environment for parties to explore emotions and enable a foundation for future collaboration.

Ideally, facilitation of these problem-solving workshops should be conducted jointly by impartial leaders and experts in the psychology of conflict management. Whereas the leader will bring substantive knowledge and international credibility to the facilitation, the expert in psychology will be able to detect emotional resistances to joint work and will be able to help facilitate dialogue that breaks through resistance. For example, Bosnian leaders may resist open dialogue about economic cooperation with Serbia. To an untrained outsider, the resistance may to be due to pragmatic economic concerns. However, a trained psychologist may note Bosnian fear of a greater Serbia that swallows up Bosnia and other Yugoslavian territory. Without adequately dealing with this type of issue, the substantive negotiation is likely to generate few options, and commitments are unlikely to be sustained over time.

Perhaps the tenuous Serbian situation today could have been prevented if efforts aimed toward addressing negative emotions were initiated along with the establishment of the international tribunal. This is not to say that the legal approach to dispute resolution has no beneficial consequences on people's emotions. To the contrary, Martha Minow notes, "The claim, and the hope, is that trials create official records of the scope of violence and the participants in it, and that guilty verdicts afford public acknowledgment of what happened, and its utter wrongfulness" (Minow, 1998). In this sense, trials move the public toward a new emotional understanding of the situation and the involved parties, the guilty are punished for their actions, and precedent is set as a warning to others who might consider enacting similar behavior.

However, litigation is legitimate only when it is not *perceived* as corrupt or biased. Unfortunately, the perception among many Serbians is that the international tribunal is biased against them—leaving no effective transitional environment in place for Serbians to deal with their negative emotions. Moreover, litigation in general does not provide a safe environment for a dialectical conversation aimed at mutual understanding and appreciation.

### Ethiopia/Eritrea

Turning to the border conflict between Ethiopia and Eritrea, we show that the framework can also be applied on a more grassroots level. Though the situation remains tenuous, the recent agreement between Eritrea and Ethiopia to work together to prevent border incidents from flaring up suggests that both sides have established a metaframe of understanding about the conflict they have faced (see "Ethiopia, Eritrea in agreement," available at http://www.news24.com/News24/Africa/News/0,,2-11-1447_1461214,00.html). Yet without a transitional environment and the realignment of their object relations, their relationship appears stuck.

*Creating a Transitional Environment*

Ethiopians and Eritreans need community-level activities to assist their transition from living in a tarnished past to building a better future. For many group members on both sides, their day-to-day space and time is congested with the fear of insecurity and the felt need to fight in order to survive. A transitional environment would replace incentives to fight with incentives to collaborate. The fabric of the groups' daily existence would encourage mutual cooperation, not the other's annihilation.

It is possible for the international community to elicit, but not impose, a transitional environment within Ethiopia and Eritrea. International monetary aid may be made available in the form of grants for communal projects that encourage cooperation between Ethiopians and Eritreans. The World Bank, the United Nations, and other international governmental and nongovernmental institutions may set aside several million dollars to fund projects created by Ethiopians and Eritreans. Funding priority would go to those projects that most clearly demonstrate the potential to encourage economic, social, and political cooperation between Ethiopians and Eritreans. Grant proposals could be developed jointly or separately by Ethiopians and Eritreans. The process of developing projects would be, in effect, problem-solving workshops that would stimulate collaboration and cooperation toward a tangible goal. Ethiopians and Eritreans would be given the autonomy to develop projects that *they* think are good for their countries. A failure to develop enough projects would result in the loss both of international aid and of a solid opportunity to help their countries toward a stable peace.

Microfinancing for development could be geared to the border region between Ethiopia and Eritrea, where there has been the most mingling between the groups. Currently, many people blame their hard feelings on the governments and the activity of soldiers. International agencies and governments could make microloans or microgrants for locally devised development projects. These projects could help people living near the border to take ownership of their process toward communal development and a stable peace.

*Realign Object Relations*

A transitional environment is not enough in constructing a stable peace between Ethiopians and Eritreans. The object relations they use to conceive of their mutual relationship need to change. If they work on cooperative projects but still see one another as "adversaries," work may get done, but tensions are ripe for escalation.

The list of ways to realign object relations can stretch as far as one's imagination. A goal of object realignment is to build both positive affiliation between the groups and a sense of mutual autonomy so that neither group feels its freedom to act is inappropriately impinged by the other. What follows are two illustrative ventures that can, perhaps, help to promote nonadversarial relations between Ethiopians and Eritreans.

*Using Metaphor as a Means for Object Realignment*

While in some circumstances it can be helpful for groups to share their personal narratives with the other group, this process is not always ideal. Each group may fear explicit discussion of their strong negative emotions toward the other. They may worry that expressing to the other the extent of their own rage, disgust, and anger may antagonize the other or cause them to lose control of their own words and actions. They also may fear the vulnerability of expressing subtle, powerful emotions such as shame, guilt, and fear. Sharing one's emotional wounds with the other side leaves one open to being attacked again on an emotional level. Hence, a dilemma arises. Although talking about emotions can leave each group feeling vulnerable, not talking about them leaves each group member at the mercy of emotions. The conflict perpetuates. What to do?

The use of metaphor can help intergroup rivals understand one another's concerns about autonomy and affiliation and to support the building of constructive relations. Exploring conflict metaphors keeps people's emotions safely distanced from their egos. Rather than openly sharing their internal emotional landscape fully—and risking emotional injury—disputants can talk about their emotions indirectly through metaphor. They can draw on some object or idea to represent the emotions involved in their conflict. Through this self-reflective process, disputants may learn new information about their own beliefs and emotions, as well as about those of others.

Consider an example. A nonprofit organization plans a conflict-management workshop for approximately 24 influential community leaders from Ethiopia and Eritrea. During the workshop, Eritrean- and Ethiopian-only groups first are tasked to create a metaphor to describe the current relations between Ethiopians and Eritreans. Are relations rocky like a ship at sea? Unpredictable like an earthquake? Is the other group like a monster breathing down our necks? After that, new groups with representatives from both sides form to share their metaphors and brainstorm creative revisions of each of the two metaphors to illustrate how relations can be improved through cooperation, collaboration, and respect for one another's autonomy and affiliation.

The final stage of this activity moves from the creative to the practical. What kind of collaborative projects may be established to "bring sunlight" to the relations between Ethiopians and Eritreans? Each group brainstorms ideas. Perhaps they might agree to explore a small joint economic project? Or maybe they decide to initiate a letter-writing campaign between youth from Ethiopian and Eritrean villages?

Working groups share their metaphors, revised metaphors, and practical action plans with the group. The facilitator may choose to have the group as a whole come to agreement about which activities they plan to pursue. The group discusses details of project development and takes action.

*Using Mass Media as a Means for Object Realignment*

Is it an unrealistic goal to promote positive relations between millions of Ethiopians and Eritreans who have hardened attitudes of the "other?" Not every Ethiopian will interact with an Eritrean, or vice versa. Yet with no intervention, the attitudes each holds of the other may transmit from generation to generation and contribute to renewed violence. Is the notion of a stable peace simply an ideal? We think not.

Mass media provides a powerful way to change the object relations of large sets of people. To be sure, the process can be slow and ineffective at times. However, the benefit of object realignment can be the prevention of violence, death, and war.

Consider an example. Two mothers, an Ethiopian and an Eritrean, may co-host a radio show broadcast across the two countries. Each week, the hosts invite mothers onto the show who share one fact in common: each lost a son in the war. The mothers individually share stories and memories about their child, including the child's hobbies, joys, aspirations, and personality. The mother also may talk about the pain of no longer having the child on this earth. Rather than reacting to the desire for vengeance, both sides together mourn the loss of human lives. Mourning the dead becomes an intergroup process. The radio show honors the children, and it humanizes each group. Healing occurs through affiliation with the deceased and with the painful and inspiring stories of the survivors. A further benefit of such a show is that its Ethiopian and Eritrean organizers work jointly on the project. The organizers develop a personal understanding of one another. They learn how to work together and to support one another. And their enhanced affiliation may have a positive impact on the way they talk about the "other group" during radio broadcasts.

## Conclusions

Vertigo can have a powerful inhibiting force on intergroup cooperation. There is a diminished ability to self-reflect. Time and space collapse. And relational categorization becomes common, leaving disputants face to face with iron fists and no attractive alternative to violence.

In this chapter, we argue that there is a clear set of phases to escape the throes of vertigo and to reduce the likelihood of intergroup violence. Parties can switch to a metaframe, create a transitional environment, and align internal object relations with external potential for cooperation. Consequently, they enhance the psychology of a stable peace.

## Notes

Portions of this chapter have been drawn from Daniel L. Shapiro's article, "Vertigo: The disorienting effects of strong emotions on negotiation," a Working Paper of the Harvard Negotiation Project (2004).

The authors are indebted to Roger Fisher and Vamik Volkan, whose wisdom established the intellectual foundation upon which this article builds.

1. On September 19, 2003, Ethiopia officially rejected the border decision of the Eritrea-Ethiopia Boundary Commission, a mediating body established to draw up a new border.

2. Consider the case of a soldier with a low to moderate biological, social, and genetic predisposition to post-traumatic stress disorder (PTSD). If the soldier experiences vertigo while in combat—fully immersing himself or herself in the visceral experience of killing the

"enemy"—the intensity of the concomitant emotions generated may be enough to trigger PTSD. For others, psychopathology may result not from the emotions experienced during vertigo, but rather from the postvertigo guilt or shame that is experienced upon reappraising the appropriateness of one's behavior while in a state of vertigo. After killing one's neighbor in the "heat of passion," the perpetrator may feel such guilt and shame that clinical depression onsets.

3. See Shapiro (2002b) for details of a theory about common "relational identity concerns" that can be used to enlist positive emotions and ameliorate the likelihood of negative emotions in a negotiation.

4. Even with amnesty, both the alleged perpetrator and victim must deal with the social ramifications of public disclosure of harmful acts.

5. The past can haunt parties. Such chosen traumas may impact the present interaction. Therefore, parties need to clarify now from then and past from present (Russell, 1998). They can deal with past grievances through mourning (Volkan, 1997) and present problems through problem solving (R. Fisher, Ury, & Patton, 1991). Either way, parties want to keep a vision of cooperation in mind.

# References

Averill, J. R., & Nunley, E. P. (1992). *Voyages of the heart: Living an emotionally creative life.* New York: The Free Press.

Balderston, A. (2002). Reflections on a summer internship in Sarajevo. *Newsletter of the International Studies Center.* Seattle: The Henry M. Jackson School of International Studies. University of Washington. http://jsis.artsci.washington.edu/programs/cis/CIS/newsletter/winter2002.pdf

BBC News. (1999, November 8). A refugee's story. Retrieved September 30, 2005, from http://news.bbc.co.uk/1/hi/world/africa/509869.stm

Bion, W. (1967). *Second thoughts: Selected papers on psycho-analysis.* London: William Heinemann.

*The Economist.* (2004, February 26). A Balkan mess. Retrieved September 30, 2005, from http://www.lexis-nexis.com

Epstein, S. (1990). Cognitive-experiential self-theory. In L. Pervin (Ed.), *Handbook of personality: Theory and research* (pp. 165–192). New York: Guilford Press.

Epstein, S. (1998). *Constructive thinking. The key to emotional intelligence.* Westport, CT: Praeger.

Fisher, R. J. (1980). A third-party consultation workshop on the India-Pakistan conflict. *Journal of Social Psychology, 112*(2), 191–206.

Fisher, R. J. (1993). Developing the field of interactive conflict resolution: Issues in training, funding, and institutionalization. *Political Psychology, 14*(1), 123–138.

Fisher, R., & Shapiro, D. L. (2005). *Beyond reason: Using emotions as you negotiate.* New York: Viking.

Fisher, R., Ury, W., & Patton, B. (1991). *Getting to YES: Negotiating agreement without giving in* (2nd ed). New York: Penguin.

Fiske, S. T., & Neuberg, S. L. (1990). A continuum of impression formation, from category-based to individuating processes: Influences of information and motivation on attention and interpretation. In M. P. Zanna (Ed.), *Advances in experimental social psychology* (Vol. 23, pp. 1–74). New York: Academic Press.

Fiske, S., & Taylor, S. E. (1991). *Social cognition.* New York: McGraw-Hill.

Friedman, M. (2000). The truth and reconciliation commission in South Africa as an attempt to heal a traumatized society. In A. Y. Shalev, R. Yehuda, & A. C. McFarlane (Eds.), *International handbook of human response to trauma* (pp. 399–411). New York: Kluwer Academic.

Fridja, N. H. (1993). The place of appraisal in emotion. *Cognition and Emotion 7*, 357–387.

Gelpi, C. (2003). *The power of legitimacy.* Princeton, NJ: Princeton University Press.

Giovacchini, P. L. (2001). Dangerous transitions and the traumatized adolescent. *The American Journal of Psychoanalysis, 61*(1), 7–22.

Grant, J., & Crawley, J. (2001). The self in the couple relationship: Part 1. *Psychodynamic Counseling, 7*(4), 445–459.

Greenberg, J., & Mitchell, S. (1983). *Object relations in psychoanalytic theory.* Cambridge, MA: Harvard University Press.

Hartley, P. (1999). *Interpersonal communication* (see pp. 96–109). New York: Routledge.

Heifetz, R. A., & Linsky, M. (2002a). *Leadership on the line: Staying alive through the dangers of leading.* Boston: Harvard Business School Press.

Heifetz, R. A., & Linsky, M. (2002b). Leading with an open heart. *Leader to Leader 26*, 28–33.

Ignatieff, M. (1997, September/October). The elusive goal of war trials. In "Articles of Faith, Index on Censorship," *Harper's*, 15, 16–17. (Reprinted from *Harper's*, 1996, March)

Kelman, H., & Rouhana, N. (1994). Promoting joint thinking in international conflicts: An Israeli Palestinian continuing workshop. *Journal of Social Issues, 50*(1), 157–178.

Kitron, D. G. (2003). Repetition compulsion and self-psychology: Towards a reconciliation. *International Journal of Psycho-Analysis, 84*(2), 427–441.

Lazarus, R. S. (1991). *Emotions and adaptation.* New York: Oxford University Press.

Levy, E., & Campbell, K. (2000). D. W. Winnicott in the literature classroom. *Teaching English in the two-year college, 27*(3), 320–328.

Lewicki, R. J., Gray, B., & Elliot, M. (Eds.). (2003). *Making sense of intractable environmental conflicts.* Washington: Island Press.

Lovallo, D., & Kahneman, D. (2003, July). Delusions of success: How optimism undermines executives' decisions. *Harvard Business Review, 56–63.*

Mead, G. H. (1934). *Mind, self, and society from the standpoint of a social behaviorist.* Chicago: University of Chicago Press.

Minow, M. (1998). *Between vengeance and forgiveness: Facing history after genocide and mass violence.* Boston: Beacon Press.

Peterson, C., Maier, S., & Seligman, M. (1993). *Learned helplessness: A theory for the age of personal control.* New York: Oxford University Press.

Phillips, A. (1988). *Winnicott.* Cambridge, MA: Harvard University Press.

Pizer, S. (1998). Facing the nonnegotiable. In *Building bridges: The negotiation of paradox in psychoanalysis* (pp. 97–113). Hillsdale, NJ: The Analytic Press.

Putnam, L., & Holmer, M. (1992). Framing, reframing, and issue development. In L. L. Putnam, & M. E. Roloff (Eds.), *Communication and negotiation* (pp. 128–155). Newbury Park, CA: SAGE.

Rogers, C. (1951). *Client-centered therapy: Its current practice, implications, and theory.* Boston: Houghton Mifflin.

Rogers, C. (1961). *On becoming a person: A therapist's view of psychotherapy.* Boston: Houghton Mifflin.

Rogers, C., & Stevens, B. (1967). *Person to person: The problem of being human; A new trend in psychology.* Walnut Creek, CA: Real People Press.

Rohrbaugh, M., & Shoham, V. (2001). Brief therapy based on interrupting ironic processes: The Palo Alto model. *Clinical Psychology-Science & Practice, 8*(1), 66–81.

Rouhana, N. (1995). The dynamics of joint thinking between adversaries in international conflict: Phases of the continuing problem-solving workshop. *Political Psychology, 16*(2), 321–345.

Russell, P. (1998). The role of paradox in the repetition compulsion. In J. Teicholz & D. Kriegman, *Trauma, repetition, and affect regulation: The work of Paul Russell.* New York: The Other Press.

Shapiro, D. L. (2000). Supplemental joint brainstorming: Navigating past the perils of traditional bargaining. *Negotiation Journal,* 409–419.

Shapiro, D. L. (2002a). Unpublished interviews. President Jamil Mahuad of Ecuador is interviewed by Daniel Shapiro.

Shapiro, D. L. (2002b). Negotiating emotions. *Conflict Resolution Quarterly., 20*(1), 67–82.

Shapiro, D. L. (2004). *Vertigo: The disorienting effects of strong emotions on negotiation.* Working Paper of the Harvard Negotiation Project.

Shapiro, D. L. (2005). Enemies, allies, and emotions: The power of positive emotions in negotiation. In M. Moffitt & R. Bordone (Eds.), *Handbook of Dispute Resolution.* New York: Jossey-Bass.

Strauss, A. (Ed.). (1956). *The social psychology of George Herbert Mead.* Chicago: University of Chicago Press.

Taylor, S., Kemeny, M., Reed, G., Bower, J., & Gruenewald, T. (2000). Psychological resources, positive illusions, and health. *American Psychologist, 55,* 99–109.

Tegen, Belen (n.d.). Entwined blood lines: A child of Ethiopia and Eritrea, Silicon Valley De-Bug. Retrieved September 30, 2005, from http://www.siliconvalleydebug.com/Story/0122/Stories/entwinedbl.html

Tutu, D. (2000). *No future without forgiveness.* New York: Doubleday.

Ury, W. (1991). *Getting past no: Negotiating with difficult people.* New York: Bantam Books.

Ury, W. (1999). *Getting to peace: Transforming conflict at home, at work and in the world.* New York: Viking.

Volkan, V. (1992). Ethnonationalistic rituals: An introduction. *Mind and Human Interaction, 4*(1), 3–19.

Volkan, V. (1997). *Bloodlines: From ethnic pride to ethnic terrorism.* New York: Farrar, Straus and Giroux.

Winnicott, D. (1953). Transitional objects and transitional phenomena. *International Journal of Psychoanalysis, 34,* 89–97.

Wood, Nicholas. (2004, February 15). Fed by anger, undercurrent of nationalism flows in Serbia. *The New York Times,* p. A14.

Young, A. (2003). *Placing peace-making back on the map.* Retrieved June 16, 2003, from www.haaretz.com

CONCLUSION

# What Can We Do?

## *Mari Fitzduff*

There has been a great deal of progress made in the study of social psychological issues of conflict and peacemaking since the field began to develop as a discipline after the horrors of World War II. Conceptually and methodologically the field continues to progress. The changing nature of war in the world—from interstate to mainly intrastate and globalized conflict—has made the contributions of social psychology increasingly more pertinent than the traditional "realist" paradigm of international relations, which is mainly concerned with power relationships between states. As these three volumes show, psychological perspectives are particularly helpful in increasing our understanding of the causes of the horrors of wars of an intrastate nature, where a government turns upon its people, a people turns upon its government, or people turn upon each other. Such perspectives can also assist us in more adequately dealing with a new and terrifying variation of war in the form of globalized terrorist actions by nonstate groups. The authors in these volumes were specifically writing in the hope that the understandings and suggestions gleaned from their chapters can help to inform the decisions of policy makers and others with a responsibility for preventing and solving intranational, international, and global conflicts. So what are their conclusions?

**(1) Politicians and other leaders need to be careful about assisting the development of the perception of "enemy" groups to facilitate their own ends. They also need to correct imbalances of resources or power between groups so as to ensure that enmities between groups do not easily arise.**

As these chapters show, there is nothing in our nature to suggest that violence and war are inevitable. However, given our tendencies to all too easily classify and identify other groups as our enemy and to support violence against another group in the face of fear or a perceived threat, politicians and other leaders need to be careful not to sectionalize their politics, thus assisting the development of the perception of enemy groups. Those in power also need to continually monitor and correct imbalances of resources or power between groups so as to ensure that enmities between groups do not easily arise.

**(2) Wars are much easier to prevent than to stop, and we should invest more resources into such prevention.**

Our understanding of how to prevent conflict has grown substantially over the last decade, and we should take conflict prevention much more seriously. In the same way as we now have worldwide heath officials, both globally and locally, who are permanently on the alert to prevent outbreaks of diseases that could become epidemics, so we should do the same for conflict and war. We now have the understanding and skills to prevent many of the conflicts emerging in the world today, and this would be infinitely less costly than trying to manage and stop such wars and than picking up the human and financial cost that they incur.

**(3) We now know a great deal about what makes for successful peace processes, so we should take such learning seriously and use it to effect greater success in such processes.**

Many of our authors have been closely studying what has worked or not worked in peace processes. The need for consensus building work to happen at all levels, and not just at the elite level, is noted as important, as is the need to include as many "voices" as possible in such discussions so as to build peace constituencies and create a vision of the future that will serve all sides well. The use of trained and experienced mediators developing official and unofficial dialogue processes and problem-solving workshops, which can assist the development of consensus possibilities, and the need for "cognitive managers" to assist a matching of cognitive styles by the differing parties are also emphasized by our authors as being critically important to the success of many peace processes.

**(4) We now know that the signing of a peace process is no longer enough. Postconflict work needs as much strategic attention as the development of a peace process, or the peace that has been gained will not be sustainable.**

The work of economic and social reconstruction and of healing and reconciliation in a postviolent situation is utterly vital if communities are to move forward together into peace. The work of disarmament and demobilization of former combatants (and particularly of child soldiers) needs to be an integral part of every peace process. There is also a need for healing processes that address the psychological trauma and social wounds of communities and for community interventions that provide support for victims and former combatants as well as refugees/returnees. Such processes should be guided primarily by indigenous personnel. If such work is not undertaken, there will likely be a resurgence of violence and the peace will fail to be sustainable.

**(5) We should particularly note the greater involvement of men in violent conflicts. We should therefore ensure that there are sufficient opportunities for their inclusion in societal and employment processes so as to diminish their inclinations to find meaning and solutions to conflicts through the use of the gun.**

While, obviously, many men become involved in violent conflict because they see a need to protect their country or community, their greater tendency, particularly by young men, to find meaning in war-related activities has been noted by various authors. Such needs should be both respected and harnessed so that they have alternative processes of empowerment available to them through which to enable them to resist destructive mobilizations, develop their need for identity and for heroism, and foster their ability to address perceived injustices through more constructive processes than those of violence.

(6) **While intergroup contact and dialogue processes are often seen as key to addressing conflict issues, such work needs the creation of optimal conditions and processes so as to ensure success.**

Intergroup contact processes are likely to be more successful if they provide physical and emotional safety, have a goal that is superordinate to the group and agreed upon by all sides, occur under equal group status conditions, and are supported by official authority. In addition, such contact work usually needs to be sustained over a period of time, and it needs to achieve leverage with the major actors in a conflict if it is to be successful. Enabling people involved in such work to find a common complementary identity may also be useful, such as a common regional or global identity, or the development of a nonethnic civic identity. The ability to enable groups to constructively confront and utilize the negative emotions inevitable in such conflict-resolution processes is also useful, as is the ability to understand and address both the conscious and unconscious anxieties of the participants in the conflict in order to ensure that they are taken account of in developing effective processes of dialogue and problem solving.

(7) **The arts and cultural work are important resources for coexistence and reconciliation work, and they warrant investment.**

War and violent conflict are rarely rational processes, and therefore rational processes alone are unlikely to be able to disentangle the various fears and enmities that are part of the processes of such conflict. Inviting artists and cultural workers such as musicians, dramatists, and storytellers to bring their talents to issues of intergroup relations, questions of contested history, intercommunal enmities, and challenges associated with envisioning a new future is likely to pay dividends if incorporated into peace-building activities.

(8) **Religions have shown a tremendous capacity to foster destructive processes of violence. They can, however, also be used to promote dialogue and empathy if they so choose.**

History has unfortunately shown the frightening capacities of almost all religions to foster gross violence at some points in their history. Given their influence throughout the world, and their spiritual connections with billions of people, there is a need for proactivity on the part of all established religions to draw attention to those parts of their beliefs that emphasize a positive regard for those of different beliefs and to use such to connect rather than divide people.

(9) **The characteristic of leadership in situations of conflict is one of the most determinant factors in the use of violence or nonviolence in situations of**

**conflict, and the need for proactive and positive leadership needs to be addressed.**

In situations of conflict, leaders and followers are often locked in a transactional process whereby leaders will usually act with a high awareness of what their followers want, and followers, for their part, often give their leaders little leeway in terms of what decisions should be taken into account in conflict situations. The need for leaders who can empathize with all sides and transcend party differences is crucial, and such inclusive leaders should be cultivated where possible.

**(10) Contextual factors such as inequitable and unjust resource distribution, corrupt and despotic governance, and the increasing availability of arms must be taken into account and addressed if wars are to be prevented and peace processes are to be sustainable.**

It is inequities (real or perceived) of a cultural, social, or economic nature that most often fuel many of the existing conflicts of today. Such inequities, resulting as they do in anger, humiliation, and a sense of exclusion, often provide the necessary preconditions for mobilization by many of today's religious and ethnocentric leaders. Currently, increasing globalization offers hope mostly to those who are already well off and only further despair and anger to those who feel themselves excluded from such benefits. The easy mobilization of such groups is made increasingly deadly by the ubiquitous availability of arms. Work that seeks to address and resolve many of today's conflicts will not be successful unless the preconditions that produce such despair and anger are addressed and the increasing ubiquity of arms is limited through national and international cooperation.

**(11) The use of terrorist tactics by nonstate actors must be understood both in terms of the local context from which they come, as well as in the context of the balance of power and resources at play in the world.**

The objectives sought by those nonstate actors who use terrorist tactics differ according to whether or not they come from a context where political debate is available or otherwise. Where there is a context of political debate, such actors are likely to pursue politically based national liberation struggles. On the other hand, a culture where political debate is weak or nonexistent produces actors without clear goals. Addressing such activities without a clear understanding of the contexts from which they spring and labeling them as a single phenomenon decrease our capacity to effectively deal with them. Such stereotyping, along with a refusal to assess legitimate grievances, the use of technical resources, and a fixation on "hard" as opposed to "soft" power processes to address the phenomenon of global nonstate terrorism, may increase the very threat factors that we are trying to avoid. Attacks aimed at deterrence must take into account the psychological consequences of such deterrence activities and their power to rebound with multiplied violence.

**(12) If we determine that we do, in fact, need to wage a military war, then we need to combine traditional military capacities with serious training about indigenous social and cultural sensitivities and develop a vastly increased capacity to assist with regime change where such change is the desired outcome.**

Wars of today, for the most part, are no longer won or lost on superior technical military and person power. While military victories can be won relatively easily by those with superior war power, postinvasion strategies, nation building, and democracy development skills need to be vastly expanded so as to ensure that they are complementary to military power, not just sequenced in as an afterthought. Such work can be significantly assisted by social psychologists and others who are aware of the importance of the sensitivity of such approaches in winning or losing victories that are other than military related.

(13) **While accepting that we need to retain a capacity to protect ourselves or intervene to protect others in situations of threat or violence, we also need to believe in our capacity to prevent, limit, and handle conflicts without violence. Allied to such a belief, we need to further develop such a capacity as passionately as we develop our military capacity.**

The more we consider war as inevitable, and the more we prepare ourselves for it through armies and more and more lethal technologies, the more likely we are to use such resources. The more our heroes are those who are soldiers rather than mediators, the more a culture of war readiness and eagerness will prevail. Various chapters in these volumes have been dedicated to demonstrating that the belief in the necessities to fight perpetual violent wars is not necessarily reflected in a substantial number of societies in today's world and to pointing out that learning from such societies can only benefit our entire world.

(14) **Conflict-resolution practitioners and psychologists who are using their research and skills in the service of conflict resolution need to consolidate their knowledge so that its usefulness can be made known in a readily usable fashion to policy makers and practitioners.**

The field of conflict resolution, in all of its manifestations, such as conflict prevention, management and transformation, peace building, coexistence work, and the evaluation of such work, is only a latecomer to the disciplinary field and is not even as yet accepted by all as a field. However, as evidenced by these volumes and many others, it has, in fact, aggregated a substantial amount of knowledge that can be brought to bear upon many of our current conflicts today. Institutional units that can use such knowledge are growing. In the last few years we have seen the development of units within the U.S. State Department, at cabinet level within the U.K. government, and within the United Nations, which are dedicated to various aspects of conflict resolution. Both the World Bank and the OSCE (Organization for Security and Cooperation in Europe) have set up units dedicated to conflict issues, as has the European Union. All of these units can benefit from an understanding of the kinds of issues addressed in these volumes, as from the distillation of the work of many other colleagues in the psychological field who have been concerned about these issues for many years.

(15) **The world today focuses infinitely less on studying nonmilitary approaches to conflict than it does on military means, and this imbalance needs to be addressed.**

Despite the growth of policy and practice conflict-resolution units within governments and intergovernmental organization, the balance of resourcing still lies heavily with those whose prime approach to conflicts today is a military one. According to SIPRI (Stockholm International Peace Research Institute), world military spending increased by 18 percent in real terms, to reach $956 billion (in current U.S. dollars) in 2003. Of this, high-income countries account for about 75 percent of world military spending but only 16 percent of world population. The combined military spending of these countries was slightly higher than the aggregate foreign debt of all low-income countries and 10 times higher than their combined levels of official development assistance in 2001. The main reason for the increase in world military spending is the massive increase in the United States' spending, which accounts for almost half of the world total. Unfortunately the huge growth in such resources has not, to any significant extent, been matched by a complementary growth in resources to those researching and implementing nonmilitary approaches to conflict, war, and peace building. If such growth is assisted, it is likely, as demonstrated by these volumes, that we could progress much more quickly and more effectively toward our common goal of a more peaceful world.

# INDEX

Accountability, 221–22
Affiliation, 320
Afghanistan, war in, 57–58, 61
Agadir Incident, 224
"Age of Genocide," 90
Agency, 271–72
Agentic state, 97
Aggression, 42–43; becomes war, 17–23; biological causes of, 10–13; and brain tumors, 11–12; genetic contributions to, 15–17; male-specific biological causes of, 13–15; and mass psychology, 20–22; and pseudospeciation, 18–20; and role of leaders, 22–23; and steroids, 13; and testosterone, 13–15, 43
Amine neurotransmitters, 76–77
Amish, the, 180, 182, 183; and corporal punishment, 189–90; nonresistance, 181; obedience to higher authority, 190; respect for others, 183
Amygdala, 11, 78–80, 81
Ancestral shadow, vii, 99–101, 103
Anti-Americanism, 58, 62
Anti-Semitism, 92–93, 95, 115, 121
Antisocial Personality Disorder (APD), 94
Antiterrorism, 62
Arafat, Yasir, 114–15, 244

Aristide, Jean, 310
Authoritarianism: and political preference, 212; in information processing, 212; *The Authoritarian Personality* (*TAP*), 95, 211–12
Autonomy, 319–20

Batek, the, 175, 189
Berlin Blockade, 224
Besod Siach, 288, 299
Bin Laden, Osama, 114, 244; on Saddam Hussein, 126
Blair, Tony, 287
Blood feud, 152, 161n.1
Blood lust, 277
Bullying, 145; definition, 162n.8
Bush, George W., 62, 244, 286; on Saddam Hussein's regime, 298

Cannibalism, 4
Carter, Jimmy, 165n.28
Cheney, Dick, 244
Chosen traumas, 313, 327n.5
Cognitive complexity: definition, 212
Cognitive manager model, 217–18

Cognitive styles, 211–12; definition, 211–12
Cold War, 51, 52, 54, 285, 286
Competing: contending, 72–73; forcing, 72
Competitive infanticide, 2–3
Conceptual complexity theory, 212; Paragraph Completion Test (PCT), 212
Conflict, 288; causes of, 2; covert and unconscious, 288; intergroup, 288, 296–99; interpersonal, 288, 290–91; intractable, 243; intractable, explore emotions behind, 239; intractable, ideology behind, 240–41; intragroup, 288, 291–96; intrapsychic, 288, 289–90; Marx's theory of, 241–42; materialist ("realist") approach to, 243; nature of, 287–88; overt and conscious, 288; protracted, causes of, 244, 245; protracted, impasse, 244; protracted, interminable quarrels, 244; protracted, resolution stages, 251–52; rationalist approach to, 245; realist approach to, 245; therapeutic approach to, 245; violent, likelihood of reoccurrence, 308; violent, survivors suffer post-traumatic stress disorder (PTSD), 308; violent, toxic emotions result from, 308
Conflict analysts: questions to ask, 296
Conflict behaviors, 72–74, 75 table; accommodating, 73; avoiding, 73; competing, 72–73; problem solving, 74
Conflict resolution: emotionally based, 287, 288; rationally based, 287
Conflict transformation, 285–302
Corporal punishment, 189–90; exempted from definitions of child abuse in United States, 187; favored by Americans, 187, 188; possible cause of adult violence and spousal abuse, 187
Cortisol, 84; cortisol-mediated responses, 80
Cuban Missile Crisis, 285, 286
Culture of cruelty, 94, 101–2, 104

Darwin, Charles, 258

De-escalation of conflict, 85; inhibition of the fear response system, 85; support the conflict parties, 85
Defense mechanisms, 289; projection, 289; splitting, 289
Disruptive stress hypothesis, 218
Dopamine, 76–77
Doubling, 98–99
Dutch family, 16–17
Dutch family: lack of MAO A gene in adult males, 113

Egalitarian societies, 41
Egalization, 149–50, 154 fig. 6.1, 155; definition, 155
Einstein, Albert, 29
Emotions, 74–75; anger the most accessible, 249; conflict affects, 75; discoveries about relevant to human conflict and peacemaking, 71; experienced on five levels, 74; peace affects, 75; vulnerable, 247, 248
Endorphins, 78, 84
Epinephrine, 76
Ethnic violence, 41
Ethnocentrism, 46, 100
Evolutionary adaptation, 258–60; definition, 258; qualifications, 259
Evolutionary environment of adaptation (EEA), 259; definition, 259
Evolutionary psychology (EP), 99

F (Fascism) Scale, 211–12
Fear response system, 76, 78–80, 85, 86–87; provides immediate, short-term, relief from anxiety, 85
Female coalitions, 3
Feuding, 178
Fisher, Roger, 320–21
Foreign nationals: restricted rights of, 295, 298
Freud, Sigmund, 22–23, 29
Fujimori, Alberto, 320–21
Fundamentalism, 109–34; American, 112; caused by prejudice, 110; Christian, 122;

dangers of, 133; definitions, 109, 116, 133; Islamic, 125–26; Islamic religious, 112; Israeli politics, 112; link to worldwide terrorism, 133; North American Protestant, 123; religious, 109, 116–17; Roman Catholicism, 123–24; Spanish Inquisition, 112

Fundamentalist: Americans against abortion clinics, 127; Confucianism, 131–33; Hinduism, 127–28; Judaism, 124–25; religious ideology, 127; Sikhism, 128–30; Theravada Buddhism, 128, 130–31

Global village, 141, 147, 150, 155–56, 158, 161; as one single inside sphere inhabited by men and women, 158

Globalization, 146, 149–50, 155, 157–58; definition, 149, 158; technology makes possible, 159; weakens gender ranking, 158; weakens gender segregation, 158

Groups, 91–92; bring out our worst tendencies, 91; encourage abandonment of the individual self, 91; moral constraints are less powerful, 91

Haredim, 124–25

Hate-prejudice, 120; definition, 119

Histamine, 76

Hitler, Adolf, 114–15, 141

Holocaust, the, 90, 93, 309; how ordinary Germans could participate in, 92–93

Homophobia, 115, 121

Honor codes, 141, 152–53

Honor killings, 140, 152, 159, 161n.4; reasoning behind, 152

Human beings: far more emotional than rational, 71

Human nature tendencies: desire for social dominance, 100; ethnocentrism, 100; powerful, innate, "animal" influences, 100–101; start in infancy, 100; universal disposition, 103; violence and war, 1; xenophobia, 100

Human rights, 137, 140, 141, 142–43, 146, 147, 153–55, 159

Humiliation, 137–61, 240, 244, 247–48, 250; collective, 245–46; definitions, 140–41, 144; and gender-selective sparing of lives, 139; and gender-selective taking of lives, 139; and honor killings, 139, 140; humiliated fury escalating to conflict, 144–45; as inflicted by institutions, 160; by lack of recognition leads to violence, 145; layers of, 162; meaning has evolved, 153–54; "nuclear bomb of the emotions," 160; result of rape, mass rapes, 138; suffered by Germany, 141–42; as violation of honor, 145; worse than being killed, 139

Humiliation Inventory, 144

Hussein, Saddam, 61–62, 126, 244; supported Taliban and al Qaeda in Afghanistan, 126

Hutterites, the, 180; and corporal punishment, 189–90

"Identerest," 51, 53–54; definition, 53

Identerest conflicts, stages of: phase one—identerest entrepeneurs, 55–56; phase two—fostering fear, 56; phase three—guided polarization and projection, 56; phase four—calculated violence, initiated by leaders, 57

Ifaluk, the, 180, 182, 190–91, 192; link peacefulness to good health, 180

In-group, 86

Ingathering, 154, 156, 157

Inquisition, 117

Inside sphere, 147–49, 150, 151–52; the new, 156

Integrative complexity, 213–15; examine leaders' archival sample texts, 213–14; groupthink, 218–19; and international politics, 214–15; precursor of peace, 224; as predictor of successful negotiation, 215; as predictor of violence, 214, 224

International community, 160–61

Intifada, 59

Iraq, war in, 57–62; turning into civil war, 59–61

Khomeini, Ayatollah Ruholla Mussaui, 126

Ladakhis, the Buddhist, 180, 182; strive for perfection of mind and heart, 181
"Love-prejudice": definition, 119

Mahuad, Jamil, 320–21
Mandela, Nelson, 141
MAO A gene, 113–15; lack of in males in a Dutch family, 113
Mediation: socio-psychological paradigm, 82, 83; structuralist paradigm, 82
Mediators, 82; handling of clients' anger, 250–51; help clients acknowledge alienation, 246; help clients acknowledge unacknowledged emotions, 246–47; need special training to detect shame, 246
Memes, 279–81; definition, 279
Men: enjoy higher status than women (are up), 148–49; inhabit the outside sphere, 147–49
Metaframe, 315–17; needed by Serbians, 322
Milgram's electric shock experiments, 23
Mobbing, 145; definition, 162n.8

Natural selection, 101
Nature of the collective. See Groups
Neanderthals, 4; cannibalism by, 4
Negotiating team, 231–32
Negotiating team: possess a high level of metacomplexity, 231
Negotiations, at an impasse: parties need to feel heard, 243
Negotiator: distinguish the different kinds of anger, 240
Negotiators: advice for, 225–28; help the parties to formulate their stories, 243; in situations of rising integrative

complexity, 219–20; mixed levels of complexity, 225; strategies for, 229; strategies to deal with vertigo, 314–21; tend to adjust to other party's complexity level, 224; wise to match opponent's negotiating strategy, 226–27. See also Integrative complexity
Nepotism, 120; definition, 120
Neurochemicals, 76
9/11. See September 11
Norepinephrine, 76, 84

Object relations: realignment of needed by Ethiopians and Eritreans, 324–26
Orbitomedial prefrontal cortex, 80–82
Ordinary people commit extraordinary evil, 89–105; readily absorbed into civil society after the killings and lived peacefully, 90–91
Ostracism, fear of, 20–21
Out-group, 86
"Outbidding," 54–55, 56
Outside sphere, 147–49, 150, 151–52
Oxytocin, 78, 84; oxytocin-mediated responses, 80

Peace: negative, 83, 84; positive, 83–84, 86; restorative, 177; separative, 177–78; sociative, 177
Peace building: negative postconflict emotions threaten, 308–9
Peace feather, 85
Peaceful societies, 175–99; Amish, the, 181; avoid engaging in war, 177; Batek, the, 189; child abuse rare, 189; committed to nonviolent worldviews, 179, 179–83; deal with conflict in nonviolent ways, 177; definition, 176, 178; human beings are capable of peace, ix, 176; Ifaluk, the, 180–81; internally peaceful and nonwarring, 178, 196–99; Ladakhis, the Buddhist, 181; nonacceptance of warfare, 194; parents portray peaceful examples for their children, 189, 191;

peacefulness/aggressiveness is not immutably fixed through time, 177; peacefulness is heart of their worldview, 182–83; peacefulness is relative, not absolute, 176; Piaroa, the, 181–82; provide valuable insights to reduce violence, 176; punishment of children infrequent and very mild, 188; respect felt and expressed in a reciprocal manner, 183–84; respect for others a core value, 179, 183–86; respect for women, 184; show that violence and warfare are not inevitable, 193; socialize children in their nonviolent beliefs, 179, 186–92, 195; socialize children to be fearful, 190–91; suggest common presumptions about violence may be false, 175. *See also* Amish; Batek; Ifaluk; Ladakhis; Piaroa

Peacefulness: result of people living their nonviolent social beliefs and ideals, 179

Peptide neurohormones, 77–78

Perpetrators: and a culture of cruelty, 101–2; and social death of the victims, 102; dispositions and personalities of matter, 101; factors that shape identities of, 101

Perpetrators of extraordinary evil: "divided self" theories, 96–99; extraordinary only by what they have done, not by whom they are, 96–97; represent cross section of the normal distribution of humans, 95–96

Personality factors: related to the heinous genocidal actions, 211

Piaroa, the, 180, 182; total rejection of competition, 181

Policy makers: advice for, 225–28; considerations in conflict situations, 299–302; questions to ask, 298–99

Post-traumatic stress disorder (PTSD), xxiii, 145, 309, 326–27n.2

Practitioners: considerations in conflict situations, 299–302; questions to ask, 296, 298–99; role of, 296

Prejudice, 110–12, 115–16, 117–22, 134, 145, 164; all humans are the recipients of, 110; all humans have, 110; causes an "us" vs. "them" mind-set, 117;

Fundamentalisms arise from, 110; hate-prejudice, 119; institutionalized, 111; "love-prejudice," 119

Prisoner's Dilemma game, 228

Problem-solving workshops, 288, 318–19; needed by Serbians, 322–23; provide safe environment, 319; unofficial meetings, 319

Projective identification, 290

Pseudospeciation, 18–20

Rabin, Yitzhak, 296

Racism, 115, 121

Religion: as social glue, 272; definitions, 274; evolution of, 270–74; intimate connection with warfare, 257–81; reduces anxiety in the face of stress, 274; tells people what they most want to hear, 275

Religious experience: and mystical experiences in warfare, 276–77; animism, 278; capacity for is an evolutionary adaptation, 258–60, 261–62; characteristics of, 276; hypotheses for the mode of transmission of the capacity for, 279; monotheism, 278; polytheism, 278; similarity to military drills and training, 276

Religious experience, capacity for: definition, 274; evolved via individual selection in the context of warfare, 274–77; objection to the evolutionary adaptation hypothesis, 280

Respect: as a core value promoting nonviolence, 183–86; as shown by the Buids, 184–85; as shown by Tristan Islanders, 185–86; core value of the Amish, 183; definition, 183. *See also* Amish

Robbers Cave Experiment, 21–22

Rorschach tests, Copenhagen: administered to test "Mad Nazi" thesis on rank-and-file Nazis, 94

Rorschach tests, Nuremberg: administered to test "Mad Nazi" thesis on Nazi elite, 93–94

Rumsfeld, Donald, 244

al-Sadat, Anwar, 125, 296, 316
Scapegoat, 117, 293–94
Security dilemma, 150
Selfish behaviors, 75
Selfless behaviors, 75
September 11, ii, 286, 295, 297, 298;
    American unity after, 298; chosen
    trauma for Americans, 249
Serotonin, 13, 76–77, 84; 5-HIAA, 13
Sexism, 115, 121
Sharon, Ariel, 114–15, 125, 244
Situational influences on decision
    makers/negotiators, 217–18;
    environmental factors, 217;
    physiological influences, 217; stress, 217
Six Cultures study, 9–10
Social control, 156–57
Societies: least violent, !Kung San, the, 6;
    least violent, Semai, the, 6–7; matrilocal,
    7; most violent, Germans of the Third
    Reich, 5; most violent, Yanomami
    (Yanomamo), the, 5–6; patrilocal, 7
"Speak Bitterness" meetings, 241
Stalin, Joseph, 114–15
Suicide bomber, 277
Suicide bombings, 297; result of Islamic
    terrorist dogmatism, 112

Terrorism, 57–62
Terrorist groups: mentality, 295
Terrorists: as distinguished from guerrillas,
    58; definition, 58; modern equivalent to
    ancient barbarians, 57–58; think of
    themselves as freedom fighters, 57
The Authoritarian Personality (TAP), 95,
    211–12
Third party, 82
Traditional societies, 151; definition, 152–
    53; men's worth in, 159; women's worth
    in, 159
Trait complexity, 215–17
Transitional environment, 317–19; needed
    by Ethiopians and Eritreans, 323–24;

problem-solving workshops, 318–19;
    qualities of, 317; truth and reconciliation
    commissions, 317–18
Tristan Islanders, 180, 185–86; and
    corporal punishment, 189–90
Truth and reconciliation commissions,
    317–18; promote open disclosure, 318;
    provide safe environment, 318

Unokais, 43–44; definition, 264; higher
    reproductive success, 264
"Us" vs. "them," 247, 295, 298; generated
    by prejudice, 117

Vasopressin, 78, 84
Vertigo, xi, 308, 309–20, 326–27;
    characteristics of, 311–14; object
    relations, 310–11, 313; recovery phases,
    315; social cognition, 311
Violence: archeological record for
    homicidal, 4; caused by jealousy, 9;
    caused by vendetta, 9; greater male
    propensity for, 1, 8–10; international
    effort to prevent, 57; male aggregations
    foster, 7–8; organized, 17; result of
    people acting on their values, 179
Volkan's collective violence theory, 247,
    249; chosen trauma, 247; chosen trauma
    experienced as a humiliation, 247;
    collective regression, 247; entitlement to
    revenge, 247; failure to mourn, 247

War: preconditions for, 45; prevention: by
    international community, 26;
    prevention: by self-knowledge of human
    nature, 30
Warfare: affects natural selection, 265;
    altruistic, 264; capacity for is an
    evolutionary adaptation, 262–70;
    constant, episodic aspect of human
    history, 265; definition, 41, 178; militia
    warfare, 262–63, 278; professional
    warfare, 263, 278; raiding, 262, 263–64,
    278; and rape, 269–70; religious,

suicide bomber, 277vies with sex for being the most significant process in human evolution, 89; winners of have greatly increased reproductive success, 269, 278

Wars: aggression escalates into, 17–23; became common over time, 45–46; capture of women is both a cause and a consequence of, 9; competition for resources lead to, xvii, 24–25; the male factor, 8–10; why they happen, 42–51, 63; why they happen, biological approaches, 42–47; why they happen, leader's decision often accepted with enthusiasm by people on the ground, 54; why they happen, materialist approaches, 47–48; why they happen, self-interest of the leader, 48, 54; why they happen, symbolic/cultural approaches, 47

Weapons of mass destruction (WMD), 61–62, 286–87

Whitman, Charles, 11, 80

Women: enjoy lower status than men (are down), 148–49; inhabit the inside sphere, 147–49

World Trade Center (WTC), 112, 286, 297, 298

Worldviews, 179–83; definition, 179

Xenophobia, 100

Yanomami (Yanomamo), the, 5, 41, 48–51, 264; unokais, 264; wars occur for reasons related to an expanding Western presence, 49; wars occur regarding access to Western goods, 49–50

Zionism, 112, 125

# ABOUT THE SERIES

As this new millennium dawns, humankind has evolved—some would argue has devolved—exhibiting new and old behaviors that fascinate, infuriate, delight, or fully perplex those of us seeking answers to the question, "Why"? In this series, experts from various disciplines peer through the lens of psychology telling us answers they see for questions of human behavior. Their topics may range from humanity's psychological ills—addictions, abuse, suicide, murder, and terrorism among them—to works focused on positive subjects including intelligence, creativity, athleticism, and resilience. Regardless of the topic, the goal of this series remains constant—to offer innovative ideas, provocative considerations, and useful beginnings to better understand human behavior.

Chris E. Stout
Series Editor

# ABOUT THE SERIES EDITOR AND SERIES ADVISORY BOARD

**CHRIS E. STOUT,** Psy.D., MBA, holds a joint governmental and academic appointment in Northwestern University Medical School and serves as Illinois's first Chief of Psychological Services. He served as an NGO Special Representative to the United Nations, was appointed by the U.S. Department of Commerce as a Baldridge Examiner, and served as an advisor to the White House for both political parties. He was appointed to the World Economic Forum's Global Leaders of Tomorrow. He has published and presented more than 300 papers and 29 books. His works have been translated into six languages.

**BRUCE E. BONECUTTER,** Ph.D., is Director of Behavioral Services at the Elgin Community Mental Health Center, the Illinois Department of Human Services state hospital serving adults in greater Chicago. He is also a Clinical Assistant Professor of Psychology at the University of Illinois at Chicago. A clinical psychologist specializing in health, consulting, and forensic psychology, Bonecutter is also a longtime member of the American Psychological Association Task Force on Children and the Family.

**JOSEPH FLAHERTY,** M.D., is Chief of Psychiatry at the University of Illinois Hospital, a Professor of Psychiatry at the University of Illinois College of Medicine, and a Professor of Community Health Science at the UIC College of Public Health. He is a Founding Member of the Society for the Study of Culture and Psychiatry. Dr. Flaherty has been a consultant to the World Health Organization, to the National Institutes of Mental Health, and also the Falk Institute in Jerusalem.

**MICHAEL HOROWITZ,** Ph.D., is President and Professor of Clinical Psychology at the Chicago School of Professional Psychology, one of the nation's leading not-for-profit graduate schools of psychology. Earlier, he served as Dean and Professor of the Arizona School of Professional Psychology. A clinical psychologist practicing independently since 1987, his work has focused on psychoanalysis, intensive individual therapy, and couples therapy. He has provided Disaster Mental Health Services to the American Red Cross. Dr. Horowitz's special interests include the study of fatherhood.

**SHELDON I. MILLER,** M.D., is a Professor of Psychiatry at Northwestern University and Director of the Stone Institute of Psychiatry at Northwestern Memorial Hospital. He is also Director of the American Board of Psychiatry and Neurology, Director of the American Board of Emergency Medicine, and Director of the Accreditation Council for Graduate Medical Education. Dr. Miller is also an Examiner for the American Board of Psychiatry and Neurology. He is Founding Editor of the *American Journal of Addictions* and Founding Chairman of the American Psychiatric Association's Committee on Alcoholism.

**DENNIS P. MORRISON,** Ph.D., is Chief Executive Officer at the Center for Behavioral Health in Indiana, the first behavioral health company ever to win the JCAHO Codman Award for excellence in the use of outcomes management to achieve health care quality improvement. He is President of the Board of Directors for the Community Healthcare Foundation in Bloomington and has been a member of the Board of Directors for the American College of Sports Psychology. He has served as a consultant to agencies including the Ohio Department of Mental Health, Tennessee Association of Mental Health Organizations, Oklahoma Psychological Association, the North Carolina Council of Community Mental Health Centers, and the National Center for Health Promotion in Michigan.

**WILLIAM H. REID,** M.D., MPH, is a clinical and forensic psychiatrist and consultant to attorneys and courts throughout the United States. He is a Clinical Professor of Psychiatry at the University of Texas Health Science Center. Dr. Miller is also an Adjunct Professor of Psychiatry at Texas A&M College of Medicine and Texas Tech University School of Medicine, as well as a clinical faculty member at the Austin Psychiatry Residency Program. He is chairman of the Scientific Advisory Board and medical advisor to the Texas Depressive & Manic-Depressive Association, as well as an examiner for the American Board of Psychiatry and the Law, as chairman of the Research Section for an International Conference on the Psychiatric Aspects of Terrorism, and as medical director for the Texas Department of Mental Health and Mental Retardation.

# About the Contributors

**BRUCE D. BONTA** is an Associate Librarian Emeritus from the Pennsylvania State University, University Park, PA, USA. He is the author of *Peaceful Peoples: An Annotated Bibliography* (1993) plus several articles on peaceful societies. His most recent project has been writing and designing a Peaceful Societies Web site (http://www.peacefulsocieties.org), which contains an Encyclopedia section with entries for 25 of the societies listed in the Appendix to the Bonta and Fry chapter in this volume.

**LUCIAN GIDEON CONWAY III** received his Ph.D. from the University of British Columbia in 2001 and is currently an Assistant Professor of Psychology at The University of Montana. His primary research interests lie in political and social psychology; he is the author of 22 articles, commentaries, and book chapters in these areas. In particular, his interests revolve around the causes of complex (as opposed to simple) thinking and the consequences of political leaders engaging in such thinking during international crises. He studies other socio-political issues as well, including how shared cultural beliefs (for example, stereotypes) emerge and persist.

**J. HAROLD ELLENS** is a Research Scholar at the University of Michigan, Department of Near Eastern Studies. He is a retired Presbyterian theologian and ordained minister, a retired U.S. Army Colonel, and a retired Professor of Philosophy, Theology, and Psychology at Oakland University. He has authored, coauthored and/or, edited 111 books and 165 professional journal articles. He served 15 years as Executive Director of the Christian Association for Psychological Studies, and as Founding Editor and Editor-in-Chief of the Journal of Psychology and Christianity. He holds a Ph.D. from Wayne State University in the Psychology of Human Communication, a Ph.D. from the University of Michigan in Biblical and Near Eastern Studies, and

Master's Degrees from Calvin Theological Seminary, Princeton Theological Seminary, and the University of Michigan. He was born in Michigan and grew up in a Dutch-German immigrant community near McBain. Following a traumatic childhood he determined at age seven to enter the Christian Ministry as a means to help his people with the great amount of suffering he perceived all around him in the Great Depression. His life's work has focused on the interface of psychology and religion.

**R. BRIAN FERGUSON** is a Professor of Sociology and Anthropology at Rutgers University and is the Founder and Director of the *Working Group on Political Violence, War, and Peace* at the Center for Global Change and Governance. Dr. Ferguson has served on the Board of Governors for the New York Academy of Sciences since 2002. His research interests focus primarily on war, including ethnohistorical reconstructions and analyses of warfare on the Pacific Northwest Coast, and among the Yanomami, and more generally on the impact of expanding states on indigenous war patterns. As an Anthropologist, Dr. Ferguson explores many aspects of war and cultural conflict, including biological theories of culture, archaeological evidence of warfare, and the idea of "ethnic violence," a term he critiques in his recently edited volume, *The State, Identity, and Violence: Political Disintegration in the Post-Cold War World* (2003). Dr. Ferguson is currently working on a book entitled "Chimpanzees, Men, and War."

**MARI FITZDUFF** is currently Professor and Director of the M.A. program in Coexistence and Conflict at Brandeis University, in Boston, USA. From 1997 to 2003, she held a Chair of Conflict Studies at the University of Ulster where she was Director of UNU/INCORE. Previous to that she was Chief Executive of the Northern Ireland Community Relations Council, the main agency dedicated to developing and funding conflict-resolution issues in Northern Ireland. She has worked on programs addressing conflict issues in Europe, Asia, Africa, and Latin America. Her previous books include *Community Conflict Skills*, now in its 4th edition, and *NGO's at the Table: Strategies for Influencing Policy in Conflict Areas*. Her book on Northern Ireland, *"Beyond Violence"—Conflict Resolution Processes in Northern Ireland*, was winner of an American Library Notable Publications Award.

**DOUGLAS P. FRY** is a docent in the Developmental Psychology Program at Åbo Akademi University in Finland and an adjunct research scientist in the Bureau of Applied Research in Anthropology at the University of Arizona. Dr. Fry is author of *The Human Potential for Peace: An Anthropological Challenge to Assumptions about War and Violence* (2006), coeditor of *Keeping the Peace: Conflict Resolution and Peaceful Societies Around the World* (2004), and coeditor of *Cultural Variation in Conflict Resolution: Alternatives to Violence* (1997).

**MELVIN KONNER,** M.D., Ph.D., is Samuel Candler Dobbs Professor in the Department of Anthropology and the Program in Neuroscience and Behavioral Biology at Emory University. His M.D. and Ph.D. are from Harvard University, where he taught before coming to Emory. He is the author of *The Tangled Wing: Biological*

*Constraints on the Human Spirit* and *Unsettled: An Anthropology of the Jews,* among other books. He is a Fellow of the American Association for the Advancement of Science, and he has written for the *New York Times* and *Newsweek* as well as *Nature, Science,* and *The New England Journal of Medicine.*

**DANA C. LEIGHTON** is an Instructor of Psychology at Tri-County Technical College, a comprehensive community college in South Carolina. He received his M.A. in Social Psychology from the University of British Columbia in 2004. His main research questions involve the social and cognitive factors people (especially political leaders) use when deciding to wage war or build peace. His most recent research examined individual responses to threats in the physical and social environments and how they affect prejudice and stereotypes toward immigrant out-groups. He is starting a new research project involving terror management theory and its subtle effects on preferences for community.

**EVELIN GERDA LINDNER** is a social scientist with an interdisciplinary and global orientation. She holds two Ph.D.s, one in social medicine and another in social psychology. In 1996, she began her research on the concept of humiliation and its role in genocide and war. German history served as her starting point. It is often assumed that the humiliation of the Germans through the Versailles Treaties after World War I was partly responsible for the Holocaust and the Second World War. Lindner is currently working on a *Theory of Humiliation* as well as developing the global network that she founded, "Human Dignity and Humiliation Studies" (www.humiliationstudies.org).

**VANESSA LIU,** J.D., is a management consultant with McKinsey & Company in Amsterdam. A graduate of the Harvard Law School, she has taught in the Negotiation Workshop there, as well as in workshops for lawyers and other professionals. She received a Hewlett Foundation Research Fellowship in Law and Negotiation to research the World Summit on Sustainable Development negotiations. After receiving her B.A. from Harvard in psychology, she was a Fulbright Fellow in the Netherlands, doing research on the International Court of Justice and the International Criminal Tribunal for the Former Yugoslavia.

**ALLEN D. MACNEILL** is a senior lecturer in Biology at Cornell University, where he teaches introductory biology and evolution. His research interests include the evolutionary basis for religion, the implications of ecology and evolutionary theory for ethics, and the evolutionary dynamics of monogamy and polygamy in humans. He is currently writing an introductory textbook on evolution and a monograph on the evolution of the capacity for religious experience.

**DOUGLAS E. NOLL** is a full-time peacemaker and mediator, specializing in difficult, complex, and intractable conflicts and is an adjunct professor of law and forensic psychology. In addition to his law degree, Mr. Noll has a Master's Degree in Peacemaking and Conflict Studies. Mr. Noll was a business and commercial trial lawyer in federal and state courts for 22 years before turning to peacemaking. He is

AV-rated and is admitted to the California Bar, various United States District Courts, various United States Circuit Courts of Appeal, and the United States Supreme Court. Mr. Noll is a Fellow of the International Academy of Mediators, is a Fellow of the American College of Civil Trial Mediators, and is on the American Arbitration Association panel of mediators and arbitrators. He is an author of the book *Peacemaking: Practicing at the Intersection of Law and Human Conflict* (Cascadia, 2002), numerous articles on peacemaking, restorative justice, conflict resolution, and mediation and is a mediator trainer, lecturer, and continuing education panelist.

**SUZANNE RETZINGER** received her Ph.D. from UCSB in 1988 and is a research sociologist. In 1988 in the California courts, she became a family mediator and worked with conflict on a practical as well as a theoretical level. In 1993 she received a second Master's in Marriage and Family Therapy and became licensed by the State of California to practice psychotherapy. For the past 25 years she has taught and has done workshops on emotions, conflict, and relationships, both here and abroad. Retzinger has worked with emotions on both theoretical and practical levels in the fields of sociology, mental health, psychotherapy, criminology, conflict, and death and dying. Retzinger has always been interested in human relationships. Her main interests are emotions, relationships, and the bonds between people—their connects and disconnects. In 2004 she served as President of the Santa Barbara Chapter of California Association Marriage and Family Therapists. Her interest here included furthering the field of therapy and building community. Currently, she is a psychotherapist in private practice and a grief/end of life counselor with Hospice of Santa Barbara. Retzinger's books are *Violent Emotions: Shame and Rage in Marital Quarrels* (SAGE, 1991), and *Emotions and Violence: Shame and Rage in Destructive Conflict* (with T. J. Scheff, Lexington, 1991). Besides these two books, she has published many articles on emotions, conflict, mental health, and relationships.

**THOMAS SCHEFF** is Professor Emeritus of Sociology, University of California, Santa Barbara. He is the author of *Being Mentally Ill, Microsociology, Emotions and Violence* (with Suzanne Retzinger), *Bloody Revenge*, and other books and articles. He is a former Chair of the section on the Sociology of Emotions, American Sociological Association, and President of the Pacific Sociological Association. His fields of research are social psychology, emotions, and collective conflict. His most recent book (1997) concerns part/whole analysis, a unified approach to theory and method in the human sciences. A book that explains and extends the work of Erving Goffman is in press.

**DANIEL SHAPIRO,** Ph.D., Associate Director of the Harvard Negotiation Project, teaches negotiation at Harvard Law School and in the Psychiatry Department at Harvard Medical School/McLean Hospital. He holds a doctorate in clinical psychology and specializes in the psychology of negotiation. He directs the International Negotiation Initiative, a Harvard-based project that develops psychologically focused strategies to reduce ethnopolitical violence. He has trained government officials in many parts of the world and developed a conflict management program that now reaches nearly 1 million people across 25 countries. His most recent book, in collaboration with Professor Roger Fisher, is *Beyond Reason: Using Emotions as You Negotiate* (Viking/Penguin, 2005).

**CHRIS E. STOUT** is a licensed clinical psychologist and is a Clinical Full Professor at the University of Illinois' College of Medicine's Department of Psychiatry and Founding Director of the Center for Global Initiatives. He served as a NGO Special Representative to the United Nations. Dr. Stout is a Fellow of the American Psychological Association, past-President of the Illinois Psychological Association, and a Distinguished Practitioner in the National Academies of Practice. He is a recipient of the American Psychological Association's International Humanitarian Award and was awarded a Global Leader of Tomorrow from the World Economic Forum.

**PETER SUEDFELD** is currently a Professor Emeritus at the University of British Columbia's Department of Psychology, as well as Dean Emeritus of Graduate Studies. His research is generally concerned with how human beings adapt to and cope with novelty, challenge, stress, and danger. He is the author of more than 200 journal articles and book chapters, and he has presented keynote addresses at many institutions and conferences in North and South America, Europe, Australia, Asia, and New Zealand. Suedfeld has served as Co-Editor of the *Journal of Applied Social Psychology* and Book Review Editor of *Political Psychology*. He is currently Associate Editor of *Environment and Behavior* and is on the editorial boards of *Political Psychology*, the *Journal of Environmental Psychology*, and the *Interamerican Journal of Psychology*. Dr. Suedfeld has been elected a Fellow of numerous national and international psychological associations, including the Royal Society of Canada and the American Psychological Association (six divisions), and he has received many awards for his contributions to the field of psychology.

**TRACY WALLACH,** LICSW, trained as a clinical social worker and worked as a psychotherapist in various organizations and in private practice for 20 years. For the past 10 years, she has been an organization development and leadership consultant based in Brookline, MA. Her clients have included manufacturing, health care, social service, and public sector organizations. She has taught extensively on the topics of group and organizational dynamics, leadership, conflict, and communication in professional, organizational, and academic settings, both in the United States and abroad. She has long been interested in the application of group relations theory and methodology to understanding societal dynamics and to conflict transformation. She is past President of the Center for the Study of Groups and Social Systems (Boston Affiliate, AKRI) and is a past board member of The A. K. Rice Institute for the Study of Social Systems.

**JAMES WALLER** is Edward B. Lindaman Chair and Professor of Psychology at Whitworth College (Spokane, WA). For 20 years, he has taught courses on intergroup relations, prejudice, and genocide studies. In January 1996, Dr. Waller developed an innovative study tour titled "Prejudice Across America." The tour drew national media attention and was named by President Clinton's Initiative on Race as one of America's "Promising Practices for Racial Reconciliation." Many of the experiences from the tour are chronicled in his *Face to Face: The Changing State of Racism Across America* (New York, Perseus Books, 1998) and *Prejudice Across America* (Jackson, MS: University Press of Mississippi). Dr. Waller's most recent book, *Becoming Evil: How Ordinary People Commit Genocide and Mass Killing* (Oxford University Press, 2002), was praised by Publisher's Weekly for "clearly and effectively synthesizing a wide range of studies to develop an original and persuasive model of the process by which people can become evil."

**Recent Titles in
Contemporary Psychology**

Resilience for Today: Gaining Strength from Adversity
*Edith Henderson Grotberg, editor*

The Destructive Power of Religion: Violence in Judaism, Christianity, and Islam,
Volumes I–IV
*J. Harold Ellens, editor*

Helping Children Cope with the Death of a Parent: A Guide for the First Year
*Paddy Greenwall Lewis and Jessica G. Lippman*

Martyrdom: The Psychology, Theology, and Politics of Self-Sacrifice
*Rona M. Fields, with Contributions from Cóilín Owens, Valérie Rosoux, Michael
Berenbaum, and Reuven Firestone*

Redressing the Emperor: Improving Our Children's Public Mental Health System
*John S. Lyons*

Havens: Stories of True Community Healing
*Leonard Jason and Martin Perdoux*

Psychology of Terrorism, Condensed Edition: Coping with the Continuing Threat
*Chris E. Stout, editor*

Handbook of International Disaster Psychology, Volumes I–IV
*Gilbert Reyes and Gerald A. Jacobs, editors*